Z
8288
H39
1982

William Faulkner:
Research Opportunities and Dissertation Abstracts

edited by Tetsumaro Hayashi

McFarland 1982
Jefferson, N.C., and London

The dissertation titles and abstracts contained here are published with the permission of University Microfilms International, publishers of *Dissertation Abstracts International* (copyright © University Microfilms International), and may not be reproduced without their prior permission. For full-text copies of the dissertations, write University Microfilms International 300 N Zeeb Rd, Ann Arbor MI 48106, or telephone 800-521-3042.

Tetsumaro Hayashi is professor of English at Ball State University, Muncie, Indiana. He has received fellowships from the Folger Shakespeare Library, the American Philosophical Society, and the American Council of Learned Societies. He is the founder, a past director, and current president of the John Steinbeck Society of America, and editor-in-chief of the *Steinbeck Quarterly*. Professor Hayashi is the author or editor of 21 books and about 90 articles on American and British literature.

Richard F. Peterson is professor of English at Southern Illinois University, Carbondale, and the author or editor of numerous studies on John Steinbeck; he is managing editor of the *Steinbeck Quarterly*. His major work on Yeats appeared in 1981.

Library of Congress Cataloging in Publication Data

Hayashi, Tetsumaro.
  William Faulkner, research opportunities and dissertation abstracts.

  Includes indexes.
  1. Faulkner, William, 1897–1962 — Bibliography.
  2. Dissertations, Academic — Abstracts. I. Title.
  Z8288.H39 [PS3511.A86]   016.813'52   82-15236

ISBN 0-89950-048-X   AACR2

Copyright © 1982 by Tetsumaro Hayashi

Manufactured in the United States of America

McFarland & Company, Inc., Publishers
  Box 611, Jefferson, North Carolina 28640

Dedicated to
LOTTE AND DIDIER GRAEFFE
and
SAMUEL AND MARILYN SCHOENBAUM
as a humble but sincere token
of gratitude and esteem

TABLE OF CONTENTS

Preface	vii
"At the Flood": Research Opportunities in Faulkner Studies (by Richard F. Peterson)	1
William Faulkner: Dissertation Abstracts	7
Author Index	305
Director Index	309
Title Index	312
University Index	322
Subject Index	324

PREFACE

Among the twentieth-century American authors, William Faulkner still commands the most attention of doctoral candidates in English and comparative literature. Although this fact has been widely known, I had not fully realized to what extent Faulkner has been the center of academic attention until I started gathering and reviewing all the available abstracts of the Faulkner dissertations accepted by universities in the United States, Canada, and England from 1941 through 1979. While over 40 dissertations on John Steinbeck and nearly 80 dissertations on Ernest Hemingway* had been completed by 1978, I discovered that at least 415 doctoral dissertations on William Faulkner had been completed in English. Not only is the figure a revelation to me, it also clearly indicates the supreme position Faulkner occupies in academic circles.

Even a glance at the Subject Index for this book will show that the same or similar topics have been explored again and again as if the doctoral candidates never knew of the existence of the other dissertations. Also impressive is the diversity of interests exhibited in Faulkner dissertations since 1941. One of the most often stated assessments of Faulkner here and abroad is that he is perhaps the most difficult novelist in American literature. In spite of such an assessment, or rather, perhaps because of it, many young scholars in English and comparative literature have willingly accepted the challenge of studying Faulkner by exploring his experimental but fascinating literature and recapturing his vision and insight.

The purpose of this reference book is to anthologize the available English-language dissertation abstracts on William Faulkner, to index them properly for the benefit of future doctoral candidates planning to write a dissertation or a book on Faulkner, and to enlighten such scholars with an essay on opportunities in William Faulkner research. I had the good fortune to have Professor Richard F. Peterson, of Southern Illinois University, who wrote a dissertation on Joyce and Faulkner, do this important essay. Professor Peterson has published a number of essays on modern novelists including Joyce, Faulkner, Steinbeck, and D. H. Lawrence.

Six dissertations on William Faulkner were completed in the 1940s, 40 dissertations in the 1950s, 122 in the 1960s, and 247 in the 1970s. Out of 415 doctoral dissertations I have discovered, 406 were written by American scholars; two by English scholars; and seven by Canadian scholars. These dissertations have been summarized by their authors in the Dissertation Abstracts, which became the Dissertation Abstracts International in 1969; however, for the sake of uniformity and simplicity, I have treated all the volumes as the Dissertation Abstracts International (DAI). Some recent volumes are identified with a volume number first and then with "A" (Humanities and Social Sciences). I have put "A" to all volumes also for the sake of uniformity.

As I completed this project, I received the support of many individuals and institutions. Although it is impossible to list all of them here, I shall

*See Tetsumaro Hayashi (ed.), Steinbeck and Hemingway: Dissertation Abstracts and Research Opportunities (Scarecrow Press, 1980).

attempt a representative list of those friends and benefactors who have made the publication of this reference book possible. I am grateful to Professor Peterson for gracing the book with his excellent essay on research opportunities. I wish to express my sincere gratitude to Mrs. Patricia M. Colling of the University Microfilm International for granting me permission to reprint with minor revisions all the available dissertation abstracts from the <u>Dissertation Abstracts International</u> and for extending to me much appreciated moral support. I also owe a debt of gratitude to my student secretaries--Miss Robin Davis, Miss Suzanne Brown, and Miss Tera Miles--for conscientiously typing and proofreading the manuscript. Finally, I want to acknowledge the head reference librarians and their associates of the following distinguished university libraries in the United States, Canada and England, who tirelessly helped me identify information missing in the DAI: Arizona State University, Boston College, Boston University, Brandeis University, Brown University, Bryn Mawr College, Case Western Reserve University, Claremont Graduate School (Claremont College, California), Columbia University, Cornell University, Drew University, Duke University, Emory University, Florida State University, Georgia State University, Harvard University, Indiana University, Indiana University of Pennsylvania, Johns Hopkins University, Kansas State University, Lehigh University, the Loyola University of Chicago, Marquette University, Michigan State University, New York University, Northwestern University, Pennsylvania State University, Princeton University, Purdue University, Rice University, St. John's University, St. Louis University, Stanford University, the State Universities of New York at Binghamton, Buffalo, and Stony Brook, Syracuse University, Temple University, Tulane University, the University of Alabama, the University of Arkansas, the University of Bristol (England), the Universities of California at Berkeley, Davis, Los Angeles and Santa Barbara, the University of Connecticut, the University of Denver, the University of Florida, the University of Georgia, the University of Houston, the University of Illinois at Urbana-Champaign, the University of Kansas, the University of Massachusetts, the University of Michigan, the University of Minnesota, the University of Nevada at Reno, the University of New Hampshire, the University of New Mexico, the University of North Carolina, the University of Notre Dame, the University of Oklahoma, the University of Oregon, the University of Pittsburgh, the University of Rochester, the University of South Carolina, the University of Southern California, the University of Southern Mississippi, the University of Toronto (Canada), the University of Virginia, the University of Washington, the University of Wisconsin, Vanderbilt University, the Victoria University of Manchester (England), West Virginia University, and Yale University.

It is to these friends, scholars, librarians, benefactors, and many more people that I wish to express my profound gratitude.

Tetsumaro Hayashi
Muncie, Indiana

"At the Flood"

RESEARCH OPPORTUNITIES IN FAULKNER STUDIES

by Richard F. Peterson

In many ways William Faulkner is the perfect subject, some might say the natural prey, for doctoral students and their dissertation directors. Among the major American novelists, he ranks first in reputation; and, for many scholars, he is the only American writer comparable to James Joyce, Marcel Proust, and Thomas Mann, undisputed masters of the modern novel.

Beyond his reputation, Faulkner offers, to borrow one of his favorite words, a myriad of attractive subjects for doctoral work. At his most daring and difficult, he is one of the most experimental writers of the modern age. The Sound and the Fury flows along in a stream-of-consciousness narrative similar to those in Ulysses and Mrs. Dalloway. As I Lay Dying, Light in August, and Absalom, Absalom! challenge the imagination with unique approaches to narrative form, the latter novel approaching aesthetic parable in its obsession with the art of story-telling. Even the later fiction, though not as compelling or accomplished as the earlier writing, presents several key critical questions and problems, especially in Go Down, Moses, the Snopes trilogy, and A Fable, Faulkner's most ambitious and disturbing, if not disastrous, failure.

Yet Faulkner, as a Southern writer, represents the region in America most closely associated with romantic codes and traditions. If there is, as Faulkner claimed, one story that his fiction tells over and over again, it is that of the young, disillusioned hero obsessed with a dramatic episode, usually both foolhardy and doomed to failure, in the history of the South or an emotionally arresting event in his personal life. Either moment is so overwhelming that Faulkner's hero cannot prevail over the distant or immediate past or survive the present. Bayard Sartoris, Quentin Compson, and the Reverend Hightower are the most prominent among a number of characters so in love with the chivalry of the ante-bellum South that they become trapped by the values of a tradition anachronistic to modern life. Others, like Addie or her son Earl, Joe Christmas and Thomas Sutpen, never overcome a single act of betrayal in their lives whether it be a broken promise, a failure to receive a punishment for real or imagined sins, or a denial of entry or passage. Not only has Faulkner given his readers some of the most interesting narrative forms in modern fiction, he has used these forms to capture one of the most compelling stories in American literary history.

Faulkner's writing has also provided doctoral students with a number of conflicting and often controversial subjects and ideas. His world is populated by tragic heroes, bumbling clowns, and rapacious villains. There are earth mothers to captivate the Jungian and outrage the feminist, poor whites, blacks, merchants, and fading aristocrats to attract the sociologist, and enough darkly pessimistic or doomed characters to excite the student of deterministic philosophies ranging from Calvinism to existentialism. And for those fascinated by the figure of the American Adam and his passage from innocence to experience, Faulkner often counters his theme of the Old South with man's primitive relationship with nature. There are not many meaningful father figures in Faulkner's stories, but Sam Fathers certainly lives up to his name in preparing Ike McCaslin for his encounter with the bear.

Another attractive feature of Faulkner is the derivative nature of his writing. Obviously, Faulkner fits well into comparative studies of Southern writers, especially like Flannery O'Connor, Carson McCullers, and William Styron. He also merits comparison to other American writers, Hawthorne and Twain, for example, and contemporaries like Sherwood Anderson, John Dos Passos, and Hemingway. Even though Faulkner was often evasive and deliberately misleading in his statements on influences, there are strong character and thematic traces from the Bible, Shakespeare, Dickens, Conrad, and T. S. Eliot in his work, and his experiments with narrative form owe far more to Joyce than he was willing to admit. Faulkner also compares well to Balzac, Proust, Mann, and Dostoyevsky, and has had his own share of influence on writers ranging from Sartre, Camus, and Butor to Ellison, Barth, and Pynchon.

Yet, even after considering the number of ways Faulkner appeals to the doctoral student and adding to that consideration the fact of the flood of graduate study in America in the 1960s and its spillover into the 1970s, it is still difficult to come to terms with the overwhelming number of dissertations written on Faulkner. Since several dissertations in the 1940s included Faulkner in their examination of Southern writers, there have been no fewer than 415 doctoral studies either studying Faulkner directly or approaching Faulkner as a contributor to some broad literary approach, theme, or tradition. During the 1950s, completed dissertations increased gradually from two or three a year to nine by 1959. In the 1960s, the number of Faulkner dissertations averaged about ten a year until the total leaped to 23 in 1968 and 24 in 1969. The flood of dissertations continued and actually increased for a time in the 1970s with 25 completed in 1970, 29 in 1971, 24 in 1972, 31, the highest total for any year, in 1973 and 1974 respectively, 27 in 1975, 25 in 1976, 26 in 1977, and 20 in 1978. There was a modest drop in production in the late seventies; in 1979, only nine dissertations were completed.

The treatment of Faulkner in the vast number of dissertations has followed predictable lines. In the 1950s, there were a number of studies on language, character, theme, and form including Olga Vickery's "The Novels of William Faulkner: Patterns of Perspective," directed by Federick J. Hoffman; Peter Swiggart's "Time and Structure in the Novels of William Faulkner," directed by Norman R. Pearson; Walter Slatoff's "Emphasis and Modes of Organization in the Fiction of William Faulkner: A Study in Patterns of Rhetoric and Perception," directed by John Arthos; John Longley's "Faulkner's Tragic Heroes," directed by Oscar Cargill; and Irving Malin's "William Faulkner: An Interpretation," directed by Richard P. Scowcrott--all destined for publication, most in revised form and with modified or shortened titles.

Also appearing in the 1950s were a number of dissertations on individual works by Faulkner. Initial honors go to Richard Eberly's critical analysis of The Sound and the Fury, completed in 1953, but by the end of the decade dissertations had been written on A Fable, The Unvanquished, and two on Absalom, Absalom! The first doctoral study of The Unvanquished deserves special mention because it was completed by James Meriwether under the directorship of Willard Thorp. Meriwether, of course, would go on to become the foremost Faulkner bibliographer and the director of a number of dissertations on textual and critical studies of individual works by Faulkner.

In the 1960s, the major increase in Faulkner dissertations firmly established certain patterns of study, but it also produced problems of duplication and repetition that would become more pronounced in the 1970s. More and more studies traced the thematic movement from the alienation and pessimism of the early fiction to the sense of responsibility and hopefulness in the later novels. Other dissertations took the opposite strategy, observing the intensity and experimentation of Faulkner's early work and the obvious decline in power and quality in his later fiction. Myth, history, and time attracted considerable attention, as did subjects like Faulkner's humor, his character types, especially his females and Negroes (the word was changed to blacks by the 1970s), and his narrative strategies.

Several more individual works, Sanctuary, Requiem for a Nun, Go Down, Moses, Light in August, and Sartoris, became the focal point for doctoral study, but there was no great increase in the quantity of single novel dissertations until 1969 when The Hamlet, The Wild Palms, and A Fable were selected for individual treatment. More evident in the 1960s were studies of special groupings of Faulkner's fiction. There were dissertations on Faulkner's short stories, his early fiction, the novels not located in Yoknapatawpha County, and the Snopes trilogy. Faulkner also instigated or appeared in a number of studies on broad literary topics, including the initiation theme, the escape motif, the use of the grotesque, the mythic method, the impressionistic or stream-of-consciousness novel, the biblical view of history, the sense of land nostalgia, obtuse narrators, fallen women, and even noble savages.

The most significant increase in the 1960s took place in the area of comparative study. Dissertations comparing Faulkner and Joyce appeared in both 1968 and 1969, while another 1969 doctoral study traced the similarities between Dubliners and Go Down, Moses. Doctoral candidates also discovered similarities between Faulkner's work and the writings of Bergson, Kirkegaard, Sartre, Melville, Twain, Zola, Conrad, and Butor as well as a number of other novelists and philosophers. There were also dissertations completed on Faulkner's wasteland period, his use of the classics, his debt to modern novelists, his relation to modern French fiction, and his position and reputation in American literary history.

While the flow of dissertations on Faulkner increased dramatically in the 1960s, especially toward the end of the decade, the doctoral work in the 1970s turned into a deluge. The familiar themes and patterns were worked, reworked, and overworked. Studies of individual novels and comparative studies proliferated. Indeed, the amount of repetition increased to the point that it was obvious even within the individual years of the decade. Character studies repeated themselves and even extended into the bizarre. There were character indexes, ten dissertations on women, seven on blacks, and at least one work and sometimes more on parent-child relationships, young males, young protagonists, early heroines, redeemers, hero-archetypes, Indians, prisoners, social outcasts, local law enforcement officers, villains, storytellers, and narrative personalities. Religious, historical, and linguistic studies also appeared frequently, and most of the philosophical and literary fads of the 1970s turned up in Faulkner dissertations.

In 1970, doctoral candidates wrote nine dissertations on individual novels, including three on Light in August, and two more on Faulkner's short stories. By the end of the decade, nearly every major and minor full-length work by Faulkner had been treated, with the obvious choices, The Sound and the Fury, As I Lay Dying, Light in August, Absalom, Absalom!, and Go Down, Moses, receiving most of the attention. In the midst of all this activity on single works of fiction, James Meriwether at the University of South Carolina directed textual and critical studies of A Fable, The Hamlet, Requiem for a Nun, Soldiers' Pay, Light in August, The Town and the Mansion, Mosquitoes, and Flags in the Dust. While the number appears excessive, some of the dissertations, emulating the success of Thomas McHaney's work on The Wild Palms completed in 1969, have eventually been published. In a period of excess, when thematic studies of individual novels were overdone, textual studies, especially those directed by Meriwether, have proven especially valuable in Faulkner scholarship.

Perhaps no area illustrates the flood of doctoral work on Faulkner better than the comparative study. Faulkner has always been a favorite target for comparatists because of the derivative nature of his fiction, but the number of dissertations and the amount of repetition of the past decade strongly suggest that the hunt has been out of control. During the 1970s, Faulkner has been compared in doctoral studies to Balzac, Hawthorne, Dostoyevsky, Flannery O'Connor, Claude Simon, Simon again, Conrad, Bergson, Dickens, Conrad again, Hemingway, Uwe Johnson, John Barth, Conrad once more, Twain, Sherwood Anderson, Mann, Dickens twice more in 1978, O'Connor again, Hardy, Hawthorne again, and Simon once more.

Besides these studies comparing Faulkner to a single writer, there were many dissertations in which Faulkner appeared as one of a number of writers sharing a common theme, narrative approach, or character type. While the regional approach, usually linking Faulkner with O'Connor, McCullers, Warren, or Styron, has been the most frequent comparative study, others have ranged over a rich variety of writers and subjects. Faulkner's villains have been compared to those of Hawthorne and Henry James, his lost ladies to Hawthorne's, James's, and Fitzgerald's, his inarticulate characters to Hemingway's and Fitzgerald's, and his families to Wharton's, Dreiser's, Cather's, and Lewis's. Studies have found Christian humanism in Faulkner, Joyce, and Flannery O'Connor, romantic individualism in Faulkner, Henry Adams, Ellison, Belyj, and Pasternak, and the romantic tradition in the works of Faulkner, Roethke, and Bellow. Others have discovered existential themes in Faulkner, Joyce, Kafka, and Dostoyevsky, a humor of frenzy in Faulkner, Dostoyevsky, and Beckett, narcissism in Faulkner, Virginia Woolf, Fitzgerald, and Graeme Gibson, and a sense of alienation in Faulkner, Woolf, and Beckett. Faulkner's female interior monologues have been studied along with those of Joyce and Woolf, his cosmographic narrators with those of writers ranging from Homer to Joyce, his multilinear novels with Dos Passos', Doblin's, and Kieppen's, his short story cycles with Hemingway's, Steinbeck's, and O'Connor's, his novels of vision with D. H. Lawrence's and Patrick White's, and his experiments on the trilogy with Sartre's and Dos Passos'. There have been comparative studies of the treatment of nature and the human body in Faulkner, Lawrence, and Mann, the rebirth motif in Faulkner, Hawthorne, Stephen Crane, Henry James, and Ellison, and the use of time in Faulkner, Wordsworth, Woolf, T. S. Eliot, and Yeats.

All that was missing in the mass of comparative studies in the 1970s was a dissertation comparing all these studies to each other. Such a study would have had little trouble showing that doctoral work comparing Faulkner to other writers had reached the saturation point by the end of the decade. In reality, Faulkner graduate studies by 1979 had reached the state where familiarity and repetition existed in all areas. This condition had taken hold in the early seventies, especially in 1973 and 1974, when the total dissertations for the two years came to 62. In 1973, there were ten comparative studies, several character analyses, as well as the inevitable dissertations on vision, myth, history, time, and narrative. In 1974, besides studies of Calvinism, the grotesque, ethics, aesthetics, and the expected number of comparative and character studies, there were several dissertations completed on individual works by Faulkner.

Obviously, the major problem in Faulkner graduate study runs parallel to the dilemma facing doctoral programs in the English profession in the 1980s. There have been simply too many dissertations, too much repetition in literary criticism, at a time when there have been too few jobs and too little opportunity to teach literature and to publish research. In 1973, the same year that 31 dissertations were completed on Faulkner, many of them on subjects already treated in earlier doctoral studies, a number of colleges and universities in America were facing the ordeal of firing faculty, even those with tenure, because of declining financial support and fading student enrollment.

This does not necessarily mean that Faulkner graduate study has reached a dead end or even that a moratorium should be declared. It does mean, however, that greater selectivity and judgment needs to be taken by both doctoral candidates and their dissertation directors. Dissertations on character, for example, have been interesting and useful and some have eventually been published. Yet there have been so many character studies already, especially on women and blacks, that future analyses should be limited--perhaps by asking the candidate to locate and read all the dissertations already completed on the proposed subject.

New proposals for thematic and structural studies need to be put through the same scrutiny. Another dissertation on Faulkner's religious quest or his journey to self-discovery would be difficult to justify as would further study of Faulkner's use of history, myth, or time. Proposed dissertations on Faulkner's experiments with narrative form, especially the Bergsonian nature of his work or the stream-of-consciousness writing in his novels, also need to be questioned. Once again, this is not to say that work on these challenging subjects should not be done in the future. The recent emphasis on new theories of language and literary form and the concentration on the relationship between the reader and the work of fiction will no doubt generate new doctoral activity in some familiar areas of Faulkner studies, at least because of the need to apply postmodern critical thought to literature. And a new approach, but one fully aware of past scholarship, should always find a place in Faulkner graduate study.

Dissertations on single novels or collections of short stories have also reached the point of saturation, even those on early or late works. Another proposed doctoral study of The Sound and the Fury, As I Lay Dying, Light in August, Absalom, Absalom!, or Go Down, Moses should take into account the great amount of work already completed on each one of these novels. Textual studies of individual works have proven fruitful in most cases, but many have already been done and several have been published. The territory is simply drying up in spite and because of the excellent work done in the past by doctoral students.

As frequent as character, thematic, structural, and single-novel dissertations have become, no area rivals the Faulkner comparative study for repetition. Already listed in this essay are the numerous ways in which Faulkner has been placed within a group of writers perceived as united by some theme or approach to writing fiction. There is always one opening, however, one constant possibility for comparative study--the influence of Faulkner on the writing of contemporary novelists. Also needed at this point in Faulkner scholarship is a book like Hugh Kenner's The Pound Era or Robert Martin Adams' Afterjoyce that places Faulkner within the context of the major movements and ideas in modern art and traces his role in influencing and possibly changing the patterns of modern literature. While this kind of study is probably too demanding for a doctoral student some of the groundwork for such a book could very well be done in a dissertation.

The basic problem today in Faulkner graduate studies, however, is not so much finding new and exciting subjects as it is limiting the number of dissertations on what has now become the too familiar patterns and approaches to Faulkner's work. Practical considerations alone, the diminishing job market and the shrinking opportunities for graduate study, argue for a significant reduction in doctoral studies of Faulkner. Simply stated, there have been too many Faulkner dissertations. Doctoral students and their dissertation directors will have to be more selective, more willing to pay close attention to what has already been done than they have been in the past.

Yet Faulkner, like Shakespeare and Joyce, remains one of the most attractive and demanding figures for doctoral work, and he will continue to excite the imagination of the beginning scholar. For these reasons alone, Faulkner graduate studies still need to be supported. The doctoral student, however, should be aware of the current trends in Faulkner scholarship, the patterns of study evident in journal publications, particularly those devoted partly or exclusively to Faulkner studies. The candidate should also take note of the recent publications of books, whether or not they began as dissertations, whether or not they break new ground or extend a controversy, debate, or study of a complex and challenging topic.

While the expansive days of the late 1960s and early 1970s are gone, the present state and future prospects of Faulkner graduate studies have their own advantages. In the 1980s there should be far less repetition and far more awareness of past dissertations. T. S. Eliot's advice in "Tradition and the Individual Talent" to a new generation of poets seems more than applicable to today's graduate student interested in Faulkner:

> what happens when a new work of art is created is something that happens simultaneously to all the works of art which preceded it. The existing monuments form an ideal order among themselves, which is modified by the introduction of the new (the really new) work of art among them. The existing order is complete before the new work arrives; for order to persist after the supervention of novelty, the whole existing order must be, if ever so slightly, altered; and so the relations, proportions, values of each work of art toward the whole are readjusted; and this is conformity between the old and the new. Whoever has approved this idea of order, of the form of European, of English literature will not find it preposterous that the past should be altered by the present as much as the present is directed by the past. And the poet who is aware of this will be aware of great difficulties and responsibilities.

WILLIAM FAULKNER: DISSERTATION ABSTRACTS

001 The Decline of the Southern Gentleman Character As He Is Illustrated in Novels by Present-Day Southern Novelists / Kenneth ENGLAND, Vanderbilt University, 1941 (Richmond Croom Beatty) no DAI entry.

002 Freudian Influence in the American Autobiographical Novel / Ruel Elton FOSTER, Vanderbilt University, 1941 (Richmond Croom Beatty) no DAI entry.

003 The Material of Abnormal Psychology in Some Contemporary English and American Novels / Thomas P. CARPENTER, Stanford University, 1946 (Yvor Winters) no DAI entry.

004 Social Attitudes in Five Contemporary Southern Novelists: Erskine Caldwell, William Faulkner, Ellen Glasgow, Caroline Gordon, and T. S. Stribling / Althea C. CATER, University of Michigan, 1946 (Joe Lee Davis) no DAI entry.

005 The Negro in Southern Fiction, 1920-1940 / Margaret J. Wormley, Boston University, 1948 (T. R. Mather) no DAI entry.

006 A History of the Recent Translations of the American Novel into Spanish / Thomas E. BERRY, University of Pittsburgh, 1949, no DAI entry.

007 The Problem of Character in the Development of Theme in the Novels and Short Stories of William Faulkner / Dorothy N. OVERLY, University of Chicago, 1950 (Walter Blair) no DAI entry.

008 America in Literature, 1920-1940 / A. F. M. WOUTERS, Cornell University, 1950 (H. W. Thompson) no DAI entry.

009 Faulkner's Conflicting Galaxies: A Study in Literary Polarity / Albert G. HOFAMMANN, Jr., University of Pennsylvania, 1951 (Mattias A. Shaaber) no DAI entry.

010 The World of War / Ward L. Miner, University of Pennsylvania, 1951 (E. Sculley Bradley) no DAI entry.

011 Some Aspects of the Treatment of Negro Characters by Five Representative American Novelists: Cooper, Melville, Tourgee, Glasgow, Faulkner / Charles Hampton NILON, University of Wisconsin, 1952 (Harry Hayden Clark) no DAI entry.

012 Immediacy, Suspense, and Meaning in William Faulkner's The Sound and The Fury: An Experiment in Critical Analysis / Ralph Dunbar

EBERLY, University of Michigan, 1953 (John Artuos).
The purpose of this study is to describe a method of criticizing fiction and to apply it to William Faulkner's The Sound and the Fury. This method consists of evaluation based upon coordinated, intensive analysis: its object is to show how the major narrative techniques used in a short story or novel affect reader-interest. The need for such a method arises from the variety and intricacy of the devices that fiction-writers employ and from the difficulty of arriving at valid judgments by considering only random aspects of fiction.

Chapter I of the study sets forth the method in detail. First, two related assumptions are presented: that fiction aspires chiefly to capture the reader's interest and that the critic can profitably use interest as a criterion. Interest has at least three major components: immediacy, suspense, and meaning. "Immediacy" is the reader's response to fictional events almost as if they were emotionally charged experiences of living persons; "suspense" is his desire for information that the novel temporarily withholds; and "meaning" is his awareness of the book's total comment upon the "actual" world. The effects of various narrative techniques upon immediacy, suspense, and meaning are described in detail. It is maintained that analysis of a novel's creation of immediacy and suspense leads directly to evaluation: the greater the immediacy or the suspense, the greater the interest. The study of meaning, however, requires two steps: first determining what the meaning is (making due allowance here for range and tone), and then evaluating that meaning. For this evaluation two criteria are suggested: complexity (the variety of aspects of human existence reflected in the total meaning of the novel, and, within each of these areas, the range and adequacy of the comment) and coherence (the integration of the various aspects of meaning and their freedom from internal contradictions).

Chapter II illustrates the method by analyzing The Sound and the Fury, a novel sufficiently complex and sufficiently controversial to provide a good test; the major narrative techniques of this book are examined in their relation to immediacy, suspense, and meaning. The examination indicates that by using specific narration almost continuously, by concentrating time, place, and means of perception, and by making skillful use of spiral movement, dialogue, and evocative detail, this novel creates a powerful immediacy. The Sound and the Fury appears less successful, however, in producing suspense; even sympathetic readers may object to certain unnecessary confusions. In its total meaning the book bids strongly for the reader's interest: by commenting upon sociological, psychological, ethical, metaphysical, and theological aspects of the "actual" world and by achieving a wide range and a high degree of adequacy in most of these areas, it gains a satisfying complexity; and (with one important exception) it interweaves its meaning coherently.

Conclusions about the value of this method of criticism will depend upon the contribution that it makes to the reader's understanding and appreciation of The Sound and the Fury and upon the results obtained when the method is applied hereafter to other books. [Order No. 5665: 206 pages. DAI, 13A (Jan.-Dec. 1953), 806-07.]

013 The Novels of William Faulkner: Patterns of Perspective / Olga Weetland VICKERY, University of Wisconsin, 1953 (Frederick J. Hoffman) no DAI entry.

014 William Faulkner: Studies in Form and Idea / Karl E. ZINK, University of Washington, 1953 (Arnold Stein) no DAI entry.

015 The World of Faulkner's Imagination / Donald Albyn DIKE, Syracuse University, 1954 (David H. Owen).

By exploring the imaginative possibilities of a restricted situation, Faulkner has created out of Yoknapatawpha County an image of mortal life which embodies the conditions of that life. His subject-matter does not reduce to the decaying Old South; it is, rather, forms of experience for which the sense of cultural crisis promotes a special awareness. The County's inhabitants are like celebrants of a mass, internal to the structure of the plenary situation whose meaning they ritually enact; they earn their identities from participating in happenings which are larger than their several motives and insights. Such participation begins as passion and defines itself through role; attitude is socialized as vocation. By performing reciprocally related roles, which mediate between private and public experience, the characters asseverate their stakes in reality, testify to the risks and commitments of being human, and recreate values out of the trammels of the present, the bequests of the past.

Faulkner's traditionalism is not in his opinions but in his sensibility, not in preference for the past but in the sense that the past is inseparable from the present and a condition of the future. In his imagination, history, a mode of time and reminder of death, is one dimension or moral identity. Complemented by an equal conviction of nature, a mode of space and image of anonymous life, this view informs all the mature work. But it is aware of alternative attitudes. Absalom, Absalom! is about a man who tries to create merely a future, to make history by denying history. This is to assume the absolute efficacy of will, its superiority to any order and freedom from any sanctions. It is to abstract from history a series of solvable problems, to pretend out of reality the power that animates it, to admit to greater evil than temporary failure.

The world of Faulkner's imagination resists such abstractions and destroys such illusions. From it, evil cannot be dismissed. The fall, nature's divestment of innocence, is history's condition. The present inherits responsibility both for and to the past, and on its discharge the future depends. Isaac McCaslin and Bayard Sartoris find that maturity obligates their redemption of paternal sins; Joe Christmas and Charles Bon, more unfortunate, must search for fathers to redeem. All four, the accepted and the rejected, are aware that their commitment is to the human family, that only by figuring in its order can they realize their meaning. The temptation to seek innocence in dissociation from mankind is great, but the responsible among Faulkner's heroes assent to their mortality: their doomed tenure in a world of unrewarding burdens, births and deaths, enigmatic change.

The dimensions of this world are both interdependent and opposed. Through history man stylizes his responses to nature, attempts to cope with a quality from which he is separated and which often seems to threaten his moral identify. In consolidating that identity, he repudiates its condition or tries to appropriate it in his own image. But by doing so he deprives his history of a relation to reality and reduces its categories to illusion. This conflict, the basis for Isaac McCaslin's relinquishments, recurs throughout the fiction and threatens to disintegrate Faulkner's world, as it does the Compson family. Yet equally strong is a centripetal impulse to reunion: of historical man with his natural source, of fathers with their sons, of action with innocence. The love and enduring capacity for sacrifice which are the core of the impulse cannot accomplish a mythical reconciliation, but they suffice for the world's continuing atonement. [Order No. 10,408; 213 pages. DAI, 15A (Jan.-June 1955), 265.]

016 Difficult Contemporary Short Stories: William Faulkner, Katherine Anne Porter, Dylan Thomas, Eudora Welty, and Virginia Woolf / Allen Wallace GRAVES, University of Washington, 1954 (Porter G. Perrin).

This study presents a new method of analyzing difficult contemporary short stories which in their obscurity read like abstruse modern poetry. It is a method of analysis which instead of approaching the obscurities through critical terms such as Atmosphere, Character, Key Moment, and Conflict, faces directly each difficulty as it appears in context in each story, and makes a direct assessment as to (1) precisely what the obscurity is, and (2) whether it is justified artistically.

One common factor in the stories under study is that they neglect the obligation of keeping the reader informed at all times as to what characters are before him and who they are; where and how they are doing it, which is in the main traditional obligation of fiction. The stories in this study deviate noticeably from this tradition. They are analyzed word by word and each time a story does not reasonably fulfill this narrative flow, the stoppage is noted. As a result of this analysis, some conclusions are possible regarding what techniques make these stories obscure, and what peculiar artistic effects are attained through the use of these obscure techniques. These conclusions furthermore suggest possible faulty techniques, and show in what areas and by what authors apparent unnecessary obscurity occurs.

The eighteen stories analyzed in this study are Faulkner's "Barn Burning," "Carcassonne," "Hair," "Red Leaves," and "Was;" Miss Porter's "Flowering Judas," "He," and "Pale Horse, Pale Rider"; Thomas' "The Burning Baby," "The Orchards," and "Patricia, Edith, and Arnold"; Miss Welty's "Asphodel," "The Burning," "Death of a Traveling Salesman," and "The Wide Net," and Mrs. Woolf's "The Duchess and the Jeweller," "A Haunted House," and "The Shooting Party."

Thirteen of these stories are chosen for analysis because they seem particularly obscure; the remaining five--one per author--are chosen for contrast as representative "easy" stories. Some of the stories are very easy, as Miss Porter's "He," in which there are no stops at all. Some are very difficult, as Faulkner's "Was," in which there are 84 obscurities or Thomas' "The Orchards," in which there are 90. Among these 18 stories there are a total of 633 stoppages of narrative flow recorded. These obscurities are grouped into 20 different types of difficulties which contribute to this slowing of narrative flow. These types fall into five categories: limited presentation of facts, abstruse grammar and structure, difficult imagery, peculiarities of psychic process, and questions of significance.

The worth of this critical method of grouping of obscurities into specific types is revealed when these types are charted for an individual story against an average curve of occurrence for all 18 stories. The charts of single stories reveal in what areas each story deviates most noticeably from the other difficult stories in this study, and also how each story deviates from traditionally "easy" prose.

A major part of this study consists of essays on the five authors, in which the obscurity of their prose under study is discussed in detail, and in which unusual artistic aims and possible lack of aims are suggested. It is concluded from these analyses that the modes of expression of realism and symbolism, long common in fiction, have in many of these stories been muted into a lyric expression which appears to be the greatest single mutation of form which the short story has lately undergone. [Order No. 10,004; 187 pages. DAI, 14A (July-Dec. 1954), 2067-68.]

017 A Study of Metaphor and Simile in the American Literary Novel and
  the American Popular Novel, 1911-1940 / Claire M. HIGGINS, New York University, 1954 (Louise M. Rosenblatt) no DAI entry.

018 An Inquiry into the Nature of Plot in the 20th Century Novel / Arthur
  HONEYWELL, University of Chicago, 1954 (Richard P. McKeon) no DAI entry.

019 The American Novel in France / Jane V. MORIARTY, University of Wisconsin, 1954 (Henry A. Pochmann) no DAI entry.

020 A Theological Critique of the Interpretation of Man in the Fiction and Drama of William Faulkner, Ernest Hemingway, Jean-Paul Sartre, and Albert Camus / Edwin A. PENICK, Yale University, 1954 (Albert Cook Outler) no DAI entry.

021 Time and Structure in the Novels of William Faulkner / Charles P. SWIGGART, Yale University, 1954 (Norman H. Pearson) no DAI entry.

022 William Faulkner and the Negro / William Clark DOSTER, University of Florida, 1955 (Harry R. Warfel) no DAI entry.

023 The World of William Faulkner / Frank Mitchell HOADLEY, University of Oklahoma, 1955 (Victor A. Elconin).

In 1950, William Faulkner was awarded the Nobel Prize for literature. In his acceptance speech for this award, Faulkner clearly stated his broad faith in humanity. "I believe," he said, "that man will not merely endure; he will prevail. He is immortal, not because he alone among creatures has an inexhaustible voice but because he has a soul, a spirit capable of compassion and sacrifice and endurance." To the casual reader of Faulkner's works this speech may seem somewhat inconsistent with his fiction. A close examination of his fiction reveals, however, a gradual shift from a pessimistic world view to one of limited optimism. His 17 novels fall roughly into three periods: in the early period man is doomed and damned; in the middle period he merely endures; and in the final period Faulkner affirms that he will prevail. The purpose of this dissertation is to trace the development and movement of this changing world view.

Although Faulkner is considered a regional writer by most critics, the reader must have an understanding of the Yoknapatawpha myth. Within the myth, the South labors under the twin curses of slavery and exploitation of the land. The present generation, corrupted by the amorality of modernism, is unable to identify itself with its cultural heritage. Unwilling to accept its moral responsibility, this generation withdraws into a suicidal pessimism and, abjuring its ethical traditions, views the degenerate state of mankind with detached irony. The few characters who retain the old values of "courage and honor and hope and pride and compassion and pity and sacrifice" are so vitiated by the curse that they are easy prey to the ruthless advance of the machine age and its attendant robots.

The ability to endure is first evident among the Negroes and poor whites. The Negroes, persecuted and exploited, have salvaged the old values and beliefs and escaped the time-compulsiveness of modern man. The poor whites, who must struggle to glean an existence from the stubborn earth, have somehow, by their contact with the land, escaped the futility of the planter-aristocrats. In Go Down, Moses, the land assumes almost mystical proportions in reclaiming man from his lost state.

The theme of atonement gradually emerges as a positive force in Faulkner's world view. If he would attain salvation, man must expiate through his suffering not only his own sins but also the inherited sins of the past, the responsibility for which he shares with his forefathers. This is the hard lesson that Temple Drake learns in Requiem for a Nun.

Finally, human and spiritual love become the forces which will elevate man above the animal and differentiate him from the machine. Only when man eliminates his racial bigotry and establishes universal brotherhood will the curse be lifted. In his final novel, A Fable, which treats the second incarnation of Christ, man is given the opportunity to fulfill himself through spiritual affirmation. The irony, however, persists, for rather than avail himself of this opportunity, man lends moral support to the second crucifixion. Yet this irony is mitigated by the fact that the crucifixion is an ambivalent symbol, superficially pessimistic, but within the context of the Christian myth completely optimistic. Christ dies that man may attain salvation. Man is no longer, as in the earlier novels, the victim of a cosmic joke, a pawn moved about by the malignant player. He is a free moral agent with the potential of reclaiming his lost dignity. Faulkner's future novels may well chronicle the way in which man exercises this potential. [Order No. 00-15453; 327 pages. DAI, 16A (Jan.-June 1956), 338.]

024 The Treatment of the Negro Woman as a Major Character in American Novels, 1900-1950 / Beulah V. JOHNSON, New York University, 1955 (Louise M. Rosenblatt) no DAI entry.

025 William Faulkner and Existentialism / Marjorie Kimball McCORQUODALE, University of Texas at Austin, 1956, no DAI entry.

026 William Faulkner's A Fable / Sylvan SCHENDLER, Northwestern University, 1956 (Richard Ellmann).
This study is an attempt to deal systematically with Faulkner's most recent and probably most misunderstood work. In Chapter I of the dissertation, the writer surveys the critical reception of A Fable. Most critics of the novel vigorously attacked Faulkner, his art, his intellect, his rhetoric, his handling of the Christ theme, and his view of history. A few cautiously hinted at the novel's significance; one felt that it was a masterpiece. It is the purpose of Chapters II through VII of the dissertation to demonstrate that most of the adverse criticism is not justified. When Faulkner's methods and purposes are understood, and when the effects he does finally achieve are correctly read, the hostile judgments of the critics can be seen to rest upon misconceptions and misreading, understandable in the case of so complex a novel. These chapters present a detailed analysis of the form and structure of A Fable, of the novel's theme, of certain important oppositions and configurations which are key to the novel's meaning, of Faulkner's use of myth, and of his satire upon the military. Despite the critics views that he is no intellectual, Faulkner's intellect can be seen to be everywhere in control of the novel. Furthermore, A Fable is no isolated phenomenon in Faulkner's work, but a novel which makes use of many of the important techniques of Faulkner's earlier work.

A Fable is an ironic version of the Christ myth. Using a thematic, or dialectical method, Faulkner develops the opposed themes through which the ethical meaning of the novel emerges. He aims at and achieves tragedy through the pattern of recognition, revolt, defeat, and renewed revolt, and through a remarkable adjustment of the serious and the grotesque, of ritual and humor. The sense of tragedy and the call to ethical action are allied, for A Fable exhorts men to act in the face of certain defeat.

Chapter VIII of the dissertation demonstrates that Faulkner's ethical thought can be understood in terms of the similarities of response, the characteristic concerns, and the modes of analysis of the human condition which are common to him and to certain existentialist thinkers. Faulkner's views are related to those of Kierkegaard, Marcel, Jaspers, Sartre, Simone de Beauvoir, and Camus to show how his thought is part of their community of belief. From existentialist thought as from Faulkner there emerges an ethics of choice, responsibility, and revolt.

Faulkner's recent public statements may be understood in terms of the ethics of A Fable, a moral position which has undergone considerable development since he wrote Soldiers' Pay. A Fable represents the culmination of Faulkner's ethical thought. [Order No. 00-19,038; 226 pages. DAI, 17A (Jan. -June 1957), 366-67.]

027 Emphases and Modes of Organization in the Fiction of William Faulkner: A Study in Patterns of Rhetoric and Perception / Walter Jacob SLATOFF, University of Michigan, 1956 (John Arthos).

The purpose of this study has been to discover and describe some of the fundamental elements which shape and define the fictional world of William Faulkner. Beyond this, the study is concerned with the implications of these elements with respect to the general nature, coherence, and quality of Faulkner's art and view of life.

In view of the fundamental disagreements in Faulkner criticism the effort has been made to discover elements whose persistence throughout Faulkner's works is unquestionable. The study is governed, also, by the belief that it is helpful to think of a fictional world as ordered and characterized by modes of perception and thought which at once shape and are evident in the rhetoric which presents that world.

Part I describes certain persistent elements of rhetoric and perception which significantly shape Faulkner's world. Summarized briefly: Faulkner continually renders a great variety of events in terms of motion, immobility, and velocity, and he persistently juxtaposes or simultaneously suggests motion and immobility, and contrasting velocities. A persistent emphasis upon sound and silence further shapes Faulkner's world. He tends to conceive of silence as a container for sound, repeatedly presents the two conditions as existing simultaneously, and often suggests them simultaneously by oxymorons. Together, the emphases upon motion and immobility and upon sound and silence form part of a more general antithesis of quiescence and turbulence which so dominates Faulkner's presentation that it must be considered a fundamental part of his vision. Whether he is describing a scene, life history, physical action, facial expression, tone of voice, or state of mind, he is far more likely to report its degree of quiescence or turbulence than any of its other characteristics. Usually these descriptions involve a tension between quiescent and turbulent elements. In general, the condition of unreleased tension, of temporarily or permanently frustrated impulse, seems to fascinate Faulkner and is perhaps the most characteristic state of being presented in his works. Above all, Faulkner's world is shaped by antithesis between entities of all kinds--rhetorical, ideological, physical, psychological. His treatment of concepts and themes, his presentation of characters both by story and rhetoric, and many of his rhetorical constructions are all characterized by varieties of antithesis, and especially by the peculiarly strained and irreconcilable qualities of antithesis and tension that exist between the terms of an oxymoron.

Part II considers the effects and implications of these persistent elements. It is contended that Faulkner's works are addressed primarily to the senses and emotions, and that they not only will not bear careful critical analysis, but are deliberately designed to prevent full intellectual comprehension of them. Faulkner's complexities of form, unlike those of other moderns like Joyce and Woolf, have an essentially evocative function. His attitudes toward art, reason, and truth are explicable and justifiable only as Romantic ones. Up to a point his works are informed by a view of life as ambiguous and complex, and by intense contradictory feelings that life and art cannot be and yet must be meaningful. These feelings help to explain his disturbing movements toward both order and chaos; his persistent use of the oxymoron, the figure which most nearly moves in both directions; and his ability to treat his art both as a plaything and a dedication. They help to explain, also, the divergent and contradictory estimates and interpretations of his works. Finally, however, Faulkner's works are governed by his temperament rather than by particular views or feelings, a temperament characterized largely by its response to tension and opposition, its urge toward profusion, and its reluctance to make choices. [Publication No.: 00-18650; 269 pages. DAI (Microfilm, 16/12 [1950]), 2461.]

028 An Analysis of the Imagery of William Faulkner's Absalom, Absalom! / Joseph Alexander WIGLEY, Northwestern University, 1956 (Wallace A. Bacon).

Imagery in this study is defined as words and word combinations which produce sensory impressions, whether in figurative language such as metaphor or in nonfigurative, "direct" images. Approximately four thousand images were listed and examined to ascertain whether through repetition they developed into meaningful patterns. An exact count of images is impossible, because, for example, a clause consisting of adjective, noun, and verb may create a single image in one context, but each of its words may in later contexts be found to cluster with separate groups. Similarly, the number of possible classification is infinite. The procedure in this study was to focus on those clusters which appear to function in rendering the meanings of the novel, while taking care not to attempt to apply any preconceived patterns of symbolism. The following report can suggest in only the most general way the findings of the study.

Religious imagery, although plentiful, does not cluster to a major theme. The parallel with the biblical David and Absalom story is chiefly effective in suggesting the contrast between the "loving" David and the "loveless" Sutpen. Christ symbolism is frequent but not focused on a single character. An opposition between liquid, symbolizing romanticism, and stone, representing coldness and impassivity, falls short of developing into a major motif because it does not continue into the denouement. The author also experiments with stone as symbolic of immortality, and with bodies of water as symbolic of time. The imagery does not support critical judgments that the novel reflects a conflict between the land and exploiting man.

Five major image clusters were discovered, each initiated in the first chapter of the novel and continuing throughout: (1) "the effort to see"; (2) "man as animal"; (3) "scent and breathing". (4) "wars"; and (5) "the guarded door." Each is created by hundreds of images that group together to create significant themes.

The effort to see involves a number of characters, but principally Quentin Compson, the twentieth century youth upon whom the Sutpen legend is projected. In its inception in the first chapter it hints at the novel's technique of piecemeal revelation. In its full development it suggests that interpretations of history may be inaccurate, and that facts cannot be understood without an understanding of man. It suggests that the vision of the South, and to an extent that of man in general, is limited and myopic.

The animal imagery is used to intensify the reader's opposition to miscegenation, the threat of which is a central concern of the novel. It also serves to remind that propagation without love is an animal rather than a human act.

The scent-and-breathing motif reminds us that the flowering of life leads inevitably to death and decay, and suggests that without love the only alternative to complete decay is the sterility symbolized by snow.

The war theme reminds the reader not only that the Civil War has colored the thinking and attitudes of the South up into the 20th century, but that all human activity involves warlike conflict which must be tempered with love and compassion.

The guarded door is a symbol of the female, the secrecy and privacy, and of status--hence of the family. In seeking the position so symbolized, which he lacked as a child, Sutpen was guilty of denying it to others; hence the ultimate collapse of his "design."

Analysis of the imagery of Absalom, Absalom! not only reveals some of the means by which the novel acquires its emotional intensity, but helps to justify the complex and unconventional structure. [Order No. 00-19607; 169 pages. DAI, 16A (1956), 2464.]

029 A Study of Humor in the Fiction of William Faulkner / Herman O. WILSON, University of Southern California, 1956 (B. R. McElderry) no DAI entry.

030 The New South and Five Southern Novelists, 1920-1950 / William M. BEASLEY, Vanderbilt University, 1957 (Richmond Croom Beatty) no DAI entry.

031 Faulkner's Tragic Heroes / John Lewis LONGLEY, Jr, New York University, 1957 (Oscar Cargill).

This dissertation is an examination of the tragic heroes of Faulkner. It attempts to dispose of the frequently-heard assertation that tragedy is impossible in the 20th century. It begins with the adjective "tragic" found in the discussions of the better, later Faulkner critics; plus the experience of katharsis in the reader. The presumably tragic characters are measured against the traditional criteria of Aristotle and later critics. In addition, an attempt is made to establish criteria for a tragic hero who is essentially modern. Of all Faulkner characters, three are found to meet the tragic criteria. These are John Sartoris, who is traditional; Joe Christmas, who is modern; and Thomas Sutpen, who meets all the criteria both ancient and modern. Most frequently the harmartia of each will consist of a gravely mistaken idea of his personal relation to the cosmos, and hubris is present, whatever its manifestation or direction may be in a given case.

Comparisons are made between Faulkner's heroes and such tragic figures as Oedipus, Agamemnon, and the tragic protagonists of Shakespeare. Once the heroes of Faulkner have been placed and evaluated, they are related to the overall pattern of the Yoknapatawpha chronicle. Here the suggestion is made that all Faulkner's heroes are a rubric or "epiphany" of his larger heroic conception: the legendary South. It is suggested that each Faulkner protagonist is symbolic of the South and thus the South is Faulkner's actual tragic protagonist. The South is then measured against the criteria previously employed in measuring the human protagonists.

Several appendices defining critical terms and tragic criteria are attached. There is a bibliography of Faulkner criticism and a larger bibliography in the area of tragedy in general. [Order No. 24,699; 128 pages. DAI, 18A (Jan.-March 1958), 1047.]

032 The Critical Reception of William Faulkner's Work in the United States: 1926-1950 / Perrin Holmes LOWREY, University of Chicago, 1957 (Walter Blair) no DAI entry.

033 William Faulkner: A Thematic Study / James L. ROBERTS, State University of Iowa, 1957 (Frank Clark Griffith).

Faulkner's early novels and stories reveal a world in which there is, or seems to be, no hope for humanity. His most recent fiction reveals a world in which there can be no lasting despair, for attention is focused on the innate greatness of mankind. As this reversal might lead us to expect, Faulkner's fiction in its overall meaning changed from a sterile world where pessimism and disillusionment are the inevitable fate of sensible men, to a more fertile world where man shall not only endure but also prevail. All of

Faulkner's fiction does not, of course, fit into the Yoknapatawpha saga. Nevertheless, even the earlier works will be found to be a part of this unified story of the changing world or the changing William Faulkner.

Faulkner's fiction reveals that he emphasized certain basic values throughout his work, and that even though his mythical world changed from hopeless to hopeful, or from a world to be viewed optimistically, the basic Faulknerian values remained a constant unifying force. These unifying values apply both to the saga and to the novels which lie outside the saga.

The individual novels and stories which make up this overall Faulkner story will reveal how his changing world affects both the technique and the final literary value of his work. During the period of pessimism, Faulkner penetrated deeply into psychological motivations and searched for the moral center of his characters' problems. He offered, however, no definite solution to the existing problems of the world. In contrast, the period of optimism is characterized by much less acute penetration and is replaced by over-simplified solutions which are not inherent in the theme of the work. Thematically, Faulkner's work may be divided into two broad categories: the period of pessimism which ends with the publication of The Hamlet in 1940 and a period of optimism which begins with Go Down, Moses in 1942. In view of achievement, however, his fiction is divided into four periods: (1) the earlier novels and sketches which depict a barren world but which are uncontrolled and inferior works; (2) the great novels and stories between 1929-1940 in which Faulkner penetrates deeply into the psychological mores of his characters; (3) the stories in the single volume Go Down, Moses, which investigate in sustained rhetoric the values man should live by; and finally, (4) the works since 1942 which are uncontrolled in their oversimplified solutions for the salvation of mankind.

Faulkner's later novels have been disappointingly inferior; therefore, to reaffirm our belief in his greatness, we must return to earlier works where we will find the vivid style, the innovations and experiments in technique, the mythical county, the vivid characters, and the universal themes which combine to yield novels of outstanding quality and which remind us again that Faulkner is one of the great creative writers of the 20th century. [Order No. 23,780; 342 pages. DAI, 23A (July-Dec. 1957), 3023.]

034 Whorls of Form in Faulkner's Fiction / Donald Hubert TRITSCHLER, Northwestern University, 1957 (Richard Ellmann).

This is a critical study of the theory and practice of indirection in William Faulkner's fiction. This analysis of Faulkner's roundabout presentation is primarily concerned with making his purposes and methods clear, but it is hoped also that this study will, by extension, illuminate a principal aspect of technique in contemporary fiction. Against the notion that Faulkner's involuted style is a kind of obscurity calculated to confound the reader is posed the thesis that the objectives in Faulkner's works can only be achieved in this way, that indirection is both a complex means and an intricate result of Faulkner's examination of the subtle condition of man.

The method is to induce the main technique of indirection from a study of certain of Faulkner's works and to test the theories thus derived by applying them to other fictional works by Faulkner. Two of the techniques examined are discontinuous lines of action that intersect as the plot develops and multiple points of view that gradually reveal character, with the attendant method of withholding information about both action and character; the third technique is symbolism that embodies and emanates thematic content. The main points of discussion are The Sound and the Fury, Absalom, Absalom!, As I Lay Dying, "Dry September," and Light in August (the last three are analyzed at length); many other works by Faulkner and some by other writers are considered briefly when relevant to the discussion of Faulkner's indirect mode.

The investigation of indirection reveals that it is not only a way of constituting experience but also represents a theory of reality that can be related to current psychological and philosophical theories that view reality as an integrated whole. For instance, the larger formal patterns achieved in and through indirection are repeated in the smaller patterns within those works. Or, conversely, the wholeness resulting from Faulkner's unification of smaller patterns within the larger one pervades the entire experience presented in a Faulkner novel. By seeming to lead the reader away from the essence of his vision, Faulkner is able to bring many related experiences to bear simultaneously upon the center of the plot.

It is this convergence upon and expansion from a single point in an action or a particular appearance of a symbol in the work that forces the reader to grasp the fictional experience as he might in life--complete and all at once. The withholding of information, for instance, permits the reader to experience the character's feelings as deepening levels of awareness are fathomed in Absalom, Absalom!. Again, multiple points of view in As I Lay Dying help the reader sense the separateness of the characters and also understand their fierce struggles to relate themselves to each other in their searches for their identities. Symbolism is another way of conveying the fictional experience--it is the significant object or act that embodies complex feelings and ideas here--and Light in August is analyzed thoroughly to demonstrate that it is on this symbolic level that Faulkner often relates the patterns of his works to archetypal patterns in human experience and thereby lends them universal significance.

The general conclusion of the study is that Faulkner's persistent use of this basic mode of fiction to unify subtle and disparate contemporary experiences represents his major contribution to literary form. Faulkner uses indirection to bring all time into the present and thereby achieves what he believes to be the goal of fiction: to arrest the continuous processes of life in the present, the IS. [Order No. 00-23,553; 308 pages. DAI, 17A (July-Dec. 1957), 3025.]

035 William Faulkner: An Interpretation / Irving Mesmin MALIN, Stanford University, 1958 (Richard P. Scowcroft).

In his review of The Portable Faulkner Robert Penn Warren suggests that we should study isolated incidents to discover the importance of compulsion and will in the work of Faulkner. But I believe that the themes of rigidity (compulsion) as a personal and social evil and the need to rebel against rigidity in order to gain freedom (will) are so important to Faulkner that he chooses to concretize them in myth. The "images" Warren mentions are, in a real sense, the underlying principles of structure in the major novels.

Faulkner calls the pattern which orders personal existence in basically rigid ways, the compulsive plan, the "design." In his novels the major characters adopt the pattern either in an intellectually conceived or in a subconsciously desired way. Faulkner's concern with the "design" is important because he can also relate the pattern of compulsion to his own Southern environment. His novels suggest that the organization of the social and religious systems of the South does not allow individual Southerners to realize their own potentialities for human completion.

Faulkner believes that he can concretize his theme of the rigidity of personal compulsion and social organization through the use of the father image. He believes that he can symbolize the rebellion against environmental evils, the quest for new values, through his use of the son.

In his novels Faulkner does not give his full attention to the many-sided problems of women because he is more interested in the conflict between father and son, "design" and quest for identity. He inspects man's world and the women who try to enter it, equating "feminine" women (those he knows least about) with nature.

The study of Faulkner's structural techniques of oppositions substantiates, I believe, my conception of his theme. His oppositions suggest the great tensions inherent in our age.

The Old Testament may supply traditional themes to his work, may lend images to his work. Faulkner is, nevertheless, a modern writer who is trying to do the same thing Joyce does in Ulysses. The very nature of Faulkner's parallelism of past and present is associated with his theme of order or--as in his major novels--the wrongness of rigidity as order. In Faulkner's myth there are two behavioral principles continually at battle with each other--flexibility (good) and rigidity (evil). Unlike the Hebrews he believes that rigidity frequently wins.

I demonstrate Faulkner's similarities to Freud in his delineation of ego and super-ego relationships, of psychological determinism in certain characters. But I try to show that Faulkner is closer to Jung than to Freud because of his concern with the "individuation process," involving meetings with "archetypes," closeness to the animal world and to the four elements, and his symbolic use of rituals.

My conclusion tries to indicate that, like most great writers, Faulkner has seen the essentially mythic qualities of his life in his art. [344 pages. DAI, 21A (July-Sept. 1960), 344. Note: To obtain copies of this thesis, Library of Congress Catalog Card No. 57-7383, please write directly to Stanford University Press, Stanford, California.]

036 The Place of The Unvanquished in William Faulkner's Yoknapatawpha Series / James B. MERIWETHER, Princeton University, 1958 (Willard Thorp).

William Faulkner's The Unvanquished is in many ways the most neglected of those of his works which deal with the imaginary Mississippi county of Yoknapatawpha. Published in a small edition in 1938 and long out of print, save in paperback, it has received very little critical or scholarly notice. No extended study of the work has previously appeared, though the need for such a study is reflected in present critical disagreement concerning both the merit of the book and its form.

In this dissertation I have attempted both to fill the need for an extended investigation of The Unvanquished and to make use of several new approaches, in that investigation, to some general problems of Faulkner scholarship. The center of the dissertation is the three chapters devoted to The Unvanquished. In the first of these is reviewed the history of the publication of the book, six of whose seven chapters had appeared first in short story versions. Also discussed in this chapter are bibliographic details of the publication of the book, foreign translations, and its initial critical reception, which was on the whole unfavorable. In the following two chapters, the "themes" of the book are discussed in detail. The emphasis here is upon the characters, particularly the members of the Sartoris family who are the principle characters of the book, and their qualities and their meaning. By showing how Faulkner revised the first six chapters from their short story versions, and by showing how the theme of the work are carefully developed and related to each other from chapter to chapter, I have tried to show that the unity of The Unvanquished requires its designation as a novel, and that most of the meaning is lost when its unity is overlooked.

The first and last chapters of the dissertation are concerned with one particular, and basic, approach to the question of the relationship of The Unvanquished to the other works of the Yoknapatawpha series. In the first chapter the members of the Sartoris family are discussed in the works which were published before The Unvanquished; in the last, these characters are discussed as they appear in the works which were published after 1938. Together, these two chapters attempt to relate The Unvanquished to the rest of Faulkner's works rather than to illuminate its meaning by discussing related works. The results of this approach, so carried out, show clearly that it is for several reasons highly dangerous to assume too great a unity in the Yoknapatawpha series, and the misreading of the individual work generally follows any attempt on the part of the critic to subordinate the unity of one work to the unity of the series as a whole.

The Appendices represent a further attempt to study The Unvanquished both in itself and in relation to the other works of the Yoknapatawpha series. Just what that series comprises is the subject of "Faulkner's Fiction: An Annotated Check List," which represents the first attempt in more than twenty years to distinguish between Faulkner's Yoknapatawpha and non-Yoknapatawpha works. The locale of The Unvanquished is discussed in "the Region," which also supplies several maps and photographs. A complete list of the characters in The Unvanquished is given in a third Appendix, with brief discussions of family relationships. The difficult question of the contradictory chronology of the book is discussed in the fourth Appendix, which offers a number of suggestions concerning possible revisions of the text which might, in a future edition of The Unvanquished, clear up many of the inconsistencies which exist in the present form of the work. [Order No. 58-7868; 216 pages. DAI, 19A (March-June 1959), 2957.]

037 A Road to William Faulkner: A Reading of Southern Fiction / Thomas Leonard MIKULES, University of California at Los Angeles, 1958 (Leon Howard) no DAI entry.

038 The Reception of the American Novel in German Periodicals, 1945-1957 / Sara E. BALLENGER, Indiana University, 1959 (Horst Frenz) no DAI entry.

039 The Single Vision: A Study of the Philosophy and the Forms of its Presentation in the Works of William Faulkner / Joseph GOLD, University of Wisconsin, 1959 (Frederick J. Hoffman).

This study attempts to trace the objectives and limitations of the moral themes in the novels of William Faulkner. This involves re-interpreting each novel with a view to its overall implications rather than emphasizing individual scenes or Faulkner's use of language or syntax. The value of my approach is that it attempts to discover a unity in Faulkner's work that has hitherto gone undetected. Insistence on such a unity naturally involves opposing the critical tendency of recent years which sees a radical change of view in Faulkner's work from a cosmic pessimism to a pronounced optimism and the assertion of moral values.

The Nobel Prize address, however, is not an anomaly. A close examination of the early work reveals that moral concerns have always been at the heart of Faulkner's novels and that only a change of emphasis and a loss of fictional control have caused the constant themes to become obvious, with subsequent surprise to superficial readers of the early work. It seems that in recent years Faulkner has come to view himself as a spokesman for modern man. The need to speak more and more directly has increased in urgency until in A Fable we witness an assertive and overtly didactic tone and a heavy-handed restatement of the need for Christian ethics.

The basis of Faulkner's beliefs, as I have tried to extract them from the novels, is an ill-defined humanism. Faulkner is part theist, part humanist. He believes in God, but has always held man responsible for his history. Man is never represented in the novels as the helpless victim of an indifferent cosmos. But Faulkner cannot explain how to take "the leap" to faith necessary to the behavior that he advocates, and he cannot reconcile his belief in free will and determinism. His work continually begs these questions and falls back on the assertion that the Christian ethic must be made the basis of a workable society. The Christian theme is an important part of The Sound and the Fury, Light in August, Soldiers' Pay, A Fable, and Requiem for a Nun.

I see three principal types of organization in the novels and therefore divide this study into three books. The first examines the novels which assert or at least clearly emphasize the "values" or "verities" mentioned in the speech at Stockholm. These are "The Bear," Intruder in the Dust, Requiem for a Nun, and A Fable. The second part examines those novels which depict a contrast between successful and unsuccessful attempts to cope with the human predicament. Such novels are The Sound and the Fury, As I Lay Dying, The Wild Palms, and Light in August. The third part deals with those novels which reject society as Faulkner sees it in its most sordid and materialistic aspects. These novels are Sanctuary, Pylon, Absalom, Absalom!, The Hamlet, and The Town. They imply that an alternative to the chaos presented must be found. Life is intolerable for victims of society like Temple Drake of Sanctuary. Faulkner tries, through such characters, to convey to the reader the horror of a valueless world. In this last group of novels, he implies the need for a humanistic alternative by emphasizing the dehumanization of society.

The appendix briefly explains the moral import of Soldiers' Pay, Mosquitoes, Sartoris, and The Unvanquished. These are not complex or difficult works, and by Faulkner's standards their artistic quality is slight. But they too bear the mark of the involved writer who wishes to improve society because he believes that it is worthy of improvement. [Order No. 59-5772; 418 pages. DAI, 20A (Nov. 1959-Feb. 1960), 2288-89.]

040 An Index and Encyclopedia of the Characters in the Fictional Works of William Faulkner / Robert Warner KIRK, University of Southern California, 1959 (Bruce R. McElderry, Jr).

Since 1926 William Faulkner has published 17 novels and 71 short stories. Most of this fiction makes use of the same locale and of families with interconnections going back for generations. Even careful readers have some difficulty in noting the minute interconnections in this fictional world; and, since these narratives include more than 900 named characters, an index is one way of plotting the author's course, of determining what he has done.

In this index the novels are listed by title in the order of their publication; under each separate story are listed alphabetically all the named characters who appear or are mentioned in that work, together with a notation of every page on which their names occur. In addition, there appears after the name of each character a brief account of his actions which are important to the story and, whenever they seem to be significant, a short description of that character's salient personality features. Immediately following, the named characters in all of the short stories are handled in like manner. Finally, there appears a master index composed of all of Faulkner's named fictional characters, alphabetically arranged with a list of every work in which their names occur.

By way of sampling the possible uses of the index, I have made a study of nine of the major characters whom Faulkner carries over from one story to another. Among these people, selected with an eye to getting as complete a range as possible, are the Negro, Lucas Beauchamp, in "The Fire and the Hearth" and Intruder in the Dust; Narcissa Benbow, in Sartoris, Sanctuary, and "There Was a Queen"; Eula Varner Snopes, in The Hamlet and The Town; and Flem Snopes, in Sartoris, The Hamlet, and The Town. My immediate approach to this project concerned itself with Faulkner's artistry in handling these important people as he grows and develops in his craft. Later treatments of the same characters show a creative awareness of the possibilities only hinted in earlier stories. In general, there is a high degree of consistency and development.

The index by virtue of its inclusiveness would have helped make possible an indefinite extension of this project; and its potentialities as an aid to various comprehensive studies would seem to be great. Even the general run of readers may find the index a valuable aid, for Faulkner's style often proves baffling to the point that a reader not concerned with intensive study and lacking some guide may miss the significance, if not actually lose the identity, of one or more of the characters. For whatever purpose the index may be used, however, an acquaintance with it may serve to make clear one important point: Faulkner cannot be understood, appreciated, or judged piecemeal. Had he been more consistently considered during the 1930s in the light of his total work, many of the one-sided criticisms set forth during that period might never have been written, and some present-day misconceptions of the man and his works thus have been avoided. [Order No. 59-5021; 421 pages. DAI, 20A (Nov. 1959-Feb. 1960), 2292-93.]

041 William Faulkner's Absalom, Absalom! / Robert Hilton KNOX, Harvard University, 1959 (Allens J. Guerard) no DAI entry.

042 Existentialism and the Modern American Novel / Richard D. LEHAN, University of Wisconsin, 1959 (Frederick J. Hoffman) no DAI entry.

043 Faulkner in Hollywood: A Study of his Career as a Scenarist / George R. SIDNEY, University of New Mexico, 1959 (Ernest W. Tedlock).

Faulkner's career as a Hollywood screenwriter has often been referred to by critics, but has never been thoroughly studied. His work in Hollywood is important biographically, for the money he earned as a scenarist enabled him to evade the economic necessity of writing for a commercial market. It is also important critically. As a scenarist, Faulkner, using his novelistic techniques, attempted to create in an alien medium. Thus his screen writings constitute a legitimate part of the Faulkner canon.

Not only was the medium alien, but the structure of the motion picture industry, during Faulkner's affiliation with it, was such that art and the artist were subordinated to business and the profit motive. The screen writer was deprived of control over his medium, denied valid material with which to work, and reduced to the status of an insignificant tooled part in an assembly line process.

Within this system, Faulkner worked for three Hollywood studios and wrote, or collaborated in the writing of 34 screenplays and treatments: nine for Metro-Goldwyn-Mayer (May 1932 to May 1933), seven for 20th Century Fox (Nov. 1935 to Aug. 1937), 17 for Warner Bros. (July 1942 to Sept. 1945), and one for an independent producer, Howard Hawks, in 1955.

For the purposes of this study, Faulkner's screen writings have been analyzed in terms of the manner in which he handled the elements of theme, character, action, and dialogue. His treatment of these elements was sometimes in the Hollywood tradition, sometimes in the Faulkner tradition, and sometimes neither preponderantly in one or the other, but rather "composite." The screenplays for which he received screen credit (Today We Live, Road to Glory, Slave Ship, To Have and Have Not, The Big Sleep, and Land of the Pharaohs) do not admit of such analysis, since they were collaborations. They do, however, indicate further the kind of work Faulkner was engaged in.

Faulkner was at his poorest when he accepted the expectations of his employers and wrote in the Hollywood tradition; his best two pieces of writing--War Birds and Country Lawyer--deal with his own characters and themes. Despite the cinematographic techniques that Faulkner uses in his novels, he was not a good screenwriter. He could not create within the standardized form of the Hollywood screenplay and the artistically debilitating Hollywood system. He worked conscientiously, but uninspiredly. He looked upon screen writing as a remunerative avocation. His value for Hollywood was, and continues to be (as the recent screen adaptations of his novels indicate), his name. [Order No. 59-6172; 384 pages. DAI, 20A (Nov. 1959-Feb. 1960), 2810.]

044 Negro Characterization in the American Novel: A Historical Survey of Work by White Authors / H. M. SMITH, Pennsylvania State University, 1959 (Arthur O. Lewis) no DAI entry.

045 The American Novel in Germany: A Study of the Critical Reception of Eight American Novelists Between the Two World Wars / Anne M. SPRINGER, University of Pennsylvania, 1959 (E. Sculley Bradley) no DAI entry.

046 William Faulkner and Mikhail Sholokhov: A Comparative Study of Two Representatives of the Regional Conscience, Their Affinities and Meanings / David Hugh STEWART, University of Michigan, 1959 (Morris Greenhut).

The purpose of this study is to juxtapose the assumptions about man and society underlying the fictional "worlds" of William Faulkner and Mikhail Sholokhov, who are widely acclaimed at the present time as the foremost writers of their respective nations. The problem is not one of influence or even resemblance and antithesis but merely affinity, and I assume that the act of joining the two in one study provides worthwhile insights into the works of each.

Since the study treats what the two authors say and evidently believe about man and society, not how they say it, a major task was to discover some reliable device for approaching the two, a device which could counter the widespread claim that an author is somehow not responsible for what is said in his books, if, indeed he says anything at all. The most reliable device was a character-type which I have labeled the "center of consciousness" and which appears significantly in every important work. A creature with divided social and cultural loyalties, this center of consciousness is repeatedly charged by his creator with the responsibility of confronting and evaluating the crucial matter of social flux with its derivative crises in the class order, in family and individual morality and behavior. After a brief discussion of the two authors (Part I), the major portion of the study (Parts II and III) is devoted to an examination of six centers of consciousness and the works in which they are dominant. Appended to the study are descriptions of the abridged English translation of Sholokhov's Silent Don and of the textual changes made over the years in Russian editions of this novel.

The examination of Faulkner's centers of consciousness reveals that they are highly egocentric, that they believe themselves to occupy special positions or play messianic roles in the social organism, and that they have the power to order the world in their own image, i. e. they are complete solipsists. These characteristics result from their inability or unwillingness to confront reality (the "glorious" past or the "ugly" present) on its own terms and account for the impression which Faulkner's works leave of transforming the real, the concrete, into illusion or even hallucination. Sholokhov's centers of consciousness, while less high-strung than Faulkner's share the preference of illusion to reality; but they are involved in a world which demands action and brings all illusions and ideas immediately to test in practice. Thus their actions symbolize methods of living in a difficult world, not escaping from it.

Several conclusions result. Implicit throughout is a clear case for the social origin and motivation behind both authors' work, despite obvious differences in literary technique. Faulkner's fictional survey of humanity in his imaginary region is evidently so displeasing that he seems constantly to wish to stop or at least inhibit any further development. Sholokhov's survey, though perhaps even less pleasing, brings him at last to endorse human existence since (as his books show) reality is by definition irreversible, inscrutable change. Both authors share and dramatize powerfully the contemporary preoccupation with the impact of swift social transformation upon the lives of the individuals. [Order No. 59-02185; 413 pages. DAI, 19A (March-June 1959), 3309-10.]

047 The Pilgrimage of William Faulkner: A Study of Faulkner's Fiction, 1929-1942 / Melvin Abraham BACKMAN, Columbia University, 1960 (Richard Chase).

This dissertation studies ten of William Faulkner's novels published in the years 1929-1942, probably the most productive and important period of his career. The relationships existing among the novels--as exhibited in the author's choice of character, situation, theme, image, and symbol--are examined in order to clarify both the meaning of the individual novels and the working of the artist's mind. The novels of 1929-1942 created the world of Yoknapatawpha, but they have recorded, too, the pilgrimage--the artistic, psychological, and spiritual journey--of their creator. By charting the artist's journey one may learn more about the world he was struggling to create.

One way of understanding the Faulkner pilgrimage may be found by studying the protagonists of the novels. The dominant type in the early novels was the lonely, alienated figure--like Bayard Sartoris, Quentin Compson, and Joe Christmas--who fled from life to death. Estranged from society, ridden by despair and guilt, these protagonists testified to "the human heart in conflict with itself." They seemed to reflect the tensions and conflicts of the author. They dominated the early novels.

From the preoccupation with the alienated self, Faulkner moved toward a growing concern for mankind and metamorphosed destructive guilt into moral conscience. On this journey Faulkner discovered his people and made the world of Yoknapatawpha. Yet, at almost the same time that Faulkner was moving outward toward the world of Yoknapatawpha, he moved inward into the conscience of the white South. As this moral exploration--in such works as Absalom, Absalom!, "An Odor of Verbena," and Go Down, Moses--reached more deeply into the Southern psyche, the estrangement between the self and society was renewed in another form.

This estrangement from the South was part of a complex, ambivalent attitude which was mirrored in the relationship between the planter of the Old South and his 20th century descendant. Guilt and conscience struggled desperately with pride and loyalty, as the descendant of the Southern planter sought to live in a society cursed by the inheritied sin against the Negro. To the suffering and despair born out of this struggle the later works of the 1929-1942 period have given eloquent voice.

But to counteract the suffering, there was the Faulknerian humor; to counteract the despair, there was the author's idealism; and to counteract the violence, there was the author's compassion. Like the world William Faulkner created, the pilgrimage of this artist has been strange and complex; sometimes it retreated and doubled back upon itself, but generally it advanced toward maturity and objectivity, although the author reached no shrine and found no resting place. To chart this artist's journey, to map the world he created, and to examine the novels of 1929-1942 in the hope of clarifying their meaning--that is the purpose of this dissertation. [Order No. 60-2010; 281 pages. DAI, 21A (July-Sept. 1960), 193-94.]

048 The Theme of Responsibility in the Later Fiction of William Faulkner / Robert Leslie BERNER, University of Washington (James W. Hall).

Traditionalist critics who have regarded Faulkner's work in terms of its relation to the "Southern legend" have apparently been unaware that this "legend" has few parallels in history; some of them have assumed that the "legend" is Faulkner's myth and that its relationship to history is thus irrelevant. Actually Faulkner's work shows that this view is much closer to the realities of history than to the "legend." The present study, therefore, ignores work in terms of his handling of the theme which has increasingly occupied his attention since his "great period" (1929-1932)--the theme of responsibility. The works of this "great period" are characterized by a kind of moral stasis: the characters seem unable to prevent events from happening as they do. This is not due to any deterministic bias on Faulkner's part, but to his dramatic method, to his handling of time, and to his characters, who are generally unable to "prevail" over their circumstances. But beginning with Absalom, Absalom! Faulkner's work shows an increasing concern with the theme of responsibility; in his later work he seems to be attempting to create a character who can consciously "prevail" without being destroyed.

Henry Sutpen and Charles Bon resemble Faulkner's earlier characters, while Thomas Sutpen's story is one of nearly indomitable will. But it is told by fatalistic narrators: this gives the novel much of its tension. Sutpen innocently believes that he can impose his "design" upon time, but this is impossible because of the human element, symbolized by the doors which the characters can only temporarily shut against each other.

The Wild Palms juxtaposes Wilbourne and the convict, as well as the flood and Charlotte's conception of love. The novel contrasts two notions of love: love as expression and as sacrifice of self. The latter is responsible to time. The Hamlet lacks unity if read in traditionalist terms as a novel about "Snopesism." But an examination of its texture shows consistent patterns of maleness and femaleness images, which symbolize man's will in conflict with his fate. Frenchman's Bend is a society in which its members are free to walk the thin line between nature and will without succumbing to either. All of the characters, even Ratliff, finally succumb.

Go Down, Moses and A Fable dramatize the same theme: man progresses inevitably from the wilderness through his present folly to future justice. Go Down, Moses suggests that brotherhood between the races will be achieved because of the inevitability of miscegenation. McCaslin senses this, but is unable to accept the consequences of it. His rejection of his birthright is thus an attempt to avoid both social responsibility and his responsibility to time. In A Fable the conflict between the general and the corporal is between man as he is now and man as he is capable of becoming.

Intruder in the Dust, The Town, and The Mansion dramatize Gavin Stevens' discrepancy between thought and action. His speeches often express Faulkner's personal views, but his inadequate actions show that he is not merely Faulkner's spokesman. The Town and The Mansion show the long process by which Flem Snopes' evil is purged by time. Gavin is a fatalist who finally realizes that because of the final impotence of villains even they are pitiful. He is contrasted with Ratliff, who lives in terms of Faulkner's present attitude toward responsibility: time and nature rectify evil, but the individual must still meet moral decisions squarely without succumbing to fatalism. [Order No. 60-04276; 231 pages. DAI, 21A (Oct.-Dec. 1960), 1561.]

049 A Study of Faulkner's Presentation of Some Problems that Relate to Negroes / Agnes Louise MORELAND, Columbia University, 1960 (Richard V. Chase, Jr.).

Although Faulkner has often shown Negro characters to be the source of problems in his fictional world, he has also shown Southern white characters and the total Southern social structure as the primary causes of the troublemaker role of Negroes. Because of crimes that white men have committed against them, Southern Negroes have been a source of problems since the days of slavery. This four-chapter study is an analysis of some specific problems that relate to Negroes.

Chapter One is a discussion of the origins in slavery of some economic, social, and moral problems that derive from the white-Negro conflict. Those early situations fostered self-destroying ideas among white men about the labor that they might perform with dignity. The slaves developed ideas of caste among themselves and were scornful of "poor white trash"; these latter developed hatred for both slaves and slaveholders. White-Negro interbreeding began during the slavery era when masters made sexual alliances with their slavewomen. Also a legacy from slavery is the hatred that some Southern white men have for Negroes as the cause of the Civil War and hatred of Northern whites as hypocrites who exploited both Southern white men and Negroes. For the Indians who held slaves, Negroes were also a problem. In depicting slavery-era relations between Negroes and white men, Faulkner has not shown scenes of physical violence toward Negroes. His white and Negro children are loyal friends in spite of their different castes. Faulkner's main concern, therefore, is with the psychological and emotional effects of slavery on the white masters and their descendants.

Chapter Two is a study of miscegenation as a major problem for the white men who fear racial mixing and for the men who have in their veins both "white blood" and "black blood." Many Southern white men define being as being white. Racial mixing that would occur when a Negro male impregnates a Caucasian female would negate being and must therefore be prevented. Children by white fathers and Negro mothers do not threaten the being of the white group. In their attempts to define themselves despite race, Joe Christmas in Light in August and Charles Etienne de Saint Velery Bon in Absalom, Absalom!--both of whom look like white men--lead tragic lives in defiance of society. Charles Bon's "black blood" precludes recognition from his white father and ordains his murder by his white brother. Lucas Beauchamp in Intruder in the Dust, who looks like a Negro, is able to rise above the conflict of "bloods." Faulkner suggests that racial conflict will end with amalgamation of the black and white races.

Chapter Three considers problems that arise in Southern society when a Negro refuses to be subservient to white men. For many white men such defiance of tradition is a threat to order; for the self-assertive Negro such defiance invites violence or death.

Various social problems, including the perversion of law when it deals with Negroes, are the subject of the last chapter of this study. Some of Faulkner's white characters are fanatical in their response to Negroes. Others are insensitive to the emotions of Negroes, which callousness intensifies racial conflict. The Southern Negro prostitute suffers exploitation greater than that ordinarily associated with the profession. However, Faulkner portrays Negro prostitutes and other Negro offenders against the law as victims of an unjust society and, therefore, not so guilty as white law breakers.

Notes toward further study suggest that Faulkner students investigate the writer's statements about Negro "endurance" and also the probability of Faulkner's Southern white men helping to lessen the race conflict. [Order No. 60-3118; 250 pages. DAI, 21A (Oct.-Dec. 1960), 1192-93.]

050 A Critical Analysis of the Fictional Techniques of William Faulkner /
Father Malachy Michael SHANAGHAN, University of Notre Dame, 1960 (Ernest Sandeen).

This thesis is a critical analysis of the fictional techniques of William Faulkner. In particular, this is an analysis of Faulkner's handling of point of view and time sequences. The works selected for study are The Hamlet, Light in August, and The Town.

The general question underlying this analysis is whether Faulkner used techniques as ends in themselves or as means toward larger fictional goals.

In The Hamlet Faulkner chose the point of view of omniscient narration. The appropriateness of the choice lies particularly in the accomplishment of the 'wide sweep' of panorama. Omniscience conveys the definitiveness of the Snopesian invasion of Frenchman's Bend better than any other strategy. Other corroborating effects thereby achieved are: a dimension of history by which the Snopesian invasion is integrated with the total Yoknapatawpha legend; a two-dimensional focus, through the characterization of V.K. Ratliff, whereby the full extent of the new social class is realized; and, a fidelity of idiom through which a "lifelong attendance to the local scene" is manifested.

The time sequences in The Hamlet are calculated to effect a dramatic tension between the "fluid" time in which Flem Snopes acts, and the "fixed" or Southern, "historical" time of the village. Suspense too is directly related to the handling of the time sequences.

In Light in August Faulkner varies the point of view between omniscient narration and authorial speculation. The total effect is a powerful indictment of society, a highly resonant moral representation of the theme of isolation. The time sequences effect a general movement from the less remote to the more remote past. The end result is interaction between past and present and the effect of this on character.

In The Town Faulkner tells his story through three first-person narrators. He achieves a comic folklore which is an admixture of native sharpness, romantic rhetoric, and youthful objectivity. Sharp delineation of character, as well as the representation of community mind and attitudes, results. The time sequences are so handled as to achieve a solid specification of the "new times" of the twentieth century. Also, there is effected an involvement of characters in the burden of history local. And, finally, a historical and geographic perspective is accomplished in which Snopesism is seen as a distinct sociological and historical phenomenon in the larger pattern of the Yoknapatawpha legend.

The analysis made in this thesis proves that Faulkner does not use technique for its own sake or in a vacuum, but rather that he controls technique and makes it serve the larger purposes of theme, characterization, and plot. [Order No. 60-1127; 239 pages. DAI, 20A (March-June 1969), 4663.]

051 Plantation and Frontier: A View of Southern Fiction / Robert D. BAMBERG, Cornell University, 1961 (William Sale) no DAI entry.

052 The Origins and Importance of the Initiation Story in 20th Century British and American Fiction / Robert S. BICKHAM, University of New Mexico, 1961 (E.W. Tedlock, Jr.) no DAI entry.

053 Religious Themes and Symbolism in the Novels of William Faulkner / Stanley Lawrence ELKIN, University of Illinois, 1961 (John T. Flanagan).

Faulkner's eclectic religious background is reflected in his novels. Son of a Baptist mother who switched to her husband's Methodism, Faulkner attended the Methodist Sunday School as a boy and went to the annual revivals at the Methodist Camp Ground where his grandfather owned a tent. These experiences made him familiar with the rural, revivalistic Protestant fundamentalism of his region while marriage in the Presbyterian Church and affiliation, through his wife, with the Episcopal Church have further enriched Faulkner's background.

Thus, diverse religious strains, from Hines' hell-fire Calvinism to Gavin Stevens' calm Episcopalianism, are accurately portrayed in Faulkner's novels, but beyond the routine accuracy of Faulkner's social documentation is a preoccupation with certain dominant religious themes.

Heavily relying upon a religious vocabulary, words like "doom," "apotheosis," and "crucifixion" are staples of Faulkner's diction. He makes frequent use, too, of biblical and church imagery, and even his method of characterization--myth-making through hyperbole--suggests the sense of awe and wonder of the religious imagination at work.

A subordinate religious symbol in Faulkner is confession. He utilizes the confession scene simultaneously as an instrument for the transmission of information and as a religious ritual replete with rich imagery of the confessional. The Byron/Hightower, Quentin/Shreve, Temple/Governor are a few examples of the confessional relationship. Opposed to the ritual of confession is the ritual of false witness in a novel like Sanctuary.

Ultimately, all religious themes in Faulkner are associated with some concept of suffering, but Faulkner's attitude toward suffering is ambivalent. This is to be seen in the endure/prevail dichotomy. Romanticizing the Negro, Faulkner gives him the capacity to endure (passively to submit to fate), presenting him as noble in his stoicism. Faulkner's heart goes out, however, not to Dilsey or Nancy Mannigoe but to characters like the Runner or Mink Snopes who engage the world by resisting it, who prevail. Nevertheless, the notion that suffering is mystically purgative is as strong a theme in Faulkner as it is in the Russian novelists (from whom he gets it), or in religion itself.

Concerned not with evil as with the individual's reaction to evil, Faulkner has developed three basic character types. These are exemplified by Quentin Compson, Thomas Sutpen, and Mink Snopes, and they react to evil either by suicide, compromise, or resistance. Repeatedly Faulkner returns to these classic types and in A Fable presents all three. (Literally all of Faulkner's religious themes are to be found in A Fable.)

Since reaction to evil is a major theme in his novels, Faulkner makes frequent use of certain biblical archetypes, notably Job and Jesus. But although Lena Grove, the convict, and Mink are Job figures, and although Cash, Popeye, Benjy, Joe Christmas, Ike McCaslin, the Corporal, and the "shavetail" are Christ figures, each is vastly different from the other. The Job figures fit into the endure/prevail motif, their reactions varying from Lena's passivity, through the convict's stoicism, to Mink's resistance. The Christ figures react within the spectrum outlined for the three character types, varying from Popeye's insane indifference to evil (his hanging being a symbolic suicide), through Christmas' many compromises and Benjy's impotent protests to the Corporal's active resistance.

The final ambivalence in Faulkner is the split between idealism and cynicism reflected in his evaluation of the disparate nature of God. God is presented as compassionate, as indifferent, as impotent, and as malevolent, his nature shifting from novel to novel. It is the malevolent God who ultimately provides the apocalyptic milieu of Faulkner's great tragic novels, who is the irreligious force behind a humanistically religious novelist. [Order No. 62-590; 417 pages. DAI, 22A (April-June 1962), 3659-60.]

054 A Handbook of Yoknapatawpha / Ewell Otis HAWKINS, University of Arkansas, 1961 (Earle Leighton Rudolph) no DAI entry.

055 William Faulkner's Rendering of Modern Experience: A Theological Analysis / John W. HUNT, Jr., University of Chicago, 1961 (Seword Hiltner) no DAI entry.

056 The Critical Reception of American Fiction in the Netherlands, 1900-1953 / Peter OPPEWALL, University of Michigan, 1961 (Arno L. Bader) no DAI entry.

057 Sports, Sporting Codes, and Sportsmanship in the Work of Ring Lardner, James T. Farrell, Ernest Hemingway, and William Faulkner / Stewart RODNON, New York University, 1961 (Oscar Cargill).

Although a pervasive influence of sports on 20th century American literature may be documented through a close examination of the work of Thomas Wolfe, Sinclair Lewis, Sherwood Anderson, John Dos Passos, and others, its effect is most profound on Ring Lardner, James T. Farrell, Ernest Hemingway, and William Faulkner. Their creative output--more than 40 novels and over 300 short stories--is permeated with frequent treatment and allusions to sports in American life. Each author, moreover, uses sports as one approach to establishing an indictment of modern American society.

Ring Lardner, masking his anger behind a sardonic, mordant wit, is essentially an iconoclast. He attacks, using a conscious technique of self-revelation of character, the personal and professional lives of various athletic "heroes." Lardner, further, obviously resents bitterly the society which sets up false idols--men whose claim to fame rests more upon superior reflexes or exceptional eye-hand coordination than upon excellencies of character.

James T. Farrell, writing in unmasked anger, creates several characters who follow a set pattern of behavior toward sports. Over-valuing athletics, his protagonists subsequently become aware that this preoccupation has aborted their adjustment to society. Farrell's people, like Ring Lardner's, are invariably competitive and inevitably defeated. His pessimistic view of American life is emblemized by the repeated pattern of failure which his characters suffer.

Ernest Hemingway similarly uses sports to demonstrate weakness in American culture. He, of course, demonstrates a morbid fascination for those sports in which violence is customary and death is ever a potential. A subsidiary use of sports serves to delineate the Hemingway hero's code of behavior for facing life. This protagonist uses the code to reduce all of his relationships to a primitive level. Whether the code is defined as "grace under pressure" or a "complex ritual," it is basically a sportsman's code.

Primitivism, too, is apparent in William Faulkner's use of sports. He frequently illustrates the point that primitivism is superior to civilized sophistication; the values of the hunt, for Faulkner, are preferable to those of an acquisitive society. Important virtues for Faulkner may be discovered especially in his view of hunting: the code of the hunter emphasizes both primitive virtue--bravery, strength, endurance--as well as more complex concepts of honor, pride, dignity, love of justice and love of liberty.

The four authors seem to use sports in a fundamentally similar manner. They are all, though each to a different degree, critical of American society. One line of development from the earlier writings of Lardner and Farrell to the later work of Hemingway and Faulkner is observed by analyzing their attitudes toward sports, sporting codes, and sportsmanship. The stream, which has as one of its sources the implicit pessimism of You Know Me, Al, develops itself in the explicit social commentary of Studs Lonigan, extends itself through the attitude of resigned acceptance in many of Hemingway's "heroes," and culminates in the affirmative optimism of Big Woods. In his works, each author's attitude toward sports offers an index to his fundamental view of life. One aspect of this attitude, it appears, is basically opposed to the material acquisitiveness of our society. [Order No. 62-3335; 197 pages. DAI, 23A (July-Sept. 1962), 634.]

058 William Faulkner: "The Waste Land" Phase / Robert M. SLABEY, University of Notre Dame, 1961 (Ernest Sandeen).

Several critics have described William Faulkner's work as a movement from early pessimism and despair to later affirmation and belief; however, a final statement has not been given on the exact nature of the "pessimism" to be found in the so-called "Waste Land" novels of the first decade. No one has presented an adequate evaluation of the relationship between Faulkner's world-view and Existentialist philosophy. Likewise, the precise "mythic" nature of the material has not been defined. My purpose in this dissertation will be to examine the "existential" and "mythic" aspects of Faulkner's work from 1926 to 1936 and to explain the counterrelationship of these two perspectives in his evolving vision of man and the world.

Faulkner's "Waste Land" phase began, somewhat uncertainly, in Soldiers' Pay (1926) and Mosquitoes (1927), with borrowed attitudes of the "lost generation," post-war despair, and the Bohemian breakdown of the old Puritan morality. Sartoris (1929) marked the start of the Yoknapatawpha series, but it was not until The Sound and the Fury (1929) that Faulkner assumed an ethically mature perspective on his Southern material and on the shortcomings of the Romantic sensibility. Sanctuary (1931) and As I Lay Dying (1930) are examinations of existential problems: the nature of existence and man's failure to come to grips with it. In his work there is the revelation of a continuing and developing interest in mythic material, especially that derived, after T. S. Eliot's example, from The Golden Bough. Light in August (1932), an example of Faulkner's superb craftsmanship, can be read meaningfully as the story of both the Existentialist's "Outsider" and the archetypal hero of mythic adventure; the novel is an enunciation of human freedom and moral responsibility. His last novel of the decade, Absalom, Absalom! (1936), offers a critique of Rationalism and a statement of faith in the poetic imagination.

The basic subject of Faulkner's writings is the struggle to be human. Man must have the existential "courage to be"; the realities of life must be faced directly, honestly, completely; the human condition is complex and difficult. Man must search for his soul, for spiritual and moral existence, in a world that no longer values such things. Faulkner asserts his belief in man's ability to "prevail" in his attempt to give meaning to life.

If the emphasis during the "Waste Land" phase is on "sin," suffering, and isolation, ultimate salvation and reunion are not impossible. Faulkner acknowledges the dark night, but he also believes that man has the courage and endurance to see him through it. Faulkner's vision is existential and mythic, and at the same time, powerful in its expression, scope, and universal significance. [Order No. 61-5456; 252 pages. DAI, 22A (Oct.-Dec. 1961), 1632.]

059 William Faulkner and the Community / William Patrick SULLIVAN, Columbia University, 1961 (Richard V. Chase, Jr.).

The community as a geographical and psychological entity is Faulkner's essential subject. This fundamental concern is shown in the consistent and developing pattern of the Yoknapatawpha cycle. No attempt to comprehend every aspect of community in Faulkner's writings has been made. Instead, three novels are studied for their special illumination: Light in August to show why a community fails; Absalom, Absalom! to show the base of community in the family and its extensions; The Town chiefly as a wished-for, trouble-free community. These special studies are set among more generalizing chapters which take up Faulkner's differences from other writers of his own generation, the meaning of the term community, the extensive interdependence of the individual and the community in Faulkner, and Faulkner's accumulating knowledge of and concern with the community.

Chapter One: During Faulkner's apprentice years American literature dealt largely with the individual. Major novels after World War I were novels of alienation, in which the pursuit of individual ends by isolated individuals was customary. Faulkner's early novels contain the usual theme of the alienated individual, but with a difference. Soldiers' Pay and Mosquitoes are more concerned with the society than with the isolated individual. Sartoris has a protagonist firmly set in a community at home; his discontent is chiefly owing to the power of the family legend over him.

Chapter Two: The ambiguity of the term community in usage permits the use of geographical and psychological criteria, together or separately. Historically, political theory relates the community to the nature of man. The South is usually viewed as a community in agreement on behavior even more than as a geographically arranged pattern.

Chapter Three: Light in August shows the need for community. Although the main characters are outsiders, the community is prominent in their lives. The community is defined by its outcasts, its racism, its religion, and its attitude toward women; it is an exclusive society. The isolation of individuals is revealed in their attitude toward the value of words.

Chapter Four: Absalom, Absalom! shows the basis for expanding the community. Even though his methods are uncommon, Sutpen has the common aspirations. His son Bon asserts the preeminence of the father-son relationship over any other. Beyond the ties of kinship individuals are identified with one another by their influence on one another and through the communal memory, which unifies the generations.

Chapter Five: The Town, normally a place of peace, innocence, and amusement in this rather idyllic view of it, undergoes a crisis of change and purgation as the Snopeses conquer the town, but are in turn conquered by it.

Chapter Six: The extensive interdependence of the individual and the community throughout Faulkner's work can be seen in his esthetic method, by which the individual is related to the group, and his view of the social effects of individual characteristics.

Chapter Seven: Faulkner's growing concern for the community is seen in his works taken chronologically and cumulatively. Taken chronologically, they deal with relatively isolated groups of people, in the early stages, but later with interrelated groups. Taken cumulatively, especially the Yoknapatawpha tales, they represent and criticize a cultural island. [Order No. 62-1931; 183 pages. DAI, 22A (April-June 1962), 4355.]

060 The Literary Faulkner: His Indebtedness to Conrad, Lawrence, Hemingway, and Other Modern Novelists / Emily Kuempel BRADY, Brown University, 1962 (Israel J. Kapstein).

In this thesis Faulkner is treated as a writer whose proper place is among the great novelists of England and America, three of whom have been singled out for detailed study. In the Preface the method of analysis and attribution on internal evidence only is discussed with reference to bibliography and terminology. In Chapter I it is argued that Faulkner was attracted to Joseph Conrad, D. H. Lawrence, and Ernest Hemingway because all four are Romantic novelists, and some attempt is made to define the modern Romantic novel.

In Chapters II and III the subject is Faulkner's indebtedness to Conrad. Two characterizations in The Sound and the Fury, Mr. Compson and Benjy, are discussed in Chapter II as being in part probably borrowed from the characterizations of Heyst senior in Victory, and Stevie Verloc in The Secret Agent. The technique of the timeshift in the Marlow narratives, Nostromo and Absalom, Absalom!, is the subject of Chapter III. In addition, A Fable is interpreted as a following out of the full implications of the time-shift technique, which probably originated in a feeling on both Conrad and Faulkner's part about scientific discoveries and human development.

In Chapter IV Lawrence's influence on Faulkner is discussed mainly in reference to Faulkner's treatment of the Christ figure in Light in August. It is argued that Christian reference and symbols in the work of both writers cannot be understood with reference only to orthodox doctrine.

The subject of Chapter V is the connection between The Sun Also Rises and The Sound and the Fury. The characterization of both Benjy and Quentin Compson, their attitude to their sister Caddy, and the speech patterns of Quentin, are probably all the result of the influence of Hemingway's novel.

The probable influence of four minor figures--Aldous Huxley, F. Scott Fitzgerald, Willa Cather, and Edward Dahlberg--which was discovered while gathering material for the main chapters, is included in a brief sixth chapter.

In the conclusion, which is Chapter VII, some attempt is made to interpret, in the light of probable indebtedness, a pattern of Faulkner's career. Not only the authors, whom he imitated, but the mode of imitation changed radically around 1926, when, it is argued, Faulkner entered a period of about three years of intense creative activity. The trilogy that began with The Hamlet represents a retreat from writing under the inspiration derived from his reading, and A Fable shares with lesser works, Pylon, for example, the idea of illusions. The Sound and the Fury, on the other hand, is Faulkner's own favorite among his works, and the novel which is most intelligently and most heavily indebted to all three of the major writers considered. [Order No. 63-1008; 236 pages. DAI, 23A (Oct.-Dec. 1962), 2131-32.]

061 Bergsonian Dynamism in the Writings of William Faulkner / Shirley Parker CALLEN, Tulane University, 1962 (Richard P. Adams).

The writings of William Faulkner embody a pervasive Bergsonian dynamism. Although Faulkner has acknowledged a direct influence from Henri Bergson, Bergson is important to this exploratory criticism rather as an articulate spokesman of a widespread 20th century philosophical view that is given concrete, artistic expression in Faulkner's writings. Both Faulkner and Bergson consider change as the universal principle of reality, and life itself as a ceaseless flow of reality. For both, perception of this reality centers upon the distinction between "clock" time and duration by which time appears truly as a continuous present in which the past is constantly influential, similarly influencing but not determining the future.

The main emphasis of this study, illustrating this philosophical view in Faulkner's works, is on content and characterization to show how Faulkner makes a dramatic dichotomy of those characters who destroy themselves and who "endure" and "prevail" by their failure or success in achieving a harmonious, meaningful relationship to time. A very important element of characterization, reflecting Bergson's views, is Faulkner's distrust of rationality and conceptualism because they rigidify and thus distort the individual's grasp of reality.

Most of Faulkner's leading characters are guilty of interpreting existence on the basis of abstractions and adopted concepts rather than their own experience so that they develop a distortion of experience and time. Despite the predominance of such negative presentation, Faulkner reveals implicitly in his commentary on them his belief in human worth and freedom. Like Bergson, Faulkner views the capacity for free choice as an indefinable quality of the whole self, existing and extending in time. Faulkner's are not fated, doomed characters who are absolved of responsibility for their actions, but are responsible and free to act in an indeterminate present and future. Their frequent concern with the past does not indicate an unbreakable bondage to it but illustrates the Bergsonian view of the unity of time and experience.

As a critical artist, Faulkner is more interested in portraying the embodiment of the evils of rigidity, stasis, and conceptualism than in affirming man's stature. In later works, Faulkner's affirmation is pronounced, but even in the most pessimistic of his earlier novels, there is usually an illustration of the capacity of the human species to endure; for Faulkner shares with Bergson a concept of an elan vital whose continuance and extension are the goals of existence. Faulkner can thus declare his belief in "the divinity of the continuity of Man, " not as an individual nor particular group but as a part of life that will endure and prevail. Faulkner's conception of endurance, like Bergson's use of the term, is an extreme flexibility which affords the ability to cope with a changing environment. Faulkner makes clear that simple enduring, as well as prevailing, depends upon an intuitive awareness of continual change in time.

This philosophical aspect of Faulkner's work is embodied not only in theme and characterization but also in form. Faulkner attempts to overcome the fixity of language and conventional form to capture in prose the unified fluidity of time and reality. His involute style and his innovations in form are intended to convey, while overcoming the difficulty of articulating, a non-verbal reality that is an elusive process of change. His greatest novels --The Sound and the Fury, As I Lay Dying, Light in August, and Absalom, Absalom!--receive extensive treatment for factors of content and form, but illustrations are drawn from practically all of Faulkner's writings to show how the various elements of characterization, structure, and style contribute to an organic unity of theme: Faulkner's belief in dynamic change and his corresponding dislike of stasis, rigidity, and conceptualism. [Order No. 62-06472; 183 pages. DAI, 23A (Jan.-March 1963), 2521.]

062 William Faulkner: Critic of Society / Glenn Owaroff CAREY, University of Illinois, 1962 (John T. Flanagan).

William Faulkner's success as an author can be attributed to several main characteristics in his fiction--virtuosity, stylistic brilliance, creative imagination, and social awareness. This study is an analytical interpretation of Faulkner's writings with emphasis on his social criticism. Faulkner is primarily an artist, not a propagandist or reformer, but his work clearly includes criticism of man and society. This social criticism is significant not only because it is related to problems in the American South and North but also because it goes beyond the South to encompass all mankind. The principal areas of this criticism include the economic, educational, martial, political, and religious. Throughout most of his writings Faulkner voices his views on war, materialism, religion, sex, and racial difficulties, as well as his condemnation of ignorance, prejudice, vanity, and hypocrisy.

Faulkner has been sensitively concerned with the post-bellum social, moral, and ethical decay of the Southern aristocracy, the rise to power of the Snopeses and their materialistic philosophy and the effects of these forces on the South and its people, white and black. Yet Faulkner also develops a wider and more important range to his fiction as he castigates the disorders of modern society and the corruption of individual man's integrity and freedom. This universality gives Faulkner's social criticism greater significance than if it concerned only the South or the United States.

Faulkner's fiction shows not only the well-known geographical unity but also an over-all creative design which includes his social criticisms and what he believes is man's responsibility to his fellow man. These criticisms generally are not intrusive on Faulkner's art as most of them advance the action of the stories. In the glaring exception, Intruder in the Dust, excessive harangues by Gavin Stevens on integration and Northern intervention in the South's affairs interfere with the story when these speeches become propaganda, not art. Usually Faulkner makes his criticism dramatically effective and acceptable by having his main characters, the responsible men, speak and act against the evils in civilization, which include the excessive distortions of religion, the futility and worthlessness of war. As examples, the tall convict in "Old Man" demonstrates primal good as he aids and almost dies for strangers; Horace Benbow, muttering "Christians! Christians!" in Sanctuary, befriends a prostitute and her common-law husband and tries to protect them from the vicious self-righteousness of Jefferson's "good" people; and in A Fable the Christ-like corporal and the battalion runner speak and take action against the mass-murder called war. Other responsible men are Byron Bunch of Light in August and V. K. Ratliff and Gavin Stevens of many Faulkner stories, who stand for the best in man.

Faulkner's social criticism is strongly integrated with the creative design of his work. The dramatic development of his social conscience is Faulkner's acceptance of his responsibility as a man and writer. This expression of one's social conscience is found in the work of the best writers, those who believe, as Albert Camus did, that the aim of art and of a man's life should be to increase the amount of freedom and responsibility in all men. Faulkner's criticism of society places him in this select group. [Order No. 62-6116; 273 pages. DAI, 23A (Jan.-March 1963), 2522.]

063 Four Critical Interpretations in the Modern Novel / Robert George COLLINS, University of Denver, 1962 (Harvey S. Gross) no DAI entry.

064 Faulkner's Comic Spirit / Bobby Ray DOWELL, University of Denver, 1962 (Stuart James).

Faulkner's comic spirit is closely linked to his world view. Generally he presents his characters entangled in a web of cosmic pessimism, but his comic spirit acts as a cushion, for himself as well as for his reader, to soften the terrifying reality of the cosmos he envisions. Faulkner sees man's sense of humor as a precious trait in his precarious game of change, for it gives him the illusion of leveling obstacles in a world of ever present and overwhelming obstacles. Such characters as Byron Bunch and V. K. Ratliff manage to maintain a balanced perspective on reality because they can look upon life with a degree of humorous detachment. They see life as something of a joke, but they are in on the joke.

However, most of Faulkner's comic characters, such as the convict of Anse Bundren, for example, are not aware of their ludicrous roles. The comic treatment, in this case, creates atmosphere by adding a more diffused focus to scenes that might otherwise become melodramatic or overly emotional; it creates a kind of aesthetic distance.

Another important function of Faulkner's comic spirit is the significant role it plays in the structure of his works. Structurally, comic elements may serve to heighten and underscore major themes of a work by setting up parallels and contrasts; or they may function as "comic relief," that is, to relieve the tensions of pity and terror. However, comic scenes are almost never merely a relaxing interlude to make way for a renewed tensing, but instead a shift to another range, a change of key without a dropping of the theme.

Thoughtful laughter is the essence of the comic. We may laugh at almost anything at one time or another, but all laughter is not comic laughter. The comic suggests laughter as the result of our perceiving a certain inconsistency or absurdity. In other words, the comic is rooted in incongruity, and it depends upon our perceiving the incongruous.

Much laughter in Faulkner is dark laughter, but it is thoughtful laughter. There is little nonsensical laughter in his works, for whether his comic spirit emanates from words, characters, or situations, it almost always has a logical point, drift, or pertinence and yields some insight into values.

Faulkner's comic spirit further evidences his affirmation of life: that man shall not only endure, but prevail. Although the comic puts incongruity in the foreground, by its very nature the comic presupposes a sense of the ideal somewhere in the background. Much of the comic in Faulkner grows out of the actions which contradict the importance of practicing what he calls, "the eternal verities of the human heart": courage, honor, pride, compassion, and pity. These verities are invaluable, says Faulkner, because they are "the edifice on which the whole history of man has been founded and by means of which he has endured this long." Faulkner's list of verities is constant to his body of work, and it serves as the basis of a latent sense of rightness, of what ought to be. This factor is significant in relation to the novelist's comic spirit. For the job of the humorist is to uncover neglected hypocrisies, illusions, vanities, and deceptions in the behavior of persons and societies. Hence, our perception of these incongruities that Faulkner exposes through his comic vision is aided by a strong sense of underlying congruence in the works themselves. [Order No. 63-1159; 191 pages. DAI, 23A (April-June 1963), 4355.]

065 William Faulkner's Literary Reputation in America / O. B. EMERSON, Vanderbilt University, 1962 (Randall Stewart).

What has been attempted in this study is a survey of the substantial body of Faulkner criticism in an attempt to define and evaluate William Faulkner's reputation in his own country. In surveying the literary reputation of Faulkner, this writer has attempted to include a cross section of critical opinions in arriving at the position that Faulkner holds in American letters today. The span of thirty years covered in this study from the appearance of The Marble Faun in 1924 through the reception of A Fable witnessed Faulkner's rise in the literary world from the obscurity of a second-rate poet to an eminence seldom attained by an American writer.

The initial reception of Faulkner was significant but not widespread. The years from 1924 to 1939 saw the publication of a considerable number of reviews and a few distinguished articles, such as Evelyn Scott's pamphlet on The Sound and the Fury in 1929. Much of the criticism of this period, particularly of the early 1930s, attempted to fit the works into preconceived categories with little effort to discuss Faulkner in his own terms or to give a general view of the writing. The first five chapters deal with Faulkner's reputation at the hands of these early critics, whose criticism may be subsumed under three headings: journalistic, naturalistic, and social.

Although this type of criticism has continued to the present, it has been overshadowed by searching and revealing studies which began in 1939, a year that marks the beginning of a symbolic or mythological approach to Faulkner's writing. After 1939, Faulkner's reputation began to grow. Responsible for this year being a turning point in Faulkner's career were articles by Conrad Aiken on Faulkner's style, and by George Marion O'Donnell on Faulkner's mythology. The sixth chapter deals primarily with these two articles. With the appearance of these articles a trend developed to approach the work as a whole, to examine the structural and philosophical aspects which give it permanent literary value, and to consider its social-moral themes. The seventh chapter deals with the criticism of the 1940s which saw the emergence of Robert Penn Warren and Malcolm Cowley as leading Faulkner critics. These two critics and others during this period interpreted Faulkner in light of the new criticism.

The eighth chapter deals with the Nobel Prize criticism which chiefly concerns Faulkner's moral vision. The ninth chapter attempts to evaluate Faulkner's literary reputation in his native region, where his reception does not differ greatly from that on the national scene. In some cases the enthusiasm that greeted his works there exceeded that of his Northern critics.

Too, the criticism was not lacking in prominent names and significant contributions. Although Donald Davidson played an important role in establishing Faulkner's reputation in the South, no single person was more important to Faulkner's career than was his friend and fellow townsman, Phil Stone, whose influence was felt in almost every area. The tenth and final chapter deals with Faulkner Studies and other special publications.

Most critics are now agreed that Faulkner has permanently changed American fiction. Faulkner's reputation, however, is by no means settled. Thus far, although his works are highly regarded both in this country and abroad, his reputation has wavered from novel to novel, from critic to critic, from decade to decade. Faulkner has said that "with the American, the last word carries weight" and that the critic "too often abuses his privilege of having the last word." But in case of Faulkner's reputation in this country, his critics will have the last word. [Order No. 62-3414; 908 pages. DAI, 23A (July-Sept. 1962), 631.]

066 They Who Endure and Prevail: Characters of William Faulkner / James Franklin FARNHAM, Case Western Reserve University, 1962 (Lyon N. Richardson) no DAI entry.

067 Faulkner's Twice-Told Tales: His Re-Use of His Material / Edward Morris HOLMES, Brown University, 1962 (Hyatt H. Waggoner).

William Faulkner has said that if he could rewrite all his work, he believes it would do it better. Often he has re-used characters and episodes in both short stories and novels. This study attempts to show how much he has re-used material, to illustrate the changes which accompanied re-use, and to indicate the effect re-use has had on his art.

Published analyses of rewritten stories in The Hamlet have shown Faulkner's style shifting from the "factual-objective" in his early short stories toward a "descriptive-definitive" manner, and a "strongly distant formality" when the tales are reworked. This tendency is apparent in the transformation of "The Hound" from a brisk, tightly knit story as first published, to an imaginatively intensified episode in The Hamlet, profuse with massed details and made almost hypnotic by complex syntax and abstract words of high associational meaning. Even when Ratliff wryly narrated the third version of "The Hound," in The Town, he uses words like outrage, despair, betrayal; and in The Mansion, the indomitable Mink Snopes is no longer so much a mean, vindictive killer as an instrument of poetic justice.

Of seven other short stories retold in the Snopes trilogy, all except "Barn Burning" exhibit a similar shift toward complexity of details, and toward an enrichment of character and mood, often with a resulting intensity of effect. Not only are they expanded to meet the needs of the novels but also are complicated in the retelling by the quietly comic moral criticism of Ratliff who shares the narration in each.

The chapters of The Unvanquished that first appeared as magazine short stories carry in the novel more than thirty pages of added material. Their pattern is familiar--an increased intensity and imaginative coloring--but also significant, for most of the additions emphasize, if not provide, the essential evidence for the book's serious, implied theme: critical examination, through Bayard Sartoris, of the older order of the South, and its failure in Rosa Millard.

Equally significant are changes in re-used material in Go Down, Moses, and The Big Woods. "The Bear"--of Go Down, Moses--merges the themes of two earlier magazine versions, "The Bear," and "Lion." Alterations in these re-used forms of "The Fire and the Hearth," "The Old People," and "Delta Autumn" sharpen the themes of injustice to the Negro and the destruction of the wilderness. These changes, and the excision of the theme of injustice to the Negro in all re-used material of The Big Woods, suggest that Faulkner's handling of these themes is conscious and deliberate.

Other re-used elements--"Wash" in Absalom, Absalom!; Miss Zilphia Gant the spinster in "A Rose for Emily"; "Afternoon of a Cow" in The Hamlet; and "Notes on a Horsethief" in A Fable--illustrate the varying degrees of success with which the writer could rework one selection and integrate it in another, the first three with excellent results; the last, with little if any success.

The evidence of re-employed material indicates that the shift in Faulkner's style toward complexity and intensification ceased after 1930; that often he has tailored short stories for magazine consumption, not hesitating to intensify mood or a disturbing theme for inclusion in a book; and that his drive to rewrite "better" than before has contributed to his Yoknapatawpha fiction some of that quality of myth which, because it is so important to man, must, with variations, be told, and told, and told again. [Order No. 63-1032; 139 pages. DAI, 23A (Jan.-March 1963), 2527.]

068 Values and Love in the Fiction of William Faulkner / Rev. Thomas Francis LOUGHREY, University of Notre Dame, 1962 (Ernest Sandeen).

This dissertation is an analysis of fifteen novels of Faulkner with special attention given to the factors of romantic and familial love as they form the basis for the continuing society. Each work is studied in a self-contained essay, giving an original reading of the novel as a whole. The central focus in all of the studies is the influence upon the lover of a tradition of values communicated to him from the previous generation. The affirmation of this ethical constant comprising recognized obligations in society and arising from natural law is found in the fifteen works studied. The particular characterizations in which the love theme appears present various violations of the values essential to the continuing society. In Sartoris the hero-image is so distorted that Bayard's imagination remains too sick to permit his articulation in a society based upon the commitment of the person in love. Quentin Compson's sickness is also in the imagination, coming, however, from a paralyzing theology of physical nature communicated by his parents. Joe Christmas has had his experience of the joy of nature terrorized from his infancy. The pre-disposition toward strife in the Bundren family is the result of Addie's violation of natural law and of her continuing antagonism towards those who have disturbed her intense romantic experience.

In most of the studies a social-psychological factor is thus found as the source of disorders in society which Faulkner studies in a method that is at once realistic and mythic. Go Down, Moses is read as a single novel with Ike McCaslin suffering from a constitutional disinclination toward marriage. The Wild Palms is seen as a realistic treatment of a double tendency in man: either to exaggerate romantic love, or to eliminate it entirely. The Snopes Trilogy is read as a three-fold assertion of the theme of man's need to make a proper response to the mystery and beauty of woman.

In all of the studies the method is inductive, the writer working through the texture toward a coherent reading. Faulkner's occasional independence of probability in the Aristotelian sense is noticed in such works as Sanctuary, As I Lay Dying, and Light in August. His use of "mind-voice" is studied in The Sound and The Fury and As I Lay Dying; his anti-chronology in As I Lay Dying and Light in August.

The reluctance of Faulkner to deal with abnormal psychological conditions except as possibilities in society is examined. A coherent reading of Requiem for a Nun shows the unity of the work, pointing out the relationship between the prologues and the dramatic sections. The texture of Absalom, Absalom! is studied with a special emphasis upon the motifs of death developed in the imagery. Throughout the novels the antinomy of realistic "problem" developed in mythic structure is noticed. The conclusion sees Faulkner as reasserting traditional human values of man's dignity and responsibility as a lover. [Order No. 62-4799; 334 pages. DAI, 23A (Jan.-March 1963), 2915.]

069 Religion in Yoknapatawpha County / C. D. McLAUGHLIN, University of Denver, 1962 (Stuart James) no DAI entry.

070 Quest for Faith: A Study of Destructive and Creative Force in the Novels of William Faulkner / Kenneth E. RICHARDSON, Claremont Graduate School, 1962 (George Wickes).

By considering the question of what dooms and saves men and women in Faulkner's fiction, one identifies the conflicting destructive and creative force which Faulkner sees at work in modern American society. The destructive force that is fundamental in most of Faulkner's tragic fiction is inflexibility and is represented by a rigid father. Men like Colonel John Sartoris, Jason Compson, and Thomas Sutpen, among others, reflect a social order that is as rigid as they are. The inflexibility of these fathers is a destructive threat to the sons when they come to question the father's authority and the values of the social order. The creative opposite of destructive inflexibility is embodied in a life that possesses an adaptability to change. In Faulkner it is the wilderness that teaches man flexibility, for it shows life to be a perpetual cyclic regeneration, a series of successful adaptations to altering conditions of hostility. The wilderness values are revealed to a son by a spiritual father who shows him meaningful rituals that lead him to the lasting truths that make civilization possible.

A second destructive force is sexual irresponsibility, generally pictured in a female. Women like Mrs. Compson, Addie Bundren, Temple Drake, and Charlotte Rittenmeyer, among others, forsake the responsibilities of motherhood in favor of a selfish and a carnal gratification; in so doing they fail men who have a need for their love and care.

The opposite creative force is mother-love, represented by such figures as the earth-mother, the foster mother, and the grandmother. These women bring forth children in love, endure the infirmities and willfulness of the young, and teach youth the truths of the heart.

The third destructive force, Snopesism, is a soulless, predatory amorality. The Snopeses ravage the village and the town through economic and rational manipulation. They are countered by the defenders, Gavin Stevens and V. K. Ratliff, who view the people in the village and the town with compassion which leads them to battle the Snopeses in order to protect their society. The defenders are men characterized by love and by faith.

Faulkner's use of antithetic destructive and creative force indicates that his fictional method is a dialectic progress toward a resolution of warring entities, the arrival at a belief that man's faith in Mankind can overcome and eliminate destructive threats. Faulkner's studied consideration of destructive and creative force is, then, an examination of alternatives in human behavior. Faulkner employs this method of examination in order to arrive at truth as he sees it.

Faulkner's study of the opposition of destructive and creative forces can be seen to be, in reality, a quest for faith. [Order No. 63-250; 228 pages. DAI, 23A (Jan.-March 1963), 3384.]

071 The Short Stories of William Faulkner / Hassell Algernon SIMPSON, Florida State University, 1962 (Griffith T. Pugh).

An introductory examination of the critical attention accorded the short stories of William Faulkner indicated that the stories generally have been overshadowed by their author's novels, and that no extensive study of the stories as stories had been made. The stories were then subjected to detailed analysis for theme, point of view, character, and image and symbol.

Faulkner's list of eternal verities in the Nobel Prize speech was found to contain the themes of the short stories, indicating that their author's practice, contrary to a common belief, had been remarkably close to his theory. Love, honor, pity and compassion, pride, and sacrifice--though often viewed indirectly--were seen in the stories to be essential factors in the human condition.

Point of view was shown to have been continually troublesome to Faulkner in the short stories. Sometimes when he failed to find a meaningful viewpoint, his stories fell into obscurity or irrelevance, but the best of the tales are successful precisely because they permit the reader to enter the fictional world at a level on which he can share fully in the narrative experience.

Character in the stories, as in the novels, was most effectively drawn when the depicted persons were unsophisticated and given to terse, pithy observation, or else to rambling narrative in the frontier-humorist fashion. Least successful have been characters of some sophistication, especially those who speak at length.

In stories published before the mid-1930s, complex patterns of images and symbols were frequently employed, especially in connection with the concepts of death and damnation. Somewhat more hopeful themes, together with an increasing subtlety, were found to be a factor contributing to the general disappearance of such image-patterns in favor of single dominant symbols in stories of later periods.

In view of the success of a large proportion of Faulkner's stories, and his skill at various narrative techniques, it is shown that his grasp of the short-story form is not inferior to his command of the novel, as some critics have suggested, but that William Faulkner is in every way a master of modern short story. [Order No. 62-4630; 215 pages. DAI, 23A (Oct.-Dec. 1962), 1709.]

072 William Faulkner: An International Novelist / Leyla Melek GOREN, Harvard University, 1963 (Kenneth S. Lynn) no DAI entry.

073 Southern Fiction and the Quest for Identity / Catherine S. HARRINGTON, University of Washington, 1963 (Andrew R. Hilen, Jr.) no DAI entry.

074 Symbolism in the American Novel, 1850-1950: An Examination of the Findings of Recent Literary Critics in Respect to the Novels of Hawthorne, Melville, James, Hemingway, and Faulkner / A. P. HINCHCLIFFE, Victoria University of Manchester, England, 1963 (Marcus Cunliffe) no DAI entry.

075 William Faulkner and the Terror of History: Myth, History, and Moral Freedom in the Yoknapatawpha Cycle / Vernon Theodore HORNBACK, Jr., St. Louis University, 1963 (Albert Joseph Montesi).

William Faulkner's Yoknapatawpha cycle of novels and stories is structured by a single, but very complex theme: destiny in time. Each of Faulkner's protagonists attempts to confront the terror of history, and succeeds or fails in terms of a demonstrable commitment to one of three concepts of time. The characters of the major works from Sartoris through Absalom, Absalom! are obsessed with the past, predominantly, and are destroyed by a commitment to a cyclical view of time, which absolves them of the guilt of their collective heritage as Southerners, but also paralyzes them, making free, responsible action in the present impossible. Some few characters reject cyclical determinism for the illusion of freedom offered by a naive linear concept of time which is based upon an unquestioning acceptance of materialistic progress. These advocates of "progress" time make of time a commodity, totally externalized and mechanical, which can be manipulated, like goods or money. The third concept of time, which Faulkner drew from Bergsonian duration and the traditional Christian view of history as the record of a linear movement in which every event is unique because of the uniqueness of the Incarnation of Christ in history, first becomes important with the publication in 1942 of Go Down, Moses. This "Christian-existential" time frees its adherents to act responsibly in time.

Bayard Sartoris, Quentin Compson, Addie and Darl Bundren, Joe Christmas and Gail Hightower, Charles Bon and others are bound to the determinism of cyclical time by the pull of Faulkner's three basic archetypes: the Grandfather, the Civil War, and the Wilderness. To a greater or lesser degree, each is defeated because he or she is unable to face the terror of history, but is driven to attempt to escape responsibility in time in a commitment to a mythologized, cyclical view of history. Jason Compson, Anse and Jewel Bundren, and Thomas Sutpen espouse naive progress time, placing their trust in the efficacy of using time for material gain, and as a consequence become destructive influences. In "The Bear," the central document of Go Down, Moses, Isaac McCaslin achieves a break from cyclical time, which is represented by the ritual bear hunt, into the moral freedom of Christian-existential time. Isaac's break is effected through the ministry of Sam Fathers, who is both high priest of the initiation rite connected with cyclical time, and as Had-Two-Fathers, a Christ-figure.

In the post-Go Down, Moses novels, Faulkner concerned himself with the development of a new aristocracy of free and responsible men committed to a Christian-existential time. The new aristocrats win their freedom by combatting racial injustice, which is the legacy of cyclical time, as in the case of Charles Mallison in Intruder in the Dust; or they learn to confront the terror of history through opposition to the amoral forces of progress epitomized by Flem Snopes of the Snopes trilogy. In The Reivers, Faulkner's last novel, Lucius Priest and his companions achieve complete moral freedom and regeneration. [Order No. 64-4254; 283 pages. DAI, 25A (July-Sept. 1964), 476.]

076 The Waste Land Tradition in the American Novel / John Michael HOWELL, Tulane University, 1963 (Richard P. Adams) no DAI entry.

077 The Literary Styles of Jean-Paul Sartre and William Faulkner: An Analysis, Comparison, and Contrast / Lewis Alva RICHARDS, University of Southern California, 1963 (Paul E. Hadley).

The purpose of this study is to analyze, compare, and contrast the literary styles of Jean-Paul Sartre and William Faulkner as novelists. In addition to the analysis of literary styles, the purpose and function of these respective styles are given when possible or immediately pertinent.

First, the subject matter treated in the novels of the two authors comes under scrutiny. The socioeconomic backgrounds as well as the physical aspects of characters appearing in the novels are analyzed in detail. Each major character is scrutinized and his normality or subnormality indicated, and the function of the subnormal or aberrant characters is stated. Then, an attempt is made to establish the realism or romanticism of these characters. In addition, the different types of humor existing in the novels of the two authors are investigated, compared, and contrasted. Faulkner's southern frontier type of humor, its function and reliance on incongruity and ambivalence, are described. This humor is contrasted with the scope and function of the refined, intellectual humor used by Sartre. Furthermore, the treatment of sex in the novels under discussion is analyzed. Sartre's freedom in the detailed description of eroticism and its function and meaning are contrasted with the relative absence of the sex scene in Faulkner's works and his equation of sex with violence and destruction.

A consideration of plot as used in the novels of both authors is the subject of the second chapter. The main emphasis is placed on kinds and functions of plots. The meaning of plotlessness in Sartre's novels is brought out and explained. Questions such as plot versus character, dialogue versus action, the flashback, the indirect method, embedded short stories, and introspection are discussed. The plot of The Wild Palms is dissected to show how intricately interwoven a few of Faulkner's plots are. Also, Faulkner's technique of time dislocation and matter rearrangement is explained.

The third chapter compares and contrasts the use of language by the two authors. The long, difficult, and occasionally involuted sentences of Faulkner are contrasted with Sartre's short, clear-cut sentences. Faulkner's type of symbolism is analyzed. Faulkner's experimentation with language, his inventions and coinage of new words are evaluated. The employment of colloquial and substandard language by both authors is also discussed. In addition, their use of vulgar and obscene language is assessed.

Chapter IV is devoted to an investigation of other stylistic devices of importance. Such devices as contrasts, repetition, the italicized passage, the embedded short story and enigmatic chapter openings are analyzed, categorized, and evaluated. The functions and purposes of each of such devices are also explained. It is noted that while Sartre uses these various stylistic devices mainly as a reflection of the meaninglessness of the universe, Faulkner expresses primarily the dilemma of the South and the predicament of man --especially Southern man. Other minor stylistic peculiarities are also discussed and their functions explained.

The final chapter deals primarily with Sartre's existential philosophy of the freedom of man. Sartre's concept of hopeful freedom is contrasted with Faulkner's apparent psychological determinism of the individual. The influence of environment and heredity on the individual, uses of symbolism, Faulkner's preoccupation with the past, and the extent to which either author is a realist or a romanticist are also discussed in this chapter. Finally, Sartre's philosophical optimism is contrasted with Faulkner's temperamental pessimism. It is concluded that both authors are concerned with the ultimate destiny of man and the question of universal good and evil, though approaching these basic issues in conspicuously disparate manners. [Order No. 64-3105; 285 pages. DAI, 24A (Jan.-March 1964), 3756-57.]

078 William Faulkner: From Past to Self-Discovery; A Study of his Life and Work Through Sartoris (1929) / Harold Edward RICHARDSON, University of Southern California, 1963 (Bruce R. McElderry).

The previous biographies concerning William Faulkner--such as those of Coughlan, Howe, Miner, and O'Connor--have presented many helpful facts about his life and offered various critical approaches to his work. As a result, anyone interested in Faulkner is in a position to know a good deal about his early life and literary development; but the information is generally fragmented, and all too often isolated segments are played up in such a way as to make Faulkner appear bizarre and his behavior unaccountable. Thus, the total impression which biographers have given of Faulkner is that of a very odd person.

A trip to Oxford, Mississippi, resulted in some new information and clarified a number of existing conflicts in the old; even more important was a clearer sense of connection between the general facts known about Faulkner and the larger context of his early life. This sense of connection seemed gradually to give shape to patternless bits of data, to make Faulkner believable as a person, and to illuminate his work in ways not previously recognized. When these relationships between life and literary work are supplied, Faulkner becomes less of an oddity and more explainable as a person. His life and early work have been approached from two viewpoints--the aesthetic and the psychological--in order that the two approaches act as reflecting mirrors, the psychological illuminating Faulkner's work and the work itself illuminating his personal attitudes and motivations during this period of his life.

The study of Faulkner's family background and the period of his life up through his special-student days at the University of Mississippi reveals the emerging themes of the past and his struggle to identity as he was drawn, on one hand, toward that past, and, on the other, toward a more personal individuation in the South of his day. The ensuing conflict of identities helps to explain some of the tensional images appearing in Faulkner's earliest published poetry and prose, and an attempt has been made to treat these images as they steadily recur. A particularly strong relationship is revealed between the young Faulkner and both his great-grandfather Colonel William Cuthbert Falkner [sic.] and his grandfather John Wesley Thompson Falkner. However, before he could transmute these familial prototypes into the consciously communicated <u>personae</u> of literary art, it was first necessary that he write poetry. "I'm a failed poet," Faulkner said. He then turned from poetry to prose, and then from his decadent phase of the mid-twenties toward an increased reliance upon autobiographical materials placed into the context of a more concrete local color. Thus, Faulkner tapped the reservoir of the past with which he could identify and, eventually, treat successfully as an artist.

The examination of Faulkner's work of this period is arranged chronologically according to composition and covers every known publication through <u>Sartoris</u> (1929). This material reveals a variety of influences at work in Faulkner's early literary development, most notably that of the French Symbolists, who were to help him become a regional writer with a difference. The study isolates, analyzes, and traces recurring images, devices, themes, and motifs, thus giving some concept of the continuing development of Faulkner's techniques during this period. The strongest contemporary influences on Faulkner-- beginning with Phil Stone as friend, Maecenas, and editor and culminating with Sherwood Anderson as friend, writer, and source--operated in ways more subtle than has been previously realized. [Order No. 64-2602; 303 pages. DAI, 24A (Jan.-March 1964), 3750.]

079 Game-Consciousness and Game-Metaphor in the Work of William Faulkner / Nicholas Michael RINALDI, Fordham University, 1963 (Ralph A. Ranald).

Faulkner's fiction is freighted with allusions to games. In almost every novel which Faulkner has written, one finds a vast complex of game-metaphors, game-similes, game-like situations, and descriptions of actual games. The significance of these game allusions has been virtually unexplored by the criticism. What is their relevance in Faulkner's fiction? Are they merely part of the surface description of the world which Faulkner has created? Or do they incorporate some broad thematic reference in his work? If the latter, to what specific layer of meaning do they relate? These are the broad, enveloping questions which have served as guidelines for this study.

The games alluded to in Faulkner's fiction are numerous and diverse, the most prominent being: chess, checkers, poker, dice, horse- and airplane-racing, the hunt, and the duel. An introductory chapter draws attention to the fact that these games, despite their seeming disparateness, have one thing in common: all of them are agonistic in character; that is, the players who participate in them possess a keen sense of contest, are driven by a passion to win, and in order to win they resort to any underhanded strategem which their cunning can devise. In dealing with Faulkner's work, the game as agon, or self-interested context, must be distinguished from the game as disinterest or "pure" play, in which the participants are not concerned about the actual outcome of the game, the profit and loss, but are entirely engrossed in the simple joy of playing. In short, the games in Faulkner's fiction are played according to a well defined ethic: winning is the summum bonum, losing is the only evil.

It is the agonistic character of these games which gives them their thematic relevance. In virtually every instance in which Faulkner has incorporated a game into the action of a novel or story, the inclusion of the game illuminates the fact that the agonistic instincts of gamesmanship have become operative in the "real life" situations which exist outside the game: morals and human values have been supplanted by game-ethics, and life itself has been reduced to the impersonal level of a contest. The characters who bring about such a reduction may be said to be motivated by game-consciousness, a quality of consciousness which injects into human relationships the instincts and impulses, modes of thought and action, which have their proper place only inside the world of games. Thus, wherever it crops up in human affairs, game-consciousness creates an atmosphere of rivalry which destroys the mutual trust and the sense of brotherhood which man must achieve, Faulkner insists, if he is to endure.

Following a general introduction to the nature of game-consciousness, this study explores in depth the functioning of game-consciousness in four of Faulkner's major novels: The Sound and The Fury, Light in August, Absalom, Absalom!, and The Hamlet. By examining the games, game-imagery, and game-like situations in these novels, this study shows that the majority of Faulkner's characters, in diverse, intricate ways, and with varying capabilities, confront life as though they were players in a game. The stakes they play for are pleasure, money, power, respectability, or any other form of self-aggrandizement, and the methods they employ are marked by the guile and cunning, and sometimes even by the violence, which are common in actual games.

To indicate the extent to which game-consciousness is operative in novels other than the four which comprise the main subject of this study, the concluding chapter presents a broad survey of the more striking instances of game-metaphor in Faulkner's other works. The study therefore broadens into an approach which may be fruitfully applied to the entire range of Faulkner's fiction. [Order No. 64-2409; 237 pages. DAI, 24A (April-June 1964), 4196-97.]

080 The Glance of the Idiot: A Thematic Study of Faulkner and Modern French Fiction / John Kenneth SIMON, Yale University, 1963 (Richard W. B. Lewis).

Our study is an attempt to trace the pattern of significant common themes in Faulkner and contemporary French fiction: the scene of apocalypse, the imagery of metamorphosis, the narrative voice divided between action and the characterization of madness. We hope that the use of As I Lay Dying as a pivotal work will succeed in indicating a more profound relationship between Faulkner and the French authors from Andre Malraux to Michel Butor who have been fascinated by him since the early 1930s.

This is not, however, a study of source. While we shall occasionally point out moments of direct Faulknerian influence (most specifically on Jean-Paul Sartre and Claude Simon), that is not our primary interest. We shall be following a literary--not rigidly historical--development. Basically, our thesis proposes a relation between the apocalyptic landscape of contemporary fiction and the preconceptual mind of the idiot figure.

The flood of As I Lay Dying and Old Man, the anthropological explorations and deadly gas attack of Malraux's Les Noyers de l'Altenburg document the pictorial theme of erupting matter, the de-emphasized human creature's conflict with the crushing, imponderable dark continents. Return to the myth of chaos suggests a purge of the complacent, civilized surface of things.

The metamorphosis is expressed in the Baudelairian imagery of eroticism and death. Sanctuary and La Nausée are comparable attempts to describe the formless, obscene nature of life, as the body cannot innocently deny its existence as flesh. Like the decomposing cadaver, insects and crustaceans, from Dostoevsky and Kafka to Malraux and Sartre, represent a vaguely fascinating, intermediary universe on the border of the inhuman and death, where the inanimate comes to life and the living is dehumanized.

Similarly, analogous to the very narrative structure of As I Lay Dying, a schism divides the objectivity of act from the subjectivity of consciousness. A schizophrenic intellectual, the contemporary French writer doubts of the significance of objects or thoughts, of the means of narration, of words themselves. He treads an uneasy balance between total collapse before the plenitude of externals and complete withdrawal into an ultimate solipsism.

Nostalgia for a natural synthesis suggests an ambivalent figure who would not recognize--and would therefore bridge--the gap between the objective existence of things and the mind in isolation. A modified reemergence of the medieval concept of sacred madness in this sense is heralded in the ambiguity of Dostoevsky's Prince Myshkin, Faulkner's Benjy Compson, of modern versions of Hamlet. The neurosis of the artist, the lunacy of his idiot character are neither to be cured nor to be naively worshipped. Rather, reflecting the chaotic landscape and attempting to harmonize the various antitheses, there simply remains in the background the primitiveness of the "natural," the reconciliation of his mute gaze. [Order No. 64-7147; 506 pages. DAI, 25A (July-Sept. 1964), 1220.]

081 Faulkner and the Negro / Aaron STEINBERG, New York University, 1963 (Oscar Cargill).

Through detailed examination of pertinent novels and stories, the attempt in this study has been to avoid unsubstantiated generalities about Faulkner's treatment of the Negro in his fiction.

In the opening chapters, those dealing with Faulkner's earlier, less important, work, aspects of Faulkner's complex attitude are discussed. (1) Faulkner's hostility to Negroes at the beginning of his career seems evident from his statements about them in Sartoris. (2) The relative nature of Faulkner's delineation of the Negro is suggested by his portrayal of Caspey in Sartoris, who is both a "good," and a "bad," Negro, depending upon the situation in which he is in. (3) Although Faulkner feels compassion for such Negroes as Nancy Mannigoe and the Negro slave in "Red Leaves," his compassion seems inextricably mixed with other, hostile, elements and must be viewed as an ambivalent response. (4) Negroes such as Nancy Mannigoe and Rider (in "Pantaloon in Black") are used as touchstones by Faulkner to "show up" white behavior.

In the chapter on The Sound and the Fury, Faulkner's relative approach to his presentation of Dilsey is discussed, as is Quentin's statement that Negroes are "not so much persons as forms of behavior ... obverse reflections of the whites around them," from which it may be suggested that Faulkner's Negroes do not have personalities intrinsically their own, but that they depend upon white persons for their energy and substance.

Detailed analysis of the internal tensions in Light in August suggests that Faulkner is not in full control of his material: that Joe Christmas is not-Negro, but that he becomes Negro in the final moments as Faulkner, yielding to the irrational "Negro-making" energies in the novel, appears to be overwhelmed by the products of his own fantasy by the novel's close.

In the chapter on Absalom, Absalom!, the relationship of Bon's "Negro-ness" to the novel's illogical structure is discussed.

Examination of both Go Down, Moses and Intruder in the Dust suggests that Faulkner is unable to solve the problem of the Negro that he wants so desperately to solve.

It seems possible to make the following generalizations about Faulkner's treatment of the Negro.

(1) Faulkner's hostility to the Negro, his belief in the Negro's inferiority, his irrational fears of blood pollution--all deeply ingrained Southern attitudes--permeate his fiction and determine the structure of those novels in which Negroes are significantly involved. Faulkner, however, does not seem conscious of his own hostility.

(2) Faulkner appears to prefer Negroes who accept the status quo. There is no evidence that he sympathizes with Negroes who attempt to better their condition by defying the established order.

(3) Faulkner seems unable to come to grips with the problem of the Negro: the more he wants to solve the problem, the more he arouses inner blood fears precipitated by the knowledge that racial barriers must be lifted for the problem to be solved.

(4) Faulkner's Negro characters seem to derive energy and substance from their relationship to white persons to whom they are juxtaposed. They are presented relatively. They do not seem to possess complex, totally self-contained, personalities.

(5) Faulkner's Negroes are not fully developed characters in the usual sense: they are either fragmented or what may be termed "synthetic" (Christmas, for example, is not really Negro). Faulkner is most brilliant in portraying particular moments in the lives of Negroes.

(6) Faulkner's Negroes are used as touchstone-catalysts to "show up" or expose white behavior or emotions; they are also used to illustrate a thesis.

(7) Through his use of the Negro as touchstone-catalyst, Faulkner has presented uncanny psychological studies of Southern life. [Order No. 66-9531; 400 pages. DAI, 27A (Nov.-Dec. 1966), 1385.

082 Faulkner's Sanctuary and Requiem for a Nun: Songs of Innocence and Experience / Pamela Anne ULREY, Cornell University, 1963 (William M. Sale, Jr.).

The original, unpublished version of Sanctuary confirms that the book is not a "potboiler," but a serious exploration of the individual's role in society. Gavin Stevens does not make "explicit" a "tamed" Faulkner's "philosophy" in Requiem, and Sanctuary and Requiem are more significantly related than critics have perceived.

Both are concerned with injustice in society and with the reasons for its being there--so that Horace Benbow who, in Sanctuary, says he "cannot stand idly by and see injustice," is quite meaningfully succeeded in Requiem by Gavin Stevens, who tells Temple: "What we are trying to deal with now is injustice. Only truth can cope with that. Or love." Both Horace and Gavin are living in the adult world of "experience" which such characters as Lucius Priest, Bayard Sartoris, Chuck Mallison are "initiated" into in The Reivers, The Unvanquished, and Intruder in the Dust, respectively. Besides the innocence of childhood, there is in Faulkner the innocence of the idiot, of those who, like Narcissa Benbow or Isaac McCaslin, shut out most of the world around them. Throughout Faulkner's work, the contrast is significant between the character who is, or somehow remains, basically "innocent," and the character who is living either successfully or unsuccessfully in the adult world of experience. For those who become "initiated," acceptance, the ability to "sing in one's chains," is crucial; and if there is to be any "sanctuary" for the individual or any "justice" in society, they will exist only because man learns to live with the home which is himself--hence the meaning of Temple Drake's name, beyond the ironic implications of Sanctuary. The original version of Sanctuary makes it clear that Faulkner, using the reflector-device of ironically paralleling certain seemingly "opposite" characters and situations, is "defining man" as private and as public creature; his responsibility to himself and to others is a problem which unites, usually ironically, the characters within the two groups juxtaposed and then connected, through Temple.

Requiem continues the "definition," but from the vantage point of history. The prose sections illustrate Gavin's statement that the past is never dead, in relation not only to Temple and her problem of acceptance, but to the individual generally. The staccato dialogue of the dramatic sections, contrasted with the flowing prose of the historical narratives, focuses Temple's drama as a "frozen moment" among the inseperable "moments" of history, most of which reveal worlds more complicated than that of Nancy Mannigoe, who, rather than a "chorus," is an "innocent," essentially, despite the "experience" which prompts Temple to employ her. Faulkner is not a "primitivist," does not want to go back to a time basically different from that of Temple Drake.

When speaking of A Fable, Faulkner explained what he called the "trilogy of man's conscience": man can retreat from "experience" if he finds it distasteful, or he can passively endure it, or he can try to make it better. All of Faulkner's novels may be said to dramatize this "trilogy," to dramatize man's battle--sometimes won, sometimes lost, sometimes ignored--to better himself and his world. His failure is always qualified by the difficulty of his quest and by his willingness to make it--an "affirmation" Faulkner ironically emphasizes when he places a Lena Grove along with the struggling Christmas, a Dilsey along with Quentin Compson, a Nancy along with Temple --or when he places Horace Benbow in a world which, like that of Miss Lonelyhearts, is so nightmarish as to remain almost totally foreign to him. [Order No. 63-8119; 204 pages. DAI, 24A (Oct.-Dec. 1963), 2043-44.]

083 The Regional Novel of the South: The Dilemma of Innocence / Joseph
    Richard WHITTINGTON, University of Oklahoma, 1963 (Victor A. Elconin) no DAI entry.

084 Man's Enduring Chronicle: A Study of Myth in the Novels of William
    Faulkner / Walter Marion BRYLOWSKI, Michigan State University, 1964 (Hazard Adams).

Myth is an important factor in Faulkner's novels on several levels. In the earliest novels it is found on the simplest level as rhetorical embellishment; but already, in the resurrection image, it portends Faulkner's later use of myth as mythos, analogues which inform theme and structure. In the middle novels Faulkner displays an intuitive understanding of the true force of myth and, for the first time, creates characters whose reality can be understood and illuminated in terms of the "mythic consciousness" as analyzed by Ernst Cassirer.

A study of myth in Faulkner's novels reveals the nature of the polarity often remarked in Faulkner's vision. As a rational empiricist, Faulkner has a view of man which embraces the folly, misery, and corruption denying the ideal view of man. On the other hand, Faulkner cannot and will not surrender his view of man as a being capable of an ideal, that ideal often presented as a transcendental unification with the spirit of man. While in the middle period of his work Faulkner makes no attempt to present this conflict in any rationalized form, the novels following upon Absalom, Absalom! reveal a change in emphasis, a change that is roughly correlative to the epistemological progress from mythical consciousness to the religious consciousness. In this ethical period there is a greater development of the rational empiric attempt to resolve the distance between the poles of man's existence. That this was not a satisfactory resolution is indicated by Faulkner's abandonment of the approach in his magnum opus, A Fable. Here the rational empiric voice no longer attempts to mitigate the transcendental theme. And, if we are to adduce the last three novels as evidence, we must conclude that A Fable succeeded in laying to rest Faulkner's "demon," the creative force that drove him on; for these last novels communicate none of the tension of their predecessors. Myth as a factor in these novels is a consciously controlled tool subordinated to a vision already realized, the problem of evil no longer endangering the survival of the "verities."

The use of the word myth in relation to the series of Yoknapatawpha novels is, I believe, unwarranted. What myth is there can largely be accounted for in terms of a mythical consciousness on the part of certain characters who interpret their regional inheritance in mythic terms. If we are to persist in the use of the term, it must be only after a careful redefinition of the word, a procedure that is unnecessary in view of the fact that the word saga already exists and would serve the purpose better. The usual approach to the body of Faulkner's work, that of dividing the novels into those with a Yoknapatawpha background and those with other backgrounds, is also misleading. I believe a consideration of the novels in the chronology of their publication to be more revealing of the author's intellectual growth if not of his artistic success.

Faulkner's period of artistic greatness manifested in the middle period and to a lesser degree in Go Down, Moses and A Fable is that of the poet of creative intuition. His distrust of language, his constant distortion of words and syntax, reveals what Maritain calls the "liberation from conceptual, logical, discursive reason," a process intended to allow scope for "intuitive reason" which is prior to logical reason. There is a high correlation here with the mythical consciousness described by Cassirer. It is my contention that the essence of Faulkner's intuition is in that realm of mythic thought which is prior to logical reason. The polar optimism Faulkner cherishes in his most pessimistic moments is an intuition directly related to myth, an intuition that allows him to transcend the world of appearances to arrive at a statement of man's indestructible spirit. It is an achievement that places him directly in the transcendental tradition. [Order No. 65-1715; 313 pages. DAI, 25A (April-June 1965), 6617-18.]

085 Sentence Patterns in The Sound and the Fury / W. C. CHISHOLM, University of Michigan, 1964, (James W. Downer) no DAI entry.

086 The Grotesque in Modern American Fiction: An Existential Theory / Ralph A. CIANCIE, University of Pittsburgh, 1964, no DAI entry.

087 The Fury and the Design: Realms of Being and Knowing in Four Novels of William Faulkner / Rocco Roberto FAZIO, University of Rochester, 1964 (Howard C. Horsford).

With his will to order and form, civilized man has become increasingly self-deprived of direct, intuitive, unmediated experience. This is a recurrent theme in the novels of William Faulkner, a theme that has been acknowledged by a number of commentators, but whose complex dimensions have not, I believe, been sufficiently explored. There is, in Faulkner's works, frequently a dialectic between being and knowing, between intuitive experience and rational formulation, which informs some of his best novels and serves as a unifying element for many of his other important thematic interests. A demonstration of his dialectic at work in some of Faulkner's best novels is important to an understanding of Faulkner's moral vision, and it may contribute to a profitable reading of his fiction. It may further suggest a corrective for those who persist in seeing Faulkner as a regional writer.

This essay explores Faulkner's handling of the being-knowing dialectic, the shifts in treatment, in emphases, and in attitude in portraying various realms of being and knowing. Between the earliest novel, Soldiers' Pay (1926), and Absalom, Absalom! (1936) Faulkner's attitude and technique undergo significant modification. The attitude and its modification are analyzed in this essay by an examination of Faulkner's imagery, character delineation, irony, metaphor, and other relevant matters in selected novels.

This essay shows that Faulkner moves from an imaginative interest in personal being and doing to an ironic, mediative interest in life and behavior in a public and social sense. It further shows that from the very indulgent prose of the first two novels, Soldiers' Pay and Mosquitoes, novels which exhibit strong sympathy for intuitive characters, Faulkner gradually moves toward more exacting literary forms and toward a more objectively critical attitude toward being and knowing. The being-knowing dialectic is dramatically realized in some of the best novels up to and through Absalom, Absalom!. The study of that dialectic ends with this novel, for by the time he writes Absalom, Absalom!, Faulkner has reached that delicately balanced point where spontaneity begins to pass over into reflection and into the too often tiresome, garrulous ramblings of the later novels.

The strategy of this essay is to begin with an examination of Faulkner's first two novels in order to establish the nature of the being-knowing dialectic. Extended treatment is then given to The Sound and the Fury, As I Lay Dying, Light in August, and Absalom, Absalom!. These novels are generally regarded as Faulkner's best fiction, and I believe that their quality derives from the demonstrable fact that in creating them Faulkner was imaginatively engaged in working out the being-knowing dialectic. These novels show a distinct progression in awareness of the dimensions of that dialectic. Other novels of the period, Sartoris, Sanctuary, and Pylon, and many of the short stories, are excluded from extensive analysis because they do not, I believe, reveal a significant progression either in structure or theme.

Faulkner's general style and technique as employed throughout the canon are briefly discussed to show their relationship to the being-knowing dialectic, but this essay does not explore the relationship in extensive analytical detail. Crucial and obvious shifts in style and technique are noted throughout, but the emphasis is on thematic shifts. [Order No. 64-9233; 202 pages. DAI, 25A (July-Sept. 1964), 1910.]

088 Levels of Maturity: The Theme of Striving in the Novels of William Faulkner / George Leroy FRIEND, University of Illinois, 1964 (John T. Flanagan).

When William Faulkner accepted the Nobel Prize in Stockholm on November 10, 1950, he used the occasion to reaffirm his faith in man's endurance. For over 20 years his major theme had been either relegated to a minor position or totally ignored; there, however, he repeated what he had been long expounding in his novels and stories: "man will not only endure, he will prevail." My primary purpose is to verify Faulkner's assertion and to show that he was not a sociologist or a psychologist, but an artist who dramatized man's striving against inherent evil and who exalted reality over romanticism and action over passivity. These are my aims: to specify some aspects of the mature personality; to examine the problem of self-realization; to determine what influence the family and the past exert upon individual development; to present Faulkner's interest in the traditional theme of initiation; and, especially by using his idea of man's striving, to indicate various levels of maturity his characters attain by their continued growth.

In the introductory section, Faulkner's emphasis on the individual and his striving is explored in terms of his belief that man tries to be better than he actually can be. Some psychological as well as moral criteria of maturity are examined, and Faulkner's own "trinity of human conscience" is used to specify three distinct levels of maturity: those who refuse to accept evil and choose death; those who accept evil yet remain passive; and those who accept evil and do something about it.

Pylon, Absalom, Absalom!, As I Lay Dying, and Light in August are then discussed as novels in which familial influences on maturation are strongly felt. The ambiguous parent, multiple paternity, and the orphan are presented as indications of Faulkner's interest in the homelessness of modern man. Pylon is seen as a search for family and identity. Absalom dramatizes a similar theme: man must be recognized by his immediate family before he can, in turn, recognize and accept the bonds of universal brotherhood. As I Lay Dying, the novel of the family par excellence, depicts Cash's maturity as all the more admirable since it is not accompanied by profound intelligence. In his striving for identity and acceptance, Joe Christmas, the complete alien, is found to attain a belated yet high degree of maturity.

Quentin Compson, Ike McCaslin, and Gail Hightower are then presented as initiates whose inordinate addiction to the past limits their degree of maturity. As negative examples, they dramatize the importance of action in the present, thereby disproving the theory that Faulkner was a primitivist.

In his use of the theme of initiation, Faulkner deviated only slightly from the traditional. The Unvanquished, for example, employs a mature perspective. Sanctuary works an inversion of the theme: neither Temple nor Popeye gains self-knowledge. Requiem for a Nun suggests that Faulkner was not content to leave Temple unregenerated. Byron Bunch and the Runner further prove Faulkner's undying interest in the theme of individual growth. From these examples, a crucial aspect of the young man's initiation is found to be his willingness to accept free will and the responsibility it places on him as an individual.

Although Faulkner chose to dramatize his theme primarily by negative examples, his presentation of man striving to be better than he can be is sufficient proof of his faith in humanity. Although some critics still read Faulkner in terms of naturalistic determinism, his frequent use of theme of striving refutes the charge that he was a cosmic pessimist. Obviously, without free will or optimism, this Bergsonian sort of striving would indeed be futile. In Faulkner, man is always existentially free to create himself. If his struggle is irresolvable, it is nevertheless bearable, resulting in a degree of improvement. There are, then, no distinct periods in Faulkner's development, for he always insisted on a mature striving to accept whatever is as the reality that must be coped with and prevailed over. [Order No. 65-2986; 318 pages. DAI, 25A (April-June 1965), 6622-23.]

089 The Failure of the Imagination: A Study of Melville, Conrad, and Faulkner / James Lawrence GUETTI, Jr., Cornell University, 1964 (Robert M. Adams).

The subject of this dissertation is the explicit concern to be found in the works of Melville, Conrad, and Faulkner, with the insufficiencies of language. This concern is most often displayed in the dramatization of a character's or a narrator's failure to compose or structure his imaginative experience or to extract from this experience some dominant metaphor, some consistent and flexible language by which his world becomes both controlled and meaningful.

By means of close verbal analyses of Moby Dick, Heart of Darkness, and Absalom, Absalom! I have tried to show that although this dramatized imaginative failure is unequivocal, it is nonetheless ambiguous, because it is expressed in a rhetorical technique peculiar to these authors--the characteristic manner in which a narrator approaches a problem by repeatedly circling it and surrounding it with disparate allusions and suggestions, never emphasizing a single suggestion as definitive and relying, at crucial moments, upon the nearly simultaneous use of separate literary vocabularies and upon similes of the greatest but vaguest significance. The essential paradox here is that while this linguistic technique has connotations largely of failure for the central characters and even the narrators of these and other novels by Melville, Conrad, and Faulkner, at the same time it is the most suggestive and powerful of the techniques of prose fiction. This paradox has its source, as I have tried to demonstrate, in the very nature of language itself, and more particularly in the nature of metaphor.

For the expressiveness of a given metaphor--as a consideration of these writers may reveal--depends upon its instability, upon its not being finally resolved or synthesized or fixed and upon its function of holding in suspension intensely different sorts of awareness, of language, of imaginative experience. This same expressiveness also depends, however, upon the illusion that the metaphor can be or will be satisfactorily resolved so as to have an ordering and a cognitive function. The expectation of order, in short, cannot be satisfied if a metaphor is to maintain its force as such, and yet the persistent denial of this expectation exposes the supposedly metaphorical juxtaposition as aimless verbal confusion.

It is this attitude toward language, I think, that lies at the heart of the unresolved paradox and open structure chracteristic of these and other works by Melville, Conrad, and Faulkner and of works by many of the most important 20th century novelists. As an attitude it is displayed in a reliance upon narrative complexity, instability, and even confusion, and in the characteristic images of the search, the hunt, and the struggle for meaning or identity, with an insistence upon the inevitability of failure, or the anti-climax of success, and upon the fact that only the process itself is meaningful, and not its consummation or issue.

Obviously the novel with which I am concerned--at least in its most striking form--is of a special sort, one that thrives upon distance from civilized contexts, upon situations that are basically unstructured. Yet once the problems that I have sketched here are recognized, it becomes apparent that they are relevant to a major tradition in the novel. It becomes clear also that Ahab and Moby Dick, Marlow and Kurtz, and Sutpen and his "design" are much more than isolated or aberrant instances of obscure tragedy. Their quests and conflicts are important not only in relation to much established prose fiction--Lawrence, Joyce, Ford, Forster, Virginia Woolf--but also, and more significant, in relation to our awareness of the problematical qualities of language, metaphor, and imagination themselves. [Order No. 64-13,805; 240 pages. DAI, 25A (Jan.-March 1965), 4145-46.]

090 The Individual and the Community: Values in the Novels of William
Faulkner / Donald Mordecai KARTIGANER, Brown University, 1964 (Hyatt H. Waggoner).

At the heart of Faulkner's major work lies a consistent and persuasive attack on many of the basic principles of Western civilization. Not only can his work be understood as a criticism of modernism, as many critics have suggested, but as an undermining of the very idea of Western community itself, that concept of existence which inevitably subordinates the individual to his society, which believes fervently in the necessities of hierarchy, repression, and the domination of the masses by the few, which accepts finally the horror of chaos and the holiness of order. Even the pre-Civil War period of the South, frequently looked upon as the embodiment of Faulkner's supreme standards of value, is portrayed in such a novel as Absalom, Absalom! as an elaborate metaphor of rigidity, convention, and oppression, in which individuals are held in check by an inhuman plantation society.

From As I Lay Dying to A Fable, during which period this anti-social theme develops and reaches its most significant achievement, Faulkner's most sympathetic characters invariably find themselves on the periphery of society, either indifferent to it, or--sometimes at the cost of their lives-- actively opposing its most basic codes. Such characters as Darl [Bundren] of As I Lay Dying and Lee Goodwin and Ruby Lamar of Sanctuary are indicative of Faulkner's growing concern for the character who may find his self-fulfillment only in a highly individualistic form of behavior, one that the community at large cannot tolerate. Such characters as Joe Christmas, Lena Grove, and Byron Bunch, Roger Shumann and his "family," Charles Bon, Charlotte Rittenmeyer, Eula Varner and Ike and Mink Snopes, Ike McCaslin, the Corporal--all are involved in forms of anti-social behavior, whether it be Mink's murder of Houston, Lena Grove's casual promiscuity and inability to be ashamed of her pregnancy, or the Corporal's attempt to overthrow the whole military structure, itself a microcosm of Western civilization. Even in the later novels, where Faulkner definitely modifies his position, tending to reconcile even the most radical individualism with community purpose, we still find such socially dangerous characters as Lucas Beauchamp and Charles Mallison, his grave-robbing savior, Nancy Mannigoe, and even the three engaging thieves of Faulkner's last novel. The predominence of such figures in Faulkner's fiction, all presented with sympathy and compassion by the author, even as he invariably assails the communities in which these figures exist as pariahs, seems significant indication that Faulkner is hardly the conservative he has too often been categorized, and that he may in fact be one of the more radical artists of our time.

Rather than community, it is a concept of communion, particularly as it is developed in Buber's theory of I and Thou, that is one of the keys to Faulkner's standard of values. Ironically enough, this communion, this meeting of individuals, where there is solidity without loss of individuality, unity without rigidity, always occurs in Faulkner outside the community code: in the unconventional love affairs of Goodwin and Ruby, Lena and Byron, Mink and his wife, the fellowship of the Corporal and his disciples, or the occasional oneness of the unorthodox flyers in Pylon and the thieves of The Reivers.

This theme seems basic in much of Faulkner's work, especially in the period from Light in August to Go Down, Moses, with the significant inclusion of A Fable from the novels outside that range. And the general decline of value in Faulkner's fiction after 1942 can be explained partially in terms of his adoption of more orthodox attitudes. [Order No. 65-2213; 233 pages. DAI, 25A (Jan.-March 1965), 4701-02.]

091 The Grotesque in Recent Southern Fiction / Lewis Allen LAWSON, University of Wisconsin, 1964 (John J. Enck) no DAI entry.

092 Humor in Faulkner's Novels: Its Development, Forms, and Functions / James Milton MELLARD, University of Texas, 1964 (Philip Graham).
Always using it functionally in the development of plot, character and theme, William Faulkner develops his humor in three stages; moreover, each stage parallels a stage in his development in the use of different fictional modes as well as one in his rise and decline in artistic power. Corresponding to the earliest stage of his emergency as a serious artist, the first stage in the development of Faulkner's humor shows an emphasis on verbal techniques--"witty" dialogue, the pun, malapropism, misspelling, anticlimax, and incongruity--although comic characterizations and humorous situations are also employed. Even the novels of this period--Solders' Pay and Sartoris, particularly--employ the humor as a "tool," as a device, used to

develop character and narrative structure, as well as to present theme. For example, in Sartoris, the best novel of this period, the humorous remarks of Aunt Jenny reveal character by contrasting young Bayard's romantic view of himself with her own more objective and realistic view. But at the same time, these humorous remarks develop Faulkner's major theme in the novel, the deleterious effects of family and regional myth, for they are based upon the assumption that those myths can compel actions and, perhaps, determine the fate of an individual--young Bayard, in this instance.

The humor of the second stage of development relies rather heavily on comic characters and episodes, while the imitative "wit," more or less absent here, is replaced by the verbal humor of folk language--hyperbole and litotes. Since this stage parallels Faulkner's "wasteland" period, 1929-1940, the shift of emphasis in comic forms is accompanied by a tremendously increased irony. As a result of these changes, the novels of this period show a progressive movement toward heavily episodic structures, culminating in the "comic irony"--using Northrop Frye's terminology--of The Hamlet. The humor of this period is more effectively satirical than that of the first, for the increased irony gives us a double vision of the characters and events lacking in, say, Soldiers' Pay. Grotesque as the humor often is in As I Lay Dying and Sanctuary, it allows Faulkner to probe beneath appearances in order to penetrate the depths of reality. Thus, for example, the humor in As I Lay Dying is central to Faulkner's central theme of disparity between appearance and reality, for it is emphasized by the chapters of the "objective" narrators being juxtaposed to those of the Bundren family.

The humor of the third and last stage of development, from Go Down, Moses to The Reivers, continues to rely on comic episodes, but the purely verbal humor, still based on exaggeration, has become diffused because of the inflated rhetoric ascribed to characters such as Gavin Stevens. Although distinguishable from the humor of stage two because of the sharply decreased irony, the humor here often retains much of the quality of that in, say, The Hamlet. Nevertheless, Faulkner's power as a humorist begins to decline, along with his power as a "serious" artist, because his experiments with Steven's rhetorical humor, which dominate many of the novels beginning with Intruder in the Dust, are generally unsuccessful and virtually obviate the effective humor of character and episode. Similarly, the weak rhetorical humor of Faulkner's last novel allows The Reivers only to approach the quality of The Hamlet and parts of The Town. Nevertheless, The Reivers completes the career of a most "serious" writer on a note of humor, the best of which is derived from Faulkner's most successful forms--comic episodes and characterizations. [Order No. 64-8022; 255 pages. DAI, 25A (July-Sept. 1964), 480-81.]

093 The Apprenticeship of William Faulkner: The Early Short Stories and the First Three Novels / Eugene MIRABELLI, Jr., Harvard University, 1964 (Monroe Engel) no DAI entry.

094 Moral Values of the American Woman as Presented in Three Major American Authors [Hawthorne, James, and Faulkner] / Maude Cardwell ROSS, University of Texas, 1964 (Mody C. Boatright).

Through an analysis of the works of three major American novelists-- Nathanial Hawthorne's The Scarlet Letter, Henry James' The Golden Bowl, and William Faulkner's trilogy: The Hamlet, The Town, and The Mansion-- I have attempted to gain an idea of what moral values have been held by American women. I assume that an individual's moral values can best be discovered by an observation of both his actions and his evaluation of these actions, and that the pattern in his moral values can be discerned in the relationship these actions have to the goal he is seeking. Because the realistic novel has traditionally attempted to portray the lives of real people as lived in their contemporary societies, there is a likelihood that good examples of this kind of novel still give information about moral codes that cannot so readily be obtained from historical documents--such as letters and diaries--and sociological case histories. Although less objective than some of these sources, a novel generally contains more intimate details than does a case history, and relates the individual more fully to his social context than does a historical document. The moral codes which I have discovered in the novels of my study need, of course, to be investigated in the light of historical evidence.

Hester Prynne, Maggie Verver, and Eula Varner--the three fictional heroines whom I study, along with their masculine associates--although adherents to different moral codes, have some principles in common. These principles I believe to be significant for American women as a whole. The principles are as follows:

First, a woman should control her own desires completely so that she can identify herself partially or wholly with others, particularly with her children or husband or father. Through this almost supernatural feat she will impress men and thus be permitted to guide them by precept or example or simply through sexual desire and its chaotic responses which she arouses in them.

Second, she should either attempt to control her spontaneous desires or assume that she spontaneously desires only to beget and rear children. In either case, she must sharply restrict her self-expression.

Third, although Hester Prynne attempts to control non-human objects, the more recent heroines--Maggie Verver and Eula Varner--believe that such control is the moral duty of men, and that, conversely, their own moral duty is to refrain from such control.

Fourth, a woman should not attempt overt control of even hostile people. Such control, like the control of nonhuman objects, is the moral duty of men. A woman may, however, employ extensive covert control. This ideally takes the form of self-control, example, and inspiration.

Fifth, a woman--particularly in the case of Maggie Verver and Eula Varner--must be more conscious of her relationship with the unknown, and more dependent upon the unknown than are her male contemporaries. [Order No. 65-4345; 201 pages. DAI, 25A (Jan.-March 1965), 5262-63.]

095 The Structural Function of the Christ Figure in the Fiction of William Faulkner / Warren Gunther RUBEL, University of Arkansas, 1964 (E. Leighton Rudolph).

In the fiction of William Faulkner one important symbolic motif, perhaps best termed the Christ figure, has received increasing critical attention since the publishing of Requiem for a Nun (1951) and A Fable (1954). Although there have been studies of the Christ figure in separate novels--especially The Sound and the Fury (1929), Light in August (1932), Pylon (1935), Requiem for a Nun, and A Fable-- and although most commentators admit the significance of the Christ figure in Faulkner's work, there has been no general study treating Faulkner's use of the Christ figure.

This dissertation represents an attempt to fulfill the need for such a study. A reading of the fiction and criticism indicates the development within the last decade of divergent critical response to Faulkner's Christ figure. One broad group (including Randall Stewart, Amos Wilder, William Mueller, and others), seeing Christ correspondences in Faulkner's work, has frequently identified the Christ figure or the Christian imagery with the Christian message. Another group (including Irving Howe, Frederick J. Hoffman, Lawrence Thompson, and others), reacting to the same correspondences, has pointed out that the Christ identities--as Faulkner himself admitted--are primarily tools Faulkner used for his own purposes as novelist and that these purposes are not necessarily related to orthodox Christianity at all. But advocates of this latter position have not fully explored either the technical uses Faulkner did make of the Christ figure or the integrated relationship of this Christ figure to important themes in Faulkner's later fiction.

If one distinguishes between Faulkner's use of Christian imagery and the Christian faith, it becomes quite evident that Faulkner used the Christ figure in a variety of ways to achieve his own artistic ends. In fact, Faulkner's use of the Christ figure developed through three overlapping distinguishable stages. In a first stage, comprising the juvenilia and the novels Soldiers' Pay (1926), Mosquitoes (1927), and Sartoris (1929), the Christ figure appears sporadically and inconsistently in the fiction. Faulkner's characters cast their own shadows, and part of their fictional environment includes a Christ and an institutional Christianity impinging on the life and language of the fictional community. These early appearances of the Christ figure anticipate Faulkner's more sustained uses of the figure in the later fiction.

In a second stage, beginning with The Sound and the Fury, the Christ figure emerges as an important though subsidiary means Faulkner used for evoking various intellectual and emotional responses in his reader--chiefly through his use of ironic analogy. This use of the figure appears in Light in August, Pylon, and the short stories "That Evening Sun" (1931), "Beyond" (1933), "That Will Be Fine" (1935), and "Uncle Willy" (1935).

A third stage marks another change in Faulkner's use of the Christ figure. Beginning with Go Down, Moses (1942), Faulkner seems to have become progressively interested not only in calling up in the reader a variety of emotive and intellectual responses but also in having the figure work for him in elucidating and reinforcing his themes. Although ironic analogies are still present, the irony is relieved by Faulkner's increasing concern for man's need to work toward meaningful ethical norms. Isaac McCaslin, Nancy Mannigoe, and Stefan Demont place their lives in jeopardy for the Faulknerian "verities"--compassion and pity and humility and pride and courage and sacrifice. And Faulkner used Christ correspondences with these characters to arouse the reader's assent to their action on behalf of man. In Faulkner's fiction it becomes clear that Faulkner became increasingly concerned with offering to men a promise of hope. The Christ figure became for him a significant token of this promise for man. [Order No. 65-1526; 328 pages. DAI 25A (April-June 1965), 5941-42.]

096 The 20th Century Impressionistic Novel: Conrad and Faulkner / Jimmie Eugene TANNER, University of Oklahoma, 1964 (A. J. Fritz and Roy R. Male).

It is the thesis of this paper that as a novelistic craftsman William Faulkner belongs more to the impressionistic tradition of Joseph Conrad than to the stream-of-consciousness tradition of James Joyce. Owing perhaps to the fact that The Sound and the Fury and As I Lay Dying are the most widely discussed of all Faulkner's novels, critics of Faulkner have frequently referred to the relationship between his techniques and those of Joyce while virtually ignoring the more illuminating references to Conrad. In the last years of his life, however, Faulkner repeatedly asserted that Conrad was one of his "masters," an assertion corroborated by John Faulkner's statements that their mother introduced Conrad to the Faulkner boys and that William was never without a set of Conrad's works.

The influence of Conrad shows up both in Faulkner's style and in his techniques. Some passages in his earlier novels, Mosquitoes, for example, read like close paraphrases of Conradian passages from works such as Heart of Darkness. And always Faulkner's style resembles Conrad's in its rhythms as well as in its dependence on sonorous Latinisms, on abstractions paired in paradoxical phrases, on word-motifs, and on "negative ultimates"--negative words of ultimate degree. Finally, the function of Faulkner's style is the same as that of Conrad's, to draw the reader into the compelling trance of the language.

In the same way, the function of the fictional techniques in the works of both Conrad and Faulkner is to involve the reader as intensely as possible in the fictional experience. To this end, Conrad in his four best novels-- Lord Jim, Nostromo, The Secret Agent, and Under Western Eyes--directed his use of such devices and techniques as the narrator, rendering the progression d'effet, the timeshift (with its consequent juxtaposition of scenes and episodes for maximum meaning and intensity), and justification. To this end also Faulkner in three of his best novels--The Sound and the Fury, Light in August, and Absalom, Absalom!--directed his use of brilliant adaptations and extensions of the Conradian techniques, for, like all great writers, Faulkner was able to convert to his own ends Conrad's technical experiments and make his novels original creations rather than derivative ones. Nevertheless, because of his adaptations of them, the Conradian techniques are keys to the structure of Faulkner's novels and the approach to these novels through Conradian impressionism illuminates them almost as much as the same procedure illuminates Conrad's own. Faulkner, was, that is, a Conradian impressionist exploiting in his fiction all the advantages of the Conradian techniques--and sharing finally with Conrad in the one great disadvantage of these techniques: the inability to depict the growth and development of character. [Order No. 64-11,006; 220 pages. DAI, 25A (July-Sept. 1964), 1927-28.]

097 The Roles of the Negro in William Faulkner's Fiction / Walter Fuller TAYLOR, Jr., Emory University, 1964, (A. E. Stone).

This dissertation attempts an assessment of the thematic and structural roles of Negro characters in William Faulkner's fiction. Negroes are given pivotal functions in the majority of Faulkner's novels, and in many of his short stories. Although the intrinsic interest of these portraits is important, their value is chiefly in their significance for his white protagonists. In the former role, they are often less effective than his whites. In the latter, they contribute strongly to his best fiction.

Faulkner stands primarily as an assimilator rather than as a pioneer in the history of Negro characterizations. His views are seldom far from traditional ones. His most important Negro characterizations are outgrowths of the traditions of the Negro as childish dependent of the white, as emotional primitive, as clown, or as tragic mulatto. Although Faulkner's white protagonists sometimes articulate--and base their own actions on--sets of characteristics which they describe as typically Negroid, Faulkner seldom dramatizes such ideas in detailed, imaginatively conceived Negro portraits. Even in Go Down, Moses, which contains his most careful fictional assessment of his concepts of the Negro's primitivism, there is very little detailed dramatization of this subject. Intimate dramatizations of racial character are obviously not a requirement in all works which portray individuals of differing races, and stereotyped or traditional characterizations are obviously not of themselves artistic failures. The problem presented by Faulkner's Negroes, however, is the means of his employment of such portraits in individual works of art. By basing many of his plots on the race issue, Faulkner throws a weight on his Negro portraits which many readers will feel they do not always sustain.

Faulkner's historical characterizations reveal him at his furthest from direct experience, and hence furnish a guide to ways in which the uncritical re-creation of traditional views of Negro character may affect his art. This dissertation begins with a study of the manner in which traditional influences are reflected in his portrayals of slaves, Negro primitives, Reconstruction freedmen and 19th century mulattoes. It then examines in detail two 20th century characterizations, Rider of "Pantaloon in Black" (1940) and Molly Beauchamp of Go Down, Moses (1942), portraits which typify Faulkner's approach to the full-blooded Negro. It ends with an analysis of two visionary representations of the meaning of Southern history, Intruder in the Dust and Requiem for a Nun. It concludes that although Faulkner's handling of the Negro is often extremely effective, the relative weakness of his Negro portraits will for many readers have the effect of subtly undermining the motivations of his more imaginatively conceived whites. For such readers, this will weaken key passages and alter in some degree the total artistic effectiveness of his novels.

It should be emphasized, however, that Faulkner's shortcomings are often redeemed by the universal suggestiveness of his imagery, and by the artistry of his dramatization of the tragedy of the Negro's social role. In the mixed cultural heritage of the mulatto, furthermore, Faulkner often finds a material for tragic and symbolic portraits with which full-blooded Negroes do not furnish him. Perhaps his most important contributions are his attempts to dramatize the meaning of the Negro for white society; in this role, Negro and mulatto characters contribute strongly to much of his best fiction. As an eclectic artist who draws together older themes and infuses them with larger meanings, Faulkner has contributed a gallery of portraits which represent a landmark in the development of Negro characterization. Few writers have portrayed the reactions of whites to Negroes with more subtlety, or explored more elaborately the total meaning of the Negro for white society. [Order No. 64-11,221; 288 pages. DAI, 25A (Oct.-Dec. 1964), 2990.]

098 Faulkner's Rhetoric / Carey Gail WALL, Stanford University, 1964, (Albert J. Guerard and Wallace Stegner).

Faulkner's characters from book to book clearly share some kind of experience despite the differences among their lives. Nevertheless, Faulkner designs his major novels--The Sound and the Fury, As I Lay Dying, Light in August, Absalom, Absalom!, and The Hamlet--to evoke a variety of moods rather than the same one again and again. In some of the novels he subjects us to the characters' experience, while in others he permits us detachment; in each of them there is a new variety of techniques. This study began in a search for a definition of the precise nature of the experience Faulkner's characters share, for relations among the moods of the novels, and for a method underlying the variety of techniques.

"Faulkner's Rhetoric" sets forth the thesis that Faulkner's major characters' lives are all shaped by a battle between the individual human spirit and the alien forces that dispose men's fates. This spiritual battle is the primary nature of human experience as it is seen through the distorting lens of Faulkner's idiosyncratic vision, his private view of our objective world. The moods of the novels dramatize the abstract spiritual experience as Faulkner locates it in many kinds of human events. The method underlying the variety of techniques in these novels is that of the impressionistic novel: distortion. The aim of Faulkner's method, in general, is both to control our responses to frequently unlikable characters and to force us to share his vision of the world; these effects are achieved by subjecting us to the characters' spiritual experience.

In order to clarify this aspect of Faulkner's major fiction--the relation between idiosyncratic vision and technique--I have found it helpful to compare his techniques with those of other impressionistic novels. A handful of books--by James, Conrad, Proust, Joyce, and Kafka--offer sufficient illustration of the impressionistic method: the dramatic impulses underlying its various techniques of distortion and the basic effects created by means of those techniques. References to these novels appear in the course of my description of Faulkner's books whenever I have occasion to define and evaluate the basic method underlying his own techniques of distortion.

The title of this study derives from that of Wayne Booth's The Rhetoric of Fiction. "Rhetoric" is used here in the larger sense, not to designate mannerisms of style alone, but to include all matters of structure and dramatization--all of which contribute to the author's control, or lack of control, over his reader's responses. I have adopted the term because it seems to me an especially valuable one in describing the formal characteristics of fiction, the art of fiction. "Rhetoric" vulgarly means bombast, a lack of honest and direct correspondence between words and ideas. But strictly it means a carefully contrived use of language, designed to control the responses of the reader or listener. By speaking of Faulkner's techniques as his rhetoric, I wish to emphasize the calculated artistry of his major novels: this is the primary indirect argument of the whole study. Rather than an eccentric rebel against the conventions of usage and control, Faulkner is a writer of strong personal vision exploring technique and style as a means of creating for others as well as himself an image of his private world. Rather than a provincial, idiosyncratic stylist, he is a highly conscious craftsman working in the milieu of the impressionistic novel. He alters and creates techniques, much as Proust and Joyce do, to adapt fictional materials and techniques toward the personal expression of lyric poetry. [Order No. 65-2906; 343 pages. DAI, 25A (April-June 1965), 5947.]

099 The Form and Meaning of the Impressionist Novel / C. L. WEINGART, University of California at Davis, 1964 (W. V. O'Connor) no DAI entry.

100 A Study of the Noble Savage Myth in Characterization of the Negro in Selected American Literary Works / Electa C. WILEY, University of Arkansas, 1964 (Rudyard Kipling Bent) no DAI entry.

101 The Biblical View of History: Hawthorne, Mark Twain, Faulkner, and Eliot / Philip Eugene WILLIAMS, University of Pennsylvania, 1964 (Robert E. Spiller).

This study seeks to define a basic underlying interpretation of history in the American literary tradition by analysis of four major works from different periods which explore different aspects of America's history. The initial hypothesis is that the controlling presuppositions of our literature are derived from a biblical viewpoint which distinguishes our tradition from ancient religious and philosophical views of the meaninglessness of history, and from positivist views of 19th century scientific determinism. The Scarlet Letter, Huckleberry Finn, Absalom, Absalom!, and Four Quartets--despite wide differences as works of art--reflect a common tradition which holds that no rational formula comprehends history's meaning but which finds positive meaning in the dialectic of time and eternity from a perspective on history as under the ruling of divine providence working through justice and love.

Erich Auerbach's study of literary theory in Mimesis has shown how the Judeo-Christian concern with historicity gave the characteristic orientation of the European literary tradition. The present study extends this critical perspective to the literature of America, noting how these masterpieces are united in their concern with the meaning of history. Scholars have shown that the Bible is a basic literary source for the work of Hawthorne, Mark Twain, Faulkner, and Eliot. This study attempts to probe this influence more deeply in terms of doctrine.

The Scarlet Letter, a symbolic "romance" in a historic setting, rejects the idealism of the Transcendentalists and the legalistic moralism of Puritans. The view of history emphasizes "ambiguity," but lifts the perspective to a plane of divine judgment and reconciliation both in and beyond time. Relations may be traced to Jonathan Edwards and the History of the Work of Redemption, treating time as the stage of God's acts in the drama of salvation bringing good out of evil, and in this pattern Dimmesdale's "saintly" death and Hester's transformation bring renewal for their community.

Huckleberry Finn stands midway between Mark Twain's early optimism about history in response to Social Darwinism and his later nihilistic rejections expressed in vehement attacks on liberal progessivism and literal biblicism. It reflects limited hopes for history, especially in the concluding chapters which win both artistic and moral vindication through the brilliant transformation of hilarious comedy wherein Huck achieves maturity, Jim shows true nobility in the working-out of one of the finest of ironies, and Tom Sawyer's callow cruelty becomes the vehicle for the fullest character revelations and reconciliations.

In Absalom, Absalom! Greek and biblical traditions intertwine but the dominant view is of God's judgment against inordinate ambition rather than of the tragedy of implacable Fate. Like Milton's Lucifer and Melville's Ahab, Sutpen appears as a Satanic figure rather than victim of "innocence" or heredity or environment. A demonic avatar, he corrupts the whole course of history in which he is involved. Slavery, murder, and all forms of social injustice including war are brought under judgment, but the subtle center of the plot is seen in the consenting of Sutpen's "interpreters" to his demonic designs.

Four Quartets, centering all "times" in the Incarnation, gives the fullest modern statement of reconciliation as the goal of history. In this study comparisons are made with a theological tradition interpreting time in three dimensions: natural or cosmic time (with the cycle as symbol), existential time (with a point for the moment of revelation), and historical time (the directional line which insists on movement from beginning to end). More affirmative--and more American--than Eliot's other poetry, Four Quartets reflects a view of human experience founded on that of the Gospel of John with its stress on transforming grace. [Order No. 64-10,442; 368 pages. DAI, 25A (Jan.-March 1965), 4159.]

102 William Faulkner's Use of the Material of Abnormal Psychology in Characterization / William Richard BROWN, University of Arkansas, 1965 (H. B. Rouse).

The study proceeds upon the basic assumption that analogies exist between the implications of psychological disorders and philosophical and religious themes in Faulkner's work. Considerable attention is given to fictional technique, but the study is predominantly thematic.

Psychologically, the approach is clinical rather than theoretical and, as far as possible, emphasizes symptomatology rather than etiology or psychodynamics. That is, characters are studied as they exhibit thoughts, words, and actions which would be recognizable to psychiatrists and clinical psychologists as resembling traits of specific mental disorders. Archetypal patterns, Freudian complexes, myth, word association, and the author's symbolic puns are, for the most part, irrelevant to the study. It is not the primary purpose to psychoanalyze the author nor to probe the content of the unconscious.

Chapter One defines Faulkner's concept of normality as the ideal of human decency. The abnormal character exists in a state of morbid equilibrium which protects against complete chaos and insanity. His inchoate aspiration to attain the ideal causes either tragedy or other catastrophe. The statistical norm, the condition of the typical man, is defined as pseudonormality and is illustrated by Flem Snopes.

In Chapter Two is discussed the analogy between psychological and theological guilt developed in Sanctuary, Light in August, and Requiem for a Nun. It is fitting that Popeye and Joe Christmas should exhibit several traits of the sociopathic (psychopathic) personality because one of the central characteristics of this disorder is an absence of a sense of guilt and because Popeye and Christmas serve the Christ-like function of scapegoats for a guilty society. Nancy Mannigoe, not specifically abnormal although a "nigger dopefiend whore," serves the same purpose.

Chapter Three concerns the ideal of honor as it is represented in the Southern tradition and in the concept of the aristocratic family, and as it is sought for in an abnormal way through Thomas Sutpen's paranoiac delusions of grandeur and Quentin Compson's semi-schizoid preoccupation with incest. These abnormal aspirations result in tragedy.

The paranoid belief that the entire environment, the entire cosmos, conspires against one is analogous to the philosophical theme of a hostile cosmos. To the characters discussed in Chapter Four, even inanimate objects appear to participate in a surrealistic conspiracy. Such characters are the prisoner in Old Man, Jason Compson, and Mink Snopes.

In As I Lay Dying, the principal subject of Chapter Five, the disparity between ideal attainment and perverted aspiration becomes so extreme as to result in surrealistic and existentialist absurdity. The autistic or paleologic thought which exists among the Bundrens and reaches the proportions of schizophrenia in Darl is analyzed, and the existence of folie à deux between Darl and Vardaman is suggested.

The principal conclusion reached is that the theme of supernatural or metaphysical evil in conflict with the ideal almost reaches the proportions of Manichaeism and is more basic to Faulkner's work than is the theme of humanistic morality which is certainly present in Faulkner but has been overemphasized and misapplied. The more extreme the disparity between, on the one hand, man's actual condition which results from the operation of evil forces, as manifested in mental disorders, and, on the other hand, man's perverted aspiration for the ideal, the more does Faulkner admire man. Such a disparity exists in all the abnormal characters and is especially evident in the mental deficiency of Ike Snopes and Benjy Compson.

The dissertation includes an appendix concerning abnormal psychology as it applies specifically to women in Faulkner. There is also a glossary defining technical terms in the senses in which they are used in this study. [Order No. 65-8441; 335 pages. DAI, 26A (July-Aug. 1965), 1036-37.]

103 Out of that Generous Land: A Study of the Scope of the Novel Based on America from Cooper to Faulkner / C.T. DIFFEY, University of Bristol, England, 1965 (A.C. Tomlinson) no DAI entry.

104 Humor in the Novels of William Faulkner / Robert Duane HARWICK, University of Nebraska, 1965 (Robert L. Hough).

During the past two decades, critics have demonstrated the pervasiveness of humor in the fiction of William Faulkner, have identified many of its kinships, and have conjectured about its significance. My purpose in this study is to examine the nature, function, and effect of the comedy in four novels spanning Faulkner's creative life: Mosquitoes (1927), As I Lay Dying (1930), The Hamlet (1940), and The Reivers (1962). Faulkner frequently asserted that the novelist's duty was to write about man in conflict with himself, his fellows, and his environment and that all the elements of fiction, including humor, were instruments to be used in performing that task. I attempt to ascertain to what extent Faulkner's fictional practice conforms to his pronounced theory.

The central purpose of the comedy in Mosquitoes is to entertain the reader and to satirize various aspects of American life, especially the denizens of the French Quarter in New Orleans. Many of the varieties of humor which Faulkner later used as instruments in creating masterful tales of man in the human dilemma are here employed less successfully. The humor of character, of dialogue, and of situation is always amusing and frequently brilliant, but it is also sometimes irritatingly self-conscious in its cleverness; the author enjoys displaying his comic capabilities for their own sake.

In As I Lay Dying, Faulkner successfully integrates various elements of fiction and makes them all functional in relating a story of man in motion. The novel is a grotesque mock epic in which all the humor supports and develops the total mock-epic structure. The merging of pathos, horror, morbidity, and perversion with comedy results in that kind of humor known as the grotesque. Even though the book does not contain every possible mock-heroic device, it does employ many of them; and the double incongruity between traditional notions of what a funeral procession should be and what that of Addie Bundren is and between the seriousness of the subject matter and Faulkner's generally comic treatment of it creates the overall tone of the mock epic.

Though most critics have praised The Hamlet, many have maintained that its structure is episodic and that the behavior of some of the characters is unconvincing. In fact, Faulkner employs one of the most venerable of all comic patterns--that of the trickster tricked--to invest the novel with both structural and thematic unity and to make the actions of the characters credible. Every incident and episode in the book is a variation of this basic humorous design, and all the actions are meaningfully unified through its use. The Hamlet is a virtuoso performance in which Faulkner displays his complete mastery of manifold fictional elements, both serious and comic.

The comedy of The Reivers is more obvious, more relaxed, and more anecdotal than that of most of the earlier novels. The ubiquitous surface humor derives mainly from the double point of view: 67-year-old Lucius Priest recollects, recreates, and narrates the adventures of one week in his eleventh year. The serious theme of the story is the initiation of a young boy into the communion of human evil. The aged narrator is obliquely relating much of what he has learned in his 67 years; and so, one may assume, is the author. One of the primary lessons learned by both is the important function of humor in illuminating and softening the human condition, in rendering human life livable. [Order No. 65-8426; 120 pages. DAI, 26A (Sept.-Oct.1965), 1646.]

105 A Contextural Approach to the Teaching of Two Novels by William
    Faulkner at College Level / Elizabeth Lorraine MEEKS, University
of Houston, 1965 (Marvin D. Sterrett) no DAI entry.

106 The Negro Character in the Fiction of William Faulkner / Raleigh
    Preston PLAYER, Jr., University of Michigan, 1965 (Robert T.
Haugh).

The purpose of this study is to investigate the portrayal of Negro characters in the novels and short stories of William Faulkner and to evaluate that portrayal in terms of the scope and variety of the characterizations, the types and importance of the roles assigned the characters, and the thematic role of the Negro character in the author's fiction.

The Introduction of the study briefly surveys the relevant literature and determines that no similar study of equal scope has been attempted previously. In Chapter I, the 165 Negro characters found in the author's fiction are considered in relation to their occupations, their connections with the white families of the fiction, and their variety as types of characters. Faulkner's fictional techniques in portraying minor Negro characters are investigated, and it is evident that the author is successful in making specific individuals of a large number of characters of similar social classes.

In Chapter II of the study, 27 intermediate characters are surveyed in four groups: (1) Figures of Loyalty, (2) Figures of Revolt, (3) Figures of

Adjustment and Manipulation, and (4) Figures of Defeat. Faulkner's fictional treatment of these varying types of characters makes evident his skill and versatility in portraying of Negro characters of widely different responses to the situations they face in the fiction. In Chapter III, 13 major Negro characters, including seven male characters and six female characters, are examined. The male characters range in age from the young boys, Ringo, Aleck, and Henry Beauchamp to the older men, Sam Fathers, and the Rev. Shegog. The female characters include Dilsey, Molly Beauchamp, and Nancy Mannigoe, all older women. It is evident here that Faulkner's fictional artistry is at its best when he is portraying the Negro character in youth and old age and that his portrayal of the older Negro woman is similar in quality to his masterly portrayals of the older white women of his fiction.

In Chapter IV of the study, six major male characters are surveyed. They include Joe Christmas, Lucas Beauchamp, Charles Bon, and Uncle Parsham Hood. Faulkner's ability to portray the Negro character in complex social situations with fidelity and understanding is demonstrated in the portrayals of these characters. The Conclusion of the study reviews the findings of the specific chapters and briefly compares Faulkner's treatment of Negro characters with that of selected white writers of fiction in which Negro characters are also portrayed. An Appendix lists the 165 Negro characters, gives a short biographical sketch of each, and indicates the novels or short stories in which each appears.

The general conclusion which can be drawn from this study is that Faulkner's portrayal of Negro characters is characterized by skill, integrity, understanding, and compassion and that his ability to portray Negro characters well is limited only by his lack of experience with Negroes of certain types. No specific thematic role of the Negro character seems evident, but Negro characters are portrayed as having some of the human characteristics that interested Faulkner, such as loyalty, family pride, and closeness to nature. [Order No. 66-6678; 131 pages. DAI, 27A (July-Aug. 1966), 483-84.]

107 The Current of Time in the Novels of William Faulkner / Agnes Schelling POLLOCK, University of California at Los Angeles, 1965 (Leon Howard).

The problem in the dissertation is the analysis of the significance of the impact of time upon characters in the novels of William Faulkner. Throughout his career as a novelist, Faulkner was engaged in the assessment of this impact. His early work reveals that he was torn between two conflicting insights. On the one hand, he saw the past as a potential guide for those of his characters who struggled toward self-recognition. On the other hand, he was keenly aware that the past might impose a fatal stasis upon the life of the present. Faulkner's attempt to resolve the conflict in these opposing insights is a central issue in his major work and a clue to the deepest motivations of his characters.

In method, the study focuses upon ten representative works: <u>Soldiers' Pay</u>, <u>Mosquitoes</u>, <u>Sartoris</u>, <u>The Sound and the Fury</u>, <u>Absalom, Absalom!</u>, <u>As I Lay Dying</u>, <u>Light in August</u>, <u>The Wild Palms</u>, <u>A Fable</u>, and the wilderness sections of <u>Go Down, Moses and Other Stories</u>. These works, selected from Faulkner's earlier as well as his later writings, illustrate a sustained preoccupation with ways in which human personality may experience and react to time.

Three directive procedures may be recognized in the dissertation. The first of these is a statement of the premise on which the study is based. This premise is drawn from Professor Hans Meyerhoff's work entitled <u>Time in Literature.</u> The fundamental assumption is that "the way one looks at time determines the whole value and status of the self." Thus if the values of time are objective, "if life is measured by what is produced and consumed," if life "is envisaged as nothing but a procession of useful moments," then the self which must exist in time has only the value "of what it is worth in the market." If, however, time is experienced subjectively as related moments "interpenetrating and flowing," the person "becomes an end in himself and his value is intrinsic."

The second procedure is an investigation of a key scientific hypothesis of the influence of time upon human personality. The third is the attempt to distinguish the characters within the novels who move in the dimension of objective time from those who achieve the "I-time" of subjective experience.

The findings of the study are that Faulkner began the development of a coherent view of the impact of time on character and personality in his earliest work. He did not fully clarify his insights, however, until he wrote The Sound and the Fury. From this point in his writing until the end, his work reflects a deepening awareness that the values of his characters were shaped by their concepts of time. These concepts of time together with the characters who reveal them are evolved, in the dissertation, under the following categories: "Time and the Search for Reality," "Time and the Arbitrary Dial," "Time and the Substance of Remembering," "Time Within the Mythical Pattern," "Time and the Universal Legend," and "Time and Discovery in Depth." [Order No. 65-4979; 227 pages. DAI, 25A (April-June 1965), 7276-77.]

108 The World Outside Yoknapatawpha: A Study of Five Novels by William Faulkner / Randolph Edward STEIN, Ohio University, 1965 (Arvin R. Wells).

The five novels written by William Faulkner which are involved with locales other than Yoknapatawpha County are examined in an effort to establish the relationship which these books bear to each other and to the remaining body of Faulkner's writing. These novels--Soldiers' Pay, Mosquitoes, Pylon, The Wild Palms, and A Fable--are generally regarded in most critical commentary on Faulkner's writing as of minor literary merit and, largely because of their exclusion from the Yoknapatawpha setting, as of negligible importance for an understanding of the Yoknapatawpha chronicle. It seems apparent, however, that when these novels are looked upon as containing a number of pointedly explicit statements on certain themes that are less emphatically treated in the Yoknapatawpha novels, these non-Yoknapatawpha books form an effective and valuable supplement to the Yoknapatawpha writings.

One of the primary conclusions of the study is that the particular settings which are developed in the non-Yoknapatawpha volumes are determined by the special thematic concerns of the individual novel. In contrast, an examination of the Yoknapatawpha novels seemed clearly to indicate that in each of these works, the setting itself became a determinant of both theme and action. The distinction between the Yoknapatawpha and the non-Yoknapatawpha novels was seen to be not only of setting, but of compositional methodology as well. The study also finds evidence of a number of particular characteristics--such as a continuing absence of specifically identified characters--which the non-Yoknapatawpha novels share and which suggest the logic of treating these novels as a related series. The non-Yoknapatawpha novels, however, are not dissociated from the Yoknapatawpha novels--they represent, rather, more complete and emphatic statements of themes and motifs that have tended to remain latent or incompletely developed in the Yoknapatawpha novels. The insistent stress in Pylon, for example, upon the sterility of a machine-dominated society can be pointed to as evidence of Faulkner's attempt to provide a more fully articulated statement of a concept that he had not developed as completely in the Yoknapatawpha novels. Moreover, the various non-Yoknapatawpha novels possess close structural and stylistic similarities to the Yoknapatawpha novels that were being composed at about the same time. The frequently questioned episodic arrangement of The Wild Palms is seen to be less anomalous when the novel is placed in a context with such other episodic novels from the same period, such as Go Down, Moses.

The conclusions of the study clearly point to the value of regarding the five non-Yoknapatawpha novels as artistically effective supplements to the themes and patterns of the Yoknapatawpha novels and as integral parts of Faulkner's complete literary achievement. [Order No. 65-10,083; 179 pages. DAI, 26A (Sept.-Oct. 1965), 2225.]

109 The Escape Motif in the Modern American Novel: Mark Twain to Carson McCullers / Samuel BLUEFARB, University of New Mexico, 1966 (Hamlin Hill) no DAI entry.

110 Patterns of Initiation in William Faulkner's Go Down, Moses / Richard Alan LAWSON, Tulane University, 1966 (Joseph Patrick Roppolo).

This study analyzes the patterns of initiation in William Faulkner's Go Down, Moses. In past criticism, critics have tended to focus on the wilderness and civilization initiations in "The Bear" rather than to demonstrate the interrelationships and the thematic unity of them with the rest of the novel. Only recently the critics have attempted an analysis of the initiation patterns that the Negroes go through. By a close reading of the text, the aim of this study is to see how each individual responds to life in terms of his quest for identity, to demonstrate the ambivalence that operates in each individual's initiation, and to show that the critics' views of the characters as failures or successes are relative distinctions.

As a result of the initiations, several characters emerge as central figures and as primary forces on the McCaslin plantation. The characters' quests for identity and their conceptions of their positions in society have enabled them to deny their better impulses. They are troubled not only about themselves, but also about the plantation they run. Isaac McCaslin, in his rejection of the plantation, goes to the other extreme by affirming the wilderness as the best possible life. The truth of his repudiation of the plantation lies in his heart's response to nature, rather than to the cultivated land his family has corrupted. His insights in the wilderness and in the commissary are perceptive and ennobling; yet they are limiting, leading to his total confusion in life. McCaslin Edmonds and Lucas Beauchamp establish a healthy, balanced position in relation to the wilderness and the plantation.

The characters' responses to change are important in their initiations. Carothers McCaslin's alliance with change operates only in the establishing of the plantation. Once it is completed, he preserves the social and economic status quo. Isaac accepts change only in the wilderness experience until he sees Ben. His repudiation of the hunt, the killing of Ben, and of the plantation is an attempt to avoid change and to find peace. He does neither; for he is left with the vision of a static wilderness afterlife as his only refuge. Cass accepts change in the wilderness and in the plantation. He has trouble with it, yet he finds peace and fulfillment. Roth wavers between Carothers' and Cass' positions. Lucas is committed to understanding and to changing the social values of the McCaslins and the Edmondses, as well as those of the town.

One aspect of the novel is that the characters come to represent types of the Southern experience: Carothers is the ruthless plantation owner, Buck and Buddy McCaslin and McCaslin Edmonds are responsible Southerners who are trying to improve human interrelationships, Isaac is the idealist of brotherhood and the realignment of men with nature, and Lucas is the embodiment of the endurance and the emergence of Negroes in white society. Each character is more than a type; for in each one's ambivalent vision of life, he cannot understand everything in his initiation. As Ike is limited in his vision of the wilderness and of civilization, Cass and Lucas move between nature and civilization with dignity and acceptance of life. The original sexual and social sins of the South continue. Characters, like Ike, hope for an Eden, but Canaan, the land developed with an awareness of change and responsibility in human relationships by the Bucks, Buddies, and Casses, is the best that men can have. [Order No. 66-10,765; 129 pages. DAI, 27A (Nov.-Dec. 1966), 1372.]

111 William Faulkner's Early Experiments with Narrative Techniques / Egbert William OLDENBURG, University of Michigan, 1966 (David H. Stewart).

Faulkner's earliest works (Soldiers' Pay, Mosquitoes, The Marble Faun, A Green Bough, and New Orleans Sketches) have received some critical attention, but little attempt has been made to analyze their technique. Already at this early stage of his career (1920-1926), Faulkner was a conscious craftsman, and his earliest work is an interesting record of technical experimentation.

In addition to the published works, an important key to Faulkner's development as a narrative craftsman can be found in an unfinished and unpublished novel, Elmer, which he composed between the publication of the first novel, Soldiers' Pay, and the writing of his second novel, Mosquitoes. An examination of the Elmer typescript reveals that Faulkner was experimenting with fictional techniques--time displacement, point of view, and interior monologue--which figure significantly in his mature work.

Faulkner's early poetry is related in technique as well as theme to his early prose fiction. The poetry, largely imitative, shows the influence of the symbolist and imagist poets; and the techniques of symbolist poetry are related, in important ways, to the techniques of impressionist prose. Faulkner's earliest experiments in prose fiction, the sketches written in 1925 for the New Orleans Times-Picayune, reveal the influence of symbolist poetry. They show, in addition, that Faulkner was being influenced by the techniques of other fiction writers--impressionists like Thomas Beer, Sherwood Anderson, and Joseph Conrad.

The influence of these impressionists is also evident in Faulkner's first novel, Soldiers' Pay, in which the narration proceeds by means of brief impressionistic scenes. There is almost no use of summary narrative in the novel, and Faulkner's treatment of time, mostly through flashbacks, is not wholly effective. Compared with Soldiers' Pay the unpublished Elmer is a much more radical experiment. The Elmer typescript reveals that most of Faulkner's attempts to revise the novel involved the treatment of time, not by simple flashbacks--as in Soldiers' Pay--but by the chronological rearrangement of large blocks of the narrative. Although impressionistic techniques are still present in Elmer, Faulkner was beginning to move in another direction. There is much more use of summary narrative, and the first traces of another influence--the novel of ideas--begin to appear.

The influence of the novel of ideas appears most clearly in Mosquitoes, a novel indebted in method to Huxley's Those Barren Leaves and Norman Douglas' South Wind. The method of Mosquitoes is more cerebral and ratiocinative than the method of Soldiers' Pay; Faulkner is obviously completing the transition from poet to novelist. In addition, Mosquitoes is a striking technical contrast to the unfinished experiment, Elmer. In Mosquitoes Faulkner returned to a straightforward and rigidly controlled time scheme. The pattern of radical technical experiment followed by reaction and a return to a more conventional method, seen first in the relationship of these two early works, is a pattern which was repeated throughout the rest of Faulkner's career. [Order No. 66-14,564; 212 pages. DAI, 27A (Jan.-Feb. 1967), 2158.]

112 Moses, Its Sources, Revisions, and Structures / Henry Alden
PLOEGSTRA, University of Chicago, 1966 (James E. Miller, Jr)
no DAI entry.

113 Such Stuff as Dreams Are Made of: History, Myth, and the Comic
Vision of Mark Twain and William Faulkner / Ben Merchant VOR-
PAHL, University of Wisconsin, 1966 (Walter B. Rideout).

Mark Twain and William Faulkner, two writers whose works occupy places of similar importance in American literature, have their most interesting similarity in the use of the comic. As has long been known in Mark Twain's case and more recently suggested in Faulkner's both authors can be regarded as writing much of the time within the tradition of Southwest humor. The widely known elements of this tradition include such things as predilection for grotesque subject matter and the use of devices of anticlimax, exaggeration, understatement, and hyperbole. The comic, however, as it occurs in these two writers' works, may be said as well to involve certain important assumptions about history and humanity.

Both the preoccupation of Mark Twain's works with types of the people, places and events from Hannibal, Missouri and the equally intense concern in Faulkner's works with the history of Lfayette County, Mississippi of the antebellum, Civil War, and Reconstruction periods represent a retrospective view of a fact central to the idea of an American civilization: the contact, on the frontier, of the often more or less Utopian aspirations of planners and builders with the hard facts of economics, terrain, climate, and--most important-- human nature. Mark Twain looked back at his boyhood Hannibal from the vantage point of the "Gilded Age," and, later in his life, from his own deep sense of personal disappointment. Similarly, William Faulkner's chronicle of frontier Yoknapatawpha County always regards the aspirations of the people who make it up as failures of one kind or another. In short, a characteristic situation in the comedy of Mark Twain and William Faulkner is that of the disappointment of Edenic hopes by the difficult circumstances of reality--a situation duplicated specifically in the experience of Hannibal, Missouri and Lafayette County, Mississippi and more generally in the larger outlines of American frontier history. The works most susceptible to detailed analysis in this regard are Huckleberry Finn and The Hamlet. Others, requiring relatively less consideration, include The Gilded Age, The Prince and the Pauper, A Connecticut Yankee in King Arthur's Court, Pudd'nhead Wilson, "The Man that Corrupted Hadleyburg," The Mysterious Stranger, "The Great Dark," Soldiers' Pay, Sartoris, The Sound and the Fury, As I Lay Dying, Light in August, and Pylon.

The supposition that historical failure is central to the situation of comedy as it occurs in the works of Mark Twain and William Faulkner is further reinforced by the examination both of critical, psychological, and philosophical theories concerning the comic and of the significance of the comic personality (typified by Falstaff and Huckleberry Finn) and the comic predicament (typified by Aristophanic drama and The Hamlet). None of this is to suggest that Mark Twain and Faulkner do not belong in the tradition of Southwest humor where so many critics have placed them. It is to suggest that the further consideration of the two writers inside the ancient tradition of the comic helps both to better define the relationship their works bear to each other and to indicate that the contact on the American frontier of Edenic hopes with hard facts was an event uniquely susceptible to comic handling. [Order No. 66-4588; 540 pages. DAI, 28A (July-Aug. 1967), 698.]

114 Coleridge's Definition of the Poet and the Works of Herman Melville
and William Faulkner / Lewis Franklin ARCHER, Drew University,
1967 (Stanley Hopper).

The examination of Coleridge's theory of the imagination provides us with a definition of the romantic poet, and it provides us with a method by which to examine works of literature in the romantic tradition. A romantic poet is one who creates symbols which reconcile extremes or struggles to do so. The romantic poet is usually a prophetic voice within his culture who calls for a transformation of the old order into new possibilities for life. But since symbolic art must remain open and rely on the observer's own response and appropriation of meaning, such works of art often fail to communicate to the popular mind. Therefore, the major terms by which to understand a romantic poet are: reconciler, prophet, transformer, and failure.

Melville provides a fruitful example of the romantic artist. His work is a prophetic demand that American optimistic innocence die and be transformed into a new form of innocence. This new form of innocence permits a man to live in the world while accepting the ever-present extremes of light and dark, good and evil, success and failure, life and death. Melville succeeded in reaching the transcendental apex of reality and looked the Absolute in the face. But this achievement did not bring him the anticipated experiences of peace and resolution. Rather, he found there a "white world" which still demanded of him a risk and a decision concerning the meaning of human life. Therefore, Melville, and his most adequate narrators, gave up the transcendental drive and returned to the work of colors, things, and daily life.

Melville's symbolic art does not grant the reader an easy solution. The form of his art is such that the reader must, like Melville in the white world, create out of himself significant meanings, and accept the possibility of failure to create a viable form in which to live.

Faulkner's prophetic vision attacked the decadent puritan world as he knew it and revealed man's irresponsibility and escape from history. The puritan members of Yoknapatawpha County do everything to avoid living creatively in the world and in the end feel time and history as a burden.

Faulkner sought to understand his tradition and give it new life by placing children and innocent Negroes in the decayed puritan world, initiating them into adult awareness, and observing how they responded. Some failed to live in the world, some constructed illusions and tried to bring them to maturity but some--though not many--gave up innocence and tried to live in the world as responsible men, accepting all their culture presented and constructing a meaningful, just, and humane life out of the cultural elements.

The form of art used by Coleridge, Melville, and Faulkner is finally the form of Western Christianity but without a commitment or acceptance of any particular content. Thus it was the "fate" of romanticism to present men with open possibilities but no answers. Romantic art refuses to "give" meaning to men's lives. Instead, romantic art presents men with a white world and the form of a religious faith. It then throws its observers back upon themselves to create an appropriate content to fulfill the form. Thus romantic art is loyal to itself only when it takes the form of parable. Both Melville and Faulkner can be fruitfully explored if the reader grants validity to these romantic presuppositions. [Order No. 67-14,370; 478 pages. DAI, 28A (Nov.-Dec. 1967), 1810-11.]

115 The Characters of Hawthorne and Faulkner: A Typology of Sinners /
Theodore Lewis COLSON, University of Michigan, 1967 (Austin Warren).

Though there is no direct influence, there are intense and comparable religious sensibilities implicit in the writing of Hawthorne and Faulkner. Their concern begins with the possibilities for fiction in the guilt historically associated with their regions, and extends to the nature of individual involvement with sin. It is striking that certain of their characters are spiritually akin--that comments about Young Goodman Brown are found to be true of Joe Christmas. And many other characters, brought together, illuminate each other.

The wholeness of unfallen man, an eternal state not easily found within time, seems the implicit goal of many of the most interesting characters--who are religious, not orthodoxy, but in their all-out attempt to achieve this ideal. But most of them evade repentance and pursue spurious ideals. The order of scrutinizing these characters seems naturally to begin with those who first make acquaintance with sin: with Caddy in the pear tree, and thence it seems right to consider groups of characters ordered according to their increasing consciousness of sin. Consequently our exploration is roughly analogous to Dante's descent in the Inferno.

Benjy Compson and Clifford Pyncheon retain a childlike innocence in adulthood, and have a limbo existence outside of time. Only Dilsey can encounter the temporal world unflinchingly because her conception of eternal values can include the transcient. (Phoebe Pyncheon and Lena Grove have convincingly good natures, but Hawthorne's and Faulkner's few other 'innocent' grownups are not very credible.)

The simplest sin is inordinate appetite: rapacity. One kind is the mere perverted bestiality of Popeye. A second kind, respectability, functions in two ways. Most simply it is sheep's clothing for the wolf who wants to be bestial, yet respected for his morality: it can, however, be used not only as a cloak for rapacity, but as its instrument. The third kind, more sophisticated and vampire-like, tries to reach the inmost core of a victim; it is quasi-religious in its demand for what is uttered.

The morally rigid are those characters who victimize themselves and others out of obsession with moralistic absolutes; their efforts are misplaced attempts to achieve insolipsistic righteousness, Hollingsworth's philanthropic design, Sutpen's dynastic ambition, Aylmer's and Charlotte Rittenmeyer's attempts to achieve perfect human love, and Joe Christmas' attacks on impurity in women and the vileness in racism are examples.

There are characters, like Owen Warland and Miles Coverdale, who strive in various ways to become "beautiful souls." While struggling for ideal life they confuse aesthetic aspirations with ethical responsibility, and infect reality with fiction. They want to make life into art, and the result is death-in-life.

The most tormented characters are the remorseful, who recognize the need for repentance, not as regret, of which they have plenty, but as the sense of feeling forgiven, accepted, by God and the world, and hence able to forgive themselves and to forget obsession with sin. There are two related kinds of remorse. In one, a person like Dimmesdale knows what his sin is but does not want to give it up despite the pain it causes, and indeed, masochistically clings to that pain. In the other, a person like Joe Christmas feels a tremendous pain of guilt incommensurate with any conscious guilt. Both kinds are tormented with anxiety, and lead to moral wildernesses where all sense of values is endangered.

Though necessarily discussed in relative isolation, all these sins thematically permeate the novels, and indeed the greater chracters range throughout much of the whole inferno--the complexity of the novels and of the characters in this respect being an indication of their magnitude. [Order No. 67-15608; 219 pages. DAI, 28A (Nov.-Dec. 1967), 2204-05.]

116 The Myth of Southern History--20th Century Variations / F. Garvin
DAVENPORT, Jr., University of Minnesota, 1967 (David W. Noble).
It has been noted by William R. Taylor in Cavalier and Yankee: the Old South and American National Character, that in the first half of the 19th century, "Southerners carried on a peculiar kind of dialogue with the nation...

[and] ... through it all they persisted in seeing themselves as different and, increasingly, they tended to reshape this acknowledged difference into a claim of superiority."

This study examines 20th century variations of this cultural mythology in five works by Southerners from 1903 to 1953: The Leopard's Spots--A Romance of the White Man's Burden (1903), Thomas Dixon; I'll Take My Stand-- The South and the Agrarian Tradition (1930), Twelve Southerners; Absalom, Absalom! (1936), William Faulkner; All the King's Men (1946), and Brother to Dragons: A Tale in Verse and Voice (1953), Robert Penn Warren. Works by Woodrow Wilson, Margaret Mitchell, W. J. Cash, John Dollard, and C. Vann Woodward have been incorporated as they shed light on the major concern which is what Taylor calls the "dynamics rather than the origins or historical authenticity" of the myth.

The myth of Southern history suggests that because the South has experienced military defeat on its own soil, military occupation by "foreign" troops, humiliation, poverty, and privation, it is in a position to render special service to the nation which has experienced only unending affluence, progress, and victory. The South is seen as having a mission to save the nation from its own misguided optimism and materialism. Thomas Dixon believed that the South, rising from the ashes of the Civil War, would save the nation from the "threat" of Negro equality. The Twelve Southerners suggested that by drawing upon the traditional "Cavalier" mythology of the Old South, the South could save the nation or at least itself from the "perils" of industrialism. But by concentrating on the myths of the Old South, they ignored the racial problems of the modern South. William Faulkner's art suggested that the South could not ignore the burdens of its history for the illusions of tradition. Robert Penn Warren--and C. Vann Woodward--underlined this and went on to find a new mission, for a South that would recognize its own problems, in leading the nation away from McCarthyism, cultural complacency, and a naive foreign policy.

Thus these Southerners are examined in a national, as well as in a regional context. As the nature of national problems change, the myths of the nation must change. But the national needs of this century have made it increasingly difficult to propose or to accept a myth of the South which condones or ignores racial injustice. This is the plight of the Southerners who would have the South offer leadership to the nation. Finally, this study suggests that the South's task in this century has not been merely to rationalize its treatment of the Negro to the nation but to explain in meaningful terms to all Americans its own treatment at the hands of history. [Order No. 68-1611; 274 pages. DAI, 28A (March-April 1968), 3666.]

117 Archetypes in the Major Novels of Thomas Hardy and Their Literary Application / Elizabeth M. DEGROOT, New York University, 1967 (Louise M. Rosenblatt) no DAI entry.

118 Land-Nostalgia in the Novels of Faulkner, Cather, and Steinbeck / John Michael DITSKY, New York University, 1967 (Gay Wilson Allen).

Land-nostalgia is a feeling for or about the land that is both intellectual and emotional, involving the presence of Nature as a character in American fiction by virtue of the special relationship between man and the land. The associations which American writers have given the land range from an attachment to property or region to a sense of identity with nation or with Nature in general. The paradoxical sense of the word nostalgia as employed here is the result of the attempt by our writers of fiction to retain past associations with the land in looking forward to an urbanized and automated future. A close reading of the works of William Faulkner, Willa Cather, and John Steinbeck discloses the existence, extent, and efficacy of the device of land-nostalgia in contemporary American fiction.

William Faulkner's basic theories of life and art have much in common with agrarian thought; his attempts to find expression in fiction culminate in his adoption of land-nostalgia as a technique. In using the land as a chronicle of human activity, he makes the attachment of a character to the land the basis for experimentation with Time. Moreover, the land serves to record human achievement and to promise human survival, and to therefore add a third dimension to events deserving the emphasis of eternity. In using the land as the basis for dynastic establishment, Faulkner treats three identifiable classes of people, the "dynasts," "anti-dynasts," and "non-dynasts." Although his interest clearly shifts from the propertied class to the unpropertied, Faulkner's whole concern with the dynastic implications of the land is far less pronounced than is usually thought true. Thirdly, in using the land as a symbol of a covenant with man, Faulkner makes acceptance or rejection of the land-covenant the central act of any Faulkner character. And in using the land as a link with the pagan past and with the "dark forces" of fertility, sexuality, and fatality, Faulkner both develops the implications of land-religion and also relates the land to the central act by which humanity is preserved and redeemed: its acceptance of cyclical renewal. Finally, in using the land as symbol of "good" and "natural" influences in human personality, Faulkner sets up personal commitment to the things of the land as his standard of human conduct.

Willa Cather's simpler, more poignant variety of land-nostalgia rests upon her attachment to the time of her own childhood, and her consequent refusal to accept the realities of a supposedly coarser world. Cather's employment of the land as embodiment of history or witness to the past is similar to Faulkner's; and although there is a weakening of her interest in the device as her career progresses, she nevertheless consistently uses the land to involve ordinary events in myth and epic. Her employment of the land as source of hope and reflection of human dreams is constant, but changes in emphasis from futurity to reconciliation with the values of the past. Lastly, her employment of the land as shaper of individual character, especially in terms of orientation to Art, illustrates a steady pattern of human development away from the land, then back to either the land or the values it represents.

John Steinbeck's employment of land-nostalgia is extensive and varied, but not the orderly and patterned formalism of Faulkner and Cather; rather, he uses several favorite devices and themes repeatedly. Steinbeck treats the land as an object of religious worship; this sacramental vision leads far too often to excessive symbolism. His career shows an alternation between success and failure at mastering the very disparity of his method, or of restraining the evident tendency to exaggerate aspects of Nature. His stature as novelist seems assuredly greater than has already been granted, but his religion of Nature seems permanently damaged by enthusiasm.

The study of land-nostalgia in the novels of Faulkner, Cather, and Steinbeck demonstrates the possibility of criticizing the whole of their output on such a unified basis, as well as of applying the principles of resemblance and dissimilarity gleaned from such study to the works of other American writers with related concerns. [Order No. 67-10,969; 454 pages. DAI, 28A (Sept.-Oct. 1967), 1072.]

119 The Fallen Women in American Naturalistic Fiction: From Crane to Faulkner / Helen Sylvia GARSON, University of Maryland, 1967 (Leonard Lutwack).

American naturalistic fiction reflects the economic, social, and cultural changes of American life after the Civil War. Large cities, slums, and poverty produced conditions which degraded and corrupted men and women. A laissez-faire attitude permeated government, big business had vast power, and society was caught between an old code and new values. Not necessarily reformers, the naturalists attempted to reveal facts about the human situation, one of which was the plight of the fallen woman. Although the subject was not new, the viewpoint and treatment were.

The early naturalist saw the fallen woman not as a sinner but as a helpless victim trapped by heredity and an uncaring mechanistic environment. With irony or pity, detachment or judgment, he exposed all the forces that destroy the innocent: economic deprivation, breakdown of family and religion, lack of love, alienation, and dissociation. The fallen woman of the pre-World War I naturalistic novel succumbs to these forces and is harshly judged by a hypocritical society which demands adherence to an impossible creed.

The first naturalists--Crane, Garland, and Norris--differed in their attitudes toward the fallen woman. Crane, detached and pessimistic, regarded woman as an absolute victim of economics, the city, and a hostile society. Garland, an optimist, saw woman as strong enough to resist the corrupting influences of the environment. Norris, philosophically ambivalent, wavered between a sympathetic view of woman as victim and a genteel Victorianism which either harshly condemned the fallen woman or cautiously abandoned her.

Although Dreiser portrayed young girls trapped by the city and uncontrollable circumstances, the fallen woman generally survives in his harsh Darwinian world and sometimes even "succeeds." Dreiser was the last naturalist to see the fallen woman in an empathic light, for the novelist of the twenties and thirties no longer regarded woman as a helpless victim but as a masterful protagonist using sex to achieve what she wanted from life economically, socially, or emotionally.

After World War I there were many changes in the status of woman. She gained new freedom, not the least of which was sexual. The old concept of the double standard, with woman as the prey of man and victim of economic deprivation, gradually disappeared. Psychological disorientation became a major factor in male-female relationships. In the fiction of Anderson, men and women became equally lost, equally displaced. The fallen woman becomes the one who fails to recognize the meaning of sex and the supportive role woman must play to help man find some values in his world. With the novels of Hemingway, Dos Passos, and O'Hara woman seems to grow stronger, more vicious, more demanding. Fallen she remains, because she continues to use her body as an item of barter. Eventually, men and women exchange roles: the female becomes a user or a seducer, and man becomes enfeebled. In Faulkner's work the fallen woman reaches the lowest level of corruption.

Despair and anger pervade post-war literature. Novelists appear to see the fallen condition of woman as symbolic of the situation to which modern civilization has come; they find a world without hope. Only Faulkner offers an alternative; it is human to sin and fall, he suggests, but one can do penance; by admitting guilt and saying "no" to further iniquity the fallen woman may be redeemed; she can survive and she can endure. [Order No. 68-7021; 290 pages. DAI, 28A (May-June 1968), 5052.]

120 Primitivism in the Fiction of William Faulkner / George William SUTTON, University of Mississippi, 1967 (John Pilkington).

One of the noticeable traits of the fiction of William Faulkner is the so-called "sickness" or "lostness" of many of his characters and the contrasting vitality of primitive types who appear to have some innate understanding of life's meaning and purpose. Such primitive characters occur throughout Faulkner's fiction in the persons of children and idiots, Indians and hunters, poor whites, and Negroes. Faulkner displays his partiality for his primitives in his depiction of civilization as founded upon rapacity--his favorite word for excessive human greed which alienates man from nature by attempting to conquer and subdue rather than to live in harmony with nature and from his fellow man by exploiting human beings with the same ruthless passion. He also displays his partiality for the primitives by allowing them to endure and thereby gain the only possible victory that Faulkner believes man can achieve; on the other hand, the "lost" moderns frequently go either the way of Quentin Compson and Joe Christmas, to alienation and death, or the way of Jason Compson and Flem Snopes, to alienation and death-in-life. This dissertation is a study of the patterns that emerge from an analysis of the primitive characters in Faulkner's fiction.

The major pattern that appears in the development of Faulkner's primitive characters from his early fiction to his later novels is a thematic conflict between innocence and morality. In his early novels Faulkner's primitives are for the most part innocent or else are seeking innocence--Dilsey Gibson is the one notable exception. The idiots, the innocent children, the withdrawing poor whites are all examples of these characters. In his later novels, beginning with V. K. Ratliff in The Hamlet and Ike McCaslin in Go Down, Moses, Faulkner's primitives become increasingly more concerned with the problems of morality. Yet even Faulkner's most moral characters enter into life somewhat reluctantly and the culmination of his "new morality," the Corporal in A Fable, chooses death rather than life. These primitive characters, therefore, concerned as they are with moral gestures, appear to reflect Faulkner's own awareness of the insolubility of many of life's problems and his own, perhaps subconscious, desire to escape into the Edenic innocence that Ike McCaslin discovers in the great wilderness.

Faulkner's primitives, however, are not life-denying forces, and that which sustains them and gives purpose to their lives is often some ritual to which they commit themselves. They resemble the existentialists of modern European fiction in their insistence upon the need for commitment for commitment's sake; they differ in that their commitments are founded upon community traditions. Faulkner is himself a traditionalist who began his career with a devotion to the traditions of the ante-bellum South. But he was realist enough to see the flaw in the plantation society--he became to realize that rapacity was the foundation for the successes of such men as Thomas Sutpen and Carothers McCaslin. Thus Faulkner, the traditionalist and seeker of meaning, turned to the primitives because they devoted themselves to life-giving rituals. Yet these primitives, these characters who of all others seem to have come to terms with life, remain outside the mainstream of modernity and seem to promise little or no help to the lost moderns who need some of their faith and endurance and love. What can modern man, lost amid his barren wasteland of doubt and despair, learn from these primitives? Faulkner envies their lot, but he also realizes that modern man cannot "go primitive." At best they embody the redeeming virtues that modern man can imitate, but a gulf remains between Faulkner's lost moderns and his enduring primitives. [Order No. 67-7999; 355 pages. DAI, 28A (July-Aug. 1967), 695-96.]

121 An Analysis of Style: The Application of Sector Analysis to Examples of American Prose Fiction / Thomas E. WENSTRAND, Columbia University, 1967 (Robert L. Allen) no DAI entry.

122 Faulkner's Doctrine of Nature: A Study of the 'Endurance' Theme in the Yoknapatawpha Fiction / Melvin Eustace Adonis BRADFORD, Vanderbilt University, 1968 (Thomas Daniel Young).

This paper is a study of Faulkner's understanding of the natural order of society and of the ontological grounds which are subsumed in his correlative affirmation of community. It proceeds from an opening hypothetical statement to a framing of that hypothesis in intellectual history and from thence to a testing of it in explication of five Yoknapatawpha novels. A concluding afterthought contains speculation on how (and with what profit) the same assumption might be applied to the remainder of the Faulkner canon.

Chapter I is a rationale for the method followed in the paper's organization. It defines terms to be employed, relation to other Faulkner scholarship, and indebtedness to other non-literary Southern studies. Chapters II and III take from Faulkner's numerous interviews, public letters, and non-fiction his use of language connected with the pivotal words "pride," "humility," and "endurance," combine this material with a brief general reference to his fiction; and set both together in a context of Western post-Renaissance conceptions of the human condition and its malleability. In brief, the two chapters distinguish the modern aggressive and impious from the traditional submissive and mytheopic conceptions of the human condition and then identify Faulkner with the latter. What the Mississippi writer affirms, it is argued here, is an acceptance of the providentially determined features of every particular mortal lot--acceptance in humility (II--before an assigning power) and pride (III-- in performing the assignment): pride and humility which, in balance, are endurance.

Chapter IV, the body of the paper, presents readings of Go Down, Moses, The Unvanquished, Intruder in the Dust, The Reivers, and Absalom, Absalom!. The purpose of the separate critiques is to translate the structure of their subjects into expository terms and to determine the extent to which a choice between endurance or non-endurance is at issue in their central tensions. The order of the readings follows logic, not time, and is disposed so as to facilitate their mutual reinforcement and illumination. Chapter V, outlining how other Faulkner fiction could be connected to this endurance theme, attempts on thematic grounds to bind together the body of his work. [Order No. 69-4623; 532 pages. DAI, 29A (May-June 1969), 3999.]

123 From Tradition to Technique: Development of Character in Joyce and Faulkner / Sister Mary Enda BYRNE, University of Southern Mississippi, 1968 (Wallace G. Kay).

James Joyce and William Faulkner in drawing upon experience for their subject matter identified themselves irrevocably with their traditions. For Joyce it was the Irish-Catholic tradition, and for Faulkner, the Southern agrarian. Both novelists in such identification revealed the influence, significance, and meaningful relationship of their inherited traditions upon contemporaneity.

Tradition includes that vast body of practices, beliefs, and statements that is handed down orally or in writing from one generation to another. Tradition is not isolated; it is extranational, international, national, racial, sectional, communal, and personal. In this respect Joyce's Dublin and Faulkner's Yoknapatawpha County are more than a particular city and section of a region. As expressions of their traditions Dublin and Yoknapatawpha are universal communities. Each fictional character (and his personal identity) serves as an interpretation of anyman and everyman in the world. Joyce's Roman Catholicism and Faulkner's Protestantism, likewise, present doctrinal and traditional religious beliefs which offer an image of man and the world in totality. Joyce's Catholicism and Faulkner's Protestantism are presented as traditional Christianity juxtaposed against present paradoxes in degenerated and institutionalized Christianity. The individuals who assess the present as an outgrowth of tradition attempt to remold that tradition to give shape to the meanings inherent in his experience. Tradition remains, then, the best framework for the individual's self-expression. Joyce and Faulkner in drawing deep from the wells of their own experience became immersed in the myths of their cultures.

Joyce's culture was a complex one: Roman Catholic in centrality, folk and sophisticated in artistry, legendary and historical in content, classical in mode, and paralytic in nature. In exploiting his religious and cultural traditions, Joyce defined his attitudes towards the social, familial, literary, and national traditions that he had inherited.

William Faulkner also drew heavily upon his native traditions. Through the agrarian, racial, and social traditions of the Old South, Faulkner expressed the tensions of the moralist conscious of those traditions in conflict with modernity, the 20th century forces of industry, commerce, and progress, and the society to which it gave birth.

Joyce and Faulkner defined, explored, and exploited their inherited traditions and the values inherent in them. The means they used to attend to their subject matter were a variety of techniques that were in many ways similar. Language, point of view, realism, mythology, symbolism, naturalism, history, and contemporaneity were used in orchestration by both novelists.

Faulkner had read Joyce's Dubliners and A Portrait before he wrote The Sound and the Fury. Though he was not to read Ulysses until a year after The Sound and the Fury, Faulkner knew of the work, and had probably read excerpts of it. He admittedly used Joyce's stream-of-consciousness technique, and in The Sound and the Fury Faulkner adapted the three styles that Joyce had used in Ulysses. In the development of character Faulkner also used moments of great illumination which Joyce called "epiphanies."

This study develops the concept that Joyce and Faulkner, using similar techniques, drew upon their respective traditions to discover and explore their experience. It also points out that Faulkner's secular tradition takes on dimensions of religiosity while Joyce's Catholic tradition takes on aspects of the profane. Each novelist created characters who manifested the tradition in their relationships to other individuals in the novels and in their reaction to society as a whole. This study evaluates the major works of both novelists in relation to their respective traditions, traces the meaning of those traditions in the lives of the principal characters in the works, and gives evidence that the novelists used similar techniques in attending subject matter. [Order No. 69-4688; 330 pages. DAI, 29A (March-April 1969), 3091.

124 On the Aesthetics of Faulkner's Fiction / Frank Ferrell CARNES, Vanderbilt University, 1968 (George N. Bennett).

By a study of his language, form, and imaginative perception of experience, this thesis traces the development of Faulkner's writing from the early sketches to the intricate art of The Sound and the Fury. Then, on the basis of principles used in this analysis, suggestions are given for a reading of Faulkner's subsequent novels.

Chapter I shows that Faulkner, at the beginning of his career, had an interest in aesthetic theory. The early sketches are neatly ordered vignettes of passionate moments, and the sketches may be considered as exercises toward the achievement of the qualities admired in "Wealthy Jew": splendor, solidity, and color. The early works are prototypes of Faulkner's mature art.

Chapters II, III, and IV give respectively an analysis of Soldiers' Pay, Mosquitoes, and Sartoris. A study of these novels reveals a growth of artistic consciousness and skill as Faulkner was trying to shape the words and to give form to the world of his imaginative vision. Soldiers' Pay shows a sensitivity to form and language, but lacks energy and imaginative depth. Mosquitoes presents a view of art as the creation of new forms revealing the very being of man as he exists among men and within time; Faulkner was taking inventory of his artistic aim and practice, and he indicated the direction his writing was to take. Faulkner came closer in Sartoris to focusing his energy and imagination on a unified experience of characters with a viable history and a memory giving continuity to cultural and personal life.

Chapter V is an analysis of The Sound and the Fury. In the still center of his imagination, Faulkner composes the flowing circle, the form of the novel, and, in his own consciousness, the reader follows the creative act: like Benjy, who builds his little islands of peace, the reader engages in the difficult discovery of harmonies. As the experience of each character is evocative for himself, so the entire novel becomes evocative for the reader. The language achieves what may be called an aesthetic radiance because each experience illuminates another, evokes another in a flowing, though intertwining, order.

The last chapter suggests that each of Faulkner's major works moves toward some passionate moment of human experience, a moment extended in memory and desire and continuous in time, evocative moments flowing and intertwining throughout the novel. That is, the other works are similar in aesthetic order to The Sound and the Fury. As examples, brief readings of As I Lay Dying, Light in August, and Absalom, Absalom! are given. [Order No. 68-12,776; 223 pages. DAI, 29A (Sept.-Oct. 1968), 894-95.]

125 Clairvoyance, Vision, and Imagination in the Fiction of William Faulkner / Rosemary Futrelle FRANKLIN, Emory University, 1968 (Floyd C. Watkins).

Clairvoyance and other parapsychological phenomena, occurring with varying frequency in almost every one of William Faulkner's works are intimately related to his ideas about time, the methods of knowing truth, and the creative process. Clairvoyance is a significant psychological phenomenon and a metaphor in its relation to characters and themes in Light In August, As I Lay Dying, and Absalom, Absalom!

Clairvoyance is a destructive force in Light in August; fanatics and bigots track down Joe Christmas with their psychic gifts. In this novel, clairvoyance, connected with determinism, reflects the conviction of Doc Hines, McEachern, the dietician, and Percy Grimm that they have a predetermined and invincible mission in life. One of the primary images in the novel, the corridor, symbolizes their constricted vision. Joe Christmas' lack of clairvoyance indicates his position as victim of the pursuers, but his insight into the future toward the end of the novel enables him to gain control of his life and convinces him that he should give himself up to the law.

Clairvoyance is not so melodramatically destructive in As I Lay Dying and Absalom, Absalom!; indeed, it seems to be a probable and effective means of communication among family members in the two novels. But it also is a destructive weapon used by Sutpen, Darl and Addie [Bundren].

Clairvoyance in Absalom, Absalom! is a metaphor for the creative imagination. The narrators who try to reconstruct the past occasionally have visions of events pertaining to the Sutpen family. Quentin and Shreve are like artists in their sensitive rapport with the past and in their imposition of aesthetic patterns on their imaginings.

Clairvoyance in Faulkner's works is similar to the creative process as he described it. He perceived his characters and stories like a clairvoyant; his method of composition involved improvisation which relied on intuition; his mulling over a character or event to search out underlying causes approximates the puzzling many of his narrators engage in. Certain characters, such as Cash and Darl Bundren, seem to mirror the artist's problems and limitations.

Clairvoyance is used for various ends, good and evil, throughout Faulkner's works. It is a potent force which transcends the limitations of language and reason. [Order No. 69-5277; 120 pages. DAI, 29A (March-April 1969), 3135.]

126 Michel Butor and William Faulkner: Some Structures and Techniques / Mary GEGERIAS, Columbia University, 1968 (Leon S. Roudiez).
Michel Butor who as a leader among the "new novelists" wrote an im-

portant essay on Faulkner's short story, "The Bear," in 1956, two years after he published his first novel, Passage de Milan, has recalled that he was still a student at the Sorbonne when he discovered The Sound and the Fury, and he admits that his first contact with Faulkner's work had left its mark on him. Although Butor acknowledges that he was inspired by the originality and the audacity of Faulkner's work, the purpose of this study is to highlight parallel structures and techniques in their novels rather than to seek traces of influence. The question of influence is a nebulous one especially since both men shared the same masters, and they had both, in their early years, been stirred by the genius of writers like Balzac, Proust, and Joyce.

Because Butor, the novelist, has also distinguished himself as a writer of critical essays which include "Les Relations de parenté dans 'L'Ours' de William Faulkner," a preliminary review of Faulkner's "old" and "new" French critics introduces this study. Likewise, a brief review of Faulkner's and Butor's backgrounds is intended to show that striking differences account for the artist's originality, but they do not alter creative vision. The main objective of this study, however, is to compare Butor's four novels (Passage de Milan, L'Emploi du temps, La Modification, and Degrés) with selected works by Faulkner ("The Bear," The Sound and the Fury, As I Lay Dying, Absalom, Absalom!), for in these works, the authors' understanding of the world as a multiverse of harmonious relationships determined early experimentation that resulted in new fictional structures and unusual literary techniques.

In general, and also more specifically in "The Bear" and Passage de Milan, Faulkner and Butor chose family bonds as their basic framework because the family unit is the source of broader relationships that find expression in complex fictional designs. Like these anthropological structures, relationships involving past and present in The Sound and the Fury and L'Emploi de temps and those concerned with the inner and outer realities of man's consciousness in As I Lay Dying and La Modification are significant because they similarly take shape in original patterns.

In Absalom, Absalom! and L'Emploi du temps special attention is devoted to the concept of le roman comme recherche in which the author's quest for his own novel parallels that of the main character in search of his identity. The development of structure is of primary interest, but these works are also important because the authors, while making an effort to supplement unusual form with theories on literary creation, ingeniously demonstrate the relationship between theme and structure, new myths and old myths, "new novels" and "old novels." [Order No. 69-12,966; 175 pages. DAI, 30A (July-Aug. 1969), 721.]

127 Darkness to Appall: Destructive Designs and Patterns in some Characters of William Faulkner / Charles Thomas GREGORY, Columbia University, 1968 (Joseph V. Ridgely).

A major re-occurring pattern in the Yoknapatawpha novels of William Faulkner is the character or group of characters who try to live by various personal "designs" or "codes." Indeed when one views the whole history of Faulkner's fictional county, one sees a portrait of a rigid, stratified society that is consumed by surface codes of honor, designs for living based only on possessions, a religion where external strict piety hides an internal corruption, and a worship of an imagined past. These people have formulated their designs, or patterns of living, to combat the massive strength of society, to protect themselves by establishing their respectability, or to build a wall between them and the world. The aggressive patterns are divided into three basic types: economic, social, and religious as epitomized by Thomas Sutpen and Flem Snopes, the Sartoris clan, and Joanna Burden respectively; while the defensive patterns are basically a retreat into the past exemplified by

Quentin Compson and Gail Hightower. Each of these attempts fails and usually leads to the destruction of the individual. These failures, although painfully personal, also represent the larger failures of the society.

As Faulkner presents these patterns, they are a destructive force in the individual and the community. These particular patterns fail because they lack a moral basis and a genuine humanity, so their results are always disruptive and destructive. By isolating these particular aggressive and defensive patterns and studying them in depth individually and as patterns in Faulkner's work, one gains a great understanding of the characters, of the novels in which they exist, and of the complexity of this theme which permeates his writing. Thus, through a study of the failure of individual characters' designs one can also understand the moral and social depth of Faulkner's criticism of society. His conservative nature, which still believes in the intrinsic merit of family, tradition, and religion, enables him to criticize distortions and corruptions of these concepts, while praising their worth, thus dramatizing the complexities of man's situation that more radical novelists often miss in their division of things into absolute right and wrong.

Comparing Thomas Sutpen and Flem Snopes in relation to their goals sheds light on both characters and their respective novels, for their design is the same given the historical shift in power from country to town, land to bank. Both men seek a mansion, a wife, a family, and power thus achieving the desired status in the community. The comparison works both ways, exposing the shallowness of Sutpen by linking him with the Snopes clan, and enhancing Flem by connecting him with the heroic Sutpen. Each is the archetype of his time and the emptiness of both ante-bellum and post-bellum society becomes more clearly defined.

The romantic code of the Sartoris family implied and dramatized in two novels and several short stories can be summarized as follows: an emphasis on the past and traditional; superiority and purity of Southern womanhood; the inferiority of the Negro; a vague noblesse oblige feeling toward the inferior ones, loyalty to family above all else; bravery; the code of vendetta and dueling, an eye for an eye; the truth of judgments obtained in trial by combat; and the concept that superior men are above the law. Adherence to these premises gives the Sartorises position and reputation in the community, but it eventually traps and destroys them because of its very rigidity and moral shallowness. In the course of the novels and short stories Faulkner examines each premise and exposes its cupidity, despite his admiration for the family's leadership qualities and personal bravery.

The lack of a moral and generous Christian foundation is also revealed in the strict religious fanaticism of many of the characters in Light in August, particularly Doc Hines, Farmer McEachern, and Joanna Burden. Their misguided and twisted missionary zeal not only helps to destroy Joe Christmas; it traps them within its loveless boundaries, preventing them from finding the love they obviously seek.

Some Faulknerian characters, however, are not strong enough to form their own aggressive patterns; instead they can barely create a shell constructed from events and imagined ideals from the past into which they can retreat. Characters like Quentin Compson and Gail Hightower live at least partially in the past or are so haunted by it that they can not be successful in the present. Instead of advancing and meeting their society boldly on its terms, they withdraw and erect defensive barriers that isolate them--and eventually destroy them.

To live by a design or pattern is not always evil and destructive in Faulkner's work. By means of hunting rituals learned from Sam Fathers and a new awareness of his heritage gained from his study of the plantation ledger books of the McCaslins, Ike McCaslin finds a new pattern, one of repudiation and personal redemption. His repudiation of his inheritance rejects not only the design of possessions practiced by Thomas Sutpen and old Carothers McCaslin, but also the Sartoris code and what it stands for. His decision to imitate Christ by becoming a carpenter while not joining any of the local churches repudiates the mercenary and missionary religion of the Burdens and McEacherns as well. Unlike Quentin and Hightower, Ike solves the mystery of the past and uses it to save himself from the corruption of the society.

Unfortunately, Ike's repudiation is not thorough enough as proved by the story "Delta Autumn" and his design ultimately fails, but he at least has realized the evils of the designs of the past and tried to reject them. That is a beginning. [Order No. 69-15,672; 236 pages. DAI, 30A (Sept.-Oct. 1969), 1565-66.]

128 Visions and Revisions: A Study of the Obtuse Narrator in American Fiction from Brockden Brown to Faulkner / James Leland GROVE, Harvard University, 1968 (Kenneth S. Lynn) no DAI entry.

129 Soldiers' Pay to The Sound and the Fury: Development of Poetic in the Early Novels of William Faulkner / Kenneth William HEPBURN, University of Washington, 1968 (William Phillips).

William Faulkner's fifth novel, The Sound and the Fury (1929), is usually considered to be the first great work of his mature period. The four novels which precede it--Soldiers' Pay (1925), "Elmer" (1925), Mosquitoes (1927), and Flags in the Dust [as Sartoris (1929)]--are generally not related closely to the production of The Sound and the Fury. Rather, the first three are viewed as apprentice novels, useful primarily for the kind of plot and character sources they provide. Flags in the Dust is useful both as the first of the Yoknapatawpha novels and as the first full attempt at a sensitive and sick hero, young Bayard Sartoris.

It is the contention of this study that Faulkner's first four novels contribute integrally to the shaping of the poetic which informs The Sound and the Fury. This poetic is constituted by two distinguishable kinds of growth: in form (structure, technique, etc.) and in impulse (what a novel should be and do). The two terms are, finally, not separable; consequently the term poetic implies both the growth that produces the changes in the individual elements and the growth that results from the interaction of these elements.

Mosquitoes is the central book; it is the work which turns the fiction outward. Prior to Mosquitoes Faulkner's work seems directed toward fulfilling an ideal conception of a work of art--or at least toward describing the conditions under which the ideal might be achieved. After Mosquitoes Faulkner seems to have adopted an expandable poetic of particularization, the emphasis of which implied that whatever universality a work might attain would be reached through a willingness to focus on the weaknesses of flawed humanity and through a care with details.

The structures and techniques of Soldiers' Pay and "Elmer" manifest the pre-Mosquitoes poetic of an ideal conception of the novel. Soldiers' Pay evolves a fairly complex structure to produce a multi-novel: there seems to be an attempt to move toward a structure which can display a full-blown novel corresponding to any one of half dozen possible heroes or themes. The unfinished and unpublished "Elmer" is a novel about a would-be artist and his first work. The key concept here is that of "compact erectness," that quality which the artist-person will need to attain before he can produce an artifact. "Elmer" is especially interesting in that, in it, Faulkner uses extensively the technique of achieved presence through memory which will be so central in the later works.

In the novels that follow Mosquitoes the structures and techniques not only build upon the earlier novels, but build in conformity with the poetic of particularization. Both of the later novels set their characters in structures of entropic quest: in Flags in the Dust all the main characters are busy defeating themselves while simultaneously pursuing some elusive object and trying to define it; and in The Sound and the Fury characters, reader, and author pursue a never recoverable Caddy Compson. Also in these later novels improved techniques from the earlier novels are used more selectively and meaningfully.

The movement from the early novels to The Sound and the Fury is one of greater scope and comfort. As a result of experience with form, but primarily as a result of a radical shift in poetic emphasis, Faulkner, in The Sound and the Fury, is possessed of a large range of techniques and materials to employ in the writing of the novel. But it is the comfort in using these tools that, finally, is the source of this novel's greatness. [Order No. 69-1180; 248 pages. DAI, 29A (Jan.-Feb. 1969), 2263.]

130 A Dialect Study of Faulkner County, Arkansas / Patricia Joanne HOFF, Louisiana State University and Agricultural and Mechanical College, 1968 (Claude L. Shaver).

The purpose of this study is to determine the speech characteristics of the people of Faulkner County, Arkansas.

First a study was made of the history of Faulkner County in order to determine influences on immigration into the area. Most of the people came from the Southern states, particularly Tennessee.

Second, 30 performants were interviewed and the responses recorded. Two of these tapes were not usable; consequently 28 informants were used in the study. The responses were transcribed into phonetic symbols and a description was given of the dialect. Although the study is primarily a descriptive phonological study, certain lexical items were examined and comparisons, primarily with Southern, Mountain, and Midland speech, were made.

The speech of Faulkner County has similarities with Southern, Mountain, and Midland speech along with great differences from all three. The great diversity in pronunciation and in the use of lexical items suggests that Faulkner County may be a transitional area. Among the evidence to support this is the following: (1) In words such as ma and pa, either the Midland pronunciation [ɔ] or the Southern [a] may be used by the same individual. (2) The Southern [ɔ] in water does not occur; but the Southern [a] is predominant in wash. (3) The Southern diphthongization of vowels and the Southern and Mountain monophthongization of [ar] are predominant; but the loss of [r] does not occur. (4) The Northern terms brook, pail, quite (spry), and (cherry) pit are common. (5) The Southern and Midland terms lightbread, clabbered, shuck, pallet, snack, pulleybone, snakedoctor, etc., are all common; whereas the Southern terms tote, turn of wood, fritters, Confederate War, etc., and the Southern Midland terms milkgap, blinds, a little piece, etc., are either infrequent or non-existent. Further studies need to be made in the areas around Faulkner County before the evidence will be clear. There are suggestions that isoglosses appear; but the evidence suggests they may be a result of the few informants used and the small geographical area studied.

There is evidence to show that certain pronunciations and terms are dying out. These include: (1) [æ] in care, chair, stamp (one's foot); [r] in cherry syrup; [ɛ] in syrup, shut; [i] in drain; [ɚ] in hearth, tushes, widow; [ju] in new due, Tuesday; [æu] in wound; loafbread; lunch (for snack); skeeter hawk; devil's horse; fritters; Confederate War; tap; stob; firedogs; fire irons; stinging lizard; fireboard; etc.

In most instances there is no difference in pronunciation or terminology between the educated informants or those from Conway, the County seat of Faulkner County, and other informants. In a few instances the educated or those from Conway did not use pronunciations or terminology of other speakers. These include: (1) loafbread; (2) lunch (snack); (3) skeeter hawk;

(4) devil's horse; (5) stinging lizard; (6) low (moo); (7) frying pan; (8) sty; (9) hog lot; (10) rounding of the vowel in sun, brush, gums, judge, shut, touch; (11) voicing of the fricative in nephew; (12) [i] in drain; and (13) [r] in wash.

Until further evidence is available it can be said tentatively that (1) Faulkner County seems to be a transitional area with influences of Southern, Mountain, and Midland speech; (2) that certain terms are dying out; (3) that in most instances the educated informants and the informants from Conway use the same pronunciations and terminology that are used by other informants; and (4) the indications of possible isoglosses will probably not be valid as other studies are completed. [Order No. 68-10,745; 282 pages. DAI, 29A (July-Aug. 1968), 247.]

131 Life in Motion: Genteel and Vernacular Attitudes in the Works of the Southwestern American Humorists, Mark Twain, and William Faulkner / Charles Martin KERLIN, Jr., University of Colorado, 1968 (Charles Nilon).

In this dissertation I trace the conflict between genteel and vernacular attitudes in the works of the major 19th century Southwestern humorists, including Mark Twain, and of the South's greatest 20th century novelist, William Faulkner. The conflict between these attitudes is dramatically depicted in works dealing with the Southwestern frontier before the Civil War. The major Southwestern humorists, A. B. Longstreet, Joseph G. Baldwin, Johnson J. Hooper, Thomas Bangs Thorpe, and George Washington Harris, tended to view the vernacular frontiersman with suspicion and alarm. Their works often reflect the genteel attitudes of the mythical Southern aristocrat who saw the frontiersman as a kind of subversive, threatening to destroy the status-quo and the Southern gentleman's stoic acceptance of it.

As the frontier expanded, however, the best of the Southwestern writers, Johnson J. Hooper, Thomas Bangs Thorpe, and George Washington Harris, began to present the vernacular subversive's flexible response to life in a favorable context. Recognition of the frontiersman's values represents their most important contribution to American literature and culture.

Mark Twain's work in the Southwestern tradition also reflects the conflict between genteel and vernacular attitudes. His ambivalence in The Innocents Abroad, Life on the Mississippi, and Roughing It results from personae in these works who represent the values of Twain's dominant culture as well as the values of the vernacular man. Twain's persona often seems at different times to be two different men. In his finest work, Huckleberry Finn, the values of the vernacular man finally triumph.

William Faulkner also develops conflicts of social change around clusters of genteel and vernacular values. Major characters who represent both attitudes appear in Sartoris, The Unvanquished, Go Down, Moses, Intruder in the Dust, Light in August, and the Snopes trilogy. These works can be examined profitably in terms of what Faulkner has called a "trinity of conscience" if a clear relationship is established between elements of Faulkner's trinity and the different genteel and vernacular values each element represents. The establishment of this relationship presents an alternative to recent criticism of Faulkner's work which emphasizes his ambivalence and his political conservatism. This emphasis clouds Faulkner's moral vision.

Critics who emphasize Faulkner's ambivalence and/or conservatism, namely Walter J. Slatoff, Frederick Hoffman, Walter J. Taylor, Jr., and Warren Beck, do so, I believe, because they identify Faulkner's own private views with the views of his major genteel characters, John Sartoris, Isaac McCaslin, and Gavin Stevens. I do not believe that Faulkner's major genteel characters represent his views. Faulkner, like Twain, tends to resolve conflicts of social change in favor of a free vernacular response to life. Major characters in his work, namely V. K. Ratliff, Charles Mallison, Byron Bunch, and many others, defy genteel, arbitrary commitments to the status-quo. They do not, as do Faulkner's genteel characters, act violently and irrationally or hide their inability to act behind abstract, stoic rhetoric. They, to paraphrase Faulkner, do more than just repudiate. They succeed as human beings.

I do not claim that this investigation of genteel and vernacular attitudes can fully clarify Faulkner's moral vision. But I do feel that this reevaluation of those genteel characters now identified as his spokesman resolves much that seems ambivalent in his work. Specifically, I show that Faulkner often treats his genteel characters harshly. In doing so, he seems to repudiate their values while emphasizing vernacular ones. Recognition of this clarifies his ethical, moral view of man. He has identified his ethical, moral view as "life is motion." [Order No. 69-4306; 159 pages. DAI, 29A (May-June 1969), 4492.]

132 Faulkner's Characters of Sensibility / David William MASCITELLI, Duke University, 1968 (Arlin Turner).

This study focuses on a series of Faulkner's male characters who are perceptive, imaginative, self-conscious, articulate, and above all highly sensitive to their environment. The basis for such an investigation is the belief that the characters are similar enough in their traits of personality and the way in which Faulkner uses them in his fiction that any one of them is more readily understood when examined in terms of the others. Secondarily, the thesis attempts to demonstrate that Faulkner's treatment of this type of character reveals a change in attitude from the merciless ridicule and sense of futility and ineffectuality with which Faulkner presents such early examples as Horace Benbow or the reporter in Pylon to the warmer and more sympathetic portrayals of characters like Gavin Stevens and Charles Mallison in his fiction written since the late thirties.

Part One isolates a series of these characters who are further bound together by the fact that Faulkner presents them to the reader primarily through their involvements with women. Ernest Talliaferro in Mosquitoes, Horace Benbow in Sartoris and Sanctuary, the reporter in Pylon, and Harry Wilbourne in Wild Palms are all presented in Prufrockian caricatures of incompetence and ineffectuality, with emphasis on the fact that they are all brought to grief by emotional entanglements with women. The section concludes with a detailed treatment of Gavin Stevens as he appears in The Town and The Mansion through his involvements with Eula and Linda Snopes. The discussion of Stevens stresses the fact that, though he shares some of the Prufrockian inadequacies of the characters previously discussed, the portrayal is a sympathetic one that balances the elements of satire with a respect for the positive qualities of Steven's cultivated imagination and chivalric sense of honor and decency. Such a treatment on Faulkner's part suggests an increased sympathy in his later years for the man of intelligence and imagination, and an increased interest in studying in detail the convolutions of a rich and complex consciousness.

The second part of the study treats three characters, Bayard Sartoris from The Unvanquished, Isaac McCaslin from "The Bear," and Charles Mallison from Intruder in the Dust, who are linked by the fact that they are sensitive young Southerners who face a crisis in their relations with their native region. Each is forced into a situation in which his own ethical code comes into conflict with that of the society in which he has been raised. Each is subjected to the anguish of reconciling a strong commitment to his homeland with a personal sense of justice that cannot accept some of its attitudes. This section of the thesis also deals with some of the ways in which the South is most useful to Faulkner as a setting for his novels, stressing particularly the variety of interesting problems, crises, and complex situations which the South offers and the firmly entrenched codes and patterns of behavior, and social stratification which at times make Faulkner works resemble the novel of manners.

The thesis concludes by using the figure of Quentin Compson as the basis for a summing up of many of the traits and problems encountered through the discussions of the other characters. Compson's role in The Sound and the Fury links him to those characters treated in Part One of the study by virtue of the fact that his warped love for his sister Caddy is one of the prime causes of his suicide and by virtue of a romantic idealism which makes it impossible for him to adjust to the hard facts of reality. On the other hand, in his appearance in Absalom, Absalom!, he resembles the characters treated in Part Two in that he too is seeking to reconcile himself to a cultural heritage toward which he has strongly ambivalent feelings. The study concludes by stressing the fact that, though Faulkner is often thought of as a kind of "primitivist" who tends to glorify instinctive, impulsive behavior based on the simpler, more straightforward human emotions at the expense of the man of ideas, the evolution of his handling of the type of character treated in this study, and his preoccupation with it over his entire career suggest a stronger sympathy toward the workings of the sensitive imaginative mind than has often been recognized. [Order No. 68-11,208; 209 pages. DAI, 29A (July-Aug. 1968), 608-09.]

133 History as Voice and Metaphor: A Study of Tate, Warren, and Faulkner / Henry Clay MOSES, III, Cornell University, 1968 (Michael J. Colacurcio).

In this study of fiction whose subject is history's imagined form, Tate, Warren, and Faulkner stand unique among modern Southern writers in their invention of personae who are self-conscious historians. Where history is subject rather than framework or attitude, in the "Ode to the Confederate Dead," All the King's Men, and Absalom, Absalom!, it is defined as the experience of certain kinds of figurative and voiced language. In each of the three central works, the persona's imaginative failure and the author's control of the fiction's form invite the reader to perceive crucial ironies and simultaneously to assume proper historical attitudes. Participation in the fiction by both reader and character results in the repudiation of nostalgia in favor of poetic form.

History is the creative act of a disintegrated self, whose symptoms are the breakdown of voice and perception. History promises to serve as the locus of unity, so the persona in each of the central works struggles to establish the proper linguistic relationship between himself and the past, in which he becomes the predicated subject. He uses language in response to the language of received history, which may come to him from several sorts of evidence, by trying to express the past and the present vocally and metaphorically. He may filter the language of documents through his own language or try to embody time's passage in a single figure of speech. The imaginative actions of the several personae sort generally into two modes: the metaphorical, which is expansive and dialectical and allows the historical object its independence from the subject, and the symbolic, which is reductive and obsessive and is the result of the thorough imposition of subject on object. Metaphorical perception discovers history spatially; and it is in the arrangement of events and the sense of resonance between them that the reader gains ironic advantage over the persona.

Tate's "Ode" is a parody of the Romantic lyric which achieves not insight but blindness. There are in situation and landscape elements of metaphor and voice, but the persona destroys perception by his pun and curse. Both situation and landscape remain vocal and metaphoric for the reader, who can rescue history from the persona.

In Warren's <u>All the King's Men</u>, Jack Burden confronts a history whose language resists his <u>impositions</u>. He abandons a figure of speech he fashions early in the novel, which is the key to his own situation, and formulates instead the law of the Great Twitch. Jack's theory, never entirely outgrown, is a parodic and reductive version of a statement by Cass Mastern which does describe the novel's crucial historical relationships.

Rosa Coldfield and Mr. Compson in Faulkner's <u>Absalom, Absalom</u>! supply Quentin with figurative language he uses once he <u>can tell his version</u> of the history, but in their narrations clusters of figures do not describe their world so much as become it. Quentin's telling transcends compulsive modes but is also, though like a lyric poem, a world unto itself. In the world of their voiced language, Quentin and Shreve perceive history in genuinely metaphorical terms, during the moments of "overpass." Quentin is the one clear instance of the disintegrated persona who "finds himself" in history.

The Epilogue of this study treats cursorily <u>Brother to Dragons</u>, "The Bear," <u>World Enough and Time</u>, and selected poems. The conviction grows that for each of the writers considered, history (and perhaps "myth") is essentially a matter of using historical evidence to create dialectically vocal and metaphoric forms, like those embodied in the actions of telling and listening, or of creating adequate metaphor. Such dialectical imagining enacts belief, admits complexity, and achieves identity. [Order No. 69-5027; 224 pages. DAI, 29A (May-June 1969), 4014.]

134 The Literature of the Air: Themes and Imagery in the Work of Faulkner, Saint-Exupery, and Gaiser / Friedrich Peter OTT, Harvard University, 1968 (Harry Levin) no DAI entry.

135 Theme and Characterization in Faulkner's Snopes Trilogy / Donald Anthony PETESCH, University of Texas at Austin, 1968 (Gordon Mills).

William Faulkner created, in the Snopes trilogy, a modern morality play. Part One of the dissertation examines Faulkner's thematic intentions; Part Two relates characterization to theme.

In Chapter One of Part One, the two major critical approaches to Flem Snopes--Flem as representative of economic force and Flem as representative of evil--are discussed. Flem Snopes is viewed as a symbol for evil in a modern morality play. Faulkner's statements on the use of symbolic figures are examined. In Chapter Two, the narrative devices Faulkner employs to create Flem as a nonhuman Devil figure are examined. In Chapter Three, Faulkner's creation of Eula Varner Snopes as an allegorical figure is discussed. The three traditional sources of image and symbol drawn on by Faulkner to develop Eula's role are examined. Qualities which Eula represents in the trilogy are contrasted with those of Flem Snopes.

Part Two of the dissertation focuses on the character of Gavin Stevens, since it is Stevens' growth to self-awareness, coupled with the temporary eclipse of Snopesism through the death of Flem Snopes, that gives man some hope in what Faulkner regards as man's most important struggle: to be better than he is.

In Chapter One, critical responses to Gavin Stevens are examined. Until recently, Stevens has been viewed as Faulkner's viewpoint character. Confusion has resulted, in part, from Faulkner's use of multiple points of view. In Chapter Two, it is argued that V. K. Ratliff is Faulkner's viewpoint character and that Stevens is an "unreliable narrator." Central issues in the trilogy are examined to show how Stevens is often wrong and Ratliff almost invariably right. In Chapters Three and Four, Stevens' relations with Eula Varner Snopes and Linda Snopes Kohl are examined to show that Stevens suffers from a failure to act, that his rhetoric conceals a failure of will.

Chapter Five traces Stevens' slow and painful growth to self-awareness. The pressure of events, the contrast of his inaction with the action of Mink Snopes and Linda Snopes Kohl, and the prodding of V. K. Ratliff force Stevens to an awareness of his failure to act. Faulkner's moral relativism is examined and the importance of self-awareness, in the absence of the old absolutes, is discussed. [Order No. 69-6202; 194 pages. DAI, 29A (March-April 1969), 3618-19.]

136 Time and Identity in the Novels of William Faulkner / Fran James POLEK, University of Southern California, 1968 (Eleazer Lecky).

This analysis of character examines the correlation of particular cognitive time patterns to the development of personal identity in five William Faulkner novels: Sartoris, The Sound and the Fury, As I Lay Dying, Light in August, and Absalom, Absalom!. Although Faulkner's characters exhibit a wide range of attitudes toward time, it is possible to divide them into two major groups: those who reflect a form of the natural cognitive time pattern contrasted to those who reflect a form of the mechanical time pattern.

Characters who are successful in establishing a satisfactory present identity align themselves with a natural (or all inclusive, circular) cognitive time vision. Time, in this sense, is circular in its basic relationship to natural rhythms: days, months, seasons, years, and epochs. Character identity, in significant part, is structured by the belief that all time (past through memory and future through anticipation), is contained in "now." Man is a free agent who, through memory and anticipation, can shape and interpret past, present, and future to his advantage. Time is his ally, allowing a personal vision both ennobling and enduring.

Characters who are unsuccessful in their quest for an effective present identity either fall by attempting to move out of any time pattern, or limiting their vision to a mechanical (linear) cognitive time pattern. Time, in this sense, is linear, moving in a straight line from an irretrievably lost past to an illusory future. Man, as a determined agent, feels victimized by time, unable to assume responsibility for past, present, or future. Time is his enemy, destroying past values, moving him inevitably toward some final "doom."

Each of the five novels selected for analysis provides characters illustrative of the basic cognitive time patterns. In Sartoris, the first work in which Faulkner's correlation between time and identity is clearly developed, both old Bayard and young Bayard are unable to move from past to present realities. Their inability is an aspect of the basic "curse" noted in many Faulkner novels. In The Sound and the Fury, forms of the mechanical pattern are reflected particularly by Mr. Compson, Quentin, Jason Jr., and Mrs. Compson. Benjamin, an idiot, lives in a "no-time" universe; only Dilsey achieves a natural cognitive vision that enables her to endure and prevail. The strange journey in As I Lay Dying is the background against which members of the Bundren family attempt to establish meaningful identity. With the exception of Cash, they all fail in their quest. Light in August focuses on the tragic attempt of Joe Christmas to solve the mystery of his identity. Joanna Burden and Reverend Hightower succeed temporarily in finding some meaning in the present, while Lena Grove and Byron Bunch form a counterpoint of pastoral innocence undefeated by time. In Absalom, Absalom!, Thomas Sutpen tries to control time and destiny by creating a "grand design," but inevitably fails. The witness-narrators of the Sutpen saga--Miss Rosa, Mr. Compson and his father, and Quentin--are all unable to accept a natural cognitive time pattern that will free them from the past.

The study reveals Faulkner's use of time as an important aspect of character delineation. Other considerations are relevant to a final evaluation of Faulkner's achievement, but the relationship between time and identity provides one key to an understanding of Faulkner's shaping vision of man. [Order No. 69-5066; 275 pages. DAI, 29A (March-April 1969), 3151.]

137 Faulkner's South: Myth and History in the Novel / Myra Jehlen RISKIN, University of California at Berkeley, 1968 (Henry Nash Smith).

The "sole owner and proprietor" of Yoknapatawpha County was no absentee landlord, habitué of fashionable cultural spas. In Oxford, Mississippi, Faulkner lived on the land and used real Southern soil in creating his fictional universe. Or, to put it another way, his language drew specifically upon the history and myths of Southern experience. Since regional myths are more apt to contradict than to complement history, Faulkner had to judge between the two in interpreting Southern life, and his ambivalence was the crucial influence upon the form and substance of his works.

The focal issue in this ambivalence is the roll of the plantation aristocracy and its conflict with an embittered poor white class which considered itself heir to the mantle of the Jeffersonian yeomanry. Faulkner's attitude to this conflict was painfully divided; the enmity between the two characters of greatest stature in Yoknapatawpha draws much of its heat from the author's personal strife. John Sartoris and Thomas Sutpen represent contradictory attitudes toward the Southern aristocracy. In Sartoris Faulkner reproves the planters only for their impracticality, the "glamorous fatality" which incapacitated them and sacrificed their rightful pre-eminence--reproaches which themselves re-affirm the essence of the plantation myth. On the contrary, Sutpen embodies a profound critique of the socio-economic background of the planter aristocracy, finding therein the cause of its downfall. Told from the point of view of the "redneck" Sutpen, Absalom, Absalom! thus reveals implicitly Faulkner's attraction to a democratic type of agrarianism. In this novel Faulkner writes as a frustrated Jeffersonian bitter at the social devastation slavery and feudalism have wrought in the South. But even here occasionally, although much more clearly in Sartoris, The Sound and the Fury, and The Unvanquished, one can sense the author's strong bond to the romantic mystique of the plantation and its cavalier.

It is this bond, an empathy which survived all Faulkner's doubts and his essentially Jeffersonian convictions, that seems to motivate the underlying question in the Yoknapatawpha stories: can its traditional rulers lead the South through present difficulties and into a viable future?

Primarily through Gavin Stevens, Faulkner tried to visualize a positive answer. Although an aristocrat, Stevens has escaped the historical guilt and ensuing decadence of his class. But in the end he can offer neither a moral nor polotical program to revive Southern civilization and only stands by helpless, making epigrams at the Götterdämmerung. Faulkner's real answer is contained in his recurrent portrayal of a young aristocrat obsessed with the smothering effect of his past. This image expresses Faulkner's sense that the aristocracy was doomed by its own history and that, for lack of a suitable successor, it must drag down all of Southern society with it into a social chaos "ordered" only by the Snopeses who represent the worst qualities of the human soul unrestrained by the moral discipline of a vital civilization. Yet it is not the death of a Sartoris but of a "redneck" which closes the sage. Mink Snopes is born as wretched as Sutpen and never rises from his abject status, but in death he becomes the apotheosis of the agrarian South to which Faulkner thus writes a final eulogy. [Order No. 69-14,975; 361 pages. DAI, 30A (Sept.-Oct. 1969), 1148-49.]

138 Motion in Yoknapatawpha County: Theme and Point of View in the Novels of William Faulkner / William James SCHULTZ, Kansas State University, 1968 (William R. Moses.)

Although many critics have remarked on Faulkner's experimentation with point of view in The Sound and the Fury and As I Lay Dying, no one has previously made a study of numerous variations of point of view over the entire range of his Yoknapatawpha novels. This study discovers a close connection between the technical problem of point of view and a theme fundamental to Faulkner's novels after 1929--human life, in all of its aspects, expressed as "Motion," and the human destiny to grow in knowledge of this Motion. It is at this point of knowing that theme and technique interlock: a chief concern in the novels is how the characters become aware, know the motion of life; point of view, the problem of how the reader knows, reinforces this theme by drawing the reader into active involvement in the motion and experience of the novel.

The second chapter examines Faulkner's apprenticeship period, demonstrating from his early stories and the first three novels--Soldiers' Pay, Mosquitoes, and Sartoris--his early interest in experimentation with various devices of point of view that enable him to expose the subjectivity of his characters. There follows a chapter on his first masterpiece, The Sound and the Fury, discussing the stream-of-consciousness techniques which have as one effect the involvement of the reader as he struggles to comprehend the highly subjective viewpoints offered him. The next chapter does the same for As I Lay Dying, also pointing out this novel's tendency away from the extreme subjectivity of its predecessor, toward a sense of the motion of communal life. The chapter on Sanctuary shows how Faulkner uses even a relatively conventional third-person point of view to involve the reader in the motion of Horace Benbow's encounter with evil.

The chapter on Light in August observes the problem of knowing made more explicit, as well as the growing significance of the town as a repository and source of knowledge about its individual inhabitants. With Absalom, Absalom!, the study shows how Faulkner involves the reader in a quest for the elusive truth about Thomas Sutpen, thus demonstrating both man's "doom" of having to seek to know and the difficulty of ever attaining objective truth.

Next, a chapter surveys Faulkner's short stories, pointing out three tendencies--the town as source of knowledge, "telling" as a favorite point of view, and the viewpoints of young protagonists who must lose their innocence of knowledge and action. The remainder of the chapter examines The Unvanquished in light of these short practices. There follows a chapter dealing with Go Down, Moses, Intruder in the Dust, and Requiem for a Nun, in which is discussed Faulkner's development of a variation of third-person narration which provides the illusion of the stream-of-consciousness of the protagonist and also suggests a later perspective by this major character.

A chapter on the Snopes trilogy discussed The Hamlet, The Town, and The Mansion as showing a logical change in point of view as the main characters grow older in years and knowledge: from the third-person viewpoint of Ratliff as representative of the community in The Hamlet, through the first-person point of view of Chick Mallison (also a representative of the town's knowledge) in The Town, to the points of view of the older Ratliff, Charles, and Gavin Stevens in The Mansion. The concluding chapter examines The Reivers as a conclusion to the Yoknapatawpha saga, yet another exposition of the human necessity to know and to lose one's innocence in the inevitable encounter with the motion that is life. [Order No. 69-4169; 286 pages. DAI, 29A (March-April 1969), 3154.]

139 Faulkner's Use of the Classics / Sister Joan Michael SERAFIN, University of Notre Dame, 1968 (Robert M. Slabey).

This study of William Faulkner's uses of Greek and Roman material demonstrates in concordance form the classical allusions in Faulkner's entire published work, including interviews. An analytical essay preceding three indexes explains Faulkner's position in the Southern classical tradition, his use of classical quotations, imagery, rhetoric, symbols, mythology, structure, values, and the influence of the "mythical-method" of T. S. Eliot and James Joyce.

Borrowing from classical civilization, history, and religion, Faulkner constructs analogies, often ironic, between the present and the past. He quotes from Horace, Cicero, Suetonius, and Vergil. Some of his characters symbolically parallel certain mythological figures--for example, the Diana-figures of Cecily Saunders (Soldiers' Pay) and Miss Quentin Compson (The Sound and the Fury), the Venus-Helen figure of Eula Varner (the Snopes trilogy), and the fertility-figures of Lena Grove (Light in August) and Dewey Dell (As I Lay Dying). Mythical pastoral images such as satyrs, centaurs, and fauns function significantly in works like Soldiers' Pay, "Black Music," and Absalom, Absalom!.

Mythical structures, too, are found in Sanctuary, which is based in part on the Persephone myth, with Temple Drake as Persephone and Popeye as an ironic Pluto. Mosquitoes, although not totally structured on a classical model, resembles The Odyssey in its voyage motif. Absalom, Absalom!, notably based on Greek tragic form, contains a number of supporting allusions to Agamemnon and Clytemnestra, for example, and to the forceful workings of Fate.

In his concern with the decay of the Southern Code because of slavery, Faulkner studies Man in terms of the universal, classical values of honor and pride and the Stoic virtues of endurance and responsibility.

The three indexes in this study are intended to evidence Faulkner's awareness of the classics and the wide range of classical references he employs to enrich his work. Index I is a novel-by-novel census of allusions and quotations in context; Index II lists and identifies classical names used for persons, places and animals, and things; Index III is an explicated catalogue of allusions, with a list of their appearances in Faulkner's work, and the critics who have discussed the function of particular allusions or myths. [Order No. 69-4080; 264 pages. DAI, 29A (March-April 1969), 3155-56.]

140 A Freight of Faith and Hope: A Study of the Quest in the American Novel / Charles F. STUBBELFIELD, University of Denver, 1968 (E. S. Twining) no DAI entry.

141 A Gallery of Grotesques: The Alienation Theme in the Works of Hawthorne, Twain, Anderson, Faulkner, and Wolfe / Barbara White SULLIVAN, University of Georgia, 1968 (Pascal Seeves).

Nathaniel Hawthorne protested against the cold, calculating, detached seeker. He felt that isolation from other men and the elevation of head over heart were unpardonable sins. Hawthorne grouped among his unpardonable sinners scientists, artists, intellectuals, reformers, ministers, and others. As fitting punishment for their evil of estrangement, Hawthorne subjected them to perpetual isolation. Hawthorne frequently admitted the nobility and idealism of the quests which drove man to separate themselves from their fellows. Within the framework of Romanticism, Hawthorne's grotesque aliens often appeared in exotic and unreal surroundings, and many of the characters bore foreign names for an effect of remoteness and mystery. Hawthorne presented the Romantic alien; Mark Twain portrayed the Realistic alien. Mark Twain's moral aliens had ordinary names like Huck Finn and Hank Morgan. His characters used the vernacular in their speech, and their everyday actions suggested those of commonplace people in small towns. Since life, realistically, is filled with hilarity as well as pain, Mark Twain's characters often found themselves in humorous situations. It remained for Sherwood Anderson to merge the two traditions. He established the "grotesque" as the new prototype of estrangement. His "grotesques" were often inwardly as bizarre and eccentric as Hawthorne's characters, and yet they appeared in a realistic small town setting. Anderson despised the "genteel" writing of Hawthorne, and yet he was clearly indebted to the Hawthorne tradition. Anderson's Enoch Robinson, for example, is a latter-day Owen Warland. The outer garments of the aliens of Anderson and Hawthorne differed, however. Hawthorne's eccentrics wore stark black coats, while Anderson's "grotesques" were clothed in humdrum brown coats. Born in a democratic, realistic age, Anderson's people were little men who lived and died unnoticed by their fellow men. They felt "queer" around others, but the real tragedy was that few people even dimly recognized the apartness of the "grotesques." Anderson influenced two young writers who similarly explored the role of the alien in the small town. Both William Faulkner and Thomas Wolfe employed lyricism and the technique of stream of consciousness to record the thoughts of their aliens, who were often Romantic figures poised against the backdrop of the realistically portrayed hamlet. Some of the characters of Faulkner and Wolfe had a striking resemblance to the dedicated, Romantic seekers of Hawthorne; Faulkner's Thomas Sutpen was akin to Hawthorne's Aylmer, and Wolfe's Gant-Webber was a 20th century Warland. Yet, the protagonists of Faulkner and Wolfe were reared in sleepy, Southern communities, and they spoke the language of real men, some more rural than others. The conclusions of Faulkner and Wolfe about the inherent worth of the alien contrasted keenly, until the voice of Wolfe began to change. In the early works of Wolfe, the tormented cry of the egocentric artist burned with fierce fire; as Wolfe matured, he began to recognize a dawning kinship with others. Faulkner's aliens were almost always seen as grotesque pariahs, however. In their own individual ways, each of the five authors agreed on a basic moral truth about isolation--that man can only end his isolation and loneliness by forgetting self and giving precedence to the love for his fellows. [Order No. 69-3485; 223 pages. DAI, 30A (July-Aug. 1969), 698-99.]

142 A Portrait of the Artist in Motion: A Study of the Artist-Surrogates in the Novels of William Faulkner / Joseph Francis TRIMMER, Purdue University, 1968 (William T. Stafford).

The thesis of this study is that despite previous critical charges to the contrary, William Faulkner has sophisticated conceptions of art and the proper function of the artist. The basis for both conceptions resides in Faulkner's preoccupation with the antithetical nature of art and that which art attempts to portray, the fluid motion of life. Life is motion, whereas art is the process whereby motion is suspended. But invariably the suspension of motion must become a distortion since if life is to be alive, it must not be arrested. In such a situation, the relationship between art and life must necessarily be at best only temporary and always subject to further reassessment.

It is this recognition of the contingency which exists between life and art which precipitates Faulkner's use of artist-surrogates. These characters are artists in the sense that in relation to the life of the novel, they maintain an attitude of speculative detachment, and sometimes even serve as the aesthetic organizers of that life. What Faulkner gains by their presence is that he can allow them to impose a stasis on the motion of the novel. They will fail in such attempts, but in the process Faulkner can both suggest the tension which exists between art and life, and explore the reasons why the successive attempts of his artist-surrogates to resolve that tension fail.

In order to uncover this relationship between art and life, between the artist and the world, this study has attempted to see the Faulkner canon as a collection of artistic assaults on a series of separate and yet finally related aesthetic problems. The study, therefore, does not consider Faulkner's novels in chronological order except in Chapters I and VII. Rather it attempts to establish an order which reveals a progression of increasing analytical complexity. The initial aesthetic problem discussed in this respect is the problem of the re-creation of the past. But because this creative attempt is based on the principle of making life adhere to a preconceived pattern, it fails to portray the reality of the past. This failure suggests the problem of the degree to which such a past may serve as an effective tool for ordering the present. Because this project also fails, the study examines the limitations and possibilities inherent in attempting to deal directly with the fluid motion of the present.

The result of this examination is the discovery that Faulkner's novels suggest a conception of art which transcends the desire to affix stasis to motion, and a prescriptive definition of the artist who must use this conception of art as his working aesthetic. What the failure of art signifies is that it too must be in motion. It must continually be open to reassessment because its subject, life, will never remain static. The true artist should not despair at the failure of his art. For those artists who do despair, the only solution seems to be isolation from life, isolation which will produce only further distortions. The solution for the artist is to accept failure as a condition necessary to his being an artist. By such failure he is free to try again. When he does, he will be able to create a "living literature," a literature which throbs with life because its life is always bigger than the art which encompasses it. [Order No. 69-7511; 221 pages. DAI, 29A (March-April 1969), 3623.]

143 "The Snopes Dilemma": Morality and Amorality in Faulkner's Snopes Trilogy / James Gray WATSON, University of Pittsburgh, 1968 (Robert L. Gale).

The unity of William Faulkner's Snopes trilogy is dependent upon the continuing conflict between morality and amorality. In this diversified work, the figure of Flem Snopes remains an undeviating point of reference as a malevolent presence, impinging upon the lives and affairs of all men. Based upon Flem's rise from tenant farm to bank presidency, the theme of ubiquitous evil operant in the moral world is iterated through the recurrence in modifying context of character, action, and event. Motivated by his insatiable appetite for money, power, and position, and mindlessly insensitive to all human appeals, Flem is the inhuman archetype of amorality. In response to his elemental amorality, men committed to the fundamental human tenets of principled existence repeatedly rise up to challenge Flem, thereby asserting their own humanity. Through the diversity and scope of such challenges, Faulkner renders reality in its multiform complexity, dramatically demonstrating the amplitude and depth of moral principles and specifying the malign nature of amorality. On the recurrent thematic contrast between rejuvenative morality and amoral self-destructiveness the trilogy is structurally poised.

The theme of moral opposition to amoral aggression is also the major source of organic unity in each of the three novels. In The Hamlet, Flem assumes the character of a visitation, and his machinations have direct consequences for the entire pastoral community. Flem dominates the economy, and his rise is accompanied by his exploitation of the elemental human passions and virtues expressed in such varying aspects as Eula Varner's sexuality and V. K. Ratliff's generous respect for human pride and fair play. Flem's amorality is evoked by contrast to the morality of those who oppose him, suggesting that his victories are only financial. In The Town, the pervasive contrasts by which morality and amorality are made mutually revealing are continued through the medium of Gavin Steven's humane idealism. In his interpretive speculations on the nature of reality and his tentative interventions against Snopesism on behalf of Eula Varner Snopes and Linda Snopes, Gavin is corrected and assisted by V. K. Ratliff, representing the point of view of the practical realist, and by Charles Mallison, the innocent youth whose unbiased perceptions mirror reality. Through their dialogue together, Flem's amorality is seen into from a multi-faceted perspective, and through their unprincipled opposition to Flem, an ethical constant is evoked which dominates the novel. The contrast between Flem and Gavin is the central factor in the thematic unity of The Town.

The steady narrowing down of sensibilities through which Flem's amorality is revealed from The Hamlet to The Town culminates in The Mansion, where the cumulative effect of Snopesian amorality is expressed in terms of the converging revenge stories of Mink Snopes and Linda Snopes. Together, the acutely personal nature of Mink's vengefulness and the philosophical remoteness of Linda's commitment to oppose inhumanity in all of its forms define Flem's archetypal amorality with new intensity and vastly increase the scope of its significance. The heights to which Mink and Linda rise as moral beings suggest the depths to which Flem has descended. The self-destructive nature of amorality is clearly suggested by the fact that Flem's death results directly from those responses elicited by his inhuman machinations in the moral world. Conversely, the regenerative nature of morality is expressed in terms of the readiness of principled individuals to continue the struggle, despite their recognition that such a course is doomed to at least partial failure. The sustention of this conflict between morality and amorality throughout The Hamlet, The Town, and The Mansion unifies the trilogy in theme as well as in structure. [Order No. 68-12,663; 239 pages. DAI, 29A (Sept. - Oct. 1968), 1237-38.]

144 The Reconstructive Mode in Fiction: A Study of Faulkner and the
French New Novel / Arnold Louis WEINSTEIN, Harvard University,
1968 (Wilbur M. Frohock) no DAI entry.

145 The Dickens World and Yoknapatawpha County: A Study of Character
and Society in Dickens and Faulkner / Thomas Henry ADAMOWSKI,
Indiana University, 1969 (James H. Justus).

In regard to characterization, social revelation, and social criticism, Dickens and Faulkner are significantly comparable authors. They have relied on various similar techniques to illustrate the forms of conflict that exist between the self and the society in which it finds its place. By reducing the complexity of human psychology to certain ruling passions, they are able to indicate how certain human impulses may be mutually exclusive of each author. They have also indicated the conflict between self and society generated by the individual's urge for autonomy. The manner in which the past may dominate and paralyze a character, putting it at odds with its world, has been presented in such a way as to indicate the co-extension of past and present in a character. Finally, by means of the mystery novel, they have found a form which allows them to explore both the urgency of moral action and the inherent irony that result from sharp class and caste distinctions.

The conflict of self with society may be seen in a number of the novels of the two authors. In The Hamlet and The Old Curiosity Shop, it is present in the form of characters who represent antithetical impulses, e.g., activity and quiescence, love and sterility, sensuality and asceticism. The urge to become autonomous is burlesqued in a number of the characters of Little Dorrit, Our Mutual Friend, The Hamlet, The Town, and The Mansion. Here such characters prey on society, seeking to appropriate it for themselves. In Dombey and Son and in the Snopes trilogy, we find a more awesome form of such an urge to autonomy in Mr. Dombey, Mr. Carker, and Flem Snopes, characters who use society for their own purposes and are nevertheless respected to the point of idolatry by their societies. And in Great Expectations, Intruder in the Dust, and Absalom, Absalom! the mystery story reveals the bonds that connect apparently separate social classes and castes. It also draws moral issues sharply because of the presence in the form of critical situations, and its pattern of connections allows it to unmask hidden relationships thus undercutting with irony the attempts of various characters to forget their own pasts. In Bleak House and Light in August, the past is presented as dominating the lives of certain characters in such a way as to make them feel alien to their worlds and indeed almost to paralyze their wills.

A basic feature of the fiction of Dickens and Faulkner is their illustration of such issues by recourse to the extreme and a willingness to eschew verisimilitude whenever necessary. The simplification of the human psyche to one ruling impulse, the method of burlesque to attack seekers of autonomy as well as the presentation of the autonomous hero as a totem-figure in his own time are other examples of the extreme. In Bleak House and Light in August the past and the present are coextensive, and in the mystery novels moral action is often founded on crisis while social givens are questioned in an atmosphere of gothicism and melodrama. [Order No. 69-21,995; 315 pages. DAI, 30A (Jan.-Feb. 1970), 2995-96.]

146 Faulkner's Decline / Brian Michael BARBOUR, Kent State University, 1969 (Howard P. Vincent).

Although the scholarship expended on William Faulkner has in recent years become voluminous, no one has paid much attention to the contours of Faulkner's career or accounted for the decline in the quality of his fiction after 1942. Criticism generally operates on the assumption to explain why.

Chapter One deals with Faulkner's relationship to the broader movement known as the Southern literary renaissance. It assesses the reasons why Faulkner and those coeval to him were able to dramatically master the social materials which had subdued previous generations of Southern writers to the demands of the Southern genteel tradition. Chapter Two traces three fundamental elements that fed Faulkner's imagination during "the great years," 1929-1936. These elements were region, history, and creative or personal becoming, and the tension between the first two and the last was both vital and constant in the imaginative shaping of the novels. Chapter Three is concerned with The Hamlet. This novel manifests a kind of Copernican revolulution in Faulkner's imaginative universe. Previously, society was poised against the self as the self was engaged in attempting to become; now the individual is viewed as potentially destructive of society. This imaginative alteration was accompanied by a shift in Faulkner's sympathies, now centered increasingly on society. Chapter Four deals with Go Down, Moses, perhaps the key text in the Faulkner canon for understanding why he declined as a creative writer. In this novel he faced head-on the problem of slavery and its heritage, the radical personal evil underlying Southern society. Counterpoised against this evil is the figure of Isaac McCaslin who tries to escape its implications by clinging to the mythic concept of the Edenic American wilderness. The chapter shows that the novel has been consistently misread by those who applaud Isaac's rejection of his heritage, a response not warranted by the text itself. It also argues that taking Isaac's views for Faulkner's own led to considerable critical confusion and has obscured both Faulkner's relationship to the South, and the reasons for his imaginative decline. Chapter Five argues that Faulkner reached a cul-de-sac in this novel. He could never settle to his own satisfaction the ethical quality of Isaac's rejection but retained an ambivalent attitude to it the rest of his life. This ambivalence was tied to his increased sympathy for Southern society and reflected a growing provincialism in his outlook. As regards his imagination, it meant that he could no longer maintain the vital tension that came from poising the developing self over against an enveloping society. Throughout the dissertation, personal becoming is related to the organic metaphor of the creative process, and Faulkner's heritage from the tradition of romantic thought, the placing of the self at the center of the work of art, is insisted on. The concluding chapter establishes an analogy with literary history, whereby Faulkner the romantic artist is subdued by the social demands usually referred to as the Victorian Compromise. [Order No. 70-11,334; 240 pages. DAI, 30A (May-June 1970), 5436-37.]

147 Kierkegaard and Faulkner: Modalities of Existence / George Chester BEDELL, Duke University, 1969 (William H. Poteat) no DAI entry.

148 The Irrational Narrator in Virginia Woolf's The Waves, William Faulkner's The Sound and the Fury, and Gunter Grass' The Tin Drum / Ralph Adolph BERETS, University of Michigan, 1969 (James Gindin).

The irrational narrators in The Waves, The Sound and the Fury, and The Tin Drum are used by their authors for purposes beyond the depiction of a particular type of personality. In each case, the author has created irrational characters who assert certain values that could not have been presented in another manner without also having created a different effect. The techniques employed to present these characters as narrators require that the reader become involved in the process of creation to complete the portrait that the author has begun to sketch. Thus, the narrator's perspective must not be viewed as the one deduced by the reader, for the reader goes beyond this vantage point to delineate a point of view that is only partially dependent on the narrator; in addition to this irrational perspective the reader should also discover other alternatives imposed by the author through use of other characters, frames of reference, language, tone, symbol, and structure. Consequently, the irrational narrator in this study is seen as that person whose vision or state of mind guides us through segments or the whole of a novel, while point of view implies that perspective of reality that the reader must deduce from the evidence provided by the narrator and the author.

Rhoda, in The Waves, is preoccupied with the problems of communication, the loneliness of the individual, and the oppressiveness of the universe. She seeks escape in her dreams, in her past, and finally in her own death. Ironically, what Rhoda is seeking--some assurance from the outside world that she does exist, that her life has a tangible meaning, and that there is something outside herself upon which she can have an effect--is denied by the very death that was to provide a resolution for her uncertainty. For the reader to come to terms with Rhoda's perspective, he must modify her views by those of the other five narrators and by the symbolism that introduces each of the chapters.

In contrast to this approach, Faulkner establishes three irrational perspectives that are measured against one another in order to determine the validity of the events being recounted. In addition, an objective perspective is added at the end of the novel to reveal a standard by which the others might be measured. In this final chapter, Faulkner also presents two different value systems from the ones that the Compsons uphold. Here we are made directly aware of the values and contributions that Dilsey makes to the pattern of the novel, and we are also confronted by the religious implications and teachings to which she is exposed. Beyond these controls, Faulkner also provides a frame within which the events of the novel are couched: these are the Easter Passion Week ceremony and the literary allusion to which the title of the novel refers. In this manner, Faulkner circumscribes the events and reactions that his readers are able to make to the material.

Grass' attitude toward the irrational is quite different and used for a different purpose from that in Woolf and Faulkner. He uses Oskar as a rational and as an irrational narrator who sometimes espouses the truth, but at other times evades this responsibility and becomes the irresponsible child that he would like to remain. Grass seems to scoff at the notion of reconciling this ambiguous situation, since he conceives of these two attitudes as being interdependent, as well as central to the responses that man makes in this irrational world. Oskar is the logical end product of the irrational tradition, for he is both sick and healthy and cannot be seen in one dimension without simultaneously recognizing the opposite one, as well.

Thus, each of these authors is engaged with the problem of what to do with a system of values that he does not accept, yet which he is forced to work in if he is to be both relevant and involved in the situations he is attacking on a philosophical, social, or psychological level. Each solves this problem in a different way, but all choose to remove their narrators from the social norm that the rational perspective has traditionally entailed. Consequently, Woolf, Faulkner, and Grass employ their irrational narrators to define an ordered point of view that one would anticipate from authors who take their literary tasks seriously. [Order No. 70-14,475; 259 pages. DAI, 31A (July-Aug. 1970), 751.]

149 The Jefferson Urn: Faulkner's Literary Sources and Influences / Joseph Edward BROGUNIER, University of Minnesota, 1969 (George T. Wright).

A common view of Faulkner abetted by some of his self-characterizations is that of an untutored genius "warbling his native wood-notes wild"; but this view is as untrue of him as of Shakespeare. The young Faulkner believed that he should set his standards by the best literature written and being written. Thus, he read widely and intensively in European literature; and with the help of his friend Phil Stone he gained a knowledge of, and was attracted to, some of the most experimental writing of the twenties. And throughout his life Faulkner returned to a group of English, American, and European writers whom he called his "masters," and, while measuring his accomplishments against their works, assimilated them and many others to his books.

Three of Faulkner's best books show that he assimilated his literary sources with versatility and skill, and that they contribute significantly to his achievement. He used his sources and influences differently and to different effect in each book, adapting them to its individual subjects, techniques, and themes,

A mass of influences from predominantly English and American, but also European, Russian, medieval, and classical literature, is intricately interwoven into The Sound and the Fury (1929). The characterization, particularly that of Quentin Compson, is most variously influenced, by writers as diverse as Shakespeare and Hemingway, Dante and Dostoevsky. The allusions and imagery are also diverse, ranging from classical sources to T. S. Eliot. The setting of the novel is sparsely influenced, though it too contains sources from T. S. Eliot, F. Scott Fitzgerald, James Joyce, and notably A. E. Housman. In style, structure, and technique the novel is strongly influenced by the techniques of Joycean stream-of-consciousness and the impressionistic novel; and the theme shows the imprint of Eliot's Waste Land, especially. Faulkner's artistry in using his sources helps make this novel his best-wrought work.

In Absalom, Absalom! (1936), Faulkner, by using the "mythical method", portrays in Sutpen an American hero of epic dimensions and tragic stature, for he draws upon the conceptions of the hero in those myths and cultures which flowed into America and shaped its idea of the hero. Sutpen is compared to the classical tragic hero because he draws his whole family into the vortex of his fall. Yet he has the scope, ambition, and vigor of the Renaissance tragic hero, and also is portrayed as a dark-willed, accursed, Gothic villain. Moreover, he inherits much of his strength and overweening pride from Melville's Captain Ahab; and, in more recent literature, Fitzgerald's Gatsby has contributed to the theme of Sutpen's innocence and the corruption of that innocence.

Go Down, Moses (1942), thematically focused on the white man's injustice to the Indian and the Negro and on his despoliation of the American Eden, draws for its few major sources largely on Faulkner's "masters." Thorpe's "The Big Bear of Arkansas" seems clearly to have influenced the plot, and Moby-Dick has influenced the characterization and texture. Faulkner's use of the "Ode on a Grecian Urn" indicates that Isaac McCaslin, in repudiating his inheritance, precipitates his individual tragedy. The social and historical tragedies that are Faulkner's themes are emphasized by the influence of Huckleberry Finn and Shakespeare; and the influence of historical materials is suggested by a comparison of a Mississippi planter's diary with the McCaslin ledger entries.

Faulkner's use of literary sources shows that though he was no doubt a genius, he was far from untutored. To his native materials and native talents he joined a skill in assimilating the literature of others, and made his sources and influences a notable part of his achievement. [Order No. 70-5635; 275 pages. DAI, 31A (Nov.-Dec. 1970), 2375.]

150 Dubliners and Go Down, Moses: The Short Story Composite / Joanne Vanish CREIGHTON, University of Michigan, 1969 (Lyall H. Powers) no DAI entry.

151 An Analysis of William Faulkner's Major Techniques of Comedy / Josephine J. CURTO, Florida State University, 1969 (Griffith T. Pugh) no DAI entry.

152 The Making of Sartoris: A Description and Discussion of the Manuscript and Composite Typescript of William Faulkner's Third Novel / Stephen Neal DENNIS, Cornell University, 1969 (Walter J. Slatoff).

By a careful analysis of textual overlaps, page numbers, inks, and paper varieties in the manuscript and composite typescript of William Faulkner's third novel, Sartoris, it is possible to separate the composite typescript into fragments from three earlier typescripts, to reconstruct many now nonexistent portions of these earlier typescripts, and to learn much about Faulkner's methods of composition and revision.

Faulkner began Flags in the Dust, now Sartoris, as the story of a wartime incident in France in 1918. Five manuscript pages, in which Evelyn (later John) Sartoris dies when his plane is shot down under the eyes of his brother Bayard, survive from this beginning. In a two-page expansion of one paragraph in these five early pages, Faulkner shifted his story's location from Europe to Mississippi, changed Evelyn's name to John, and began to shift his emphasis from Evelyn/John to Bayard.

Later Faulkner began Sartoris again, with a rambling disquisition on the name "Sartoris" and the past of the Sartoris family. Otherwise, with the exception of new location for two Civil War tales and old Bayard's trip to the attic of his house, the Sartoris manuscript, as now arranged is followed closely by the novel's printed text.

While Faulkner was still at work on the manuscript for his novel, he began typing a first typescript from the manuscript. This fact contradicts the previous assumption that Faulkner did not prepare a typescript for a novel until he had completed that novel's manuscript. While the Sartoris manuscript was still unfinished, Faulkner decided to shift the scene of Horace Benbow's arrival in Jefferson to a later position in the novel (originally it had come almost immediately after the garden scene between Narcissa Benbow and Miss Jenny). Faulkner therefore set aside, in both manuscript and typescript, the pages filled by the scene. Later, when he had once again included this scene in the manuscript and typescript, he experimented with further positionings of the scene in his typescript but not his manuscript. Faulkner's decision to delay the scene of Horace's arrival shifted the novel's focus definitely to Bayard from whatever joint focus there may have begun to be on both Bayard and Horace.

After completing his manuscript and first typescript, Faulkner prepared a separate second typescript, which he later revised to make a third typescript. For this revision he expanded a number of passages from short descriptive paragraphs into full scenes with action and conversation. The second and third typescripts were probably submitted to publishers, and the first may have been.

At an undetermined time and for a reason which is not clear, Faulkner combined his first and third typescripts to produce the existing composite fourth typescript of Sartoris, a typescript that was almost certainly not submitted to publishers. Faulkner probably prepared from the composite typescript the typescript that was submitted to and accepted by Harcourt, Brace. This fifth typescript, the novel's setting copy, has not survived. The setting copy was cut for Faulkner, to an extent that cannot be determined, by his literary agent Ben Wasson.

There is evidence that while writing Sartoris Faulkner was modeling Jefferson on Oxford, Mississippi, though the published text of Sartoris is less explicit about geography than the novel's manuscript. According to evidence provided by people who knew the young Faulkner, several early unpublished short stories, and the incomplete early novel "Elmer," Faulkner may have begun to create Yoknapatawpha (originally "Yocona") County as early as World War I.

Faulkner twice re-used material from "Elmer," a novel begun in Europe in 1925. In Mosquitoes he revised a surrealist fantasy, and in Sartoris he began to describe a character in "Elmer" but almost immediately transferred this character's attributes to Horace Benbow. Faulkner started to use some material deleted from Sartoris in the original version of Sanctuary.

A substantial part of the study is devoted to a thorough description and analysis of the various stages in the development of the manuscript and composite typescript of Sartoris. [Order No. 70-5792; 226 pages. DAI, 31A (July-Aug. 1970), 384.]

153 To Move in Time: A Study of the Structures of Faulkner's As I Lay Dying, Light in August, and Absalom, Absalom! / Barbara Nelle EWELL, Florida State University, 1969 (Laura Jepsen).

The purpose of this study is to analyze the technique of structure and to relate this technique to the narrative content of three novels by William Faulkner: As I Lay Dying, Light in August, and Absalom, Absalom!. The thesis is that the form of these three novels--the literal order in which chapters appear, through which action progresses or stops, and by which passages develop--comes from the life of a character who is not the protagonist of the novel. Through an analysis of this basic technique, the study concludes that Absalom, Absalom! best succeeds in complementing content with form.

In Chapter 40 of As I Lay Dying, Addie Bundren explains her belief that words and deeds are never related to each other: "words go straight up in a thin line, quick and harmless, and ... doing goes along the earth, clinging to it. ..." The incongruities that occur during her last moments of dying and on her funeral journey to Jefferson and the ironic framing of these two events with words by Darl parallel Addie's statement describing her own life. Darl, who can function only on the level of words, attempts to act when he burns Gillespie's barn. His failure to go from "words" to "doing," his commitment to an asylum, proves Addie's statement that "the two lines are too far apart for the same person to straddle from one to the other...."

In Chapter 11 of Light in August, Joe Christmas tells Joanna Burden that he is part Negro. When she asks how he knows that, he replies, "I don't know it.... If I'm not, damned if I haven't wasted a lot of time." Occupying the central chapters of the novel, surrounded by the steady rhythm of Lena Grove, which begins and ends this novel, Joe Christmas functions as a retardation in time necessary for Lena to resolve her quest to find a husband/father.

Quentin Compson controls the telling of Absalom, Absalom! through his remembering what he has heard and through his conjecturing what he does not know. The form of the novel is dependent upon the shape of his memory. Quentin believes "nothing ever happens once but like ripples maybe on water after the pebble sinks...." He sees these ripples going from the original pool in concentric circles, through "a narrow umbilical water-cord," to another pool which assumes the same ripple movement though this second pool has a different temperature and temperament and though it has not even seen the pebble that began the "old ineradicable rhythm." The two sections of the novel (Chapters 1-5 and Chapters 6-9) represent these two "pools" with Quentin as the "water-cord" connecting them and connecting the story of Sutpen's Hundred with his own.

Of these three characters, Quentin Compson has the most effective control over the content of the novel whose form he dictates. Because his own uncertain affections for his sister Caddy have resulted in his inability to act, he cannot accept the idea that incest is the motivation for Henry Sutpen's act of murder. Quentin fabricates the "fact" that Henry fears miscegenation and possibly the "fact" that Charles Bon is Thomas Sutpen's son. Believing nothing ever happens only once and unable to face the incest in Sutpen's story, which he sees his own life repeating, Quentin Compson tells the story of Absalom, Absalom! over and over in a desperate attempt to escape the indictment of his own voice. [Order No. 70-3818; 191 pages. DAI, 30A (March-April 1970), 3940.]

154 Style and Dialect in Light in August and Other Works by William Faulkner / Alvin Lanier GREGG, University of Texas at Austin, 1969 (Archibald A. Hill).

The study of style in literature requires an understanding of style in both language and art. Since even outside literature there are many varieties of language including geographical and social dialects and situational styles, the discussions of language variety by linguists will throw light on style in literature. Significant language variations can be related to extralinguistic contexts. Although the definitions of Hill and Enkvist provide the means for an objective approach to describing the distinctive features of a style, the human response to these features must also be considered.

Literary style, though partly linguistic, involves larger matters of form and content. Linguistic style in literature is controlled by social, conventional, and aesthetic factors, all of which are involved in a reader's global response to the features of a style.

Defining "style" as "characteristic manner," we can then specify its special domains. Thus, an "individual style" is the variety of language peculiar to one author. And the variations in this style--in passages of narration, exposition, description, and dialogue--are also stylistic. So Faulkner has an "individual style," consisting of several substyles. A profile of Faulkner's own stylistic features--such as favorite words--can be compiled from critical studies of his style.

Faulkner's dialectical styles can be compared with actual Mississippi dialects by means of evidence from modern dialect studies and from the literary dialects in works by other Mississippi authors, but they are also influenced by aesthetic factors. His representations of various social levels of Negro and white dialects differ from those of other authors, but there are also differences in his own works. Generally, dialect features are represented most meticulously in the earlier works like Sartoris. In The Sound and the Fury, dialectal styles differ according to the point of view of the reporting characters. In the trilogy about the Snopeses, Ratliff's dialectal styles differ from novel to novel, apparently by accident.

It is possible to differentiate at least five dialectal styles in the white speech of Light in August, ranging from that of the cultured speaker to that of the rustic speaker. There are also at least three styles of Negro dialect-- those of the town dweller, the country resident, and the Negro slave. Such classifications are complicated by factors such as the length of a dialect passage and idiolectal differences among dialect speakers. Furthermore, Faulkner sometimes heightens these dialects for artistic reasons by using fewer features than usual and by including typical features from his own narrative style. [Order No. 69-21, 820; 411 pages. DAI, 30A (Jan.-Feb. 1970), 3009.]

155 William Faulkner's Narrators / John Henry HAFNER, University of Wisconsin, 1969 (Walter B. Rideout).

This study is a consideration of Faulkner's narrators from three perspectives: technique, theme, and characterization. Faulkner emphasized the importance of his narrators to an understanding of his work by explicit comments and by his conscious emphasis of the narrator's role (rewriting "That Evening Sun," for example to emphasize Quentin, or having the narrators of The Town contradict each other). With this awareness of Faulkner's emphasis of the role of narrators, I have examined the technical aspects of his use of narrators as they increase the air of verisimilitude in his fiction, as they contribute to Faulkner's manipulation of aesthetic distance, as they allow for irony, for comprehensiveness, for authorial freedom in handling his materials with ease and effectiveness. These technical matters range from the fairly obvious sense of realistic authority associated with the spoken voice to the extremely complex subject of audience involvement in art, of distance between reader and work of fiction. My contention is that a major technical device which accounts for Faulkner's artistic effectiveness is his use of narrators, and this aspect of my subject is treated in Part I of my dissertation.

His use of narrators is also crucial to Faulkner's expression of the major themes in his work. As he investigates the nature of history, literature, and myth, as he illustrates and comments on the limitations of the individual human, as he presents that individual with his limitations in a search for truth, Faulkner uses narrators to show man explicitly searching, explicitly investigating in an attempt to learn about life. Man's knowledge of his past is crucial to an understanding of the present, and Faulkner's narrators, recognizing this, try to understand that past through, first, the methods of history and, then, the creation of literature. When their investigation produces results which can become a part of man's systems of belief, those results reach the level of myth. Thematic concerns are discussed in Part II of my dissertation.

The success of the thematic investigation is reflected in the relative importance given to several characters in Faulkner's world. The central characters of that world act as narrators and their characterization is often accomplished by their narrative activity. Quentin Compson, Gavin Stevens, V. K. Ratliff, and Charles Mallison are major inhabitants of Yoknapatawpha County. Their status is largely due to their ability to tell stories and, in doing so, to reveal man in his attempt to live a meaningful life, to act as spokesman for man as he lives that life. Quentin is the early speaker for the

sensitive man who tries to cope with life, but Quentin fails because he is too
repulsed by life to be able to come to grips with it. Gavin Stevens is more
successful but he tends to get lost in abstract thought and high-flown rhetoric
and thus he too is finally unsuccessful. But when Gavin joins with V. K. Ratliff, who brings sound, common-sense knowledge of concrete man to the combination, then the two have greater success, though that success is still limited. Their student, Charles Mallison, is the most successful Faulknerian narrator-protagonist in understanding life and insisting on its meaning in the
worth of the individual man. Faulkner seems to intend Charles as a spokesman for modern man, as a character who combines the intellectuality of Gavin
with the warm humanity of V. K. in a successful union which is capable of asserting the traditional human values of courage and honor and pride and love
in a modern, mechanistic society. These matters relating to characterization are discussed in Part III of my dissertation. [Order No. 69-22,395; 343
pages. DAI, 30A (May-June 1970), 5445.]

156 The Bible as Novel: A Comparative Study of Two Modernized Versions
of Biblical Stories, Zola's La Faute de l'Abbé Mouret and Faulkner's
A Fable / Elizabeth Lowther HODGES, University of Georgia, 1969 (Calvin S.
Brown).

Emile Zola's La Faute de l'abbé Mouret and William Faulkner's A
Fable share the distinction of being perhaps the only novels which are modern
analogues of Biblical narratives. La Faute is a 19th century version of the
story of Adam and Eve in the Garden of Eden and A Fable is a 20th century
version of the New Testament. In undertaking to modernize a story, an author encounters certain problems. The first problem is to discover a milieu,
a social, a cultural, a geographical, and an historical setting in which to
place action, a setting which will correspond with or suggest the social, cultural, geographical, and historical setting of the action of the original story.
Another problem is to create a character who, by his occupation, by his situation in life, by his personality, by his action (thought and deed), will suggest
his prototype. A third problem is to find equivalents for the events of the original story, a problem which is more difficult to solve when the original is a
Biblical narrative in which supernatural events are integral.

This thesis is a study and an evaluation of La Faute de l'abbé Mouret
and A Fable as modernized versions of the stories on which the novels are
based. Five chapters are given to the presentation of Zola's and Faulkner's
solutions to the particular problems common to the writing of a modern analogue, id est, those of finding equivalents for the setting, the characters, and
the events of the original. The final chapter is an evaluation of each novel as
a modernized version of the story on which each is based. La Faute de l'abbé
Mouret is judged specifically on the effectiveness of Zola's presentation of a
modern Fall of Man and on the appropriateness, in view of the story which the
author tells, of the reference to the story of Adam. A Fable is judged on the
effectiveness of Faulkner's presentation of a modern Salvation of Man and on
the appropriateness of the comparison of his story to the Christ story. Whereas the parallels between Adam and Serge (Zola's Adam) are justified by the
existence of an essential similarity in meaning between the stories, the parallels between Jesus and the corporal (Faulkner's Christ figure) are useless
ornamentation. For this reason and for the reason that Zola's vision of Man's
Fall is far more intelligible than is Faulkner's vision of Man's Salvation, La
Faute de l'abbé Mouret is more successful as a modernized version than is A
Fable. [Order No. 70-10,196; 164 pages. DAI, 30A (May-June 1970), 5447.]

157 The Rhetoric of Multiple Points of View in Selecting Contemporary
Novels / Mithcell A. LEASKA, New York University, 1969 (Louis M.
Rosenblatt) no DAI entry.

158 William Faulkner's The Hamlet: Its Revisions and Structure / Donald Jay LEVIT, University of Chicago, 1969 (James E. Miller, Jr.). no DAI entry.

159 Chronicles of Children: William Faulkner's Short Fiction / Anthony Peter LIBBY, Stanford University, 1969 (Alfred Apple, Jr.).
Faulkner's short stories, all but ignored by critics, provide new insights into Faulkner and are important in their own right. This study begins by examining them in relation to the pre-Civil War school of Southwestern humor. With the tall-tale authors Faulkner shares extravagance of plot, characterization, and style, and a central interest in the world of children and childlike men, psychological regressives. Faulkner's simplest stories are tall tales very close to the Southwestern tradition. They involve the same balance between realism and fantasy, often the same settings, and the same world of childlike adults at play. Psychological childhood is presented as a common and generally pleasant state. In these stories Faulkner differs from the traditional humorist only in his narrative skill and in the quality of his humor. While the humor of the earlier, aristocratic writers was based on condescension to their clownish lower-class characters, Faulkner's is based on affection for characters deliberately rendered charming.
Faulkner's humor can be dark as well as light, however, and while the light humor ignores moral problems, the black humor focuses on them. The moral awareness apparent in Faulkner's more complex stories differentiates him from the Southwestern humorists, although the more serious stories retain the trappings of the tall tales. Children still dominate, but childhood, especially the psychological childhood of adults, is no longer considered an escape from the unpleasant complexities of the world. In the stories concerned with the problem of justice, Faulkner creates men who become self-destructive children in their obsession with odd versions of "justice." The view of humanity is pessimistic.
Pessimism also dominates the stories of sex, and so do children, actual or psychological. Sex is generally seen as a destructive force. More destructive, however, are mothers, generally depicted as obsessed dominators. The sexually developing child must rebel against this domination, ultimately an attempt to keep him forever in the world of childhood, now considered a trap.
Rebellion as a struggle between male child and tyrant mother becomes a metaphor to describe other types of rebellion. The rebel never really wins, though he is permitted to make magnificant gestures. Faulkner sympathizes with him, but Faulkner the political conservative refuses to contemplate the possibility of successful rebellion of any sort, and insists on regarding rebels of all ages as children rebelling against parents.
All social interactions are viewed in terms of the child-parent relationship. Social stability is depicted as analogous to family stability. Faulkner is a traditional conservative, but the tone of his conservatism varies between extreme pessimism and optimism about society. This is especially evident in his stories about American wars, which indicate that his pessimism is genuine, whereas his optimism is largely a matter of self-delusive rhetoric.
The society-family analogy is particularly relevant in stories of Negroes and Indians, which examine the contradiction of the "paternalistic" oppressor. Faulkner sometimes depicts the Negro as a child to be fathered by white society, but sometimes parodies paternalism or describes the rebellious Negro playing the childish role for his own purposes.
Faulkner's children are most interesting as they move toward maturity, in his stories of the hunt, which again show the direct influence of the Southwestern tradition. The hunting stories also embody his ultimate pessimism about society, racial problems, and the possibility of reform, though "The

Bear" balances actual pessimism with rhetorical optimism. In "Red Leaves" Faulkner honestly examines the implications of his pessimism, and finds a sort of triumph at its heart. [Order No. 69-17,438; 327 pages. DAI, 30A (Sept.-Oct. 1969), 1568.]

160 William Faulkner's The Wild Palms: A Textual and Critical Study / Thomas Lafayette McHANEY, University of South Carolina, 1969 (James B. Meriwether).

The published text of William Faulkner's eleventh novel, The Wild Palms (1939), differs greatly from the author's final typescript version of the book. Due to editorial intervention or oversight and printing errors, there are over 650 differences between what Faulkner wrote and what appeared in print. Chief among these is the emended title. Faulkner conceived the unusually structured novel as "If I Forget Thee, Jerusalem," a reference to Psalm 137. His editor substituted "The Wild Palms," taking what had stood originally only for the story of the runaway lovers. More than 50 substantive revisions, made by editor or proofreader, destroyed or altered the meaning of Faulkner's sentences. His logical innovations of style disappeared under the wholesale addition and alteration of punctuation and spelling. Further, the publishing history of the book does not show it being treated any better than it was during preparation for the press. The Wild Palms has never reached the public in the form it was intended to have; frequently it has been issued only piecemeal.

Since the first reviews in 1939, critics and scholars have expressed puzzlement over Faulkner's intention and method in writing a novel composed of two separate unconnected tales in alternate chapters. There can no longer be any doubt that he wrote the novel just as he said he did--in the alternated form. Manuscript evidence for that fact is everywhere supported by a close critical reading. The parts, conceived under the pertinent title, cohere.

The major thematic connection between "Wild Palms" and "Old Man" is the motif or "eternal return" expressed in recurring real and symbolic births and deaths; in successions of dawn, noon, and twilight; in cycles of the moon and of the seasons; in the rise and fall of the flood; in circular voyages of experience. This theme is expressed in the context of the philosophy of Arthur Schopenhauer, evoked by name in the fifth chapter, and Frederick Nietzsche. Much of what Harry Wilbourne says--and the tall convict does-- can be found in The World as Will and Idea. The convict's rejection of womankind at the novel's end, as he embraces the peace and solitude of prison, is a Schopenhauerian denial of the will, by which he escapes the cycle of pain and ennui that is, according to the pessimistic German and also according to the convict's recent adventures, the staple of life. Harry, on the other hand, having learned the same things about life as the convict, accepts the "eternal return," taking the alternative to Schopenhauer advanced by Nietzsche in Thus Spake Zarathustra; and he affirms the will and life.

Ten chapters of this study are a chapter by chapter reading of the ten sections of The Wild Palms. The themes and philosophy mentioned above are discussed in detail, as well as further connections of character, event, dialogue, and imagery. The analysis includes frequent reference to allusions to Faulkner's own work and to the writings of Robinson Jeffers, James G. Frazer, Freud, Dante, Ernest Hemingway, Edgar Lee Masters, Sherwood Anderson, and others. The 11th chapter gives evidence that Faulkner drew heavily upon his reading and memories of both Hemingway and Anderson. This includes the use of Anderson's second wife as a model for Charlotte; the borrowing of images out of Dark Laughter (1925); a portrait of Hemingway taken from Anderson; and many more references to Hemingway than have been noted before. Appendices include detailed tables on the treatment of the text, a survey of criticism, a chronology of the two tales, and an accounting of Harry's funds. [Order No. 69-20,111; 336 pages. DAI, 30A (Nov.-Dec. 1969), 2540-41.]

161 The Influence of William Faulkner on Michel Butor / David Dean McWILLIAMS, University of Oregon, 1969 (Roland C. Ball).

Michel Butor, one of the most important and experimental novelists to appear in France in recent years, has on several occasions acknowledged publicly the importance of William Faulkner in his own literary formation. The purpose of this thesis is to explore the nature and extent of Michel Butor's debt to William Faulkner.

Butor's interest in Faulkner is reflected in the important essay, "Les relations de parenté dans 'L'Ours' de William Faulkner," which Butor devoted to Faulkner in 1956, as well as in the numerous references to Faulkner in other of his essays and interviews. The purpose that Butor finds in Faulkner's fiction, a desire to increase his reader's freedom by making him more conscious of his situation and of the social and cultural forces which created that situation, is quite similar to the purposes Butor ascribes to his own fiction. Granted this kinship that Butor felt with the American author in the basic objectives of his literary art, it is not surprising to find striking similarities between the techniques Butor studied in Faulkner and the techniques practiced by Butor in the three novels which follow his essay on Faulkner. These three novels are: L'Emploi du Temps (1956), La Modification (1957), and Degrés (1960).

This thesis divides these technical similarities into four categories: mode of narration, including radical limitation of point of view, interior monologue, second person narration, and multiple narrators; methods of organizing the chronological sequence of the narrative; sentence structure and prose style; and devices such as patterns of family and mythic relationship which are used for the description of a situation. A comparison of the use of these techniques in the novels by Butor mentioned above and their use in Go Down, Moses, Absalom, Absalom!, Sanctuary, and The Sound and the Fury, novels by Faulkner studied by Butor, reveal many important similarities. The conclusion that the adoption of these techniques is the result of Faulkner's influence is strengthened by the fact that most of these techniques are not found in the novel by Butor, Passage de Milan (1954), which preceded his essay on Faulkner.

Although certain aspects of Butor's portrait of the United States in Mobile (1962), notably the Negro and Indian theme, are indebted to Faulkner, Butor has with this work abandoned the novel and has, therefore, entered a stage of his career where the example of Faulkner is of little use. Faulkner's influence seems then, for the time being at least, at an end.

The study of William Faulkner proved to be exceptionally fruitful for Michel Butor, providing a wide variety of techniques that Butor found useful during the phase in his career when he was trying to refine the novel as instrument for the transformation of the reader's consciousness. Butor's use of Faulkner is more than a mere borrowing; he adapts these techniques selectively and creatively to his own purpose. [Order No. 70-14,229; 231 pages. DAI, 31A (Sept.-Oct. 1970), 1282-83.]

162 Faulkner's Females: The Thematic Function of Women in the Yoknapatawpha Cycle / Tom Malcolm MASSEY, University of Nevada, 1969 (Robert A. Hume).

It is now generally recognized that the novels and stories of William Faulkner having Yoknapatawpha County as a setting constitute a world of recurring characters, events, themes, and values. An examination of this world, which Faulkner called his "keystone of the universe," reveals what might be called Faulkner's Moral Overview, and the fullest understanding of any particular work results from placing it in the context of his total vision. Faulkner's definition of the proper role of women in this world and their thematic significance in their separate stories is the subject of this study.

Reality and truth in Faulkner's world are best apprehended by intuition, or the heart, rather than by reason and intellect, and since women live closer to their emotions than men, his female characters are often the vehicles of positive thematic statements. His good women are those who follow their hearts and act in harmony with Nature by bringing life into the world and sustaining the "eternal verities of the heart": courage, compassion, sacrifice, and endurance. His bad women reject their natural functions and thus cause discord, chaos, despair, and death. On the basis of their roles in their particular stories and their relationship to Faulkner's Moral Overview, the good and bad women are classified into general categories. The good women are grouped as follows: "The Grand Old Ladies"--Rosa Millard, Jenny Du Pre, Dilsey Gibson, and Miss Habersham; "The Earth Mothers"--Lena Grove, the pregnant woman in "Old Man," Eula Varner, and Linda Snopes Kohl; and "The Social Outcasts"--Ruby La Marr, Nancy Mannigoe, Corrie, Miss Reba, and Candace Compson. The bad women, judged by the same standards, are classified as follows: "The Young Bitches"--Temple Drake (in Sanctuary), Belle Mitchell Benbow, her daughter Narcissa, and Elly (in "Elly"); "The Perverted Mother Figures"--Charlotte Rittenmeyer, Mrs. Compson, Addie Bundren, and Temple Drake Stephens (in Requiem for a Nun); and "The Victimized Spinsters"--Joanna Burden, Miss Emily Grierson, Rosa Coldfield, and Minnie Cooper.

"The Grand Old Ladies" operate as the chief forces of affirmation in their stories, personifying those qualities which sustain life and the family and enable man to endure adversity. "The Earth Mothers" passively follow their deepest instincts and perpetuate the species in harmony with nature and counterbalance the forces of negation and despair. "The Social Outcasts" demonstrate that intuitive goodness often transcends the rigid moral standards of society.

All of Faulkner's bad women, in denying their natural function as females, bring despair and death to their lovers, husbands, and children; all are incapable of responding to love and compassion.

Faulkner's work viewed as a whole stands as an affirmation of those qualities in man which make him immortal as a species, and it is in his good women that these qualities most notably manifest themselves. [Order No. 70-1,928; 188 pages. DAI, 30A (Jan.-Feb. 1970), 3468.]

163 Woman in the Works of William Faulkner / Sally Rigsbee PAGE, Duke University, 1969 (Arlin Turner).

"Woman in the Works of William Faulkner" is an examination of the patterns of meaning which Faulkner develops through his characterization of woman and his delineation of the role she plays in the fictional world he creates. Woman is extremely important in Faulkner's works; not only has he created a large number of female figures who are vivid and effective fictional characters, but, more significantly, woman is of major thematic importance in many of Faulkner's novels and stories. This study focuses on those works in which Faulkner is directly concerned with woman's special nature and role in human life.

Faulkner's intense interest in woman and man's need of her is the primary impetus of his first published work, The Marble Faun, and of his two apprentice novels, Soldiers' Pay and Mosquitoes. In these works the essential impotence of man in the face of death is indicated by the frustrations of sexual love. Man's desire for woman and his idealization of her virgin beauty express his quest for freedom from the bonds of mortality. However, woman's imperfections and the perversion of her natural role indicate the limitations of human existence.

In Faulkner's early fiction there is a gradual movement away from an emphasis on the sexual allure of young women to an emphasis on the human need for the qualities of maturity, self-sacrifice, and commitment to the sustenance of life which Faulkner embodies in the woman as mother. The Sound and the Fury depicts the tragedy and the chaos of a family whose mother has refused the responsibilities of motherhood and has thus destroyed her children's capacities for normal affection and creative living. In Sanctuary Faulkner portrays the decay of a whole society which has refused the responsibilities of maturity. Sanctuary demonstrates that individual families and society as a whole desperately need the moral order wrought by the unselfishness that characterizes motherly love. Evil flourishes in these two novels because men and women cling to their childishness, their selfishness, and their naivete. Dilsey's character illustrates those qualities of maturity, unselfishness, and devoted service to the sustenance of life which the Compson family lacks. Ruby Goodwin is the only character in Sanctuary who is able to bear the responsibilities of maturity.

Woman's sexuality is important in Faulkner's fiction because he employs perverted sexuality to display evil and the life-destroying forces in the human being. At the same time he uses woman's submission to the natural sexual process and her commitment to the nourishment of human life to illustrate the nature of virtue and the pattern of survival. Women characters in "Elly," "Dry September," "A Rose for Emily," Miss Zilphia Grant, Idyll in the Desert, and Absalom, Absalom! present forcefully Faulkner's equation of the misuse of sexuality with death itself. When women, such as Addie Bundren (As I Lay Dying) and Charlotte Rittenmeyer (The Wild Palms), attempt to use sexuality as a means of escaping the reality of life's limitations rather than as a means of reproducing life, they align themselves with the forces which destroy life, and ironically, in a search for life's vitality they embrace death and decay.

Lena Grove, the heroine of Light in August, and Eula Varner, the heroine of the Snopes trilogy, provide a needed counterpoint in Faulkner's fiction to his image of woman as death. These women symbolize the possibilities for fertility, creativity, serenity, and abundance which human life offers to mankind. Light in August and the Snopes trilogy display the conflict between the male and the female--the former representing the human drive for self-assertion and personal freedom and the latter the human need for submission to the on-going process of life. In these works the male drive is depicted as destructive and suicidal, whereas the female drive is creative and sustaining. Though the conflict of the male and the female is forever unresolved in Faulkner's fiction, the capacity for life displayed by Lena Grove and Eula Varner Snopes indicates the author's faith in the ability of humanity to survive and to sustain life. [Order No. 70-20,281; 288 pages. DAI, 31A (Nov.-Dec. 1970), 2396.]

164 The Structure and Meaning of William Faulkner's A Fable / Philip Edward PASTORE, University of Florida, 1969 (Harry R. Warfel).

The Failure of both sympathetic and disparaging critics to discover a cohesive structure in William Faulkner's A Fable has led to a misunderstanding of the novel's meaning. A Fable exhibits a clearly unified structure if viewed from the proper perspective, but one cannot attain this perspective by equating surface correspondences between A Fable and the Christian Passion with particulars of Christian theology, nor by relating resemblances to incidents in World War I to a particular interpretation of history. One must go below the surface texture of A Fable to discover its structure and meaning.

A key to the sub-structure of A Fable may lie in Henri Bergson's influence upon his thinking. Bergson's idea of the intelligence and intuition as conflicting modes of interpreting and ordering experience, what I term the "deep structural dialectic," is the unifying structural element in A Fable. This "dialectic" follows a pattern which occurs in the main conflict between the Corporal and the Marshall and again in all the "disparate" episodes in modified form. The pattern is roughly this. Authority, representing the intelligence, is challenged by an individual, representing the intuition or a variant of it, who "mutinies." Order is disrupted, but authority frantically attempts to restore the previous condition. The mutineer is eventually defeated and the status quo restored but in a slightly altered condition. This parallel pattern becomes a commentary upon the main action when an episode is viewed in its entirety in relation to the main action. By changing the "environment" in which the basic pattern occurs, Faulkner's total effect is a definition of the human condition, since the episodes all concern men engaged in the same basic opposition.

Chapter I briefly reviews some represenative criticism. Chapter II describes Bergson's extensions of the intelligence and its status morality as it is manifested in the "closed society" and "static religion." These ideas describe various characters and actions in A Fable. The Marshall is the highest representative of the intelligence and the closed society, which is portrayed through three major segments, each having its symbolic projection: the military--war; the civilian--city; static religion--historical Christianity and the clergy. The static nature of the closed society is emphasized through imagery of immobility or meaningless motion. Each segment is also described in terms of the other to emphasize its essential sameness.

Chapter III describes the Corporal's character and function. He resembles Bergson's true mystic, the rare man who has reimmersed himself in the elan vital, the life force (Bergson's approximation of God), and revivified the "vague halo" of intuition which surrounds the intelligence. The Corporal functions as the highest representative of the intuition. As such he represents the radical, as yet unrealized potential that exists in man. He represents the extensions of the intuition also, the "open society" which seeks a universal brotherhood, and "dynamic religion," a religion without historical precedent, without ritual, without verbalization. In this role he must overpower the Christian legend which looms behind him.

Chapter IV demonstrates the total structural unity of A Fable by examining in detail the many parallels and contrasts of character and action in the various episodes. The major episodes are seen in a new relationship. The "Notes on a Horsethief" episode is viewed as an expression of "Eros," or, idealized but desiring love, in contrast to the "Agape," or selfless love of the Corporal.

The definition of man which finally emerges from A Fable is a complex one which is also an affirmation of man's ability to prevail within the context of failure and doom. [Order No. 70-12,255; 285 pages. DAI, 31A (July-Aug. 1970), 397-98.]

165 Names of Characters in Faulkner's Mississippi / Frances Willard PATE, Emory University, 1969 (Floyd C. Watkins).

This study of the names of William Faulkner's Mississippi characters is designed to illuminate a seldom explored aspect of Faulkner's art. All literatures boast characters whose names are significant, either because they are descriptive or because they provide a sense of culture. But William Faulkner, alone among moderns (and possibly among ancients as well), seems to have successfully sustained a combination of these two functions of names.

Names that are descriptive of individual characters fall into four basic groups. On the most elementary level, names obviously refer to dominant character traits, physical characteristics, or patterns of behavior. Goodhue Coldfield, Joanna Burden, Dewey Dell Bundren, and Gail Hightower are examples. A second group is made up of ironic names. Byron Bunch, for example, is a solitary figure who prefers to keep to himself rather than become involved in a group, or "bunch," of people. The descriptive element in some names lies in the root meaning. Examples are Charles Bon (good) and Amodeus (beloved of God) McCaslin. Faulkner also uses names that are allusions to delineate character: Isaac McCaslin and Benjamin Compson, like their Biblical counterparts, are sacrificial figures; Gavin Stevens, like the Gawain who sat at King Arthur's round table, is something of a chivalric knight.

Often, though not always, the names in this latter group seem to take on added dimensions. They sometimes serve to bring sharply into focus Yoknapatawpha's link with the past, often the mythological past. These names, in effect, juxtapose past and present and thereby help to achieve a sense of the continuity, the universality of human experience, while, paradoxically, often illuminating the gap that exists between the wholeness of the past and the decay of the present. Bayard, for example, reveals the kinship between the Sartorises and Chevalier de Bayard of medieval French legend; yet the comparison forced by the name also underscores the foolhardiness on which the Sartorises sometimes base their concept of bravery.

Faulkner's skill with names is not limited to his descriptions of individual characters. He has also used names to help link his Yoknapatawpha works together. Frequently recurring names--Sutpen, Sartoris, McCallum, Stevens, and so on--provide a sense of continuity to Faulkner's novels and stories and, thereby, indicate how they are interrelated.

Within these works, names further help to create a sense of a believable culture. The names and naming practices used within Faulkner's mythic culture are, like the culture itself, thoroughly rooted in the South. Like actual rural Southerners, Faulkner's characters have Biblical names (Job, Rachel, Samson, and Matthew) and classical names (Jason, Quentin, Clytemnestra, and Dilsey). They also follow other Southern naming practices: they seldom use a Negro's surname; they tend to preface the given name of a white "lady" with Miss.

Yet Faulkner oversimplifies many of these Southern naming practices or, more often, gives them specific connotations with his myth. For example, he tends to use surnames of Scottish origin (McCallum, Gowrie, Muir) to indicate the most fiercely independent of his characters; he tends to use corrupted surnames (Manigault to Mannigoe, Grenier to Grinnup, Ratcliffe to Ratliff) to indicate a decline in social status. Faulkner, in fact, wields names and naming practices in such a way that they become devices to describe and classify the populace of Yoknapatawpha. The net result is that names and naming practices serve as reminders that Yoknapatawpha is Faulkner's mythic region as well as a mirror of the rural South.

(Because almost every name in Faulkner's works is significant--either culturally or symbolically--the bulk of this study consists of an alphabetical listing of all the names in the Mississippi works, with important information given for each. An introductory essay summarizes Faulkner's art of naming.) [Order No. 69-17,721; 326 pages. DAI, 30A (Nov.-Dec. 1969), 2036-37.]

166 Time as Character in the Fiction of James Joyce and William Faulkner / Richard Frank PETERSON, Kent State University, 1969 (Bernard Benstock).

Both James Joyce and William Faulkner have long been recognized as writers committed to the study of time as an integral part of the literary study of man. Physical and psychological time play essential roles in the thematic unity of a major portion of their works. Structurally, aspects of both external and internal time place significant restrictions upon the physical dimensions of their works, yet often these restrictions are utilized in such a way that the depth and scope of experience depicted within a limited time span often border on timelessness. In effect, no phase of time is excluded from the fiction of Joyce and Faulkner. Watches tick and clocks chime; yet thoughts flow chaotically onward and myths and cycles begin, disintegrate, and begin again.

In the fiction of Joyce and Faulkner characters appear who represent widely divergent views on time. Some of these views seem by their very nature alienated from the world view of the artist. Others are so intensely expressed that it is difficult to disassociate those views from the time theory of their creator. In several instances, characters created by Joyce and Faulkner, as they revolve within their temporal worlds, bear strong, often striking, similarities to each other. Their closeness "in time" allows us to view them both from the perspective offered within the individual work and from the broader viewpoint available when time concepts of an artist's work are examined in relation to those of another artist, particularly when there is already general agreement as to the possible influence of one artist on another.

Manifestations of the temporal concerns of Joyce and Faulkner generally fit into three basic categories: physical, psychological, and eternal. The Joycean or Faulknerian character usually succeeds or fails in life according to how he responds to one or more of these categories. Those characters who commit themselves to either physical reality or psychological time are usually denied any meaningful relationship with life. Physical reality cannot be denied, but a mechanical existence in itself provides no balanced viewpoint beyond the world of clocks and calendars. Psychological time is also inescapable, but it is insufficient for providing a meaningful existence beyond an excessive and at times obsessive concern for self. Only the Joycean or Faulknerian hero who reaches a compromise with time manages to either retain his sense of humanity or can provide the means for a younger, less experienced character to realign himself with the community. This sense of equilibrium in time had to be achieved so that the time-worlds created by Joyce and Faulkner could be expanded both through the active world of the male and the passive world of the female to include the more acceptable external reality to be found in mythical and historical patterns.

The diverse directions that Joyce and Faulkner pursued in the later period of their artistic development are not so much a comment on their time-worlds as a statement on the eventual dimension achieved in their works. The "slowing-down" of Faulkner in his own time does not lessen the achievement of his earlier career. Joyce's depiction of time and reality proved as winding, expanding, and inevitable as the river that became his ultimate symbol of life. With Faulkner we must allow The Sound and the Fury, As I Lay Dying, Light in August, and Absalom, Absalom! to stand tree-like at the center of his career and further allow ourselves to be subsumed by their vitality. [Order No. 70-11,355; 267 pages. DAI, 31A (Sept.-Oct. 1970), 1285-86.]

167 Man in His Struggle: Structure, Technique, and Theme in Faulkner's
    Snopes Trilogy / Irma Anne POWELL, Florida State University, 1969 (Griffith T. Pugh).

With the exception of Flem, who is pure evil, the Snopeses represent all men; thus Faulkner's theme is broader than the conflict between good and evil--it is man in his struggle. The purpose of this study is to analyze the narrative structure of Faulkner's Snopes trilogy and to examine the techniques of characterization--both in relation to this theme. The thesis is that there are relationships among form, techniques, and function which add a special dimension to Faulkner's theme of the necessity of moral action.

In the narrative structure events are determined by characters, and the development takes place in parallel movements. The plots remain discrete except when external forces bring together characters in moments of violence. Coherence among plots is sustained by the narrator-actors. The continuous sequence of action is discernible in the structure of the whole. There, fluctuations of a moment in time appear as incidents in a continuous flow of positive action largely determined by the character of Eula Varner. Dramatic tension is weak because the characters who exert the greatest moral strength are the least effective dramatically. However, the intensity of moral action is implied by the structure of events; for after Eula's suicide all action flows towards Flem in a motion which becomes as significant as its static object.

In addition to being separated by discrete plots, characters are isolated by techniques which render them as individuals. Symbols, mythic allusion, and impressionistic details create figures who are psychologically consistent and distinguishable according to their capacity for life.

Because they are isolated by nature, for all characters except Mink Snopes the venture into the realm of social action is difficult. Thus Faulkner presents a central paradox of man in his struggle: to remain apart from the human realm is to invite destruction; however, to join the social realm by means of moral action is also to invite destruction, or at least further isolation in a higher morality.

Techniques and themes similar to those in the trilogy are found in Faulkner's short story "Barn Burning." In all of Snopesdom there is no integrity--personal, social, or moral--without action; and all action is rewarded by some efficacious change. Nor does Faulkner rest the burden of moral action with any particular segment of the community. The Snopes saga records an unfailing belief in man and a moral vision which is constant. [Order No. 70-16,345; 136 pages. DAI, 31A (Sept.-Oct. 1970), 1287-88.]

168 Creation of Atmosphere in the Novels of Hawthorne, Faulkner, and
   Julian Green / Marie-Antoinette Untereiner ZRIME, Harvard University, 1969 (Wilbur M. Frohock) no DAI entry.

169 The Human Comedies of Honoré de Balzac and William Faulkner:
   Similarities and Differences / Roxandra Illiaschenko ANTONIADIS, University of Colorado, 1970 (Vivian Mercier).

The thesis views the novels of Honoré de Balzac and William Faulkner as exhibiting a number of striking similarities in the authors' vision and fictional representation of "the human comedy." Important differences between their works are evident as well; they point, nonetheless, to a similar attitude toward man's possibilities of fulfillment in the modern world.

The study begins with a discussion of the similarities in the overall design of Balzac's Comedie humaine and Faulkner's Yoknapatawpha series together with their narrative techniques: both design and techniques proceed from the authors' stated purpose to reduce the passion of human experience to literature. Similarities in design include the depiction of a complete society in a series of cyclical novels; the use of reappearing characters and the faithful rendering of place serve to unify further the social drama portrayed. The narrative techniques of Balzac and Faulkner are based upon an attention to detail, and what might be termed its correlative, a disjunction of chronological time. Both authors thus break with the linear method of narrative.

Chapter II treats the conservatism of Balzac and Faulkner as the basis for their tragic vision of modern society: material standards of success corrupt the generous impulses of the imagination and heart and alienate man not only from his fellows but from himself.

Chapter III is concerned with differences in the authors' overall designs. Balzac had a more rationalistic approach to his work than did Faulkner, whose attitude was instead more pragmatic. This fact accounts for their dissimilar approaches to the criticism of society; for Balzac's specific attempts to probe the nature of the creative process, as in Le Chef-d'oeuvre inconnu; for Faulkner's stronger emphasis on the moral significance of the work of art.

Chapter IV opens with a discussion of the cultural heritages and political loyalties of Balzac and Faulkner as they help to explain the former's mystique of the City, the latter's mystique of the Land. Modern Paris provided Balzac's universe with its dominant spatial reference, with a symbol of the author's very aesthetic, and with a basis for subsidiary themes revolving about the principal theme of money as the symbol of passion, of passion, that is, as finally destructive of life. Faulkner's sense of belonging to a particular place and tradition may in part account for his concentration upon Lafayette-Yoknapatawpha County, where it is the Land that shapes men in its own image. The bond between man and the Land is studied in Go Down, Moses, in which the hunt is viewed as Faulkner's central symbol, embodying the vital ethic by which kinship and mutual responsibility may be restored to the human community.

Chapter V treats the two authors' aspirations and expectations for the future of humanity. Balzac's mystique of the City reflects a social aestheticism by which the progress of the artist from aristocrat to anarchist is realized. Balzac's Thirteen points to a new order of men, to the exceptional individual whose impulse goes beyond the City in his search for singular destiny; freed from the inhibiting influences of the social order, he is projected into a new spiritual sphere: Vautrin, Goriot, Balthazar Claës, and Louis Lambert are examples. Faulkner, as we may see by juxtaposing Flem Snopes to Thomas Sutpen, views the evils of present society as a perpetuation of those of the past. Through Go Down, Moses he recreates an ideal time: its lesson for modern man is renewal of the heart's virtues. Balzac's perception of reality is primarily aesthetic, Faulkner's primarily ethical. Both arrive at definitions of a new innocence by which selfhood may be achieved.

The Conclusion notes further areas of possible comparison between the two authors. [Order No. 71-5864; 233 pages. DAI, 31A (March-April 1971), 4753.]

170 A Critical and Textural Study of William Faulkner's A Fable / Abner Keen BUTTERWORTH, Jr., University of South Carolina, 1970 (James B. Meriwether).

This dissertation is a comprehensive study of Faulkner's A Fable. The first part of the Introduction traces the compositional history of the novel from its inception in 1943, through its various vicissitudes, to its publication in 1954. This history utilizes manuscript and typescript materials of the Alderman Library, University of Virginia; Faulkner's unpublished correspondence with his agent Harold Ober; and some other unpublished materials and published material from a number of sources. The second part of the introduction traces the novel's critical reception to the present and attempts to point out the faults of much of the existing criticism. It also demonstrates how Faulkner's use of the Christ story in a wartime setting has caused many readers to assume automatically that it is a pacifist novel, which it is not. The dissertation holds that the corporal is not the moral center of the novel, but rather, the marshal represents the center and the two poles, the individual and authority, are represented by the corporal and Gragnon. The marshal is responsible for civilization itself, the forms and guides of which the masses can not do without.

The body of the dissertation consists of eight chapters, which generally deal with the divisions of the novel. However, each chapter also focuses on a single character, or two characters, to demonstrate the wide range of sympathies Faulkner displays in the novel. For all his sympathy, though, Faulkner realized the necessity of making judgments; consequently, he reveals the limitations of the Quartermaster General, the runner, Levine, and others. The dissertation holds that Faulkner's affirmation of humanity is manifest in both the corporal and the marshal. The marshal has accepted responsibility for all of civilization, a terrible burden to bear. The corporal has accepted martyrdom in order to assert man's spiritual aspirations. They both desire reconciliation, and a kind of reconciliation takes place at the Arc de Triomphe in the final scene, but there is no solution to the conflict in which they are caught; consequently, the runner's outburst breaks the momentary truce between the individual and authority and the conflict begins again.

The dissertation has two appendices. The first is an essay on the criticism of A Fable. It attempts to evaluate the various treatments and place them in context with the others. The second appendix is a textural study based on collations of the typescript setting copy with the first American printing, of the American edition with the British edition, and of several printings within the American edition. There is a list of emendations to the text, which attempts to restore a number of Faulkner's original typescript readings that were changed by editors at Random House. [Order No. 71-9708; 211 pages. DAI, 31A (March-April 1971), 5390.]

171 Faulkner's Late Short Fiction / William Frank CANTRELL, University of South Carolina, 1970 (James B. Meriwether).

This dissertation attempts to provide as complete a record as possible of Faulkner's achievement in short fictional forms in the late stages of his career. It utilizes the records of the author's literary agent, Harold Ober, to date the composition of the late stories in a way which differs significantly from that indicated by publication information. Thus, it has been possible to limit the study to works actually composed after Faulkner completed Go Down, Moses.

Detailed examinations are presented of the eleven stories and two fictional essays the author wrote from 1942 on. Two of the stories--"Knight's Gambit" (different from the title story of the 1949 volume Knight's Gambit) and "Snow"--are unpublished works. The other nine stories ("Two Soldiers," "My Grandmother Millard," "Shall Not Perish," "A Courtship," "Shingles for the Lord," "A Name for the City," "Mr. Arcarius," "Race at Morning," and "By the People") have all been published though only five appear in Collected Stories. The two fictional essays ("Mississippi" and "Sepulture South: Gaslight") are also published works.

These 13 generally ignored works are examined critically and an attempt is made to determine their merit relative to the author's other short fiction. [Order No. 71-9709; 175 pages. DAI, 31A (March-April 1971), 5391.]

172 William Faulkner's Short Stories / James B. CAROTHERS, University of Virginia, 1970 (J. C. Levenson).

Each of Faulkner's short stories is a self-contained, unified work of prose fiction, describing a significant change in the life of the story's central character. The specific nature of this change, the ways in which it is brought about, the character's response to it, and the implications of the change for the characters and the storyteller all contribute to an implicit value judgment of the characters and their world. Faulkner's early stories, like his early novels, project a fictional world of comedy and romance. This development is gradual rather than sudden, and it can be observed in Faulkner's consecutive treatments of single characters such as Gavin Stevens and Flem Snopes, and in consecutive treatments of themes and situations such as social justice, sexuality, time, Negro identity, and the relation of the Southerner to his heritage. Faulkner's short stories and novels at first imply a resentful attitude toward a universe which is indifferent to the prosperity of evil or antagonistic to the virtuous, but the later fiction demonstrates Faulkner's qualified acceptance of things as they are, and shows his capacity to appreciate the occasional benevolence of Providence, nature, and humanity. Short stories are useful in describing this development, for they show more accurately than the novels Faulkner's outlook at a given point in time.

The short stories are related to the novels in the Faulkner canon as structural units of entire novels, structural units of single episodes in novels, extracts from novels-in-progress, sequels to novels, and sources of analogues and allusions to characters, situations, and events developed in novels. The differences between single short stories and related novels show that in writing and reworking his short stories Faulkner was always concerned with the work in hand, rather than with an extrinsic notion of mythic design, morality, technique, or style.

The Unvanquished and Go Down, Moses are often discussed as collections or cycles of autonomous short stories, but they are better approached as novels constructed from revised short story material. Knight's Gambit is a collection of stories about a single character who is conceived differently in consecutive renderings. Big Woods shows Faulkner's attempt to impose unity on a disparate body of material. Collected Stories is a carefully organized volume which includes many of Faulkner's best stories, but it does not include some of the stories which had been worked into novels and other collections, some stories which did not apparently fit the design of the volume, and some stories which are distinctly inferior.

Faulkner held the short story in high esteem, calling it the most demanding of literary form, after poetry. The care which he devoted to individual stories and the attention he gave to the arrangement of story collections substantiate his interest in the form. Though each of his short stories can be understood without recourse to his other works, the connections among the short stories and novels provide a means by which the apparent paradox of simultaneous autonomy and interdependence of Faulkner's works may be understood and appreciated. [Order No. 71-6626; 244 pages. DAI, 31A (March-April 1971), 4757.]

173 The Role of the South in the Fiction of William Faulkner, Carson McCullers, Flannery O'Connor, and William Styron / Samuel Chase COALE, V, Brown University, 1970 (Hyatt H. Waggoner).

The purpose of the thesis is to examine the changing role of the South in the fiction of William Faulkner, Carson McCullers, Flannery O'Connor, and William Styron and to explore the nature of the Southern imagination as revealed in the fiction. The rural background of this imagination, the heightened awareness of its moral polarities, the resulting Gothic and grotesque nature of its fictional fulfillment, the depth of its religious awareness, and the mature emergence of it in the Southern "Renaissance" are examined in the first chapter. The Southern imagination is much more than a mere revelation of the "mindlessness" which W. J. Cash has charged in his book, The Mind of the South. The thesis attempts to reveal the limitations of Cash's book as suggested by C. Vann Woodward in his illuminating article, "W. J. Cash Reconsidered."

The image or role of the South changes from Faulkner to Styron and accounts for the varied styles and artistic concerns of the four writers. Faulkner's is an aristocratic, dying South; his artistic consciousness is tragic, his style a retrospective, rhetorical hymn to loss in the manner of myth. McCuller's is a milltown, wasteland South; her artistic consciousness is tragic also, her style an introspective, objective hymn to loss in the manner of the fable. O'Connor's is a "hillbilly," Bible-belted South, her artistic consciousness is comic, her style an inspective, objective examination of the mysterious workings of God's grace in the manner of the allegory. Styron's is a suburban, self-indulgent South; his artistic consciousness is tragic, his style similar to Faulkner's own, though altered by an existential awareness of isolation and expatriation, often in the manner of a religious parable.

Faulkner's South was his personal demon but raged sanctuary; McCullers' was both a Gothic wasteland and a childhood retreat; O'Connor's, a burned-over district and religious asylum; Styron's, a self-indulgent world torn between existent guilt and existential awareness. The role of the Negro, the different attitudes toward society and the individual, the knowledge of man's limitations and the recognition of infinite and unknowable powers, the primitive and romantic attitudes toward the land and its people, the unending battle between the head's intellect and the heart's emotion--these and related ideas are explored in the works of the four authors.

The thesis concludes with final comments on the Southern consciousness, an attempt to summarize the various literary and cultural attitudes which characterize this regional experience as seen in the fiction of the four writers. The author assumes that a sense of place is important in the best of modern American literature and has written the thesis with that basic assumption in mind. [Order No. 71-13,848; 388 pages. DAI, 31A (May-June 1971), 6596-97.]

174 The Trilogy as Form in Modern American Fiction / Joseph Michael COULOMBE, Purdue University, 1970 (William T. Stafford) no DAI entry.

175 Parent-Child Relationships in the Works of William Faulkner / Albert J. DEVLIN, University of Kansas, 1970 (Edward F. Grier).

Commentators have not dealt satisfactorily with an important aspect of Faulkner's work: his frequent portrayal of victimized children, particularly within the context of problematic parent-child relations. This is not to imply that the entire issue of childhood has been overlooked, but to suggest that critics generally have failed to appreciate either the frequency of victimization or the severity of its effects. The latter involves a crucial concept--psychological determinism--which can be briefly defined as the causal and paralytic impingement of past upon present, and which can be used to explain the seeming immaturity and failure of so many Faulkner protagonists.

Chapter I--"Faulkner's Children: A Survey"--establishes the frequency with which careless, loveless, or simply absent parents wound their children. Bayard Sartoris, Quentin Compson, Darl Bundren, Temple Drake, Joe Christmas, Charles Bon, and a number of lesser figures from Faulkner's later fiction demonstrate not only the frequency of victimization but also the causal relationship between personal immaturity and unsatisfactory childhood experiences.

Chapter II--"Titania Mitchell and Jack Shumann as Victims"--focuses upon children who figure rather prominently in Sanctuary, Sartoris, and Pylon. Belle Mitchell, Horace Benbow, and Laverne are examined as parents who fail to meet the normal needs of their respective children. In the course of the chapter it becomes clear that this parental failure frequently develops out of severe personality disorders. Horace Benbow's fear of sexuality contributes to the promiscuity of his stepdaughter.

Chapter III--"Isaac McCaslin: A Revaluation"--views Isaac McCaslin's rejection of his patrimony and dedication to the wilderness as a failure to participate in what Faulkner termed "motion." Sophonsiba and Buck McCaslin, his parents, and Sam Fathers, a guide and mentor, have an impact upon Ike which infixes a fear of sexuality, a pattern of retreat from the demands of mature, adult life.

Chapter IV--"Pseudo-Normality: The MacCallums"--questions the traditional interpretation of the MacCallum episode (Sartoris). The MacCallums supposedly represent a healthy alternative to the wasteland which surrounds but does not engulf them. Upon close examination, however, the family manifests a sterility and perversion which evoke wasteland motifs prominent in other sections of the novel. Virginius MacCallum, the family patriarch, has a debilitating impact upon his six sons, one which explains their immaturity and unsatisfactory sexual adjustment.

Chapter V--"Normality: Lucius Priest"--attempts to understand the close relationship between the successful initiation of Lucius Priest and the stable familial environment to which he is exposed. Alison and Maury Priest, as well as Grandfather Priest, provide the love, acceptance, and wise guidance which are so frequently lacking in the case of Faulkner's earlier heroes, Quentin Compson, Joe Christmas, Charles Bon. Special emphasis is placed upon Lucius' successful adjustment to his own sexual potential, an adjustment which Quentin Compson, for example, is unable to make.

The most fundamental conclusion involves a realization of the pervasive role which psychological determinism plays in Faulkner's work, particularly in the realm of parent-child relations. Any attempt to see Faulkner as an existentialist thinker is undercut by the intense determinism which he posits. His fictive heroes certainly do not possess the kind of freedom which Sartre requires. [Order No. 70-25,322; 219 pages. DAI, 31A (Nov.-Dec. 1970), 2916.]

176 The Achievement of Gavin Stevens / Mary Montgomery DUNLAP, University of South Carolina, 1970 (James B. Meriwether) no DAI entry.

177 Faulkner's Light in August: Sources and Revisions / Regina Kobacker FADIMAN, University of California at Los Angeles, 1970 (Blake R. Nevius).

Although William Faulkner disliked being called a literary man and occasionally referred to himself as a farmer, the revisions in the manuscripts and typescript of Light in August testify to the fact that he was a careful craftsman who revised the novel with scrupulous attention to the most minute detail. In the manuscript at the University of Virginia Faulkner left evidence of the later stages of composition. The manuscript is of particular interest primarily because it illustrates the structural alterations which changed the total meaning of the novel.

The study examines the genesis and revisions of Light in August. In a detailed description of the documents which precede the published novel, it not only illustrates the author's work habits but also traces the kinds of revisions he made and the stages through which the novel evolved. The conclusions are drawn from the external and internal evidence in the Virginia manuscript and typescript, the four-page manuscript at the University of Texas, and the published text. The last contains a number of inconsistencies which provide further evidence for the conclusions reached.

External evidence reveals that Faulkner wrote and revised the episodes of the narrative present separately from those of the Christmas flashback. In integrating these two major sections of the novel he made a series of extremely important changes affecting the intention and direction of the work. In making these alterations he: (1) expanded the Christmas flashback, adding the episodes of Christmas' affairs with Bobbie Allen and Joanna Burden with the result that Christmas dominates the novel; (2) revised the sections in which Christmas was definitely part Negro, and introduced ambiguity about his racial heritage; (3) changed his intention to open the novel with Gail Hightower by adding the present Chapters I and II; (4) reordered the time-structure of episodes which were written chronologically, so that they now appear as flashbacks, remembered or recounted by certain characters at highly significant moments; (5) rearranged many chapters dealing with the events of the narrative present to include episodes from the two parallel stories, the Lena-

Bunch-Hightower plot in the narrative present and the Christmas story; (6) increased thematic counterpointing by the addition of parallel actions which frequently evoked antithetical responses; (7) inserted the Burden family history into the story of Joanna's and Christmas' romance and revised the history to appear to be recounted by Joanna Burden; (8) drew material from two different endings, thereby introducing a series of contradictions of narrative fact, and rearranged the order of the episodes and certain of the chapters after the scene of Christmas' capture; (9) deleted transitions between the events of the narrative present and the Christmas flashback; and (10) compressed and unified the novel by shifting the settings, narrative point of view, and levels of time.

The revisions changed the novel from a chase story in which three characters are inadvertently caught up in and affected by the search for a mulatto murderer into an investigation of how man apprehends experience--his own and that of his fellows. In understanding his own experience, each man registers the information his senses provide and stores it in his memory to become the foundation for his most basic beliefs. These beliefs, underlying all that man knows, frequently conflict with reason. Ultimately, the novel reveals that in trying to understand experience, "man knows so little about his fellows." [Order No. 71-16,312; 417 pages. DAI, 32A (July-Aug. 1971), 427.]

178 The Fatal Illusion: Self, Sex, Race, and Religion in William Faulkner's World / Jewell Handy GRESHAM, Columbia University, 1970 (Robert A. Bone).

This study of William Faulkner of Mississippi proceeds from a point of departure which challenges traditional critical views wherever these would tend to eliminate or negate history as a legitimate factor to be considered in serious analysis of an artist's works.

Whatever the nature of existing theories of aesthetic criticism held by students and critics of literary experience, it is felt that the ultimate principle which must hold in any case is that serious analysis must begin where the artist begins--that is with the unique experience projected in the works. It is that experience, of which the form it is rendered is an integral part, that signals most strongly the critical approaches apt to be most effective in the examination of the creation.

In the Yoknapatawpha series, Faulkner has accomplished what no other American author has equaled or even attempted in quite the same fashion: a systematic treatment of his society on a scale of immensity and of depth designed to reveal the hidden or disguised corners of it and the secret hearts of the men and women who are its members. In treating a small corner of Mississippi thus, the author inherently makes use of the cultural and historical circumstances of his region as both the framework and focus of his creations. In the light of this, it is felt that an extended understanding of Faulkner requires awareness of the significant historical and cultural forces which produced him.

A major purpose of this study is to attempt to illustrate that a prototype exists for the Old South culture, and that the structure of Faulkner's Yoknapatawpha world, characterized though it is by certain notable distinctions of its own, reflects the earlier model more than coincidentally. The system to which we refer is medieval chivalry, which proved a potent prototype for those instrumental in building the world of the Old South and for the latter's apologists thereafter. Thus the fictional world created by Faulkner is overlaid, as it were, by two layers of the past: the Old South past, and behind it, the feudal past.

Though the 15 novels and assorted short stories of the Yoknapatawpha series form the basic corpus for this study, four key works have been selected to illustrate the basic thesis set forth here: Sartoris, The Sound and the Fury, Light in August, and Absalom, Absalom!.

The precise method of investigation utilized in testing the hypothesis set forth is what might be called a "relativistic" or "symbolic" approach in which the attempt has been made to survey the basic images, patterns, and motifs as they occur singly or in combination with others in an effort to determine whatever it is that the author sets forth in primary rank. Those ideas or concepts which emerge as central motifs around which all else is shaped are set forth here as subtitle of this treatise: Self, Sex, Race and Religion in William Faulkner's World.

Throughout the series, the author demonstrates, both implicitly and explicitly, the society's constant concern with the inherited Chivalric myth. The point of his works, however, is that it is a false Camelot which betrays the Chivalric dream of honor and valor even as its members structure a cultural facade paying homage to that dream. The author portrays the toll enacted by a society which is guilty of such betrayal. In keeping with the extent of that price, this study is entitled: The Fatal Illusions. [Order No. 71-8959; 268 pages. DAI, 31A (March-April 1971), 5402.]

179 The Diaphoric Structure and Unity of William Faulkner's Go Down, Moses / Carol Ann Clancey HARTER, State University of New York at Binghamton, 1970 (John V. Hagopian).

This study attempts to make three distinct but related observations about William Faulkner's Go Down, Moses: (1) that this "collection" of "short stories" is in fact a novel--a uniquely structured and unified work; (2) that its structural principles are spatial rather than temporal and that primarily by means of diaphoric structure--i.e., by varied juxtapositions, counterpointing symbolic patterns, repetition, parallelism of phrase and image--meaning emerges; and (3) that Faulkner thoroughly and painstakingly revised the original short stories for inclusion in Go Down, Moses with the express purpose of creating a spatially organized, diaphorically structured and unified entity.

These three characteristics of Go Down, Moses are confirmed by a detailed examination of each of the "stories" in the novel together with its original version (either in previous publication or in manuscript.) A comparison of the often lengthy and always significant changes Faulkner made in the originally self-sufficient stories to integrate them into the larger entity makes clear that in Go Down, Moses Faulkner was experimenting with a novelistic form which, while it frequently eschews traditional cause-effect relationships, nevertheless creates a series of analogues which produces, in the words of William James, "emotional congruency." In short, by means of the revisions, Faulkner yoked together originally disparate stories into a unified structure which embodies a complex network of interrelated human experiences.

The dramatic foci of Go Down, Moses are most easily perceived when the stories are grouped according to this emotional congruence. While Faulkner employs a plethora of narrative modes in the novel--burlesque, comic, tragic-ironic, mythic, and philosophical--there are certain primary relationships among particular "stories" which exist despite the differences of mode and which develop the novel's foremost themes. For example, the first and last stories, "Was" and "Go Down, Moses" establish a socio-historical framework within which the events of each of the stories takes place and against which the various visions of time and history are juxtaposed. "The Fire and the Hearth" and "Pantaloon in Black" also form a complementary pair of chapters in that, through utterly dissimilar modes and ostensibly disconnected characters and events, they develop the single most important "presiding image" of the novel--the "fire and the hearth"--an image which embodies the positive values of marriage and family in the societal context. "The Old People," "The Bear," and "Delta Autumn" form another narrative unit whose milieu is the wilderness and whose protagonist, Isaac McCaslin, seeks personal fulfillment and freedom from the moral corruption of his family's history and his Southern heritage.

Ultimately, the "domestic" group of stories and the wilderness group are synthesized by three primary experiences symbolically embodied, in different ways with varying emphases, in each of the stories. These three major motifs are: (1) man's relationship to the land, whether the wilderness or the "tamed" land; (2) man's relationship with other men in the context of a racially oriented society; and (3) man's capacity for transitory stability in an existential cosmos--his potential for establishing a community defined by "human coherence and solidarity" by means of a real or symbolic marriage and family.

And while each of the stories deals with all of these themes to some degree, the separate threads and symbolic strands of the novel culminate in "The Bear," the most complex single chapter in Go Down, Moses. In this story Faulkner juxtaposes the mythic-moralistic vision of Isaac McCaslin's wilderness and self-created history against the frenetic, richly textured and cryptic world of the commissary and McCaslin Edmond's cynical, existential view of experience. In this chapter a static, aesthetic vision of history and life is counterpointed with a fluid, atemporal continuum of experience. Finally "The Bear" makes it clear that in isolation from the human community, man is ineffective, self-deluded, and emotionally sterile; he is incapable of attaining the values implicit in the fire and the hearth. [Order No. 71-13,433; 195 pages. DAI, 31A (May-June 1971), 6057-58.]

180 Narrative Forms in the Modern Southern Novel / Mark Robert HOCHBERG, Cornell University, 1970 (Robert Elias) no DAI entry.

181 A Study of the Text of William Faulkner's The Hamlet / James Everett KIBLER, Jr., University of South Carolina, 1970 (James B. Meriwether.)

A Full-length study of the text of The Hamlet, this dissertation seeks to establish, as nearly as it is now possible, the novel's text. It reports complete collations of typescript, the three American editions (1940, 1956, and 1964) and the English edition (1940) in order to isolate all differences. Each variant is considered individually for the proposed edition and the reasons are given for accepting or rejecting it. The object is to arrive at the reading Faulkner desired. Faulkner's obvious errors, compositor's errors, and editorial tamperings are thus eliminated. Because the editor's hands played the largest role in introducing alien readings, space is devoted to discussions of Saxe Commins and Albert Erskine of Random House. A knowledge of their editorial principles reveals why certain readings not present in Faulkner's typescript appear in the first edition (1940) and third edition (1964).

The most important change of this nature occurs in the third edition, in the novel's last chapter. Here, the time of the novel is moved ahead by 20 years. This alteration is rejected because it was Faulkner's editor and not Faulkner who originated it. It is found that this third edition corrects many objectionable readings in the first two, owing to a consultation of the typescript for its preparation, but also introduces many corruptions by means of house-styling and the above-mentioned change of setting. Its text is thus not reliable. Likewise imperfect, the first edition text was also house-styled and contained many significant typographical errors. In addition, Saxe Commins made emendations of his own--in grammar, punctuation, spelling, and capitalization. The second edition, in which Faulkner likely had no hand, corrects a few of the more obvious typing errors of the first but adds a good many new corruptions to those already appearing in the 1940 edition (as this was used for setting-copy). The second edition is still published as the Vintage paperback. It is the most widely used text of the novel, and, for all but the last chapter, the most unreliable.

Section II of the dissertation is a list of changes that should be made to the first edition to bring it into line with Faulkner's wishes and to eliminate unsound readings. Each suggested change is then discussed separately in Section III. Section IV lists reasons for not making some changes in the first edition which might possibly be called for. Section V establishes the readings for all words divided at the ends of lines in the typescript and the first edition. Section VI tabulates all the differences (both accidental and substantive) among typescript and the three editions. In the first appendix, Faulkner's typing errors are listed along with the typographical errors in the three editions. The second appendix is a detailed 22-page study of the chronology of typescript composition.

The 69-page Introduction which prefaces the study gives, without the benefit of Faulkner's correspondence, what can be said of the novel's inception, composition, and publication and discusses The Hamlet texts: the manuscript, rejected typescript pages, short story versions, typescript used for setting-copy, carbon of the typescript, proof copies of the first edition, printings of the first edition, the English edition, and the three American editions. In addition, changes in the texts of The Town and Sanctuary are also discussed when they shed light on some of the problems in The Hamlet. [Order No. 71-9718; 300 pages. DAI, 31A (March-April 1971), 5407.]

182 Faulkner's Grecian Urn / Joan Smolin KORENMAN, Harvard University, 1970 (Joel Porte) no DAI entry.

183 A Darker Freedom: The Villain in the Novels of Hawthorne, James, and Faulkner / Milton Herbert KORNFELD, Brandeis University, 1970 (Peter Surggart).

The aim of this dissertation is to discover what kinds of changes have taken place in the characterization of villainy and depiction of evil in American literature during the past century, and to determine what effects these changes have had upon the fictional representation of moral and psychological reality. Works by Hawthorne, James, and Faulkner were chosen because they are of sufficient moral and psychological complexity to provide valid materials for analysis. This study is not meant to be exhaustive, in terms of either the problem under analysis or the authors chosen for investigation, but is an attempt to chart the beginnings of what might be an unexplored trend in American fiction, and to test some of its implications.

The primary focus for this change is the state of consciousness, the level of self-awareness, of characters suspected of playing villainous roles. The villanous consciousness, as I define it, is one which is self-regarding in a negative, enclosed, contripetal way, one which doesn't expand or grow with experience but remains rooted, fixed, sterile, and rigid in its response to experience. In American fiction the villain is the archetype of a freedom, the Kurtzian freedom of unrepressed, uncivilized desire and untrammeled appetite; a freedom which is rarely expressed with the honesty of a Kurtz, but is exercised behind the benign and protective forms of the American dream and its limitless possibilities.

In Hawthorne the villain is still capable of apprehending the horror of his actions and fully experiencing guilt; but in James the villain's consciousness is characterized by an increasing insensitivity and occasional ambivalence to the graceful brutality which epitomizes the darker side of the Jamesian world; in Faulkner the problem of the consciousness of evil has been solved by the villain through its total annihilation. The villain is so incapable of perceiving his own evil that Faulkner must locate a center of moral consciousness and conflict outside his villains, a shift which seems to imply a complete depersonalization and dehumanization of villainy, and indicates the kind of difficulty found in any modern attempt to evaluate behavior from a moral point of view.

Treating people as a means to an end, exploiting them, restricting them for selfish purposes, these are the components of villainy that appear in different guises in each author. Chillingworth and Ethan Brand are villains motivated by perverse idealizations of themselves: Chillingworth conceiving of himself as the agent of retributive justice, and Brand as a searcher for scientific truth and the knowledge of ultimate evil. The Jamesian villain is not a distorted idealist, but intensely pragmatic and opportunistic, having replaced the Christian and Faustian imperatives with a completely secular desire for power. Dr. Sloper, Kate Croy, and Gilbert Osmond want power that is negative, repressive, graspingly manipulative, and materialistically concrete. Faulkner's villains are also interested in power, but they operate without the civilized urbanity, the refined and distorted consciousness of James' characters. Popeye, Jason Compson, and Flem Snopes represent a brutal, exploitive insensitivity characteristic of the gangster-businessman in his most vulgar, debased, and sometimes comic form.

Each author explores the epistemological problem of how evil can be known. For with the normalization of villainy, the shifting of its goals into the realm of the ordinary, the identification of evil becomes more difficult. By confronting villainy and the problem of evil these authors test the limits of our moral vocabulary, our impulses to punish, criticize, and understand, and force art to perform its most challenging function, to humanize its audience. [Order No. 70-24,643; 158 pages. DAI, 31A (Nov.-Dec. 1971), 2883.]

184 Hawthorne and Faulkner: The Continuity of a Dark American Tradition / Eleanor Marianne LANG, Lehigh University, 1970 (James R. Frakes).

This study of the literary relationship between Hawthorne and Faulkner makes a detailed comparison of the three major works of each writer, The Scarlet Letter and Light in August, The House of the Seven Gables and The Sound and the Fury, and The Marble Faun and Absalom, Absalom! in an attempt to show the continuity of certain character types and situations in the fiction and consciousness of America. The dynamism of Hester Prynne and Lena Grove is set against the static abstraction and masochism of the false clergymen, Arthur Dimmesdale and Gail Hightower, against the refusal of the blackness inherent in human existence by the insidious persecutors, Roger Chillingworth and Doc Hines, and against the moral annihilation of the children of evil, Pearl and Joe Christmas, who are trapped at the point of impact between the life and death forces. The organic wholeness of Dilsey and Phoebe challenges the disengagement from reality and fragmentation of the family caused by the false pride of Hepzibah Pyncheon and Mrs. Compson, the greed of Judge Pyncheon and Jason Compson, and the estheticism of Clifford Pyncheon and Quentin Compson. Both The Marble Faun and Absalom, Absalom! turn on the acceptance of the element of darkness in man, which darkness precipitates the eternal fall; that fall can be fortunate if acknowledged but unfortunate if denied, and the refusals of Hilda and Quentin, as harbingess of the future, to affirm their own participation in the Adamic descent permeate both works with a nihilism that is relieved solely by any reconciliation the reader may make to the timeless parables of historical responsibility that Hawthorne and Faulkner present. And to express these cosmic conflicts, both authors employ stylized characters in a pattern of opposition and balance, playing out the primal scheme; that is to say, Hawthorne and Faulkner write prose romances.

Both writers fit Leslie Fiedler's definition of a Gothic novelist as "one who makes terror rather than love the center of his work, knowing all the while, of course, that there can be no terror without the hope for love and love's defeat." This is what joins Hawthorne and Faulkner in the dark mainstream of American literature, this and a cosmic pessimism lightened only after the fictional fact by their own accomplished act of the imagination which is a leap in the darkness of the human heart. [Order No. 71-10,517; 160 pages. DAI, 31A (March-April 1971), 5410.]

185 Faulkner's Young Protagonists: The Innocent and the Damned / Gladys Welch MILLINER, Tulane University, 1970 (Joseph Patrick Roppolo).

In his young protagonists' view of the world and in the influence of the world upon them, William Faulkner expresses his criticism of society. Using the theme of initiation into maturity, Faulkner presents the conflict between tradition and change, between an artificial social code and a personal moral code. From the viewpoint of the young, he examines the values, the good and the evil, of their world. Some pass successfully into maturity, rejecting the evil, preserving the good, and adjusting to the changes that must come, while others never achieve maturity and are crushed by the experience. Faulkner comments upon society in the comedy and the tragedy of his younger generation of the innocent and the damned.

In his depiction of the experience of conflict within the young, Faulkner reflects the experience of the South in the conflict between tradition and change from the time of the Civil War to the mid-20th century. That conflict can be traced in Faulkner's works from the time when the young Bayard Sartoris of The Unvanquished rejects the old Southern code of honor and violence to the time when Chick Mallison learns a lesson in Negro pride and human dignity from Lucas Beauchamp and helps to teach a lesson in equal justice to a Southern town. The young Bayard Sartoris of Sartoris destroys himself in an effort to live up to the Southern social code. Ike McCaslin, however, passes successfully through initiation into two worlds--the world of the wilderness and the world of Southern society. Quentin Compson accepts the code of the past so completely that he is unable to live in the present and commits suicide. In varying ways the other Compson children are influenced by their society. Caddy, who rebels against social conventions, is punished. Jason, who accepts the materialism of a changing, industrial South and rejects the past completely, is doomed to a life of sterility and isolation. Only Benjy is not affected by society because in his innocence and idiocy he is unaware of its restrictions. Faulkner uses Charles Mallison as the "mirror of truth" in The Town and to reflect the attitudes of white society toward the Negro in Intruder in the Dust. Finally, in The Reivers Lucius Priest takes a journey into maturity along the open road, away from the closed society.

In his life and in his public statements, there is evidence that indicates Faulkner's attitude toward young people. Biographies of Faulkner and memorabilia reveal associations between young Faulkner and the young people in his novels. In his remarks he frequently expressed respect for their perceptions of man and his world.

The thoughts and experiences of Faulkner's young heroes reveal Faulkner's criticism not only of Southern society but of all society. Through the questioning eyes of some of his young characters, Faulkner looks at the world from a moral viewpoint, while in the experiences of others he dramatizes that vision. It is a vision that gives insight into the effects of established and changing social patterns and attitudes upon men. [Order No. 70-24,539; 206 pages. DAI, 31A (Nov.-Dec. 1970), 2928.]

186 A Critical Study of Faulkner's Early Sketches and Collected Stories / Philip MOMBERGER, Johns Hopkins University, 1970 (Charles R. Anderson.)

Faulkner's short fiction dramatizes his abiding concern with man's need for communal involvement. Throughout Faulkner's early sketches and Collected Stories, we see the detached and isolated individual as lost, self-destructive, and finally dehumanized. Only by integrating his separate existence with the lives of others can the protagonist achieve a viable identity.

In "The Hill" (1922) Faulkner's first prose sketch, the protagonist's initial situation is defined with poetic economy. Alone on a hilltop, the "tieless" hero discovers his profound estrangement from nature, from God, and from his fellow men. At the end of his meditation he resolves to descend the hill and enter the village below, for he can complete himself only through participation in some form of human community.

In Faulkner's New Orleans Sketches (1925), his next venture in short fiction, the tieless hero enters society and begins his quest for an authentic identity. But he finds that the modern urban world offers him no sense of involvement in a cohesive social order. Faulkner's New Orleans is a chaotic realm of moral and physical violence. Entering this anarchic world only heightens the protagonist's sense of isolation. Completely sundered from one another, the inhabitants of this urban wasteland are dehumanized. Faulkner's depiction of social chaos, however, implies its opposite: the ideal of an organic community within which the individual would find, in his ties with others, the ground of his own status and growth as a human being.

This contrast between communal order and anarchic violence underlies the structure of Faulkner's Collected Stories (1950), the artist's own summing up of his achievement as a writer of short fiction. The volume's six-part structure, as Faulkner described it, is "contrapuntal in integration."

In the stories of sections I and II, "The Country" and "The Village," Faulkner juxtaposes the organic society of the first with the fragmented world of the second. The farmers of the Country are born into a traditionally ordered community based on common values and a shared way of life. But this harmonious union of self and society is exploded in the Village where, as in Faulkner's New Orleans, the collapse of the communal spirit leaves the individual adrift and unable to complete his identity. Sections III and IV of the collection, the Indian tales of "The Wilderness" and the stories of World War I subtitled "The Wasteland," form a second "contrapuntal" pairing in which this basic contrast is intensified. Wilderness and Wasteland are dramatically heightened versions of Country and Village. The Indians' commitment to the primitive integrity of their culture magnifies the farmers' sense of participation in a firm social order, and the violent world of the Wasteland carries the social and personal disintegration witnessed in the Village to its absolute culmination.

The protagonist of section V, "The Middle Ground," inhabits a neutral territory between the extremes rendered in parts I-IV. He is free to establish bonds with others and thus to affirm the possibility of social and personal wholeness represented by Country and Wilderness. Conversely, he can reject the imperative of communal involvement and so move toward the dehumanizing fragmentation dramatized in Village and Wasteland. The choice is his own. And as is confirmed in part VI, subtitled "Beyond," a choice is unavoidable. The protagonists of these stories discover that not even the final certainty of dying can absolve the individual of his need to search for communal ties. From his early sketches to the great stories of his artistic maturity, this quest is the thematic center of Faulkner's short fiction. [Order No. 72-28, 967; 308 pages. DAI, 33A (Nov.-Dec. 1972), 2386.]

187 The Visual Imagination of William Faulkner / Robert Kirkland MUSIL / Northwestern University, 1970 (Jean H. Hagstrum).

After a review of criticism, "The Visual Imagination of William Faulkner" pursues the thesis that William Faulkner's attention to Aubrey Beardsley,

John Held, Jr., the popular arts of the 1920s, and to his own practice of the visual arts contributed to the pictorial quality of his fiction. The dissertation discusses this influence in ten of the novels which divide into four areas.

Chapter One discusses Faulkner's relationship to the visual arts from his fascination with his grandmother's chalk drawings at Sunday school to his acquaintance with magazine cartoons and stereotypes of the day, and his admiration for the works of the American cartoonist John Held, Jr., and the English decadent, Aubrey Beardsley. Because the works of Held and Beardsley influenced Faulkner's art work and his fiction to a great degree, they are illustrated and described in detail.

Faulkner's own description of his creative process is discussed, highlighting his frequent mention of visual mental images or pictures that were the germs of his stories. That his artistic background and these visual mental images are carried into the prose is shown by a number of graphic art works that have been produced based on Faulkner's text, and by Faulkner's frequent reference to the terminology of the visual arts, art techniques, and artists in his work.

In order to determine what pictorial style infuses his imagination, Faulkner's own published art works are illustrated and thoroughly discussed. Finally, terminology for his style is developed and explained.

Chapter Two shows that in his early period, Faulkner frequently presents pictorial scenes for their sheer visual fascination. Progressing from New Orleans Sketches to Soldiers' Pay, Mosquitoes, and Sartoris, Faulkner gradually shifts from the more conscious Art Nouveau and Jazz Age stereotypes of Beardsley and Held to the Yoknapatawpha descriptions at which he is more adept. In addition, it is shown that the work of the early years is a time of growing sophistication both in relating pictorial passages to themes and in varying the timing and purpose of a character's initial cartoon for rhetorical effect.

Chapter Three introduces Faulkner's major aesthetic strategies for using pictorial presentation. The first, stereotyping an individual by the use of cartoon exteriors and then revealing his true human "heart" through interior monologue or flashbacks, is discussed in The Sound and the Fury, Light in August, and Absalom, Absalom!.

Chapter Four discusses Faulkner's mixture of multiple exterior cartoon views and inner revelations in As I Lay Dying and Sanctuary. In these worlds, public comedy and private tragedy become equally meaningful. There are no stable values and ultimately no justice.

Chapter Five analyzes Faulkner's use of cartoons and rapid comic-strip action in The Hamlet. In this novel our focus remains on the exteriors of the characters and, in general, we are not so upset about the misfortunes that befall people. We can laugh at them and the human fate that we all share.

The final chapter compares the 1934 version of the short story "Mule in the Yard" with its revised version in The Town, published in 1957. Then the revised version of the story is compared with the remainder of the novel. This comparison reveals some decline in Faulkner's use of pictorialism, the destruction, in its revised form of the original comic purpose of the short story and a lack of any pictorialism that reveals his artistic background in the remainder of the work.

Appended to the dissertation are 24 plates of the art work of William Faulkner, Aubrey Beardsley, John Held, Jr., and selected cartoons of the 1920s. [Order No. 71-1926; 306 pages. DAI, 31A (Jan.-Feb. 1971), 3558.]

188 Motion and Status Theme as Structuring Principle in the Art of William Faulkner / Robert L. NADEAU, University of Florida, 1970 (Gordon E. Bigelow) no DAI entry.

189 Plot Manipulation and Kaleidoscoping of Time as Sources of Tragic Perception in William Faulkner's Absalom, Absalom! / Sister Mary Dolorine PIRES, St. Louis University, 1970 (Maurice Basil McNamee).

Because man's knowledge of human nature has been remarkably increased, it must be conceded that some aspects of Aristotle's otherwise insightful theory of tragedy are no longer relevant. Modern tragedians realize that the magnitude he required in the tragic hero must include values emphasized by democratizing processes and psychological research--the inner and outer tensions experienced by the total person, and the consequent fine play between human responsibility and chance. In narration, too, his concern with a clearly defined beginning, middle, and end yields to experimentation with distorted forms sharply delineating contemporary man's plight. The connection between technique, perception, and pleasure points to a definition of catharsis not as purgation (relief from the emotions) or purification (refining of the emotions) but as a deepening of these emotions, climaxed in a sympathy derived from the superior knowledge afforded the reader by the author's structuring of events. This process of empirical enlightenment provides new insight into the mystery of suffering and evil, in turn according the reader that pleasure which derives from the acquisition of empathetic understanding, an eminently humanizing experience.

In Absalom, Absalom! Faulkner brilliantly exemplifies the possibilities opened up for modern tragedy. Showing a deep concern for the aristocracy of the human person, he reveals the struggle his characters endure within their own psyches and against outer tensions. Utilizing a cinematographic style, he skillfully manipulates events in the overall structure so as to effect simultaneously plot progression, character revelation and reader perception. By kaleidoscoping time, he brings the past and future into focus in the present, allowing a closer study of causes and effects, guilt and exoneration, evoking a well-founded compassion.

Employing several narrators, he views the tragic hero from different, often contradictory angles, revealing Sutpen as both sinned against and sinning. Presenting him first as an ogre, Rosa's account defeats itself by her distraught exaggerations betraying prejudice. Mr. Compson's lengthy narration counters this with a vision of Sutpen as a determined hero doomed by capricious Fate. In the strategically located, italicized central chapter, Miss Coldfield epitomizes an essentially human judgment when she appraises Sutpen as "... villain true enough, but a mortal, fallible one less to invoke fear than pity." In the interpretive second half of the novel Quentin, a young Southern collegian, and Shreve, a Canadian outsider, try to conjecture a synthesis, highlighting the lack of knowledge which compounds the difficulty of decision-making and lessens the guilt in seemingly completely malicious behavior. Their exploration ends in their own "overpassing to love"--underscoring Sutpen's tragedy as his failure to exercise a love that could include the part-Negro son which cold ambition and regional bias refused to countenance as adjunctive to his grand design.

This novel exhibits an ingenious structural unity and extraordinary but appropriate textual richness, bearing testimony to literary artistry. As a brief analysis of Picasso's Girl before a Mirror and Chagall's White Crucifixion indicates, Faulkner's use of multiple perspectives can be likened to that of synthetic Cubist painting and the manifold psychological images of Surrealism. [Order No. 71-3287; 313 pages. DAI, 31A (Jan.-Feb. 1971), 4176.]

190 As I Lay Dying: A Study of the Poor White in Faulkner / John Brown ROSENMAN, Kent State University, 1970 (Thomas F. Marshall).

Despite increasing interest in Faulkner, critics still overlook the primary significance of his poor whites, and the fact that As I Lay Dying is his most representative and relevant work largely because it constitutes his most comprehensive, concentrated treatment of them. This dissertation, based upon an analysis of the novel, attempts to modify such "misapprehensions" by establishing the following points. First, as a seminal source for studying Faulkner, As I Lay Dying is the only work which provides a capsule representation both of the poor white and of the full range and gamut of his drives, desires, nature, and goals. Second, as the most important class in Faulkner, poor whites, especially as they are presented in As I Lay Dying, not only pursue more goals than other groups, but also, because of these goals, are unrivaled in the extent to which they prefigure or elaborate upon other characters, regardless of the classes to which they belong. Third, largely because Faulkner sees in poor whites those qualities he values, they are the ones he draws upon most often in depicting characters of nobility, honor, and purpose.

Following the Introduction, which defines "poor whites" and discusses Faulkner's significance as a "naturalistic" portrayer of them, Chapter One focuses upon the two Bundrens who made Addie's burial journey possible. In it, Cash's stoic suffering is seen as linking him with numerous characters such as Dilsey in The Sound and the Fury and Mink Snopes in The Mansion, who are able to "endure." In turn, Jewel, Faulkner's first significant furious poor white, is considered in relation to provincials whose fury and envious resentment of the rich he anticipates.

Chapter Two, "Addie, Jewel, and Vardaman: Secular Trinity," discusses three Bundrens whose roles are conceived in Christian terms. Also, it examines the nature of Faulkner's recurrent method in using Christian, pagan, and Southern myths and legends in order to dramatize the ceaseless "now" of existence.

Chapters Three and Four are concerned with the states of innocence and experience. Addie, a victim of the fallen world and the first Faulkner character who seeks revenge, is shown as one who anticipates those like Bayard Sartoris, II, Mink Snopes, and Thomas Sutpen. Again, her son Vardaman, the first "boy-symbol," is related to other boys, both poor whites and aristocrats, who face the "real" world--and the male's need to define it-- for the first significant time.

Chapter Five considers Dewey Dell. Involved with the role of childbearing, and demonstrating the woman's (rather than the man's) concern with practical, unromantic issues, she resembles other "eternal females" like Lena Grove, Eula Varner, and Caddy Compson. Also, since Dewey Dell is the first woman in Faulkner who undertakes a long journey, and embodies natural values which he frequently contrasts to the debilitating ones of town and city, she furnishes yet another indication of As I Lay Dying's relevance.

Chapter Six, which concludes the study, is intended as a balance to the first chapter. Unlike Cash and Jewel, who embody the ability to act which Faulkner so admires in poor whites, Anse and Darl share an inability to accomplish anything. Anse, the father, ruled by "common sense" and laziness, escapes commitment by selfishly exploiting others and by looking after his own interests like Flem Snopes and Thomas Sutpen. Moreover, his reliance on words suggests the empty verbiage that Faulkner presents in other characters. In kind, the "mad" Darl, because of his preoccupation with intellectual abstractions and his awareness of cosmic absurdity (an awareness that pervades Faulkner), displays an incapacity for life found in those as divergent as Gavin Stevens, Joe Christmas, and Joanna Burden. However, despite his psychic paralysis, Darl's reflections are the most poetic in the novel and epitomize Faulkner's enduring tendency to heighten poetically the inarticulate thoughts of his provincials. [Order No. 71-10,861; 223 pages. DAI, 31A (May-June 1971), 6069-70.]

191 The Design of Faulkner's Light in August: A Comprehensive Study / Don Noel SMITH, University of Michigan, 1970 (Robert F. Haugh).

This dissertation undertakes a more comprehensive study of William Faulkner's Light in August than has yet been attempted, through a systematic and integrative approach to the novel and criticism of it. Although the study is devoted specifically to Light in August, long considered one of Faulkner's finest and yet most problematic works, it does relate this novel to the total context of Faulkner's thought, methods, and materials. The study has assumed not only that Light in August is in itself a work of art worthy of careful attention but that a close examination of it cannot fail to illuminate further the entire Faulkner canon.

Chapter I of the study presents a review of current attitudes toward Faulkner and his work and of the criticism of Light in August in particular, delineating the central critical concerns and various critical approaches. Chapter II offers a general conceptual frame of reference; it makes a distinction between Faulkner's artistic vision and its moral context and discusses the assumptions about art, life, and consciousness that seem to underlie his works. Chapter III offers an extensive technical frame of reference; here are examined the structure, the imagery, and the mythic and Biblical parallels, which provide subtle commentary on the action. Chapters IV-VI contain a close exegesis of the distinguishable actions and their relation to each other, set against the conceptual and technical frames of reference already established.

The last chapter attempts broadly to evaluate the success and significance of the novel, concluding that Faulkner is a master of the modern methods he chose to use but that those methods perhaps have certain intrinsic limitations that must be considered in any final assessment of his achievement; this chapter also finds that Light in August is itself an ingenious but rewarding work, sometimes sacrificing dramatic clarity to elaborateness of texture, and that, like the other Yoknapatawpha works, it yields the kind of richly evoked reality that is the mark of a major talent. [Order No. 70-21,791; 262 pages. DAI, 31A (Nov.-Dec. 1970), 2402.]

192 The Fourteenth View: A Study of Ambiguity in William Faulkner's Light in August / Mary Therese STRAUSS, University of Pittsburgh, 1970 (Robert L. Gale).

The diversity of critical interpretations of the novels of William Faulkner is largely due to his heavy reliance on ambiguity. Both definitions of the word "ambiguity" apply to Faulkner's fiction: many aspects of his work have two or more possible meanings, and some of Faulkner's meanings, it appears to me, are indefinite and unclear.

I have chosen Light in August as the focus of my study because it is one of Faulkner's most richly paradoxical novels and because the devices employed in it are typical of Faulkner's ambiguous method.

The first chapter of my study presents a detailed analysis of Faulkner's presentation of Joe Christmas. From the very first reference to the character in the novel, Faulkner presents him ambiguously: "He looked like a tramp, yet not like a tramp either." Joe Christmas is simultaneously compared to both a flower and a snake: this juxtaposition of disparate images is, in miniature, a reflection of Faulkner's whole method of presenting Joe Christmas. Faulkner presents both negative and sympathetic qualities of Christmas. The author's use of multiple viewpoints and his manipulation of esthetic distance actively engage the reader in trying to apprehend the "true" personality of Christmas. Ambiguous aspects of his presentation such as Christmas' Negro status, the degree of his personal responsibility, and the significance of his death and of the Christ parallels are examined in detail.

The second chapter analyzes the characterization of Gail Hightower, Lena Grove, Joanna Burden, and the other characters in Light in August. It reveals that Faulkner employs many of the same ambiguous methods in presenting these characters that are observable in his characterization of Joe Christmas.

The third chapter studies the presentation of the community, the general tone, and the unity of Light in August. These analyses reveal that the community is regarded ambiguously, that the general tone of the novel elicits a dual response, and that the unifying theme is, in the final estimate, ambiguous.

This study demonstrates that Faulkner intentionally imbues every aspect of Light in August with ambiguity: the imagery, symbolism, characterization, tone, structure, and theme of the novel elicit a dual response from the reader. In addition, the ambiguity of Light in August and of Faulkner's greatest fiction actively involves the reader in helping Faulkner to create his novels. Faulkner "makes" his reader by forcing him to participate in apprehending the "true" view of the characters, events, and themes in his works. Most importantly, Faulkner's heavy reliance on ambiguity provides a realistic view of the complexity of human motivation and behavior, the difficulties involved in determining why people behave as they do. Faulkner's recognition of the dualities and complexities of human existence is mirrored in his entire method in Light in August. The ambiguity of his art reflects the ambiguity of life itself. [Order No. 71-13,223; 206 pages. DAI, 31A (May-June 1971), 6074.]

193 The Commitment of Self in the Works of William Faulkner / Andrew Jackson WESTBROOK, University of Texas at Austin, 1970 (Thomas B. Whitbread).

William Faulkner's characters in The Sound and the Fury, Absalom, Absalom!, Light in August, The Hamlet, The Town, The Mansion, As I Lay Dying, and Go Down, Moses, although necessarily distinct from actual humans in that they are discovered by the author in his mind and presented with artistic selection in his fiction, enjoy a participation in the human situation to the extent that they can be seen to have definable Selves and personal worlds. The personal world consists mostly of the values held by a character, and his Self is the free agent that has no choice but to deal with the problems of his nature and those problems appropriate to his dealing with the community of men. This lack of freedom to be not free makes demands on the Self regarding value judgments. As the Self makes these judgments through action it defines itself, and further defines the nature of the character. Any crucial decision, i.e., when some high matter of morality or other important value is at stake, amounts to a commitment. The Self, further, being terribly alone in all this, cannot resist the desire to be relieved of tension in some freeless, Edenic residence, but since a person has to live in the actual world, he is necessarily condemned to be free. By their nature, Faulkner's characters, like actual human beings, must act when circumstances force them to, and they must act consistently with their nature, and their nature is at any given time predominantly an accumulation of commitments the Self has made. Any new commitment further defines and broadens both that Self and the character's nature. Faulkner's approach to the writing of fiction was grounded in his keen interest in the human problems which he saw in terms of the characters in his head, who, once created by him, assumed their own natures and made demands on him that their stories be told. Apparently, the combination of recognized universal conflicts and the imaginative presence of self-defining characters resulted in Faulkner's art. His use of language is, in a broad sense, poetic, in that it serves as an effort to discover realities in the human situation that reside beyond the actuality of the words themselves. The demand, made by the poetic on the language that discovered it, is that the language dismiss itself as an object of concern by means of its own power. [Order No. 71-210; 112 pages. DAI, 31A (Jan.-Feb. 1971), 3568-69.]

194 The Past in the Works of William Faulkner / Bill Kaler ADDISON, University of Minnesota, 1971 (C. Turpie).

William Faulkner's intense longing to understand the past generated both his ways of viewing the past and his efforts to suit the form to the particular view. And although Faulkner never found the one view by which he could best understand the role the past plays in our lives, his drive to discover it led him to create works of genius. This dissertation discusses five important ways Faulkner saw the past and describes the forms that reveal them. Chronological structure, Faulkner's vision of Southern history, the past as determiner, the past as present, and the present as past designate the views of the past that Faulkner conceived in the major novels and stories of the Yoknapatawpha saga.

Among the few novels in which Faulkner produced the past in a straightforward manner, The Unvanquished (told in person) charts a bildungsroman of a boy growing into responsible manhood while Sartoris, an early work, for the first time incorporates doom and disaster and the ghost of the past-motifs that begin to transform Faulkner's presentation into something other than a simple retelling of events. Faulkner's vision of Southern history perhaps came closer to enabling him to understand the past. It is a tragic, guilt-centered view deriving from the South's violation of what he considered the inviolable land and from slavery's profanation with its twin curses of denial of kinship and deprivation of human status: a view that in its encompassing defeat and frustration and in its moral implications, to some degree or other, informs everything he wrote. This vision opened to his consideration "the problems of the human heart in conflict with itself which alone ... is worth writing about, worth the agony and the sweat." In its essays before the acts, Requiem for a Nun contains the quintessence of Faulkner's vision of Southern history. The past as determiner of the present describes another view to which Faulkner responded--a highly controversial one if we judge by the conflicting critical opinion of the topic of determinism in Faulkner's work. This dissertation proposes that Light in August and Absalom, Absalom! deeply explore determinism; that the multiple points of view Faulkner used in Light in August evolve out of Freudian psychology with its revelations about the agonized effect of the past on the behavior of characters; and that Absalom, Absalom! told by narrators sifted through a central intelligence, derives determinism metaphorically by relegating Southerners to an inescapable ghost status in a dead South. In The Sound and the Fury Quentin Compson, whose extreme introspection makes him prey to what he sees in the past, actually relives his past in the present. Recurrence is the name I have given to the technique by which Quentin's past materializes in his present. In yet another variant, Sanctuary at significant moments shows the present become the past. The three methods by which this happens include spatial temporal distancing, instantaneous conversion, and occurrence off the scene.

All these views and techniques center on the most profound truth that Faulkner posited: his belief that there is no immunity from the past. For, irrespective of how the past reveals itself, as far as Faulkner was concerned, it abides. He makes us realize (and herein we discover the universality of his work) that man has no deeper struggle than that of grappling with the respiteless past in the attempt to see its effect on our lives. In Faulkner's striving to see and to portray what the multifarious everlasting was, the grappling became his art. [Order No. 71-28,204; 188 pages. DAI, 32A (Nov.-Dec. 1971), 2669-70.]

195 Faulkner's Readers: Crosscurrents in American Reviews and Criticism, 1926-1962 / John Earl BASSETT, University of Rochester, 1971 (Howard Horsford).

Though not the first study of William Faulkner's critical reception in America, this is the most comprehensive. A selective but broadly based search of American book review sections, supplemented by both the Random House files and the Linton Massey Collection at the University of Virginia, stands warrant for the generalization about contemporary reviews. An extensive examination of literary histories, anthologies, and general essays on fiction, plus a search of the unindexed little magazines, has unearthed much commentary rarely if ever considered. Necessarily random coverage of literary biographies and collections of letters has revealed a number of comments by Faulkner's fellow writers. From this wealth of material several different Faulkners emerge. One is the idiosyncratic Mississippian whose strange books sold poorly, whom many Americans knew only as "the author of Sanctuary" or the purveyor of degenerates. A second is the novelist often (though certainly not invariably) reviewed quite favorably by American newspaper and magazine critics, generally not profound but displaying a broader and more open imagination than their own readers. Just as regardful of his accomplishments were fellow writers like Hemingway, Aiken, Wolfe, Anderson, and the Vanderbilt Fugitives. Yet another Faulkner is the morbidly pessimistic curio portrayed by several literary historians and academic critics of the thirties and early forties, the hard-boiled Southerner wasting his talents on sadists and morons (this Faulkner, however, underwent the greatest change after World War II). The composite picture is one of an original and difficult novelist, whose popularity and critical success were limited by his difficulty at a time when "style" was more often than not a term of opprobrium; whose symbolic and mythic structures were often opaque to many critics impressed by physical realism and social didactic; whose seeming morbidity and nihilism dismayed readers looking for more optimistic visions in a depression-torn world; yet whose rich fables of both tragic resonance and comic vitality were to a substantial group of sensitive readers a major contribution to imaginative literature.

Following a preface on methodology and an introduction outlining the main currents of Faulkner criticism, each chapter deals with a significant chronological period. Between 1926 and 1930 cautiously encouraging reviewers granted Faulkner's apprentice novels reserved praise and his first two masterpieces a surprisingly sympathetic reception. In the early thirties, despite favorable responses to Sanctuary and Light in August, anti-Faulkner sentiment increased among varied groups who found his subject matter morbid, his social consciousness undeveloped, or his prose unintelligible. American literary historians badly underrated Faulkner during the mid- and late thirties, and even the reviewers were perplexed by the demands of Pylon and Absalom, Absalom! but his other novels were well received, and at the same time French writers and critics began to praise his fiction abroad. Between 1939 and 1943 Faulkner studies flourished; and despite the scarcity of wartime essays, this attention was again in evidence after 1946 (at times revolving around but not completely the result of Cowley's Portable Faulkner). The transition period in Faulkner criticism can be somewhat loosely defined as the two years on either side of 1950, when he received the Nobel Prize: a whole new generation of university scholar-critics canonized him as a major American novelist; the Swedish award symbolized and accelerated his recognition and made him a public figure; gradually he became a semi-popular author whose fiction brought him a substantial income. During the fifties, when Faulkner himself was a tired novelist whose fiction declined in power, criticism and scholarship proliferated, his readers no longer intent on arguing the merits of his novels (those having been accepted) but concerned with explaining the novels and their creator. [Order No. 71-22,282; 682 pages. DAI, 32A (Sept.-Oct. 1971), 1502.]

196 The Monument and the Plain: The Art of Mythic Consciousness in William Faulkner's Absalom, Absalom! / Oliver La Fayette BILLINGSLEA, University of Wisconsin, 1971 (Walter B. Rideout).

This work examines in depth the thesis that Absalom, Absalom! is a novel about the nature of reality, that its concern is epistemology, and that what William Faulkner sought to create was a cosmos of spatial and temporal phenomena in which man must face the universal problem of the "human heart in conflict with itself"; it attempts to show, rather simply, that the only solution to this spiritual conflict will be the development of a "system" by which the individual can be accommodated to his fellow man. Clearly illustrated is the fact that Faulkner's cosmology can best be understood typologically: that the basis for Faulkner's art is a "mythic consciousness" inherent in all mankind, and that although each character in his own limited way fails to understand reality, the reader is able to approach the cosmos with some certainty of understanding the greater issues of the human spirit. The theory is advanced that like most of Faulkner's tragedies, Absalom, Absalom! seems at first that "frantic steeplechase toward nothing," but is, nevertheless, also a reassertion of humanity in defeat: a "life motion" toward a dreamed-of perfection. Throughout, Absalom, Absalom! is seen as a book about the history of man and about his attempts to order the universe into rational, and sometimes irrational, systems.

As part of an inexhaustible stream of history, Thomas Sutpen is pictured as "Author" of those who seek to understand him, a Creator of the Past and Shaper of the Present through which each narrator and we, in turn, perceive all that can be known about the Past. His "design" is envisioned an attempt to implement a system of order upon a world which lives by empirical diversity, a world in every way diametrically opposed and "negative" to his own unaccommodating dream. Seen as Emerson's god unto himself, he is pictured as being inflexibly rigid in carrying out his phallic-oriented vision of the "monument on the plain," tragically creating but another world of barrenness in the midst of what is already seemingly a wasteland. An investigation is given the relationship between Sutpen and Quentin and between Quentin and his own father, especially in respect to the decisive effect the Past has on Quentin's feeling of impotence.

Examined is the novel's form and mode of narrative development: its structure and what may be defined as its technique of "complementary reality" through which the reader is forced to focus again and again on the fictional product through an active participation in its artistic process: sharing in an art not representational, but presentational. A book about the creative process itself, Absalom, Absalom! is necessarily also a book about language which serves a single thread in the spider-web of human consciousness; the relationship between language and reality is, consequently, explored in depth.

Its several narrators are examined in detail, a measure of validity granted each in respect to the perspective afforded him by his mythic consciousness--the mode by which he seeks to comprehend the empirical diversity he encounters; and an entire chapter is devoted to the hitherto almost neglected authorial intrusions of Faulkner himself, especially in respect to his providing an interpretive counterbalance, his desire to create an aesthetic distance between event and reader, his corroboration of the "mythic consciousness" out of which the novel's metaphysical truth evolves, and the numerous instances in which he insinuates that we experience what may be no more than a complement of reality in respect to any given incident. Attention is regularly given the novel's imagery as it clarifies the various perspectives through which the Sutpen story is revealed. The result is a close textual analysis, and, hopefully, a demonstration of the creative awareness Faulkner expected of his readers in faith that the best of them would supply that "fourteenth image of the blackbird," that epistemology of hope and affirmation of the human spirit, even in defeat. [Order No. 71-25,711; 365 pages. DAI, 32A (Nov.-Dec. 1971), 3293.]

197 The Reality of Gothic Terror in Faulkner / Ruth Annette Huntington Hartmann BRADY, University of Texas at Austin, 1971 (John G. Varner).

Modern American Gothic writers have been interested in psychological and pathological dangers, but they have been unable to resist the temptation of aping some of the older Gothic devices to lend weight to the newer effects they hope to create. More recent American writers, especially Southern ones, transcend their European ancestry to find a terror which changes a mere titillating and romantic thrill into a horrible reality that contemporary affairs and new psychological discoveries authenticate.

William Faulkner finds in the South elements which terrify, and more often than not he finds them in the aberrant mind. Yet he does employ traditional Gothic devices found in earlier works. Among these are Oriental implants, black slavery, religious fanaticism, insanity and idiocy, incest, murder, rape, loneliness, isolation, sterility, the American version of the castle, cemetaries, yawning vaults and open caskets, journeys, decomposition, disease, blood, ghosts, tombstones, sounds, odors, colors, and sometimes, but not often, the sentimental heroine fleeing to preserve the jewel of her chastity.

To establish my thesis, I have chosen to discuss one representative short story, "A Rose for Emily," and five representative novels: As I Lay Dying, Sanctuary with its sequel, Requiem for a Nun, Light in August, The Sound and the Fury, and Absalom, Absalom!

In several instances in Faulkner, the old Gothic journey becomes a journey through aberrant minds. "A Rose for Emily" explores the title character's mental aberrations, a kind of amalgamation of the Oedipus complex and necrophilia; yet her warped psyche hides beneath a thick veneer of aristocratic Mississippi virtue. Quentin Compson, in stream-of-consciousness revelations from his watery grave, explains how his obsession for family honor has led him to suicide. And Rosa Coldfield unknowingly reveals herself as a vengeance-ridden, pious racist in her dramatic monologue.

Often Faulkner has transferred evil to woman. Aristocratic Emily Grierson is a murderess-necrophile. Addie Bundren rejects all members of her family except the illegitimate son Jewel. Temple Drake states bluntly that she likes evil. Pious Narcissa Benbow helps lynch an innocent man. Loveless Caroline Compson repudiates all of her children except ruthless Jason. And tradition-bound Rosa Coldfield thrives on hate and revenge and ferrets out evil in everyone except herself.

Occasionally Faulkner introduces a terrible irony into his stories. A backward family forcibly commits a sensitive, perceptive son to an asylum. Traditional bulwarks of justice, such as religion and law, shelter corruption. Rural Southern communities become one of the worst terrors, with their violence, racism, and religious fanaticism. One victim of these qualities is brutally castrated because he has killed a white woman and is said to have Negro blood.

Although Faulkner has borrowed from tradition, this enigmatic genius merely uses these devices as a part of regional settings which he merges with his characters who, if not always normal, do exist. Faulkner's greatest contribution to the Gothic novel stands in this character development and in structure, where he has created a suspense that the early Gothic could not anticipate. [Order No. 72-11,317; 188 pages. DAI, 32A (March-April 1972), 5774-75.]

198 Duality in the Novels of William Faulkner and Fyodor Dostoevsky / Emil Stanley BRICKER, University of Michigan, 1971 (Lyall H. Powers).

My dissertation compares three internally divided characters in Faulkner's novels--Quentin Compson, Darl Bundren, and Joe Christmas--to the doubles in Dostoevsky's fiction. Part One deals with the religious, psychological, and social sources of the tensions that cause duality. Pride, self-willed isolation, and the inability to love, drive the dual personality or "double" toward absolute egoism. But these solipsistic tendencies are balanced by the double's desire to love others. Some of the split personalities in Dostoevsky's work (Raskolnikov and Versilos) are eventually able to unify their divided souls by devoting themselves wholly to love, but none of Faulkner's seems capable of doing so.

The psychological phenomenon of duality is traced to origins in narcissism, latent perverse sexual drives, and autoscopic hallucinations. Profound alienation from all mankind, combined with failure to discover a meaningful role in life, leads the double to criticize civilization severely. Dostoevsky's internally divided characters offer possible solutions to society's problems; Faulkner's less articulate doubles are employed as symbols of society's flaws.

The second part of my study treats duality in four of Faulkner's novels. Quentin Compson in The Sound and the Fury, like Dostoevsky's philosophical suicide Kirllov and the would-be suicide Ippolit Terentyev, expresses ambivalence toward God, death, resurrection, and time. His psychological condition and social circumstances are much like those of Arkady Dolgoruky, who worships his cynical father, and simultaneously loves and hates his unmarried, pregnant sister.

Darl Bundren in As I Lay Dying manifests a duality between thought and act, as does Dostoevsky's Underground Man, who wishes to revenge himself on life but cannot. Joe Christmas in Light in August, a murderer as is Dostoevsky's Raskolnikov, is split between his own deterministic beliefs and his desire for freedom, and finally renounces his duality, as does Dostoevsky's hero.

Quentin Compson in Absalom, Absalom! is torn between love and hatred of his Southern heritage. His growing awareness of the evil in the South, and his personal acceptance of responsibility for the Sutpen's deeds are compared with Ivan Karamazov's gradual recognition of his own guilt for the murder of his father.

In the conclusion of my work, I suggest that Faulkner turned away from duality in many of his later works because his novelistic interests gradually shifted from preoccupation with the plight of the individual to a concern with the community as a whole. The doubles in Faulkner's novels are not magnificent in stature as those in Dostoevsky's. The scope of their free will has been limited (though free will has not disappeared in Faulkner's work); they are victims of life as well as tragic heroes. [Order No. 72-14,815; 327 pages. DAI, 32A (May-June 1972), 6413-14.]

199 Abstraction and Insularity in the Fiction of William Faulkner / Panthea Reid BROUGHTON, University of North Carolina at Chapel Hill, 1971 (Weldon Thornton).

Even the most casual reader of William Faulkner's fiction might hazard a guess that "outrage" is Faulkner's favorite word. Certainly Faulkner has created myriad characters who are repeatedly outraged by experience. But a perhaps less obvious observation is that there is a whole system of other words which, as corollaries to "outrage," are used almost as much and certainly as significantly; these terms imply retreat, disengagement, attempted invulnerability; among them are "sanctuary," "immunity," "insulation," "imperviousness." They are corollaries to "outrage" because, with Faulkner, outrage results from being forced to encounter the undefined, the unsettling, or the uncontrollable situation. His fiction details repeated instances of characters who use the fixity of an abstraction either consciously or unconsciously, as a sanctuary from experience. To such characters a strict and static point of view toward life seems to afford "insulation, isolation, ... the unchallengeable immunity" from existence itself; thus they attempt to fix human relationships or to raise to absolute status the past, or authority, or a code, or a single interpretation of reality. The attempt is a denial of the flux of experience and, to William Faulkner who believed that "life is motion" is both futile and pernicious.

Faulkner felt, of course, that codes, rituals, and abstract ideals can afford invaluable enrichment of existence and that they are necessary to order and to sustain life. He saw, however, that in the South especially all too often they become absolute and devitalized and therefore distort rather than enhance man's existence. His fiction emphasizes the negative, rather than the positive, aspects of codes-and-abstractions because he is acutely aware of and concerned over their misuse. This dissertation focuses upon the negative effects of abstractions, then, because Faulkner did. The theme is chosen, furthermore, because its pervasiveness has gone largely unnoticed in critical commentary.

Awareness of the insulatory effect of abstractions is implicit in much that Olga Vickery says in The Novels of William Faulkner, but she does not focus upon it or isolate it as a major theme running throughout the canon. There have been various studies of motion in Faulkner's fiction, but none concentrates upon stasis itself or clearly defines it in terms of an abstract and fixed point of view toward life. Richard P. Adams in Myth and Motion equates stasis with sterility and lifelessness but does not isolate his discussion of stasis or, in fact, define the term itself. Walter Slatoff in his Quest for Failure examines Faulkner's use of the terms "motion" and "stasis," finding in their juxtaposition, as in the oxymoron, little more than a refusal to be coherent. From Slatoff's point of view, Faulkner regarded "too much coherence as a kind of failure." Slatoff, then, excuses himself from discovering the coherent and consistent awareness behind Faulkner's concern with stasis. Warren Beck in his Man and Motion examines the motion motif in the Snopes trilogy. His study does not concern itself with an examination of stasis itself, however. The subject, then, remains largely unexplored.

This dissertation is an incipient attempt to redress the balance. Although the theme of evasion and insulation through abstractions dominates The Sound and the Fury and Light in August, it appears as early as Soldiers' Pay and is never wholly absent from any novel. Limiting the dissertation to any particular group of novels could be somewhat arbitrary and would obscure the theme's pervasiveness. Therefore, the dissertation is organized around patterns or evasion as they are found throughout the fiction. The concern is chiefly with the novels, but examples from the short stories have not been excluded. The dissertation will deal with characters who evade experiential reality by erecting an insular barrier of fixed abstractions between themselves and experience. Only the most salient examples are discussed; the dissertation makes no pretense of being all-inclusive. [Order No. 72-10, 693; 235 pages. DAI, 32A (March-April 1972), 5220.]

200 The Religious Symbolism in Faulkner's Novels / Winifred CLARK, University of Tulsa, 1971 (Manly Johnson).

William Faulkner grew up in the Christian tradition, and in his later life expressed the belief that his religious training had become an inextricable part of his being. No man succeeds in writing and ignoring the well of information formed by his early years from which his imagination draws, and

Faulkner did not try. Religion, with its macrocosmic world of good against evil, permeated every corner of Faulkner's microcosmic world.

Faulkner wrote about many kinds of people. Some were evil, such as Flem Snopes, Thomas Sutpen, Jason Compson, Temple Drake, or good like Gavin Stevens, Ratliff, Dilsey, and Miss Habersham. The majority of his characters, however, were a very human mixture of good and evil. Regardless of the category in which they fell, Faulkner presented them with a semi-detached and benign tolerance, making no judgment nor condemnation of their behavior.

Faulkner's belief in man's striving to be "better than he is," shows in all his works. He confronts his characters with challenges and they either rise to overcome them or fail in their efforts to overcome them or, worst of all in Faulkner's eyes, refuse to admit that there are challenges in life and remain inactive.

The most persistent religious symbols appearing in Faulkner's novels concern the dichotomy of man's nature shown by his inner struggle against evil; the Christian virtues that are possessed to some degree by all who are not avatars of evil; the person crucified either because of religious, moral, environmental, or political reasons. Faulkner shows that crucifixion is either sought by the individual or it is forced upon him by others.

The worst evil to Faulkner is, as it was to Hawthorne, the violation of the human heart. War, oppression, injustice, slavery, and racial prejudice are some other evils that challenge the best of men to battle them. Faulkner depicts these men as having some or all of the "verities of the human heart": compassion, aspiration, courage, endurance, self-sacrifice, and love.

In all his writings Faulkner reveals his deep concern with the betterment of mankind, man's inherent ability to cope with the evil in the world, and the hope that humanistic man will become a better creature by his striving to improve his own lot as well as that of all peoples. [Order No. 71-24, 259; 148 pages. DAI, 32A (Sept.-Oct. 1971), 1506.]

201 Faulkner's Un-Christlike Christians: Biblical Allusions in the Novels / Jessie Alma COFFEE, University of Nevada, 1971 (Robert D. Harvey).

This dissertation offers the first full-length study of William Faulkner's use of Biblical allusions (as distinguished from general religious references). The work is in two parts: Part II consists of a classification and explication of the 379 verses or combinations of verses identifiable both in the King James Bible and in one or more of the 19 novels. The Faulkner allusion is explicated in the context of the original Bible reference. Tables showing the distribution of the verses and other statistical information are given in three Appendices. Part I is a critical study, based on the Concordance and Commentary, showing Faulkner's philosophical approach to Biblical usage, his usage of Biblical patterns (the Bible reference, an entire passage or story, or a group of related references), and his variations on the patterns. An understanding of Faulkner's Biblical patterns and variations is essential for the appreciation of his novels: for example, the paradox of his un-Christlike Christ figures occurs because of a combination of the Hebraic-Christian and the pastoral traditions

Faulkner's Biblical allusions deal for the most part with the basic tenets of the Christian faith--sin, vicarious atonement, and salvation. The majority of the Scriptures touch on the following theme: Patriarchs, Sons, and Siblings; Patrimony, Sacrifice, and Salvation. Sons and daughters are shown inheriting a patrimony of sin for which they are obliged to make a sacrifice to obtain some kind of salvation either for themselves or for others. Man is not only heir to the ravages brought about by the mutability of time but, because of the continuity of the races, a person may inherit guilt from Adam, Eve,

Cain, Ham, or some more recent progenitor. Guilt often concerns irregular family relationships, or a combination of the two.

Innocent characters who might be termed sacrificial lambs include Isaac McCaslin (Go Down, Moses), who tries to atone for his grandfather's guilt; Henry Sutpen (Absalom, Absalom!), who becomes a murderer and a fugitive when his father's sins "come home to roost"; and the corporal (A Fable), the illegitimate son of a general, who insists on his own execution in opposition to the father who has finally acknowledged his existence. All these characters are (relatively) innocent victims.

Other piaculars, however, are like the sacrificial goat of Leviticus 16: they are sinful, but, paradoxically they are innocent victims. Such sacrifices are Mink Snopes (The Mansion), Nancy Mannigoe (Requiem for a Nun), Benjamin Compson (The Sound and the Fury), and Joe Christmas (Light in August). These characters, all murderers but one and he an idiot, are sympathetic because they are presented more in the pastoral tradition, as defined by such 20th century critics as William Empson, than in the Hebraic-Christian tradition.

Faulkner's one allegorical book A Fable, is unique among the novels in that it follows Biblical allusions with some degree of exactness. Consequently the important characters, the ones who re-enact the story of Passion Week, are unrealized artistically.

This dissertation proposes, then, that Faulkner used allusions from the King James Bible to a greater or lesser extent in all his novels. The predominant Scriptural pattern is that of the patriarch who bequeaths a patrimony, usually one which requires a sacrifice, to his descendants. Only in A Fable, however, does Faulkner follow Biblical patterns exactly. A study of the novels shows that Faulkner's usual method of composition--imagination--Biblical pattern--pattern changed to fit imagination, was for him the road to literary artistry. [Order No. 71-24,375; 235 pages. DAI, 32A (Sept.-Oct. 1971), 1506.]

202 The Quest for Sacred Space: Setting in the Novels of William Faulkner / Edward L. CORRIDORI, Kent State University, 1971 (Thomas F. Marshall).

Critics have often focused attention on the "realistic" aspects of William Faulkner's Yoknapatawpha setting, noting that his mythical county tends to mirror the actual county of Lafayette, Mississippi. However, the conscious artistry with which Faulkner employs his native materials reveals a much deeper kind of "realism" in his work. For Faulkner, the setting, or element of space, becomes an instrument of meaning, a structural and thematic device in his novels. He uses the setting as a framework for his complex narratives; he incorporates the setting into the patterns of imagery which predominate in his style; he exploits the setting for its symbolic value within the work; and he employs the setting to evoke certain archetypes and suggestions of myth. This utilization of the element of space indicates a level of conscious artistry for which Faulkner is not always given credit. Moreover, this emphasis on setting suggests the importance of its role in Faulkner's vision.

This deliberate stress on the setting reveals a significant Faulknerian theme underlying much of the fiction. This theme, which may be termed a "quest for sacred space," is the portrayal of the individual's struggle to make an apparently meaningless world meaningful. It expresses itself in the individual's attempt to find, create, build, or hold on to some particular sacred place. This "sacred space" is analogous to T. S. Eliot's "still point" in that it is a space, qualitatively different from other space, that provides a contact point with the deity or some transcendent order of being. As such, it provides a point of orientation and a center of value in an otherwise chaotic world. In religious terms, the sacred space sanctifies the world making it holy, or meaningful and real. It is "real" in the sense that it opposes the unreality or formlessness or uncreatedness of chaos. Thus, Faulkner's work may be termed "religious," using that term in its broadest and, perhaps, most fundamental sense. His work explores the relationship between man and the cosmos he inhabits. The struggle for a sacred space, a struggle for orientation or faith in an external order, is a religious struggle.

The quest for a sacred space is a consistent theme in Faulkner's work. Characters like Ike McCaslin and Lucas Beauchamp sacrifice everything they possess in order to retain that space which is sacred to them. Horace Benbow searches desperately for a similar center of value. The Compsons, cut off from contact with the sacred earth, suffer bitter alienation and dissolution. Thomas Sutpen goes through the motions of sanctifying his mansion, but his own spiritual emptiness dooms it to be a sterile and hollow temple. And Flem Snopes, who personifies an amoral rapacity, usurps the sacred space for his own profane ends, only to have the earth exact its retribution from him. In each of these stories, Faulkner stresses man's need for a sacred space, a still point in which contact with a transcendent order of being is possible. Through this experience of the sacred space, man is able to perceive his proper relationship with the natural world and with his fellow man. That is, by virtue of contact with the sacred space, man comes to understand the order of creation. Without his experience, as so many of Faulkner's characters testify, orientation is impossible and man faces the social and personal consequences of a chaotic existence.

In creating Yoknapatawpha County, Faulkner was establishing his own sacred space. Hence, the "realism" of his work can be seen as something far deeper than the resemblance of his mythical county to any actual geographic locale. It is real because it is founded on a deep-seated and enduring faith in the act of creation. It ritualizes the creation and is, therefore, a cosmos, a sacred space. This is the meaning of Faulkner's continual recourse to his mythic soil. In an era in which man is beset by alienation, uprooted from his proper attachment to the earth and its natural cycles, and severed from any meaningful contact with his Creator, Faulkner sought, through the ritual of his art, to restore man's rightful relationship to the cosmos. By providing the reader with a sacred space, a repository and citadel of the values and traditions which make life real (Faulkner called them the "old verities of the heart"), Faulkner sought, in his own way, to restore order to the chaos of modern times. [Order No. 72-9251; 173 pages. DAI, 34A (March-April 1972), 5224.]

203 William Faulkner, V. K. Ratliff, and the Snopes Saga (1925-1940) /
Roger Lewis DAVIS, University of California at Los Angeles, 1971 (Philip C. Durham).

Most critics generally understand Faulkner through his tragic heroes, the ones unable to cope with themselves, their environment, and other people. Those who seek affirmation in Faulkner tend either to infer the positive from these negative examples on the basis of Faulkner's public statements, Nobel Prize speech, and interviews or they look to Faulkner's primitives--idiots, children, Indians, Negroes--and to Ike McCaslin who merely repudiates and does not affirm. These misdirections have led to more misinterpretations of Faulkner than perhaps any other single factor.

Faulkner's most positive character, the only character in the works themselves to approach the kind of affirmation common in Faulkner's public statements--V. K. Ratliff--has been almost universally either misunderstood or overlooked. Faulkner everywhere stated that he was not writing about history, sociology, or ideas but about people. He has said that it was V. K. Ratliff, along with Dilsey, he liked best in all of his own work, and further remarked that he was all along writing for those "some, not necessarily many, who do and will continue to read Faulkner and say 'Yes. It's all right. I'd rather be Ratliff than Flem Snopes. And I'd still rather be Ratliff without any Snopes to measure by even.'" What Faulkner does affirm cannot be truly appreciated other than by fully understanding his most positive character.

Examination of the unpublished Faulkner manuscripts and typescripts on deposit at the University of Virginia Alderman Library reveals that the Ratliff character (originally called Suratt) had been conceived contemporaneously with the Snopes clan as part of the same story and that Flem Snopes never appears in any work which does not include Ratliff. Thus far, criticism has largely lacked either the will or the opportunity to thoroughly investigate the unpublished material and has totally missed the central structural and thematic role that the Ratliff character played in the genesis of the Snopes saga and in the fusion of its early pieces into The Hamlet. By taking these factors fully into account an entirely different picture of the genesis and development of the Snopes saga (in fact, of Yoknapatawpha) emerges than has always been assumed from the published short stories and novels alone. By focusing heavily on Ratliff as a starting point an entirely new critical perspecive is also achieved which renders more consistent and plausible interpretations of the individual short stories (1925-1939), their incorporation into The Hamlet (1940), and The Hamlet itself. Almost inevitably a rather unique picture emerges of the developing mind and craft of William Faulkner as he struggled with the same material in a variety of forms over a 15 year period. [Order No. 72-1472; 363 pages. DAI, 32A (Nov.-Dec. 1971), 3300.]

204 Christian Historical Analogues in the Fiction of William Faulkner and Flannery O'Connor / John Francis DESMOND, University of Oklahoma, 1971 (Victor A. Elconin).

The Christian vision of history has traditionally been identified as an integral part of Southern fiction. This study is an analysis of the Christian conception of history as an analogical dimension in Southern fiction, particularly in the works of William Faulkner and Flannery O'Connor. Two fundamental problems are treated: (1) how a Christian conception of history is used typologically in their fiction; and (2) how this conception of history is rendered dramatic through their fictional techniques. The underlying premise of this study is that these problems are one and indivisible--that is, that the typological use of a Christian conception of history by these writers, rather than evoking Christian history simply as mythic background, constitutes a fictional act of continuing revelation from a Christian standpoint. In short, this study asserts that the imaginative and creative rendering of history by these two writers is both formally and thematically incarnational--and as such rooted in a historical incarnation.

This study initially describes some central themes in the Christian conception of history used analogically by these writers. It begins by discussing the typological relationship between classical mythology, Old Testament and New Testament revelation. Certain basic themes in the Christian incarnational vision of history are elucidated. They are: the redemptive conception of history; the belief in mystery; the incarnational view of spirit and matter; the word and the act; the theme of time and eternity; the concept of place; the theme of spiritual motion; and the theme of community. Following this, the negative counterparts of these same themes are elucidated: the contemporary assault on mystery; the erosion of historical sense; and the themes of displacement, dissociation, and immunity.

Having outlined the basic themes of the Christian historical vision, the study then analyzes manifestations of this vision within the American historical framework, in particular, the Providential design of Puritan New England, the post-Civil War "fallen" world of the South, and in contrast the modern anti-Christian temperament both within and without the South.

The study then proceeds to analyze the formal problems of how a Christian historical sense actually works within the creative act to dramatically bring that vision to life. Relationships are drawn between the metaphysical principle of the analogy of being and the operation of the historical sense within the creative act, so that a fundamental unity is seen to exist between the author's conception of history, certain formal techniques of typology used by the author, and an "incarnational" sensibility which brings history "to life" in the work.

Finally, the Christian historical analogues are examined specifically in the major works of these two writers. Works by Faulkner examined are: "The Bear," Absalom, Absalom!, Light in August, The Sound and the Fury, and A Fable. Most of Miss O'Connor's complete canon of novels and short stories is examined in detail. [Order No. 72-3384; 196 pages. DAI, 32A (Jan.-Feb. 1972), 3994-95.]

205 The Grotesque in the Fiction of William Faulkner / Robert Clark FERGUSON, Case Western Reserve University, 1971 (George Kummer).

The term grotesque has been variously defined and applied throughout modern literary criticism. Frequently it is used merely to designate anything bizarre, outlandish, or distorted. However, some scholars like Wolfgang Kayser, Lee Byron Jennings, Warren Beck, Lewis Lawson, and William Van O'Connor have gone further in actually defining the term and analyzing its function as an indicator of the writer's attitudes toward life and the changing world. With an indebtedness to these men, the grotesque as defined in this study is viewed as a hybrid mode of characterization in which there is a mingling of various degrees and proportions of the comic and serious ranging from the humorously horrible or tragicomic to the comically grave and sober. The dominant effect of horror or comedy depends on the proportions of each in mixtures of the fearsome and ludicrous, humorous and terrible, clownish and solemn; but always the combination arouses mixed reactions of fear and amusement, laughter and pain in the observer.

In light of this definition, the present study distinguishes two major kinds of grotesque in Faulkner's writing and analyzes their functional relationship to his essentially optimistic philosophy of man. The first type, the noble grotesque, enables Faulkner both to dramatize man's moral struggle against impossible odds and to attack the dehumanizing influence of middle-class values and sensibilities. The second type, the ignoble grotesque, used merely for atmosphere, shock, or sensation, develops from the writer's whimsy rather than from any serious moral or social commitment. It engages the reader only on an emotional level of fright or amusement.

The dominance of the noble grotesque in Faulkner's writing is ample testimony to his prevailing belief in man. Such characters as Quentin Compson, Joe Christmas, Emily Grierson, Anse Bundren, Mink Snopes, and Lucius Priest reveal in either largely comic or tragic grotesqueness the striving spirit of man in the persistent struggle for fulfillment in life. Optimism is also pronounced in the gradual mellowing and eventual disappearance in the later works of fearsome grotesqueness used to criticize modern society. In particular, the consuming threat of Snopeses' materialism is diminished in The Town and The Mansion by Faulkner's rendering both Flem and the lesser Snopeses as genial grotesques. By the time Faulkner had come to believe in the doctrine of motion, he was able to accept Snopesian evil as simply a part of change and alteration in the course of human events.

Further evidence of Faulkner's optimism is indicated by the noticeable increase in geniality in the grotesques, both noble and ignoble, after The Wild Palms. The shift reveals that Faulkner, at this stage in his career, felt compelled to state his philosophy of man in unequivocally affirmative terms. Gavin Stevens, Mink Snopes, and Lucius Priest are more comical than despairing in their strivings. Even such ignoble grotesques as Eula Varner, Miss Reba, the McCaslin twins, and Butch Lovemaiden inspire more delight than terror. [Order No. 71-22,800; 174 pages. DAI, 32A (Sept.-Oct. 1971), 1508.]

    206 The Mystery of Significance and the Enigma of Time: An Analysis of the Thematic Structures of Faulkner's The Sound and the Fury and Claude Simon's L'Herbe / Diane Leonard HINKLE, University of North Carolina, 1971 (Eugene H. Falk) no DAI entry.

    207 William Faulkner and Claude Simon: A Stylistic Study / Monique Raymonde HYDE, Indiana University, 1971 (Robert Champigny).
    This study attempts to examine in detail the similarities between the styles of Faulkner and Simon by closely comparing and analyzing extracts from their works. The first chapter deals with the structure of the sentence. The two writers make a consistent use of the following devices: coordination rather than subordination, appositions, absolute constructions, anacoluthon, unconventional punctuation, parentheses, extended comparisons, and reflections. The result is a sentence which is loosely constructed, linear, juxtapositional, protracted, and stylistically ambiguous.
    The second chapter analyzes the components of the sentence, the parts of speech preferred by Faulkner and Simon. A massive stylistic effect is obtained through the heavy use of clusters of nouns, verbs, and adjectives, and through the technique of redundancy, which involves repetitions, pleonasms, alliterations, and enumerations. The result is accumulation.
    The other components of the sentence can be classified under the headings of approximation and immobilization. Approximation makes use of grammatical terms which weaken or cancel a suggestion by introducing an alternate, complementary, or opposite suggestion. Conjectural terms and alternative suggestions express doubt, hypothesis, and inconclusiveness. Negative terms describe the object by suggesting its positive qualities through the evocation of its negative characteristics.
    The use of approximation shows a desire to shy away from a direct description of the object. It stems from two sources: the reconstitution of past events by narrators relying on hearsay, memory, and imagination; and the desire to suggest the ineffable character of what they attempt to describe.
    The parts of speech which contribute to immobilization are the present participle and substantive heavily used by both novelists, whose style is nominal rather than verbal. Present participles, having no temporal value in themselves, detemporalize the event by obliterating the sense of temporal sequence. Substantives, especially when used to describe violent actions, play a similar role.
    The function of the noun and the present participle is to "essentialize" the process of becoming by arresting activity at certain points. We find numerous examples of Faulkner and Simon of "frozen moments" and of the immobilization of actions into tableaux, stemming from a desire to halt the destructive process of time. [Order No. 72-12,959; 211 pages. DAI, 32A (March-April 1972), 5740-41.]

    208 Silence and the Impeccable Language: A Study of William Faulkner's Philosophy of Language / Paul Ramond LILLY, Jr., Fordham University, 1971 (Richard Giannone).
    Faulkner's best fiction dramatizes the phenomenon of language, and this study will attempt to extrapolate a philosophy of language from certain of his most linguistically complex novels. The Sound and the Fury, As I Lay Dying, and Absalom, Absalom! are informed by a paradoxical attitude toward verbal language as a medium of art, and this sense of paradox stems from

Faulkner's desire to achieve the timelessness of art by means of the transient medium of language. In Faulkner's mind, the poet alone is capable of resolving the paradox. The poet, he says, speaks an "absolutely impeccable" language. What the poet says is eternal, because his language is.

Faulkner's notion of poetry as an absolutely perfect art-language is an index to his philosophy of language. His earliest efforts with verse display a deepening interest in achieving the illusion that the actual words on the page hint at a purer, wordless language beyond the edges of the actual poem.

Soldiers' Pay and Mosquitoes, the subject of the first two chapters of this study, represent Faulkner's attempts in prose to dramatize the paradox of art-language. Both books articulate assumptions about language that later on give life to his best novels--issues like the virginity of language, virgin speakers who are poets, the tension between language and silence, and the struggle of the verbal artist with his medium.

The Sound and the Fury, As I Lay Dying, and Absalom, Absalom!-- analyzed in the last three chapters of this study--address themselves to the special problem of the verbal artist confronting the medium of words. Quentin, Addie, Darl, and Rosa are the speaker-poets of these novels. They represent variations of the verbal maker caught up in the crises of creation. Each is obsessed by the word "virginity" and by the virginity of the word. Challenged by the transience of language, they demand a pure, impeccable language, one free from the pecca of accumulated and changeable meanings. They are moral and linguistic absolutists, and their quests for the impeccable language of silence are failures. But their failures are also poetic utterances and these utterances probe the paradox of Faulkner's art.

Quentin and the other speaker-poets articulate Faulkner's faith in and deep skepticism of the creative energy of the word, his conviction that a literary artifice is equally timeless and transient, his reverence for the vitality of the actual word and for the hypothetical purity of silence, his belief that the word in the act of utterance is both a symbol of process and a mode of escape from the consequences of process. If Faulkner's philosophy of language is a paradox, it is because he sees paradox in the behavior of words and as a condition of the experience language expresses. [Order No. 71-20,178; 221 pages. DAI, 32A (July-Aug. 1971), 973.]

209 Faulkner Studies in France: 1953-1969 / Peter Landers MAKUCK, Kent State University, 1971 (Howard P. Vincent).

In the mid-1940s, William Faulkner's works were nearly out of print in the United States; few Americans recognized his genius. In France, however, Faulkner's reputation was reaching its peak. His rise to literary fame there began in 1933 with the translation of Sanctuary prefaced by André Malraux. From 1933 until the outbreak of war in 1939, each year there appeared a new translation of one of Faulkner's novels, followed largely by a wave of favorable criticism. Although no new novels were published from 1939 to 1946 because of German suppression, the French immediately following the war resumed translation of Faulkner's novels and short stories. Numerous critical studies again appeared. When Faulkner won the Nobel Prize in 1950, the French began to boast that they had discovered him.

There are only two books which attempt to survey the critical writing on Faulkner in France: one is by Ward Miner and Thelma Smith and entitled The Transatlantic Migration; the other, written in French, is William Faulkner en France: 1931-1952 by Stanley Woodworth. Both books selectively describe the trends of criticism to 1952. Since 1952, however, eight more of Faulkner's novels have been translated and published in France: Absalom, Absalom! (1953), Go Down, Moses (1955), Requiem for a Nun (1956), A Fable (1958), The Hamlet (1959), The Town (1962), The Mansion (1962), and The Reivers (1964). The chapters of my dissertation are determined by the focus of post-1952 criticism which is on As I Lay Dying (the only pre-1952 novel published in France to hold a major interest for the French), Absalom, Absalom!, Go Down, Moses, Intruder in the Dust, and Requiem for a Nun. Material which cannot properly constitute a chapter is briefly discussed in the conclusion.

Since 1952, Faulkner studies have been to a certain extent a reaction to and a qualification of the early essays written by Sartre, Coindreau, Malraux, and Mme Magny. However, unlike the critics of the 30s and 40s who were largely concerned with "la métaphysique faulknérienne," the critics of the 50s and 60s have combined an interest in Faulkner's techniques and metaphysics with an interest in the social and political problems of the South. In many cases, these critics attack Faulkner's politics and see his notion of history as antithetical to social progress. Still another group of critics contributes original absorbing essays which deal with Faulkner's imagery. But perhaps the most enlightening criticism of this period is in the realm of comparative study where Faulkner is examined in light of Dostoevsky, Camus, Proust, Balzac, Beckett, Robbe-Grillet, and the new novelists.

Stanley Woodworth stops his survey at 1952 because the years following, he says, "ne vont pas ajouter grand-chose à l'image qui est déjà dessinée." Perhaps Woodworth is right in saying that the years following would add little to Faulkner's already-established image, but surely, in the 17 years since, the quality and maturity of French criticism has increased appreciably. The important early voices of Sartre, Malraux, Mme Magny, and Le Breton have been replaced by those of Weisgerber, Gresset, Bleikasten, and Mme Nathan. In view of their pioneer articles, the range and depth of their understanding of his work, the French can claim to have discovered Faulkner and to have played an important role in establishing his literary reputation. Though Faulkner studies in the United States matured rapidly in the 1950s, a statement made by Michel Butor after Faulkner's death is not without some validity: "Son pays a mis long temps à le comprendre." [Order No. 71-30, 515; 263 pages. DAI, 32A (Nov.-Dec. 1971); 3314.]

210 Syntactic Features of William Faulkner's Narrative Style / Norma Lee MEYER, University of Nebraska, 1971 (Curtis W. Hayes).

Although much has been said regarding William Faulkner's style, very little has been done in the way of technical analysis. This is because (1) improved methods for analysis have only recently been made available, and (2) critical comments have been largely impressionistic and frequently negative. This study provides a survey of such comments as well as of developments in modern stylistics.

The study itself is devoted to application of techniques of generative-transformational grammar to textual samples from Light in August, Absalom, Absalom!, and A Fable in an effort to determine the syntactic choices underlying the "full" style. Samples were limited to omniscient-author narration in order to eliminate, as much as possible, the influence of fictional circumstances (such as the representation of dialogue or of abnormal mental states). Syntactic features were considered a central element of any style, remaining much the same from book to book and helping to make the style readily recognizable as that particular author's.

It was determined that the syntactic aspects of the style could best be described by the oxymoron "condensed-expansion." The techniques developed by Faulkner for sentence expansion can be applied almost indefinitely, and yet the structures added are largely reduced forms. Noun compounding, parallel, embedding, multiple coordination of constituent elements, and reduced relative embedding all contribute to a condensed style, while a strong reliance upon post-position of participle phrases, absolutes, appositives, and subordinate clauses as well as object clauses and chained-embedding allows successive "appendages" to follow the sentence matrix, which is most often kept basic in form. Structural complexity is thus avoided even though each sentence is packed with information. In the sense of maximum information carried by a minimum of structural framework, the style is highly economical.

Extended noun phrases and non-finite verbal phrases are responsible for a large amount of sentence length, resulting in a highly verbal nominal style. The abundance of information, the techniques for structural continuity, and the structural overlapping contribute to making the style multi-impressionistic in effect. Because nominalization, conjunction, and right-branch embedding--all central elements of the style--are natural tendencies in English, it was suggested that Faulkner succeeded in stretching the language into new accomplishments because he was stretching "with the grain" structurally. [Order No. 72-16,003; 196 pages. DAI, 32A (May-June 1972), 6406.]

211 William Faulkner's Trilogy / Nancy Rife NORRIS, University of Pennsylvania, 1971 (Daniel Hoffman).

Most criticism of William Faulkner's trilogy--The Hamlet, The Town, and The Mansion--has been restricted to the sociological and moral implications of the legendary rise and demise of Flem Snopes. In the only chapter in which I discuss this level of the action, I suggest that a three-volume "chronicle" allowed Faulkner to develop, more fully than had been possible in his novel-length works, the complex psychological motivation for, and the consequences of, revenge on a ruthless man who betrayed his kin to further his career. Flem's own consciousness is not portrayed; the moral changes during the course of three volumes occur within V. K. Ratliff, Gavin Stevens, and Chick Mallison, who, in narrating the legend of the Snopeses, learn to cope with the quality of "Snopes" in themselves.

As in Absalom, Absalom!, the moral theme provided only the outer structure within which Faulkner rendered the "Orestean" theme of incestuous wishes, murderous aggressive feelings, and the resultant anxiety about psychotic breakdown. It is these psychological "events" of the trilogy to which I devote most attention.

Although the revenges of Linda Snopes Kohl and Mink Snopes upon their kinsman Flem involve their complex associations to him as a father figure, the more intense fantasies of the trilogy concern a mother and sister figure. In fact, parallels between the unpublished manuscript of "Father Abraham" (the earliest extant evidence of Faulkner's work on the trilogy) and Quentin's section in The Sound and the Fury lead me to conjecture that Faulkner's anxiety about the psychological theme contributed to his 34-year delay in completing the trilogy, some of its structural weaknesses, and the displacement of Jody Varner's feelings about his sister Eula to the fantasies of Labove, Ratliff, and Gavin.

Since it was Eula who committed suicide, and since none of her feelings were directly expressed, her suicide seems, on one level of narrative fantasy, a displacement for the disintegration of Labove, Ratliff, or Gavin. On still another level, it represents the need to "kill off" their source of anguish. Yet Eula seems more credibly characterized than has been generally recognized as the kind of mother who would have sacrificed herself for the sake of her daughter, as well as the kind of daughter who would have turned the anger at her father in upon herself.

It is my hypothesis that ultimately the trilogy's themes of sex and aggression are not separate, but rather different levels of Faulkner's "one story." The narrators' panic about the Snopeses seems out of proportion to their actual evil because the Snopeses' literal acting-out of the impulse of greed functioned as a narrative displacement for the sense of being overwhelmed by "forbidden" incestuous and sadomasochistic impulses.

It is through the significance of sexual symbols like the horse and cow, repeated words and images, patterns of association in the episodic structure, and character displacements that I attempt to analyze the dark and complex theme at the heart of the trilogy. [Order No. 72-17,406; 171 pages. DAI, 32A (May-June 1972), 6994.]

212 The Signboard for New Hope: Faulkner's As I Lay Dying / Charles Arthur PEEK, University of Nebraska, 1971 (Lee T. Lemon).

Death has been a subject of major interest for the last three-quarters of a century; witness the number of titles of books in religion, culture, and literature that suggest this theme. Ironically this makes our age much like those "darker" ages which lived under the death's head that they had created. But what does someone make of death who considers man indestructible? If he begs the question, he is not artist, no thinker. (Kierkegaard tells the story of a philsopher who spent his life constructing proofs of immortality but was afraid to die.) If he is an artist, then death with all its finality must be a reality, must be an end of something. And, since even Socrates was a mortal (as the logicians remind us), it is an end of something for all of us... we all lay dying. What that is like is the subject of Faulkner's novel; and what this dissertation tries to do is to suggest, on the basis of many factors (Faulkner's relationship to the thought currents of his day, the novel's relationship to its historical tradition, and the relationship of image and theme to their source), how the novel might best be read. In addition, it offers "readings" of the novel as it has been read in the past and an annotated bibliography of the extant criticism on the novel. [Order No. 72-3074; 186 pages. DAI, 32A (Jan.-Feb. 1972), 4015.]

213 The Ritual of Survival: Landscape in Conrad and Faulkner / Richard Philip PINDELL, Yale University, 1971 (Martin Price).

Conrad finds in "the immensity" and Faulkner finds in the earth a working version of that unlimited deity which is necessary to man's survival of a hostile, unpredictable world in full possession of his humanity. The search for the perfect interlocutor ends in a landscape whose magnitude and energies repeatedly require man's appraisal of his inwardness. In a fundamentally experimental art the landscape is both the reflector and the reserve of various modes of accommodation. It serves to embody the whole which is at once the actual and potential sum of human experience and an ideal composite self which presides over the effort to construct a place to realize that self. Against such a whole Conrad and Faulkner test their alternative selves as they are embodied in their characters. The latter mediate between the author and the whole, to which at some point they are sacrificed. The author's bold manipulation and frequent destruction of his characters to create a space where knowledge can occur present him as a type of that genius loci most visible in his work as a passage figure. Acting as a medium of self-entry, landscape acquires an important expressive function that both explains and vindicates the failure of the language. The collapse of noetic frames and the elusiveness of any firm symbolic scheme draw the reader into a creative partnership with the author, who himself models the protagonist best able to cope with crisis. [Order No. 71-31,095; 265 pages. DAI, 32A (Nov.-Dec. 1971), 3324.]

214 A Textual and Critical Study of William Faulkner's Requiem for a Nun / Noel Earl POLK, University of South Carolina, 1971 (James B. Meriwether).

It is the central thesis of this study that Temple Drake Stevens, rather than Nancy Mannigoe, is the moral center of Requiem for a Nun. She is the admirable figure in the novel, since it is she alone who chooses to face bravely the anxieties of life, consciously accepting the responsibility for her sins. Quite opposed to her are Gavin Stevens and Nancy Mannigoe, who are established as idealists who have retreated into abstraction in order to escape the need for moral deliberation and choice; their intense idealism separates them from human suffering, from the realities of life, and they are therefore void of any form of compassion or pity. The civilization which is seen developing in the historical prologues is not to be construed as the unnecessary wasting away of individual freedom, but as the inevitable forward motion of time, which is life. The complexities of civilization--of living in the present with full consciousness of the past--thus become a metaphor for the human burdens of guilt and anxiety, which Temple, but not Nancy, chooses to bear.

The method of this study is an act-by-act analysis and explication of the text. It draws upon the Requiem manuscript and typescript material now in the Faulkner archive in the Alderman Library at the University of Virginia. The dissertation also includes a textual appendix, which presents a table of variants based upon a collation of the typescript setting copy with the first printing, which restores many of Faulkner's original readings that were editorially altered. These tables, in effect make Requiem for a Nun available as Faulkner wrote it. The study concludes with an annotated checklist of criticism of the novel. [Order No. 71-21,851; 325 pages. DAI, 32A (July-Aug. 1971), 980.]

215 Coordinate Structure in Four Faulkner Novels / William Currie
RAMSEY, University of North Carolina at Chapel Hill, 1971 (Weldon Thornton).

Discussions of the structures of Faulkner's novels reveal considerable scepticism and much vague praise from critics. A few excellent studies exist, but they lack a systematic conceptual framework that would relate the works to one another and relate the whole corpus to fictive traditions. "Coordinate structure" can supply the basis for such a framework.

The concept of coordinate structure is partly a derivation from that simplification of Eugene C. Falk's Types of Thematic Structure: The Nature and Function of Motives in Gide, Camus, and Sartre (Chicago, 1967). Falk analyzes at length the significant linking, by juxtaposition, leitmotif, or "material similarity," of major motifs whose thematic implications substantially modify or supplement one another. Patterns of parallel and contrast create interpretive contexts, embedded in the narrative, by which events and characters must be judged.

Faulkner parts from the subjects of Falk's study by quite openly letting thematic structure supplant plot, rather than merely supplement it. The Sound and the Fury, as Sartre observed, does not try to tell a story. Instead it tells four stories, whose narrators and subjects are quite distinct. Four different orientations toward life delineate themselves in their appropriate, respective settings. Such major motifs as journeys, and almost innumerable minor coordinations signalled by leitmotifs, point out elaborate patterns of comparison and contrast. Each major character is finally measured against his fellows and against his own words and actions.

The Hamlet, from its consistent third-person perspective, presents a fuller range of human attitudes and obsessions. The protagonists of its various episodes range themselves along a scale whose extremes are Ike and Flem Snopes, representing selfless love and loveless self-interest, respectively. As a whole, The Hamlet approaches the novel of manners, ruthlessly analyzing the values and institutions of an irresponsible community. Leitmotif is used more subtly than in The Sound and the Fury, and coordination is more often signalled by material similarity or simple juxtaposition of motifs.

The Unvanquished comes closer than the aforementioned books to a consecutive narrative, but there is a sharp discrepancy between the narrator's pessimistic tone and the overtly optimistic pattern of events. Coordinating analysis resolves the problem by reading the book as a sympathetic but unreliable confession. Finding only a personal solution to a community problem, the narrator senses but never understands the dimensions of his weakness.

The Wild Palms goes farthest of all, juxtaposing by alternation of chapters two outwardly self-contained novelettes. Previous studies have found many parallels but no convincing rationale for this structure. Coordinate analysis reveals that the two stories constitute plot and subplot of one design, developing themes in a sequence that is lost if the stories are read separately.

These books represent the range of Faulkner's achievements. The coordinate method applied to them does not displace other approaches, but alternately supports and modifies existing interpretations. It also makes clear Faulkner's links to the past. His use of leitmotif resembles the use of fire imagery in the Iliad. Innumerable writers, from Augustine to Aldous Huxley, have founded structures upon parallel and contrasted motifs. In sum, Faulkner must be considered one more of the major experimenters who receive and skillfully modify important traditions. [Order No. 72-18,444; 223 pages. DAI, 33A (July-Aug. 1972), 283-84.]

216 A Chronology of William Faulkner's Yoknapatawpha County / Richard Allen REED, Emory University, 1971 (Floyd C. Watkins).

Within the 13 books and more than 50 stories in which William Faulkner developed the history of Yoknapatawpha County, there is a broad sweep of time that spans the years from 1699 to 1961. Although the works cover many generations with a basic chronological consistency, the time system of the fiction is always complex and often inconsistent. In some places Faulkner is intensely concerned with dates, and in others he provides no dates at all; time is treated specifically at one place and then only generally at another; distinctions between past and present are sometimes blurred; there are conflicting dates for single events; and there are bewildering inconsistencies in otherwise well-ordered schemes of ages, dates, and times. Such complexity and inconsistency were caused by Faulkner's forgetfulness, his disdain of factual detail, his concept of time, his deliberate attempts to complicate chronology, his manner of composing and publishing the fiction, his re-use of characters and events, and his dynamic conception of this apocryphal county and its people. First recognized by Faulkner himself, the chronological difficulties posed by that Yoknapatawpha fiction have received an increasing amount of critical attention; however, all of the studies published to date consist either of random observations on miscellaneous dates or of restricted studies dealing with the particular problems of individual works. What is attempted in this dissertation is a study that conveys the whole of the Yoknapatawpha chronicle, its inconsistencies as well as its essential unity. The numerous problems in chronology preclude the existence of a single, consistent, unified chronology, but it is this very impossibility that makes a chronology so desirable and so necessary. A sound sense of the time systems in all the works is essential to comprehending the totality, the complexity, and the artistry of the Yoknapatawpha chronicle. [Order No. 71-27,793; 372 pages. DAI, 32A (Sept.-Oct. 1971), 2101.]

217 The Role of the Negro in William Faulkner's Public and Private Worlds / Evalyne Carter ROBINSON, Ohio State University, 1971 (Wilfred Eberhart).

As a historical inquiry concerned specifically with Faulkner's delineation and depiction of the Negro, the central purpose is to explicate further those aspects of Faulkner's life important to his literary career by considering the significance of that data to his response to the Negro, individually and as a race, in the factual and fictional worlds of which he was a part.

The discussion has been limited by three general stages of Faulkner's career: (1) the period of apprenticeship (1924-1929); (2) the "time of genius" (1929-1936); and (3) the period of consolidation and affirmation (1940-1962). Accordingly, three groups of Faulkner's works of varied chronology and genre have been considered and cited, and concentrated and final emphasis has been directed to those works in which Negro characters and themes of racial conflict are proportionately important.

Chapter II presents a rationale for a reading of Faulkner's fiction appropriate to this study and for establishing the validity of the relationship of Faulkner's public and private worlds. Yoknapatawpha County is introduced, and its social classes, myths, and themes are reviewed. Chapters III and IV include a discussion of the place of Negroes in Southern life and their functions in Faulkner's fiction as they are employed in their several relationships to the South and to other ethnic groups--as moral and social catalysts, as important elements in the development of Faulkner's moral perspective, and as a means toward a more universal statement regarding the South. Chapters V and VI include a synthesis of the study and the conclusions.

The findings of this study warrant the general conclusion that although Faulkner's moral view of the Negro varied at different age levels and career stages, and his efforts to characterize the Negro were reflected in an uneven progression, there is a continuity in his rational speculation of the Southern "condition" manifest in his early and later works, as well as in the relationship of this speculation and the philosophical and religious representations that form the foundation for the speculation. [Order No. 71-27,547; 320 pages. DAI, 32A (Nov.-Dec. 1971), 2704.]

218 The Family in the Novels of Wharton, Faulkner, Cather, Lewis, and Dreiser / Frank Wilsey SHELTON, University of North Carolina at Chapel Hill, 1971 (C. Hugh Holman).

Although the family was a very important institution to the initial settlers of America, early American fiction did not emphasize how central it was to the life of the individual. Only with the rise of the realists in the latter half of the 19th century did the family as a social entity begin to play an important role in American fiction. 20th century novelists have continued this concern for the family, but their work reflects the fact that, as the country has moved from being predominantly rural to urban in nature, the family as an institution has weakened.

The five novelists dealt with are treated thematically, with the aim of discovering how they regard and employ the institution of family in their fiction. Selected representative novels of each are analyzed in detail to determine the novelists' view of the relationship between modern society and the condition of the family. Each author concentrates on a different segment of society, and taken together they provide a wide diversity of backgrounds. Edith Wharton and William Faulkner deal with traditional, highly organized societies, and though their geographical settings are different, family is central to these societies and thus important to their novels. Much of Willa Cather's work focuses on pioneers of various kinds who attack great importance to family. Sinclair Lewis deals with the small town or small city, and family is often depicted as one of the important aspects of social life there. Theodore Dreiser concentrates on city life, and in his work can be seen most clearly the effect of the urban environment on family.

An analysis of the fiction of these writers reveals that all regard close family ties as characteristic of American life of the past, and that they see the weakening of the family to be one of the characteristic elements of modern life which contributes to the isolation and alienation of the individual. Each novelist to some extent writes against the background of a remembered past, and though they recognize that the family can be restrictive, they see its weakening as having a detrimental effect on the individual. The mother is generally viewed as the center of the family and the determining factor in its degree of stability, and each writer concentrates heavily on the effect of the family on the children, who are the characters most in need of its support. Beneath the diversity of their subject matter, approach, and technique, these novelists maintain strikingly similar ideals. Though most of the novels discussed emphasize the dissolution of the family and the consequent helplessness of the individual, all five writers regard the family as one possible source of that human contact and communal life which they feel is lacking in modern society, and yet is necessary to the individual's well-being. [Order No. 72-10,771; 384 pages. DAI, 32A (March-April 1972), 5244.]

219 A Study of Tensiveness in Selected Novels of William Faulkner / Myron Duane WEYBRIGHT, Northwestern University, 1971 (Lillia A. Heston).

This study analyzed "tensiveness" in As I Lay Dying, Light in August, and The Hamlet by William Faulkner. Terms were defined in Chapter One and novels analyzed individually in Chapters Two, Three and Four. A summary was presented in Chapter Five. Tensiveness was defined as the pull between opposing forces created by conflicts, strains, resistances, and expanding associations in a novel. The analysis investigated tensions developed in the narration, within and between characters, and in the plots of these novels.

In As I Lay Dying, tensions arise from the conflicting perspective of events, the paradoxical union of stillness and motion, and the strain between language styles within the narrative accounts of the 15 character-narrators. Tensiveness is also produced in the narrative of Light in August by language which develops conflicts between levels of thought within characters and through contrasting narrative perspectives of character and event. Present-tense passages depicting important changes within Bunch, Christmas, and Hightower suggest the narrator's approval of characters who can live in the immediate moment free from negative restrictions of the past. Major tensions in The Hamlet caused by differing perspectives of character and event were found within Ratliff as his understanding of Flem Snopes changes throughout the novel. The tensive qualities of language employed in the Isaac Snopes and the spotted-horses episodes demonstrate Isaac's unique perception and the tensiveness of arrested motion in the horses.

The richest source of tensiveness was found in the tensions within and between characters. A central tensiveness in As I Lay Dying is created by conflicts within and between the Bundrens as they struggle to adjust to Addie's death and burial journey. Tensions in characters outside the family are created by conflicts between their urge to assist the Bundrens and their criticism of the family. Tensiveness within and between characters in Light in August develops from conflicting responses to Lena Grove and Joe Christmas. Tensions within Bunch and Hightower lead Bunch to responsive participation in life and Hightower to avoid involvement. Tensions within Christmas develop from his conflicting attitudes toward religion, women, and the mixed blood he believes he possesses. Many of the tensions within and between characters in The Hamlet are initiated by Flem Snopes and Eula Varner. Flem is successful because he creates within Varner, Ratliff, and the peasants enfeebling tensions which destroy their ability to resist his schemes and they are defeated by Snopes. Eula inspires enormous desire and lust but her oblivion to the passion she evokes drives those who approach her to madness and frustration.

Finally, the analysis revealed tensiveness arising from the plots of these novels. Tensions are formed in As I Lay Dying by a tensive blend of comic and painful events as the Bundren's journey is resisted by Darl, members of the community, and natural catastrophes. Contrasting responses of characters and oppositions among juxtaposed accounts serve to clarify the tensions of the burial journey. A central tensiveness in the plot of Light in August grows from the arrangement of events in the center of the novel which stresses the tensive connection between Christmas' past actions and his present life. Tensions in the plot of The Hamlet are established by Ratliff's resistance to Snopes and by the arrangement of events which blends comic with somber events, juxtaposes scenes of sexual frustration with sexual conquest, and contrasts affirmative with negative relationships between man and nature. The tensions developed by these conflicts suggest that the elimination of humor and sympathy from relationships among people may lead to successful business transactions but produces impotence and sterility on the human dimension. [Order No. 72-7857; 299 pages. DAI, 32A (March-April 1972), 5389.]

220 The Existential Absurd in Faulkner's Snopes Trilogy / John Owen WHITE, Arizona State University, 1971 (Wilfred A. Ferrell).

Faulkner's Snopes trilogy, The Hamlet, The Town, and The Mansion, expresses a perception of a purposeless universe in which man must act to establish meaning for himself. Faulkner's vision of the existential absurd is one in which man denies his own humanity by living an "inauthentic life," by acting automatically and mechanically, and by doing what is expected of him rather than asserting himself as an individual. His portrayal of the existential absurd is a warning of what man may become if he does not assert his humanity and consciously choose that course of action which assures a meaningful existence.

In recognizing man's predicament, Faulkner is in the mainstream of the tradition of western literature, but his recognition has generated a significant technique for expressing the absurd. By isolating, exaggerating, and distorting everyday, commonplace reality, by dramatizing a vision of life which is grotesque though real in its essence, Faulkner clearly renders the absurdity of the meaningless life. And, as he does so, the technique he uses becomes especially important as it both embodies and springs from theme.

Faulkner's method of implementing theme is very similar to the dramatic technique of the Theater of the Absurd. The point is not that either genre influenced the other, but that both use techniques which are generated from a similar perception of the human condition. Since the technique of the Theater of the Absurd is the most obvious and conspicuous example of distorted exaggeration to reveal the absurd, a comparison of this technique with that employed in the trilogy allows added insight into Faulkner's thematic implications. Both magnify the trivial and banal in everyday reality, and strip away the protective camouflage of familiarity.

The techniques of the absurd are apparent in Faulkner's characters who are exaggerated and one-sided to represent and call attention to various traits in man, most of which interfere with the authentic life. Flem Snopes and Eula Varner, the most obvious symbolic figures, are not the only ones who are distorted; most of the characters in the trilogy represent one or another human trait that can take control of a life. To see them as naturalistic selections from a realistic environment is to obscure the themes of the novels.

Most of Faulkner's characters are mechanical in their actions and are controlled by the rigid forces of reason, emotion, and/or convention. Action is merely reaction as they have forfeited all meaning in the banality of their automatic lives. This absurdity is apparent even in affairs of love. Faulkner explores the range of human relationships and provides, in his spectrum of love, a view of those factors which limit the potential of love and affection.

As part of the Absurdist technique of exaggeration, Faulkner employs dramatic tableaux, stop-action scenes which unite and assemble the thematic elements and provide nearly visual impact to reinforce thematic meaning. He also uses the tall tale in a distinctive way by focusing less on the extravagant humor than on an undercurrent of concern with man, the victim.

Faulkner thereby expresses his perception of man in the existential absurd, and his feeling for the technique which best expresses man's predicament. And it is this technique, and this perception, which unites the trilogy-- not the threat of invading Snopesism, which is actually just the reactionary crusade of Gavin Stevens and Ratliff. A study of Faulkner's technique, and an understanding of his perception of the existential absurd, reveals the themes implicit in the novels and allows a fuller understanding of the Snopes trilogy as a whole. [Order No. 72-1589; 222 pages. DAI, 32A (Nov.-Dec. 1971), 3336.]

221 The Endless Jar: "Contraries" in William Faulkner / Agnes Akiko YAMADA, University of Oregon, 1971 (William J. Handy).

In The Marriage of Heaven and Hell, William Blake develops the theme of "contraries," or poles which gain their strength one from the other, as well as their meaning and their significance. The concept of the Blakean contraries implies not a synthesis of the two opposing poles, as in Hegel's dialectic, or the seeking of a truth somewhere between the two extremes, as in Aristotle's concept of the Golden Mean. Blake chose to keep the polarities sharp and differentiated, insisting on a double vision in which the two contraries never merge but, instead, give rise to a truth which encompasses both poles. They not only always exist in conflict, including each other rather than forming pairs of mutually exclusive oppositions, but they, together, form the only wholeness in which meaning can begin to mean. The two poles of Blake's contraries are essential to each other; one needs the other to exist and to push against. Each partner of the married contraries retains his individuality and integrity while gaining new and added significance and meaning as he defines and redefines himself in the light of his relationship with the other.

I do not wish to imply that Blake had any conscious or unconscious influence on Faulkner; but there is discernible, in Faulkner's works, a vision which is as concerned as is Blake's with polarities. Ulysses, in Troilus and Cressida, speaks of "right and wrong, /Between whose endless jar justice resides." "Right and wrong"--here are the contraries, each needing the other. It is of them and of "the endless jar" that I propose to treat in this examination of four novels of William Faulkner. These novels were selected from three of the four periods of creativity posited by Frederick Hoffman: The Sound and the Fury and Light in August from the major second period; The Wild Palms from the pre-third; and A Fable from the third. The first period, which includes Soldiers' Pay and Mosquitoes, was not considered since these works are uniformly inferior to Faulkner's later novels and since the purpose of this dissertation is not to study the development of Faulkner's vision but to describe its workings in his novels.

It is the double vision of Faulkner that accounts for the basic tension in his works. That this tension is, in the final analysis, irresoluble is not evidence of weakness or indecision but is, on the contrary, evidence of his uncompromising determination to present the world as he sees it, in all its contradictory and paradoxical aspects. What Faulkner sees, of course, is conflict. And that conflict is celebrated not only because it is, but because it is necessary to man's growth and development.

Characters like Quentin and Jason Compson, Joe Christmas, and Charlotte Rittenmeyer are presented as head-bound beings whose chief failing is their having substituted something--absolute answers and certainties, the order and idealization of literature--for man. What characterizes all of them is single vision. Driven by their private needs, obsessions, and compulsions, they fail to see that flux characterizes life, and that while order and meaning are indeed desirable and necessary, that order and that meaning may not be used to deny the looseness and seeming chaos of life.

Life changes, but it also endures. Both continual change and unremitting continuity are aspects of life. For Faulkner, it is only the seer with double vision who can cope with the eternal contradictions of life. [Order No. 72-9561; 161 pages. DAI, 32A (March-April 1972), 5249.]

222 Soldiers' Pay: A Critical Study of William Faulkner's First Novel / Margaret Janis YONCE, University of South Carolina, 1971 (James B. Meriwether).

Soldiers' Pay has not attracted the attention that one might expect to be given to the first attempt of a major writer at the genre in which he subsequently achieved his greatest mastery. Faulkner's first novel has customarily been dismissed as an apprentice work of negligible intrinsic worth. This study attempts to show that the novel does have merits of its own which have been misunderstood or overlooked; for example, the abundance of apparently gratuitous allusions is not merely awkward decoration, as has been assumed, but an attempt by the young writer to create a web-like tissue of cross references connecting and unifying the work. Of more importance, however, this study examines Soldiers' Pay for evidence of embryonic techniques which were later developed by the mature artist. The result is that one perceives Faulkner's early efforts to create the effect of simultaneous actions, to employ multiple narrators, and to use myth to extend the dimensions of his work.

One of the concerns of his study is to uncover some of the sources and purposes of allusions in Soldiers' Pay. Eliot's Waste Land and two of its sources, The Golden Bough and Jessie Weston's From Ritual to Romance, are shown to have precipitated one of the major motifs of the novel--that of the dying fertility god of the vegetation myths. Donald Mahon is seen to be a manifestation of the wounded Fisher King and the action of the novel reflects the mythic quest for the Holy Grail which will restore life and vitality to the wounded deity.

Although a textual study is not included, the typescript of Soldiers' Pay has been examined and collated with the published text with the result that interesting differences are shown to exist which shed light on some of the compositional and thematic problems of the work. Also included is a study of unpublished poems and short stories which are precursors of the novel. Much of Faulkner's published verse is also examined in relation to the novel. An annotated bibliography of criticism of Soldiers' Pay is included as an appendix. [Order No. 71-21,856; 300 pages. DAI, 32A (July-Aug. 1971), 991.]

223 The Barrier of Words: A Study of William Faulkner's Distrust of Language / Lynn Marie Lipphart BERK, Purdue University, 1972 (William T. Stafford).

The relationship between language and human experience is necessarily a central concern of any serious creative writer. Words are his artistic tool, and he must understand their strengths and weaknesses as a communicative medium. Until the 20th century most American writers expressed a profound faith in the powers of language. They tended to believe that language could communicate the mysteries of life, that it had an integral connection with reality. However, Darwinism, behaviorism, and linguistic science undermined the mystique of words. The American writers of the post-World War I era began to distrust language both as a communicative medium and as an accurate reflection of reality. No post-war writer was more sceptical regarding the relationship between words and reality than was William Faulkner. At the same time, none was more successful in manipulating language to illustrate its own inadequacy.

The most obvious manifestation of Faulkner's distrust of language is his thematic treatment of the problem of words. The relationship of language to human experience is touched upon in nearly all of his prose works and constitutes a major thematic concern in many. Even his very early sketches affirm the deed and question the reliability of the word. This distinction between doing and saying is amplified in his first novels, Mosquitoes being devoted almost entirely to this theme. But while the limitations of language are thoroughly exposed in Faulkner's early works, neither their style nor structure reflects this preoccupation.

The novels of Faulkner's "great middle period," The Sound and the Fury, As I Lay Dying, and Absalom, Absalom!, explore the problem of language with far greater complexity and subtlety. In these works Faulkner explores the impact of words on a myriad of character types and dramatizes their varying responses. These novels also examine the dilemma of the creative writer who is of necessity committed to language. Style and structure work to reinforce theme. Faulkner's conviction that one cannot depend upon what people say is manifested in his unique experiments with point of view. The unreliable narrator is characteristic of these novels as is the technique of frequently contradictory, multiple narration. Style, too, contributes to the complexity. Faulkner tends to heighten rather than minimize the ambiguities inherent in the English language by employing grammatical constructs and words which, through their apparent obscurity, force the reader to create his own reality.

These stylistic and structural peculiarities are also carried over into Faulkner's later novels and stories. In these works his preoccupation with the pitfalls of language is generally focused on a single character--Gavin Stevens. He exhibits all of the deleterious effects of an excessive dependence on words--isolation from human involvement, substitution of the word for the deed, the mistaking of language for truth. In Knight's Gambit, Intruder in the Dust, Requiem for a Nun, and the Snopes trilogy, all of the problems raised in the previous volumes are re-examined by Faulkner through this one ubiquitous character.

But whereas Faulkner insists that language has its serious limitations, he by no means suggests that it is irrelevant. He recognizes man's utter dependence on words and suggests both thematically and stylistically the ways in which language can be a useful tool. If one is cognizant of the grave limitations of language, he should be able to exploit its potential without succumbing to its pitfalls. This is precisely what Faulkner succeeds in doing when he communicates his own distrust of language to his reader. [Order No. 73-5989; 199 pages. DAI, 33A (March-April 1973), 5163-64.]

224 Six Grotesques in Three Faulkner Novels / Edward Depriest CLARK, Sr., Syracuse University, 1972 (David H. Owen).

An analysis of three novels by William Faulkner suggests that the theory of the grotesque the old writer in Sherwood Anderson's Winesburg, Ohio, explains is also a structural-thematic device Faulkner uses to present Quentin Compson and Jason Compson in The Sound and the Fury, Joe Christmas, Joanna Burden, and Gail Hightower in Light in August, and Thomas Sutpen in Absalom, Absalom!.

Quentin Compson's inordinate concern about the meaning of honor, justice, and love eventually renders him incapable of any effective action. His inability to accept his sister's loss of virginity and the sense of despair he derives from his father's cynical philosophy help reduce him to a spiritual grotesque. Jason Compson IV acknowledges a genuine allegiance to no one, evaluates occurrences only as they affect him. His insatiable quest for the golden fleece renders him a grotesque.

When Joe Christmas learns that he might have some Negro blood and what that means in the Deep South, he establishes rigid patterns of order to retain his individuality and to gain a sense of inner harmony. Efforts by others to violate the order Christmas vows to maintain cause him to react through grotesque behavior. Joanna Burden feels that the curse of the white race is the black man, so she attempts to eradicate the stain by aiding Negro colleges and benevolent agencies. Her failure to integrate her sexual, her racial, and her religious activities leads to grotesque conduct. Reverend Gail Hightower confuses religious truth with the galloping cavalry of Civil War glory to the extent that he drives his congregation away, his wife to adultery and suicide, and himself into exile, where he rehearses his memories of the past.

To overcome completely a humiliating rejection he experienced during his childhood, Thomas Sutpen works to establish a superior estate and family. He becomes so obsessed with the desire to complete his grand design that he becomes oblivious of ethical or humanitarian behavior. His perverted sense of justice and paternal devotion and his compelling and undeviating drive make him a grotesque.

It is concluded that the six protagonists do emerge as grotesques because of their pertinacious and blind adherence to private versions of truth. Further, many of the other important characters associated with them are to some extent grotesques because they, too, become slaves to their individual ideas about truth. The thoughts of most of the persons in the novel's focus on some concept of truth, and their reactions to these truths provide the major tensions in the works. Hence, the theory of the grotesque is an important structural-thematic link in all three novels. [Order No. 72-20,317; 215 pages. DAI, 33A (July-Aug. 1972), 302.]

225 Eschatological Thought in Faulkner's Yoknapatawpha Novels / Margaret Mary Mulvehill CULLEY, University of Michigan, 1972 (Robert F. Haugh).

In his Yoknapatawpha novels Faulkner has created an entire world, a world that had a genesis and is moving toward an end. Faulkner's "sense of the ending" is one aspect of his thought informed by the Judeo-Christian mythology which was his heritage. His fiction reveals the same tension between apocalyptic eschatology and "realized" eschatology that his formative scriptural sources do. At times, when his anxiety about the shape of the age to come is intense, he projects, "the end" to an indefinite point in the future marked by a cosmic, cataclysmic event. Most often, however, the eschata, or "ultimate things"--usually thought ot as death, judgment, heaven and hell-- are embodied in the present moment.

Faced with the "ultimate things" in the present moment, man chooses his destiny by his response to them. If he chooses to affirm the "verities of the heart," he will endure and "be nearer the figure that we mean when we say God." If he chooses to deny the "communal anonymity of brotherhood," if he chooses Snopesism, he risks "ending the world, effacing it from the long annual of time and space." Thus the seeds of a man's judgment lie in his present choices; he becomes what he chooses, he makes his "own heaven or hell in this world."

To say that Faulkner is an eschatological writer is to shift the focus from his concern with the past to his concern with the present and the future. Just as the consequences of past choices live in the present; so, too, the consequences of present choices will shape the future. Faulkner's conviction that man will endure reveals his commitment to that future, and his very act of writing is his way of saying "No" to death, of making a gesture toward the future.

The absence of a personal God in Faulkner's vision does not seem to undercut his eschatological anticipation; rather, it increases it. His search for the values once embodied in the absent God leads him to focus on man and his destiny. Faulkner's comic-horrific vision of hell-on-earth will, hopefully, turn man from a Snopes-destiny of his own choosing toward the true kingdom, the kingdom of man. This kingdom bound by the "verities of the heart" exists unobtrusively among the powerless, the victims of the world. The clearest sign of the presence of the kingdom is the reality of suffering, suffering which must be affirmed if one is to enter the kingdom.

Thus the present moment is the eschatological moment, the moment in which man chooses his judgment and his destiny. In Faulkner's words, "There is only the present moment, in which I include both the past and the future, and that is eternity." [Order No. 73-6810; 172 pages. DAI, 33A (March-April 1973), 5167.]

226 Essays on Faulkner: Style, Use of History, Film Adaptations of His Fiction / E. Pauline Sutta DEGENFELDER, Case Western Reserve University, 1972 (David D. Galloway).

Yoknapatawpha Baroque: A Stylistic Analysis of As I Lay Dying: Among the 15 characters in the novel, there are degrees of communicability, depending on relative integration in the community. Through linguistic analyses, such as generative and transformational grammar, it is possible to define styles. Cora's passages exemplify the colloquial style: those of Darl, the baroque. Between these is the carpenter Cash, who achieves a balance of styles, between stasis and motion. The balance is demonstrated through the principle of "beveling," for which Faulkner offers a prose equivalent.

From the Actual to the Apocryphal: Faulkner's "History" of the Poor White in Absalom, Absalom!: The subject of the poor white provides a starting point for determining Faulkner's use of both historical facts and legends, such as the Cavalier thesis, and for assessing his imaginative re-shaping of these materials. Faulkner frequently disregards historical fact such as the absence of antagonism between the poor white and the planter, in order to construct a revenge tragedy. Absalom, Absalom! departs from the genre of the historical novel because it disrupts temporal continuity and because it gives priority to the narrators' limited interpretation rather than an omniscient view. The device of multiple narrators creates a simultaneity of past and present and an emphasis on history as a continued reevaluation.

A Marriage of Art and Technology: The Film Adaptation of William Faulkner's Fiction: Although Faulkner adapted only one of his own works, there have been a total of nine film adaptations. Six films are discussed in this essay: Intruder in the Dust, The Reivers, The Story of Temple Drake, Sanctuary, The Long Hot Summer, and Today We Live. The first two are "faithful" adaptations; the other four are "loose" adaptations. The essay assesses these films as popular art, as an interpretation of Faulkner's fiction, and as a transposition of novelistic techniques into cinematic equivalents. [Order No. 73-6285; 209 pages. DAI, 33A (March-April 1973), 5169.]

227 Faulkner's Sense of History: Criticism of the Magnolia Myth in the Novels of William Faulkner / Elizabeth Ann DOWNEY, University of Denver, 1972 (Robert E. Roeder).

One of William Faulkner's great literary concerns is the South's perception and use of its past. Faulkner's own attitudes differ significantly from the South's traditional view of its past--a view embodied in the magnolia myth. The magnolia myth describes the antebellum South as a land of cultured aristocrats who lived in harmony with their happy slaves and lesser white neighbors. Forced into Civil War by the rapacious North, the gentry fought and died heroically, and thus gave later generations a pattern for noble action.

Faulkner's Yoknapatawpha novels reveal that especially in northern Mississippi the magnolia myth seriously distorts and misrepresents the actual past. Old Mississippi was not the land of a cultured aristocracy, but was the frontier west. Its society was rough and uncultured, its life primitive and violent. Early inhabitants were primarily plain folk who came west seeking escape or opportunity. Many obtained their land unfairly and tamed it with their own and slave labor. Frequently they compounded the evils of forced labor with the evils of forced miscegenation.

In this view of the old South, the Civil War could be regarded as merited punishment for the evils of Southern society. Faulkner believes, however, that the South would have been better off left along to solve its own problems peacefully. He deplores the needless destruction of life and the distortion of values that the War brought, though he cherishes the bravery and sacrifice which it often prompted.

The tragedy of the creation and persistence of the magnolia myth is that it encouraged values which are harmful to the post Civil War South. The lives of many of Faulkner's major characters reveal the destruction which the magnolia myth may bring. Young Bayard Sartoris and Quentin Compson retreat into the past because they cannot cope with rapid, apparently senseless change. Their view of the past, however, is so distorted that it increases their frustrations and hastens their destruction. Furthermore, those ancestors whom they admire most experienced similar failure. Rosa Millard, Colonel John Sartoris, his brother Bayard, and Thomas Sutpen all died tragically and unnecessarily because they refused to accept the passing of the old society. The lives of Joanna Burden and her family, suggest, moreover, that distortion of and inflexible adherence to any particular interpretation of the past may bring destruction.

John Sartoris' son Bayard and Isaac McCaslin are only slightly more successful than these characters. In their youth they assess their heritage and recognize the fallacies of the magnolia myth and the corruption at the base of Southern society. Although they repudiate the evils of the past, they cannot sustain their independence. They end their days as impotent, ineffectual old men.

While Faulkner illustrates the dangers of the magnolia myth, he does not feel that it makes the past deterministic. Success or failure is ultimately a product of the individual will. Some of Faulkner's characters, like Chick Mallison, successfully resist the romantic attractions of the magnolia myth. To a certain extent, even the doomed characters demonstrate man's freedom and capacity for growth. Gail Hightower and Joe Christmas both find peace, and possible redemption, by coming to grips with the past, by rejecting or accepting certain aspects of it. The early failure and the later limited success of Hightower and Christmas capsulize Faulkner's belief that man can prevail only by balancing the claims of past and present. But, he insists, those who look toward the past alone are looking, like the statue of the Confederate soldier in Jefferson, for reinforcements that can never come.
[Order No. 72-33,049; 194 pages. DAI, 33A (Jan.-Feb. 1973), 3534.]

228 A Critical and Textual Study of William Faulkner's Light in August /
 Carl Frederick Wilhelm FICKEN, University of South Carolina, 1972
(James B. Meriwether).

Chapter I of the dissertation discusses the unity of the novel. Faulkner worked carefully with theme, characterization, narrative perspective, parallel imagery, and structure to make Light in August a single story. In describing the complex lives of the four major characters--Lena Grove, Byron Bunch, Gail Hightower, and Joe Christmas--Faulkner established an unmistakable forward motion, as well as an interplay with the past, and moves these four characters toward a climactic August Monday. While no simple structural pattern appears, it is possible to think of the novel in units comprising common time periods, point of view, and action.

Chapters II through IV of the dissertation deal with the first three units of the novel. Chapter II covers the first unit (the first chapter of the novel) and focuses on the emphasis there on Lena Grove, her association with an older civilization, the light-dark contrast, and the imagery of the road, the wheel, and the wasteland. The third chapter deals with the mounting tension of the novel's Chapter II over the Burden fire and over the relationship between Byron and Lena, as well as with the theme of estrangement brought on with the introduction of Joe Christmas. The fourth chapter presents the third unit (Chapters III and IV) with its unified Sunday night action; the discussion centers on the introduction of Hightower and the major question of his involvement in the lives around him. Hightower's history serves as a preparation for what the reader will later learn about Joe Christmas.

The next two chapters of the dissertation analyse the two flashback units (Chapter V, Chapters VI-XII). The fifth chapter deals with the suspension of the forward direction of the novel; this suspension occurs as the action returns to the Friday of Lena's entry--now with a description of Joe Christmas in three intrachapter sections which, with their movement from darkness to daylight and back to darkness again, expand the light-dark imagery, give the novel a deeper emotional level, and impart a stronger sense of impending tragedy. This brief flashback prepares the reader for the longer journey to the early life of Christmas; Chapter VI, then, demonstrates how, in these six chapters of the novel, Faulkner is consistently developing parallels to and reminders of other portions of the narrative, thereby weaving the various actions into a single piece.

Chapters VII through X deal with the final four units of the novel. Chapter VII covers the sixth unit (Chapters XIII and XIV) and shows that when the narrative returns to the present time action, the lives of the main characters are on a similar course: Hightower is now in flight; Byron has ceased his flight and has come to a new confidence; Christmas has a moment of self-understanding which enables him to accept the inevitability of death and to surrender. The seventh unit, on the events of Friday through Sunday (Chapters XV and XVI), is discussed in Chapter VIII with an emphasis on the way these chapters fill in further background for the character of Joe Christmas and move Hightower to a harsh rejection of the involvement which is being forced on him. Chapter IX presents the climax of the story, a climax which is spread over four of the novel's chapters (XVII-XX) and has to do with the crisis in the life of each major character; on this Monday each of them has some overwhelming experience: Lena in the birth of her child and in the recognition of her love for Byron; Christmas in his second flight and death; Byron in his fight with Brown; Hightower in his successful delivery of Lena's child and then in his painful awareness of the course of his own life. Chapter X covers the final unit and final chapter of the novel and stresses the way this humorous extension of the action carries the story beyond the tragic week in August and into a broader world. The dissertation's last chapter suggests that the novel is not to be limited to a single theme but that here Faulkner is writing about a variety of people--about people in motion--and about the forces in their own lives and in their society which shape and control them.

The appendices conclude the study. A textual appendix describes the manuscript and typescript and includes tables with the results of a collation of the typescript and first edition; these tables provide the readings necessary to correct the errors in the first printed edition of the novel. The second appendix presents an annotated checklist of Light in August criticism. The third is a chronology of the entire action of the novel, including the flashbacks. [Order No. 73-3597; 393 pages. DAI, 33A (Jan.-Feb. 1973), 4411-12.]

229 The New Rhetoric of Faulkner's Heroes in His Later Work / Joseph Weldon FLORY, Indiana University of Pennsylvania, 1972 (David L. Young) no DAI entry.

230 William Faulkner's A Fable: A Fragmented Christ / David HOCHSTETTLER, Syracuse University, 1972 (David Owen).

William Faulkner's A Fable chronicles the reappearance of Christ in the trenches of France in 1918. The reappearance is no conventional incarnation, however. It is accomplished through processes which I call fragmentation and synthesis.

One of the novel's characters explains that when a man passes from physical existence into mythic existence he continues only as "fragments." The fragments are distributed among various "custodians," and the myth figure can become manifest only in the "mutual confederation" of the custodians.

The characters of the novel illustrate such fragmentation and synthesis. While the corporal is an ostensible Christ, he lacks certain fragments. The details of Christ's youth are paralleled in that of the old general. Christ's role as spokesman for truth is assigned to the Rev. Sutterfield. Other characters work miracles and descend into hell. No one character is Christ's complete manifestation. Conversely, the novel's characters are composites of several mythic figures. The old general, for example, is Satan, Pilate, and Caesar as well as Christ.

As another way of understanding the same process, another character sees man's archetypes as "intersections" which contemporary men "pass through." Thus the characters of the novel may be understood as passing, at various moments, through each of several archetypes and becoming avatars of them. Whether expressed in terms of fragmentation or passing-through, Faulkner's interest is in multiple incarnations both simultaneous and sequential.

The first three chapters of my study establish that awareness of fragmentation is essential to an understanding of the novel. Chapter Four discusses the ideas which emerge once fragmentation is observed.

Faulkner's Christ serves not to advocate, nor even to exemplify, the values central to A Fable. He functions to expose evil, making overt that which has been covert. Confronted with overt evil, people can ignore it and live mindlessly as A Fable's masses do. One can acknowledge the reality of evil and respond by killing himself in disillusionment, by passively enduring, or by acting heroically to reject evil. These three responses are illustrated in the "trinity of conscience" figures. At rare moments many men may confederate for a time in an heroic struggle against evil. This occurs in A Fable's two mutinies.

To prevent facile romanticizing about common men who confederate, Faulkner relies on several patterns of images. A Fable's masses are as mindless as waves or as any of several beasts (principally the earthworm). Their sounds, again implying mindlessness, are contrasted with the sounds of war (guns and bugles) and the sounds of nature (principally the lark). A color motif (blue) serves to identify those who are able to hope.

Although Faulkner regarded A Fable highly, the consensus of critics remains harsh. My final chapter discusses several charges made against the novel and shows how my analysis of fragmentation serves to answer some misconceptions about it. The charge that A Fable's Christology is perverse seems unwarranted, in view of the composite Christ presented. The charge that it violates the standards of realism has some merit, but such violations are to be expected in fabulistic literature. Confusion about A Fable's opposed forces has led to mistaken theories about the nature of the novel's central conflict. It is not primarily concerned with pitting advocates of war against those of peace, nor with setting spokesman for individualism against spokesman for authority.

A Fable does not affirm the triumph of either good or evil in time. It does affirm the possibility of an authentic human existence. The measure of that authenticity is man's "splendid failure to do the impossible." [Order No. 73-9531; 206 pages. DAI, 33A (March-April 1973), 5724-25.]

231 William Faulkner; A Study in Spatial Form / John Michael LANNON, University of Massachusetts, 1972 (Arthur F. Kinney).

Faulkner's Yoknapatawpha fiction has often been regarded as a metaphor for any number of more encompassing social, philosophical, or psychological statements about the nature of man. Instead of viewing the Yoknapatawpha fiction as a vehicle for some extrinsic, pre-existent meaning, this study considers the internal relationships which distinguish Faulkner's imaginative world. Faulkner is, above all, an artist, not a moral philsopher. With this assertion as a point of departure, I try to comprehend Faulkner's achievement accordingly.

It is not the story, but the way in which it is told, which is of primary importance to Faulkner. The artist himself has described his creative process as "telling the same story over and over, which is myself and the world." Faulkner strove for perfection of expression rather than range of subject matter. Throughout Faulkner's fiction there recurs the principle of potential meaning which is "myself and the world." This is a life-principle which Faulkner attempts to make sensible by casting it "over and over" within an art-principle, a specific design. Each new attempt to find the perfect form in which to render an imperfect human existence represents a new way of seeing--a spatial mode of organizing the creative imagination.

Spatial form is a basic element of structural organization in the Yoknapatawpha works. Assuming that spatial form is a kind of deep structure of Faulkner's art, contiguous with the perceptual patterns contained by the artistic consciousness (a "world-view"), I attempt to re-think my way back to such a deep structure from the narrative and dramatic surface of the text. This study considers individual novels in an attempt to reveal the dual nature of spatial form in Faulkner's fiction: it is an element of narrative organization and experimentation and also an abiding factor of thematic structure.

Virtually all of the Yoknapatawpha novels are unified by a recurring artistic design; in our examination of it, this unifying design is manifested in the perceptual structures of Faulkner's imaginative world which are a function of spatial form. Each major chracter and event is an aspect of the artistic consciousness attempting to grasp for itself the meaning of the relationship of self and world. Uniting the diverse characters and events of the Yoknapatawpha sequence is a structure of contiguity which provides a revealing view of the underlying artistic imagination. In each novel, a metonymous progression, or substitution, is repeated as the personal psychology of the respective characters inevitably becomes a subordinate aspect of the human landscape. The abiding reality of each situation is never, finally, the subjective consciousness of any individual. No single posture is ever adequate in Faulkner's world. Again and again, subjective consciousness is objectified and resolved into the immanent space of the human landscape. The world as immanent space is always more real than the singular sensibilities of the fictive avators who unsuccessfully attempt to encompass it. Faulkner's imaginative world consists of a series of radical experiments in technique imposed upon a fixed and unchanging artistic vision which underlies the world of each novel. I am concerned with structure, not for its own sake, but instead, as a primary source of meaning embodied in spatial form. Without attempting to reduce Faulkner's complex achievement to a single determining feature, I look for a fundamental way of organizing our aesthetic perceptions of Faulkner's art.

My study is restricted to a detailed consideration of six novels which span much of Faulkner's career: The Sound and the Fury, As I Lay Dying, Sanctuary, Light in August, Intruder in the Dust, and The Reivers. Together, these six novels test my approach in two dissimilar and fairly discrete parts of Faulkner's canon. In Chapter I, I include a brief discussion of those Yoknapatawpha novels which are not explored in detail. I have dealt only with the Yoknapatawpha fiction because that is the imaginative space to which Faulkner most often returns. [Order No. 73-6692; 168 pages. DAI, 33A (March-April 1973), 5184.]

232 Not Only to Survive but to Prevail: A Study of William Faulkner's Search for a Redeemer of Modern Man / Benjamin Wright McCLELLAND, Indiana University, 1972 (J. Albert Robbins).

In the last two decades several distinguished literary scholars have made contributions to the delineation of the moral order in and theological vision of Faulkner's fictional world. The most useful study in this area is John W. Hunt's William Faulkner: Art in Theological Tension (1965). In his analysis of the theological complexity of The Sound and the Fury, Absalom, Absalom!, and "The Bear," Hunt shows a tension between Christian and Stoic visions in the fiction.

I have applied Hunt's mode of analysis to characters in four novels which he did not use in his study: Light in August (1932), The Hamlet (1940), A Fable (1954), and The Reivers (1962). Hunt's basic thesis is valid, but there is a significant shift in the balance of the tension in the fiction over the years.

Faulkner makes several attempts at creating a redeemer for modern man, a man who would sacrifice himself in order to save his fellows and the world from the doom caused by the modern industrial state. Hunt has shown the failures of the tragic figures, Quentin Compson, Isaac McCaslin, and Thomas Sutpen; those in my study are comic figures, who, unlike the tragic figures, are relatively successful in redeeming their world.

One of Faulkner's earliest characters to demonstrate a religious tension is V.K. Ratliff of The Hamlet. Basically, Ratliff lives according to stoic principles of benevolence to but aloofness from his fellow man; however, his allegiance to these principles is challenged by his penchant for gambling and his inclination toward having Christian compassion for his fellow man.

In Light in August Byron Bunch withdraws from active participation in the human community until falling in love with Lena Grove, an ideal stoic character, through whom, paradoxically, Byron experiences Christian love, which enables him to become compassionately involved in the lives of others. Byron plays a significant part in Gail Hightower's late but admirable decision to rejoin the sacrficial act of love.

A Fable is Faulkner's modern version of the passion story in which the Corporal, the Sentry, the Runner, and Reverend Sutterfield, each attempt various acts of Christian redemption. The Corporal is the perfect stoic who fails to incorporate man's finitude in his being; also as a purely rational thinker he admits to no transcendent powers, divine or demonic, in man's history. The Sentry, the Runner, and Reverend Sutterfield, all products of a mixed (Stoic and Christian) religious tradition, play multiple roles. In one instance one of these characters may participate in an act of redeeming another, while in a later instance, he may exhibit a diabolical nature and be in need of redemption by another.

Faulkner realized his greatest success in creating a redeemer figure in his last novel, The Reivers. In Ned McCaslin Faulkner has combined the saintly and devilish qualities of Sutterfield and the Sentry; Ned draws Lucius Priest and Boon Hogganbeck into a gambling scheme which turns out to be a sacrificial act of redemption for them and Bobo Beauchamp. That Faulkner was concerned throughout his career to tell a modern version of the redeemer myth is evident from studying these early and late characters who portray in various ways the redeemer of modern man. [Order No. 72-15,919; 172 pages. DAI, 32A (May-June 1972), 6438-39.]

233 The Non-Yoknapatawpha Novels of William Faulkner: An Examination of Soldiers' Pay, Mosquitoes, Pylon, The Wild Palms, and A Fable / Duane Johnson MacMILLAN, University of Wisconsin, 1972 (Walter B. Rideout).

Among the non-Yoknapatawpha novels of William Faulkner, Mosquitoes is probably the weakest work in the canon, A Fable is easily the most complex, and Soldiers' Pay, Pylon, and The Wild Palms are acknowledged to be minor Faulkner in comparison with the great works such as The Sound and the Fury, Go Down, Moses, and Absalom, Absalom!. Certainly, the non-Yoknapatawpha novels have remained critically less popular than those set inside the author's "postage-stamp" of native soil in northern Mississippi. In writing the non-Yoknapatawpha novels, Faulkner may have gained superficial or mechanical advantages by using settings outside Yoknapatawpha, but the themes, characters, and situations dealt with in these five works link them securely to the rest of the canon. The novels of William Faulkner are all of one piece: they result from the same literary imagination and a consistent world view.

The non-Yoknapatawpha novels are examined individually in order of publication, and the same method of approach is repeated for each book. A brief biographical context for the novel is followed by acknowledgment of the reviews. A fairly exhaustive critical survey of pertinent existing scholarship precedes a fresh examination of the work itself.

Soldiers' Pay is seen to be an extended inquiry into the best way of enduring the human condition, particularized in the returning soldier situation. Mosquitoes examines the results of irresponsible conduct in a microcosmic artistic milieu. Pylon is Faulkner's ultimate treatment of themes and ideas he previously worked out in several short stories. The Wild Palms is a tour de force in which the author uses seemingly disparate stories in concert to study the concept of love. A Fable is the capstone and justification of a career that earned Faulkner the Nobel Prize for Literature. This novel is his credo, his magnum opus, and--possibly--his greatest achievement.

But it is not so much the conclusions reached about these books individually that are so important as it is their total implication. This dissertation states that, taken together, the non-Yoknapatawpha novels present a viable approach to and a valid means of assessing Faulkner's overall literary output. That which most unites these five novels one with another and also ensures their deserved place in the Faulkner canon is the author's basically "pro-life" attitudes of pity, pride, compassion, and understanding toward mankind in general. The non-Yoknapatawpha novels present man in peace and in war, in cities and in virgin territory, in groups and in isolation. In the moments of crisis Faulkner chooses to illustrate those momentary flashes between the dark of eternity; there stands forth clear and distinct his overwhelming faith in the ability of man to endure and to prevail. [Order No. 72-15,369; 359 pages. DAI, 32A (May-June 1972), 6986.]

234 The Bystander in Faulkner's Fiction / Kenneth Douglas MacMILLAN, University of British Columbia (Canada), 1972 (Elliott Gose).

In much of his fiction Faulkner used a type of character which one might call the "bystander." The bystander is important not as a participant in the action of a novel or short story, but rather as a witness to the actions of other characters, the protagonists. Frequently, however, the focus of the author's attention falls upon the perceptions and feelings of the apparently irrelevant witness instead of upon the ostensible action of the work. Faulkner analyzes closely the effects the action has upon the bystander who may become involved in events which, strictly speaking, should not concern him. Reciprocally the protagonists very frequently are conscious of the watching eyes of the bystander (or bystanders) and adapt their actions to placate or defy the watching consciousness. There is, therefore, a complex relationship between the two types, protagonist and witness.

Many critics have seen individual bystanders in Faulkner's fiction as mouthpieces of the author, but this dissertation attempts to refute this interpretation. The first four chapters of the dissertation consider the choric or collective bystanders, the problem, important to Faulkner, of perception and the subjectivity of vision, the use of irony in treatments of the bystander, and the use of the youthful bystander. Each of these topics reinforces the assertion that Faulkner views the bystander figure inevitably as limited and fallible and not as an authorial spokesman. Because Stevens appears more frequently in Faulkner's work than any other bystander figure, and because he has attracted more adverse criticism than any other character in Faulkner's fiction, the last five chapters focus upon him and discuss in detail the works in which he appears. The dissertation shows Faulkner's portrayal of Gavin Stevens to be complex and effective, not the failure it is often claimed to be.

Indeed, a discussion of the bystander casts new light upon several of Faulkner's less famous works and indicates how those works extend the treatment of themes recognized in the major successes of the 1930s. The influence of the town in Soldiers' Pay and Sartoris, the significance of the mysterious figure of the Reporter in Pylon, the importance of the experiments in Knight's Gambit, all appear by means of this investigation. Similarly, this dissertation shows how bystander figures play important parts in nearly all of Faulkner's novels and in many of his short stories.

The dissertation reveals Faulkner's continued interest in the passive bystander who only witnesses the actions of the protagonists but who yet exerts a powerful influence upon their actions. Thus the treatment of this type in Faulkner's fiction indicates both the powers and limitations of perception. The bystanders are frequently sympathetic, intelligent, and morally aware, but they are, at the same time, ineffectual, passive, or escapist. Furthermore, because Faulkner's stance as an artist is often that of the non-involved witness, a study of his use of the bystander leads ultimately to a consideration of problems central to his conception of fiction. [For microfilm copy, order from the National Library of Canada at Ottawa. DAI, 34A (July-Aug. 1973), 783.]

235 The Cavalier Spirit in Faulkner's Fiction / Richard Allen MILUM, Indiana University, 1972 (James H. Justus).

The presence of a cavalier myth in Southern culture and of William Faulkner's participation in it have long been acknowledged. This study attempts a general, although not exhaustive analysis of the nature and significance of the cavalier tradition in Faulkner's work.

Chapter I examines first of all the transmittal of Scottish cavalier values via the ancestry of Faulkner's Mississippi hill people and the novels of Walter Scott. The contribution of French cavalier culture is next traced primarily through contact by the inhabitants of Faulkner's Mississippi frontier with characters of French descent (Louis Grenier, the Chevalier Soeur-Blonde de Vitry, Thomas Sutpen's French architect), and with centers of French culture such as New Orleans, the West Indies, and France itself.

Chapter II traces the main outlines of the tradition in the life style of Faulkner's aristocrats, focusing principally upon four major families: Compson, Sartoris, Benbow and Stevens. Whereas the original cavalier possessed a balanced mixture of physical, intellectual, and spiritual attributes, centuries of decay have left Faulkner's cavaliers hopelessly fragmented. Having long since lost their essential spiritual base, their flamboyant physical deeds lead only to public annoyance and self-destruction, while their most refined intellectual endeavors serve only as a means of escape from responsibility. Such difficulties are further intensified by the prevailing and restrictive Calvinistic atmosphere which condemns cavalier excess in all its forms, charging the climate with perpetual conflict. The chapter further identifies the principal cavalier values which survive as sources of motivation and patterns of behavior and which exert an influence not only upon its logical aristocratic inheritors, but upon the entire Yoknapatawpha social scale including Indian, Negro, and poor white.

Chapter III treats the horse as a major element of the cavalier tradition in Faulkner's work. Basically, the horse (and its metaphorical extensions, the automobile and the airplane), represents an irresistible temptation, and inevitably leads Faulkner's modern-day cavaliers into varying degrees of mischief and misadventure. The horse and a character's relationship to it, functions simultaneously for Faulkner as a dimension of character, an element of plot, and as a literary symbol of the chivalric age.

Chapter IV examines the propensity of Faulkner's characters for battle. Sharing the cavalier's characteristic employment, Faulkner's warriors are dedicated either to a Lost Cause or to no cause at all except self-glorification. Faulkner's treatment of the attitude ranges all the way from a light-hearted satire of their youthful enthusiasm to a sombre rejection of the romantic instinct for death, stressing particularly the purposeless sacrifices of life and the mental anguish of those (especially the women) who are left behind.

Chapter V analyzes the behavior of Faulkner's lovers, placing them in the tradition of romantic love as described by Denis de Rougemont in Love in the Western World. As such, their efforts involve no fruitful cause, no ideal of marital contentment, but a search for passion which increases with separation and denial and finds its ultimate extension in death.

Chapter VI concludes the study by examining the collective contribution of the cavalier heritage among the unlikely cast of Light in August. Functioning significantly in each major plot line, the excesses of cavalier behavior (especially those stemming from the tradition of romantic love) are confronted by the repressive demands of American Calvinism, thereby providing the major source of dramatic conflict in the novel. [Order No. 73-9770; 268 pages. DAI, 33A (March-April 1973), 5737.]

236 Perspectives on William Faulkner: The Author and His Work as Reflected in Surveys of American History, Works on Southern Life and History, and Works and Comments by Mississippians / Robert Henry MOORE, University of Wisconsin, 1972 (Walter B. Rideout).

Although William Faulkner's stature among literary scholars is well-established, little attention has been given to how his writing has been received by readers other than scholars and students of literature. This dissertation complements formal "literary" opinion by describing and examining the response to Faulkner's work as it is reflected in the following sources: in general surveys of American history; in studies dealing specifically with the culture and history of the South; and in the documented opinion of a cross-section of Mississippians.

In general surveys of American history published before 1950, Faulkner's writing received only cursory attention. But by the end of the 1950s, stimulated at least in part by Faulkner's Nobel Prize, historians became increasingly concerned, if not altogether sympathetic, with Faulkner's reputation as a celebrated literary figure. As the explicit revisions of their earlier texts reveal, these historians though troubled by what they saw as a convoluted literary style and an obsession with morbidity, were increasinly inclined to concede Faulkner's stature as a major American regionalist. Not until the

1960s, however, did most of these historians begin to assert that Faulkner's writing offered, not simply a depiction, but rather an incisive analysis of the South or that his convoluted style, which was formerly denigrated as liability, was a positive aspect of his consummate literary artistry. By the end of the 1960s many historians were contending that Faulkner had created Yoknapatawpha County, not for its own sake, but as a microcosm of the larger world and that Faulkner was addressing problems common to all men.

This same pattern in Faulkner discussions--a movement from relative indifference to critical approbation--is generally characteristic of those studies dealing specifically with the culture and regional history of the South. More importantly, these regional studies unlike the broader historical surveys are especially significant because they are understandably preoccupied with the specifics of how Faulkner's work illuminates a way of life that is indigenously Southern.

This conception of Faulkner as preeminently a "Southern" writer is a major focal point in the third and perhaps the most revealing of the dissertation's three distinct sources: the body of data which represents the documented cross-section of Mississippi opinion on William Faulkner and his work. The first part of this section draws upon a limited number of select sources to establish a bench mark for considering the wide variety of Mississippi response that was generated by my research. These select sources are works on Mississippi and comments made in personal correspondence with me by Mississippi historians, journalists, and public officials. Once the bench mark is established, the study turns to an analysis of responses elicited in 1969-1971 in a statewide survey of newspaper editors and Mississippians of various backgrounds from Oxford and other Mississippi communities. The resulting discussion provides a unique account of the history of Faulkner's readership in the state. This account suggests that despite the fact that most literate white Mississippi adults have read little if any Faulkner, they are hostile to his work. However, a sizable minority of these Mississippians have been belatedly, but substantially, influenced by the Hollywood filming of Faulkner's work and his national and international fame, to at least read his writing. Such people frequently comment favorably on specific aspects of Faulkner's work although many report having to overcome an initial impatience with Faulkner's artistic techniques and an annoyance at what they tend to regard as the author's obsession with atypical elements of North Mississippi life. But far more significant than these general patterns of response is the fact that the individual survey responses, which are reproduced verbatim in a series of appendices at the end of the dissertation, constitute the most extensive record we have of the complex dynamics of contemporary Mississippi attitudes toward William Faulkner and his work. [Order No. 72-4290; 590 pages. DAI, 32A (March-April 1972), 5798-99.]

237 "And By Bergson, Obviously": Faulkner's The Sound and the Fury, As I Lay Dying and Absalom, Absalom! from a Bergsonian Perspective / Susan Dale Resneck PARR, University of Wisconsin, 1972 (Walter B. Rideout).

In a 1952 interview, Faulkner noted that he had been influenced "by Bergson, obviously." Although this interview contains what appears to be his only public acknowledgment of Bergson as one of his possible sources, a consideration of Faulkner's major fiction, in particular The Sound and the Fury, As I Lay Dying, and Absalom, Absalom!, in a Bergsonian context proves extraordinarily fruitful in terms of both Faulkner's formal and thematic accomplishments. For instance, Bergsonian thought proves relevant to Faulkner's own explorations of the relationship between reality and man's perceptions of that reality and between such perceptions and man's expression of those perceptions. Even more specifically, Faulkner's consideration of the effects of time's fluidity on the individual and his concern with the relationship of the past to the present, of memory to perception on the one hand, and his dramatization of the vagaries inherent in point of view and of both the power and the limitations of conventional usage of logic and language, on the other, all take on new meaning when viewed from a Bergsonian perspective. Moreover, Bergsonian analogues often facilitate new insights into the motivations, the values, and even the sanity of a great many of Faulkner's characters and into his concern with the relationship of the individual to society while other analogues prove relevant to Faulkner's use of multiple narrators, of ambiguity, and in at least one instance, of a mixed mode of comedy and tragedy. Finally, this dissertation also demonstrates how Faulkner's major fiction fulfills one of Bergson's most important criteria for successful art in that it exposes to the reader what Bergson calls the "fundamental absurdity" inherent in any artistic attempt to communicate reality, while simultaneously and paradoxically it succeeds in lifting the veil that Bergson sees as normally existing between man's perception of reality and reality itself. This in turn allows the reader to participate in, to experience for himself, that reality.

Chapter I of the dissertation documents Faulkner's concern, as revealed in his published essays and interviews, with those metaphysical, epistemological, and aesthetic concerns which do have Bergsonian analogues. This chapter also surveys the Faulknerian scholarship relevant to this approach. Chapter II outlines the appropriate Bergsonian analogues. The emphasis of Chapter III on The Sound and the Fury is Faulkner's dramatization of the power and limits of language, of certain problems of point of view, and of the importance of memory to perception. Of particular concern also is Quentin's suicide which takes on new meaning when viewed from a Bergsonian perspective. The subject of Chapter IV, As I Lay Dying to an even greater extent than The Sound and the Fury, employs what Bergson calls a "cinematographical" method in its presentation of characters and events. Although As I Lay Dying also dramatizes the relative nature of truth and the limitations inherent in any point of view, it at the same time suggests the opposite view, that truth may not be relative after all since individuals with independent angles of vision are often able to perceive reality in identical or nearly identical ways. The dissertation concludes with Absalom, Absalom!, for it is here that Faulkner's questioning of language, perception, and reality reach fruition. Interestingly, it is here too that for the first time Faulkner not only dramatizes his views but also employs an unidentified narrator who explicitly articulates certain important aspects of the novelist's aesthetic. Absalom, Absalom! is also significant in that it extends the scope of an individual's memory beyond that dealt with in the earlier two novels and beyond that with which Bergson is specifically concerned, for here, Quentin must come to terms not only with his memories of a personal past but also with his larger cultural heritage. [Order No. 72-13,991; 243 pages. DAI, 32A (May-June 1972), 6996.]

238 A Study of William Faulkner's As I Lay Dying Based on the Manuscript and Text / Catherine Mary PATTEN, New York University, 1972 (John R. Kuehl).

This dissertation offers a new critical evaluation of As I Lay Dying by examining the extant manuscript and changes between it and the published book. The Introduction documents the need for such a study and describes the manucript itself. Moreover, it concludes that Faulkner revised as he wrote and that this manuscript is the first draft of the complete novel. An appendix documents the evidence upon which these statements are based.

Each chapter deals with a specific technique in relation to the overall effect of the novel. In Chapter One the narrative management of the novel is found to be complex and experimental. In examining the temporal sequence the author finds a threefold framework for the book: chronological linear time; a "plot" form centering around the triptych; a developing psychological conflict between Darl and Jewel and Dewey Dell.

A study of the characterization in Chapter Two focuses on the Bundrens who are present to the "now" of the novel, especially Darl, Vardaman, Dewey Dell, and Jewel. It examines in detail the psychological conflict between the children which parallels the physical journey to Jefferson.

In contrast, Chapter Three deals with the atemporal Cora/Addie/Whitfield triptych and its role in the novel. Subsequently this chapter studies the imagery of the book, much of which takes on new meaning after the Addie section.

Humor and irony and the means Faulkner uses to achieve them are the subjects of Chapter Four. Here a study of Anse and Cash illustrates how Faulkner distances various characters and uses them to reinforce humorously and ironically themes treated more seriously elsewhere.

Chapter Five discusses the role of myth in As I Lay Dying, explores some of the sources of Faulkner's myth, and suggests that Eliot and Joyce were his main inspiration. It concludes that the Odyssey, the Agamemnon and Demeter/Persephone stories, and Joyce's Ulysses are the primary parallels, and that Faulkner used these traditions to write about contemporary life in mythic terms.

The author concludes that As I Lay Dying fits the aesthetic category of the grotesque as defined by Wolfgang Kayser in The Grotesque in Art and Literature. [Order No. 73-16,566; 277 pages. DAI, 34A (July-Aug. 1973), 331-32.]

239 Faulkner's Initiation Stories: An Approach to the Major Works / Henry Wooten PEABODY, University of Denver, 1972 (Stuart B. James).

This study is based on the following theory: an examination of the initiation pattern in The Unvanquished, Intruder in the Dust, and The Reivers can offer significant dividends for readers of more challenging novels like Go Down, Moses, Light in August, and Absalom, Absalom!. What one gains from the initiation stories is best described as a perspective that reveals unifying patterns in the major work, but the kind of perspective that one gains can be suggested by at least five distinct patterns in the initiation stories:

1. Each boy moves from the security of his community's use of behavior to a moment when that code is no longer adequate.

2. Each boy reaches maturity in a crisis when his heart is in conflict with itself.

3. Each boy concludes that his internal conflict is insoluble but that he must never quit trying.

4. Each boy matures to a point where he can accept Faulkner's tragic view of life.

5. In each novel Faulkner's pattern of development is based on juxtaposition. Sometimes characters are compared or contrasted implicitly; sometimes events are played off upon one another; and sometimes paired chapters are used to evoke the opposing forces in the protagonist's internal conflict.

The conflict between family-community loyalty and the demands of individual vision plays a large part in all three major novels, and of course the "human heart in conflict with itself" is always important in Faulkner's novels. Norms for behavior in Faulkner's world are extremely hard to find, but when one is conversant with the idea that people "must not stop," he can often find characters who are tempted to "stop," characters who yield to that temptation, and characters who refuse to yield. The three major novels treated in this study are filled with characters of all three types; they are more understandable for one who is familiar with this norm. Faulkner's tragic view of life is certainly important to readers of his fiction, but the explicit comments that one finds in records of Faulkner interviews are extremely cryptic; so a logical strategy might well be a careful study of those works in which his treatment of this tragic sense of life is most nearly didactic. In The Wild Palms Faulkner showed how far he could go in experiments with juxtaposition, his most distinctive technique. It plays a major role in all of his novels. In the relatively simple initiation stories one is able to see Faulkner using this technique in the service of fairly obvious purposes. The relationship between Faulkner's means and his ends is more clear than it is in his major work; so one can see, in these minor novels, the things that he must be alert for in those novels that are famous for their complexity.

The application of the foregoing theory is carried out in six essays, one on each novel. The unifying patterns of the novels are suggested by the chapter titles: (1) "The Unvanquished: The Power of the Dream and the Power of the Tradition"; (2) "Intruder in the Dust: The Community and Individual Vision"; (3) "The Reivers: Integrity as a Continuing Struggle with Duality"; (4) "Go Down, Moses: Freedom from a Cursed Family in a Cursed Land"; (5) "Light in August: Light, Darkness, and the Harsh Gale of Living"; and (6) "Absalom, Absalom!: The Tragic, Shadowy Ground between Cynicism and Belief." The ironic "freedom" in Go Down, Moses is a dream that Chick Mallison repudiated in Intruder in the Dust; the problems of duality in Light in August are related to the problems that Lucius Priest struggled with in The Reivers; and Absalom, Absalom! develops according to a pattern of opposing forces that is used in The Unvanquished. [Order No. 72-33,054; 172 pages. DAI, 33A (Jan.-Feb. 1973), 3663.]

240 Earth, Air, Fire, and Water: The Elements in Faulkner's Fiction / Constance Mae PIERCE, Pennsylvania State University, 1972 (Philip Young).

The body of Faulkner's fiction is characterized by a pervasive use of symbolism and imagery derived from the four elements: earth, air, fire, and water. A close reading of individual works indicates that the elements function rather consistently on several levels, both thematic and structural, and that the interrelating and counterpointing of the imagery and symbolism is connected with many of Faulkner's more prominent concerns--the attempt to create order out of chaos, the revelation of knowledge, the assertion of sexuality, to name a few. Although Faulkner's pattern is ultimately revealed through the ways in which the elements relate to one another, the heaviest emphasis is placed on fire, which appears with significance in almost every work.

In keeping with the Promethean myth, fire provides a symbolic pride not only for Ab Snopes, as explicitly stated in "Barn Burning," but for Faulkner's other oppressed and alienated characters as well. The destructive power of fire allows Joe Christmas, Benjy Compson, Wash Jones, Mink Snopes, Clytemnestra and others to claim momentary recognition from a society that otherwise would ignore them, thus illustrating the dual nature of the element that is both creator and destroyer. Fire is also extended to include sexual pride, and for Faulkner's sexually ineffectual characters, such as Flem Snopes and Popeye, the element functions almost as a surrogate virility. Further the technological extensions of fire (the automobile, the gun, the airplane) operate in a similar manner, ironically enough, since it is technology which is in part responsible for the impotence of Faulkner's men.

It is with regard to sexuality that the other elements come fully into play. In keeping with various traditions, the elements divide, earth and water aligning with the female principle, air and fire with the masculine. The sexual conflicts so prominent in Faulkner's works are reinforced by a comparable warring of the elements as male and female elemental images are pitted one against the other. Similarly, as conflicts are resolved and order is achieved, the elements often exhibit harmonious relationships, suggesting that Faulkner is making use of the Renaissance notion that world order depends on the concordance of earth, air, fire, and water. In fact, Faulkner's use of the elements most often can be viewed as relative to literary and philosophical traditions. He appears to draw from Platonic and Pythagorean thought, from classical mythology, from the Bible, from Freudian psychology, as well as other, more obscure, sources.

It seems apparent, then, that definite contexts can be established for the elements as they appear in Faulkner's fiction, that his use of them is far from random. Indeed, he often times appears to be moving within various traditions or reinterpreting these traditions in terms of their modern significance. But perhaps most importantly the intricate structuring of the elemental images and symbols amplifies his themes and adds artistic power and cohesion to his work, thus, along with the traditional associations, increasing the profundity of his art. [Order No. 73-14,038; 144 pages. DAI, 33A (May-June 1973), 6927.]

241 A World of Voices: "Talking" in the Novels of William Faulkner / Stephen Moodey ROSS, Stanford University, 1972 (Thomas C. Moser).

In this dissertation, fictional "talking" refers not only to quoted dialogue, but also to any dramatic illusion of people speaking to one another-- as when a narrator talks to his readers, or when a character narrates a story to other characters. Faulkner's novels and stories contain strikingly large amounts of talking: time and again he lets his characters share in the telling of a story, or he lets them expostulate at great length about what events mean. The most important scenes in Faulkner's fiction, scenes that become almost archetypal within his world, are those in which a young man (like Quentin Compson) listens to someone tell of the past and of the young man's heritage.

The presence of so many voices in Faulkner's world emphasizes what he has said himself, that he conceives of fiction more as told story than as written artifact. Living in a Southern community in which oral modes of discourse--conversation, story-telling, preaching, oratory of various kinds-- retained tremendous social and cultural authority, Faulkner understandably adapted Southern oral traditions to his own artistic purposes. He acquired many of his stories, and many of his techniques, as much through listening as through reading. He felt the impact of certain attitudes which tend to be reinforced by vital oral traditions: a strong sense of the individual's place in his community, a vivid awareness of the past as it affects the present, and a perception (and re-creation) of the world as an organic whole rather than a sum of discrete parts.

I examine the nature of talking as it helps form the techniques and themes of Faulkner's four major works through 1936. After preliminary consideration of talking as a subject in Mosquitoes, and of the presence of voices in the background of Sartoris, I describe three kinds of talking individual voices, the community voice, and the voice of the Southern past. In The Sound and the Fury, Faulkner bases his version of stream of consciousness on story-telling that is distorted to reflect psychological states; he also builds the Compson brothers' monologues largely out of remembered talk, such as Quentin's confrontations with his father and with Caddy, or Jason's conversations with his mother. The community talk of the average citizens of Yoknapatawpha County first appears in some of the monologues in As I Lay Dying; it is developed further in the short stories about Jefferson, and finally assumes moral dimensions in the voices we hear in Light in August. In Absalom, Absalom! Faulkner extends the impressionistic method (derived from Joseph Conrad) by drawing on the tradition of Southern oratory; he employs the cumulative and extravagant rhythms of oratory to evoke an overriding voice that each narrator speaks in; he constructs the novel in a carefully contrived pattern similar to the persuasive rhetoric of oratory. [Order No. 72-16,783; 301 pages. DAI, 32A (May-June 1972), 7002.]

242 Cinematic Techniques in the Novels of William Faulkner / Sister Paul Christi SAVARESE, St. Louis University, 1972 (Joseph George Knapp).

The relation between literature and the film is, at the present time, the object of increased attention among many people engaged in higher education and in literary criticism. However, actual studies of writers who may be "cinematic" are all to few. This dissertation examines the novels of William Faulkner in an attempt to establish his position as a cinematic writer.

Two factors contribute to the presence of film techniques in Faulkner's work: his own unique visual imagination which bears a strong affinity to the visual emphasis found in film production and, more specifically, his actual experience in Hollywood as a scenarist over a long period of time which gave him a first-hand knowledge of cinematic techniques used in the film industry.

The examination of his novels in relation to film is divided into four categories: time, space, editing, and sound. Understanding how time is treated in the film leads to a clarification of Faulkner's use of time in his novels. The film techniques of flashback, flash-forward, slow motion, and stasis are explained and illustrated by passages from Faulkner's novels. The space continuum, presented filmically by the camera, reaches the viewer in a variety of camera shots, literary equivalents of which can be found in Faulkner. Similarly, the editing process by which different movie scenes and sequences are put together involves such devices as straight cuts, dissolves, and fades. These, too, appear in Faulkner as transitions between scenes, chapters or main parts of a novel. Montage, related to editing but in reality of far greater thematic importance, is also present in Faulkner's work.

Finally, Faulkner's use of sound, intensified by his acute aural sense, resembles the way sound is used in a film. The sound track of a motion picture is used not only to match dialogue with the visual image but also to increase the realistic rendering of a scene. In addition, sound is often used metaphorically in a film. The function of sound in Faulkner corresponds to the way a sound track is used in film production.

Though Faulkner may not have consciously used literary transpositions of cinematic techniques in his writing, they are there in abundance and contribute substantially to that special quality of his work which simultaneously perplexes and delights readers and critics. The presence of cinematic techniques in Faulkner's novels enhances his work in several ways which are discussed in the conclusion.

Since Faulkner's style often obfuscates a clear understanding of his work, it is suggested that he be studied "cinematically." Familiarity with film aesthetics is constantly gaining momentum in the academic world. Using the film as an avenue of approach to a difficult writer like Faulkner would provide a new method for elucidating and appreciating his complex style. An example of "cinematic reading" is provided in the appendix to illustrate one way of using a filmic approach to literature. [Order No. 72-24,011; 162 pages. DAI, 33A (Jan.-Feb. 1972), 1179.]

243 William Faulkner and The Search for Lost Time: Three Aspects of Literary Deformation / Margaret Christine Trieschmann SCANLAN, University of Iowa, 1972 (David Hayman).

The appreciation the French have accorded William Faulkner's novels, even when he was out of print in the United States, is well known. Less familiar is a fact which may help to account for this appreciation: Faulkner's affinity for French literature, expressed in his translation of Symboliste poems and his repeated praise of Proust. Sufficient attention has not been paid to the analogues between Proust and Faulkner. Like Proust, Faulkner created a coherent and "realistic" fictional world, yet deformed that world through post-Symbolist techniques and vision. In both instances, historical materials are used to establish a reality, style, and the creation of novelistic myth to extend and stipulate its meaning.

Rémy de Gourmont declared that popular speech and poetry characteristically deform language. In Proust and Faulkner we see both types of deformation. Both are interested in dialect, which Proust uses to mythicize Française and to suggest the mutability of language, while Faulkner uses a "spelling dialect" in Sartoris to reinforce a condescending attitude toward his uneducated characters. In <u>The Sound and the Fury</u> Faulkner exploits the poetic suggestiveness of deviant speech. He later creates for the Snopes trilogy an artificial language which blends dialect with educated speech. Both writers use long fluid sentences which deform syntax and contain a "double" vision of individual consciousness and society. But Proust tends to resolve conflicts intellectually whereas Faulkner underscores them.

<u>Un amour de Swann</u> is closely linked to the rest of <u>A la recherche du temps perdu</u>. Deformation of frame is signaled by conventional forms of authorial intervention, allusions to the narrator, and metaphors of sickness which come from the narrator's own consciousness. The "mythic" quality of the story resides less in allusion than in structure, especially (Levi-Strauss) in the "double" time structure. The story is not only Swann's but a model for all of the other stories to which it is linked. In <u>Absalom, Absalom!</u>, we see another self-conscious imitation of myth. Each of the narrators is unreliable, but when they tell the Sutpen story they use a common narrative voice, which unifies the narration and suggests the possibility of personal transcendence. A repetitive, circular narrative technique helps to create the "timeless" world of myth. As in Proust there is considerable interpenetration of narrator and story, which is reinforced by images which suggest the theatrical quality of life ordinarily lived and its reality when imaginatively re-created. A comparison with Wallace Stevens underscores the notion that, while valuing the imagination, Faulkner and Proust use it, not to posit a separate <u>mundo</u>, but to re-create a personal or regional past.

"Openness to <u>event</u>" extends to the use of historical materials. Both writers use these realistic materials but deform them to fit the fictional world. Proust's treatment of the Dreyfus Affair is in many respects conventional, but he ignores its political implications to concentrate on changes in <u>le monde</u> and on psychology. He demonstrates the instability and irrationality of even the most enlightened politics. The narrator concludes that neither politics nor society can provide the enduring reality which he finds only in art. In the Snopes trilogy we see the gradual disintegration of a fabulous world. Where Proust used one or two major historical events, Faulkner portrays the more diffuse effects of world wars and social change. In <u>The Hamlet</u> there are already hints that the fabulous world has been created to be destroyed. In The Mansion Faulkner re-creates Mink's timeless world and opposes it to Linda's world of historical time. Linda and Mink together kill Flem; thus he dies at the hands of two orders to time. Unlike Proust, Faulkner refuses to transcend historical experience. [Order No. 72-26,732; 205 pages. DAI, 33A (Sept.-Oct. 1972), 1741-42.]

244 The Search for Identity of Faulkner's Black Characters / Frank Howard THOMAS, III, University of Pittsburgh, 1972 (Thomas L. Philbrick).

The characters dealt with in this thesis have, or are thought to have, black ancestors. Moreover, excepting Sam Fathers, their primary roles in their fictional contexts define them as black characters. These characters are examined in order to understand their individual searches for identity and, particularly, the role of race in their development. Unlike other studies of William Faulkner's black characters, this study does not attempt to apply the perspective of Faulkner biography to the fictional evidence. My contention is that the characters will be seen most accurately in terms of their fictional context alone.

This dissertation reaches no single conclusion about the search for identity of fictional black characters, but rather reaches as many conclusions as there are characters under consideration. In fact, the diversity of revealed personalities among the principal figures considered attests to Faulkner's fine sensitivity to the many forms (of behavior, values, self-awareness) of black humanity. The central figures are Simon Strother (Sartoris); Ringo Strother (The Unvanquished); Old Job, the Deacon, and Dilsey (The Sound and the Fury); Molly and Lucas Beauchamp (Go Down, Moses and Intruder in the Dust); Nancy Mannigoe ("That Evening Sun" and Requiem for a Nun); and Sam Fathers (Go Down, Moses and "A Justice"). My introductory chapter explains the principles of inclusion and exclusion.

Brief discussion of two of these characters' analyses will indicate this study's specific concerns and methods and the shape of its conclusions. Simon Strother, the old family retainer of the Sartorises in post-World War I Jefferson, has constructed his identity not only in harmony with but also often in outright mimicry of the values and traditions of the white Southern aristocracy that surrounds him. Since Simon has discovered, well before the time-present of Sartoris, an identity in which he is confident and secure, the means by which Simon maintains his self-image and the image others have of him are this chapter's main concerns. What little evidence Sartoris gives of Simon's background serves as a clue to the impetus for and process of Simon's identity formation. But his main importance in the novel, in the Yoknapatawpha saga, and in the chapter devoted to him is the meaning of his role and personality for the modern world that has defined him, and many like him (even including old Bayard Sartoris), as hopelessly out-of-step and therefore unworthy of full respect or concern.

The analysis of Joe Christmas is this study's most exhaustive and its pivotal chapter in terms both of theme and of method. The evidence of Light in August takes the reader from the circumstances, however dubious, surrounding Joe's conception to the moment of his death. There is more specific raw material by which to examine Joe's search for identity than is available for any other black character in Faulkner. The psychological workings, in Joe, of the unsubstantiated, unprovable belief that he has inherited a drop of black blood are the focus of this part of my analysis. It is Joe's reaction and the reactions of others to this questionable aspect of his make-up that constitute the driving forces in, as well as the major obstacles to, his efforts to achieve a dependable and consistent identity.

Seeking such an identity--along with, ideally, the autonomy of a Lucas Beauchamp--is a process involving many of Faulkner's characters. Blackness, however, brings its own special problems and results for characters engaged in the search. A goal of this study is to reveal Faulkner's broad and deep contribution to an aesthetically provocative and socially crucial matter: the identity struggles of black people in America. [Order No. 73-13,250; 307 pages. DAI, 33A (May-June 1973), 6935.]

245 William Faulkner's Yoknapatawpha: The Land of Broken Dreams /
Evelyn Joyce THOMPSON, Texas Tech University, 1972 (J.T. McCULLEN, Jr).

The physical earth has been from the beginning of Southern history a vital force at work in the lives of Southern people. Sociologists, notably Howard W. Odum, and Southern writers, especially members of the Agrarian Movement, have emphasized the strong ties between Southerners and their land. Of all the Southern writers, William Faulkner makes the greatest use of the land to reflect the condition of the South and its people. Concentrating on his imaginary Yoknapatawpha County in Mississippi, Faulkner tells the story of the people who inhabit the area. Of primary importance in telling this story is the story of the land which serves as the foundation of aristocratic wealth and power.

The five original aristocracies of Yoknapatawpha County--the Greniers, the Compsons, the McCaslins, the Sutpens, and the Sartorises--approach a virgin wilderness to take land on which they attempt to give concrete form to their dreams of grandeur. Although all of the original settlers are momentarily successful in their designs, the land ultimately rejects those who have abused it; and the dreams of a perpetual dynasty, which the first gentlemen nurtured, crumble as their descendants renounce their heritages and allow the land to pass out of their hands.

One can see the fate of the land which originally belonged to these families as long as he can trace the history of the families themselves, and he can see the parallel relationship between the situation of the families and the condition of their land even though the land often acquires new owners. As the families--the Greniers, the Compsons, and the Sutpens--age and wane, the land which they have owned also falls into disuse and ruin. As the Edmondses, the descendants of the original McCaslin's daughter, turn to industrialized exploitation of their land, they become alienated from it. Although the land remains in the legal possession of the Edmondses, it grudgingly yields its fruit to unsympathetic hands. As the Sartoris family passes into dignified old age, its land passes into peaceful productivity. Faulkner pictures, unmistakably, in his portraits of these families and their land, the enduring ties which exist between Southerners and the land which sustains them. [Order No. 73-4079; 162 pages. DAI, 33A (Jan.-Feb. 1973), 4435-36.]

246 Jeffersonian Agrarianism in Faulkner's Yoknapatawpha: The Evolution of Social and Economic Standard / Gerald Fred WEBB, Florida State University, 1972 (Griffith T. Pugh).

Faulkner's examination of the South focuses, in part, on the dual abuses of the South's economic system: the violation of man's proper role as caretaker of the earth and his violation of human dignity through the institution of slavery. From the Yoknapatawpha Indian who is gradually corrupted by European concepts of land possession to the 20th century Snopes who uses the land for economic exploitation as a commodity of trade, the Southerner's record is largely one of systematic exploitation of land and people.

The first whites to enter the Yoknapatawpha are men of vision but the vision is flawed. Carothers McCaslin and Jason Compson seek to establish family lineage. The wealth necessary to establish and maintain a family line is to be taken from the land which the exhaustive plantation system demanded in vast, expendable quantities. To wrest from the land its natural wealth, great quantities of labor are needed and thus, in nurturing and expanding the slave system, the Southerner's peculiarly tainted dual heritage is completed. A later arrival, such as Sutpen, only accentuates and intensifies the errors of the South, for time is foreshortened in the shadow of an impending Civil War.

The Civil War terminates legal slavery, but spawns what is for Faulkner an equally repulsive set of circumstances with the rise of the commerce oriented, "New South" Snopesism. Men and land are still exploited; the restraining web is now economic.

Thus, in an important sense, Faulkner rejects what may be viewed as the dominant currents of the South, past and present. The Compsons, the McCaslins, the Sutpens, the Varners, and the Snopeses err by abnegating man's fundamental responsibility to the earth and to his fellow man. The only individuals in the South Faulkner draws with a positive consistency are the yeoman farmers. Guilty of neither the moral abuses of the past nor the commercial abuses of the present, the yeoman holds viable and temporary title to the earth in quantities sufficient for the subsistence of himself and his immediate family. The fierce economic, political, and moral independence seen in Faulkner's yeoman reflects an intellectual position substantially identical to that of Thomas Jefferson whose tenets Faulkner may simply have assimilated from his society. A second, influential source for Faulkner's fictional portraits may be found in the frequently overlooked, but always present, small farmer indigenous to Southern society.

Whatever the impetus and sources of influence, there is little question that it is the yeoman who represents for Faulkner the pattern of life which is most substantive and meaningful in the 20th century. In the Yoknapatawpha County the McCallums, the Tulls, the Bookwrights, the Hamptons, and the Griers culminate man's potential for social, political, and economic virtue through a type of Jeffersonian agrarianism wherein they are the caretakers and conservers of the earth and the defenders of republicanism. In Faulkner's presentation of the yeoman can be found a succinct, positive, intellectual position containing no taint of "cosmic pessimism" and affirming long before the Nobel laureate address the qualities which enable man to endure and prevail. [Order No. 73-9388; 162 pages. DAI, 33A (March-April 1973), 5754.]

247 Faulkner's Absalom, Absalom! and Dickens: A Study of Time and Change Correspondences / Louis C. BERRONE, Jr., Fordham University, 1973 (John V. Antush).

A review of the primary texts and the canon of Faulkner-Dickens criticism indicated that correspondence between fixed attitudes towards time and change in characters in Absalom and correlative attitudes in characters in Dickens' fiction constitute an analogical way of knowing how disastrous such fixed attitudes can be. For example, analogues between young Tom Sutpen and young Pip in Great Expectations help the reader to understand Tom's transformation of character and his commitment to the future. Both boys are victims of class and class-child prejudices. Tom is humiliated by the black butler when he is the poor white "boy-symbol at the door" to the manor house. Pip is humiliated at the door to Satis House. Both boys compensate for their feelings of inferiority by projecting grandiose plans into their distant future to emulate their oppressors. The analogues with Dickens suggest that Faulkner touches upon a universal feeling of inferiority in young Tom and that his attempts to compensate for those feelings by controlling the future are not isolated examples of Southern experience, but are, rather, representative exempla of similar attempts in other places and times. The analogues throughout Absalom seem to add new insights into the archetypal nature of the characters.

Analogues with Paul Dombey, Sr., in Dombey and Son provide insights into Sutpen's hardened determination to control the future by means of a son and heir. Daughters for both Sutpen and Dombey are less prestigious than sons. Both men also mistreat their wives. After his sickness Dombey does feel remorse for his misdeeds against women, and he does relinquish his dreams for dynasty to express his love for Florence, her husband, and her child in the present. Sutpen never feels remorse, his dreams for dukedom remain unflagged, and his attitudes towards women never improve.

Sutpen like Lady Dedlock in Bleak House manifests Faustian traits when he sells his soul for the glittering future of high class status. He repudiates his first wife and son because they have "a drop" of Negro blood in them: a stigma that prevents them from being accepted as "aristocratic" gentry in the South. Lady Dedlock repudiates her first lover and her daughter by him because she wants to marry into the aristocracy. The immorality of social taboos against miscegenation and their effects on Sutpen's mulatto son and his descendants is represented by their contracting yellow fever, similarly as the immorality of social taboos against the lower classes and the effects of those taboos on Esther and her friends is represented by their contracting the slum-bred disease of smallpox.

Analogues between Sutpen and Compeyson in Great Expectations focus on their harsh treatment of women. Rosa Coldfield withdraws into a darkened house and wears black for 43 years and Miss Havisham withdraws into her darkened house and wears her white wedding gown for 25 years to sustain past-haunted hatred against the villainous fiances who injured them. Eulalia Bon acts out a kind of Havisham Complex against Sutpen when she unleashes her son for revenge against him, even as Miss Havisham unleashes Estella against all men. Quentin Compson's predicaments are in some ways similar to those of Richard Carstone's in Bleak House in that he cannot disentangle himself from the Wiglomerations that confuse him as an emotionally-involved party to the case of Southern history. As the reader comes to understand such correspondence between characters in Absalom and in Dickens' fiction, he enlarges his perspective on how Faulkner's characters lose sight of love and piety in the present because they are possessed by inordinate future expectations or past traumas. [Order No. 74-2492; 258 pages. DAI, 34A (Jan.-Feb. 1974), 5158.]

248 Point of View as a Mode of Thematic Definition in Conrad and Faulkner/ Hae-Ja Kim CHUNG, University of Michigan, 1973 (Lyall H. Powers.)

Some modern novels have affinity with Symbolist poetry in their metaphysical vision and the narrative technique used to express it. In these novels, the concrete object of sense-perception does not comprise reality in itself, but serves as a symbol for the imaginative truth of the individual mind. Since the imaginative truth is subjective and multifarious, no arbitrary authority on objective truth, such as the omniscient author, can be present in the novel; instead, it is imperative to make the reader participate actively in the novel, to lead his cognitive process into a deliberate but rewarding dilemma by creating confusion in his mind through the controlled medium of point of view. The assumption of this study is that in Conrad and Faulkner the technique of point of view is an organic part of the novel, a mode of thematic definition.

The ultimate meaning of the imaginative truth differs in the two writers, reflecting their respective moral perspectives. In Conrad, no positive universal truth can be revealed to man and thus life is founded on the created values of man's consciousness, what Conrad calls, illusion. Lord Jim is in a sense Marlow's understanding of Jim's imaginative truth, a dream of heroic responsibility; Nostromo is an examination of material interests in terms of several imaginative truths of the various characters. In Faulkner, life is self-revealing when one lives by cyclical time--by the truth of the heart. The individual mind constantly tries to construct the continuum of cyclical time in its consciousness while assessing the real value of the past. However, an individual, like a fraction of the continuum, is able to see only one phase of the truth and tends to make it a personal matter, often turning the imaginative truth into an obsession or a perversion of truth. The Sound and the Fury contrasts the perverted, imaginative truths with the truth of the heart; Absalom, Absalom! best dramatizes the cognitive process of conceiving imaginative truth in one's consciousness; The Wild Palms sets the truth of the heart against the self-destructive imaginative truth of the mind.

Both Conrad and Faulkner dramatize the effects of "the confusion between the imaginary world and the real" in the first-person or eye-witness narrators and a further confusion between the perceptions of different minds in multiple point of view. Presenting each point of view as partially unreliable makes the reader experience confusion and compels him to search for the truth on his own. However, since in Conrad the search for truth is to reveal what is behind appearance, the different perspectives mostly serve as ironic contradictions and commentaries on each other; whereas in Faulkner, universal truth can be revealed by the sum of different consciousnesses and each of the different perspectives represents one phase of the total truth. Conrad and Faulkner used the similar technique of point of view to reflect their metaphysical vision, but their difference in moral perspective is inevitably implicated in the ultimate meaning of the imaginative truth and point of view. [Order No. 74-15,649; 174 pages. DAI, 35A (July-Aug. 1974), 442-43.]

249 The Serpent of Lust in the Southern Garden: the Theme of Miscegenation in Cable, Twain, Faulkner, and Warren / William Bedford CLARK, Louisiana State University and Agricultural and Mechanical College, 1973 (Darwin Shrell).

Throughout its history, this nation has been deeply race-conscious, and, as a result, the concept of miscegenation has generated a profound influence upon the American literary imagination. Quite naturally, this influence has been felt most forcefully by writers in the South, where the question of sexual relations across the color-line is still surrounded by sinister associations of horror, guilt, and outrage of a particularly virulent sort. Despite the persistence with which Southern writers have returned to the theme of miscegenation, however, little has been done to explore the reasons behind their fascination with mixed blood, and few critics have addressed themselves to a systematic consideration of the unique literary potential of the theme.

In an effort to correct this situation in part, my dissertation begins by defining the dimensions of the theme of miscegenation through an analysis of a paradigmatic short story, Joel Chandler Harris' "Where's Duncan?". A careful reading of that story yields four fictional motifs that appear repeatedly in the works of other Southern writers: (1) a basic narrative pattern involving the progression from guilt to retribution; (2) a tendency to identify the particular "sin" of miscegenation with the racial "sins" of the South as a whole; (3) the portrayal of the character of mixed blood as both victim and avenger; and (4) the question of the mulatto character's crisis of identity. I offer a hypothetical explanation for each of these aspects of the broader theme based on a survey of abolitionist tracts, anti-slavery fiction, and antebellum travelogues treating the question of miscegenation in the South. I then proceed to trace the theme in the works of George Washington Cable, Mark Twain, William Faulkner, and Robert Penn Warren.

In works like "Tite Poulette," Madame Delphine, and The Grandissimes, Cable uses the plight of the New Orleans quadroon caste to point up the dehumanizing aspects of the South's inheritance of racial wrongs. Twain's Pudd'nhead Wilson is a novel which begins as an indictment of specific Southern shortcomings and ends as a bitter satire on the "damned human race" in general. It points toward the author's final conviction that "the skin of every human being contains a slave." Faulkner's Absalom, Absalom! and Go Down, Moses stand as the two most successful novels growing out of the theme of miscegenation and are dealt with in some detail. The final chapter of this study concerns itself with the way in which the identity crisis of the mulatto character prefigures the situation confronting contemporary man who is increasingly faced with a sense of alienation and uncertainty regarding who and what he is. Faulkner's Joe Christmas in Light in August and Warren's Amantha Starr in Band of Angels are remarkable cases in point.

Although this study is by necessity limited in focus, one of its purposes is to suggest the breadth of the tradition in question and to demonstrate the range of its literary potential. [Order No. 74-7213; 190 pages. DAI, 34A (March-April 1974), 5958-59.]

250 Faulkner's Vitalistic Vision: A Close Study of Eight Novels / Peter Glenn CROW, Duke University, 1973 (Victor H. Strandberg).

This study shows how Faulkner's fiction is antithetical to the sense of despair over lost values and over deflated human stature associated by many writers with the modern era. Implicit in Faulkner's fiction is the belief that value resides primarily in vitality rather than ethical imperatives. Because in the modern world of fluid mores ethical imperatives are difficult both to define and to maintain, the possibilities for a full life through the exercise of personal vitality are all the more important.

To illustrate Faulkner's view, I have chosen eight Yoknapatawpha County novels. Four of those represent four modes of vitality identifiable throughout the author's work. They are: As I Lay Dying (comic-cyclical pattern of vitality), Absalom, Absalom! (Tragic-linear pattern of vitality), Light in August (tragicomic suspension from vitality), and The Hamlet (pattern-free vitality). Two novels, Sanctuary and Go Down, Moses, represent respectively a general retreat from vitality through despair and idealism. Finally, two novels, The Sound and the Fury and The Reivers, present the full spectrum of vitalistic modes in extremes of obsessed atrophy and reminiscent glory.

Faulkner associates certain characteristics, values, and limitations with each mode of vitality. The vitality of linear characters such as Boon Hogganbeck and Jewel Bundren originates in will and moves uncompromisingly toward specific objectives. Taken to an extreme, this kind of vitality becomes tragic, as exemplified by Thomas Sutpen and Joe Christmas. The tragic character, during his lifetime, achieves a sense of individual identity and provides a focus of interest for people who know him. After his death, he becomes a legend. Yet his life is a lonely one, and his goals prove ultimately to be elusive.

The vitality of cyclical characters such as Everbe "Corrie" Corinthia originates in instinct and moves in a recurring pattern usually related to regeneration or work routine. In fullest measure, this kind of vitality becomes comic (in the "old Greek" tradition of the term), as exemplified by fertility figures such as Lena Grove or Eula Varner. The recurrence of these figures in Faulkner's works as manifestations of archetypes is appropriate to their communal rather than individual proclivities. The value of the comic mode is the preservation and perpetuation of life and motion. The main limitation is a lack of individual recognition.

Tragicomic suspension from active involvement in life is illustrated by the irreconcilable conflicts between ideals from the past and imperfections of the present experienced by Gail Hightower, Quentin Compson, and Emily Grierson. As a permanent state, such a suspension has no value other than a sort of indomitable immobility which is essentially the antithesis of vitality. As a temporary state, however, it provides detached perspective during periods of both growth and reminiscence.

When detachment is combined with vitality, pattern-free behavior becomes possible. This is the mode of vitality open to those lacking in (male) vigor or (female) bustline and disinclined to accept limited linear or cyclical fulfillment. The pattern-free characters, exemplified by Flem Snopes, V. K. Ratliff, and Ned McCaslin, are the most unconfined in their actions, but they do not experience either the emotional intensity of the tragic-linear characters or the depth of fulfillment of the comic-cyclical characters. Because of their capacity through manipulation to channel the behavior of other people toward their own ends, the pattern-free characters command great potential for producing happiness when their motives are altruistic, for causing pain when their motives are selfish, and for getting into mischief when their often intricate schemes backfire.

This investigation demonstrates that Faulkner is more versatile in his outlook on life and more consistent in presenting that outlook throughout his career than has heretofore been acknowledged. [Order No. 73-19,470; 329 pages. DAI, 34A (July-Aug. 1973), 764-65.]

251 Lost Ladies: The Isolated Heroine in the Fiction of Hawthorne, James, Fitzgerald, Hemingway, and Faulkner / Sharon Welch DEAN, University of New Hampshire, 1973 (Philip L. Nicoloff).

The plight of the lost lady is captured in Hawthorne's The Marble Faun when Miriam Schaefer cries out that "when women have other objects in life, they are not apt to fall in love." In much of the best American fiction, women do not have other objects beyond the domestic. The source of the lost women's dilemma, however, is that even the domestic role is denied her. Because she is a sexual threat or because love is impossible in a wasteland society, she is exiled by women who conform more than she, by men, and by the world as a whole. As a result of her exile, she seeks an impossible escape from isolation, most often via an illicit love relationship. When this fails, she accepts --or even chooses--her isolation and in doing so practices some form of martydom as the only role left her.

Such a woman appears frequently in the works of Hawthorne, James, Fitzgerald, Hemingway, and Faulkner. She is represented specifically by Hawthorne's Hester Prynne (The Scarlet Letter, 1850), Zenobia (The Blithedale Romance, 1852), and Miriam Schaefer (The Marble Faun, 1859), by James' Kate Croy (The Wings of the Dove, 1902) and Charlotte Stant (The Golden Bowl, 1904), by Fitzgerald's Gloria Gilbert (The Beautiful and the Damned, 1922) and Nicole Diver (Tender Is the Night, 1933), by Hemingway's Lady Brett Ashley (The Sun Also Rises, 1926), Catherine Barkley (A Farewell to Arms, 1929), and Maria (For Whom the Bell Tolls, 1940), and by Faulkner's Caddy Compson (The Sound and the Fury, 1929), Laverne Shumann (Pylon, 1935), and Charlotte Rittenmeyer (The Wild Palms, 1939). The elements of sexuality, isolation, and sacrifice are the dominant characteristics of these women. They reveal not just the author's vision of womanhood but also his vision of life. For Hawthorne and James, the social order must survive and the woman who threatens to destroy this social order, most often by ignoring its laws against adultery, must atone for her sin. The Hawthorne and James lost woman, therefore, accepts isolation for society rather than continuing to seek isolation from society. On the other hand, Fitzgerald does not so clearly endorse the value of the social order; his heroine pays tribute to the isolated moments of love and practices her renunciation more for an individual than for society as a whole. Like Fitzgerald, Hemingway believes in the worth of the isolated moment, but like Hawthorne and James, he sees also that this isolation can destroy. Where the Hawthorne and James woman sacrifices for the social order which is valuable and the Fitzgerald woman sacrifices for the individual, the Hemingway woman sacrifices for her lover because the social order is necessary if a male is to live productively. Finally, in Faulkner, the value of society is neither asserted nor denied; when Faulkner's lost woman renounces, she does so in order that someone else, most often a child, may at least have a chance for survival in society if he chooses this over isolation.

Hawthorne, James, Fitzgerald, Hemingway, and Faulkner all use the lost lady as a vehicle for exploring the conflict between isolation and society. She is an especially appropriate vehicle because of her limited feminine role. Where the man may live his life, the female must surrender hers. Where the man may find fulfillment outside of love, the female may not and, what is more, either loses the love that temporarily sustains her or never finds love at all. By forcing his lost lady into this kind of plight, the writer stresses the importance of maintaining male and female uniqueness. He finds inspiration from his heroine and yet keeps her always at an idealizing distance so that she cannot demand too much of him or plunge him into the inertia a perfect love relationship might engender. More important, the heroine, by suffering and sacrificing, attains the necessary depth needed for tragic stature. The lost woman is remembered precisely because she is left with nothing but pain and because she selflessly endures this pain with humility and with dignity. [Order No. 73-25,782; 254 pages. DAI, 34A (Nov.-Dec. 1973), 1616.]

252 Towards a New Objectivity: Essays on the Body and Nature in Faulkner, Lawrence, and Mann / John Clark ELDER, Yale University, 1973 (Charles Feidelson, Jr.).

In its three essays, this dissertation discusses treatments of the human body and nature in certain novels of William Faulkner, D. H. Lawrence, and Thomas Mann. For each of these novelists, the body is both the most immediate manifestation of the physical world and a primary symbol for the entire natural order. It is also the vehicle of true knowledge of the world, as opposed to the mind's abstract understanding. Thus, for all three writers bodily consciousness represents a goal: the assimilation into the individual subjectivity of the body's direct awareness of the world. This increased clarity of experience could provide additional guidance for human behavior, and make possible the reduction of obliviously destructive actions. For this reason the human will, in its various manifestations, is an important related subject in the essays. For the question of types of will is ultimately a matter of varying perceptions of the individual being's place in the larger natural order.

The first essay looks at three novels which form their own cycle within the larger development of Faulkner's fiction. That aspect of As I Lay Dying is emphasized which reveals the basic disjunction between human consciousness and physical reality. In the section on Absalom, Absalom! the story of Sutpen's Hundred is treated as revealing the extravagant will that is the corollary of human isolation from nature. Finally, Go Down, Moses is discussed as an attempt to escape from the pattern of isolated human consciousness, to harmonize man's life with the larger flow of life in the wilderness.

The essay on Lawrence begins with a short section on Sons and Lovers, designed to show Lawrence's relation to the main themes of English Romanticism; those themes are also important to the shape of the later novels, where they may not always be as evident. The Rainbow and Women in Love are at the main focus of the essay. Through a reading of these novels as being in essential continuity, two main categories of human will are developed: the rooted will and the isolative will, corresponding to the organic and mechanistic aspects of nature. In this connection, the essay examines the complex meaning of sexual love for Lawrence, since it leads in the novels both to the most intense experiences of human rootedness in nature and to the worst abuses of the isolative, manipulative will.

Disease is at the center of Mann's treatment of nature and the body. The final essay begins with Der Tod in Venedig, as an ironic version of Plato's "divine madness." It discusses the way in which disease is able to tie together Aschenbach's disintegration and his transcendent experience of love and beauty. In the treatment of Der Zauberberg the emphasis is on the concept of receptive existence. The warmth of decay and the fever of love are one in the novel, and in abandon to them one approaches the secret of life. Doktor Faustus is presented in part as Mann's alienation from his own ironic fascination with disease, but is also seen as the culmination of his attempt to import objective reality into the isolation of human subjectivity. [Order No. 74-10,669; 214 pages. DAI, 34A (May-June 1974), 7228.]

253 William Faulkner's Literary Reputation in Britain, with a Checklist of Criticism, 1929-1972 / James Randolph FITZGERALD, University of Georgia, 1973 (Rayburn S. Moore).

This dissertation is primarily a bibliography of approximately 1,000 entries charting William Faulkner's literary reception in Britain from 1929 when he received his first press notice there to 1972, ten years after his death. Entries include articles in British newspapers, magazines, journals, and trade publications, as well as critical notice in books either published in Britain or written by Britishers or both. There is also included a listing of Faulkner's British editions.

The accompanying essay traces the history of Faulkner in Britain, discussing how he first achieved recognition there through the efforts of Richard Hughes and Arnold Bennett, and disputes British claims that that recognition played a large part in Faulkner's subsequent appreciation in America. The essay explores the main areas of concern in the British criticism, finding them to be quite similar to the American emphases, as in Faulkner as moralist, Faulkner as regionalist, Faulkner as fatalist, etc. Particular books and articles are singled out for appraisal, including several books on Faulkner by British scholars, the three prefaces by Richard Hughes to Soldiers' Pay, The Sound and the Fury, and Mosquitoes, and the famous 1934 attack on Faulkner by Wyndham Lewis.

Faulkner's standing in Britain is found to be respectable but not of the first rank. Some theories as to why he is less popular there than in the United States or France are British displeasure with his "gauche" attention to sexual and physical matters and with the preponderance of violence in his works, the Southernisms that make him doubly difficult for the British, his stylistic innovations, and his use of the English language in a precedent-setting way.

Writers to whom Faulkner is most often compared by British critics are Joyce, Hardy, Dickens, Conrad, Huxley, and Lawrence. British influence on his writing is not seen as a major aspect of the British criticism, but comparisons are frequently made. Neither is Faulkner seen as a major influence on contemporary British writing. He is accorded special recognition as a master detective story writer and as a master at creating believable English characters.

There are indications that Faulkner's reputation in Britain is on the upswing. He is gaining attention in academic circles, is being taught at more universities, is appearing in more scholarly journals. He is also the subject of more British theses and dissertations in the past few years, becoming, in fact, the most popular American writer for such research. Since he was awarded the Nobel Prize, his book sales have increased significantly, particularly in the paperback editions.

Critical attention to Faulkner has always been extensive in Britain, and with the recent contributions of Professors Millgate, Mottram, and Tanner, among others, it is becoming of better and better quality. [Order No. 74-4796; 114 pages. DAI, 34A (March-April 1974), 5965-66.]

254 William Faulkner's Absalom, Absalom!: An Exercise in Affirmation / Donald James FORAN, University of Southern California, 1973 (Charles B. Berryman).

Absalom, Absalom! is one of Faulkner's most complex and brilliant works. Unfortunately, however, literary criticism has not produced a comprehensive interpretation of the novel which takes Faulkner's vision of life and his concept of the artist's vocation into consideration. This study explores the interrelationship of structure, imagery, and style in Absalom, Absalom!, and draws upon Faulkner's appreciation of man's and the artist's capacity for affirming rather than repudiating flawed humanity. This affirmation is the statement of the novel as a whole. It is made even in the face of specific failures of characters and societies in the story narrated.

Any comprehensive treatment of Absalom, Absalom! depends upon an analysis of three distinct levels of meaning: the Sutpen tale, the telling of that tale (and its effect upon those who tell it), and the aesthetic organization of the novel by its author. There is no spokesman for Faulkner's point of view in the novel (unlike other complex works like Go Down, Moses where Cass McCaslin articulates many Faulknerian themes), but the French architect is a type for the kind of artist who is able to curb the magnificence of his design, and create an artistic victory out of the stuff of past defeats.

Faulkner uses a wide variety of weighing and balancing images to establish Thomas Sutpen's utterly logical and incredibly innocent approach to reality. Sutpen adopts the very methodology of the system he wishes to rival. The novel's narrators, especially Quentin and Shreve, also weigh and balance, accept or discard the dead facts which they exhume but fail to breathe life into. They so abstract upon the horror of Sutpen and Sutpenism that Quentin becomes overwhelmed by the tale, and, forgetting that Sutpen was human and radically innocent, repudiates the elements of the Southern past which have sapped his vitality and dried up his interest in living. Quentin's tragedy is as profound as Sutpen's.

Absalom, Absalom! abounds in livestock and animal imagery. Victims and victimizers are literally reduced in humanity by abstract, inhuman designs. Further, persons come to be considered as chattel by those whose arbitrary "ownership" is guaranteed by a stratified society. Finally, the oppressed are often described as existing in a state of suspension, as weightless. Faulkner's concern that humanity might be "vanished from the animal called man" is brought forcefully home in this novel. The human spirit alone survives, and will ultimately prevail, but Faulkner employs another strand of imagery to suggest a solution which is at hand for characters in Absalom, Absalom!, but not embraced.

Touch, the one thing which cuts through the channels of ordering and establishes relationship, is the alternative to abstraction. The touch of flesh with flesh, if love is present, is more powerful than the shibboleths of caste or color.

Time, which elapses as the Sutpen and Quentin tragedies unfold, is not the enemy which Sutpen thinks it is nor the context for tragedy which Quentin concludes it must be. Time is the context for affirmation for those who can accept human failures without rejecting humanity.

Faulkner is arguing from absence; he organizes his material so that the reader might see the ramifications of the failure to touch and the folly of repudiation. He involves the reader in the beauty and the horror of the human situation. Faulkner makes us see that every man has the capacity for affirmation or repudiation, and that if men are in touch with the truths of the human heart, their choice will be one which upbuilds rather than destroys the human race. [Order No. 73-31,641; 212 pages. DAI, 34A (Jan.-Feb. 1974), 4259.]

255 Uses of Time in Four Novels by William Faulkner / Daniel Gordon
FORD, Auburn University, 1973 (Carl Benson).

This is a study of the varieties of temporal awareness in William Faulkner's The Sound and the Fury, Sanctuary, Light in August, and Absalom, Absalom!. The purposes of the study are: (1) to analyze the use of clock, calendar, and psychic time; (2) to assess the artistic values of Faulkner's temporal manipulations; and (3) to attempt an adequate expression of Faulkner's tenuous but profound vision of time.

The study argues that while Faulkner is deeply interested in the accurate creation of clock-calendar structure in the four novels, he is equally interested in creating a sense of non-mechanical, fluid time. Presenting evidence that Faulkner was influenced by Henri Bergson's idea of duration and Marcel Proust's idea of involuntary memory, the introduction examines what we know of Faulkner's metaphysics of time. A split in his conception of time is identified and temporal idioms from Bergson, Proust, and others are charted under the headings of clock time and psychic time.

The second chapter surveys the best criticism of Faulknerian time and establishes useful terminology for the analyses which follow. The four sections on the novels present detailed analyses of clock-calendar structure, of character and narrator psychic time, and of the thematic and organic contributions of time. The conclusion explores Faulkner's vision of time as durational. It reviews the evidence that Faulkner affirms the potential of the human heart to see "the first and the last" of human experience from an atemporal perspective. [Order No. 74-19,376; 179 pages. DAI, 35A (Sept.-Oct. 1974), 1654.]

256 Problems of Perception in the Modern Novel: The Representation of Consciousness in Works of Henry James, Gertrude Stein, and William Faulkner / Sheila FRIEDLING, University of Wisconsin, 1973 (John O. Lyons).

A basic premise of this study is that the representation of consciousness in 20th century fiction is linked to ways of perception that are both cultural and individual. Part I attempts to establish cultural forms of perception by defining crucial transformations in philosophy, aesthetics, and the theory of fiction. Especially significant is the shift from idealism to subjective empiricism in the late 19th and early 20th centuries, as expressed, for example, in the ideas of William James and Henri Bergson concerning the categories of time, space, substance, causality, perspective, language, and the self. To define forms of representation, I consider the relationship of art to epistemology, particularly developments in aesthetic theory and the visual arts in the late 19th and early 20th centuries culminating in Impressionism and Cubism. Here an analysis of the categories of perception in terms of their aesthetic counterparts indicates that modernist art forms express a temporal and spatio-temporal rather than spatial view of reality, and disregard traditional ideas concerning formal pattern, perspective, aesthetic distance, frame, and iconography. In exploring the influence upon fiction of epistemological skepticism, I focus upon the methods and aims of the psychological novel. Discussing its divergence from fictional romance and "formal realism," I examine particularly the altered modernist treatment of plot, character, time, point of view, and symbol.

The second part of the study explores individual modes of literary perception by examining specific works of Henry James, Gertrude Stein, and William Faulkner that illustrate my theoretical assumptions and demonstrate as well the evolution of form and ideas in literature. In their attempt to represent consciousness, these novelists become involved with the "epistemological theme," and the problematic relationship of seeing and knowing, intuition and representation that is at its heart.

I present detailed analyses of The Portrait of a Lady and The Sacred Fount, with reference also to The Golden Bowl, to illustrate Henry James' representation of consciousness in terms of the spatial imagination. In the earlier work, James makes plot and ethical context the primary vehicles of thematic expression; architectural imagery defines the self and society as reciprocal forces in a world governed by traditional values and expressed in spatial forms. In the later works, James uses spatial imagery to define the substantive, symbolic aspects of the stream of thought. In this context, I discuss the relationship of Henry James' portrayal of the nature of truth, perception, and consciousness to the ideas of William James.

In contrast to James' spatial representation of consciousness is Gertrude Stein's portrayal of temporal modes of consciousness and narration. I first examine her criticism and aesthetic theory, which emphasizes the significance of seeing or primitive perceptual knowledge as opposed to the conceptual knowledge she identifies with spatial forms and symbols. Then, I discuss Three Lives to illustrate how Stein's representation of pure time and the durational self reflects the ideas of William James and Henri

Bergson about time, self, and language, especially the problematic relationship of language to the representation of "asymbolic" experience or the transitive aspects of the stream of thought.

I have selected The Sound and the Fury and Absalom, Absalom! as William Faulkner's most effective experiments in extending the boundaries of fictional form through exploration of epistemological themes. In these novels, Faulkner portrays the conflict of idealist and empirical modes of perception, of analysis and intuition, and offers a fictional interpretation of the relationship of time, self, and language that is indebted to the ideas of Bergson. However, unlike Gertrude Stein, Faulkner does not conceive of temporality or durational consciousness as a subjective absolute, isolated from a historical, social context and from the chronological dimensions of time. Because his subject is the temporal self as historical product and consciousness, he makes use of the spatial and symbolic forms that define intellection, conscience, society, and the social self. In this context, I refer to Faulkner's creation of spatio-temporal forms as fictional counterparts to Cubist and cinematic modes of perception and representation. [Order No. 73-20,992; 694 pages. DAI, 34A (Nov.-Dec. 1973), 3391.]

257 The Indestructible Woman in the Works of Faulkner, Hemingway, and Steinbeck / Mimi Reisel GLADSTEIN, University of New Mexico, 1973 (Hoyt Trawbridge).

American male novelists, according to the critical commonplace, have difficulty creating fully human females. Critics indict Faulkner, Hemingway, and Steinbeck as prime examples of this deficiency. Though their works represent distinct styles, focuses, and subject matters, these three writers do have some striking similarities beyond their alleged inability to allow full humanity to their female characters. They all express a pervasive disillusionment with contemporary society and project generally pessimistic world images. However, each author has certain optimistic undertones: mankind's ability to endure is one of them. A recurrent manifestation of this theme is the indestructible woman.

The indestructible woman, a figure present in the works of all three men, functions positively as a symbol of hope for the future. She is, in part, a product of the primitivism and the naturalism present in Faulkner, Hemingway, and Steinbeck. But, more importantly, she illustrates their inability to come to terms with the Otherness of woman. The reaction to this Otherness results in highly ambivalent characterizations which are a mixture of attraction and repulsion.

The female characterizations of each author are studied separately. While the differences among the authors dictate a somewhat different methodology for studying each, the general thrust is to examine the mythic framework within which each artist operates.

Faulkner's characterizations of women are a result of the integration of regional and universal myths. His indestructible women are manifested in three patterns: earth goddess, Demeter-Persephone, indomitable crone. Hemingway's indestructible women are likewise mythic, corn goddesses and bitch goddesses; they reflect the mother figures in his life who became progressively less threatening. The indestructible women in Steinbeck's works are the nurturing and sustaining cells of the group animal which is Steinbeck's biological conception of the human species. In all three authors the female's endurance suggests a positive force for human survival.

It is true that these authors seldom present really believable female characters. Many critics, however, give this deficiency undue significance. For, in fact, the mythic nature of their works makes unrealistic characterizations predictable and even pardonable. [Order No. 74-20,336; 214 pages. DAI, 35A (Sept.-Oct. 1974), 1655.]

258 Men of Thought, Men of Action: A Pattern of Contrasts in Faulkner's
Major Novels / Daniel Vernon GRIBBIN, University of North Carolina
at Chapel Hill, 1973 (Louis D. Rubin, Jr.).

The object of this study is to identify and analyze a pattern of characterization which runs through Faulkner's novels during the period of his greatest creativity, from 1928-1936. At the heart of each novel from The Sound and the Fury through Absalom, Absalom! is a central contrast between two sharply opposed protagonists. On the one hand, we find men of thought like Quentin Compson, Horace Benbow, and Gail Hightower, characters whose idealistic principles induce them to withdraw from the trials of life into a thought-world of order and stasis. These men of thought are contrasted against men of action like Jason Compson, Joe Christmas, and Thomas Sutpen, aggressive characters who share a common urge to establish their self-sufficiency and vindicate themselves in the eyes of the world by using whatever means possible. Faulkner supplies background information to show how these men became twisted in their approach to life, detailing the traumatic shock to their youthful expectations which sets each of them in violent motion.

In analyzing individual novels, we find that the implicit or explicit opposition between a man of thought and a man of action contributes substantially to the growth of each work. Faulkner used men of action to motivate his plots and to provide a totally different perspective on stories like that of the Compsons in The Sound and the Fury. Moreover, as we proceed chronologically through this group of novels, we notice that Faulkner reacted to his frequent difficulties with the men of thought by emphasizing more and more the roles of the men of action. Hence the emergence of Joe Christmas as the chief protagonist of Light in August, and the appearance of a magnificent hero like Sutpen in the last novel of the period, Absalom, Absalom!. Studying the interplay between the men of thought and men of action leads to a deeper appreciation of how Faulkner's best novels grew and how they achieve their marvellous effects. [Order No. 74-5921; 237 pages. DAI, 34A (March-April 1974), 5969.]

259 William Faulkner's Uses of Elaboration and Multiple Story Lines /
Terry L. HELLER, University of Chicago, 1973 (Sheldon Sacks) no DAI entry.

260 Images of the Negro in the Novels of William Faulkner / Lee Clinton
JENKINS, Columbia University, 1973 (Dean M. Schmitter).

Some of the major conflicts and tensions of Faulkner's art are generated out of a conception in which the patterns of life existing before and after the Civil War are contrasted, the war constituting the crucial event in which the continuity of antebellum life, the conception of its commitment to certain ideals of integrity and humane behavior, is destroyed or enters upon a period of inevitable decline. This social upheaval is viewed as an injustice as much imposed upon a proud and defiant people as it is deserved by them, in retribution for their sins and those of their ancestors.

The consequences of the South's dilemma are seen in the perversion of human and social relations, among blacks and whites as well as among the whites themselves. Faulkner's attitude toward the blacks is marked by a strong ambivalence, though he has nevertheless proved incapable of being content with traditional preconceptions, attempting to create new images which accommodate an expanding vision of the reality which originally gave rise to the stereotype. This development has been slow and tortuous, never wholly successful.

This dissertation is an examination of three phrases in Faulkner's development and of the characters which epitomize them: Dilsey of The Sound and the Fury, Joe Christmas of Light in August, and Lucas Beauchamp of Intruder in the Dust and Go Down, Moses. [Order No. 73-29,841; 217 pages. DAI, 34A (Nov.-Dec. 1973), 3403.]

261 The Hunting Metaphor in Hemingway and Faulkner / Mary Jim JOSEPHS, Michigan State University, 1973 (Russel B. Nye).

This comparative study of Hemingway and Faulkner focuses on the hunting metaphor as a means of perceiving and comparing the value systems of the two writers. The method of the study is close analysis of individual works within the context of the writer's other works on the same theme. This study concludes with comparative readings of The Old Man and the Sea, and "The Bear," considering these works as typical of each writer and, therefore, as an appropriate basis for comparing the two value systems through the uses made of the hunting metaphor.

Both these writers portray many characters for whom hunting and/or fishing is a central life-long activity. Hunting is portrayed by each of them as a ritual of self-renewal in times of trauma, as a pattern for moral growth and development, as the basis of a set of moral standards which can be transferred to other aspects of life, and as an arena in which man can prove his masculinity without getting involved with women.

Hunting, fishing, and bullfighting--the ritualized killing of animals--create, in Hemingway's works, the occasion for the individual to live more intensely in the present moment. Killing is a private experience for the one who kills, not something to be shared with others, as can be seen in many of Nick Adams stories or in bullfighting stories like "The Undefeated." For Hemingway's hero there is an isolation of the individual in a present activity which allows him to block out all past and present unpleasantness and dominate himself (in the sense of controlling his responses and even his emotions) as well as the beast he faces. Tradition, in the usual sense, is not an important factor in the killing experience for the Hemingway character; he does not seek or find a link to the past except in the sense of a union with the person he was in the past, in a recreation of his own youth and a reexperience of himself free from present fears and pain.

For the Hemingway character, the highest ethical value is "killing cleanly," as Hemingway explains in The Green Hills of Africa, striking a careful balance of fair practices in relation to the animal of quest, creating an even competition, and never topping the balance by cheating on the rules. These rules do not serve an abstract concept like "honor," however, they serve to protect the quality of the hero's own experience. The virtues most respected are discipline and courage, yet, again, there is never an abstract insistence on their value. These are simply the qualities most frequently required in the concrete situations that are important to the hero.

Hunting, for Faulkner, is a traditional activity in which a man unites himself through shared activities and a shared reverence for the wilderness with his ancestors and with his neighbors, as can be seen in stories like those of Go Down, Moses and Big Woods. Hunting is a ritual which spans the space of time, both vertically and horizontally, creating a sense of brotherhood not only in a cherished and shared activity, but also in a common set of absolute values, an ethical code derived from the activity itself. Since there are rituals, a network of absolute values, and persons who exemplify and teach those values, hunting takes on the function of a religious system in the lives of Faulkner's characters. Because the system is grounded to the past by tradition and thus requires learned attitudes as well as learned techniques, an elaborate initiation phase is an important element of the mystique. Faulkner frequently focuses on this initiation phase of hunting and on the relationships of the hunter to the hunted and to the wilderness. It is everywhere implied in these works that these relationships are the mark of a man's sense of responsibility to his fellows, and, consequently, the measure of his moral worth. And even when unspoken the abstract absolute values ring out like echoes in the woods: truth and honor and pride and endurance....

For both these writers the values demonstrated here through the metaphor of the hunt are the same ones dramatized in other ways in other works. In Hemingway's war stories or love stories the qualities of the soldier or the lover are the same as those of the bullfighter or fisherman, and the emphasis is always on the intensely personal experience of the individual in a moment of crisis. In Faulkner's other works he portrays a farmer, a lawyer, or a sewing machine agent with the same earthy qualities as the hunter, and the emphasis is on a character as he functions in relation to his fellow man and as he is influenced by his cultural heritage.

Hemingway and Faulkner give us two very different images of the American experience and the contrasts posed are as rich in possibilities as the minds of two great writers and as the parameters of our national consciousness: individual man vs. social man, existential man vs. essentialist man, international man vs. national or regional man. Each writer, however, presents man as committed to the preservation of his own dignity and to that of the human race, although they define that dignity by different criteria. [Order No. 73-20,357; 264 pages. DAI, 34A (Sept.-Oct. 1973), 1282-83.]

262 The Fiction of William Faulkner and Uwe Johnson: A Comparative Study / Sara Jane King LENNOX, University of Wisconsin, 1973 (Arthur E. Kunst).

By examining in detail the stylistic and thematic similarities between Faulkner and Johnson, this study attempts to show that a fundamental affinity exists between them. Both condemn modernity and look back with longing on the social consensus which existed in a traditional society, and both seek formal innovations to portray this insight.

The dissertation begins with an examination of previous criticism relating Faulkner and Johnson, the availability of Faulkner's works to German writers, and Johnson's encounter with Faulkner's novels.

Chapter One considers similarities in style at the sentence level. Examining their employment of commas, colons, lengthy parentheses, long series of adjectives, and marathon sentences, the study determines that both writers qualify and elaborate upon events and objects because they can no longer assume generally agreed-upon definitions. Considered in their entirety, however, the writers' sentences display a basic difference. Faulkner's hypotactic sentences imply the existence of an ordering mind. Johnson's paratactic sentences present their information sequentially, denying the possibility of organization.

In Chapter Two the study examines point of view. To avoid the use of an authoritative narrative voice, both writers employ interior monologue to illuminate a central character and dialogue as the structural framework of their novels. They further challenge the possibility of an unequivocal version of truth by juxtaposing the perspectives of various individuals, by throwing the reliability of the traditional narrator into doubt, by depicting an unsuccessful search for truth, and by showing the achievement of a truth based on speculation which is subjectively satisfying though possessing no ultimate intersubjective validity.

Chapter Three discusses the two writers' handling of time. Though they use certain similar techniques like the incremental revelation of information when considering subjective time, their treatment of objective time differs drastically. Faulkner attempts to deny the existence of movement through time, while Johnson insists on a chronological presentation of information; Faulkner emphasizes the presentness of the past for his characters, while Johnson stresses his characters' awareness of historical change. Faulkner structures his novels so they will be understood as a totality only in one final instant of time. Johnson's major novels employ a double chronological sequence, his characters recalling a past which they recount in chronological order. Faulkner's additional emphasis on his characters' relationship to myth and to natural rhythms and their subjection to fate underlines their powerlessness to change their lives. Johnson's insistence on his characters' existence in historical time, however, preserves for them the freedom to act in time.

In Chapter Four the study considers Faulkner's and Johnson's portrayal of a traditional society and its loss. Employing the similar techniques of recurring characters and a constant geographical base, Yoknapatawpha County and Jerichow, the two writers show that though their societies retain important human values, they are flawed by racism. Both societies are further in a state of dissolution. Johnson shows the society's loss through a geographical shift which demonstrates that the modern world has produced developments which the old society cannot contain. Faulkner's analysis of the decline, though profound, is limited because he restricts his consideration to Yoknapatawpha County, thus cannot examine the characteristics of modernism which are really responsible for the society's destruction.

The study concludes that the loss of the homogeneity of the traditional society which the two writers chronicle has forced them to employ formal techniques which both examine and attempt to overcome the lack of socially agreed-upon meaning.

The dissertation also includes a genealogical table of the Papenbrock-Cresspahl-Niebuhr families in Johnson's works. [Order No. 74-488; 498 pages. DAI, 34A (March-April 1974), 6647.]

263 William Faulkner: The Heroic Design of Yoknapatawpha / Lynn Gartrell LEVINS, University of North Carolina at Chapel Hill, 1973 (C. Hugh Holman).

In the Yoknapatawpha novels Faulkner is using materials that remind the reader, either consciously or semiconsciously, of a world of heroic ideals. He juxtaposes the events of his fictional locale--a community essentially of hill people and small tenant farmers--against scenes from and echoes of myths, classical drama, epic poetry, chivalric and historical romance. For example, in As I Lay Dying the funeral procession through flood and fire from Frenchman's Bend to Jefferson is to be viewed as an epic journey. The episode of Ike and the cow in The Hamlet suggests in both event and tone the medieval romance. Defending the object of his love--called at once Astarte, Juno, Troy's Helen--from water, fire, and "dragon," Ike Snopes is to be seen as a modern day protagonist of the knightly tales of valor. Although the tone is by no means romantic, still the subject matter of Old Man is essentially chivalric, and the tall convict and the woman in the tree become the counterpoint not only to Harry and Charlotte in The Wild Palms, but also to the couple in medieval literature who sacrificed all for love. The point is that Faulkner, in each case, is not parodying traditional literary modes by focusing on the grotesque diminution of legend and myth in Yoknapatawpha County; but rather he is writing in As I Lay Dying and Old Man and The Hamlet of the fulfillment of an ethical obligation, and when the obligation is accomplished in spite of temptations to abandon it and difficulties to thwart it, then the action of Anse Bundren or the tall convict or the idiot Ike Snopes approaches heroic proportions.

By setting the actions of his Yoknapatawpha characters within the framework of Greek tragedy, as he does in Absalom, Absalom!, or chivalric romance, or the epic, Faulkner adds to his fictional southern region a mythical dimension, which is to be distinguished from, say, the John Sartoris myth, or the making of a wildly extravagant romanticism. Behind the chivalric framework of the tall convict's actions, behind the Bundren pilgrimage as epic journey or the identification of Thomas Sutpen as the old Greek tragic hero lies the concept of the existence of an heroic ideal, which for Faulkner is representative of what people are capable of--both the baseness and the grandeur. This juxtaposition of the present with an older heroic age is the same artistic technique which T. S. Eliot uses, but Eliot will at times employ it to contrast the contemporary scene with a more glorious past--to reduce significance instead of expanding it. For Faulkner, however, the juxtaposition is an affirmation of some principle of continuity which ties our era with a past that presupposes the greatness of man. In his Yoknapatawpha canon Faulkner is rejecting the image of the wasteland as the proper aesthetic projection of the modern age and, instead, asserting his belief in a world where the heroic is still possible. [Order No. 73-26,201; 253 pages. DAI, 34A (Nov.-Dec. 1973), 2635.]

   264 Ontological Implications in Faulkner's Major Novels / Ruth Thompson LINCOLN, Indiana University, 1973 (James H. Justus).
   Throughout his major period, Faulkner is concerned with the relationship between the esemplastic imagination and contingent reality. Sanctuary establishes the poles of his dialectic: the imagination possessed by myths is divorced from the reality of natural process.
   In The Sound and the Fury, Faulkner suggests that a decreative act must precede the creative acts by which we humanize reality. Through such decreations, gestalt and ground, kairos and chronos may remain in an uneasy correspondence. In this novel, dehumanized reality becomes a sexual figure, dissolving identity in a chaos of potentialities. Hence sexuality is terrifying to the rigid idealistic imaginations of the masculine characters.
   In As I Lay Dying, we find a new tolerance for the insufficiency of human fictions. Faulkner suggests that our fictional gestalts defend "the clotting that is you" from dissolution into the "myriad original motion."
   Sanctuary, however, again argues for realism as opposed to myth. Here the imagination possessed by second-hand fictions is wholly destructive.
   The extreme antitheses of Faulkner's dialectic become, in Light in August, the source of Joe Christmas' oscillation between masculine and feminine, light and dark, the rigid form of the urn and the liquid it contains, "deathcolored and foul." Centering on the image of the Grecian urn, Faulkner extends his antithesis of myth to reality, kairos to chronos, into a dialectic between beauty and truth. He suggests a resolution in fictions which are inabsolute and self-conscious, as opposed to the "fine, dead sounds" of myth.
   In Absalom, Absalom!, Faulkner further resolves the polarities of his earlier novels. Here he conceives of fictions which are open-ended and continually creative. Such paradigms need not be preceded and succeeded by decreative acts; their own temporal transformation is intrinsic to them. Contingent reality is suggested by the unresolved multiple narrations, but a concordance among them is established not through dialectic and final synthesis, but by an unfinished process of inclusion and organic growth which Quentin calls "overpassing to love." The mode of narration itself becomes a mode of mutuality rather than the mosaic juxtapositions of earlier novels. This narrative mode, like Faulkner's characteristic oxymoronic style, transcends the dialectic opposition of beauty and truth, form and fact, man and world. In Absalom, Absalom! the esemplastic imagination discovers humanizing forms which are asymmetrical, inclusive, and energetic. Thus it recovers a "loving" rather than an alienating faculty, uniting creation with discovery, poet with realist. [Order No. 73-19,742; 233 pages. DAI, 34A (Sept.-Oct. 1973), 1286.]

   265 History as Perception, History as Obsession: Faulkner's Development of a Theme / Hubert Horton McALEXANDER, Jr., University of Wisconsin, 1973 (Walter B. Rideout).
   This study traces Faulkner's development of a bi-partite theme--the idea that history for any man is most fundamentally determined by his own

perceptions of the past and the linked idea that some men allow these perceptions of the past to become their obsessions. This study locates the outlines of that theme in Sartoris, it examines Faulkner's focusing and refining of his presentation in the Gail Hightower sections of Light in August, and it explores Faulkner's development, his ultimate statement of both parts of the theme in Absalom, Absalom!.

Sartoris presents clear outlines of the theme, but it presents outlines alone because the novel exhibits flaws which serve to undercut any truly consistent and coherent rendering. The major flaw is the strange split in the characterization of young Bayard--one side, the scion entrapped by his family's past; the other, the rather representative Lost Generation figure suffering an intensely private trauma. The secondary fault is the inconsistency of the narrative voice, a factor which blurs the issues of both perception and obsession.

In the Gail Hightower sections of Light in August, Faulkner focuses that theme so diffusely suggested in Sartoris and here, particularly because of his stricter control of the narrative voice, renders the theme with greater clarity and power. Hightower, however, like Bayard, is presented as a disturbingly split character--a man capable of both a grotesque obsession with the past and a profound insight into life. As a result, Faulkner has still failed to tie theme to character in a fully convincing and compelling way.

Absalom, Absalom! owes a significant debt to these two earlier novels, a debt which critics hitherto have not acknowledged. But while drawing from these novels, Faulkner went far beyond those only partial renderings of the theme to present his ultimate statement in Absalom, Absalom!. Here Faulkner builds an entire novel around the idea that history is what one perceives it to be. And through the intricacy of the novel's structure, he dramatizes the idea from a variety of points of view. The last point of view which the novel in fact creates is the response of the reader. And from a survey of reader response (the criticism), one gauges the full artistry with which Faulkner has rendered his statement. For in the variety of critical judgment on the particular historical context which the novel presents, one finds a still further demonstration that history is basically perception.

Enclosing the rendering of Faulkner's idea of the nature of history is the author's most powerful dramatization of the idea of history as obsession. In Quentin, Faulkner has worked out those problems of characterization found in the earlier obsessive figures. Quentin is a split character, but one whose two selves--the boy of the present and the boy obsessed by the past--clearly cannot share an uneasy co-existence. They must do battle, and it is, indeed, the progress of this battle and of Quentin's torture (to which Shreve is not only witness, but party) that both unifies the novel and lends the particular intensity to the final half. It is not, however, until one registers the final powerful effect of Absalom, Absalom! that one charts Faulkner's full development of both parts of the bipartite theme. For the nature of Quentin's obsession can be given full definition only through the perceptions of the readers of the novel. [Order No. 73-28,932; 158 pages. DAI, 34A (March-April 1974), 6596-97.]

266 The Theme of Revenge in the Fiction of William Faulkner / Albert
James MEMMOTT, University of Minnesota, 1973 (George T. Wright).
More than any major American writer since Melville, William Faulkner makes use of revenge themes and situations. Concentrating upon Absalom, Absalom!, The Unvanquished, The Hamlet, The Town, and The Mansion, the purpose of this study is to locate and analyze Faulkner's revenge patterns, to show the depth and complexity of his use of revenge, and to suggest connections between his attitude toward revenge and his broader discussion of private versus public responsibility.

Beginning with a brief review of the revenge theme in American literature, the dissertation moves to analysis of the conflicting revenge designs in Absalom. Rosa Coldfield attempts to take revenge upon the dead Thomas Sutpen; Sutpen designs to get back at the land-owning class by aping it; and his children try to repay him for his neglect of them. The heavy influence of revenge literature upon Absalom is shown. Sutpen follows Euripedes' Jason and Melville's Ahab; Rosa Coldfield repeats the attempts of Dickens' Miss Havisham to stop time and wreak revenge, and Henry, Charles, and Judith mirror in their lives the Biblical revenge triangle of Absalom, Amnon, and Tamar.

Study of The Unvanquished shows the novel's depiction of revenge as ritual and/or game. The war begins as a game-like and essentially harmless confrontation; it fast becomes real and harmful. Bayard's barbaric killing and mutilation of Grumby in revenge for his grandmother's murder represents, not the ultimate disintegration of society, but, instead, the necessary sacrificial exorcism of evil, the ritualistic and moral initiation of a period of reconstruction. Bayard's later rejection of blood-revenge upon Redmond is shown to be a son's assertion of his own independence from his father and his simultaneous acknowledgement of his duty to avenge his father's death.

The Hamlet and The Town are discussed in this study as novels of settlement in which newcomers test and generally defeat the communities' moral and civil codes. Finally, in The Town, a buried moral force begins to exact justice upon the Snopeses, but it cannot punish Flem Snopes, who seems immune to the revenge instinct himself. Flem finally pays for his sins in The Mansion, and his death represents the affirmation of the laws of family and marraige which he abused. Analysis of his death shows that Flem's and the novel's endings are consistent with The Mansion's melodramatic structure. This last volume of the trilogy is a deliberate revenge melodrama: Faulkner changes facts and simplifies issues to give a sense of significant, socially conclusive, ending to his study of the Snopes family.

Review of the major revenge novels and the other novels and stories employing revenge themes reveals that Faulkner usually describes situations in which his characters decide to take revenge rather than to defer their vengeance to God as the New Testament advises. Furthermore, the civil law is described as irrelevant to their concerns. They worry about when, not about why or how--the revenger's persistent problem is to conquer time and distance so he might succeed. Once the victim is apprehended, the revenge is simple and unadorned. The revenger in Faulkner seldom compromises the justice of his act by becoming artful; his primary interest is moral, not aesthetic. Throughout his fiction Faulkner sees revenge as a reflection of the moral vision of the individual. This vision may be warped and paranoid, but it often affirms the traditional values which unite society and, according to Faulkner, give meaning to life. [Order No. 74-726; 259 pages. DAI, 34A (Jan.-Feb. 1974), 4273-74.]

267 Faulkner's Indians / Marc Anthony NIGLIAZZO, University of New Mexico, 1973 (Leon Howard).

From the publication of "Red Leaves" in 1930 to the creation of an Indian background for Boon Hogganbeck in the 1962 novel, The Reivers, the Indian element is consistently alive in the works of William Faulkner. Short stories, background allusions within novels, and occasional topical preludes such as those in Requiem for a Nun and Big Woods give accounts of the Indians and emphasize their significance. However, no extensive critical study has been made on the Indian in Faulkner. Individual characters have received attention as have some individual works, but there has apparently been no effort to correlate the total Indian element within Faulkner's Yoknapatawpha saga and to study its artistic validity.

This dissertation offers such a study as it first attempts an identification of Faulkner's major Indian stories and a formulation of them into a chronological sequence. In this sequence, the Indian presence can be more easily understood as it extends from the earliest history of Yoknapatawpha into the 20th century. Second, Faulkner's knowledge of the Mississippi Indians is explored within the context of historical background, and his personal comments upon the historical Indians and his fictional creations are considered. With the establishment of a chronicle of Indian stories and Faulkner's awareness of the context of history, a thorough critical analysis of individual stories within the chronicle is made, especially in terms of theme and symbol. A clarification of major character contradictions within the chronicle brings the study to an end.

The conclusion drawn from this study is that the Indian stories, when viewed as a unified chronicle, find validity as literature and as a subject of critical study. The Mississippi Indian is artistically depicted in a semi-primitive state by Faulkner and then he is drawn, through the degrading mire of greed, artificiality, and insensitivity, to his ultimate destruction. Throughout the progression Faulkner projects both a sense of nostalgia for the past, the noble existence when men and nature were one, and a sense of tragedy in the almost deterministic demise of the red man, who often sees, even voices his predicament, but who can never completely release himself from it. That close analysis of the Indian stories can reveal some parallel of fiction with history, as indicated in the second part of this study, is useful for an understanding of the structuring of the stories and for judgment about historicity, but this parallel becomes incidental to Faulkner's portrayal in his chronicle of the very character and perhaps soul of a people dispossessed. [Order No. 74-8662; 128 pages. DAI, 34A (March-April 1974), 6650-51.]

268 Psychological Rebirth in Selected Works by Nathaniel Hawthorne, Stephen Crane, Henry James, William Faulkner, and Ralph Ellison / Gordon Duncan REYNOLDS, University of California at Irvine, 1973 (Murray Krieger).

Certain major literary works by Ellison, Faulkner, James, Crane, and Hawthorne are characterized by significant use of a pattern which this study terms psychological rebirth. The pattern is related to myths, initiation rituals, religious rites, and psychological phenomena described by such theorists as Joseph Campbell, Mircea Eliade, and Carl Jung. However, in this study psychological rebirth is defined ultimately by the literary works. The pattern includes the breaking down of a character's immature, inadequate mental identity, aberrations in perception, and other mental processes, the appearance of guides, entrance into a deathlike state, awakening to a new mode of perception of the familiar, suggestions that the character is a new or newborn person. The psychological rebirth tends to make the character more mature and more self-confident, a potential leader. In the particular literary contexts, however, such favorable tendencies may be at least partly offset by psychological or situational complexities. This study describes the specific working out of the psychological rebirth pattern in the selected works. [Order No. 74-13,835; 447 pages. DAI, 34A (May-June 1974), 7719.]

269 The Vanishing Community: Studies in Some Late Novels by William Faulkner / Carol Anne Roscoe RIGSBY, University of Toronto (Canada), 1973 (Michael H. Millgate).

Although the increased attention paid to Faulkner's later novels in recent years has resulted in some excellent studies of individual novels, the notion persists that during the latter half of his career Faulkner retreated into intellectual and artistic conservatism and impaired the quality of his work thereby. Much criticism has focused on the character of Gavin Stevens, who has often been seen as a spokesman for Faulkner's ideas and evidence of his inability to incorporate those ideas into the novels. Yet a review of Stevens' earlier appearances demonstrates that Faulkner's attitudes toward and uses of the lawyer were never quite so simple and straightforward and suggests that a re-examination of the novels in which he is a major character might be the basis of a fresh evaluation of Faulkner's concerns and techniques in the late novels.

Between the publication of Go Down, Moses (1942) and Intruder in the Dust (1948) Faulkner published only a few short stories, but Malcolm Cowley's Portable Faulkner made portions of his earlier works known and available to large numbers of new readers. Cowley's emphasis on what he considered the saga of Yoknapatawpha, though it slighted the integrity of individual works, may also have had the effect of drawing Faulkner's attention to a unique opportunity presented to him by the nature of his earlier writings. Because he had created a body of legend and history which defined a particular community, he was able in his later novels to use what he had written to explore some questions of increasing interest to him--the nature and value of community in general and the possibility of its survival in the modern world.

Although Intruder in the Dust, Requiem for a Nun, The Town, and The Mansion are linked by their concern with the community, they by no means present a single view of it. Intruder in the Dust reflects the belief that a stable community, whatever its faults, can be an important source of strength for the individual and that much will be lost if such communities are destroyed by technological change and modern American mass culture. To a large extent, this has already happened in Requiem for a Nun. The historical preludes describe the movement of Jefferson and Jackson away from frontier individualism toward the conformity of the 20th century. Yet the final prelude suggests that something of the past endures and that a leap of the imagination may enable modern man to escape his sense of isolation by re-establishing the link between himself and those who have gone before. The drama of Temple Drake provides an example of an individual as yet unable to escape her moral isolation or to find comfort in the abstract solutions offered by reason (Stevens) or faith (Nancy). In The Town the community is presented not as a possible source of strength but as the embodiment of those hypocritical attitudes which allow Flem to prosper while Eula is driven to suicide. The Mansion depicts a world in which the community has dwindled into irrelevance. Mink and Linda must look elsewhere for strength and stability.

Just as Faulkner's changing attitudes toward the community demonstrate his continued intellectual flexibility, the variety of narrative techniques he employs in these novels demonstrates his continued creativity. With a wide range of methods at his command, he was able in Intruder in the Dust, Requiem for a Nun, The Town, and The Mansion to choose those which allowed him to develop most fully the significance of his materials. [To obtain a microfiche copy order from the National Library of Canada at Ottawa. DAI, 36A (Sept.-Oct. 1975), 1509-10.]

270 From Genesis to Revelation: The Grand Design of Faulkner's Absalom, Absalom! / Maxine Smith ROSE, University of Alabama, 1973 (O. B. Emerson).

This study purports to show not only that Faulkner makes occasional use of biblical parallels in Absalom, Absalom! but that parallels based on biblical characters, themes, events, places, language, and cadences provide vital sources of style, structure, and technique. A close point-by-point examination of scriptural and fictional patterns is maintained throughout.

Chapter I examines the background of the writer and attempts to establish the fact that the Bible had an early and lasting influence on Faulkner.

Chapter II focuses on the powerful personalities and the essential thematic concerns of Absalom, Absalom! which have their roots in biblical characters and themes. Though the Davidic parallels, which give the novel its title, dominate the book, various other parallels--e.g., Sutpen as Jehovah, King David, Adam, Abraham, the demon, the dragon of the Apocalypse, and Bon as Absalom-Amnon and Christ--bring new dimensions to the scope and power of the novel, in each case providing thematic and structural links, as well as illuminating character.

Chapter III surveys the biblical imagery of Absalom, Absalom!. Sutpen is identified with images of the Old Testament: images of warfare, iron, stones, smoke-fire-altar, suggesting hardness, coldness, inflexibility. Bon, as a bringer of a new covenant of love, is portrayed in images more characteristic of the New Testament: images of seeds, sower, vines, connoting fecundity, fulness, pleasure. Clusters of images related to vines (wistaria), warfare, sparrows, letters, lamp, key, cup, brimstone, smoke-fire-altar, sickle, door, stones, iron, clay, dust, numbers, structures, and patterns are related to biblical patterns, and are explored in terms of the unity they bring to the novel.

Chapter IV attempts to show through specific passages from Absalom, Absalom! that in rhetoric and cadence the style echoes the stylistic qualities of the Bible, especially the King James Version. This chapter shows that Faulkner's rhetoric frequently falls into biblical rhythms, that his ideas are frequently expressed in a grammatical and rhetorical parallelism which corresponds to biblical poetry, and that everywhere Faulkner uses words (diction) that are normally associated with the King James Bible.

Chapter V explores the narrative modes in Absalom, Absalom!. The earliest narratives reflect the antediluvian age. Following this age, the Old Covenant is reflected in the inflexible code of Sutpen. The rise of the monarchy, with David as the model king, provides far-reaching parallels for the Sutpen legend. The era of wisdom literature with its humanistic concerns is echoed especially in Mr. Compson's narration. The prophets, as moral gadflies, reflected in Miss Rosa and in Quentin, in varying degrees, serve as the conscience of Israel--the South. Quentin is also somewhat like St. John, who in Revelation is endowed with new ways of looking at time and space. Shreve offers a priestly interpretation. General Compson, as an indirect narrator, represents the Judges, particularly Samuel.

Thus, the architectonic structure of the Bible provides the major patterns of Absalom, Absalom!. In addition to the conflicts in the Davidic dynasty, the two major antagonists, God-Jesus and Satan-demon-dragon, offer powerful cosmic parallels for Sutpen and Bon, with possibilities for divine and human qualities, and paradoxical God-Satan combinations. Bulging parallels allow Faulkner the freedom he wants, while giving the characters and action the bigness they demand. The biblical parallels which provide the skeletal framework for Absalom, Absalom! span the history of Israel from the time before the creation through the end of the created world. Not only do they cover the span of the whole human race, but the divine parallels extend the scope to heaven and hell and the time to eternity. Thus, Absalom, Absalom! becomes Faulkner's own Bible, reshaped and recreated, from Genesis to Revelation. [Order No. 74-9382; 262 pages. DAI, 34A (March-April 1974), 6656.]

271 The Story of All Things: Faulkner's Yoknapatawpha County Cosmology by Way of Light in August / Michael Perry ROUTH, University of Wisconsin, 1973 (Walter B. Rideout).

"Beginning with Sartoris," William Faulkner said late in his career, "....I created a cosmos of my own." This essay explores the implications of Faulkner's own definition of himself as cosmological writer in the sense that the Biblical poets and Skakespeare--Faulkner's two most influential sources--Milton, Blake, and the like are cosmological writers.

The study begins with an attempt to achieve a workable definition of "cosmology" as symbol system and as literary art. Theories of macrocosms and microcosms are related to symbolic cosmologies, showing how man as the "little world" is considered to contain within his very being the "great world," the exterior universe. Further, the notion that a vitalistic impulse similar to Aristotle's "originative power," Schopenhauer's "World Will," Bergson's elan vital, Hans Driesch's "entelechy," and G. B. Shaw's "Life Force" is inherent in a symbolic cosmology as that element which makes a cosmology "live."

In terms of literature, generally speaking, a cosmology provides a symbolic scaffolding within which the writer can tell a story of the widest possible implications--indeed, can tell the story of all things.

Four chapters contain a detailed analysis of Light in August as a model for study of Faulkner's cosmology. The novel is considered in terms of a tremendous Armageddon between the vitalistic impulse--the Life-Force-- and the forces of death in the context of an ambiguous world. There is, first, a long discussion of ambiguity as theme and as technique. As theme, ambiguity constitutes the state of a world in which right perception of reality is extremely difficult. As technique, ambiguity becomes a literary strategy whereby Faulkner as author strives to duplicate in his narrative mode problems of perception similar to those his story-characters must face.

There are discussions of Lena Grove as representative of the Life-Force and of Joe Christmas and several others as representatives of the forces of death. Broadly speaking, the Life-Force is an innate impetus, an instinct perceivable only by way of intuition, carrying life within itself. If a character, like Lena, follows his intuitions and is true to his instincts, he will achieve fulfillment. If, on the other hand, a character, like Joe, is taught to mistrust his instincts and intuitions, he learns to hate life and therefore to hate also himself; he becomes afflicted with what is called here "Quentin's disease," in which the life-drives invert and the sick soul quests not for life but for death. The novel's climax, it is argued, is contained in a scene virtually ignored by previous readers. In this scene Lena's fidelity to the Life-Force is most fully tested.

The last chapter moves in the opposite direction from the chapters analyzing Light in August, radiating outward to link all 14 Yoknapatawpha novels to cosmology on the thesis that Yoknapatawpha County represents a Mesocosmic Being (like Blake's Albion in English literature and, in American literature, Whitman's Full-Size Man) whose history (i. e., the South's) repeats the archetypal journey of the soul through life. Light in August, then, is really only a chapter of what is in fact one long novel. [Order No. 73-30,344; 245 pages. DAI, 34A (March-April 1974), 6657-58.]

272 Strange Textures of Vision: A Study of the Significance of Mannered Fictional Techniques in Six Selected Novels of D. H. Lawrence, William Faulkner, and Patrick White, Together with a Theoretical Introduction on "The Novel of Vision" / William Gerald SCHERMBRUCKER, University of British Columbia (Canada), 1973 (Lee M. Whitehead).

The purpose of this dissertation is to present, by theory and example, a critical approach to a certain type of 20th century novel, described as "the novel of vision." The approach is intended to enable critical readers to experience the aesthetic impact of such novels most directly, in contrast to the indirect experience produced by those approaches which import concepts or terminology to the text from external sources, such as schools of psychology or theories of genre. The approach follows the basic dogma of New Criticism, in treating each novel as a self-contained work of art requiring close textual scrutiny for its illumination; external glosses are rigorously avoided, and specific stress is placed on strange or distorted elements in the language and structure of each novel, by which the novelist chiefly communicates his particular vision of reality.

The first section of the dissertation consists of a theoretical rationale for the critical approach adopted in analyzing the six novels which are the main subject. By way of defining what is meant by "a novel of vision," brief passages are quoted from such novels, which contain the typical characteristics distinguishing this kind of novel from other kinds. Chief of these characteristics is a startlingly mannered prose texture. "The novel of vision," having been defined by textural characteristics, it is then argued that such a novel functions as a cultural medium through which the novelist engages in dynamic interaction with his society, offering society his vision which is usually in conflict with conventional values and norms of perception. Next, a definition is given of a useful role for the critic, as an illuminator of the artist's vision, rather than interpreter or judge of it. Finally in this section, typical techniques of "the novel of vision" are discussed, and a few convenient terms for referring to these techniques are suggested.

The main body of the dissertation consists of six analytical chapters in which the present writer plays the role of critic defined earlier, and tries to illuminate the vision of the artist in D. H. Lawrence's The Plumed Serpent and The Man Who Died, William Faulkner's As I Lay Dying and Absalom, Absalom!, and Patrick White's The Aunt's Story and The Vivisector. Each of these chapters begins with a brief contrast being drawn between the present approach and typical approaches of other critics. It is noted how certain critics have brought preconceived concepts and terminology to the texts in order to make sense of them, and it is argued that these approaches tend to avoid the artists' strange visions in these texts. Each chapter then proceeds at greater length to employ the critical approach here suggested, confronting each text on its own terms.

No attempt is made to relate "the novel of vision" to the history of the novel generally, nor to such trends in literary history as Expressionism, Symbolism, or Futurism. Nor, in the analyses of specific novels, are they related to other works by the same author, in order to show the development of techniques of vision in the canon of an author.

There is no implication that the three authors studied are the only or even the best examples of "novelists of vision"; rather, these three writers provide convenient and well-known examples by which to demonstrate the critical approach in three quite different literary contexts. The term "novel of vision" is believed to be original, as is the critical approach to such novels here offered. [To obtain a microfilm copy order directly from the National Library of Canada at Ottawa. DAI, 35A (July-Aug. 1974), 473.]

273 Some Romantic Elements in the Works of William Faulkner / Kearney Isaac SMITH, University of Georgia, 1973 (James B. Colvert).

Several attitudes implied in Faulkner's fiction are essentially the same as those expressed in the writings of the English Romantic Movement, although these attitudes in Faulkner are not usually put as directly or theoretically as they are in the poetry and prose of the romantics. Romantic attitudes in Faulkner make themselves evident in embodiment of idea in imagery, character, and action. In his work romantic assumptions about man and nature are given expression through his use of natural imagery and through the feelings, action, and speech of character. Sometimes they are also suggested through Faulkner's rhetorical narrative style which can have the effect of casting a mythical aura about events and creating an atmosphere conducive to romantic beliefs.

Implicit in Faulkner's fiction is a confidence in man's subjective powers and his primitive virtues. These virtues can be and are too often corrupted by man's forfeiting his moral sense in his pursuit of material good and factual certainty. The simple virtues do remain firm in some characters who keep in touch with the natural world, a world with the same benevolent powers attributed to it by Wordsworth in "Tintern Abbey." The city, usually Memphis in the Yoknapatawpha stories, becomes symbolic of the evils of modern life in its rapid pace, its emphasis on the acquisition of things, and its reliance on mechanisms. Also, the city is capable of harboring great corruption partly because of the anonymity of life there.

At the same time, Faulkner's fiction suggests that there are spirits or powers moving in the lives of men which can be only dimly perceived. Much of this power may be ascribed to memory, as in many of the characters there is a pervasive sense of the past and the Old South. For example, in Sartoris, Colonel Sartoris' presence is felt in Jefferson years after his death. Other more mysterious manifestations of this spiritual power like extrasensory perception are not so easily explained in naturalistic terms. Usually this kind of power and perception is purposely left dim and unexplained.

Faulkner's hints on the supernatural are often maintained in a relatively realistic fabric by the indirectness of his narration. Supernatural power is suggested in the portraits of characters like McEachern, Hines, and Grimm in Light in August. Rosa Coldfield's calling Thomas Sutpen "demon" works in a similarly suggestive way, as does the narrative technique of supposition in Absalom, Absalom!. More like Melville than Poe or Hawthorne in this regard, Faulkner is able to maintain a credible naturalistic fabric of narrative while the incidents and characters of his fiction take on larger-than-life dimensions. The accoutrements of literary Gothicism, rhetorical devices, and thematic echoes, are used by Faulkner to create and maintain this illusion. [Order No. 73-31,968; 126 pages. DAI, 34A (Jan.-Feb. 1974), 4286.]

274 William Faulkner: The Dynamics of Form / Gary Lee STONUM, Johns Hopkins University, 1973 (Laurence B. Holland).

Faulkner's public statements about his work suggest that he conceives of form as a dynamic process of continual formings. The achieved work is generated out of a conflict between the arresting force of the writer's shaping imagination and the forces of motion in the vitality of his subject matter. The artist's intention becomes the engendering in language of this vitality in such a way as to depict the continual flux of time and change and the permanent "verities of the human heart" which exist within the flux.

As I Lay Dying focuses directly on the existential consequences of life within a universe of rapid and frantic motion. The Bundren family's burial journey dramatizes the yawning discontinuities which can open up between the self and its past and its environment. In this novel Faulkner assumes the privilege of direct entry into the consciousness of his characters, although they are continually thwarted by the otherness of other selves and even of their own past selves. The author also interrelates his characters' minds by means of a systematic pattern of imagery. The result is that the novel's form is curiously static, in spite of the tumult of the world displayed. The novel presents itself as already arrested motion, as a form already constituted as a totality.

In Absalom, Absalom! the focus is on that process of arresting and designing which As I Lay Dying takes for granted. The narrators and the protagonist are all trying to design the future or to discover the design of the past. The postures of each character towards his material and towards the designing process prove inadequate in some way. The contrasts between them, however, are articulated in such a way to gesture towards an ideal designing posture which might include them all in paradoxical harmony.

The Snopes trilogy as a whole attempts to generate an adequate existential response to the conflict between the tumult of recent social history and the need of both individuals and communities to erect and codify forms of behavior. The Hamlet and The Town portray the breakdown of established forms of community in the face of the economic and sexual forces centered in Flem and Eula. Social and economic forms are discovered to possess no potency other than what the individual is able to infuse into them. In The Mansion Mink Snopes, who has been stripped of his place in any community, is nonetheless able to create an existence for himself without depending on external forms. Out of the wreckage which ensues from Mink's murder of Flem, Gavin Stevens is able to achieve a compassionate acceptance of life. This compassionate acceptance becomes the cornerstone of the trilogy's ultimately elegiac vision. The forces of arrest and of motion are seen at once in sorrow and celebration as aspects of a single, indomitable, human energy. [Order No. 73-28,435; 285 pages. DAI, 34A (Nov.-Dec. 1973), 3433.]

275 Youth and Innocence in the Novels of William Faulkner / Michael J. TUMULTY, St. John's University, 1973 (James HaFley).

This study confines itself to an examination of the theme of youthful innocence in Faulkner's Yoknapatawpha novels. "Youthful innocence" as used in this study is defined as "a state of ethical and moral becoming which is readily susceptible to adult influence and termines in virtue or vice because of repeated choices of good and evil" (p. 19).

The study demonstrates that the first six works develop a theme of the general tendency of youth toward destructive behavior because of adverse adult influence. Aunt Jenny is revealed as being mainly responsible for the reckless disregard of human life manifested by her nephews John and Bayard in Sartoris. The Sound and the Fury and As I Lay Dying are analyzed as dramatizations of the roles played by morally deficient parents in contributing to the tragedies that befall the Compson and Bundren children. Faulkner's care to account partially for Popeye's viciousness in terms of a broken home and Temple Drake's ready corruptibility in terms of an over-indulgent family is shown in the treatment of Sanctuary. Light in August is studied as a dramatization of the multiple corruptive adult influences largely responsible for the emergence of Joe Christmas as a dynamic force of destruction. Faulkner's final treatment of the theme of corrupted youth is traced through the intricate design of Absalom, Absalom! which cords Thomas Sutpen's youthful disorientation by a materialistic society and his pursuit of an amoral design which results in his corruption of youthful innocents through three generations.

Drawing attention to The Unvanquished as a pivotal novel, the study proceeds to examine the later Yoknapatawpha novels as dramatizing the beneficent effect favorable adult influence can have in enabling youthful innocents to develop into dynamic agents for good. Rosa Millard's role as moral mentor to Bayard Sartoris is traced in the study of The Unvanquished. The necessary qualifications are made before treating The Hamlet as depicting Eula Varner as an especially endowed youth who achieves an easy victory over Labove, and Go Down, Moses as recording the influence exerted by Sam Fathers in motivating Isaac McCaslin to free himself from a corrupt tradition.

Faulkner's continued use of this new theme in the last five Yoknapatawpha novels is explored in examinations of the following roles played by mature adults in assisting youthful innocents to counteract evil: Lucas Beauchamp's and Gavin Stevens' motivating Chick Mallison to initiate effective action against Southern prejudice in Intruder in the Dust; Nancy Mannigoe's bizarre use of Temple Gowan's infant daughter to save Temple's marriage in Requiem for a Nun; Gavin Steven's successful effort to liberate Linda from the pernicious influence of Flem Snopes in The Town; Ratliff's ability to use two boys as instruments to effect the removal of Senator C. Egglestone Snopes from public office in The Mansion; Lucius Priest's parents' and grandfather's so supervising his upbringing that he emerges as the liberator of the prostitute Everbe Corinthia in The Reivers.

The final chapter of the study considers the question of the possible superiority of the Yoknapatawpha novels written prior to The Unvanquished. An examination of Faulkner's richly evocative treatment of Quentin Compson on the day of his suicide, as depicted in the second section of The Sound and the Fury, is contrasted with the undeniably attractive but less intense depiction of Chick Mallison's growth in moral awareness, as dramatized in Intruder in the Dust. The conclusion is drawn that it seems possible that Faulkner "is more deeply stirred to dramatic detail by the victimized than by the victorious" (p. 285). [Order No. 73-29,983; 299 pages. DAI, 34A (Jan. - Feb. 1974), 4292.]

276 Faulkner's Young Males: From Futility to Responsibility / Willis Earl WEEKS, Arizona State University, 1973 (Winifred A. Ferrell).

William Faulkner's novels often present young males searching for individual identity, for communication with others, for meaning in existence. During his career as a novelist, Faulkner altered his attitude concerning young men's roles in facing problems in society: from an early sense of futility to a later sense of responsibility. His portrayal of young men divides into three periods, closely paralleling the general world view projected in his fiction.

In the first period, pessimism predominates in his characterizations of young men. In his first novel, Soldiers' Pay (1926), the major young males face the problem of futility in the "waste-land" era following World War I. With Sartoris (1929), Faulkner depicts Bayard Sartoris and Horace Benbow futilely attempting to assume vital family roles upon their return from the war. Buddy MacCallum, the one "healthy" young man, appears late in the novel and does not actively develop any major theme. Then, in The Sound and the Fury (1929), all three Compson brothers--Benjy, Quentin, and Jason--have such significant limitations that they cannot help resurrect their their dying family.

In the middle period, Faulkner's presentation of young men was so varied that neither optimism nor pessimism prevails. In As I Lay Dying (1930), the three oldest Bundren brothers strive to find individual identity: Darl is unsuccessful, Cash is successful, but Jewel's success is uncertain. In Light in August (1932), alienation is the young men's common problem, one result being the brutal killing of Joe Christmas by the perverted Percy Grimm. Yet Byron Bunch overcomes his personal alienation, counterbalancing their negative characterizations. In Absalom, Absalom! (1936), the problem of repudiation confronts young Thomas Sutpen in the antebellum South, his sons Charles Bon and Henry Sutpen in the Civil War period, and finally Quentin Compson in the post-war South. Quentin's divided feeling about the South is partially offset by Shreve McCannon's "outside" influence that forces Quentin to face the past's ugly truths. Finally, Go Down, Moses (1942) presents several young men coping with racial injustice, ranging from the generally hopeless or helpless young blacks and the frustrated Ike McCaslin to the more positive figure of Lucas Beauchamp in his young manhood.

In the third and final period, with the adolescent male protagonists of Intruder in the Dust (1948) and The Reivers (1962), Faulkner finally made optimistic fictional statements about young males' potentialities to improve society. Chick Mallison (Intruder in the Dust) and Lucius Priest (The Reivers) both appear ready to assume responsible roles in adulthood following their experiences.

Since Faulkner's most memorable works appeared before his "optimistic" phase, however, some readers overemphasize the earlier novels' more striking pessimistic elements. Hence, the "negative" young men in those novels probably contribute much to interpretations that Faulkner's fiction is fatalistic. Faulkner's overall thematic intention was not negative, though, because alongside the most hopeless situation or character he usually placed an affirmative counterpart.

Faulkner used some young men to represent the frustrated aspects of man's striving for meaning and purpose, but others represent man's capacity to find direction despite overwhelming problems. His young men therefore play key roles in developing an ambivalent attitude in Faulkner's writings. Transcending this ambivalence was his deep belief in mankind expressed in his 1950 acceptance speech for the Nobel Prize: "Man will not merely endure; he will prevail." Faulkner's fiction indicates that with the proper guidance the young man can play a responsible role in helping man prevail. [Order No. 73-21,899; 236 pages. DAI, 34A (Nov.-Dec. 1973), 2663.]

277 William Faulkner and the Mythology of Woman / David Larry WILLIAMS, University of Massachusetts, 1973 (John J. Teunissen).

Faulkner's view of human destiny is of greater consequence than the memorable platitudes of the Nobel Prize address would suggest. The poet's voice," if it is to help man prevail, must answer the despair of those created males who regard the world as an inhuman mechanism. Certain of Faulkner's women offer a vitally non-rational answer; there are numinous properties in these women which suggest, at the very least, that the life-dominating forces are both nonhuman and organic. The latitude of their powers is much more comprehensive than the "earthmother" concept has been able to suggest; they have a crucial bearing upon material and artistic creation, upon the psychologies of "consciousness" and "culture," and upon the end--or endurance--of human life. These women (who are an authentic expression of the anima, the feminine-in-man) incarnate the Archetypal Feminine; they possess the ability to touch their world with the value of existence or to make it bankrupt. The plight of Faulkner's males then, is not the purposeless condition of pessimistic naturalism; it is the volitional condition of man confronting myth.

Since the archetype is incarnated in verbal form (myth), it is also of fateful importance for art. To that end, it has been my purpose to offer a new synthesis of what myth means--both in significance and process--to literature. By definition, the archetype is a dynamic as well as a structuring factor; if literature is to be actively mythic, these two factors must coincide. Symbol, the more affective element, refers to an image-complex with an unconscious input; mythos, the formal element, concerns the structural ordering of numinous power in human form. Mosquitoes offers certain proof that Faulkner was cognizant of the myth of the Feminine. "Archetypal" contents have little to do, however, with the quality of art produced; the artist who is gripped by an archetype will reveal its effect in dynamic form. Faulkner's apprentice works contain this unformulated potential but they are not totally informed by the archetype. The four works published between 1929-1932 are all variations on the same continuing theme, but they become true myth because in every case mythos and symbol have matured and fully merged. The major portion of this study is an attempt to analyze their varying formal resolution. By the time of the Snopes trilogy, a kind of mythic degeneration is taking place. Eula Varner retains something of the character of authentic symbol, but the mythos of The Hamlet is a record of the myth's defeat. In The Town and The Mansion, the mythos is further debased while a frantic counterattempt to save the symbols occurs. In The Reivers, the old compelling mythos is finally revived; its only mythic weakness consists in excessive mentalizing of the novel's major symbol. Throughout much of Faulkner's work, then, the emergence of the Feminine archetype has an absolute effect upon the process of artistic form, as well as upon the prospect of human destiny. [Order No. 74-8646; 379 pages. DAI, 34A (March-April 1974), 6610.]

278 Faulkner's Psychology of Individualism: A Fictional Principle and Light in August / Steven Early BALLEW, Indiana University, 1974 (Robert Eugene Gross).

Like American writers of the 18th and 19th centuries, Faulkner has an overriding concern with the state of the human psyche. While participating in the American Puritan tradition which emphasizes the way that the past molds and even twists the psyche, Faulkner also draws upon the Emersonian tradition of optimistic, self-reliant individualism, which undercuts the seemingly inescapable influences of the past and asserts the self-directing potential of every man. Faulkner's definition of the modern self-reliant individual turns on the problem of freedom and fate. True individuals must understand themselves and others as free men and women--a stance which brings together a man's cognitive and affective qualities and makes change and growth possible. Hence, the self-reliant individual must become alienated from communities like Jefferson which demand uncritical and undeviating acceptance of communal norms.

Taking an essentially subjectivist position, Faulkner considers both freedom and fate as aspects of consciousness; according to this view, freedom means overcoming the automatic nature of one's conceptions, perceptions, and emotive responses, while fate means passively repeating them. Faulkner's self-propelling man desires his independence yet simultaneously fears the consequences of defining his own values; in this figure, Faulkner reformulates the dialectic of freedom and fate in terms of the psychological tension between hope and fear and, so, transposes the dialectic of the American Puritan tradition from the absolute realm to the relativistic.

Faulkner's approach to self-determination in terms of an internalized dialectic between freedom and fate informs his creation of character types and affects his thematic emphases and narrative procedures. Light in August paradigmatically represents the effects of Faulkner's understanding of individualism in his novels, and his characters can be distinguished by the quality of self-knowledge and self-assurance they achieve. As the various types of characters struggle to achieve or avoid self-insight, their effort becomes the basis for the narrative unity in a Faulkner novel. While the substance of any single character's decision is dependent upon his own specific past and while the outcome is dependent upon his own fortitude, the psychic process of growth is shared by all the characters. Even when Faulkner presents the pattern of growth non-chronologically, the structural organization is nonetheless based on a developing personality. The many separate narrative sections cohere into a formal unit as parts of a single development. The basis of their coherence is a principle of shared identity--each narrative block being itself a step in the developmental process that Faulkner dramatizes. Since Faulkner's psychology of individualism suggests a broad temporal structure based not so much on Christian mythic patterns as on a generalized pattern of human growth toward self-definition and self-direction, his orientation to the problem of freedom and fate is always responsive to both the multiplicity and the universality of human experience. Thus, while Faulkner is able to use the lack of connections between many narrative units to suggest the informing influences of the past, the many temporal and spatial shifts also emphasize the disjointed, fragmentary nature of even the most significant events in the characters' lives; in this way, he insists upon the need to create a meaningful design from the mélange of past experiences by conferring a personal order to time and space.

Because his novels reflect a radical subjectivity in which self-validation is totally contingent upon personal values, Faulkner is able to evolve the 19th century tradition of romantic individualism so that it not only encompasses a notion of steady growth and process but also contains an organic definition of evil and of community. While the Faulknerian struggle for personal freedom takes place in different terms from those of the 19th century, Faulkner preserves the traditional American battleground--the individual psyche--as a plain on which a man can win and rewin the joy and responsibility of self-direction. [Order No. 75-8927; 190 pages. DAI, 35A (March-April 1975), 6700.]

279 William Faulkner's Use of the Tragic Mulatto Myth / Fay Elizabeth BEAUCHAMP, University of Pennsylvania, 1974 (Robert F. Lucid).

Between 1931 and 1942 Faulkner repeatedly emphasized racially ambiguous characters in his major fiction. His use of characters such as Joe Christmas, Charles Bon, and Sam Fathers has caused debate among critics. Irving Howe, for instance, believes Faulkner emphasizes "mulattoes" because of unconscious racist feelings; Robert Penn Warren stresses symbolic importance. This dissertation begins by examining Faulkner's raw materials: facts about "mulattoes" and tri-racial isolates, myths held by Southerners about these people, and, most important, a literary tradition which already used these facts and myths.

Chapter I draws upon criticism by Sterling Brown and Northrop Frye to discern two archetypal patterns in the literature concerning "tragic mulattoes." The first pattern involves the female "tragic mulatto" whose African inheritance becomes a barrier to marriage. The woman is rejected so utterly by her society that she commits suicide or accepts exile. Authors such as Dion Boucicault, William Dean Howells, and Charles Chesnutt used this story to expose social injustice. The second pattern concerns the male "tragic mulatto" who is often described in terms of internal dichotomy with "white blood" conflicting with "black blood." The story climaxes when the male "mulatto" murders a close kin, often a brother. Like the female, he also ends in exile or suicide. Southern myths seem to identify the male "mulatto" with Cain.

Chapter II explores the psychological implications of the male pattern. Twain's Pudd'nhead Wilson, Conrad's Heart of Darkness, and Jean Toomer's Cane suggest that the "black blood" represents the subconscious world while the "white blood" represents the world of laws and restraint. Paul Green, whom Faulkner met while writing Light in August, uses this dichotomy ironically in In Abraham's Bosom.

Chapter III shows how Joe Christmas follows the pattern of the Cain archetype. Faulkner tried to repudiate the racist implications of the myth by using it for psychological symbolism without supporting it on a literal level. Faulkner disparages the "white" part of Christmas more than critics have perceived. Insight into Christmas' dichotomy is gained by comparing him to Hightower, Joanna Burden, and Lena Grove.

Chapter IV analyzed Charles Bon in terms of the female "tragic mulatto." The Cain myth is only used ironically since the white brother is the fratricide. Novels in the "tragic mulatto" genre which can be fruitfully compared to Absalom, Absalom! range from Jane Eyre to Thomas Dixon's The Sins of the Father. If Faulkner attacks those who are cruel because of their fear of miscegenation, the novel also seems to show that miscegenation is inevitably unfortunate.

In Go Down, Moses Faulkner makes his ambivalence on racial issues a central subject and objectifies it in the character of Isaac. Chapter V focuses on the scene of Old Ben's death. Significantly, all those present, with the apparent exception of Isaac, are half-breeds: Sam Fathers, Boon Hogganbeck, Tennie's Jim, and even the animals Lion and the mule. An analysis of these characters leads to a consideration of Isaac as internally divided, caught in a dichotomy objectified in the division between the world of the woods and that of the plantation. While Light in August emphasizes psychological dichotomy and Absalom, Absalom! emphasizes social injustice, Go Down, Moses combines the two motifs.

The study concludes that while it is most illuminating to pursue the symbolic importance of the "mulatto" figures, Faulkner does not totally disassociate himself from racist implications of the myths in Light in August, Absalom, Absalom!, and Go Down, Moses. In Intruder in the Dust and The Reivers, however, he does repudiate the myths of the isolated, divided, sterile, and suicidal "mulatto," but these novels lose force as a result. [Order No. 75-14,538; 295 pages. DAI, 36A (July-August 1975), 297-98.]

280 I. Sir James Frazer's "Homeopathy" and "Contagion" as Archetypal and Structural Principles in William Faulkner's Go Down, Moses. II. The Auditory Dimension in Arnold's Search for a Distinctive Poetic Voice: Prosodic Commentaries in Selected Poems of Matthew Arnold. III. Images of Women in Recent Speculative Fiction / Christopher James BOND, Rutgers University, State University of New Jersey, 1974 (David R. Weimer).

I: Understanding the relations between "The Bear" and its context Go Down, Moses improves our critical estimate of William Faulkner. Using Victorian anthropologist James Frazer's analytical notions of "homeopathy" --the idea that like produces like--and "contagious magic"--the idea that things once in contact continue to act on one another--I consider Faulknerian character crises, or ceremonies, of repudiation and possession in Go Down, Moses. By such magical ceremonies Faulkner's characters discover they can exist vividly only in couples, inviolate, Godlike, and innocent.

We find a powerful unity of "Frazerian action" combined with a variety of textures permitted by Faulkner's diction and allusions. But "unity of action" does not preclude enlivening structural tensions: Frazer's two principles, although logically interdependent, may also be projected throughout the book as antagonistic or opposed modes of perception. In particular, "Pantaloon in Black" will be examined as a prototype for several stories in the book.

II: Arnold's restless experiments in poetic technique and his early-ended career represents a (largely unsuccessful) search for a voice of his own which could soothe others as Wordsworth's voice had often soothed Arnold. This search is often represented metaphorically as a search for the buried river of the self (as in "The Buried Life"), a river endangered by the "unplumbed, salt, estranging sea" which drowns efforts to communicate, and sometimes less metaphorically as a search for a Wordsworthian "healing" voice amid contexts of noise imagery and discord.

To understand adequately Arnold's replies to Wordsworth, we must attend not only to the direct statement in such poems as "Memorial Verses," but listen with the close attention of prosodic analysis for the more hidden Wordsworthian echoes in such poems as "Dover Beach" or "The Buried Life."

Arnold also engages and attempts, through prosodic devices, to represent other voices such as Byron's, Goethe's, or that of Thomas Arnold. And in "Resignation" and "The Strayed Reveller" Arnold considers, or projects, an ideal poetic voice.

We may at the same time analyze Arnold's prosodic devices and auditory imagery to evaluate the prosodic enactment of his critical prose remarks about Wordsworth's dialogues with nature, and we may better understand Arnold's remarks about the potential of meter as a poetic technique.

III: Recent speculative fiction threatens us with a reign of terror through literalized metaphor. The science fiction genre is one terminal case where literalized images have become paraphernalia rather than the stuff of dreams intended by Shelley, Wells, Capek, and others.

Between the extremes of technological man and animal man traditionally set up in speculative fiction, we now find, very often, hysterical heroines, tormented women, ideal victims as in Ballard's "Plan for the Assassination of Jacqueline Kennedy" or Pyncheon's Oedipa Maas in The Crying of Lot 49. Doris Lessing's sailor's narrative in Briefing for a Descent into Hell reads like a sexual melodrama about a fastidious heroine's fears. Technological conspiracies which once threatened the ideal victim from outside become, in Durrell's Nunquam, the very fine-woven artificial skin of the heroine/robot.

Both Lessing and Durrell borrow, self-consciously, science fiction conventions such as robots, telepathy, or "death machines." They combine the old stereotype of the mad scientist with the new stereotype of the "space fiction" writer to create the frightening portrait of an artist who literalizes metaphor in space fiction, and then factory-manufactures his images. [Order No. 74-27,589; 204 pages. DAI, 35A (Nov.-Dec. 1974), 3725.]

281 The Development of Women Characters in the Works of William Faulkner / Mattie Ann BURNS, Auburn University, 1974 (Carl Benson).

William Faulkner understood and appreciated the complexities of the human being, and his understanding and appreciation allowed him to create many complex, unpredictable, and well-rounded men and women. The men in his novels and short stories have long been the subjects of critical analysis, and Faulkner's ability to create individual men has been praised. The women, however, have been categorized and shelved, praised by critics for their adherence to the "womanly roles" or damned for their "unwomanly deviation" from those roles, but seldom discussed in terms of their functions as well-created fictional characters.

A study of his major and minor characters, as well as of the innumerable portraits of women sketched into the background of his works, reveals that the women, as well as the men, profit from Faulkner's creative genius and that they too are strong forces in his works. He understood well the strictures and boundaries imposed on men and women by a traditional society, and he understood the attempts by both men and women to formulate stereotyped notions about each other. Of ultimate significance, however, is the fact that he understood the complexities of the human heart and created characters who, because they are individuals in given situations at given times, grow beyond these strictures and stereotyped notions to become strong, living creations. In order to consider the women as well-developed fictional characters, this dissertation deals with them as major and minor characters in the works in which they appear, with special attention to Faulkner's development of them as individuals who, like the men, defy categorization and who stand along with the men as proof of Faulkner's creative ability. [Order No. 75-551; 234 pages. DAI, 35A (Jan.-Feb. 1975), 4502-03.]

282 Told By an Idiot: Toward an Understanding of Modern Fiction through an Analysis of the Works of William Faulkner and John Barth / Dante Kenneth CANTRILL, University of Washington, 1974 (Richard Blessing).

There is growing interest in the concept of the fiction-maker as one who self-consciously fulfills a role by creating a world that is neither more nor less fictional than the one in which he writes. According to this view, reality, once thought to yield only to imitation in art, is actually only a framework of the individual imagination; every person is a poet, a fiction-maker, to the extent that he is imaginative, and the appropriate symbol is no longer Daedalus but Arachne, weaving from her bowels a life-sustaining fabrication. This concept can and should be related to the metaphysical premises of modern relativism that emphasize the hypothetical and subjective nature of all conceptual frameworks, and especially to the rather poetic attitude that there is little, if any, difference between hypotheses and fictions. Among the consequences of these premises is the dilemma facing the author and critic alike that the worlds of tale, teller, and reader are equally real, or equally fictional, for if all knowledge is a fictional construct then every tale and every interpretation must be said to be a subjective, but necessary "reversion" of the tale of life. The creation of a viable fiction becomes the concern of both author and reader, who, in a sense, is also the author of every story that he reads.

To gain a clearer understanding of the implications and ideas that are involved in this phenomenon, I have done an analysis of the fiction of two American writers, William Faulkner and John Barth. My intention has been to demonstrate how this attitude toward fiction-making has been promoted by the writing of each in his own way, and, correlatively, how the fiction of each can be interpreted in terms of the relationship between the concepts of reality and fiction and between fiction and the fiction-maker. Using Barth as a representative figure, I have tried to show the historical and philosophical conditions that best explain his novels, and have counterpoised this with a similar examination of Faulkner's novels. Thus, in arranging my dissertation in this fashion, I have tried to image as well as describe the subject of my study, thereby acknowledging the implications for criticism of this concept of fiction-making. [Order No. 74-29,384; 264 pages. DAI, 35A (Jan.-Feb. 1975), 4505.]

283 William Faulkner: The Calvinistic Sensibility / Mary Dell FLETCHER, Louisiana State University and Agricultural and Mechanical College, 1974 (Otis B. Wheeler).

William Faulkner's vision is essentially religious: men struggle constantly, wrestling with the forces of good and evil, to assert their will. When he referred in his Nobel Prize acceptance speech to conflicts of the human heart, Faulkner was speaking primarily of the struggle between good and evil, a struggle which becomes in many of his characters a flesh-spirit battle. Although the conflicts that Faulkner portrays are so powerful, so elemental, that they assume universal significance, his fiction is structured largely in terms of the Christian interpretation of history. This interpretation, strongly modified by Calvinist Protestantism, provides Faulkner with a concept of man's nature and condition which he does not completely accept, but which, nevertheless, shapes his artistic vision and infuses his writings with both vitality and gloom.

The influence of Calvinism on Faulkner is not to be found, however, in a literal application of Calvinistic dogma, but rather in images, allusions, and analogues that show moral attitudes persisting long after beliefs are gone. The concept of original sin pervades the entire body of Faulkner's works. Although there are no systematic references to the Fall, his entire vision suggests that man is fallen, that his spiritual condition is a result of original sin. Isolated, these "hints" are perhaps not too meaningful, but taken in totality, they form a pattern that shows Calvinistic tensions in both Faulkner and his characters. Many of his characters exhibit traits so extreme that they seem to function allegorically as pure evil or innocence. Others undergo an initiation which is analogous to the Fall. His most fully developed women characters when viewed through the eyes of the male seem to spring from Eve: they do not fall into evil but rather are born with an affinity for it. In both theme and technique Faulkner demonstrates an emotional commitment to the paradigm of the Fall as a way of representing the human sense of isolation and alienation.

Ideas suggesting Faulkner's connection with Calvinism are contained in varying degrees and in diverse expression throughout his major fiction. Some works like Go Down, Moses are shaped entirely by the idea of man's fallen nature which manifests itself in Anglo-Saxon rapacity and exploitation of Negroes. Other works such as Absalom, Absalom! are concerned not only with the doom man has brought on himself but also with the excesses of secularized Calvinism. In nearly all of the works the characters are polarized-- the artificial and rigid representing man's negative aspects and the natural representing, if not the ideal, at least a more harmonious relationship with nature. This study is centered on the three major novels that best exemplify Faulkner's relationship to secularized Calvinism: The Sound and the Fury, Sanctuary, and Light in August. Both the concept of woman as the instrument of man's fall and man's impoverished view of nature are secular manifestations of the theological tenet of original sin. The Doctrine of Predestination also finds unique expression. The idea of "election" is embodied in a belief in white supremacy, an inflexibility in morals, and in an almost fanatical emphasis on respectability. Another aspect of this doctrine is dramatized in characters who, believing themselves to be damned by the curse of the past, exhibit a fatalistic attitude. [Order No. 75-1923; 245 pages. DAI, 35A (Jan. -Feb. 1975), 5400.]

284 Faulkner's Changing Vision: Narrative Progress Toward Affirmation / Doreen Ferlaino FOWLER / Brown University, 1974 (Hyatt H. Waggoner).

An examination of Faulkner's canon in chronological sequence reveals the gradual stages of development inherent in the change in Faulkner's world view from the despairing idealism of the early novels to the call to practical commitment that characterizes the later works.

In Faulkner's early novels, Soldiers' Pay inclusive of As I Lay Dying, man is presented as the helpless pawn of the forces of time, sex, death, and circumstance. Repeatedly in these novels the same procedure is pursued to the same end. Faulkner establishes the uncompromising standard of the idealist and arrives at an assessment of humanity by rationally reviewing the empirical data. The conclusion that human existence lacks all meaning is the inevitable result.

In Sanctuary Faulkner veers from this format. A despairing estimation of human existence is reached in Sanctuary, not as a result of man's subjection to natural and physical forces, but because of the realization of man's inherent inclination to evil.

Having confronted the nadir of despair in Sanctuary, in successive novels Faulkner examines the premises and methods of evaluation which have led undeviatingly to this despairing assessment of the possibilities of human existence. In Light in August, Absalom, Absalom!, and Requiem for a Nun, Faulkner questions the authority of fact and logic and concludes that the rationalistic-empiric method is an inadequate guide to the truth of human experience.

Faulkner now also questions his former attempt to define human experience in terms of rigid categories. The idealist's standard of perfection, which Faulkner had presented sympathetically in early novels, especially in The Sound and the Fury, is severely criticized in later novels (Light in August, The Unvanquished, The Wild Palms, Go Down, Moses, Intruder in the Dust, The Town, The Mansion, The Reivers) as life-denying and antagonistic to that commitment to the human community which Faulkner now sees as essential to the improvement of the human condition.

In the transition novels, Light in August through Go Down, Moses, new themes and ideas, the characteristics of the world view of the later novels, emerge. Whereas formerly Faulkner had emphasized man's limitations, now Faulkner stresses man's capabilities. In Light in August and Absalom, Absalom! Faulkner explores the enormous power of human belief to shape reality and the potential of human suffering to efface evil. Faulkner also examines the awesome capacity of human endurance in these transition novels. And, most importantly, in Light in August, Absalom, Absalom!, The Hamlet, The Unvanquished, and other novels, Faulkner becomes gradually aware of the fundamental unity of the entire human race.

The realization of the oneness of all men leads to new insights into those issues which were sources of despair in Faulkner's early novels--

human evil, man's ephemerality, man's subjection to death. In the transition novels Faulkner asserts that because the human race is interrelated the suffering of one man can efface the evil of his fellowman, that no human act is ever ephemeral because such actions affect the lives of all members of the community of man, and that every man who is a part of the one everlasting life of man lives forever.

Many of Faulkner's later novels return to the themes, or the characters and settings of the early novels, and attempt to view the old situation from the perspective of a new world view. Thus Go Down, Moses, Intruder in the Dust, and The Reivers deal with the central theme of Sanctuary--the introduction of human evil to the uninitiated. Both Requiem for a Nun and The Reivers return to the characters and the setting of Sanctuary. A Fable explores the conflict between a hopeful and despairing estimation of human existence--a conflict which characteristically appeared in Faulkner's early novels, and The Town and The Mansion scrutinize the idealist figure who played a prominent role in the early novels. In each of these cases the situation of the early novel is seen from the perspective of Faulkner's recently won insights into human existence so that the anguish and despair which characterized the early novels is replaced by a new tranquillity and acceptance. [Order No. 75-9149; 195 pages. DAI, 35A (May-June 1975), 7302-03.]

285 Implausible Motion: Generation and Regeneration in the Novels of William Faulkner / John Joseph HINCHEY, Harvard University, 1974 (Warner B. Berthoff) no DAI entry.

286 Affirming the Void: Futilitarianism in the Fiction of Conrad and Faulkner / Philip Loring HUTCHEON, Rice University, 1974 (Wilfred S. Dowden).

Chapter I introduces the central problem: the tendency of critics to interpret the great works of Conrad and Faulkner as affirmations of human capacities; with Faulkner this tendency is almost always accompanied by reference to his assertion in his Nobel Prize acceptance speech that man will "prevail." Properly viewed, these writers at their best belong in the modern tragic tradition, the theme of which, as Leslie Fiedler and Murray Krieger have shown, is the futility and meaninglessness of human existence. Zola's Germinal is a prominent example of a novel falsified at its end by an effort to "affirm"; the thorough pessimism which overrides the unjustified ending of Zola's novel is carried by Conrad and Faulkner into the 20th century, and this profound philosophical affinity, as much as their technical innovations, links the most powerful fiction of these two supreme modern novelists.

Chapter II treats the most apparently affirmative of the major works of each novelist. The Nigger of the 'Narcissus' and Light in August were spoken of as affirmations by their authors. Conrad's novel, however, is not the simple affirmation of solidarity that some critics have called it; it presents in fact a mixed judgment of man which belittles him as much as it praises him. Light in August presents a genuine affirmation in the Lena Grove-Byron Bunch story, but the tragic Joe Christmas counterplot proves the sentimentality of the later Faulkner's sweeping generalizations about the unlimited capacity of one man to save another.

Chapter III focuses on key nihilistic passages in Heart of Darkness, Lord Jim, "Youth," As I Lay Dying, and The Sound and the Fury and rebuts the critical tendency to exaggerate the affirmativeness of such aspects of these works as Marlow's lie to Kurtz's intended in Heart of Darkness and Dilsey's role in The Sound and the Fury.

Chapter IV compares the tragic fates of Charles Gould and Fidanza in Nostromo with the fate of Thomas Sutpen in Absalom, Absalom!. The defeat of the individual of extraordinary aspirations and abilities, whose obsessive quest for his goal causes him to forfeit human fellowship, is the ultimate exemplar of the futilitarian ethos at the core of the finest fiction of Conrad and Faulkner. [Order No. 74-21,284; 187 pages. DAI, 35A (Sept.-Oct. 1974), 2271.]

287 Faulkner and the Concept of Excellence / Alma Aquilino ILACQUA, Syracuse University, 1974 (David H. Owen).

The idea for this dissertation came to me during a summer of intensive investigation in the early period of American literature. As I studied the writing of men such as Bradford, Winthrop, Williams, the Mathers, Hooker, Samuel Sewall, and Jonathon Edwards, it occurred to me as it has to others that Puritan patterns of thought are not limited to the 17th and 18th centuries. Rather, they constitute a continuing strain in American literature.

One major exponent of these Puritan patterns of thought is William Faulkner, whose native South is greatly influenced by white, Anglo-Saxon, Protestants firmly grounded in the American Puritan heritage. This modern novelist seems as concerned with conflicts between good and evil, liberty and license, love-of-humanity and self-love as the early New England formulators of American Puritanism. A particularly significant and pervasive Calvinistic strain in his fiction is the concept of excellence. Many of Faulkner's major works contain one or more characters who seem to possess excellence.

Although a number of early Puritan theologians were concerned with the idea of excellence, few treated the concept as extensively as Jonathon Edwards. Because his definitions are so copious, consistent, and precise, and also because he is a major figure in American letters, I have relied in this study on Puritan patterns of thought as developed by Edwards.

Use of Edwardsean definiitions is in no way intended to imply that Faulkner studied Edwards or to suggest a direct influence of Edwards on Faulkner. Limiting definitions to those of one major theologian is intended merely to facilitate comparisons. Indeed, the only assumption made by this study is that Puritan patterns of thought are part of our American heritage and, as such, infiltrate, perhaps unconsciously, the work of American writers. In this paper, I hope to trace the idea of excellence as it appears in representative novels and short works by Faulkner. The works I propose to analyze include The Sound and the Fury, As I Lay Dying, Light in August, Absalom, Absalom!, "Spotted Horses," "Old Man," "That Evening Sun," "The Bear," "Delta Autumn," and A Fable. [Order No. 75-13,995; 293 pages. DAI, 36A (July-Aug. 1975), 314.]

288 Faulkner's Crime Fiction: His Use of the Detective Story and the Thriller / Peter Wilson JORDAN, University of Connecticut, 1974 (John D. Seelye).

Although scholars have begun to explore Faulkner's debt to popular crime fiction, none has done so in depth. This dissertation demonstrates the profound influence on Faulkner by the two major forms of crime fiction-- the thriller and the detective story--especially by the latter.

The first two chapters establish background. The introductory first chapter demonstrates that Faulkner as a young man was sifled creatively because he consciously attempted to produce highbrow, fin de siècle fiction. Although he was still to discover the strength of crime fiction conventions, only in Sartoris when Faulkner began to work with popular conventions did he begin to discover his power. The second chapter defines the terms thriller and detective story and briefly surveys the forms available to Faulkner when he began his most creative period at the end of the 20s and the beginning of the 30s.

The third chapter explores Faulkner's thrillers, Sanctuary and Light in August, focusing on Sanctuary and proving that it not only has the general structure of a thriller but also is directly influenced by Frank L. Packard's 1929 potboiler, The Big Shot. Faulkner also toys with detective story and hard-boiled conventions in the novel.

The fourth chapter demonstrates that the six detective stories collected in Knight's Gambit are second- and third-rate productions primarily because Faulkner failed to take the requirements of the detective story seriously. They are bad stories because they are bad detective stories.

The fifth chapter proves Absalom, Absalom! a detective story not only in the broad pattern of its plot but in almost every one of its details as well. The power of the novel can be directly attributed to the fact that Faulkner transmuted formulae of the detective story for serious purposes. An examination of the novel as detective story also helps elucidate such oft-debated questions as when Quentin learned the truth about Henry Sutpen's motivation for fratricide and to what extent Quentin's ratiocinations are to be accepted by the reader.

The sixth chapter shows Faulkner in Intruder in the Dust forgetting the lessons of Absalom, Absalom! and stifling an inherently powerful detective story with a didacticism directly opposed to the lessons of the plot.

The use and misuse by American novelists of popular fiction has often been an important key to their success and failure. Faulkner is no exception. This study of his use of the conventions of popular crime fiction offers an explanation not only of his failures but also of his greatest success: when Faulkner regarded those conventions as a mere money-making game, as in Knight's Gambit, he failed, but when he took them seriously, as in Absalom, Absalom!, he produced his most powerful work. [Order No. 73-28,518; 220 pages. DAI, 34A (Nov.-Dec. 1973), 2630-31.]

289 Faulkner the Storyteller / Blair Plowman LABATT, Jr., University
    of Virginia, 1974 (Jacob C. Levenson).

William Faulkner thought of himself as a craftsman in stories. As a storyteller, Faulkner makes something happen. His events are usually connected not only to their causes but to the changes in the relations of communities; his stories are journeys from equilibrium to equilibrium. In The Sound and the Fury, Faulkner's most modernist anti-story, the seeming events are dismantled, disconnected: causes are multiple and contradictory, effects are mostly blunted or balked. Absalom, Absalom!, on the other hand, seems a prototype of how to tell a story anecdotally: one basic event is withheld and embellished, and the cause which actually fits the central event appears only in the last, most elaborate conjectural embellishment. Throughout his career, Faulkner shows his great inventiveness at making stories, sequences of cause and effect. He makes things happen in his shortest stories, and in his longest--the Snopes novel-cycle.

Even in his short stories Faulkner shows versatility in emphasizing and deemphasizing, complicating and simplifying events. Some of the stories ("That Will Be Fine") include an anecdote which is not at the center of the reader's attention. But in others Faulkner successfully violates the prescriptions of other practitioners of the art, the warning that short stories are better off without plot. "My Grandmother Millard..." concentrates our attention on so continual and complex a reorientation of characters as to make it unprofitable to try to say where one event ends and another begins. "Mountain Victory" has the form of a much simpler anecdote, yet in fact deceptively conceals a really inextricable complexity, a dynamic conflict of human wills. Apparently the irreducible plot is built simply on the separateness of people.

The form of The Hamlet requires the reader to focus his attention on both the governing incidents and the separateness of those other things with which they coexist. For a proper sense of the plot of collision and recoil, we need to be aware of the non-plot--episodes of exposition, verbal wit, and fantasy. We need not be without discrimination in distinguishing episodes of manifest independence and plenitude from contrived relevance and from wasted or unexploited material. The plot and the nonplot form a coexistence in which the ultimate authority of the one does not inhibit the momentary independence of the other, and in which the constant interplay of the two makes for moments of contemplation in the middle of the chain of reactions.

Plots depend on characters at odds, and in The Town Faulkner greatly complicates his conflicts by increasing the number of his independent actors. But human interaction requires both independence and communication, and Faulkner emphasizes this combination in the intricate dialogue enacted between the novel's narrators. The dialectic of communication is implicit even in the complicated form of the episodes, which carry within them an entire tradition of telling and retelling, the storyteller's dialogue with himself.

The plot of The Mansion is simpler than that of The Hamlet or The Town. As a novel in its own right, it seems to be all ending. The conclusion of the novel, though strongly foreshadowed, does turn out to conceal new complications until the end. But the very success of the final revelations depends on an almost total restraint beforehand. The major part of the novel is contemplation, the reconsideration of old characters, an act of faith on Faulkner's part in the freedom and the complexity of his human actors.

Series of local conflicts which give pattern and plot to a massive chronicle; causation, and isolated actions; collision-and-recoil, and longstanding strategies--Faulkner uses all these tools in shifting proportion, demonstrating the storyteller's multiple ways of showing the almost-infinite things people do to other people. [Order No. 74-12,672; 248 pages. DAI, 34A (May-June 1974), 7761.]

290 The Function of Stock Humor and Grotesque Humor in Faulkner's Major Novels / Justine M. MANLEY, Loyola University of Chicago, 1974 (Thomas R. Gorman).

Humor pervades all of Faulkner's work; it is even apparent in novels not normally considered comic. This humor falls into two categories: stock humor is a traditional type of humor which results from mistaken situations, exaggerated actions, and stock characters such as the Southern gentleman or belle, the faithful Negro servant, the dandy, and the fool; grotesque humor is a more hurtful thing which is recognized by its characteristics of: (1) delicate subject (such as death, love, sex, religion, politics); (2) the extremity to which the circumstances are taken; (3) the unnaturalness of the situation; (4) the resulting tension and the vacillation of tone between sympathy and criticism; (5) the response of laughter linked with horror; and (6) the detachment of the audience and the author from the circumstances of the grotesque humor. In Faulkner's work, stock homor is a gentle thing used to produce comic relief and to underline theme. Stock characters, although humorous, and stock situations of comedy are more than just comic relief; they are always given significance beyond that normally assumed appropriate for a stock comic character or situation. This stock humor reflects Faulkner's love and faith in the South since whenever he treats a circumstance or a character with stock humor, he indicates his desire that we commend or emulate those characteristics. In contrast, grotesque humor is the theme of the novel and is most important to the communication of that theme. The grotesque humor and its function as theme reflect Faulkner's other attitude toward the South: his criticism and hate and annoyance with it. This is not to say that the only way Faulkner might express criticism is through humor of any sort, but grotesque humor always expresses criticism.

The early novels such as Soldiers' Pay, Mosquitoes, and Sartoris are purely stock humor especially in a tall tale kind of way since so many of the incidents of these novels follow that format of a sophisticated teller, exaggerated circumstances, and an abrupt trick conclusion. The Sound and the Fury is not a predominantly humorous novel although there is a lot of stock humor in the characters of the Negroes, especially Dilsey and Luster, of Mrs. Compson, and of Jason; the stock humor is linked to the theme of the novel concerning the fall of a family and of the South. As I Lay Dying and Sanctuary are both entirely grotesque humorous novels; the humor is intended to be a major technique in the novels and is the theme itself. Hypocrisy, wayward justice, phony rituals, and false standards of action are all criticized in these two novels through the grotesque humor. Light in August and Absalom, Absalom! include both types of humor although that humor is never obvious and always quite subtle; here the stock and grotesque humor are decidedly secondary to the serious theme of the novels although that humor is apparent on careful investigation. The Snopes trilogy of The Hamlet, The Town, and The Mansion again includes both types of humor although much more obviously than any earlier work. The Hamlet is a predominantly comic novel using both types of humor while The Town and The Mansion display only minor humorous incidents of both types. Finally, The Reivers is again a completely intended comic novel although now the humor is strictly stock humor coming from the characters and the boy's point of view. [Order No. 74-16,956; 458 pages. DAI, 35A (July-Aug. 1974), 1111.]

291 The Role of Women in Three of Faulkner's Families / Collin Gilles MATTON, Marquette University, 1974 (Joseph M. Schwartz).

The purpose of this study is to examine the roles played by the female characters in three of Faulkner's families. The families have been arbitrarily chosen on the basis of their typicality and importance in the Faulkner canon. Within the family unit, the women in Faulkner's world achieve significance by their ability to physically sustain the human race. In cases where women are unable to bear children, the females acquire dignity, not by exceptionally heroic deeds, but by providing a sense of stability for the members of the family and by reminding them of their past. The women in Faulkner's world ideally become guardians of the family unit in either perpetuating or in sustaining the race. Those women who embody the characteristics of the guaradians of the family achieve a degree of serenity and tranquility not found in the men who are often too occupied with rash schemes. Certain female characters emerge in some families, however, who do not adhere to their charge. Some women destroy the family by their neglect or selfish behavior. Yet, even these women are significant in defining the role of women in that they point to the virtues they ought to possess.

This study begins with an examination of the critical response which has been afforded William Faulkner. Through a survey of existing criticism, we find that Faulkner's reputation has shifted considerably since the 1920s but has consistently elicited a great deal of study. Yet, the attention devoted to Faulkner has generally not included a great deal of material on the subject of his female characters.

The bulk of this study focuses on three families in the Faulkner canon-- the Sartoris, Compson, and Snopes families. In the Sartoris family, Faulkner creates an example of strength and virtue in Aunt Jenny. Surrounded by reckless men, Aunt Jenny defines her position in the Sartoris family as a raconteuse whose stories of the past glorify the family. Aunt Jenny does not herself further the race, but she provides the example of love to the other Sartorises and, in so doing, gives them a moral center. In contrast, Narcissa Benbow and Drusilla Hawk emphasize Aunt Jenny's virtues by their failing to possess her qualities.

The Compson family is in serious decline in the 1920s because no women in the blood family possess the love and wisdom of Aunt Jenny. The three Compson women--Mrs. Compson, Caddy, and Miss Quentin--each fail to understand the power of love. Mrs. Compson in particular shows the decline which surrounds a family unsustained by love. By her failure, Mrs. Compson destroys the basic social order and precipitates the final doom of the Compsons. In contrast to Mrs. Compson, Dilsey Gibson, the faithful black servant, demonstrates a basic understanding of love in her relationship to the Compsons. Dilsey is used to exemplify the qualities a woman ought to possess and to highlight the failures of the Compson women.

The Snopes women, like Aunt Jenny and Dilsey, possess a sense of tranquility. They go about their tasks with little concern for the hectic life around them. With some of the Snopes women, Faulkner enlarges his imagination to consider the mythic dimension to his characters.

This study ends with a brief notice of areas not yet explored by Faulkner critics and with a view of possible areas for further study in a consideration of the female characters in the fiction of William Faulkner. [Order No. 74-22, 296; 108 pages. DAI, 35A (Sept.-Oct. 1974), 2283.]

292 Tricked by Words: Syntax and Style in Faulkner's As I Lay Dying / Trudy Kehret MURRAY, University of Washington, 1974 (Donald Kartiganer)

The intent of this study was to investigate in a systematic way and in a specific literary context some of the assumptions about language and literature which underlie modern stylistic studies. The three assumptions which I chose to investigate were: (1) that form is content, i.e., that formal linguistic structures have psychological functions; (2) that a communication model of language provides a sufficient basis for narrative theory; and (3) that a reader's ability to understand sentences is primarily a matter of competence, i.e., that grammar is at the center of all linguistic behavior and that abstract linguistic structures are directly mapped onto speech perception and production. I chose to investigate these assumptions by asking about their consequences for the interpretation of a particular literary work: Faulkner's As I Lay Dying.

The larger question of whether form is content, whether linguistic structures have psychological functions, became the specific local question of what a fictional character's characteristic syntactic choices "mean": whether for example, these choices correlate with personality or point-of-view.

The larger question of whether a communication model of language provides a sufficient basis for narrative theory became the specific local question of how to account for "non-narrator" (nonexpressive, nonreportive) passages within a communication theory of language. (Non-narrator passages in As I Lay Dying appear in the passages describing Darl's clairvoyant experiences.)

The larger question of the explanatory adequacy of syntactic accounts became the specific local question of whether a reader's processing of adjectives and negatives can best be accounted for grammatically or via perceptual strategies (i.e., whether this processing is a matter of competence or performance.)

My conclusions call all of the above assumptions into question. With respect to the assumption that linguistic structures have psychological functions, I argue that linguistic facts mean differently in different circumstances, and that, to quote Stanley Fish, the explanation for that meaning "is not the capacity of syntax to express it, but the ability of a reader to confer it." Chapter Two, which identifies the syntactic idiosyncracies of certain characters in Faulkner's novel, finds the significance of these idiosyncracies, not in any inherent psychological symbolism, but in the structure of expectations within which they function and which moves the reader to assign them a value. This chapter identifies two basic "styles" in the novel, one adjectival, one predicative-subordinative.

With respect to the assumption that a communication model of language provides a sufficient basis for narrative theory, I have suggested in Chapter Three, following Kuroda and Banfield, that there is in fact no linguistic reason to invoke such a theory unless the grammar itself assumed a communication setting, i.e., unless we encounter discourse in either a reportive or expressive narrative mode. This permits us to acknowledge the existence of "narratorless" passages, and to account for the strangeness of such passages when they occur in the context of narrated fiction. I suggest that in the case of Darl's clairvoyant experiences, the narratorless mode is precisely right, producing a sense of events not directly perceived but simply "there." I further suggest that since the adjective style and the narratorless mode are uniquely characteristic of Darl, we tend to interpret the assumptive quality of the adjective style and the "I-less" nature of the narratorless mode as evidence of Darl's having a means of access to objective, "I-less" reality, and as evidence of the price he pays for that access: horror, astonishment, and the eventual annihilition of the "I" that is Darl.

With respect to the explanatory adequacy of syntactic accounts, I argue in Chapter Four for the usefulness of Emmon Bach's suggestion that "the facts of interpretation [are] better explained by assuming an interaction of grammar and interpretive strategies that would be needed in any event." [Order No. 75-28,409; 166 pages. DAI, 36A (Nov.-Dec. 1975), 3660.]

293 Knowing in the Novels of William Faulkner / Thomas Edmund PERRY, University of Rochester, 1974 (William Rueckert).

This thesis is an attempt to study the novels of William Faulkner as renderings of epistemological problems. It examines various aspects of knowing in the novels in order to establish both the nature and the importance of Faulkner's epistemology, which is best treated as an artistic method rather than a philosophical system. The thesis comments upon acts of knowing, the boundaries of the knowable, the sources of knowledge, obstacles to knowledge, covert structures of reality, recurrent types of knowers, the nature of perception, and narration as an act of discovery and disclosure. The study begins with a general discussion of knowing in Faulkner's works, then uses aspects of knowing as a critical tool in explication of a number of individual novels.

Part I, "Knowing," is a preliminary discussion of acts of knowledge in the novels. The first chapter proposes a redefinition of event, the basic structural and conceptual unit in the novels, as a cumulative knowledge relation between mind and occurrence. The second chapter illustrates the tentative nature of the assertions of characters and narrators. The third chapter is a discussion of the relationship between time and knowing. The last three chapters of Part I are descriptions of three representative ways in which knowledge is obtained: the emblem or frozen tableau, the types of ratiocination customary in the detective story, and the visionary knowledge of dream.

Part II, entitled "Structures: The Discerning of Meaning," consists of four chapters which view the structures of events as vehicles for conveying covert meanings. The Sound and the Fury is examined as a structure of unheard narratives designed to reveal the unknowable. Go Down, Moses is treated as an interplay of competing theories concerning the structure of events. Chapter IX attempts to illuminate As I Lay Dying by comparing it with structures from elsewhere, the recurring structures of human action posited in the writings of Norman O. Brown. Chapter X examines the relationship between words and their referents in a discussion of Faulkner's modes of entitlement.

"Investigation and Discovery," Part III, contains four chapters concerning the processes by which individuals come to know about events in the novels. A chapter on the implications of the act of exhuming corpses in Intruder in the Dust is followed by a chapter on narration as an act of discovery and disclosure in Absalom, Absalom!. Another chapter discusses A Fable as a study of revelation and its effects. Another treats Requiem for a Nun as a way of tracing hidden causation backward through time.

Part IV, entitled "Confrontation with Event," examines various mental operations in which characters engage in order to alter the immediate data of sense, or to overcome gaps in their knowledge. Included are chapters on the division of the self into actor and knower in Sanctuary, forms of translation in the dichotomized world of Pylon, the displacement of human acts to created contexts in The Wild Palms, the opposition of knowledge and acknowledgement in The Reivers, and the perception of masks in Light in August. Part IV ends with a discussion of The Hamlet, The Town, and The Mansion as renderings of the mind's struggle to clarify ambiguity and enigma. [Order No. 74-22, 620; 370 pages. DAI, 35A (Sept. -Oct 1974), 2289.]

294 Faulkner's Style: A Syntactic Analysis / James Louis RADOMSKI, Kent State University, 1974 (Yoshinobu Hakutani).

Syntax is the most revealing aspect of a writer's style, and transformational-generative grammar has enabled us to analyze it in a more precise and rigorous manner. Since Faulkner's prose appeals to stylistic analysis, the present study attempts a transformational account of several passages from Intruder in the Dust and "The Bear." The investigation has led to the indentification of his major stylistic features and suggests a theory of language Faulkner might have used to portray character, plot, setting, or tone.

Chapter One discusses Faulkner's syntax and diction in general. I have surveyed some of Faulkner's earlier critics and evaluated objections and observations made about his style. I have also introduced the work of Chomsky in linguistics and Ohmann in the theory of style, and discuss a method of analysis. Because the styles of Hemingway and Faulkner lend themselves to comparison, Chapter Two uses several statistical studies to emphasize the chief syntactic devices of each author. The advantages and disadvantages of statistical investigations are also pointed out. Chapter Three, then, provides an analysis of two comparable passages from Hemingway and Faulkner (100 line passages from Intruder and A Farewell to Arms,) resulting in the identification of Faulkner's major syntactic choices. The analysis shows that conjunction, relativization, nominalization, and participial constructions are the means Faulkner uses at once to suspend the narrative and embed material into his sentences, thereby making his prose more economical and efficient.

Chapter Four analyzes six more 100-line passages, four from Intruder and two from "The Bear," in order to illustrate how Faulkner uses syntax to enhance other elements of his fiction. For example, a statistical comparison of the three passages from Intruder (which serve to reproduce the thought of Chick Mallison as he reflects on Lucas Beauchamp and his alleged murder of a white man) indicates that Faulkner uses conjunction, relativization, nominal compounds, and certain participles in order to describe the confusion and anxiety of the young man. Although subordination is a consistent device here, coordination is also found significant. Contrary to common knowledge, Faulkner's relativization does not go beyond a certain level of complexity, nor does it interfere with comprehension. Finally, Faulkner uses participles to lend to historical report or on-going action.

The examination of prevalent transformational choices in Intruder and "The Bear," therefore, has led to the discovery of Faulkner's major stylistic techniques used to achieve aesthetic effects and psychological insights. This analysis might serve as an introduction to Faulkner's style; moreover, it could be extended to other works by Faulkner or to works of comparable writers. The study goes beyond the mere labelling of Faulkner's prose as "stream-of-consciousness," and suggests, in fact, the nature of Faulkner's code, the means by which the reader learns to unravel meaning and "re-create" experience. [Order No. 75-7096; 204 pages. DAI, 35A (March-April 1975), 6154.]

295 An Application of Script Analysis to Four of William Faulkner's Women Characters / Suzanne Renshaw REIRDON, East Texas University, 1974 (James M. Lacy).

Purpose of the Study: The purpose of this study is to apply the principles of Eric Berne's script analysis, which has evolved from transactional analysis and which provides a method whereby a therapist can predict human destiny, to four women characters from Faulkner's novels: Lena Grove and Joanna Burden in Light in August and Candace Compson and Dilsey in The Sound and the Fury. Further, the purpose of this dissertation is to illuminate the characterizations of these women by giving the reader an insight into the compulsions which drive each of the women to her individual and ultimate destiny.

Procedure: The study begins with the establishment of the criteria from Berne's theories from which a delineation of the characterizations of the women can be made. After development of the criteria, the organization of the paper is designed by categories, which are winners, losers, and autonomous persons. The criteria are then applied to each of the women characters which are selected for analysis from Faulkner's canon.

Findings: The findings indicate that Lena Grove in Light in August is a winner because she receives a blessing from her Parental influences. However, because Joanna Burden in Light in August receives a curse from her Parental influences, she is a loser with a tragic ending. Like Joanna Burden in Light in August, Candace Compson in The Sound and the Fury receives a Parental curse and becomes a loser with a tragic ending. Dilsey, in The Sound and the Fury, alone of the four women, meets the criteria which determine that she is free of Parental influences and is free to control her own destiny.

Conclusions: The significance of this exercise is in learning that script analysis can be effectively utilized as a tool of literary analysis. Although the method of script analysis has been used in drama criticism, its application to fiction is yet unplumbed. Also, any method which will explain the tortured characters in William Faulkner's novels is not without merit. [Order No. 75-1600; 196 pages. DAI, 35A (Jan.-Feb. 1975), 4549.]

296 Faulkner's Flags in the Dust and Sartoris: A Comparative Study of the Typescripts and the Originally Published Novel / Melvin Reed ROBERTS, University of Texas at Austin, 1974 (Gerald Langford).

This study provides: (1) a critical commentary on the significant differences between Flags in the Dust (the typescript version of Faulkner's Sartoris) and the novel as originally published and (2) a list of the omissions from and the additions to the content of the narrative as it was altered in revision. The central conclusion reached in the commentary is that the final product, Sartoris, emerged as a clearly superior dramatic structure, but that there was considerable loss: severe restrictions were placed on the thematic scope and the detailed character development of the original novel. The most striking and extended revisions are related to three major characters--Bayard Sartoris, Narcissa Benbow, and Horace Benbow--and to a minor character, Byron Snopes. A chapter in the commentary is devoted to each of these characters, and the same general procedure is followed in each discussion: first, a discussion of one or more problems in Sartoris which can be solved or alleviated through reference to Flags; second, an examination of those passages which either give a new insight into a character or else provide a basis for questioning familiar critical responses. The initial chapter explores the thesis that, whereas in Sartoris the sources of young Bayard Sartoris' terror are "localized," in Flags his ghosts remain ambiguous so that he remains susceptible to the cumulative force of the legendary specters of the Sartoris past. The result is that Bayard's character, as it emerges in Sartoris, is less relevant to the "Sartoris game" than it was in Flags. The chapter on Narcissa Benbow reveals that her curtailed presentation in Sartoris has produced a number of misreadings of her character. Flags not only provides careful foreshadowing for her ultimate surrender to Bayard but also emphasizes the central conflict underlying her outward serenity. The sources of Horace Benbow's indolence and despair, intimated in Sartoris but fully explored in Flags, are discussed in Chapter Three. Through an extended presentation of Horace's relationship with Narcissa and Belle Mitchell, Flags supplies vital motivation for Horace's consistently "messy" involvement with women. The following chapter on Byron Snopes shows how the portrayal of his anguish in Flags was sacrificed in Sartoris to subordinate his role to a clearly functional status. The result is that in Sartoris Snopes inspires more contempt than pity. A final chapter is concerned with a number of revisions not directly related to specific characters, additions to the text of Flags which supply local-color details and intensify the conditioning environment depicted in the novel published as Sartoris. [Order No. 74-14,754; 202 pages. DAI, 35A (July-Aug. 1974), 471.]

297 Work in Counterpoint: Faulkner's The Wild Palms / Ann Doniger ROWER, Columbia University, 1974 (George Stade).

In the case of The Wild Palms, William Faulkner's fourteenth novel, the history of its critical reception is of particular interest since it appears to have affected the publication history as well. For in between the original 1939 Random House edition and the most recent ones, the publishing industry consistently took the work, which is made up of alternating chapters of two separate stories, "Wild Palms," and "Old Man," apart, either publishing the stories separately or, even more frequently, reprinting only "Old Man."

And so this study, which takes The Wild Palms as a work typical of Faulkner's conception of complex form, in its simplest form--the two-in-one-- begins by examining some of the instructive difficulties other critical readers have had answering the question of whether the two narratives, ten years in time, involving different groups of characters and two separate series of events had any connection with each other. While the early reviewers tended to dismantle the original whole (the form in which Faulkner submitted it for publication and in which it was, presumably, composed) and to regard the method of alternating chapters as a "technical" failure, many later critics, even those more committed, on principal, to preserving the unity of the original conception, still tend to misread the relation between the two stories as one of simple ironic contrast.

We are, it is perfectly true, made aware of contrast, but not merely because the narrative shuttles back and forth between the two stories. The contrast which focuses the meaning and value of the work keeps up so continuously and so variously that it holds the whole together, working simultaneously and alternately with and against the pendulum-like alternations of plot. For the work we read is not two stories but "the one story" Faulkner has said on many occasions it is, the series of alternations simultaneously progressive, interlocked. This is the only direct experience any reader can have of the work and in it the awareness of the reader is made to focus not on contrast only but however subconsciously, on some deep prior matching, some original unity out of which all contrast emerges, into which it, in time, returns and of which it is absolutely the inverse.

The remaining four chapters therefore examine four ways in which The Wild Palms is "the one story, the story of Harry and Charlotte" that Faulkner says it is. One way is to see, as Chapter One, "Being in Motion," suggests, the way everything in both stories--the two plots, the journeys, the characters, their situations, even the atmosphere, the ground--presents itself as being in relation to being in motion in which the wholeness and continuity of "the one story" is like the motion of the two journeys, the characterization of the "people in motion" separately or taken together, as a balancing of motion and rest or motion and not. In the same way, "parallel but in reverse," character, situation, and atmosphere appear as repeated variations of the same situation of which the issue is not simply motion itself but motion humanized, as the possibilities for human freedom, in which the unifying value lies in how what is done is chosen, which is the subject of Chapter Three "Being Free."

"Being an Other," Chapter Four, considers the way (and the way of this work might well be typified as inversion) these situations which present themselves to the reader as variations of being in motion and being free are both themselves part of an even more encompassing pattern in which everything in the whole work presents itself in relation to, as self and other which anything needs to be whole or free. Like the continuously opposing and reinforcing "other" story, everything in this work insists on being regarded in relation to an other which is always both complement and nothing, lover and enemy, is, finally, simply, the truth which being faces. This chapter focuses on the position and function of the "others" in the two stories, particularly the plump convict, the middle-aged doctor, and the two women, one in each story, as they relate to the two protagonists, Harry and the tall convict, and to each other.

Finally, the form of the whole work is shown as being itself the same as its subject: the couple, the one, the two-in-one, in which the two parts, the two separate stories, like any two particulars in this work, are seen as parts of necessity and the whole is seen as needing the two to be whole, in Chapter Five, "Being Whole/Being There." [Order No. 75-9307; 193 pages. DAI, 35A (March-April 1975), 6731.]

298 The Unalterable Doom: Horror as an Element of Tragedy in Four Novels of William Faulkner / Bernice J. RUDENSKY, University of Chicago, 1974 (Sheldon Sacks) No DAI entry.

299 A Textual and Critical Evaluation of the Manuscripts and Typescripts of William Faulkner's Intruder in the Dust / Patrick H. SAMWAY, University of North Carolina at Chapel Hill, 1974 (Louis D. Rubin, Jr.).

William Faulkner wrote Intruder in the Dust during three months in the winter and spring of 1948. From his correspondence with his agent, Harold Ober, and his editor, Robert Haas, it is clear that he had been thinking about this novel during the previous eight years, part of which he spent in Hollywood writing film scripts and struggling over what he considered his masterpiece, A Fable. The actual composition of Intruder took place immediately after he had finished the racehorse episode in A Fable. The Alderman Library of the University of Virginia contains 609 pages of manuscript and typescript which comprise the two versions of the novel: the original draft and the setting copy. As far as can be determined, there are no other Intruder manuscript or typescript pages elsewhere. Faulkner wrote six chapters of the original draft (the last is incomplete) before putting this draft aside to write a final draft which became the printer's setting copy. Faulkner wrote the original draft chapter by chapter, making few corrections or modifications. His second draft, however, greatly expands the first as he rewrote sections and shifted pages about. The first two chapters of the setting copy were written as one in the original draft. Also, Chapters Nine and Ten of the setting copy took considerable time and energy to compose. The novel as it presently exists is in an imperfect state, not only because of a number of typographical errors, but because Faulkner sent his editors, after the novel was published in September 1948, two pages to be inserted in the second printing into one of Gavin Stevens' speeches. Unfortunately, this was never done. What is unusual about this new material is that in it Faulkner refers to himself and makes a direct allusion to Absalom, Absalom!. Intruder reflects two of Faulkner's interests: the black man's struggle to obtain his civil rights and the Chick Mallison-Gavin Stevens murder mysteries which Faulkner had been writing during the 1940s and which were eventually collected into the Knight's Gambit volume. Faulkner maintained that Intruder was based on a "whodunit" he had read, but a search of the murder mysteries at Rowan Oak does not reveal a definite source. Rather, there seems to be a number of influences at work in the composition of Intruder: murders involving black men that happened in and around Oxford, Mississippi; Faulkner's outside reading, particularly Dickens and Twain; characters and events in Faulkner's earlier short stories and novels which are more fully developed in Intruder. In Intruder, Lucas Beauchamp, a Negro, has allegedly killed a white man and it takes an old woman, Miss Habersham, and two boys to prove to the Jefferson community that Lucas is innocent and that their preconceptions about him are wrong. The novel is essentially a Bildungsroman as young Chick, aided by Miss Habersham, Gavin, and Lucas, grows in his awareness of his obligations to the black people of his community and to the South. What Gavin philosophically professes, Chick dramatizes through action; Chick reveals and surfaces, to an extent, the psychological dimensions of the Southern mentality. Though Intruder has not been generally regarded as one of Faulkner's better novels, it remains an important, imaginative transition between Go Down, Moses and Requiem for a Nun. [Order No. 75-15,693; 529 pages. DAI, 36A (July-Aug. 1975), 328.]

300 William Faulkner: Myth-Maker and Morals-Monger; Esthetics and Ethics in Yoknapatawpha County / Otto Norman SCHLUMPF, University of California at Santa Barbara, 1974 (Lawrence Willson).

The greater part of William Faulkner's fiction forms itself into a myth. The myth of Yoknapatawpha has certain marked characteristics in its esthetics, its ethics, its major component parts, and its thematic elements.

Faulkner created the Yoknapatawpha fiction from an esthetic consciousness that can truly be labelled myth-making. Among the characteristic manifestations of such a consciousness is what can be called a telescoping of time, space, and character. The "inconsistency of details" noted by many of Faulkner's critics is due to such telescoping rather than to Faulkner's carelessness. He was, in his own words, trying to put all of human experience "on the head of a pin," an endeavor that led him to concern himself with the consistency or integrity of the whole of his vision rather than with that of its parts. His emphasis on an esthetic unity that supersedes the artificial unities of time, space, and character is expressive of Ernst Cassirer's description of mythical thought.

The ethics which the myth embodies is a complement to the esthetics. One of the major ethical principles according to which Faulkner judges his characters is their willingness to escape from what Mircea Eliade calls "the terror of history." That is, Faulkner expects his characters not to be bound to the past with emotional, psychological, social, or ritual chains, but to find new ways of expressing timeless values in a world that is constantly changing. He himself was constantly refining his understanding of how those values are to be expressed. Thus, his ethical judgment of certain of his characters changed as time went on, or, as he put it, as he "found out more about them."

For the purpose of a critical re-examination of the Yoknapatawpha fiction, Absalom, Absalom! is understood as paradigmatic of the esthetic and ethical principles expressed. The major component parts of the rest of the myth can be labelled from titles of Faulkner's choosing: (1) the old people, (2) Sartoris, (3) the town, (4) the hamlet, (5) intruder in the dust. Although each part overlaps, each deals with either a specific time, a specific place, or a specific set of characters as its focus. Each has its particular triumph and failure. Each has its particular villain and hero, esthetically and ethically speaking. Often there is more than one point to be made, thus more than one esthetic or ethical focus.

The thematic elements of the myth, springing from the ethical concerns, stand in the same relationship to the parts of the myth as the ethics do to the esthetics: they run through every part, linking them to each other and showing them as complementary. Some of the major thematic concerns, with which each generation and each sub-culture must come to terms, are: (1) nature vs. civilization, (2) innocence vs. guilt, (3) a dead vs. a living conception of honor, (4) despair vs. hope, and (5) love vs. perversion or perverseness.

The conclusion that emerges from evaluating Faulkner in the terms expressed is that he is ultimately an optimist in both his esthetics and ethics. Artistically, he was his own severest critic, painfully aware of his shortcomings. Ethically, he was a harsh judge of human immorality. But in the final analysis he was satisfied with both his art and with man, knowing, on the one hand, that he had done his best and believing, on the other, that man will prevail. [Order No. 75-11,497; 272 pages. DAI, 35A (May-June 1975), 7327.]

301 **The Evolution of an Artist: A Genetic Study of William Faulkner's The Hamlet** / Barbara Booth SERRUYA, University of California at Los Angeles, 1974 (Leon Howard).

This dissertation is a genetic, textual, analytic study of William Faulkner's The Hamlet, the first volume of the Snopes trilogy. While there are several critical interpretations of this novel, there has been no thorough study of its composition. This study, then, is to fulfill a critical need in at least two ways. First, by attempting to understand Faulkner's own intentions in writing the novel, the study provides fuller insight into The Hamlet and a basis for evaluating it as a novel. Examination of the early prototypal works, such as "Father Abraham" and "The Big Shot," as well as of the early manuscript and typescript drafts of the short stories and The Hamlet, shows that Faulkner had formal and conceptual problems in writing the Snopes saga. For example, the idea for the novel began in a series of tall tales of a satiric nature in which there was no thematic depth or dramatic unity. Moreover, the two protagonists of The Hamlet, Flem Snopes and V.K. Ratliff, originated as rather similar comic redneck businessmen. Faulkner was only gradually able to work out the dramatic, narrative, and moral implications in these characters and their relationships to make them structural and thematic centers of The Hamlet. The novel, then, is the product of focusing and fusing many diverse tales and defining characters. The final form of The Hamlet becomes clearer if we understand this genesis.

Second, this study provides insight into Faulkner's artistic aims and methods and his development as a writer. The Hamlet evolved over a fifteen-year period, from 1925 to 1940, concomitant with the writing of his major works. The changes this early material underwent reveal not only Faulkner's mastery of his art over the years, but the process of symbolic perception, the open-ended nature of the creative act that generates its own new forms and themes. Faulkner worked from the concrete, local, and humorous to the universal and tragi-comic as he discovered the symbolic truth implicit in his tall tales. He also enlarged his idea of the Snopes chronicle from the satiric story of how the peasant Flem makes good to encompass the life of a whole community and the extremes of human passion. This process generated in particular Eula's, Ike's, and Mink's tales, all of which were later additions to the original idea of the novel. Systematic, diachronic study of the manuscripts allows us to see the various stages of this development and the shift in focus of his aims and perceptions. [Order No. 74-22,962; 248 pages. DAI, 35A (Sept.-Oct. 1974), 2298.]

302 **Faulkner's Black Characters: A Comparative Study** / Roslyn SIEGEL, City University of New York, 1974 (Charles C. Walcutt).

Alexis De Tocqueville says of blacks and whites in Democracy in America that "These two races are attached to each other without intermingling, and they are alike unable entirely to separate or to combine."* Faulkner attempts to come to terms artistically with this problem which no one has been able to solve socially or politically. In his struggle to clarify relationships, to examine the intricate ties between the races on a philosophical, social, and biological level, he concentrates on black characterization with an intensity and seriousness unknown in earlier white American fiction. George Washington Cable, Joel Chandler Harris, Herman Melville, Mark Twain, and Ellen Glasgow all use black characters in their works. But Faulkner's blacks are outstanding in originality, stature, and structural significance.

Faulkner begins by drawing on the southern plantation tradition, giving us the familiar mammy, loyal servant, and tragic mulatto types. These conventional characters, however, grow into something quite different in the hands of Faulkner who turns the loving mammy into a prostitute dope-addict-murderess, the loyal servant into the proud and stubborn half-brother of his master, the tragic mulatto into a tortured and despised image of Christ.

Although Faulkner begins by drawing on the surface realism and nostalgia of Southern literary tradition for his presentation of black characters, he enriches their portraits by borrowing elements from the symbolic tradition of New England. Like Hawthorne and Melville, Faulkner investigates the philosophical and religious implications of the color black. Thus we find his symbolic use of the black man as the "shadow" of original sin and at the same time as sufferer who expiates that sin. Similarly, Faulkner uses his black characters as visual and moral contrast to the white characters, emphasizing differences in personality traits, and using the black to test and evaluate the actions of the white. In Faulkner's works, as in Melville's, "Black" designates not only a person in a definite social and historical situation, but also a state of being.

Although Faulkner's characters stem primarily from southern and New England literary types, they also are influenced by the modern literary tradition. Consequently they often function as symbols of modern man who suffers from social alienation, physical isolation, and loss of identity.

Most important in the depiction of black characters, however, is Faulkner's personal vision and particular psychological makeup. His nostalgic longing for idyllic childhood friendships, his attachment to his own mammy, his Calvinistic preoccupation with guilt and redemption, and his adherence to agrarian doctrine, greatly transform and color his characterizations.

Faulkner presents a whole range of black figures who function on many different levels and differ greatly amongst themselves. Some characters are relatively simple, having interest on a realistic level only, while others function symbolically and some even mythically. In his stories involving black-white relations, Faulkner has given new meaning to the suffering of human beings, has tapped the unconscious of both races, and found new value in the old relationships. Merging a southern and northern literary tradition while embodying a highly personal vision, Faulkner produces black characters who come from the past and challenge the future. They are unique in American fiction. *Alexis De Tocqueville, Democracy in America, 3rd ed. (New York: D. Appleton & Co., 1904), p. 361. [Order No. 74-19,487; 401 pages. DAI, 35A (Nov.-Dec. 1974), 3009-10.]

303 Inarticulate Characters in Modern American Fiction: A Study of Fitzgerald, Hemingway, and Faulkner / Paul N. SKENAZY, Stanford University, 1974 (Ian P. Watt).

Inarticulate characters in American fiction often experience or represent conflicts of individual and community beliefs. A character's preference for silence indicates his commitment to a non-verbal state of experience while, in his speechlessness, the inarticulate figure challenges the assumptions of his environment, especially as they are represented in its language patterns.

Writers like Crèvecoeur, Crockett, Thoreau, Melville, Stein, and Anderson relate inarticulateness to a primary, instinctual mode of thought which is associated with nature, physical experience, and a lack of training in social or linguistic forms. Such characters as the wood-chopper in Walden, Billy Budd, Huck Finn, or Melanctha Herbert express their powerful emotions more directly than their articulate counterparts, often through actions rather than words. They tend to view life as a timeless whole--a fact which is often represented by their associations with transcendental ideals, or with the cycle of the seasons.

Melville's treatment of silent characters like Benito Cereno and Bartelby suggests the enigmatic, fatalistic qualities of life. The complex series of speculations and projections through which Captain Delano and the narrator of "Bartelby" try to understand these figures reveals the difficulties of moral and ethical judgments in a world framed by ambiguity and uncertainty.

In The Great Gatsby, Fitzgerald portrays the attitudes and values of the Eastern rich through the projections of other characters upon Gatsby's activities. Gatsby's silence is associated with his Platonic dream, and reflects the lack of "manners" which separates him from the Buchanans and Nick Carraway. As Nick tries to explain Gatsby's longing for a timeless, silent reunion with Daisy, he comes to recognize his own inarticulate romantic yearnings, and is able to express them within the forms of perception and understanding his language provides.

Hemingway portrays inarticulateness as an intuitive contact with elemental experiences--nature, sports, one's own mortality--and as a mute protest against the life-denying rhetoric of the community. The reticence that characterizes his heroes emerges from his awareness that language often destroys one's ability to apprehend these elemental actualities. Hemingway's uneasiness with all but the most rudimentary words issues in a style geared to the precise transmission of sensory experience, and reinforces his pervasive anti-intellectualism.

In Faulkner's works, we are confronted with the paradox of an extremely eloquent, often verbose, writer who characteristically expresses his fury at the human condition in simple, inarticulate figures whose atrophied minds function by intuition rather than thought. Like Hemingway, Faulkner uses silence to represent a protest against social institutions and inhuman, unrealistic rhetoric. Inarticulateness is associated with an atemporal, intuitional recognition of incomprehensible powers which propel men, often against their wills.

Faulkner explores many of these themes in Ike McCaslin, a man who undertakes the impossible task of uniting his family legacy of ownership with the timeless experience of the ritual of the hunt. Inarticulateness is an image for the values inherent in the wilderness: values which surpass man's powers of apprehension or expression.

After Fitzgerald, Hemingway, and Faulkner, American novelists like Steinbeck, McCullers, Hammett, Kesey, Bellow, and Pynchon retain the associations of inarticulateness with a life lived by the promptings of the instincts and the heart, and with a belief in experience which cannot be expressed in language. The silent figure continues to be portrayed as an object of projection, and as a symbol of social protest. [Order No. 74-13,691; 335 pages. DAI, 34A (May-June 1974), 7783.]

304 A Study of William Faulkner's A Fable / John Howard SLADE, Stanford University, 1974 (Thomas C. Moser).

A Fable is the work in which William Faulkner attempts to express most explicitly and completely his view of mankind's condition. The novel examines the tension between man's desire to be a free individual, determining for himself his system of values, and his desire to submit himself to authority, thus escaping from the responsibility for his own and others' welfare. This duality within human nature is represented primarily by two characters, the corporal and the old general. The corporal is a messiah who teaches soldiers on both sides of the trenches in World War I to rebel against their officers and to work for peace. He shows them through his own actions, including his death, that in order to attain that peace, each man must accept responsibility for his own welfare and that of all others. The old general is the supreme commander of the Allied Forces, and thus the ultimate military authority over three nations. He commands his troops according to the traditional regulations of warfare. His soldiers, and the civilian population, obey him because they believe he will save them from Germany, and because their nations have taught them obedience. His soldiers willingly comply with his orders because, by deferring to him, they can escape the responsibility of being their brothers' keepers. Faulkner thus examines two conflicting necessities: the individual's psychological need for security within society, and society's vital need, especially during wartime, for individual responsibility.

Many critics have felt that the novel is less successful than Faulkner's other work; some even believe the novel to be a failure. Their complaint is that A Fable is too much from the mind and not enough from the heart, that it is predominantly an intellectual allegory portraying the conflict between authority and freedom, rather than an emotional experience, as are most of Faulkner's Southern novels, in which the lives of complex, realistic characters are dramatized. A major purpose of this study is to show that A Fable is written as strongly from the heart as any of Faulkner's other works. It further argues that the other characters are as richly complex as any of Faulkner's Southern figures.

Another purpose of this study is to examine the theme of fear as it is developed in each of the characters. The corporal and the old general, the two major figures, respectively represent the acceptance and the fear of responsibility. Certain characters prove able, through acceptance of responsibility, to believe in the corporal and follow him. Other characters place their faith in authority. One other character, a British pilot, proves unable, however, to believe either in authority or in any potential good, and therefore commits suicide. The theme of responsibility is dramatized also through a large cast of minor characters who seem to represent humanity in general; included in this group are those who do not understand the corporal's message that men are able to, and must, accept individual responsibility, and those who understand him but are unable, primarily because of fear, to sustain their faith in him.

An appendix contains a comparison between the events in A Fable and the historical events on which the novel is based, and a detailed plot summary. [Order No. 75-6927; 183 pages. DAI, 35A (March-April 1975), 6160.]

305 "You Smart Sheriffs and Such": The Function of Local Peace Officers in William Faulkner's Light in August and Intruder in the Dust / Shelby Dean STEPHENSON, University of Wisconsin, 1974 (Walter B. Rideout).

Concentrating on the administration of law at the grass roots, this dissertation investigates the function of local peace officers in William Faulkner's Light in August and Intruder in the Dust. Chapter I of the dissertation uses The Sound and the Fury as a test case which concludes that in Quentin's section Faulkner satirizes the efforts of local lawmen to keep the peace and through such satire points up in the novel a central theme of social and regional prejudice. In Jason's section Faulkner uses the sheriff's refusal to help Jason to emphasize Jason's own foolishness or, worse, his villainy.

Chapter II, on Light in August, first examines Sheriff Watt Kennedy's attempt to apprehend Joe Christmas and concludes that Kennedy is a well-rounded though minor character who is inclined to act justly and even-handedly in his official capacity but, because of his race prejudice, too often acts to reinforce and to protect the established white power-structure. This chapter also analyzes the function of "games" imagery in the description of the pursuit of Christmas and especially examines Percy Grimm's extraordinary role in the legal situation. Accepting the fact that Grimm is a racially prejudiced person and that prejudice is involved in his motivations to capture Christmas, such prejudice, it is argued, is less important than his militarism in establishing why he thinks and acts as he does. In short, all of Grimm's actions in the novel, except the butchering and mutilation of Christmas, are motivated by his militarism, his boyhood dream to be the soldier he never was. Grimm's belief that "the white race is superior to any and all other races" is subsumed by his militaristic principles; his belief that the "American is superior to all other white races" suggests that nationalism goes beyond racial differences. Through Grimm, Faulkner dramatizes the truth that in the South and in Yoknapatawpha County white-black conflicts may not depend solely on racial prejudice.

Chapter III, on Intruder in the Dust, emphasizes Faulkner's dramatization of Sheriff Hope Hampton as the completely competent sheriff, less rounded and ambiguous in characterization than Watt Kennedy. The Jefferson community's response to Lucas Beauchamp's involvement in the Vinson Gowrie murder is rendered essentially in social terms, unlike the legal situation in Light in August. In Light in August the assumed black man is a man of ambiguous racial and ancestral heritage, a true, all-time fugitive from justice, a man, in short, whose actions may baffle yet impress the reader as well as Sheriff Kennedy and his deputies. In Intruder, the prisoner is a black man whose racial and ancestral heritage is known in detail by his community, and who is put upon by his white neighbors. Further, Chapter III concludes that the legal situation works to demonstrate the mental and moral development of the novel's "center of consciousness," Chick Mallison. His thinking progresses from an attitude of prejudice--similar to the prejudiced members of the community--to an enlightened, independent view of black-white relations. Finally, Chapter III examines Gavin Stevens' mental development. With his nephew's influence he becomes willing to act, to try to re-educate himself to human relationships rather than limit himself to legal and intellectual matters.

The dissertation concludes with a short Chapter IV which supports the accepted judgment that Light in August is aesthetically superior to Intruder in the Dust. Such judgment is primarily deduced from the observation that in Light in August the local legal situation is presented as more baffling and ambiguously complex than the neater, more schematized legal situation in Intruder in the Dust. [Order No. 74-19,358; 279 pages. DAI, 35A (Nov.-Dec. 1974), 3012.]

306 Confronting the Ghost: Quentin Compson's Struggle with His Heritage in Faulkner's Absalom, Absalom! / Morris Owen WEE, Boston College, 1974 (Andrew J. Von Hendy).

Quentin Compson feels an intense ambivalence toward the story of Thomas Sutpen which he hears and tells in Absalom, Absalom!. He identifies strongly with the story, because it has always been part of his heritage, and consequently, part of him. But he also shuns the story, because it reminds him of his failure to protect his sister and of his inability to control his destiny.

To fully understand Quentin's aversion to the story, we must study The Sound and the Fury. In that book, we see his obsession and guilt concerning his sister's sexual relationships, and the analogy between his situation and Henry Sutpen's defense of Judith. These concerns are the sources of the tension which governs Absalom, Absalom!. Quentin's resistance to the story helps shape the novel, for he alters his narrative to avoid thinking of Henry. But the story is so much a part of Quentin that he cannot escape it. The Sutpen story seems to become autonomous and to force itself into Quentin's narrative against his will.

Quentin's heritage communicates to him both the ideas and the language of its predominantly fatalistic world-view. But Quentin desperately wants to believe in his power to determine his course and to avoid living out the destiny for which he fears he was "fated." A close study reveals Quentin's dependence on the inherited ideas and words, as well as his attempts to alter them to reduce their fatalistic implications.

Quentin's narrative describing his confrontation with Henry epitomizes his intense ambivalence toward the story. He continually tries to avoid the visual image of Henry until he stands outside the door "saying 'No. No!' and then 'Only I must. I have to!'" (p. 372.) To the very end, his two impulses-- to escape the story and to identify with it--remain in conflict.

Rather than accept the control of his past and live out the role it dictates for him in the moral confusion of the twentieth century, Quentin continues to search for escape where none is available. Unable to resolve his tension, he finally seeks peace "in the caverns and grottoes of the sea." [Order No. 75-5970; 54 pages. DAI, 35A (March-April 1975), 6166.]

307 Psychological Approaches to the Narrative Personality in the Novels of William Faulkner / Charles Francis WHITAKER, Purdue University, 1974 (Margaret Church).

Faulkner's acceptance speech for the Nobel Prize emphasizes his belief in the potential of man and affirms his faith in man's future. Faulkner's attitude here is reflected in his fiction, and this dissertation considers that fiction from psychological perspectives in order to see the reasons manifested in his novels for his image of man. The study discusses five novels by Faulkner: Soldiers' Pay, The Sound and the Fury, As I Lay Dying, Absalom, Absalom!, and The Reivers, from the theoretical and therapeutical viewpoints of Freudian, Jungian, and Existential psychologies.

The study begins with a discussion of critical theory and introduces a rationale for the significance of interdisciplinary study. Drawing a distinction between Lockean and Kantian models of "theories," the Introduction considers the criticism of Northrop Frye and Frederick Crews as representative of these models and also considers the similarity of these two "models" to S-R and Humanistic psychologies. The rationale concludes that interdisciplinary studies are effective in responding to the Kantian model, a model which emphasizes the importance of "a pair of glasses" to man's ability to determine meaning.

The study then considers Faulkner's novels from the basis of this Kantian model. The central concern of the study is to explore the importance of a dialectical image of man in Faulkner's work as revealed by the "Kantian glasses" of Freud, Jung, and Existentialists such as Binswanger, Boss, and May. The approach to the fiction is through personality, and thus the study focuses upon the "narrative personality" of Faulkner's novels. Using what is termed Faulkner's "thematics of form" as a means of revealing "inside narratives" in the fiction, the study discusses the personality dynamics of the novels. In a method analogous to that of psychotherapists, the study considers style, structure, characterization, and point of view as means through which the reader can understand and participate in the "inside narratives" of the fiction. The study emphasizes the importance of the theme of freedom in Faulkner's work and concludes that that theme is significantly related to Faulkner's dialectical image of man.

The first and last chapters of the study are devoted to Faulkner's first and last novels. In these novels, one notices Faulkner's reliance upon dreamlike narrative devices, which lead the reader to a clear view of Faulkner's dialectics and emphasize the importance of freedom in those novels. The middle three chapters discuss a separate novel from three different psychological viewpoints. The "lead" section of each chapter is a more extensive consideration, the intention being to suggest the broad potential for each of the psychological approaches selected here. The two other sections in each chapter focus upon the critical problem raised in the first section but from the viewpoint of the two other psychologies. The study is therefore concerned with presenting potential methods of integrating literature and psychology, as well as seeing the artistic development of an image of man in Faulkner's novels. [Order No. 75-10,982; 290 pages. DAI, 35A (May-June 1975), 7276-77.]

308 Faulkner's Style and Its Relation to Theme: A Stylistic Study of Two Stories from Go Down, Moses / Carol Ann Groening WINKEL, University of Delaware, 1974 (Ronald E. Martin).

Faulkner has long been recognized as a literary master, whose readily identifiable style is intrinsic to his greatness. Yet while many critics have admired the appropriateness of Faulkner's style to the kind of world presented in his works--the heightened rhetoric, the complex and involuted sentence structure, the dislocations of narrative structure and point of view--their critical analysis has generally consisted of quoting illustrative passages rather than characterizing his style in non-impressionistic terms.

I have taken two stories by Faulkner from his collection Go Down, Moses, "Pantaloon in Black" and "Delta Autumn," both of which attest to Faulkner's greatness, are representative of his style, and yet seem to be contrasting stories in the kind of thematic experience they convey to the reader. I have looked closely at Faulkner's style as it is manifested in these two stories, in order to account for the effectiveness of these stories stylistically, to characterize the variable elements in Faulkner's style, and to demonstrate the correspondence between style and theme.

"Pantaloon in Black," subjected to close reading to establish a basic interpretation, is a story with a strong narrative drive, that kinesthetically involves the reader through the dominant paradox: Rider's need to conquer the physicality of his body as it demands air and food to fuel the strength that serves as barrier to reunion with his now spiritual Mannie. This kinesthetic narrative constricts in the second part to the deputy's detached account of Rider's lynching. The deputy's confined and limited point of view is metaphoric parallel to the confinement of Rider in his physicality, which he strives to transcend and finally breaks free of in his death. In the same way, during the climactic resolution of the deputy's narrative the reader breaks free of the deputy's perspective and, whole again, sees Rider with his own eyes.

The kinesthetic involvement and narrative drive of "Pantaloon in Black" contrast strongly with the other story studied, "Delta Autumn," in which an old Isaac McCaslin returns to the Big Woods for his last hunt. This story, revised extensively for inclusion in Go Down, Moses, sets lyrical descriptions of the woods and old times against the laconic and cynical dialogue of the hunters accompanying Ike. Ike's failure as moral guide for those who follow and the inadequacy of his wilderness heritage in a real world of human relations are crucial thematic elements that are clarified by the careful distancing of the narrator in revision and the expanded material of the revision.

Having established the contrasting natures of the two stories, I have sought confirmation of these mostly intuitive interpretations of style and technique in the words by which these stories are conveyed. In almost all counted elements--nouns, verbals, function words, grammatical sentence patterns-- the two stories are remarkably similar, attesting to the consistency of Faulkner's style regardless of theme. But more discriminating classifications reveal stylistic differences, confirming the felt differences in the two stories. As a story highly dependent on narrative drive and involvement, "Pantaloon in Black," while no more verbal than "Delta Autumn," has a higher proportion of sentences with a structurally simple core along with interior subordinate clauses and sentences in which the free modifiers are predicative participial and absolute phrases rather than, as in "Delta Autumn," more static noun adjuncts. These objectively defined and verifiable stylistic differences, manifested in the narrative pace that is determined by differences in sentence development, validate the intuitive judgments of literary analysis and confirm the correspondence between style and theme in these two Faulkner stories. [Order No. 74-26,108; 194 pages. DAI, 35A (Nov.-Dec. 1974), 3017.]

309 Joyce, Faulkner, O'Connor: Conceptual Approaches to Major Characters / David Hubert AIKEN, State University of New York at Stony Brook, 1975 (Jack Ludwig).

In spite of the voluminous criticism on James Joyce, William Faulkner, and Flannery O'Connor, the significance and identity of some of their major characters remain problematic. This dissertation is a series of related critical essays on three of those characters: Leopold Bloom, Jason Compson, and Asbury Porter Fox, O'Connor's satiric representation of Stephen Dedalus. The critical perspective of the whole study is Christian humanism.

The first two essays analyze two diametrically opposed modalities of existence. The critical ambiguity toward Bloom and Jason Compson can, it seems to me, be partly settled by examining these well-wrought characters from the conceptual depths of our culture. Søren Kierkegaard's Fear and Trembling and The Sickness unto Death provide illuminating analytic paradigms.

Ulysses grows out of the fundamental roots of Western culture: Greek and Hebrew. The key to Bloom's heroism is his unique personal freedom, and at its deepest level that heroism is Hebraic rather than Greek; the most revealing model for Bloom's modality of existence is not Homer's Odysseus but rather the biblical Abraham. Kierkegaard's poetic analysis of Abraham is strikingly similar to Joyce's dramatization of his petit bourgeois Dubliner. Both Kierkegaard's Abraham and Joyce's Bloom experience a particular relation with the infinite dispensing with every form of mediation, an infinite resignation regarding the finite things of this world, a reverse movement in which they again dwell in the finite, and what Kierkegaard calls the fearful teleological suspension of the ethical.

The second essay is an analysis of Jason Compson, who, like Milton's Satan, will serve no one nor anything other than himself. Although named after Euripides' debunked argonaut, Jason is ultimately modelled on the demonically defiant Macbeth; and in this last male head of the Compson household Faulkner develops the novel's most significant parallel to Shakespeare's tragedy. Jason's humor, feigned indifference, self-contradictions, and egotism are the result of what Kierkegaard calls a despairing willingness to be oneself. This peculiar despair, rather than self-love or petty materialism, is his major characteristic. In the Easter morning sermon in Section IV of The Sound and the Fury, Faulkner makes a theological comment on this revengeful creature of defiance. The imagery of the sermon, paralleling the imagery of Jason's Sunday morning chase after his ruined niece, provides the norm from which we are invited to view the final doom of the Compson family.

The analysis of O'Connor's satire of Stephen Dedalus emphasizes her literary perspective, shows misunderstanding if not weakness in her criticism of Joyce, and serves to illustrate the great differences between Joyce's young hero in Portrait and the Stephen of Ulysses. The younger Portrait Stephen is triumphant from the first. He has the requisite talent, and after his vocational epiphany his friends and superiors proclaim him an artist. The older Stephen of Ulysses, however, comes home from his self-imposed exile a lapwig. To Stephen's failure as an artist, Joyce adds a new dimension of personal failure in Stephen's loveless, hyperborean disposition. Although Asbury, the central character in "The Enduring Chill," sees himself as the triumphant Stephen Dedalus, O'Connor satirizes him as the loveless failure of Ulysses. [Order No. 75-26,149; 174 pages. DAI, 36A (Nov.-Dec. 1975), 3680-81.]

310 Neither We from Them nor They from Us: An Interpretation of Go Down, Moses / Warren AKIN, Bryn Mawr College, 1975 (Earl Ramsey).

Go Down, Moses displays some of Faulkner's most brilliant writing and most sustained exploration of concerns which are central to his fiction. This work has, however, been treated piecemeal or without full regard for the unifying structure, tones, and themes. The unity of Go Down, Moses can best be understood by examining the conversation of Part 4 of "The Bear" as a framework for the novel, the juxtaposition of the chronological and sequential time frames, and Isaac McCaslin as protagonist. In the conversation in which Ike explains his relinquishment of the land, Ike and McCaslin arrive at the major issues of the novel: relations between blacks and whites, Ike's relation to the wilderness, and the "freedom" of Ike's later life. Thus, the argument of Part 4 explains and is in turn explained by the other sections of the work.

Also, the action of the novel is constantly enhanced by a tension between the information and tone of individual stories and a chronological reconstruction of the history of the McCaslin-Beauchamp-Edmonds family. We see sequentially, before the presentation of Ike's relinquishment, events from relations between blacks and whites in "The Fire and the Hearth" and "Pantaloon in Black" which occur chronologically after the relinquishment. These events suggest that Ike has freed few of "His lowly people." And the continuing struggle between the Beauchamp and Edmonds families and Rider's plight indicate the operation of the "curse" up to the present of the novel. In the first three stories we are also led to realize the "normal human feelings" of blacks--an insight which reaches its fullest manifestation as Ike's humane consciousness struggles to author the facts and meaning of his family's history.

Implied in the first two approaches, Ike McCaslin's life determines the work's form and defines its themes. He clearly grasps the sin recorded in his family's history, a sin which epitomizes the inability of whites to realize the humanity of blacks. The motivation for Ike's response--relinquishment--to his understanding of the wrong derives from his particular relation to the wilderness. In "The Old People" and "The Bear" he is initiated into "life" through the wilderness and into a special relation to the wilderness. He learns virtues associated with the hunt and of change and death as aspects of life as he witnesses and accepts the deaths of Old Ben, Lion, and Sam and as he acknowledges the snake. Instead, however, of using the wilderness' lessons to cope with the evils of the "tamed land," Ike responds to a level of initiation which admits him to an inheritance from Sam Fathers and the old people, a changeless, timeless realm.

The mode of "ideal" perception engendered by this realm causes Ike to feel that he must either eradicate the evil in the tamed land or escape it entirely. His vision of providential history in Part 4 is an attempt to cancel the evil. When this fails, however, he believes he can live within the wilderness' "freedom." But this "freedom" insures that he will have no son, literally or symbolically, and thus no place in history. And in "Delta Autumn," the curse enters the wilderness, and Ike is stripped of his remaining illusions. The final story, "Go Down, Moses," leaves Ike's immediate life and presents, along with a continuation of the curse, some of the more hopeful elements in this history: the "comedy of life, the symbol of the fire and the hearth, and, above all, further insight into the humanity of other people--attitudes which presage more than an endurance of the wrong in later novels. [Order No. 76-6003; 277 pages. DAI, 36A (March-April 1976), 6094.]

311 William Faulkner as a Literary Naturalist / John Vernon BELLUE, Wayne State University, 1975 (Joseph Prescott).

For almost three decades the naturalistic aspects of Faulkner's works have been ignored--from about 1941 until 1950--because Faulkner himself was essentially ignored by American critics, and after 1950 because his being awarded the Nobel Prize apparently caused critics to avoid expressing opinions resembling those of the "Cult of Cruelty School," whose hostility toward Faulkner was largely responsible for his failure to achieve widespread recognition in America as a major writer during the thirties and forties. The paucity of criticism devoted to the naturalistic elements in Faulkner's works is evidence of a post-Stockholm tendency among American critics to make only favorable statements about Faulkner's fiction and to avoid expressing views resembling those of the early critics, who repeatedly deplored Faulkner's "unmitigated naturalism."

Yet Faulkner constantly tried to achieve naturalistic objectivity, frankness, and amoral detachment in his narratives. His practice of narrating obliquely either by representing the stream of consciousness of various personae or by using such choral commentators as V. K. Ratliff and Gavin Stevens to evaluate or interpret the actions of his protagonists was not a violation but a refinement of the conventions of naturalistic narration. By such means he anchored his fiction as deeply as possible in the realities of individual mental experience, maximized his authorial detachment, and avoided the direct moralizing or editorializing that is anathema to literary naturalists. Furthermore, the themes which Charles Child Walcutt, in American Literary Naturalism, A Divided Stream (Minneapolis: Univ. of Minnesota Press, 1956,) classified as typically naturalistic--survival, violence, taboo, and determinism--are among the central themes of Faulkner's fiction. Other major Faulknerian themes, such as his emphasis on human powers of endurance, are corollaries or equivalents of those listed by Walcutt. Yet despite an abundance of evidence, extracted from the texts of Faulkner's works and from interviews with the author, that Faulkner was a literary naturalist, most critics have for a quarter of a century shied away from an investigation of naturalism in his works, preoccupied themselves with secondary themes or technical aspects of his fiction, and ignored the issues which were of vital concern to his early reviewers.

Analysis of Faulkner's greatest works--The Sound and the Fury, Absalom, Absalom!, Light in August, and "The Bear" from Go Down, Moses--reveals that naturalistic themes and tendencies permeate his major fiction. And his lesser works--Sanctuary, As I Lay Dying, and The Wild Palms in particular-- are even more conspicuously naturalistic. There is no better example of the themes of survival, violence, and determinism than the portion of The Wild Palms entitled "Old Man." And there is no better instance of the theme of taboo than Faulkner's treatment of Popeye's affair with Temple Drake in Sanctuary.

A demonstration of the prominence of the naturalistic elements in Faulkner's works is necessary because of the extent to which most book-length criticism of Faulkner has become rarefied, disembodied, or tenuously related to the central implications of Faulkner's fiction. Without significant truncation or distortion of the text of Faulkner's works, a naturalistic reading of Faulkner accommodates the implications of such standard focusing devices of modern literary naturalists as "mythic" parallels, symbolism, imagery, and the conventions of Aristotelian tragedy. In the interest of critical balance and accuracy, the early view that Faulkner was a literary naturalist should be restored to respectability, although by no means should the early vilification of Faulkner for his "unmitigated naturalism" be repeated.. [Order No. 76-10,915; 242 pages. DAI, 36A (May-June 1976), 7417.]

312 Faulkner's Military World / Arthur Hadfield BLAIR, University of
   North Carolina at Chapel Hill, 1975 (C. Hugh Holman).
   William Faulkner frequently alluded to military material in his prose fiction much as he used any other body of material in the creation of his fictional world. His fiction is filled with characters who have military backgrounds, and he used actual or plausible military events to emphasize appropriate charac-

teristics of his major figures. The sources of his military material were his Southern environment with its Civil War heritage, his own limited military experience, his observations of veterans of all the wars in his lifetime, and his extensive reading of fiction and history.

His perspective on war and soldiers seems to progress from a romantic view to a realistic view and finally to an idealistic one. His point of view toward war is always pejorative, but his comments upon soldiers reflect a tension within himself that varies from a romantic approval to a realistic horror of the acts soldiers sometimes perform in war. In all instances, however, Faulkner does not separate soldiers from the rest of mankind nor war from the normal course of human events. [Order No. 76-9220; 212 pages. DAI, 36A (March-April 1976), 6679.]

313 Quentin Compson as Narrative Voice in the Works of William Faulkner / May Cameron BROWN, Georgia State University - School of Arts and Sciences, 1975 (Thomas McHaney).

This dissertation is a full-scale chronological investigation of Quentin Compson's function in the six Faulkner works in which he serves as the principal narrative voice: The Sound and the Fury, "That Evening Sun," "A Justice," "Lion," Absalom, Absalom!, and "A Bear Hunt" (Big Woods). Existing scholarship on Quentin has concerned itself with Quentin as character but fails to address itself to the specific problem of Quentin as narrative voice. There have been general studies of Faulkner's narrative technique as well as studies of Quentin as a character in specific works. There has not been, however, a comprehensive study of the thematic and structural functions of this character in all six works which he narrates.

The stories which Quentin successfully narrates (Although Faulkner identifies him as the narrator of "Lion" and the 1955 "A Bear Hunt," the voice is not Quentin's.) are pessimistic tales of a deteriorating aristocracy, unresolved racial conflict, sexual promiscuity, injustice, pain, death, and, above all, the destructiveness of time. His obsession with time determines the structure of his consciousness, which functions on several levels of complexity and accounts for the unique quality of his voice. The simplest levels of expression, those which occur in his conscious mind and consist of complete ideas presented in simple syntax, include his perceptive and rational descriptions of his environment, his conversations in the present, his direct narrative and non-judgmental reports of events from the past, and his accounts of his own mechanical actions in the present. The more complicated aspects of his voice are revealed through his stream-of-consciousness, in which his unconscious, triggered by a word or an object or a sensory impression in the present, replaces his conscious thoughts. These memories may be recollections of complete scenes from the past and are thus logically and chronologically arranged. In his most complicated level of expression, however, Quentin's mind engages in associations within associations, characterized by ambiguous pronouns, inverted word order, and fragmented sentence structure.

"Voice," taken broadly as the vision of experience which Quentin represents, is a subtle but sharp focus on specific aspects of human reality; it underscores and interprets the important factual, tonal, and symbolic elements of the stories with which it is concerned. As a character haunted by a past to which he is inadequate, dogged by a present he cannot face, and doomed to no future, Quentin, through his diction and general point of view--both what he speaks and what he thinks--dramatizes a modern yet universal sensibility. The allusions which occur in the context of his voice are invariably appropriate to him and to the subject matter which fascinates him. The syntax of his thoughts and observations and memories shows by turns the uncontrolled possession of a madman and the carefully controlled behavior of the wounded contemporary hero. Faulkner allows us to realize these qualities almost simultaneously by the subtle alternation of memory, event, reflection, speech, and outburst in Quentin's section of The Sound and the Fury; by the pathetic, image-laden memory of Nancy and Jesus and the ominous ditch which separates the white and black lives of Jefferson, Mississippi, in "That Evening Sun"; by the significant recollection, from among all the stories Sam Fathers must have told, of one entitled "A Justice," concerning miscegenation, betrayal, ambiguous parentage, and abandonment; and by the complex weaving of memory, history, hearsay, and obsession in Absalom, Absalom!. As one of the most memorable and fully-realized voices in the canon, Quentin is a phenomenon, one who remains as proof of Faulkner's achievement in narrative technique. [Order No. 76-2526; 162 pages. DAI, 36A (Jan.-Feb. 1976), 5291-92.]

314 The Genesis and Unity of Faulkner's Big Woods / David Leroy BURGGRAF, Ohio University, 1975 (Carol Clancey Harter).

William Faulkner's Big Woods, ostensibly an anthology of his hunting stories, was published in 1955, and the nine sections which comprise the book include four stories, a prologue, three interludes, and an epilogue. Although Faulkner re-uses previously written material, most sections of the book show considerable re-writing; furthermore, examination of Big Woods in relation to the source materials reveals that, as he was revising, Faulkner focused on the themes of mutability, morality, and the relationship in the ritual hunt between the pursuer and the pursued. Ultimately Faulkner produced a unique and aesthetically unified work when he created Big Woods.

Pursuit is the central metaphor of Big Woods; it focuses on and magnifies the tensions between life and death, past and present. Ritual pursuit follows a consistent pattern: in Big Woods, pursuit symbolically equals life and is therefore inescapable; everyone chooses to be a pursuer, not realizing that everything is mutable and that the pursuit itself alters the pursuer. Time changes the pursuer into the one pursued; the pursued one ideally recognizes the inevitability of mutability and mortality.

The first four sections of Big Woods can be characterized as tragic, epic, individualistic, and romantic. The prologue relates the historical and cultural evolution of Mississippi from unalien Indian to ululating city-man. The prologue also introduces the man who cannot or will not adapt to civilization's changes, the renegade, the pariah, the murderer crouched in his last thicket. Isaac McCaslin, the central character, repudiates the age in which he lives because of his hatred of basely used money, mechanistic technology, and cultural diminishment, and tries to reverse the movement of history and civilization presented in the prologue. Isaac, by the end of "The Old People," creates a strategy for life which he believes makes him as unalien as the Indian in the wilderness: memory and imagination, romantic individuality, and negation of mutability and mortality become the staples of his vision.

The second four sections of Big Woods can be characterized as comic, humanistic, anti-romantic, and communal; they present alternatives to Isaac's escapist resolution of the need to synthesize the past-present and wilderness-civilization dichotomies. Doom, although Machiavellian, possesses wit and adaptability. Ratliff, although a game-player, moves comfortably between the women of the town and the men of the hunting camp. However, Mister Ernest, the farmer-hunter, emerges in Big Woods as the man who most embodies a humanistic ethic of pursuit; his ethic is based on skill, humility, clear positioning in space and time, respect and honor for the pursued, a belief in "touch and let go, never satiety," generosity, and a comfortable insecurity about the unpredictable future.

In the epilogue, Isaac McCaslin makes his "last stand," realizing the inevitability of the disappearance of the big woods; his seventy-year love for a dead wilderness finally turns to grief. Throughout the book, Isaac acts as moral spokesman excoriating the evils of exploitation, but his own life, based on repudiation rather than engagement, precludes his being a moral agent. Isaac hates modern civilization and loves the natural wilderness life; yet Faulkner's characters in Big Woods who are closest to the "natural" life are all obsolete, dispossessed, anachronistic, destroyers, accursed, possessing "no bowels for compassion or avarice or forethought," amoral; they manifest only endurance, hatred, and will-power.

On the other hand, the civilized men, those who try to live as best they can in their own ages, are characterized by forethought, potency without need for proof, respect, wit, and understanding of mutability and mortality, and an acceptance of the need for social engagement in man's ongoing destiny. The stories in Big Woods ultimately fuse into an artful paradox: man must be engaged in the present; he must also feel compassion for his mutable heritage. [Order No. 76-8847; 168 pages. DAI, 36A (March-April 1976), 6679-80.]

315 Courtly Love in the Writings of William Faulkner / Anderson Aubrey CLARK, Vanderbilt University, 1975 (Herschel Gower).

It is a long way from the France of the twelfth century to the Mississippi of William Faulkner, but one continuity is the medieval formulation of a view of male-female relationships traditionally called "courtly love." This view reverses the Adamic roles of the sexes; the woman is placed on a pedestal, and the man becomes her adoring servant, the slave of love. Such a concept pervades the "Old South" myth.

This thesis analyzes the writing of William Faulkner from the vantage point of courtly love. Three characteristics of courtly love are helpful in interpreting Faulkner's use of this tradition: worship of woman, doctrinaire free love, and sublimation of love into chivalric activity. In the first chapter, I define "courtly love," examine its tradition in several writers between the twelfth and twentieth centuries, and consider Faulkner's attitude toward the "Old South." In the remaining four chapters, I consider five characters from Faulkner's corpus as courtly lovers. Obviously, the woman, the "pursued," the "mistress," "the goddess," is important; however, for the study, the lovers are the keys to understanding Faulkner's treatment of the courtly tradition and his attitude toward romantic love.

The four main chapters follow a continuum of the emotional stability of the lover at the end of his affair. In Chapter II, Byron Bunch (Light in August) is Faulkner's nearest approach to courtly love rewarded, pointing to the possibility of a future stable relationship in marriage. In Chapter III, Gavin Stevens (the Snopes trilogy) spends his life in search of romantic fulfillment through the ritual of courtly love, only to realize and accept in his later years that no permanent satisfaction is available through his efforts. In Chapter IV, Quentin Compson (The Sound and the Fury,) a young courtly lover, particularizes his love for the ideal in his sister, and when he can no longer sustain his illusion, he commits suicide. In Chapter V, my last two analyses consider Faulkner's two lovers Ike Snopes (The Hamlet) and Harry Wilbourne (The Wild Palms.) These two men represent distortions of traditional courtly love. Ike, mentally defective, represents the purest impression of courtly love, but the object of his adoration is a milk cow. This grotesque relationship operates on multiple levels. Harry Wilbourne is an embarrassingly weak courtly lover, who, in effect, becomes the "pursued" rather than the "pursuer." Harry's inversion of roles with his mistress is especially important because of Faulkner's conscious separation of chivalric and courtly behavior in the two short novels which compose the single-titled volume.

Faulkner uses the conventions of courtly love as a means of creating tension in his characters between the ideal of an earlier culture and the present reality. Moreover, he employs its rhetoric and ritual thematically in defense of those virtues when they are kept within the range of human limitations. Faulkner's primary technique is situational and dramatic irony by which he satirizes

those whose view of romantic love--including its attendant ritual and rhetoric--
takes them away from a realistic appraisal of human romantic emotions. With
dramatic sympathy, Faulkner creates realistic characters who by virtue of
their complexity as human beings stand larger than any code or philosophy.
[Order No. 76-94; 311 pages. DAI, 36A (Jan.-Feb. 1976), 4482-83.]

316 William Faulkner's Romantic Heritage: Beyond America / Charles
Wilbur DEAN, University of Massachusetts, 1975 (Arthur F. Kinney).

Critics have recurrently noted parallels between William Faulkner's
mythic saga of Yoknapatawpha County and the Romantic movement in nineteenth-
century Europe and America. But with the exceptions of John Keats, Nathaniel
Hawthorne, and Sir Walter Scott, little extended attention has been given to
Faulkner's Romantic affinities. "William Faulkner's Romantic Heritage: Beyond America" attempts to develop, more fully than has previous criticism, a
view of Faulkner's fundamentally Romantic sensibility.

Faulkner's relation to European Romanticism demonstrates more consistently attitudinal confluences than verbal influences. Faulkner, unlike Eliot,
utilized a process of "creative borrowing" rarely. But his ideological fraterni-
zation with the major English Romantic poets--particularly those of the second
generation--is pervasive.

My methodology in this essay is fairly straightforward. The introduction offers a brief survey of Faulkner's relationship with some modern writers
who are recurrently considered major "influences" upon his art--Mann, Proust,
Joyce, Conrad, and Henry James--and a rejection of these great modern writers
as formulators of Faulkner's basically Romantic Weltanschauung.

Chapter Two develops the theory of Romanticism, largely derived from
Morse Peckham, by which I classify Faulkner as a Romantic sensibility in the
remaining chapters of this essay. My major departure from Peckham consists
in a rejection of his view of imperfection as a positive value in Romantic art.

Chapter Three examines parallels between Faulkner and certain European Romantics, particularly Honoré de Balzac. The lack of marked connections with Continental writers outside of France is explained by Faulkner's
lack of foreign languages other than French.

The fourth chapter discusses Faulkner's affinities with the first generation Romantic poets in England, particularly Wordsworth and Coleridge. These
poets are treated collectively because they provide philosophical and ideological
insights into Faulkner's works, but are rarely quoted or invoked specifically.
But I have also attempted to demonstrate that Faulkner quotes Wordsworth's
"Intimations Ode" more often than any other single Romantic work except Keats's
"Ode on a Grecian Urn," and shares with him a similar view of nature.

Chapters Five and Six offer closer, empirical demonstrations of connections between Faulkner and--respectively--Byron and Keats. The burden
of each of these chapters is a comparison of specific works; Cain with Light in
August, and Endymion with The Sound and the Fury. Comparison between Absalom, Absalom! and works by the other Romantic writers are recurrent, for
I contend that Malcolm Cowley was correct when, in 1936, he asserted that--
of all Faulkner's works to that point--Absalom was "the most romantic." This
assertion is not compromised by any of William Faulkner's later works.

Because English Romanticism is generally viewed as a poetic movement,
I have limited my consideration to major poets, ignoring--for the most part--
such writers of fiction as Jane Austen, Scott, and the Bronte sisters. In a
brief Appendix, however, I have responded to Michael Millgate's provocative
discussion of Jane Eyre as an influence upon Faulkner's Absalom, Absalom!.
[Order No. 75-16,550; 335 pages. DAI, 36A (July-Aug. 1975), 885-86.]

317 Stream-of-Consciousness Narration in Faulkner: A Redefinition / Norma
LaRene DESPAIN, University of Connecticut, 1975 (Charles A. McLaughlin).

This thesis attempts to define stream-of-consciousness narration as a set of rhetorical devices employed in rendering the flow of consciousness of a first-person narrator and to explore the power of that definition to distinguish the variety and subtlety of Faulkner's narrative techniques in The Sound and the Fury and As I Lay Dying. These are the only works found to depend heavily on stream of consciousness in Faulkner and the dissertation explores the reason for his abandonment of the device in later works. The qualities Joseph Warren Beach identifies as being responsible for the "disappearance of the author" are shown to find final development in stream of consciousness, that type of narration in which the last vestiges of the author's narrating voice--formal exposition, explicit transitions, and other rhetorical guides--have disappeared. Adapting Beach's discussion to first-person narration shows that the narrating voice disappears there also when narrating time draws close enough to experiencing time that the narration is indeed the act of experiencing--a tendency that eventuates in the internal monologue. Hence, as Faulkner uses it, stream of consciousness is a first-person mode in which the narrating I is personified by a minimal or non-existent time lag between narrating and experience, in which there is little explicit context, and in which mental processes are portrayed by associational juxtaposition.

Applied to The Sound and the Fury this formula demonstrates that the three monologues constitute a continuum stretching from Jason's relatively coherent "monologue of justification," through Quentin's more clearly stream-of-consciousness section, which, though it retains a surprising amount of traditional narration, relies heavily on interweaving of fragmentary scenes, to Benjy's where the narrating and experiencing I's have merged completely due to Benjy's complete lack of time sense.

Analysis of As I Lay Dying identifies three types of narration: traditional narrative, stream of consciousness (either soliloquy or internal monologue depending on relative coherence,) and a third rhetorical mode peculiar to Darl. In all these cases the nature of the narrative becomes a characterizing device. Thus, the narrators (e.g., MacGowan, Armstid, Samson) tend to be outsiders who see only what happens, while the soliloquists (Anse, Cora, Whitfield) respond to happenings and words, but turn everything inward, usually seeking moral justification for themselves. The monologuists (Addie, Jewel, Dewey Dell) want to get below surface words and actions, but seem confined by their own perceptions. Darl has sections that correspond to all these types, for he can see both action and meaning, but for him Faulkner has developed a peculiar non-naturalistic, formally rhetorical voice which places his sections outside the stream-of-consciousness mode. Faulkner uses this voice to indicate Darl's search for meaning beyond words and beyond the prison of his own perceptions.

The final chapter shows that this voice, developed in a stream-of-consciousness mode for Darl, is used in a third-person context in subsequent books to portray consciousness. In Light in August, Absalom, Absalom!, and "The Bear," three works often called stream of consciousness, use of this Darl voice shows how each is outside that mode, yet retains close links with it. [Order No. 76-14,288; 159 pages. DAI, 37A (July-Aug. 1976), 306-07.]

318 The Relationship of Storyteller to Community in the Tales of the Southwest Humorists, Mark Twain, and William Faulkner / Sonia Grace GERNES, University of Washington, 1975 (Martha Banta).

Counter to studies of various literatures which have remarked upon the theme of the artist alienated from community, this thesis examines a current in American literature, particularly that which in some way stays close to the folk culture and the storytelling traditions of the old Southwest frontier, in which the artist, as exemplified by the storyteller-character, uses his art and position as artist as a means of coming into relation with a human community.

He may use his artistic talent to gain entry into the already existing community, to form a new community, to influence, alter, or improve it, to solidify his position in it, to distinguish the qualities of various communities, and sometimes to judge them.

Chapter I examines briefly the nature of the frontier which brought forth a humor so full of violence and physical brutality that critics have called it a "laughter of despair." Although it is impossible at this point in time to separate the intermingled oral and written tale traditions, it would seem that for the frontiersman, the swapping of oral tales was a communal means of asserting his dominance over the environment by exaggerating his exploits, and of assuaging the brutality of existence by reducing it to laughable proportions. When outsiders to the frontier community let the frontiersman show how uncouth he was, the storyteller defended his community by creating a fantastic and brutish self-caricature with which to gull the self-righteous intruder.

Chapter II discusses the role of the storyteller in the tales of the Southwest Humorists (circa 1830-1860), a group of amateur writers who made literature of the frontier tale. George Washington Harris, Thomas Bangs Thorpe, and others frequently used a vernacular narrator surrounded by a frame-tale. This device displayed not only the tale but the interaction of the storyteller with his audience. In telling his tale, which often involved a "catch" or verbal contest, the vernacular raconteur could be observed using his skills to form a community, to prove his right to belong to or retain a position in an already existing community, to protect it by keeping out undesirables, or to aid, cheer, or build closer bonds.

Mark Twain began his career thoroughly embued with the Southwest Humor tradition--a tradition he took to its greatest heights in his "Celebrated Jumping Frog of Calaveras County." His subsequent career, however, took him away from the frontier, and, to a large extent, from the Southwest Humor tradition. His major works form a rough chronological pattern backwards in time (from the present to the Middle Ages); corollary to that backward gaze is an increasing pessimism about the possibility of viable human community. Chapter III examines Twain's storyteller figures up through Huckleberry Finn and traces the shifting attitudes toward community that they express.

William Faulkner's characters exist in a world of motion and chaos, but a world in which some combination of "human verities allows man to endure and occasionally to prevail." His storyteller figures, like his favorite V. K. Ratliff, catch occasional glimpses of this balance between the need to be for oneself and the need to join communally in being for others. Throughout most of the Snopes trilogy, which forms the basis of Chapter IV, Ratliff functions as the typical Southwest raconteur with all the tricks of deadpan, conning, and "catching." Like his Southwest predecessors, he uses tales to maintain his place in the community and to sustain, alter, or defend it. He also uses his art to probe the mystery of man's endurance and shares the results, however partial and infrequent, with the community he would have prevail. [Order No. 75-28,353; 239 pages. DAI, 36A (Nov.-Dec. 1975), 3685-86.]

319 Faulkner's Narrative Voices in The Sound and the Fury / Linda Gerson
    GILL, University of California at San Diego, 1975 (John Stewart and Roy Harvey Pearce).

The Sound and the Fury, consisting of the original four sections (published in 1929) and of the "Appendix" (published in 1945,) is a study in both point of view and narrative technique. The five sections are each related by a different narrator; uniting the five perspectives, however, is the view of one implied author whose norms and values pervade the entire work. Each narrator creates his own narratee to whom he addresses himself, while the implied author creates an implied reader who may judge, laugh at, or endorse the diverse perspectives of the narrators. The various narrative techniques determine the way each actual reader will relate to the implied reader who is created by the text itself.

In the Benjy section, Faulkner has created a narrator who cannot speak. By so doing he calls the attention of the reader to the narrative function itself. Benjy's section is not "stream of consciousness," an untransmitted flow of the narrator's consciousness, but a transcription by a writer. Quentin's section is presented partially in the stream-of-consciousness technique. It consists of an asyntactical presentation of his thought or pre-thought processes presented in contrast with an objective and syntactically normal description of his external actions. This dichotomy establishes the split in Quentin's personality in which his inner life has become more real than his outer. Jason's section is a soliloquy presented to an audience, a narratee-listener, whom Jason attempts to influence. Like the Quentin section, however, it is based on a dichotomy. The remarks not in quotation marks are directed only to Jason's narratee, not to other characters. A study of Jason's quoted remarks and those not in quotation marks reveals that Jason presents himself to his narratee-listener as brave and bold while his actions and quoted remarks show him to be a coward and a bully.

The fourth section of The Sound and the Fury is, in contrast to the three previous sections, presented by an omniscient narrator who views the Compsons sub specie aeternitatis and relates their everyday world to that of the cosmos. While it does not present positive affirmation, the section does give the reader a sense of a broader perspective in which the world of the Compsons is but a part of a larger whole. It is not Dilsey who gives us this view, however, but the omniscient narrator, whose perspective is above the merely human ones of the first three sections or of any of the characters in the book.

The "Appendix," published sixteen years after the original four sections, presents a fifth perspective on the Compsons. The narrator of the "Appendix" is, moreover, no more William Faulkner than the other narrators; Faulkner called him a "Garter King-at-Arms." He is a town-historian telling the story of the Compsons from the perspective of one who thinks he is being objective but has his own partial and slanted view of the Compsons.

Faulkner experimented both with several points of view and with several techniques in The Sound and the Fury, each of which is sufficient to tell a part of the Compson's story, each of which is insufficient to tell the entire story. Like the perspectives of the various narrators, the various narrative techniques are not to be weighed as inferior or superior to each other. Just as no one perspective can give the whole truth, no one narrative technique is per se more effective than any other for fiction. [Order No. 75-29,437; 254 pages. DAI, 36A (Jan.-Feb. 1976), 4489.]

320 A Study of the Early Versions of Faulkner's The Town and The Mansion / Nancy Eileen GREGORY, University of South Carolina, 1975 (James B. Meriwether).

This study is largely based on an examination of typescript material for The Town and The Mansion in the Faulkner Collection at the University of Virginia. Existing are a nearly complete typescript of The Town, located among recto pages of an incomplete typescript (154 pages) of The Town and verso pages of an early typescript draft of The Mansion, and that early draft of The Mansion itself. This dissertation draws upon evidence from these early typescript versions of the two novels, from additional fragments of Town and Mansion material on versos of two typescripts, and from early short stories incorporated into the novels, to explore the intent of the author as revealed in revision and alteration of material.

Also existing among versos of the incomplete (154 pages) Town manuscript and of the early Mansion typescript are fragments and complete drafts of a number of essays, speeches, published and unpublished letters, and of two short fictional works. The appendices of this dissertation analyze these two typescripts, describe the various material to be found among pages of each, and publish significant data from both rectos and versos of the typescripts. The dissertation is supplemented by my article "Faulkner's Typescripts of The Town," published in the Mississippi Quarterly in the issue for Summer 1973. [Order No. 75-28,985; 323 pages. DAI, 36A (Nov.-Dec. 1975), 3686-87.]

321 The Self as History: Studies in Adams, Faulkner, Ellison, Belyj, Pasternak / Anne Miller HEDIN, University of Virginia, 1975 (David Levin).

These five American and Russian modernist novelists and autobiographers are grouped because of their pursuit of a common literary aim: the need to reconceive the representation of character in accord with a critique of Romantic individualism. The following works are analyzed in this light: The Education of Henry Adams, William Faulkner's Absalom, Absalom!, Ralph Ellison's Invisible Man, Andrej Belyj's Petersburg, and Boris Pasternak's Doktor Zivago. The thesis proposes that each author makes communal history the central constituent of personal identity (and thus of character); the structure of experience in these works is historical, not personal, given, not improvised. However, the history which character internalizes contains serious breaks or fault-lines which are faithfully reproduced in the fragmented identities of the protagonists. The most common device for representing character in this dilemma is a radical reworking of the Romantic convention of the doppelganger. The chapters devoted to separate works concentrate on the use of the device of doubling, showing how, by borrowing from Romanticism, it retorts upon its literary source and criticizes the obsession with individual uniqueness, while also tracing fragmented modern identity to a historical crisis which broke the organic relationship of self and contemporary society which character represented in the nineteenth-century realistic novel. Adams, Faulkner, and Ellison take the Civil War as the breaking point in their country's history; for them the "self-made man" (or their protagonist's attempt to become one such) marks the crucial intersection between historical process and personal experience because he provides a scale model for the American experiment in democracy and rational social ordering. For Belyj and Pasternak respectively, the revolutions of 1905 and 1917 (also civil wars) appear as partial analogues for Peter the Great's Westernizing revolution and for Christ's incarnation, betrayal, and passion. Belyj and Pasternak juxtapose the charismatic figures of the social revolutionary and the "holy fool" (jurodivyj) of the Russian Orthodox kenotic tradition. The juxtaposition explores the conflict between worldly and other-worldly striving, between individualistic and archetypal conceptions of selfhood. Introductory and concluding chapters attempt briefly to place these five writers within their respective literary traditions and to draw some tentative connections between American and Russian novelists' concern with giving form to history. [Order No. 76-14; 272 pages. DAI, 36A (March-April 1976), 6074.]

322 Faulkner's Study of Youth / Connie Ranck KONDRAVY, Lehigh University, 1975 (James R. Frakes).

This study of As I Lay Dying, The Unvanquished, Go Down, Moses, Intruder in the Dust, and The Reivers proposes that Faulkner believed that the movement from innocence to experience--the thematic center of his canon--could be delineated most clearly through the use of a child/ adolescent as protagonist. In each of these novels (and in several short stories as well) Faulkner suggests that the youth's transition from boyhood to manhood captures the essence of mental, physical, and emotional innocence. Hence, each protagonist--Vardaman Bundren (As I Lay Dying,) Bayard Sartoris (The Unvanquished,) Ike McCaslin (Go Down, Moses,) Chick Mallison (Intruder in the Dust,) and Lucius Priest (The Reivers)-- undergoes an initiation experience, replete with qualified testers, an initiation testing ground, and ritual in varying degrees. Usually Faulkner depicts this "coming of age" through a motif analogous to the journey of life; therefore, the initiation figure moves through stages of growing awareness until he reaches a threshold experience. Faulkner suggests that if the youth meets this crisis with intellectual flexibility, he achieves moral maturity and accepts adult responsibility--Bayard, Chick, and Lucius represent this category; if the initiation figure fails because he cannot reconcile life's dualities to his code for living, he does not achieve his place in society--Ike McCaslin is one such doomed individual (although too young to comprehend the significance of his initiation experience, Vardaman exhibits his potentiality for moral maturity.)

Hence, Faulkner has made the innocent child the archetypal symbol of man: the youth's journey to understanding suggests the incalculable exposures to unfamiliar situations that each adult encounters throughout his life. Thus, the child's initiation becomes applicable to all human experience. Faulkner's continuing interest in the "coming-of-age" process over a period of thirty-two years indicates the complexity he found in this subject. Moreover, his overwhelming absorption with the young protagonist, especially the youth who successfully adjust to life's dichotomies demonstrates in the earlier works as well as the later ones an optimism many critics have failed to recognize. [Order No. 76-5092; 240 pages. DAI, 36A (March-April 1976), 6100-01.]

323 Faulkner and American Humor: Traditions and Innovations / Matthew Wood LITTLE, University of Chicago, 1975 (Hamlin Hill) no DAI entry.

324 Humorous Characterization and the Tradition of the Jonsonian Comedy of Manners in William Faulkner's Early Fiction: New Orleans Sketches, Soldiers' Pay, and Mosquitoes / James Barlow LLOYD, University of Mississippi, 1975 (John Pilkington).

By looking at the existing body of criticism of William Faulkner's individual novels, one might logically conclude that the very early works-- New Orleans Sketches, Soldiers' Pay, and Mosquitoes--are somehow not so much worth being considered, somehow not so important, as the later ones. And, this is true in the sense that they are not great literature and do not seem to bear so directly on what Faulkner called "the problems of the human heart in conflict with itself." Yet to put forth such a bland generalization invites refutation. For works like Soldiers' Pay and Mosquitoes, which are obviously not so important to an overview of American literature as The Sound and the Fury or Absalom, Absalom!, are at least important to an understanding of Faulkner's artistic methods as the later works, perhaps more so precisely because they are not so well done. They are, to borrow Faulkner's metaphor, the "badly sawn planks" which the apprentice carpenter produces before he becomes a master. Yet, since they are not so well put together, one can better see the individual parts, how they function, and how they fit together than one can in a well-made work which tends to be of a piece.

When one turns to the early work with an eye to discovering formal patterns and methods of characterization, and if one happens to be familiar with Elizabethan drama, one might be struck--without wishing, particularly, to pursue any direct line of influence--by the similarity between some of Faulkner's characters and Ben Jonson's humorous characters and the Overburian types. And, upon consideration, one might further be struck, even considering the difference in genre, by the structural similarities between the works of Faulkner and Jonson, particularly in a novel like Mosquitoes in which Faulkner, like Jonson, depicts the manners and and morals of a particular sophisticated, and insular segment of the urban population.

A young artist, in short, must practice, must experiment with the methods which he will later perfect; hence the best place to examine those methods is in the early work where his hand is most visible. After Mosquitoes, Faulkner's novels, of course, are vastly different, since with Sartoris he began working what he called his own "little postage stamp of soil," Yoknapatawpha, a county peopled by the yeoman farmers, aristocrats, and Snopeses who made him famous. But, an artist does not abandon his apprentice work easily, and by the time he had finished Mosquitoes, Faulkner had achieved some degree of competence as a creator of comedies of manners after the style of Jonson. Thus, though New Orleans Sketches, Soldiers' Pay, and Mosquitoes may not be his best work, their relative importance to the student of Faulkner has been underrated, since in them one can clearly see Faulkner the artist experimenting with Jonsonian forms and methods of characterization which continue to appear in the later work. [Order No. 76-455; 187 pages. DAI, 36A (Jan.-Feb. 1976), 4493.]

325 Land-Character Relationships in Selected Works of Faulkner's Yoknapatawpha Sage / Helen H. MALLONEE, University of South Florida, 1975 (Jack B. Moore).

Analyzing the interplay between the land and the characters in major works of Faulkner's Yoknapatawpha saga, this dissertation explores the role of the land as basic both to those who abuse the land and suffer the tragic consequences of their actions, and to those who cherish the land, work it, and receive nourishment from it, both physically and psychologically.

The Sartoris, Compson, and Sutpen families are examined as family dynasties that fall, owing to basic human defects. Opposed to these are Faulkner's earth-mother figures, such as Caddy Compson, Lena Grove, Eula Varner Snopes, Linda Snopes, as well as many Negroes, such as Lucas Beauchamp, who offer their love or patient endurance in contrast to the false pride of the aristocrats. Of particular importance in Faulkner's land-character relationships are the Snopeses, who overrun Yoknapatawpha by their sheer multiplicity and cunning survival drives. Flem Snopes, leader of the tribe, is portrayed by Faulkner as the rodent-like animal who takes over the land but does not cherish it. Symbolically, however, Flem does provide for a strengthening of the land, for as scavenger, he demands that those who overpower him develop a strength greater than his own.

The study concludes that Faulkner presents the treatment of the land as a major index to character analysis and family stability. His Yoknapatawpha saga demonstrates his realization that the land is timeless, that it will endure, and that Man himself, to be whole, must accept the land as vital to a full social, psychological, and humanistic relationship with life. [Order No. 75-17,833; 155 pages. DAI, 36A (July-Aug. 1975), 890.]

326 A Study of William Faulkner's Informal Dialect Theory and His Use of Dialect Markers in Eight Novels / John Wilson MURPHREE, Jr., Ball State University, 1975 (Charles L. Houck).

The purpose of this study was two-fold: (1) to establish William Faulkner's informal theory by comparing interview statements which he made on the subject of dialect with Sumner Ives' formal theory and (2) to uncover broad patterns in Faulkner's use of dialect markers from the beginning to the end of his literary career by making a rigorous statistical analysis of his use of dialect markers in eight Yoknapatawpha County novels written between the beginning and the end of his career.

Chapter I is an introduction to the study. Chapter II contains a review of literature in the field of dialect study in recent years and examines the main relationships between those studies and this one. Chapter III discusses the basic principles of Sumner Ives' formal dialect theory, particularly as they may be applied to William Faulkner's use of dialect. Chapter IV compares Faulkner's informal dialect theory, as it was expressed in various interview statements which he made on the subject of dialect, with Ives' formal theory. Chapter V describes the data gathering procedures for the statistical analysis of Faulkner's use of dialect markers, and Chapter VI gives the results of the analysis. Chapter VII presents the conclusions for the entire study.

The comparison of William Faulkner's informal dialect theory and Sumner Ives' formal one reveals that they were, in their broad outlines, essentially the same.

For the purpose of analyzing Faulkner's use of dialect markers, his works were divided into three periods--early, middle, and late--with the following novels selected for analysis in these periods: early, Sartoris (1929) and The Sound and the Fury (1929); middle, Light in August (1932), The Unvanquished (1938), and The Hamlet (1940); and late, Intruder in the Dust (1948), The Town (1957), and The Reivers (1962). In all 3,714 dialogue passages were analyzed in the eight novels; these dialogue passages contained 83,619 words.

Also for the purposes of analysis, a dialect marker was defined as either a phonological spelling or a nonstandard grammatical construction. The statistical analysis of Faulkner's use of dialect markers was an analysis of variance involving seven independent variables and six dependent variables. The independent variables were the numerical order of the literary period in which they were grouped with other novels in the study and the age, sex, class, race, and location of the characters who spoke the dialogue analyzed. The dependent variables were the percentages of words used as dialect markers per utterance under the categories "total," "verbs or auxiliaries," "nouns," "adjectives or adverbs," "pronouns or demonstratives," and "others."

The analysis of Faulkner's use of dialect markers revealed that he made significant change in that use from the beginning to the middle, but not from the middle to the end of his career. It showed that the greatest part of that change was a decrease in marker use by lower class characters rather than middle or upper class characters and by black characters rather than white characters. It also showed significance change on a sex basis with a larger decrease for male than female characters and a significant difference on an age basis with children and old adults using higher percentages of their words as dialect markers than young or middle aged adults. On a parts of speech basis, the analysis indicated that Faulkner's most frequently used and most consistently used dialect marker was the verb. [Order No. 75-21,463; 234 pages. DAI, 36A (Sept.-Oct. 1975). 2177-78.]

327 Prisons and Prisoners in the Works of William Faulkner / Eric Luther NEWHALL, University of California at Los Angeles, 1975 (Philip Durham).

This study attempts to explain the surprisingly frequent occurrence of prisons, jails, and prisoners in the works of William Faulkner. Prisons, jails, and prisoners play a significant role in Sanctuary (1931), Light in August (1932), The Wild Palms (1939), The Hamlet (1940), Go Down, Moses (1942), Intruder in the Dust (1948), Knight's Gambit (1949), Requiem for a Nun (1951), A Fable (1954), The Mansion (1959), and The Reivers (1962), or in other words, in more than half of Faulkner's novels and in a significant number of his short stories. The actual convicts treated in these novels were certainly not the only sort of prisoners in whom Faulkner was interested. His works abound with characters who, although they never see the inside of a jail cell, can be said to be prisoners in that they are trapped, confined, repressed, compelled, or limited by various personal (conscience, psychological obsessions,) sociological (racial prejudice, lack of money, societal mores,) and metaphysical (time, necessity or fate, the pull of the earth) forces which restrict their freedom. Every character in the Faulkner canon fits into at least one of these three categories.

Faulkner uses the prison as both a thematic and a structural device. The relevance and applicability of the prison to his thematic concerns is not difficult to see. In very general terms, he uses prisons to symbolize any and all forces in the modern world which are antagonistic to human freedom and fulfillment. The prison becomes an objective correlative used to evoke all of the sterile, repressive, and aggressive forces represented in Faulkner's novels by Flem Snopes, Jason Compson, Popeye, spokesmen for conventional morality, and modern industrialism in general. Faulkner saw that the prison and all it connoted could serve him well in developing such themes as the isolation and alienation of modern man; the failure of human beings to communicate meaningfully with each other; the repression of individuals by powerful authorities and by a puritanical society; man's ability to endure hardship and deprivation; guilt, punishment, and expiation of sin; the relationship between legal and moral justice; the sterility (lack of regenerative power) of the modern world; and finally, the meaninglessness (the sound and the fury) of modern life.

As a structural device the prison fits nicely into the dialectical pattern Faulkner most frequently employs. Nature and freedom is his "thesis"; civilization, modernism, and the absence of freedom (symbolized in the prison) form the "antithesis." The synthesis is what Faulkner's characters attempt to work out for themselves. Increasingly cut off from nature, and trapped in a hostile modern world which seems to leave no room for love and humanistic values, they try to find peace in the middle ground between the anarchy of nature (Faulkner was not a primitivist) and the regimentation and enforced conformity of civilization. As a structural device the prison is often used contrapuntally, as in The Wild Palms, in which the plight of an actual convict is used to comment by juxtaposition upon the plight of Charlotte Rittenmeyer and Harry Wilbourne. Faulkner frequently juxtaposes separate and discrete blocks of material in order to achieve the sort of internal thematic reverberation which is one of his trademarks. Frequently this process involves placing a chapter or episode dealing with a jailed prisoner side by side with a chapter or episode which treats one of the sorts of "prisoners" mentioned earlier.

After a biographical section in which there is an attempt to document Faulkner's concern for individual freedom, I discuss the sources of his interest in and knowledge of prisons, and briefly suggest several relevant literary influences (I find Freud's influence on Faulkner to be particularly significant,) I move to a discussion of The Wild Palms, The Sound and the Fury, Sanctuary, The Reivers, The Mansion, Intruder in the Dust, Requiem for a Nun, and A Fable, eight novels in which prisons and prisoners play an important structural and thematic role. The result, I think, is more than simply a narrow imagistic study. Faulkner's concern with human freedom was central to both his life and his work. A study of the prisons and prisoners in his novels leads to a greater understanding of his view of man, his view of civilization and its effect on humanity, and his conception of human possibility and limitation. [Order No. 76-3049; 297 pages. DAI, 36A (Jan.-Feb. 1976), 5300.]

328 A Question of Responsibility: The Villain in the Yoknapatawpha Fiction of William Faulkner / Linda Scott RANDOLPH, University of Mississippi, 1975 (John Pilkington).

Although the term villain conjures up a world of easily recognized absolutes of right and wrong conduct, nothing could be more alien to the fictional universe of William Faulkner, who presents the inextricable tangle of good and evil of a world in continuous flux. In spite of its limitations, the term villain can serve as a point of departure in investigating and illuminating the nature and the source of evil as Faulkner sees it.

In this study the villains are identified by the traits they hold in common. Villainy is identified as a state of consciousness derived from the subject-object metaphysical system characteristic of Western rationalism. This orientation toward life leads to "bad faith," an existential concept which involves the failure of a two-fold responsibility involved in authentic living. Instead of constantly reevaluating his ever-changing experience, the villain substitutes an intellectually conceived "design" which relieves him of the necessity of choice and anguish of freedom. He exhibits the inflexibility of a closed consciousness which precludes self-recognition. At the same time, he perverts the responsibility that he should exercise toward mankind; he exploits Man and Nature. Characterized chiefly by his role as exploiter, he displays a lack of capacity for love. The inversion of love, Pride or self-love, motivates him to inflict harm willfully upon others or to perpetuate a pattern of evil. Moreover, he serves as a reflection which constitutes an indictment of society. Although the villain is both victim and creator of a pattern of evil, his main role is that of victimizer rather than victim.

Faulkner's most accomplished villains are Flem Snopes, Jason Compson, Thomas Sutpen, Anse Bundren, Popeye, and Percy Grimm. Lesser villains include Narcissa Benbow, Caroline Compson, old Carothers McCaslin, Doc Hines, Simon McEachern, Eustace Graham, Gowan Stevens, and a trio of Snopeses--Clarence, Lump, and I.O.

Underlying and fostering the bad faith of the Faulkner villain is an extreme and destructive rationalism characteristic of modern Western man. An outlook on life oriented by rationalism leads to both the inflexibility and exploitation which constitute the bad faith of the Faulkner villain. Since the tradition of rationalism identifies truth with an intellectual construct, it encourages the adoption of a design or pattern as a guide for living rather than emphasizing a constant reevaluation of ever-changing experience. The villain does not see that his design simplifies and therefore falsifies the dense complexity of existence. He underestimates the irrational--a term which describes the greater part of life. The dualistic subject-object metaphysical system which is an integral part of the rational tradition promotes the villain's chief role of exploiter by emphasizing a dichotomy instead of a unity between Man and Nature. The villain views all of Not-me--that is, Man and Nature--as objects to be controlled. He cannot see that he is intimately related to that which he manipulates and transforms. In the case of the villain the detachment has become so great that he has lost touch with humanity. The central and most fundamental characteristic of the Faulkner villain is the abstractedness that results from a rational orientation toward existence; his life is so dominated by intellectual constructs that he has almost lost touch with experiential reality. The villain is the reductio ad absurdum of rationalism.

Although the villain has been identified chiefly through his failure of responsibility, his "bad faith," Faulkner balances the concept of free will by making a strong case for determinism. As always, the reader must return to the basic issue of free will versus determinism, on which turns the question of personal responsibility. To what extent have forces unrecognized by the villain formed the character out of which decisions which perpetuate evil are made? Is the villain responsible for his attitude or state of consciousness out of which his actions arise? Can the villain be held responsible for the exercise of bad faith? Herein lies the age-old question of personal responsibility: Is man to be regarded as a sinner who perpetuates evil through choice, or is he merely an imperfect creature whose flaws result from the finite nature of man? Implying that there is some truth to be found in both poles at once, Faulkner presents the issue as a tension between the two opposed concepts, alternately tipping the balance between either pole.

When the reader considers the totality of Faulkner's work, he can conclude, in spite of Faulkner's public utterances to the contrary, that the author shifts the balance in favor of determinism. This conclusion can be supported by the fact that the characters Faulkner admired most, his "primitives," derive a moral orientation toward life from their environment, from their relation to nature. Moreover, they accept life as it is rather than try to reform it or to construe meaning out of life's richness. Faulkner's belief in man's finitude and his compassion for mankind also lend support to the contention that Faulkner tips the balance in favor of determinism. The tension between the two forces, however, cannot be finally resolved, for Faulkner sees paradox and ambiguity as the essence of life. [Order No. 76-11,737; 227 pages. DAI, 36A (May-June 1976), 7425-26.]

329 The Uses of the Past in the Novels of William Faulkner / Carl Edmund ROLLYSON, Jr., University of Toronto (Canada), 1975 (Michael H. Millgate).

This dissertation deals with the past in Faulkner's novels as it is perceived and used by the author and his characters. Those novels which are specifically set in the past and which project a general idea of history are the focus of discussion. In the Introduction Faulkner's nonfiction statements on his general conception of time and his sense of the past are treated in order to elaborate the principles on which his works are grounded. A brief summation of the critical work on Faulkner to which this dissertation is indebted and of the criteria used in the selection of the novels studied is provided as a way of stating an overall view of his uses of the past.

Chapter One centers on young Bayard Sartoris in Flags in the Dust, the first Yoknapatawpha novel in which Faulkner discovers but does not entirely define a clear and consistent attitude toward the past, and on Bayard Sartoris (young Bayard's grandfather) in The Unvanquished in which Faulkner explicitly demonstrates but does not convincingly dramatize the evolution of his main character's conception of the past. Chapters Two and Three attempt a thorough exploration of the structure of Absalom,

Absalom!, a major novel in which the characters' reinterpretations of the past result in a rich and complex view of history. Particular attention is paid to the creation of history as the product of human imagination, with the various accounts of the Sutpen story--and more specifically Quentin's and Shreve's discovery that Charles Bon is Sutpen's son and has Negro blood--compared and contrasted with the statements of historians on the study and the making of history. In Chapters Four and Five a similar approach is taken toward the structure of Go Down, Moses, in which Ike's discovery in the commissary books that his grandfather old Carothers had conceived a child upon his own Negro daughter is thoroughly examined and placed within the context of what historians have said about the interpretation of historical documents and about the more general question of the reconstruction and recreation of the past.

Chapter Six compares and contrasts The Unvanquished, Absalom, Absalom!, and Go Down, Moses with Henry Esmond, Redgauntlet, and Nostromo so that Faulkner's uses of the past may perhaps be understood as both extensions of and experimental departures from the view of history provided by the distinguished historical fiction of his predecessors. Chapter Seven and the Conclusion seek to build upon the argument of previous chapters by setting out and interpreting Faulkner's specific nonfiction statements on the relationship between historical fact and historical fiction in his work, and by discussing examples from The Sound and the Fury, the Compson Appendix, and Requiem for a Nun in which his attitude toward the past and his more general idea of history seem to be most clearly exemplified. A final assessment of the novels and their relation to the work of historians and historical novelists is meant to highlight both the traditional and the innovative aspects of his uses of the past. [DAI, 37A (March-April 1977), 6488.]

330 Classical Myth in the Novels of William Faulkner / Robert H. SOLOMON, Pennsylvania State University, 1975 (Philip Young).

Beginning with the poem, "L'Apres-Midi d'un Faune" in 1919, Faulkner assembled a limited and consistent body of classical myth-figures, which appear in his poems and many of his novels. This study examines the sources and interpretations for the most significant of these myth-figures: the male figures of violence and sexual license, including fauns, satyrs, Pan, Poseidon; and the female figures of love and fertility, Aphrodite, Io, and Persephone. Bulfinch and Robert Graves are cited as apparent sources for several allusions; and Faulkner is revealed as heavily indebted to contemporary anthropological interpretations of myth as disguised fertility ritual.

The poems are examined for the earliest use of the myth-figures, and the ideas of the anthropologically-oriented critics. The pivotal moment in Faulkner's steadily growing understanding of myth is seen as the summer of 1919, before he could have read T. S. Eliot or Mrs. Sherwood Anderson's copy of The Golden Bough. The effect of Faulkner's education in classical myth, literature, and culture is evident in the poems. The mature art is examined to see how the myths were interpreted and utilized in Faulkner's prose. The longest borrowing is the Phaethon-Apollo myth, which Faulkner took from Bulfinch and used as the model for the flight of the Bundrens in As I Lay Dying. Identifying the parallels changes the emphasis of the novel, unifies it better than has been possible before now, and places it clearly in the development of Faulkner's art from 1919 to 1962.

In The Hamlet, Ike Snopes' romance of Houston's cow is told as the rape of Io, in the form of a cow, by Zeus. The "Spotted Horses" section is told as the parodic circus of centaurs, half-men and half-horses.

Eulah is revealed as a cow-honey goddess, sharing the qualities of Aphrodite Erycina. The Snopeses are seen as a collective figure of Hermes. The novel is about the sexual wasteland of post-reconstruction Mississippi, where the Hermetic Snopeses destroy normal love of crop and man.

Ares appears as the "protagonist" of the Christ-like runner in A Fable, making that novel's comic subplot important to its main action for the first time. In The Reivers, a pattern of Hadean images identifies the book's symbolic setting and its major statement about the necessary cohabitation of evil and good within each man's heart. The bee-goddess aspect of Aphrodite explains the role of Everbe Corinthia in the action and thematic statements of the novel.

Faulkner's body of myths lies beneath puns, often; it is pointed out by "signposts" we have missed until now. Faulkner used the theories of the anthropological myth-critics because he believed that man was a victim of a pattern of sacrifice of life and limb for brute fertility. He layered the myths from Greece with myths from other areas and eras; he displaced or condensed mythic figures in the manner we know from dream analysis. The classical myths indicate that the human heart was in an eternal conflict with a nightmarish half of itself. The myths are the most important element in much of Faulkner. [Order No. 76-10,793; 296 pages. DAI, 36A (May-June 1976), 7428-29.]

331 The Cosmographic Strain in Narrative: From Homer to Faulkner, Joyce, and Butor / Khachig TOLOLYAN, Brown University, 1975 (Robert Scholes).

We think of narrative as a literary form in which a temporal syntagm made up of subject and action, with a beginning, middle, and end, is regarded as the best way of integrating details into an order which bestows coherence and meaning on man's experience. I use "cosmographic narrative" to refer to works which do tell a story but which also suggest that there are many elements that are needed to narrate and explain the human situation but cannot be satisfactorily incorporated into the story. These elements are arranged by other orders which either complete or compete with the order of narrative; they serve to represent a world-model (a "cosmos") even as they make the writing of the fiction ("graphos") a possible task.

The first chapter of the dissertation surveys major cosmographic narratives in the western tradition from the Iliad to Bouvard et Pécuchet. I develop Havelock's arguments in defense of encyclopedic narrative to show that catalogues, ecphrases, paradigmatic digressions, and similes are all in the service of cosmography, but enhance rather than subvert the main narrative. In the Odyssey, Invention as well as Memory contribute to the catalogues, the correct recitation of which assumes symbolic rather than mnemonic importance. In Hesiod's work, ecphrasis, enumeration, and catalogues help to explain the world by creating genealogies which are both narrative and categorical. In Herodotus' Histories, narrative is torn between the need to tell the story of history of an action and the desire to depict a cosmos which deserves to be surveyed both in its own right, and because it helps to explain events. Epic models control Herodotus' use of narrative and catalogue. Vergil's Aeneid is the cosmography of Rome. It uses topical and textual allusions to encompass the totality of a cosmos which is conceived of not only in terms of geography and history but also, for the first time, in terms of a literary culture.

Medieval narratives unite the world and the book by trusting to analogies between a divine artificer and the author. The explosive growth of Europe's boundaries and literary technology during the Renaissance, combined with the collapse of Christian authority, forces the adaptation of cosmography to new uses. Instead of representing the cosmos as assured totality, Rabelais records its fragmentation, and uses language as an object which can be manipulated at will, in order to question other orders and institutions beside the linguistic. Burton's Anatomy reflects a similar dilemma: books can record details but not endow them with coherence.

The second chapter explores Faulkner's attempts to make the creation of a world and the narration of a story coextensive. In Go Down, Moses and Requiem for a Nun he uses genealogy, geography, and history to create a cosmos which can and must be interpreted as though it were a text. The third chapter focuses on Ulysses, especially on "Nestor" and "Oxen of the Sun," to show that Joyce uses competing orders, each of which arrange details differently, but in such a way that they prevent narrative from asserting itself as the primary pattern of sense-making in a cosmos that encompasses the real spaces of Dublin and the metaphorical spaces of Western literature.

The last chapter focuses on Butor's Degrés. It demonstrates the influence of Joyce and Faulkner on this work, and gives a reading of it from the perspective provided by cosmographic narrative. Butor's teacher-hero intends to create a re-unified cosmos through the accumulation of genealogical, historical, and cultural detail, but he is doomed to fail. His failure constitutes an education for the reader. [Order No. 76-15,731; 240 pages. DAI, 37A (July-Aug. 1976), 303.]

332 Myth and Dream in the Novels of William Faulkner / William Leigh TROWBRIDGE, Vanderbilt University, 1975 (T. D. Young).

This study describes and traces the development of one of Faulkner's most effective fictional techniques, that of setting a mythic dimension of reality against a dream dimension to create an epistemological and ontological counterpoint. It is suggested that this counterpoint is a major stylistic device employed in the production of some of his best novels, influencing structure, characterization, plot, action, and setting.

Faulkner's use of the mythic mode has received a great deal of attention in recent years. Therefore, though not neglected, this subject is treated in less detail than that of his employment of the dream mode. Examination of Faulkner's use of the dream mode reveals that it corresponds, much more extensively than previous studies have indicated, to Freud's explication of dreams, especially as found in The Interpretation of Dreams.

Most of this study focuses on the novels written between 1928 and 1932: The Sound and the Fury, As I Lay Dying, Sanctuary, and Light in August. These are the works which seem to be the most enlightening in an examination of Faulkner's use of the myth-dream counterpoint.

In The Sound and the Fury the counterpoint emerges almost fully developed from the occasional and relatively insignificant uses of the mythic and dream modes in the earlier novels. This counterpoint consists of a mythic dimension of reality, associated with Dilsey, set against a dream dimension, centered in the mind of Quentin.

As I Lay Dying and Sanctuary show Faulkner experimenting with two different implementations of the counterpoint, both of which result in a less balanced version of it than the one in The Sound and the Fury. In As I Lay Dying the mythic dimension is located almost exclusively in the setting, rather than being associated with a character; too the dream dimension emerges gradually out of the consciousness of Darl instead of appearing fully developed from the start as it did in Quentin's case. Because Darl's character seems to lack the requisite depth and intensity, the dream dimension seems somewhat overshadowed by the powerful mythic one. Sanctuary, on the other hand, shows a radical shift of the balance in the opposite direction, with the dream dimension centered in Horace and Temple dominating and obscuring the underdeveloped mythic one embodied in Ruby Lamar.

Light in August seems to represent the culmination of Faulkner's use of the myth-dream counterpoint. The mythic dimension emanating from Lena is balanced against the dream world of Joe, with Byron and other members of the community providing an empirical center-point and bridge between the two non-empirical dimensions of reality.

With a few notable exceptions, the myth-dream counterpoint becomes much less significant in the novels following Light in August. This development seems a consequence both to Faulkner's continued use of new techniques and of his increasing tendency towards a discursive rather than a dramatic presentation of his material.

The contribution of this study to existing Faulkner criticism is basically threefold. First, it provides a means of sharpening and unifying a number of diverse critical perspectives on the nature of Faulkner's reality. The meaning of such frequently applied terms as Faulkner's "mythic mode," his "nightmarish" or "gothic" characters, and his "surrealistic" imagination not only may be more precisely understood in themselves, but they also may be seen as relevant to a single, organically unified artistic vision present in some of Faulkner's best novels. Second, the dream mode, heretofore given comparatively scant critical attention, is shown to be a major stylistic element in these novels. Finally, additional insight is provided into the development of Faulkner's artistry during his most productive years. [Order No. 76-126; 263 pages. DAI, 36A (Jan.-Feb. 1976), 4498-99.]

333 The Role of Women in Faulkner's Yoknapatawpha / Maureen Anne WATERS, Columbia University, 1975 (Robert A. Bone).

An understanding of the women characters in William Faulkner's novels and short stories is central to an understanding of his art and to the view of life that emerges from that art. One of his recurring themes, for example, is that woman as child bearer is in harmony with the natural world and therefore constitutes a kind of superior moral force. Cultural disintegration, on the other hand, may be associated with the failed mother or with a promiscuous woman.

In creating women Faulkner tends to reflect what Eric Neumann terms the Great Good Mother and the Terrible Devouring Mother, which are fundamental components of the Feminine Archetype. The Good Mother sustains life and reflects the benevolent forces of nature; the Terrible Mother, with whom are associated the seductive figures, Aphrodite, Lilith, Cybele, is seen as a threat to male rationality and consciousness. This is not to suggest that Faulkner's characters may be reduced to simple archetypes. Faulkner's is a rich and diverse world, but because of his great mythopoeic powers, his feminine characters tend to reflect the deepest fears and desires of the male psyche.

In Yoknapatawpha women are seldom distinguished by powers of intellect. One of the assumptions underlying the novelist's portraits of women seems to be that they are by nature "intuitive" rather than "rational" beings. Faulkner reinforces this assumption by insisting on a dichotomy between the mind and the heart. Thus the male becomes the embodiment of the rational principle with its defects, its tendency toward "cold abstractions"; the female is aligned with the emotions and so rendered mysterious, unpredictable, and "other." Faulkner's younger woman is rarely allowed to exist in or for herself; a pure male fantasy, she is

usually represented as helpless in the sway of her deepest biological impulses.
While maternal figures are associated with harmonious and enduring values, women who venture outside their traditional sphere are usually masculinized like Drusilla Hawks or Joanna Burden, and they tend to be associated with violence and bloodshed. Women who do not marry are frequently made into sterile and dangerous spinsters. Virtually all of the women who are sexually attractive are also inherently dangerous to men.

In Faulkner's work the idealistic man is often victimized by an older or more worldly woman who appears as the other face of Eve, the temptress. Embracing her is to experience the death of reason, the fall from grace. Faulkner revives one of the most ancient and enduring myths of western civilization by associating women with the unconscious mind and, even more fundamentally, with devouring or castrating images of death.

Faulkner's treatment of women and his description of sexual experience reflect the influence of Calvinism. Physical passion is either treated as a matter for broad country humor or it becomes painful, deadly, grotesque. No other important American writer is so obsessed with the concept of virginity. "Ladies" who allow themselves to be seduced are represented as corrupted or as "slain flowers." Human intercourse is linked with crude or brutal images of animals. In Light in August the sexual impulses of Joanna Burden are described as a foul sewer drawing the protagonist to his death.

As a writer Faulkner reflects as well as criticizes the values of the southern, agrarian, and patriarchal culture in which he had his roots. Those values encouraged him to formulate a maternal ideal, while underestimating or condemning other facets of feminine nature. [Order No. 75-15,765; 205 pages. DAI, 36A (July-Aug. 1975), 332-33.]

334 Short Story Cycles of Hemingway, Steinbeck, Faulkner, and O'Connor / Harlan Harbour WINN, III, University of Oregon, 1975 (Christof Wegelin).

In modern fiction, writers have combined the aesthetics of the novel and the short story to construct groupings of inter-related stories that are too finely patterned to be described as a mere collection of stories and too dependent on individual components to be described as a novel. Among the names proposed for this new genre, Forrest Ingram's suggestion of "short story cycle" in Representative Short Story Cycles of the Twentieth Century (The Netherlands, 1971) most clearly represents its nature. In this dissertation the theoretical principles of this recently acknowledged genre are advanced and illustrated through the analysis of four short story cycles: Ernest Hemingway's In Our Time; John Steinbeck's The Pastures of Heaven; William Faulkner's Go Down, Moses; and Flannery O'Connor's Everything That Rises Must Converge. To establish a context in which these cycles can be discussed, the introduction describes both the external and internal techniques used to construct cycles to suggest both the autonomy and interrelationship of the stories. External devices can include individually entitled stories, consecutively numbered stories, correspondence between the title of a cycle and one of its stories, correspondence between the title of a cycle and one of its stories, epigraphs, prologue, and epilogue. Internal means for interconnecting stories involve recurrent use for cumulative effect of point of view and tone, setting, characters, structure, motif, symbol, and theme.

In the four body chapters of the dissertation the explication of each of the short story cycles includes such points as its compositional method, its author's stated intention, its publication history, its treatment by critics, and its interconnecting devices. The cycles analyzed demonstrate the different organizational techniques and degrees of unity within the spectrum short stories and the combination of linear and associational development in Hemingway's In Our Time; the recurrence of protagonists tied together by common locality and the emergence of a more general theme for the cycle that does not occur in any one story in Steinbeck's The Pastures of Heaven; the juxtaposition of protagonists descending from three different genealogical branches within the same family and the counterpointing of the past and the wilderness with the present and civilization to advance the history of the South in Faulkner's Go Down, Moses; the recurrence of similarly treated themes in varied contexts and the ordering of the final story to reiterate and conclude patterns of thematic concern developed throughout the previous stories in O'Connor's seven-story cycle, Everything That Rises Must Converge.

The Conclusion speculates that reasons both central and extraneous to the internal development of literature can explain the emergence of this new genre. For example, experimental use of fictional techniques would be attractive to authors who write both short stories and novels, for the short story cycle combines the essential difference between the two prevailing genres: each individual story within a cycle focuses upon a single moment of peculiar significance in the life of its protagonist, yet the sequence of stories traces a number of peak moments in a series of events. In addition, such reasons as the demand of publishers that fictional works be novel length and the growth of the American magazine in the twenties can also account for the growth of the short story cycle. To speculate why the short story cycle has flourished in America particularly, the Conclusion also traces the influence of Sherwood Anderson's model in Winesburg, Ohio on subsequent American writers. [Order No. 76-983; 183 pages. DAI, 36A (Jan.-Feb. 1976), 4500.]

335 Self-Communion: The Early Novels of William Faulkner / Laurence Michael YEP, State University of New York at Buffalo, 1975 (Leslie A. Fiedler).

Faulkner once wrote, "I am telling the same story over and over, which is myself and the world." While this is true of any author, Faulkner's statement suggests a particularly useful approach to his early work. The dissertation describes the ways in which he explores the relationships between himself and his external world on at least two levels. Faulkner does this first by creating special interpersonal relationships between his fictional surrogates and their external world. Such early heroes as Donald Mahon, Bayard Sartoris, Horace Benbow, and Quentin Compson display increasingly more complex and abstract interpersonal strategies, ending finally with the artist-like methods of Quentin Compson in dealing with others.

On the linguistic level, this search for special relationships becomes involved with the language by which Faulkner actually created his fictional surrogates and their world. Just as there is a basic pattern to the relationships of Faulkner's imaginary characters, there is a similar pattern in the relationships between Faulkner and his readers. Using Norman Holland's model for the dynamics of literary response, the dissertation tries to show how Faulkner manipulated the conventions of language and of literature to achieve a unity with his readers on his own terms. Quentin's section in The Sound and the Fury is used for this purpose.

Faulkner also comes to realize that this search for a special relationship has analogues on the aesthetic level. The final chapters of the dissertation show how Absalom, Absalom! represents the culmination of the interpersonal strategies Faulkner was trying to create for his heroes and of his own artistic strategies. It is in this novel that Faulkner partially recognizes that art alone provides the special type of relationship which he seeks. [Order No. 75-18,858; 295 pages. DAI, 36A (Sept.-Oct. 1975), 1513.]

336 Levels of Consciousness: Women in the Stream-of-Consciousness Novels of Joyce, Woolf, and Faulkner / Betty Jean Edwards ALLDREDGE, University of Oregon, 1976 (William J. Handy).

The primary purpose of this study is to examine how levels of consciousness are presented in three major stream-of-consciousness novels: James Joyce's Ulysses, Virginia Woolf's Mrs. Dalloway, and William Faulkner's As I Lay Dying. The findings of this examination are then focused on the central women characters in the novels: Molly Bloom, Clarissa Dalloway, and Addie Bundren.

The argument of the dissertation is twofold: (1) that an understanding of the techniques by which levels of consciousness are presented leads to a more comprehensive character analysis of these characters than has heretofore been possible and thus to a new understanding of each novel as a total thematic image by making the thematic implications demanded by the technique; and (2) that women's changing roles and their concept of self in the twentieth century are contributing factors to the fictional techniques of the stream-of-consciousness novel as part of the "turning inward" of the novel which occurred in the first half of this century. The increased gap between a woman's individual needs and wants and her continued expected conventional role in society accelerated the presentation of a separate inner world for women characters. The stream-of-consciousness novel functions to create this inner reality and thus to establish the tension of these novels by means of the often ironic contrast between inner and outer reality.

The first chapter of the dissertation reviews and synthesizes the work of earlier critics--primarily Humphrey, Friedman, and Edel--and also of more recent attempts to define stream-of-consciousness fiction. This study establishes stream-of-consciousness fiction as a subgenre of modern fiction which subsumes various techniques, including internal monologue. The central chapters of the study present a theoretical analysis of the techniques involved for the individual author and follow with an applied analysis of the woman character and an interpretation of the novel as a whole. The chapters include a close examination of levels of consciousness as reflected in language, structure, point of view, time-space relationships, characterization, and finally thematic images of the novel (including both formal and sociological-cultural aspects.)

The Joyce chapter deals with the parallel patterns observable in the consciousness presentations of Stephen and Bloom with movement into internal monologue reflecting levels of consciousness. The chapter then concentrates on the Molly Bloom internal monologue which ranges over several levels of consciousness. Levels are primarily reflected in changes in scene structure and increasing fragmentation within the monologue. The Virginia Woolf chapter analyzes several key scenes in Mrs. Dalloway, with the conclusion that levels of consciousness are reflected in patterns of imagery. The Faulkner chapter notes the most clearly discernible levels of consciousness with three distinct levels of character presentation in As I Lay Dying--soliloquy, internal monologue, and narrated consciousness.

The conclusion summarizes the findings and presents a brief discussion of the work of two post-war American novelists who have written novels in the Joycean stream-of-consciousness tradition: William Styron's Lie Down in Darkness and Ken Kesey's Sometimes a Great Notion. The study concludes with an assessment of women characters in stream-of-consciousness fiction from Molly Bloom to Viv Stamper. [Order No. 76-27,623; 197 pages. DAI, 37A (Nov.-Dec. 1976), 3610.]

337 Possibilities of Place: The Fiction of William Faulkner / Christopher Edward ARTHUR, Cornell University, 1976 (James R. McConkey).

William Faulkner's work has often been commended for its sense of place and of community. But the use he makes of that sense is something radically different from the kind of sociological accuracy or meticulous description or regional pride more usually associated with the term. His places are metaphysical constructs rather than objects to be described; his sense of place is as much a part of his world view as his sense of time.

To Faulkner and to his characters, places are a counter to the forces of time. They endure: they were there before a person was born and they will be there long after he is dead. For this reason, they are larger than any individual: to find a place and to belong to that place is to find a way of escaping the isolation of modern life and become a part of a whole. But places do not obliterate the individual in the way time does: they are the carriers of memory. The soil is itself the dead: the towns they lived in, the buildings they built, the trees they planted, the places where they lived all serve as memorials to them.

Faulkner's perception of these meanings arises from an understanding of traditional beliefs in the significance of places. The ancient practices of establishing a sacred center and of making pilgrimages to it are examples of these traditions; Jerusalem, for instance, has long offered believers the chance to participate in a reality beyond everyday life and to remember great moments and great people of the past. The American tradition is deeply rooted in such beliefs in a significant place, especially in the belief that America is the promised land. The American tradition differs from earlier ones in emphasizing the importance of seeking out a significant place, and in finding the most sacred places to be those which individuals have chosen as their homes. Many American architects, for example, developed a philosophy of the importance of one's home that reflects this tradition. Faulkner has not always been as closely associated with the mainstream of American tradition as he should be; the kind of significance he accords to place indicates the depth of his roots in that tradition.

His novels do not simply describe that tradition; rather, they comment on it. His characters travel considerably in search of some better place; he finds their travel to be successful only when they surrender their will and no longer know exactly where they are going. Only then can they listen to the earth and its people and hear what they have to offer. His characters seek to participate in a world beyond themselves and to become immortal, either by mingling with the earth and its rhythms, by experiencing the timeless wilderness, or by getting close to the sacred center, Jefferson and its courthouse. He finds all the variations of this process to be uncertain; place offers no sure way to conquer time. But he values the effort. Most importantly, his characters try to establish a sense of belonging to a home or a homeland. Again and again they fail, finding their country and the homes which embody their identities to be "dark houses" of fear and hatred. Faulkner finds that to succeed, a home--and by implication, America--must not be a monument to a single man or a single ideal and must be willing to open its doors to all: it must be a place of love. Only then can it fulfill the possibility of place to mean. [Order No. 77-19,985; 387 pages. DAI, 38A (Sept.-Oct. 1977), 1383-84.]

338 Kenneth Burke's Structuralism: A Structural Description of Narrative and Technique in Faulkner's Fiction of the Southern Aristocracy / Gary Edwin BARRICKLOW, University of New Mexico, 1976 (Roy Pickett).

Objective description of literary technique is an aspect of literary criticism which has largely been ignored, in part because of the influence of the Formalist school of literary criticism which insists that all critical reading is necessarily subjective and that intention--an integral element in any examination of literary technique--is impossible to isolate or define. Contemporary structuralists disagree.

Structuralists believe that the "system" of literature, like any other language system, is comprised of both performance and competence. That is, the structuralists assume that, to read a text as literature rather than as sentences, the reader must first internalize a "grammar" of literature--the value system, conventions, symbolic logic, and purpose of literature in general. In other words, they assume that there is a certain universal, innate and hence objective sense of structure which lies behind the construction of any literary text. Structuralists, however, tend to ignore the purpose behind a specific literary structure.

Kenneth Burke, though not a self-identified structuralist, patterns his critical apparatus in a similar fashion, except that his concern is almost exclusively for motive and purpose. Burke's theory of symbolic action which is grounded on certain biological-neurological universals of the human experience, is similar to the structuralist's theory of literary competence, and his critical apparatus, the "dramatistic pentad," posits these extrinsic functions as integral units of a literary structure in much the same manner as the structuralists consider competence to be an integral function in performance. This combination of Burke's theories of motive and purpose with the structuralist's theories of narrative operations provides an ideal means of dealing objectively with prose narrative technique. Additionally, this combination provides an apparatus which allows the critic to discuss the purpose, motive, and effect of a literary structure by noting how an individual artist manipulates the various universals of literary structure. Moreover, because the apparatus shows conclusively that motive and purpose are immanent in the structure itself, the critic has a means of recovering the artist's intention and thereby the efficacy of the process.

By approaching a text in this manner, one can uncover certain meanings and motives which lie buried in the text and which are not recoverable through any of the purely intrinsic approaches to literary structure. The concluding chapter of the dissertation demonstrates that, when seen through the perspective of Burkean structuralism, William Faulkner's Go Down, Moses, which many critics feel lacks a unifying theme, reveals a definitely unified thematic structure and shows a theme which recurs in many of Faulkner's novels of the Southern aristocracy--the destructive nature of extremes. Moreover, such an approach affords the critic a means of discussing not only how the text is constructed, but why--not only the act of construction, but the drama as well. [Order No. 76-25,653; 204 pages. DAI, 37A (Nov.-Dec. 1976), 2856-57.]

339 Pylon: The Doomed Quest. A Critical and Textual Study of William Faulkner's Neglected Allegory / Helen Moore BARTHELME, University of Texas at Austin, 1976 (Gerald Langford).

A critical and textual study of Pylon, William Faulkner's eighth novel, this work is an attempt to find in the novel a totally coherent scheme integrating characterization, plot, narrative strategy, and tone. Although earlier critical studies have contributed to the understanding of the novel, the present study is the first effort to provide a comprehensive reading which resolves significant problems and ambiguities in Pylon. The study shows that the novel, which has been previously neglected since its initial reception, is neither the failure nor the puzzle which most critics seem to find it. As an ironical allegory in which a quest motif provides structural wholeness, the novel gives us an integral vision of the possibilities of myth and religion in man's attempt to sustain his humanity in the mechanistic and dehumanized world of the twentieth century.

Significant in what it reveals of the author's attitude toward man's relationship to the past and the necessity of the recognition of sin and guilt in an otherwise amoral world, Pylon is related to the Yoknapatawpha novels, especially Absalom, Absalom!, in that it illuminates by contrast the moral order of that world. The central figure of the novel, the Reporter, embarks on a quest for mythical consciousness, for the life and spirituality or "truth" which it will bring, and it is in what happens to him that the reader learns of Faulkner's attitude toward the present. The Reporter's search leads him to the death and permanent entombment of the pilot as a symbol of the loss of the Christian god, a black irony which is rather intensified than relieved by the ludicrous figure of the newspaperman. Nevertheless, the survival of man in spite of the failure of the quest is implicit in Faulkner's vision.

The first chapter discusses major critical problems and shows how they can be resolved if Pylon is read as ironical allegory. Three stages of the manuscript have been used for this study: the holograph, typesetting typescript, and galley proofs. These materials are used throughout in the development of the critical argument.

Chapter II is an analysis of narrative strategy and shows how Faulkner's vision, a bold departure from the thematic material of the Yoknapatawpha novels, emerges from the narrative structure. Chapter III is devoted to a full discussion of the actions of the Reporter as the seeker in the quest. Formerly symbolic of Death itself, the Reporter is now attempting to escape the novel's "City of the Dead." In the analysis of the symbolic patterns of the quest for a mythical consciousness, corresponding mythic patterns established by anthropological and psychological scholarship have been explored. The study examines the characters and the meaning on the two levels of the rational-empirical and the allegorical. The two levels, though unified for the most part, are a source of one of the difficulties confronting the reader.

Chapter IV is a discussion of the family of fliers and shows how they move from the mythic realm to the human realm. Shumann is examined as a Christ figure and as a symbol of man's spirituality. In Chapter V, relevant textual materials not already examined in the preceding chapters are explored. The chapter also examines evidence that Faulkner was compelled to finish the novel quickly, an important point in considering the problem of tone and organic wholeness in the final chapters. The significance and value of Pylon are discussed in the concluding chapter. [Order No. 77-29,125; 198 pages. DAI, 38A (Jan.-Feb. 1978), 4163.]

340 The Demonic Paradox: Studies in Faulkner's Imagery / Lynn Dillon
    BUCK, State University of New York at Stony Brook, 1976 (Sallie Sears).
    In his successful works, Faulkner uses carefully constructed antithetical image sequences to make an aesthetic statement reflecting his comic view that acknowledges an inherent polarity in the universe. The paradox that life is, in essence, a preparation for death provides the basis for his tension of opposing generative and demonic images, along with images of light and darkness and of the grotesque. When Faulkner adheres to his aesthetic principles, his fictional world pulses with vital energy. This is evident in three of his early novels--The Sound and the Fury (1929), As I Lay Dying (1930), and The Hamlet (1940). But when his image patterns disintegrate, the novels lose their vitality, as in the last two volumes of the Snopes trilogy, The Town (1957) and The Mansion (1959).

In The Sound and the Fury patterns of light, shadow, and darkness reveal the characters' inner natures and create special textural dimensions. Firelight and sunlight suggest goodness and beauty, particularly that of Dilsey and Caddy. Jason's conflict with the sun accentuates his evil tendencies. Quentin demonstrates his despair through the parade of shadows following him from sunrise to sunset, then moves into darkness and death. Dilsey, in a progression of light--from gray dawn to bright noonday sun--interprets life as a natural cycle. The dual patterns of darkness and light emphasize the unresolved theme and counter-theme: suffering and negation of life as opposed to suffering and affirmation of life.

As I Lay Dying presents Faulkner's world at its most paradoxical. In an absurd universe, who is truly sane--the person who adjusts or the one who, like Darl, refuses to adapt and is thereby judged insane? Demonic forces are at work against the Bundrens' struggle to survive their agonizing pilgrimage to bury Addie. Against a backdrop of the grotesque and the demonic, however, are superimposed images of beauty (such as Jewel on his horse) which reveal astonishing vitality and emotion, asserting Faulkner's eternal "dilemma of the human heart."

The Hamlet is a rich and paradoxical blend of generative and demonic forces. Animal and vegetable imagery place many characters in the subhuman category; and characters' relationship to sun and fire reveals their inherent goodness or evil. Ike Snopes is garlanded by a splendid crown of sunlight. Mink Snopes' murder of Houston is committed in darkness of a "moonless night." Eula Varner, a Persephone figure, is envisioned as a goddess "on a sunwise slope of Olympus." Flem Snopes is characterized by flames of Hell. Interludes of Ratliff's humor soften the horror, but ultimately the demonic is victorious.

The Town and The Mansion suffer from a scarcity of imagery. Except for two early short stories, "Centaur in Brass" and "Mule in the Yard," inserted as chapters, and the account of Eula's death, The Town is a monotony of words. Its texture is thin; settings are barren; characters are abstract, one-dimensional people. Flem is transformed from evil incarnate to an ordinary man, obnoxious but not fearfully grotesque. Even Ratliff is less funny. Gavin Stevens and Chick Mallison monopolize much of the narration with banalities. Linda is a sexless, cardboard figure. The Mansion, too, is inexplicably dull, except in passages involving Mink (which surge with energy in the old Faulknerian style.) Many events are recapitulated from previous works, and with each retelling more imagery disappears. Because of poorly controlled images, Linda is a weak caricature of the powerful heroine she might have been. A comparison of these two novels to the previous three demonstrates a diminishment in the rich complexity of Faulkner's world directly related to the deterioration of his patterned imagery. [Order No. 76-28,049; 515 pages. DAI, 37A (Nov.-Dec. 1976), 3620.]

341 An Exploration of the Literary Relationship Between Sherwood Anderson and William Faulkner / Mary Ellen BYRNE, Temple University, 1976 (William Rossby).

This study of the literary relationship between Sherwood Anderson and William Faulkner explores areas of influence in the works of Faulkner which can possibly be attributed to Anderson and affords an insight into the formation of Faulkner's literary method. Through a discovery and exploration of those qualities in Anderson which recur in Faulkner and an analysis of Faulkner's handling of them, this study reveals the possible indebtedness of Faulkner to Anderson and the probable effects of Sherwood Anderson's influence on William Faulkner's writing.

From "the father of my generation of American writers" Faulkner could have gained much. Anderson used simple but extremely effective images and symbols. His natural symbols, such as birds, plumes, hands, speak for the natural free, good life Anderson espoused; his man-made symbols, such as the barriers of walls, windows, rooms, and doors, convey a denial of these possibilities. For Anderson darkness seems the time his characters, usually futilely, seek release from lives denying passion, sensuality, and love. Anderson's tableaux, images of stasis, attempt to stop the moment "dead still," to capture a crucial moment, a moment often depicted in Biblical or religious terms. Faulkner expanded Anderson's images and symbols for his own purposes. He contrasted similar natural symbols with man-made symbols. Darkness signifies more than denial and frustration; it also signifies evil. His images of stasis, frozen moments, incorporate a concept of time with the graphic, pictorial qualities of Anderson's.

Anderson's theory of the grotesque in the preface to Winesburg, Ohio, in which a spiritual deformity results from adherence to one "truth," could have been suggestive to Faulkner in the creation of some of his greatest characters, Sutpen, Colonel Sartoris in The Unvanquished, the Generalissimo in A Fable, Quentin Compson in The Sound and the Fury, Horace Benbow, Joe Christmas, Joanna Burden, and Gail Hightower, who adhere inflexibly to an extreme of a "truth" and thus sacrifice human relationships. Anderson's adolescent whose transition to manhood involves violence and brutality and a surrender of childhood innocence and illusions is a typical figure in Faulkner. For both the adolescent is often an orphan. Faulkner's creation of the character of the town with its Puritanical repressions, its violence, its condemnation of the eccentric individual owes much to Anderson's concept of the town. Mysterious strangers disrupt both writers' towns. Both give a narrative voice to the adolescent and the town.

Faulkner's experimentation in the novel-short story form, evident in The Unvanquished, Go Down, Moses, The Hamlet, The Wild Palms as well as Light in August and Absalom, Absalom!, could have been stimulated by Anderson's example in Winesburg, Ohio and Poor White and his theory that the novel needed more freedom, greater complexity, and more looseness of form. Finally the vision of man alone and lonely, isolated from his fellows, yet still seeking love and brotherhood while wrapped in darkness, is common to both. Both Faulkner's characters have greater strength amidst a greater horror.

Hopefully this paper is a contributing chapter to ongoing scholarship toward a definitive study of Faulkner's literary method and the literary influences which shaped it. Until this final all-encompassing work is done, it appears that the totality of evidence assembled here argues for Anderson's influence. [Order No. 76-11, 986; 274 pages. DAI, 36A (May-June 1976), 8055.]

342 The Development of Narrative Technique in the Apprenticeship Fiction of William Faulkner / Ronald Lloyd CORWIN, Brandeis University, 1976 (Peter Swiggart).

Although there has been a great deal of critical work on Faulkner's major novels and the novels which lie within the Yoknapatawpha Cycle, until the last decade the fiction of his "apprenticeship" period has been passed over as derivative and inferior to his best work. This fiction may be derivative, but it is also experimental, and it does set the stage for the appearance of such brilliant and technically accomplished early novels as The Sound and the Fury and As I Lay Dying. Several recent studies of Faulkner's apprenticeship have demonstrated that Faulkner, if not very successful as a novelist during these years, was much more a conscious artist than has been supposed. These studies may be divided into two sorts.

In the first, critics have treated Faulkner's early work as the proper object for studies of influence. Not much is to be hoped from further work along these lines, since we are hampered by the lack of direct evidence that Faulkner borrowed from his reading anything except the most general ideas and images. These studies do help to document the wide range of Faulkner's reading and his familiarity with the experiments and ideas of his contemporaries.

In studies of the second sort, critics contend that, even in his apprenticeship fiction, Faulkner is a conscious artist who grows in both sensibility and skill. Two studies have appeared which treat this growth in some depth. Of the two, one spends much time in plot recapitulation and fails to take into account the existence of some important materials. The study also construes the idea of narrative technique so narrowly that it includes only the manipulation of point-of-view and time-sequence. The other study does take fully into account the available texts, unfinished drafts, criticism, and biographical material. However, since it is the primary purpose of the second study to place Faulkner in the company of impressionists Conrad, Thomas Beer, and Sherwood Anderson, much of the discussion of narrative technique is directed to this end.

Further study of Faulkner's early fiction is in order. In addition to the increasing sophistication in his treatment of point-of-view, Faulkner's early work shows important changes in such areas as the depiction of character, the use of ironic juxtaposition, and the uses to which sources and models are put. His understanding of the medium of fiction and of the relationship of the author to his work also seems to be in flux during the pre-Yoknapatawpha years.

Materials treated in this study are the Double Dealer and Times-Picayune stories and sketches which appeared in the spring of 1925; Soldiers' Pay; the unfinished novel Elmer Hodge; and Mosquitoes. The typedraft of Elmer Hodge and prepublished drafts of the two novels with corrections in Faulkner's hand on deposit in the University of Virginia's Alderman Library are examined and discussed. Fragments of unpublished short stories have also been taken into account. [Order No. 76-25,298; 237 pages. DAI, 37A (Nov.-Dec. 1976), 2869.]

343 Faulkner's Early Short Story Career / John Peyton CRIGLER, III, Yale University, 1976 (Cleanth Brooks).

The famous novels that Faulkner planned and wrote during the late 1920s and the early 1930s have received a great deal of scholarly attention. The large number of short stories he wrote during the same period have received almost none. This dissertation examines Faulkner's early short story career and a number of critical questions which that career poses.

The first chapter discusses the relationship between Faulkner's jealously guarded private life and his fiction. It argues that the short stories reveal the passionate individualism that underlies all of Faulkner's work.

The following chapter makes theoretical and historical distinctions between the short story, the novel, and the orally told story and attempts to explain precisely what Faulkner meant by his repeated assertions that he was "a storyteller."

Succeeding chapters survey the early short stories, giving special attention to the 1925 series of New Orleans stories and to These 13, Faulkner's first collection of stories. While examining particular short stories in detail, these chapters elaborate earlier speculations about Faulkner's conception of the short story and about the capacities and limitations of the short story form.

A concluding chapter considers the relationship between Faulkner's short stories and the rest of his literary career. It outlines a number of ways in which the short stories may illuminate the novels, particularly the "story novels" of Faulkner's late career; and it argues that the short stories play an important part in Faulkner's creation of a narrative fiction capable of fully representing the conflict between the flickering private world of subjective and cultural experience.

Appendices collect and organize bibliographical information about the short stories. [Order No. 76-29,827; 223 pages. DAI, 37A (Jan.-Feb. 1977), 4352.]

344 Faulkner's Negro: Art and the Southern Context, 1926-1936 / Thadious Marie DAVIS, Boston University, 1976, no DAI entry.

345 William Faulkner's Compleat Woman / Mary Ellen Marshall GOODENBERGER, University of Nebraska at Lincoln, 1976 (James L. Roberts).

This study attempts to show that Faulkner's complete roster of women characters includes all the qualities and characteristics that have accrued to the concept of woman down through the years, that he presents a realistic picture of the development of the human female, and that his view of women is a positive one. A brief introduction describes the common misreading which leads to the belief that Faulkner had a negative attitude toward his women characters and also sets the stage for the development of the thesis. The first chapter includes a descriptive list of representative women of mythology and the Bible. It also reiterates pertinent ideas from such authorities as Margaret Mead, Sigmund Freud, Jean Piaget, and Lawrence Kohlberg. The second chapter deals with Faulkner's "emergent woman" with all her variations. She may be a descendant of Diana, or she may be a miniature Venus. She may have the maternal qualities of young Miriam guarding baby Moses, or she may be a Delilah.

The third chapter examines Faulkner's women who have become effective mates and mothers, beginning with exemplars who are likely to be black women, poor white wives, or former prostitutes. The fourth chapter assesses his large group of women who are defeated by life, who go awry for some reason, who may become destructive, but who still are likely to endure. Within

Chapters II, III, and IV, parallels are drawn between Faulkner's women and their Biblical and mythological antecedents. Attention is called to his female characters' verisimilitude as supported by the findings of the behavioral and social scientists. The fifth chapter reviews the lives of Faulkner's matriarchs, the wise observers of society, the grandmothers and surrogate mothers who represent woman fully matured and fulfilled. The conclusion summarizes the study's findings about the comprehensiveness and realism of Faulkner's view of woman and about his belief that she has positive qualities which are urgently needed to complement man's basic nature. [Order No. 7732120; 269 pages. DAI, 38A (Jan.-Feb. 1978), 4827.]

346 Pastoral and Parody: The Making of Faulkner's Anthology Novels / James Michael GRIMWOOD, Princeton University, 1976 (Carlos H. Baker).

Most of Faulkner's novels of the late 1930s and the 1940s are "anthology novels"--hybrids of novels and short story collections. They belong to a transitional period, when his writing displayed an impulse to self-parody. One reason for this development was his growing awareness of the inconsistencies inherent in the pastoral character of much of his art--in the application of comparatively literate and sophisticated perception to the rendering of comparatively illiterate and simple experience.

The alternating construction of The Wild Palms creates divisions between levels of society and between the author and his literary constituency. Upon the bourgeois protagonist of the title story, Faulkner projected an autobiographical concern with the impediments to his artistic vocation. He implied that the convict of "Old Man," who typifies the rural poor about whom he frequently wrote, stood in the relationship of reader to author with the autobiographical character in "Wild Palms." By combining them gratuitously in the discontinuous form of the whole novel, Faulkner emphasized their separation, representatively denying upward mobility to ambitious poor whites who threatened to displace him. Also, by disconnecting his authorial figure from his figure of audition, he revealed a sense of his own artistic failure.

The Hamlet developed out of Faulkner's alarmed reaction to the "rise of the rednecks." He employed in it the techniques of Southwestern Humor, a tradition conservative Southerners founded a century earlier to preserve their hierarchical prerogatives. These techniques, involving the use of genteel narrators to contain the democratic energies of vernacular characters, led Faulkner to replicate in the texture of his prose the complex relationships among the segments of his community. In the counterpoint between his "literary" voice and his impersonations of sharecroppers, he came to question his own stylistic identity. The Hamlet consequently comprises a series of self-conscious performances, in which Faulkner attempted to define himself in terms of the lowly people about whom he wrote.

In Go Down, Moses, he pursued that effort further, defining his art in terms of people he perceived as impervious to it. Writing about Negroes, he adopted the formulae of the plantation novel, invented a century earlier to repress conflicts between races rather than classes. Go Down, Moses reflects his ambivalence about a central symbol of Southern culture, the plantation estate as a pastoral sanctuary of the mind. In writing about illiterate blacks, he came to realize that his subject was not their illiteracy but the suspicious nature of his own eloquence. The book that began as an investigation of his relationship to blacks ended as a confession of his inability to write faithfully about anyone.

Faulkner manifested a similarly suspicious attitude toward his art in Knight's Gambit. Between the first five stories, written afterward, the doubts he expressed in his book about Negroes entered his fiction generally. In other works of the same period, notably A Fable, he continued to dramatize the futility of his authorial enterprise. [Order No. 77-4788; 473 pages. DAI, 37A (March-April 1977), 5828.]

347 William Faulkner's Theory of Fiction / Bobby Wayne HAMBLIN, University of Mississippi, 1976 (John Pilkington).

That William Faulkner was a conscious craftsman, keenly interested in the aesthetics of fiction, is evidenced throughout his career--from his early prose and poetry and apprenticeship novel, Mosquitoes, to his later correspondence with Malcolm Cowley and post-Nobel Prize interviews, conferences, lectures, and essays. These sources, in conjunction with his actual practice in the many novels and stories, provide the basis upon which Faulkner's theory of fiction may be established. This story involves the nature of art and the artist, the sources of the writer's materials, and each of the traditionally designated components of fiction, that is, character, plot, viewpoint, style, symbolism, and theme.

Recognizing, as he said, that "the aim of every artist is to arrest motion, which is life, by artificial means and hold it fixed," Faulkner prefers a "living literature" faithful to both the flux of experience and the stasis of artifact. The permanence of such art provides a means of "saying No to death" and of recording the struggle of man to endure and prevail. Faulkner insists, however, that great literature of this type may be produced only by the artist who is willing to humble himself completely before his art and who is self-reliant enough to experiment constantly and to risk censure, neglect, even failure.

According to Faulkner's theory, literary genius is both inherent and acquired. Time and again Faulkner identifies the sources of fiction as "observation, experience, and imagination." His own fiction bears out the accuracy of this statement, while it simultaneously supports Faulkner's notion that the most important of the three ingredients is the writer's imagination.

The principal component of fiction, in Faulkner's view, is character. As demonstrated in his work, the major emphases in Faulkner's theory of characterization are a concern for variety in both range and type of character: a deliberate attempt to mirror the complex, even paradoxical, nature of man; a desire to depict (though with considerable allowance for the willful and irrational) convincing motivation for character behavior; and an inclination to fuse realistic techniques with an extensive use of the grotesque.

Faulkner's theory of plot involves a method which employs radical shifts of scene, frequent disruptions of chronology, and unique applications of restrictive viewpoint to ensure a suspensive unfolding of story and theme. The Sound and the Fury and Absalom, Absalom! are, among other things, masterpieces of suspense. Another important aspect of Faulkner's theory of plot is his expressed fondness for counterpoint. This device provides the unity often denied Faulkner by his unorthodox handling of time and viewpoint.

Perhaps Faulkner's principal contribution to a theory of fiction is his concept of viewpoint. While he employs almost all of the various points of view, he displays a special interest in first-person narration and the use of multiple narrators. In such approaches the reader is required to view the material from different angles and then construct his own "truth" about the characters and event. While this technique does not necessarily deny the existence of absolute truth, it does suggest that man's pursuit of that truth is always circuitous and difficult.

Faulkner's theory of style is linked to his views concerning language, time and death, and truth. The use of an expansive vocabulary, accretional detail, and multitudinous figures of speech are logical outgrowths of Faulkner's belief in the ineffable quality of experience, as of his attempt to master time and death by "trying to say it all in one sentence, between one Cap and one period." Faulkner also believes (and demonstrates to perfection in The Sound and the Fury) that style, like the perception of truth, must change according to the particular viewpoint in a given story.

Finally, Faulkner insists that all great literature is symbolic, particularly in its use of local elements to express a small body of universal truth.

This theory, which links Faulkner to the basic tenets of mythic criticism, is supported by the frequent use of the "initiation" motif and by various adaptations of biblical archetypes, especially the Eden and Christ stories. Such identification with ancient and familiar patterns underscores Faulkner's contention that the only genuine concerns of great literature are the timeless verities of the human heart.

The delineation of Faulkner's theory of fiction not only provides a useful approach to the Nobel Laureate's practice in the various novels and stories but also enhances his position as one of the great experimentalists in the history of fiction. [Order No. 76-20,524; 560 pages. DAI, 37A (Sept.-Oct. 1976), 1546-47.]

348 The Decomposing Form: Studies in Faulkner, Woolf, and Beckett /
Nancy Williams LAMPL, Case Western Reserve University, 1976
(Roger B. Salomas).

The transformation of the novel in the twentieth century is often seen in terms of loss. We have lost the traditional character in fiction; he is no longer rooted in a solid, external reality, and has frequently lost his features, his name, and his very sense of selfhood. We have lost coherent plots constructed according to familiar, sequential chronologies. And we have lost the guidance of the author who, if not omniscient, at least provided a privileged perspective on the text. These losses reflect a cultural and philosophical anguish stemming from the modern awareness of the absence of God and the disillusionment with language as a means of describing reality. Critics of art and culture speak of "The Loss of the Self," the "Disintegration of Form," and the "Dehumanization of Art."

For the modern writer, the forms of language cannot capture reality because reality is relative, shifting and multifaceted. The attempt of novelists to reflect both this shifting reality and their awareness that no form can capture it has resulted in novels structured to allow multiple viewpoints to coexist and coincide in ever-changing combinations. The stability of the old novel form has been replaced by the mobility of open-ended works from which no one form or meaning can be extracted. The structures of these novels no longer reflect the hero operating in the external world, nor the inner life of the character, but the processes of consciousness by which the mind grapples with the inaccessible reality. The novel has become a process reflecting upon itself.

Faulkner, Woolf, and Beckett are transition figures in the metamorphosis of the novel. Despite vast differences, each writer confronts similar problems and develops new forms to express his recognition of what is beyond expression. Each writer scrutinizes his own creative processes and holds his own work suspect.

In The Sound and the Fury and As I Lay Dying Faulkner attempts to hold in balance the mind in the process of formulating experience and a reality that exists beyond the deformities of consciousness. By Absalom, Absalom! the balance has shifted; the novel has become a self-enclosed system of multiple and contradictory fictions with no access to reality. In To the Lighthouse Virginia Woolf maintains a traditional theme and setting within a structure that insists upon multiple readings of that "reality." But even that "reality" is absent from The Waves. The intricate structure and metaphorical language of The Waves precludes a realistic reading, and yet provides the most variable and fertile portrayal of consciousness in the act of shaping experience into forms. For both Faulkner and Woolf reality is flux, and the attempt to form against that flux is both heroic and absurd, tragic and creative.

Beckett, too, is concerned with the problem of form. But for Beckett there is neither heroism nor tragedy--there is only futility. The ceaseless process of formation and dissolution that is life itself is anathema to Beckett. In his trilogy, he examines the forms of Western Civilization in order to destroy them. For Beckett, the novel is a self-negating process, an act against itself.

In these three writers, then, we see not only the death of the old forms and the development of the new, but a questioning of the very nature of form itself. An examination of their works provides insight not only into literature, but into the deepest philosophical questions at the heart of twentieth-century art and culture. [Order No. 77-12,011; 305 pages. DAI, 37A (May-June 1977), 7735-36.]

349 Creative Responses to Time in the Novels of William Faulkner / John Thomas MATTHEWS, Johns Hopkins University, 1976 (Laurence B. Holland).

As Jean-Paul Sartre early demonstrated, Faulkner's novels repeatedly dramatize the human conflict with time. Sartre finds the characters of Faulkner's novels helpless victims, benighted in what he considers the "indefinable present," prone to the "sudden invasions of the past." I agree with Sartre that the characters of the early novels, through The Sound and the Fury, are unable to fabricate imaginative forms which might successfully defend the mind from time's deprivations. The symmetry of Benjy's idiocy, Quentin's reducto ad absurdum of suicide, Jason's desperately affirmed sanity, and Dilsey's comfortable eschatology, may all be read as extreme placations of the dispossessing forces of time. But in subsequent novels, several imaginative forms emerge as creative responses to a variety of temporal dilemmas. The forms--primarily language, myth, and ritual--share a respect for both the sovereignty of time and also man's need to reply to temporal chaos with order and continuity.

In Absalom, Absalom! the past is in danger of being ignored and forgotten, and Faulkner presents language as an instrument for recreating it, commemorating it, taking revenge upon it, and forging continuities with it. In the narratives of Rosa, Mr. Compson, and Quentin and Shreve the word allows temporary recreation of the past and also affirmation of individually designed meaning, largely through parodic fictions that simultaneously respect the alienness of the past and the importance of translating it into a contemporary and personal idiom. The narrators' success in dealing with the past contrasts at significant points with Sutpen's imaginative failures, which derive from his innocence of the capacity of language to respond to temporal crises.

As the deliberate acts of memory in Absalom betray Sartre's conception of a past that is oppressively "hard, clear, and immitable," so The Hamlet's interest in the future depreciates Sartre's belief that Faulkner has "decapitated" the future. The Hamlet raises the relationship between cultural transformations and the need for continuity. The novel questions the capacity of traditional myths and rituals to predict what the future under Snopesism will be like. Flem Snopes, who merely synchronizes himself with the advancing present, and Ratliff, who seeks to preserve the fabric of the hamlet's past, present, and future conflict over the relevance of the historical imagination. Ratliff's opposition to Flem rests on his attempt to rally the community's resistance by exposing that Flem seeks to overthrow the values, rituals, and myths that compose the hamlet's tradition and confirmed links to the past.

Having looked to the obsolescence of some cherished values and modes of behavior in The Hamlet, Faulkner investigates actual moments of dispossession in Go Down, Moses. The seven stories of the novel share a crisis of loss. From the rotten-to-the-touch splendor of the Old South in "Was" to the final solemn burial of a last McCaslin child in "Go Down, Moses," each story dramatizes characters who seek to translate the past into the present in order to modify the acute sense of dispossession.

The inability of the imagination to counter change and loss accounts for the moving despair of The Sound and the Fury; but that despair is partially redeemed by the capacity of human creativity to reply to the temporal dilemmas of the past, future, and present in Absalom, Absalom, The Hamlet, and Go Down, Moses. [Order No. 77-7747; 411 pages. DAI, 37A (March-April 1977), 6486-87.]

350 Rhetoric of Loss: An Analysis of Faulkner's Perceptual Style / Gail Linda MORTIMER, State University of New York at Buffalo, 1976 (Leslie A. Fiedler).

William Faulkner's narrative style reflects a configuration of perceptual assumptions that tells us a great deal about the world he has created. His fictional world is largely an expression of a particular way of being-in-the-world, a style which in the details of its elaboration is unique to Faulkner. My central assumption in this study is that a significant correspondence exists between the prose structures and contents which direct a reader's perceptions and the psychological structures and contents which comprise an author's distinctive modes of perceiving reality.

Faulkner's perceptual style is evident in his characterization of Joe Christmas in Light in August, whose difficulties in establishing a viable sense of identity reflect a bifurcated view of reality. The qualities attributed to women and black people in Faulkner's prose are perceived as radically distinct from those of the Southern white male. Joe's ignorance about his own blackness or whiteness leaves him completely ambivalent about qualities which he experiences both as "alien" and as "self." This problem of identity is at bottom a problem of definition; and Faulkner's definitions and descriptions of objects, people, and concepts alike reflect a spatialized, visual, and polarized view of things.

While Faulkner's manner of spatializing the entities he describes has the effect of separating and controlling them, his fictional universe nevertheless reflects the transience of a world in flux. Faulkner expresses the ongoing metamorphosis of objects which exist through time by focusing on surfaces which alter or flow into new entities. There is a rhythm of emphases in Faulkner's descriptions between moments when boundaries cohere and are firm and moments when they blur or fade away.

In part because of a preoccupation with the past, Faulkner's world consists to a significant degree of objects whose importance lies in what they say about things or people that are absent. Objects become traces of things which once existed and perpetuate the feeling of less which pervades his stories. They are perceived as containers, holding (actually or potentially) the things they signify. Indeed, Faulkner's writing as a whole can be seen as a trace, a container, a way of dealing with and compensating for a world in which transience is the major fact and, as a consequence, loss is the dominant emotion. Faulkner's rhetorical strategies, his thematic concerns, and the structures of his stories are all expressions of a style of perceiving reality that involves holding on to things of value which threaten to go away. [Order No. 76-17,034; 194 pages. DAI, 37A (July-Aug. 1976), 971-72.]

351 Against the Limitations of Rationalism: Undercurrents in the Works of William Faulkner / Martha NOCHIMSON, City University of New York, 1976 (Robert A. Day).

Although reams have been filled by the critics of The Sound and the Fury, Light in August, and Absalom, Absalom!, much about their structure and unity remains a mystery. Is it the limitations of our western culture that makes it so difficult for readers to understand these novels? When we dispense with our culture's Cartesian, dualist bias, the discontinuous structures of these novels make complete sense. By breaking rationalist conventions of time and space, these novels allow the reader an unorthodox perception of both idealist Christian morality and materialist theory as false and, what is more, destructive evasions of immediate life. All of the characters in these novels structure their lives with the grid of some form of dualist, rationalist thought--either idealist or materialist. They are all in conflict, but the structuring of the novels makes it possible for the reader to cease to ask which one is right. The rational criterion of correctness is made irrelevant as the radical structures of the novels place the reader in a position to give priority to immediate experience and living energy, as the characters cannot.

Faulkner never claimed an anti-dualist bias. Indeed it is present in only eight of his novels: Sanctuary, As I Lay Dying, Pylon, The Wild Palms, and A Fable, in addition to the above mentioned three. Considering the rarity of outspoken western anti-dualists, it is not strange that Faulkner never declared what he showed in eight of his novels. Lacking Faulkner's authorization for any interpretations of the nightmare world he showed the world to have become under the domination of dualism, the critic is aided in discussing what he sees by a comparison between Faulkner's creation and the works of a unique, avowed western anti-dualist, William Blake.

Blake is optimistic about the human struggle with dualism and Faulkner is essentially pessimistic. There are interesting parallels, however, between Blake's Ulro, also a product of the perversions of dualism, and Faulkner's nightmare world. The resemblances between Blake's consciously avowed creation and Faulkner's underscore the crucial essence of anti-dualism in Faulkner's radical work, on which he never commented himself.

The reinterpretations of The Sound and the Fury, Light in August, and Absalom, Absalom! in an anti-dualist light, with the aid of Blake's spectacles, are intended as paradigms for reinterpreting all eight novels that belong to Faulkner's radical group. [Order No. 76-20,846; 359 pages. DAI, 37A (Sept.-Oct. 1976), 1551.]

352 Faith, Identity, and Perception--Three Existential Crises in Modern Fiction and Their Artistic Reconciliation: A Comparison of the Fiction of Dostoevsky, Joyce, Kafka, and Faulkner from the Perspective of the Works of Sartre and Camus (Volumes I-III), Donald Emanuel PALUMBO, University of Michigan, 1976 (James Gindin).

There is a remarkable similarity in the works of Dostoevsky, Joyce, Kafka, and Faulkner that may not be immediately apparent because the fiction of these authors is in so many ways so unique and so uniquely different. Yet each repeatedly utilizes his literary artistry to explore the complex reality of man as he exists in modern society and to examine within the individual, as deeply as prose narrative can, those anxieties, paradoxes, problems, frustrations, and enlightenments that are inextricably linked with his existential situation. Although its orientation within the context of the works of each author is quite different, each author does grapple with the crisis of faith that is the root issue of the existentialism of Camus and Sartre: the question of God's existence. This crisis is also a crisis of perception, as it radically concerns man's conception of the universe he inhabits; and both are crises of identity, as a change in man's conception of his environment must necessitate a change in his conception of his relationship to that environment and a consequent confusion in the perception of the self. One broad indicator of the actual indivisibility of these crises is the fact that the various reactions to them posited by these authors--rigidity, suicide, and acceptance--cannot affect one without influencing the others. The aim of this dissertation is simultaneously to explore this similarity on a variety of levels (from the juxtaposition of specific details to a correlation of a broad apprehension of each author's implicit world-view) and thus to develop a comparison of the works of these four authors. The method is first to analyze the philosophical and literary works of Camus and Sartre to evolve a coherent, highly integrated system that will then be used as the framework and organizational principle of this comparison.

The crisis of faith itself takes various forms in the works of each of these writers, yet in the case of each it both precipitates and is precipitated by crises of perception and identity. In the eyes of many of their characters the denial of the unifying idea of God leads to a non-unified, disjointed view of the world in which things seem to exist independently of one another, each in a separate reality of its own. This feeling finds its antithesis in a feeling of epiphany, a brief moment of understanding or integration. The crisis of faith also sparks the realization that man is free; yet men find this freedom oppressive and attempt to escape it through assuming rigid views of themselves and their world by which they can exist (in bad faith) as defined, non-contingent beings. For many, the idea that God may not exist deprives their world and their lives of any sense of absolute meaning they might otherwise have had, and these characters come to view their reality as absurd. These authors employ irony to emphasize and reveal the world's absurd aspect, but also employ it to suggest that limited meanings may be discovered or created in the vacuum of absolute meaninglessness. Alienation from the idea of God also either produces or symbolically manifests itself through an all-pervasive alienation from fathers and father figures, nature, other human beings, one's country, culture, and past, and the self. Paradoxically, those who suffer freedom are plagued by inescapable guilt, which stems from their alienation and the feeling that they are de trop, and which they cannot evade because of their keen sense of a lack of contact both with others and with a higher authority who might absolve them. Many consider or accept suicide as an avenue of escape, but each of these authors suggests the existence of the more positive alternative of a direct confrontation with and creative acceptance of life and its limitations. Significantly, in this creative manner the very form of these authors' works offers a limited solution to the problems posed in their content. All fiction is an ordered restructuring of reality in which all elements have artistic as well as semiotic meaning; and, as the existential dilemma springs from the concept of God's nonexistence, of the absence of any organizing and meaning-giving principle, it is solved symbolically through being treated in a fictional format in which meaning and order are implied. [Order No. 76-27, 564; 911 pages. DAI, 37A (Nov.-Dec. 1976), 3616.]

353 The Sound and the Fury: An Archetypal Reading, Theresa Lee PEARSON, University of New Mexico, 1976 (David M. Johnson).

Though The Sound and the Fury has received considerable critical attention since its publication in 1929, certain issues have yet to be resolved. Primary among these are the related issues of the novel's unity and of the possibility of an optimistic theme. The theory of archetypes postulated by C. G. Jung provides a model that helps to solve these problems. Archetypes are patterns of human experience though, as Jung insists, they can never be "reduced to a simple formula." However, one can speak of models that parallel the literary experience. The model that parallels this novel is that of an archetypal, psychological journey from chaos through a realm of adventure and peril to a condition in which conflict is resolved and wholeness and peace restored. This model is most closely paralleled in human experience by the "rites of passage" which Arnold Van Gennep describes in three stages: separation, transition, and incorporation. In other words, in The Sound and the Fury the reader, like the primitive initiate, is separated from everyday reality, lives through trials and transitions with the characters, and reemerges with a broader understanding of life and a fuller range of experience.

The first section, "April Seventh 1928," corresponds to separation. The removal of the initiate from his customary surroundings is analogous to the disorientation the reader experiences upon entering the mind of the idiot. Two motifs supplement this experience: the motif of separation represented by the section's time scheme, the changes in the Compson world, the eccentric method of narration, and the imagery of passage; and the motif of reconciliation embodied in images of light and trees which symbolize illumination and rebirth.

"June Second 1910" and "April Sixth, 1928" parallel the transition stage.

Though Quentin and Jason are unsuccessful in passing the trials of initiation, their sections provide the basic terms of the initiation paradigm through which a person must work: the shadow (whatever is within ourselves, what we do not wish to accept and so project onto others) and the encounter with the archetypal feminine (physical life in both its positive and negative aspects).

In the final section, "April Eighth 1928," through a series of oppositions and transformations that symbolize the reconciliation of paradoxes by active participation in symbol and rite, we complete the trials and are "incorporated" into the vision of the novel. The final scene completes the experience by providing a symbol of unity and wholeness--the mandala or magic circle, the ultimate symbol of Oneness which at once epitomizes the completeness of the novel and "closes" our initiation into the mystery of The Sound and the Fury.

This framework makes it possible to propose a new reading of this novel that provides some answers to issues left unsettled by previous readings. If, for instance, we look at the four sections as phases in an initiation journey traced by the reader, we are able to talk about unity without denying the individuality of the fragments. In addition, an archetypal approach gives us a way to talk about the meaning of the novel in the light of the optimistic purpose Faulkner asserted in his Nobel Prize Speech. The pattern suggested here is inevitably optimistic because it confirms our sense of the unity and imperishability of all being. [Order No. 77-6566; 175 pages. DAI, 37A (March-April, 1977), 6487.]

354 The Yoknapatawpha World and Black Being / Erskine Alvin PETERS, Princeton University, 1976 (Carol Baker).

The purpose of this dissertation is to investigate the significance of the black characters in William Faulkner's fictional world. One major objective is to bring together the most significant details and characters in order to see how they influence the general character of the Yoknapatawpha community.

Chapter One, "The Youthful Sensibility and the Cultural Heritage," is a chronological investigation of all Faulkner's published writings from the poetry of his teens (1916) through the novel Flags in the Dust (1929). The chapter focuses upon the young writer's use of themes and images which have implications for his later concerns with black character and situation. It specifically examines the imagery of "white and black" and "light and dark," and explores the subject of time as it is related to the mythic past, the historical past, and eternity. This chapter also gives a considerable amount of attention to Faulkner's early awareness of the more universal ramifications of issues involving race, and to his early difficulties with the creation of black characters.

Chapter Two, "The Historical Context of Black Existence in Yoknapatawpha County," provides a chronological account of the facts of black history as Faulkner presents them throughout his works. The chapter seeks to establish Faulkner's own sense of the background against which he was creating his saga.

Chapter Three, "The Tragedy of Human Distance," treats the manifest violence and psychological division inherent in the Yoknapatawpha racial situation. Particular attention is given to the forceful character of the community and its response to the black predicament.

Chapter Four, "Three Mulatto Crises: One Man's Imagination, Another Man's Dilemma," focuses upon the peculiar psychological problems which result from the obsessive fear of miscegenation. The discussion deals mainly with the lives of Charles Etienne Saint-Valery Bon, Charles Bon, and Joe Christmas. The major thematic concern is with the formulation and destruction of their personalities by the community.

Chapter Five, "Comic Maneuverings and Gestures of Confrontation," deals with numerous individuals and the manner in which each conducts himself in his associations with the community. Emphasis is also placed upon each character's originality and self-perception. Attention is given to the social rituals of racial encounters, and to the way in which certain characters defy those rituals in their efforts to assert their individualities.

Chapter Six, "Dilsey: Her Touch with Time," is a discussion of the character of Dilsey Gibson in The Sound and the Fury. It examines her spiritual essence and her relationship to absolute, relative, and mechanical time. She is also discussed with reference to the major characters of the novel and in relation to what she suggests about Faulkner's ultimate beliefs.

The Appendix, "The Compassion and the Grief: Life Outside the Fiction," is a chronological interpretation of Faulkner's extrafictional remarks about the racial situation. The focus is upon the development of Faulkner's public attitude toward blacks. [Order No. 77-4796; 308 pages. DAI, 37A (March-April, 1977), 5831.]

355 Black Characters in Faulkner's Fiction / Janet Leah Steffen PIEPER, University of Nebraska at Lincoln, 1976 (James L. Roberts).

In Faulkner's fictional Yoknapatawpha County, blacks outnumber whites in a ratio of nearly 3:2 (there are 9,313 Negroes and 6,298 whites); yet of the nearly thirteen hundred named characters created by Faulkner, only about one hundred and fifty are black. Most of these are cooks, gardeners, porters, or other menial laborers. Faulkner obviously reflected his white Southern milieu; he said every writer had to write "out of what he knows. . . . It has nothing to do with how much of it I might believe or disbelieve--it's just there." Although Ralph Ellison has praised Faulkner for breaking away from the Negro stereotypes, a close study of black characters reveals that Faulkner's attempts to individualize Negroes were infrequent and not always successful.

Faulkner's description of Lucas Beauchamp's temporary change from Negro to "nigger" (Lucas became "not Negro but nigger. . . enveloping himself in an aura of timeless and stupid impassivity almost like a smell") serves as a point of departure for discussing black characters. Negroes--fully developed fictional characters--are rare in Faulkner's work; most of the Blacks are unobtrusive "niggers," using Faulkner's description of Lucas. Often these "niggers" are stereotyped with cliché references to rolling white eyeballs, a characteristic smell, or a frightened look. Faulkner left many black characters nameless (while he named a larger proportion of white characters), and he also used black characters more often than whites in groups--almost like herds of animals to be shifted about like masses of puppets.

When Faulkner did avoid stereotyping, some interesting characters emerged. Joe Christmas in Light in August, who never finds out if he has any black blood, nevertheless suffers the psychological and physical consequences of extremists' actions--both racist and antiracist. Sam Fathers, who has both black and Indian blood, seems to epitomize a primitivism not usually found in Faulkner's white characters; he is almost a high priest of the wilderness. Other "primitive" Blacks exhibit different traditional--almost cliché--characteristics: child-like speech and habits; animal-like tendencies; supposedly "natural" sexual responses; unusual reactions to grief and fear.

The most fascinating black characters, however, are the "superblacks." Lucas Beauchamp is one example. He is referred to as a better man than his white employers, and in "The Fire and the Hearth," he succeeds in a superhuman effort to cross flood-swollen rivers to get a doctor for Zack Edmonds' wife, only to find that Zack's wife has died in childbirth and Lucas' wife has moved to the plantation house to nurse the motherless baby as well as her own baby. Lucas is patient for six months; then he demands that his wife be returned to him, though he has to risk being shot at by--or having to shoot-- Edmonds.

Dilsey in The Sound and the Fury is another example of superpatience, and she also has a religious faith that gives her a sense of eternity ("I seed de beginnin, en now I sees de endin") exhibited by no other character--black or white. Other examples are Nancy Mannigoe, martyred former "dopefiend nigger whore" in Requiem for a Nun, who murders Temple Drake's baby to keep Temple from running off with a lover; Ned McCaslin in The Reivers, who stands up to the police and watches over Lucius Priest; and Parsham (Possum) Hood in The Reivers, who can talk to heaven "as one man of decency and intelligence to another."

When Faulkner developed black characters in any detail, he sometimes over-emphasized either primitive or super-human racial elements. He could not, after all, avoid the white Southern attitudes that existed in Mississippi.

An Appendix lists the black characters and gives a brief description of each. [Order No. 76-25,887; 149 pages. DAI, 37A (Nov.-Dec. 1976), 2877.]

356 The Raging Impotence: Humor in the Novels of Dostoevsky, Faulkner, and Beckett / Assunta Sarnacchiaro PISANI, Brown University, 1976 (Arnold L. Weinstein).

This dissertation is an analysis of humor of frenzy of implosion and explosion, in the novels of Dostoevsky, Faulkner, and Beckett. It is organized in three main sections each dealing respectively with the three authors, preceded by an introductory chapter on definitions for humor and the comic, and followed by a discussion that brings the three writers together. Dostoevsky's The Devils, Faulkner's The Hamlet, and Beckett's trilogy (Molloy, Malone meurt, and L'Innommable) are used as paradigms for the study; such an approach provides both a separate, in-depth reading of the novels in question, and the basis for an approach to the works of the three authors in this light.

Though the well-known classifications and definitions of humor and comedy--especially those of Pirandello, Bergson, Freud, and the German romantics--are taken into account, the main concern of this study is to look at humor in its relationship to impotence and to the tension and rage that result from it. Aside from its philosophical and psychological implications, humor is thus seen as becoming an increasingly physiological phenomenon, in some ways regaining its ancient and Renaissance dimension.

All three novelists work mainly with different levels and manifestations of impotence, generally to a degree that informs every aspect of their novels. The impotence and the resulting rage gives rise to the characters' frenzied style of living and expression. Their failure to communicate, to establish meaningful human contact is the most central manifestation of impotence in these novels. In Dostoevsky this is shown both as a failure on a private basis of exchange between two people and as a public failure in the scandal scenes. Characters are rejected and ridiculed and this causes a state of implosion in many, especially the dignified characters, and explosion in others, especially the buffoons, who generally provoke scandals and turn serious meetings into carnivals.

Communication becomes more problematic for Faulkner's characters and here impotence results predominantly in implosion, with fewer carnivalistic occasions to provoke an explosion. Generally, Faulkner's characters are a further elaboration of Dostoevsky's dignified characters; they exist in a state of impotent rage throughout, without the possibilities of release.

In Beckett, failure of communication reaches the well-known extremes of resorting to a sign language to express need for the very minimal objects of survival. Beckett's characters, like Dostoevsky's buffoons, choose explosion as an outlet for the rage to which their physical and mental impotence gives rise. They are involved in fabulation not only, like the buffoons, to the extent that it becomes their reason for being, but also to the point that their very existence comes to depend on it.

Comic and humorous effects are achieved as a result of the tension and rage, the implosion and explosion of the characters. The comic effects, generally seen as the temporary release of tension for the reader, in the frantic atmosphere of the novels are subsumed by the humorous effects which work, instead, in accumulating tension. This tension is gradually or suddenly relayed to the reader who becomes an increasingly greater victim of it as fiction moves from the 19th century with Dostoevsky to the 20th century with Faulkner and Beckett.

The direction of attempted communication and contact, on a character-to-character basis in Dostoevsky, is transformed in Faulkner and especially in Beckett into a character-to-reader exchange, where the clowns, unlike Dostoevsky's buffoon, cannot profit from an immediate audience. Thus the reader of Beckett's works replaces entirely the audience of a Dostoevskian scandal. The release of humors, which depended on the internal workings of the text in Dostoevsky, comes to depend increasingly through Faulkner and to Beckett on an exchange between text and reader. [Order No. 77-14,176; 277 pages. DAI, 38A (July-Aug. 1977), 248-49.]

357 Characters in Crisis: Communication and the Idea of Self in Faulkner / Deborah Lynn ROBBINS, Northwestern University, 1976.

Several of Faulkner's protagonists are engaged in a crisis of self-definition. Loss, rejection, or the failure of codes of value have shaken characters like Joe Christmas, Quentin Compson, and Darl Bundren out of a sure sense of who and what they are; exposed, and desperate for external confirmation, these characters in crisis strive to achieve a validating contact beyond the self. Their fundamental motivation is to make a mark on minds that will testify to their own unique existence.

In the world of the novels such contact is virtually impossible, not just for the alienated protagonists, but for all Faulkner's people. The individual is trapped in the isolation of subjective consciousness; the experience he is moved to express to others is ineffably personal. The failure of communication is a persistent motif in As I Lay Dying, The Sound and the Fury, Light in August, Absalom, Absalom!, and The Hamlet. Words, actions, gestures-- all prove to be inadequate to close the distance between self and self. Faulkner is more interested, however, in the psychology of his obsessive talkers and gesturers than in whether they succeed or fail in their efforts to communicate. He uses his characters in crisis to explore the process of communication as a means of dynamic self-creation.

Following an introduction, Chapter I, "The Tellers and the Tale," considers the narrators of Absalom, Absalom! as articulate competitors in a contest for self-validation. In telling Sutpen's story each narrator in effect tells his own and seeks to win recognition from his audience. Language is on trial in Absalom, Absalom! as a medium for effecting such a vital contact, and this chapter examines Faulkner's own attitude toward the power and limitations of his medium.

In Chapter II, "Trying to Say," the efforts of Benjy Compson, Ike Snopes, and Jim Bond to break through the barrier of idiocy are seen as primitive attempts toward self-definition. Idiocy becomes a metaphor for the isolation of all of Faulkner's characters, and the struggle of the idiots to assert themselves in contact with other people serves as a paradigm of the urgent need for and immense difficulty of communication in the novels.

Chapter III, "Language as Bulwark and Barrier," interprets Quentin Compson and Darl Bundren as beleaguered speakers who use words to establish and defend concepts of self and world. The self-justifying rhetoric of Gail Hightower and others is shown to block the awareness of vulnerability that compels the characters in crisis to seek ratifying communication.

Chapter IV, "The Faulknerian Gesture," presents Joe Christmas, Addie Bundren, and others as enactors of jeopardized identities, while Jewel Bundren is shown to be a man of action who is incapable of the focused gesture of self-definition. The final chapter, "The Eye of the Storm" considers Lena

Grove and Dilsey Gibson as serene foils to these characters in crisis: their tranquil natures provide a tonal resolution in novels where a genuine resolution is not possible. The experiential, imaginative, and, in Lena's case, moral limitations of the two reflect Faulkner's commitment to his characters in crisis and to the idea of self-creation dramatically embodied in their struggles to communicate. [Order No. 77-10,084; 230 pages. DAI, 37A (May-June 1977), 7132.]

358 The Evolution of Patterns of Characterization from Faulkner's Soldiers' Pay (1926) Through Absalom, Absalom! (1936) / Stella P. SMITH, Texas Tech University, 1976 (Mary Sue Carlock).

Although Soldiers' Pay has received little attention from scholarly critics, it is a seminal novel in which Faulkner developed patterns of characterization which have served as prototypes for characters in the ensuing decade. In Soldiers' Pay, Faulkner created eight patterns of characterization, and they fall into three groupings.

First, there are the male supporting characters: the good men in motion, the good men in stasis, and the villain. Since motion, energy, change, the good man in his novels is often a man of energy who fights evil. Joe Gilligan is the prototype for such a man, and Cash Bundren and Byron Bunch are developments of the same idea. The three are small, nondescript men, kind, unassuming, and humble, capable of selfless love. They exemplify the Christian virtues. Also good men are Dr. Mahon, Horace Benbow, Jason Compson III, and Gail Hightower; but they are ineffectual. Highly educated, with an affinity for the traditional, they are at a disadvantage in an antitraditional society. Dr. Mahon loves his rose bush and his church spire, Horace his almost perfect little vases, Mr. Compson his Latin poets and bottle of bourbon, and Gail Hightower his fabricated vision. The third category, the villain, is personified by Januarius Jones, who anticipates the characterizations of Byron Snopes, Jason Compson IV, and Popeye Vitelli. Jones denies the human and desecrates nature, as do the others.

Second, there are the women: the flapper, the brave young war widow, the unsophisticated child of nature, and the enduring servant. Cecily Saunders, the flapper, is the prototype for Temple Drake. Margaret Powers' characterization anticipates those of Drusilla Hawk and Judith Sutpen. Emmy, the unsophisticated child of nature, is a naiad (a water nymph) and a tomboy, and from this pattern in the future come Patricia Robyn, Dewey Dell Bundren, and the incomparable Lena Grove. The last of the patterns for women is that of Callie, Donald Mahon's Negro mammy, who is surely taken from Faulkner's own Mammy Callie, and who is the prototype for Louvinia and for his most admirable creation, Dilsey.

Finally there is Donald Mahon, the returned soldier, the young man with the mortal wound, whose character is created with the help of three metaphors: the faun, the centaur, and the gull. Mirroring his faunlike qualities are the Civil War Bayard Sartoris and the First World War Johnny Sartoris, and Gordon the sculptor. Participating in the metaphor of the mechanized centaur are the Civil War John Sartoris and the First World War Bayard Sartoris. Those characters coming after Donald who are also gulled by Time and Circumstance are Quentin Compson and Thomas Sutpen.

Faulkner's central concern in Soldiers' Pay, as it was throughout his work, is the problem of evil. His characters define themselves in their reaction to evil and its subsequent grief and suffering. Good consists in those old verities of the human heart listed in the Nobel Prize speech; evil is in their opposites. Man prevails by his acceptance of suffering and his affirmation of the dignity of the human spirit. [Order No. 76-23,907; 244 pages. DAI, 37A (Nov.-Dec. 1976), 2881.]

359 The Darkening Window: Four Problematic American Novels / George Edward TOLES, University of Virginia, 1976 (Alan Howard).

The novels examined in this dissertation are Charles Brockden Brown's Edgar Huntly, Herman Melville's Pierre, Mark Twain's Puddn'head Wilson, and William Faulkner's Sanctuary. Each of these works, with the exception of Edgar Huntly, has received a great deal of intelligent critical attention, and the recognition that these novels are somehow "problematic" is by no means a new one. Leslie Fiedler and other critics have suggested that the novels I'm treating have a similar status as "flawed, but interesting" experiments within the respective careers of their authors. While I would not disagree with this assessment, I would nevertheless question its implication that our awareness of the flawed elements in any of these novels can be clearly separated from our response to what we find interesting and valuable in them. My method of dealing with novels I judge to be "problematic," therefore, departs from that of other critics in my efforts to show how it is precisely the unstable, disordered material in them--what T. S. Eliot, in his Hamlet essay, referred to as the "intractable stuff" that hasn't quite been "manipulated into art"-- which gives them their power and peculiar fascination.

Throughout this study, I attempt to do justice to the mysterious intensity and beauty of certain kinds of failure in a work of art. My starting point is the assumption that each work under consideration was the product of a creative period of exceptional stress, in which the writer's mind was brought close to the breaking point, unable to find a vocabulary or imaginative situation expansive enough to fully render (much less resolve) the mass of contradictory impulses it was struggling with.

All four novelists are centrally concerned, in their different states of crisis, with the failure or inadequacy of a particular mode of vision. Brown's Edgar Huntly, the first American novel to discover the full potential for Gothic horror lurking in the woods and caverns of the virgin landscape, restlessly fluctuates between two equally extreme and distressing forms of "seeing": nature is either viewed from a state of utter passivity, in which case it appears as a vague, undifferentiated mass, or it overstimulates the eye, so that isolated features of the landscape achieve an obsessive clarity which gives them too strong a hold on the imagination, and permits nothing beyond themselves to register there. Melville's Pierre depicts a kind of gorgonizing vision in which all human relations, "abstract faiths," and spiritual ideals are gradually turned into stone. Twain's Puddn'head Wilson dramatizes the author's partly unconscious relinquishing of his romantic vision of the Hannibal world of his childhood. Finally, Faulkner's Sanctuary established the twisted vision of the impotent voyeur as the appropriate, and perhaps inescapable, way of "seeing things" in an affectless modern cityscape.

With each of these novels, I attempt to distinguish carefully between these conflicts and forms of imaginative tension which serve a clear function, either thematically or stylistically, and those which seem to block or seriously interfere with the emergence of a coherent fictive world. I argue that the creative vision in each of these novels is both deformed and "necessarily incomplete," and that a sensitive examination of these "flaws in the crystal" is absolutely essential to understand what the works are communicating. The chapters of the dissertation are conceived not as fully unified interpretations, but as lengthy meditations on (or, to be more precise, exploratory probes into) a series of problems raised by certain representative passages in each novel. [Order No. 76-22,880; 211 pages. DAI, 37A (Jan.-Feb. 1977), 4378.]

360 A Methodology for the Study of Philosophy in Literature: Philosophy and Symbol in Selected Works of William Faulkner and Thomas Mann / Richard Evan ZIEGFELD, University of Texas at Austin, 1976 (A. Leslie Willson).

The dissertation is divided into four sections. In the first section a brief historical sketch delineates rampant critical confusion which has produced no organized and tested methodology for studying the philosophy that is contained in some literature. Definitions of terms (philosophy, literature, and symbol) and methodological suggestions follow.

Symbol is suggested as a methodological key for explicating such literature. Although symbol sometimes functions only as a representation of a concept that has already been presented explicitly (it reflects), the symbol may also crystallize abstract material, provide essential material where a dearth previously existed, or function as a catalyst between the material that is to be embodied and the embodiment. To whatever extent symbol functions as a bridge between subject matter and embodiment (or the abstract and the concrete) it is an outstanding tool, because the relationship between philosophy and literature is often characterized in the same terms.

The methodological suggestions are tested in selected works of two authors who write profoundly but in noticeably different fashions--William Faulkner and Thomas Mann. The second section (Chapter Two) focuses on the inchoate discovery of philosophy and symbol in the early works. The fourth section (Chapter Seven) focuses on the later works in which a startling development occurs: the author's symbolic techniques continue to develop, but the philosophies do not. An evaluation of the methodology is also included in the fourth section.

The third and most important section (Chapters Three through Six) concerns the stage of mature control in which philosophical issues are incorporated in masterful fashion. The four texts selected for close scrutiny include The Sound and the Fury; Absalom, Absalom!; Light in August; and The Magic Mountain. The third section is divided into chapters on time, epistemology, reality, and man's state (free will, the nature of being, and the attitude toward death). Some of the symbols under investigation include broken watches, the mountain location, letters, x-ray photographs, shadows, snow storm, snow, dreams, circles and paths, séances, style and narrative structure that function symbolically, and doors that open and shut (include and exclude).

The discoveries about particular symbols such as shadows and doors demonstrate an axiom: in numerous instances these writers render their philosophical conceptions in such an indirect fashion (through a symbolic statement that unifies the writer's conceptions) that if the reader does not explicate symbol he is left with isolated fragments of the writer's position. Symbol may be used to reveal the philosophical content of a literary text, or it may be used as a heuristic device to study how philosophy and literature interact. Moreover, given that an author's symbolic technique usually evolves, the critic may also use symbol to investigate the evolutionary development of the philosophy that is incorporated into various texts during an author's career. Symbol functions as an essential tool for the study of the philosophical element of the works of two prominent writers and may consequently be considered successful within a particular paradigm. [Order No. 77-4005; 294 pages. DAI, 37A (Jan.-Feb. 1977), 5105.

361 Faulkner's Early Heroines / Philip Dubuisson Castille, Tulane University, 1977 (Richard P. Adams).

The Sound and the Fury, William Faulkner's fourth published novel, has been judged by many critics to be his best work. However, none of the three far less accomplished novels which Faulkner wrote before it seems to anticipate its achievement. The relation of The Sound and the Fury to these three apprentice novels is a major problem in the study of Faulkner's work and career, and it is this critical issue which I examine in my dissertation.

The most crucial character in The Sound and the Fury is Candace Compson, whom Faulkner regarded as the heroine of the book. Caddy's story is at the core of the narrative and her actions are the mainspring of the plot. I believe that Faulkner's breakthrough in The Sound and the Fury is directly related to his success in characterizing Caddy and in dramatizing her ruin. In this dissertation I try to clarify the nature and function of the role she plays in The Sound and the Fury by viewing her in relation to her predecessors, the heroines of Faulkner's first three novels. I argue that Caddy's characterization bears a close kinship to the characterizations of Emmy in Soldiers' Pay, Jenny Steinbauer in Mosquitoes, and Narcissa Benbow Sartoris in Flags in the Dust.

All of these female characters share mythic traits and properties. Faulkner endows each of his early heroines with attributes associated with the ancient fertility goddesses of western Asia Minor. He draws upon sources as Sir James George Frazer's The Golden Bough in order to enrich their characterizations. Like Eliot and Joyce, Faulkner uses "the mythical method"-- the technique of establishing ironic parallels between the significant past and the chaotic present--to portray the disorder and decay of contemporary life. In the world of Faulkner's early novels the modern goddess of life and love is neither acknowledged nor reverenced, but is in fact denied and abused. As a result her potential for creating and sustaining life is severely restricted, and the modern community falls into decline and desolation.

My purpose in this dissertation is to show that, even from the beginning of his career as a prose writer, Faulkner portrayed heroines who are at odds with their culture. By examining The Sound and the Fury in relation to Faulkner's first three novels, I try to show that the story of Caddy Compson represents a crystallization of Faulkner's efforts in his apprentice fiction to depict the plight of vital women trapped in a sterile society. [Order No. 77-20,200; 201 pages. DAI, 38A (Sept.-Oct. 1977), 2121.]

362 Faulkner, Stasis, and Keats' "Ode on a Grecian Urn" / Hilayne E. CAVANAUGH, University of Nebraska at Lincoln, 1977 (Charles W. Mignon).

According to William Faulkner's Paris Review interview, which Malcolm Cowley believes was less an "interview" than a piece composed by Faulkner alone for his friend Jean Stein, the aim of the artist is to arrest motion and hold it fixed so that it might be preserved to move again in the future. Elsewhere in the "interview," Faulkner acknowledges, as he does in a number of other statements, the importance of Keats' "Ode on a Grecian Urn." Since Keats' poem is in fact an example of motion and life arrested and preserved for future contemplation, it is not difficult to see why Faulkner valued the Ode or why he refers to it so frequently in his work and why it appears often as a model for the imagery of stasis.

In the introduction to this study, the various references to the "Ode on a Grecian Urn" that occur in Faulkner's poetry, short stories, and novels are identified. While there is no consistent pattern of imagery or allusions to the Ode, it is to be found, with varying concentration, in "The Hill," "Poem X" of A Green Bough, "Out of Nazareth," Mosquitoes, As I Lay Dying, Light in August, Requiem for a Nun, The Hamlet, and The Mansion.

Chapter One examines the composite portrait of Narcissa Benbow Sartoris, who appears in Flags in the Dust, Sanctuary, and "There Was a Queen." In Flags Narcissa is called by her brother Horace "the unravished bride of quietude," which links her with Keats' Ode and identifies her as a personification of the Urn itself. Unique in Faulkner's writing, Narcissa is developed through three works with increasing complexity, at first somewhat ambiguously as "serene" and consuming in Flags, then as a shrewish commentator on the morality of others and as part of the pattern of total moral degeneration in Sanctuary, and finally in "There Was a Queen" as a thorough hypocrite determined to preserve at any price her self-concept as an honorable woman. But because of the early association of Narcissa with the "Ode on a Grecian Urn," she must be measured against the truth and beauty concept of the poem. What emerges from the three works is a rich, brutal, and ironic portrait of a selfish and self-destructive woman.

In the second chapter, Isaac McCaslin in Go Down, Moses, is analyzed in light of Keats' Ode, which is read to him as a young boy by his cousin McCaslin Edmonds. More than anywhere else in his writing, Faulkner makes integral use of the Ode in Section IV of "The Bear," and to a lesser but important extent in "The Old People" and "Delta Autumn." Appropriately, much of "The Bear" and its two companion stories are rendered in static imagery. In addition to the moral and aesthetic importance the Ode has on Ike's life, it influences him to halt and preserve the significant moments in his life, in particular the hunting experiences he has with Sam Fathers, and lock them in his memory. What begins as a consolation for Ike's not having killed the bear, the message of the Ode, which he misunderstands, becomes a way to resist the forces of life. Ike's stultifying obsession with his woods experiences so paralyzes him that he is prevented from performing any important action in his life, even though his youthful humanitarian impulses suggest that he will assume a role of moral leadership. Like so many others in Faulkner's fiction, Ike as an adult can do nothing but dwell on the past, resist the present, and disregard the future. The paradox of the "Ode on a Grecian Urn" is resolved with regard to Ike McCaslin in recalling Faulkner's words that "life is motion," thus showing that the message of the Urn and the frozen life it portrays is literally negative and dead. [Order No. 77-23,129; 136 pages. DAI, 38A (Nov.-Dec. 1977), 2783-84.]

363 The Secular Imagination: The Continuity of the Secular Romantic Tradition of Wordsworth and Keats in Stevens, Faulkner, Roethke, and Bellow / Allan Richard CHAVKIN, University of Illinois at Urbana-Champaign, 1977 (Jack Stillinger).

The study explores the continuity of a major English romantic tradition, the secular romanticism of Wordsworth and Keats, in four major twentieth-century writers. A detailed discussion of the seminal works of Wallace Stevens, William Faulkner, Theodore Roethke, and Saul Bellow shows how these writers assimilate, transform, and extend the romantic sensibility of Wordsworth and Keats. The first two chapters define and explain this secular romantic tradition, its difference from the two other romantic traditions of existential romanticism and visionary romanticism (Chapter I), and the renovating power of the secular imagination and the functioning of "spots of time" in "the poem of the mind in the act of finding what will suffice" (Chapter II), while subsequent chapters take up the individual twentieth-century writers, briefly noting their specific debts to Wordsworth and Keats but mainly concentrating upon their dynamic absorption of the two older writers. "Sunday Morning," "The Idea of Order at Key West," "No Possum, No Sop, No Taters," Absalom, Absalom!, "Meditations of an Old Woman," and Herzog are examined in Chapters III-VI.

We are still suffering from a warped view of twentieth-century literature as a result of the lingering anti-romantic prejudice of T.S. Eliot, Ezra Pound, and the imagists, who, in their zeal to revitalize a literature stagnating in late Victorian imitation-romanticism, caricatured romanticism as softminded, thereby causing subsequent critics to ignore the crucial role of English romanticism in the development of modern literature. The present essay helps correct this distorted view by showing the centrality of the concept of the Wordsworthian non-transcendental imagination throughout the twentieth century. Since the purpose of the Wordsworthian imagination is to search for an earthly affirmation in an earthly manner, I call this imagination the secular imagination, and writers who use this imagination, secular romantics. The secular imagination renovates the individual in "spots of time," heightened moments in which the mind creates meaning in an intrinsically meaningless world and illumination blazes up from "the dreary intercourse of daily life." The mind has the awesome power to transform reality into something emotionally satisfying as well as defend itself against its own abysmal depths of extreme self-consciousness, existential nothingness, and madness. [Order No. 7803954; 204 pages. DAI, 38A (March-April 1978), 6129.]

364 Sinbad in New Orleans: Early Short Fiction by William Faulkner--An Annotated Edition / Leland Holcombe COX, Jr., University of South Carolina, 1977 (James B. Meriwether).

The central purpose of this edition is to make available certain early prose writings by William Faulkner in a more reliable text than has heretofore been possible. Rather than reprint all of Faulkner's prose compositions up until the publication of Soldiers' Pay--his first novel--in 1926, it was decided to limit that present edition to a body of early short fiction which Faulkner himself conceived as a series, the separate parts of which first began appearing in the Sunday supplement to the New Orleans Times-Picayune and in the Double Dealer little magazine in 1925. The titles of the stories comprising the series were subsumed at different times under two general titles: "Sinbad in New Orleans" and "The Mirror of Chartres Street." The first of these general titles appears to have been an editorial invention. Thus, "Sinbad in New Orleans" has been retained as the title for this edition.

To give some indication of the breadth and depth of Faulkner's reading at this early stage of his career--as well as to provide a literary, historical, and cultural backdrop against which his early short fiction may be read--all of the seventeen stories that are printed here have been annotated. Further, as a corrective to what has become a critical commonplace among the scholars who have given their attention to the wellsprings of Faulkner's career as a novelist--that his early writing is either mere hack work or significant only in its anticipation of later fiction--a general introduction to the stories has been included. No exorbitant claims are made. Rather, the argument is advanced that, upon reasonably close examination, these seventeen stories appear to have some intrinsic artistic merits of their own.

The typescript and manuscript authority upon which this edition is based is outlined in the textual introduction and the note on the text. Detailed textual data are contained in textual appendices A through E. The reader seeking opportunities for further study in the field--and their number is legion--is referred to the bibliographies of manuscript and typescript material, and of the literary, historical, and philosophical works which have been examined as possible influences on William Faulkner's early writings. [Order No. 77-22,404; 364 pages. DAI, 38A (Sept.-Oct. 1977), 2122.]

365 William Faulkner: The Search for Reality / Patrick Gerald EAGLIN, Harvard University, 1977 (Alan Heimert), no DAI entry.

366 Plot Materials and Narrative Form in Faulkner's Early Fiction / Jeffrey Jay FOLKS, Indiana University, 1977 (James H. Justus).

In his early fiction William Faulkner arrived at an aesthetic conception of narrative form which was heavily shaped by the specific nature of plot material which he was incorporating. While Faulkner had always sought to imitate the unity and organic form of the dramatic novel, he was also pursuing his interests in the direction of popular culture, local storytelling, and extra-literary sources. In this dissertation the effect of the introduction of diverse narrative materials on Faulkner's aesthetic conception of plot is traced. Although the primary purpose of this study is not to investigate sources and influences, numerous sources for Faulkner's plots are discussed in an effort to arrive at a critical understanding of the aesthetic conception of plot and action in the early fiction.

Within the formal requirements of the dramatic novel William Faulkner consistently incorporated subliterary and extraliterary materials, thus extending the range of the dramatic novel beyond its previous limits with regard to certain types of plot and character. The study of plot materials and narrative form in the early fiction establishes a continuous interrelationship between literary form and subliterary material, and it demonstrates that the process of shaping an aesthetic conception of narrative to include both dramatic novel form and diverse plot material had been taking place since the beginning of Faulkner's apprenticeship. The partial failure of Mosquitoes and Soldiers' Pay is shown to result, in part, from the author's inexperience at incorporating diverse plot materials into a dramatic novel structure, but also from the absence of an aesthetic conception of dramatic novel which incorporates subliterary and extraliterary materials. However, the attempts to shape an aesthetic model for the introduction of diverse narrative materials within a conventional literary form are studied in order to provide critical insight into the structure of Faulkner's early fiction.

This study of the apprenticeship fiction concludes that William Faulkner was drawing more heavily on American subliterary and extraliterary sources, and on those American literary figures who also drew on diverse plot materials, than he was on European fiction, which may have provided models for innovative fictional techniques but not for the incorporation of diverse narrative materials. Soldiers' Pay is treated as a novel in which conventional fictional plot structures are employed alongside subliterary and extraliterary plot material, but in this first novel plot material does not adequately determine narrative form. Mosquitoes continues to introduce a large number of subliterary and extraliterary elements, yet the plot structure is only slightly affected by the material. Only with Flags in the Dust does Faulkner begin to resolve sufficiently the problem of incorporating diverse plot material within the formal structure of the dramatic novel. [Order No. 7805631; 261 pages. DAI, 38A (May-June 1978), 6724.]

367 Changes in the Novel: A Structuralist Comparison of Middlemarch, The Confidence-Man, and Absalom, Absalom! / Sarah Holland HOLDEN, Rice University, 1977 (Walter Isle).

Between mid-nineteenth century and early twentieth century, the British and American novel changed drastically. Using an approach that focuses on the reader's experience, this thesis closely analyzes three novels--Middlemarch, The Confidence-Man, and Absalom, Absalom!--to describe changes in structure, in concept of language and stylistic practice, and in the author-reader relationship.

Following an introductory chapter, the second chapter compares the structures of the three novels. Ferdinand de Saussure's distinction between paradigmatic and syntagmatic structures points to some differences. One sees a shift from the primarily syntagmatic structure of Middlemarch to the paradigmatic structures of The Confidence-Man and Absalom, Absalom! Although Eliot develops her characters using a blend of syntagmatic and paradigmatic structures, her emphasis is on the syntagmatic. The Confidence-Man can be seen as a transitional work in that it shows characteristics of both centuries; however, even though it was written before Middlemarch, its paradigmatic structure is closer to twentieth-century structures. Another concept useful in discussing structure is Gerard Genette's identification of three levels in narrative discourse--histoire, récit, and narration. His terminology helps distinguish between the structures created by the author and those created by the reader; the récit is the work of the author, while the histoire and the narration are abstractions constructed by the reader as he tries to make sense of the novel.

Changes in style and concept of language also create more responsibility for the reader. Chapter III discusses how words, for Eliot, are referential while for Melville and Faulkner they are symbolic and transformational. Syntax also changes: Eliot's syntax is clear and direct; Melville's is confusing and involuted; Faulkner's is innovative and idiosyncratic in its use of repetition and oxymoron. The sophistication of technique in twentieth-century novels is an end in itself; by contrast, in Middlemarch technique is always subordinate to character development.

Changes in the author-reader relationship, as Chapter IV shows, also lead to more decision-making from the reader. Eliot's authorial narration directs the reader, controlling his vision of the novel's meanings. Through constant qualification and contradiction, Melville's voice confuses the reader, making him search for meanings. The third person narrator of Absalom, Absalom! is impersonal; he does not seem aware of an audience and suggests no moral applications to the reader's world. As a consequence, the reader decides whether to apply his experience of the novel to his life. Eliot clearly shows her own moral values while The Confidence-Man's darkness shows a lack of certainty which creates ambivalence in the reader. Rather than giving his personal judgments, Faulkner seems interested in showing how characters (and, by implication, people) come to create their own sense of what is true and real.

What changes most in the transition from nineteenth-century to twentieth-century modes of writing is the reader's responsibility for making decisions about meaning. Changes in structure, in concepts of language, and the author-reader relationship contribute to the change. [Order No. 77-19,264; 181 pages. DAI, 38A (Sept.-Oct. 1977), 1409.]

368 Endure and Prevail: Faulkner's Social Outcasts / Evelyn JAFFE, University of Colorado at Boulder, 1977 (James K. Folsom).

This dissertation investigates William Faulkner's use of socially outcast characters to develop themes of endurance. It came to my attention when reading criticism of Faulkner that there was no significant work on Faulkner's notions of "endure" and "prevail" (that dominate his Nobel Prize Acceptance Speech, other late oratorical statements, and A Fable.) I decided to study the development of these ideas through his career, and found that Faulkner's view of endurance underwent significant changes between Soldiers' Pay and The Reivers, with the positive Nobel Prize Speech sentiments emerging after the Second World War.

In my introduction, I trace the different facets of endurance that develop between the Waste Land years and the post-Hiroshima, apocalyptic ones. I also discuss the influence of the tension between Modernism and American Romanticism on Faulkner's ideas about man's ability to survive, endure, or prevail. This unresolved tension, which dominates many novels and characters, leads to a multi-sided view of endurance in Faulkner's fiction as opposed to the primarily positive statements upon receiving the Nobel Prize.

With the problem of endurance defined, I turned to a study of character to see how the individual, in his day-to-day life, can meet the challenge of modern life. In looking at Faulkner's novels and short stories, I found that his ideas about man's ability "to endure" and "to prevail" are unified by people outside mainstream society. By studying Faulkner's presentation of poor whites, criminals, Blacks, and women separately, I discovered that these people could be linked together thematically. Like the fool in King Lear, the outcast senses the weaknesses in society's structure but is powerless to correct them. The suggestion is that if society could see itself through the eyes of the outsider, it could better itself. But society rejects the outcast because the pain of recognizing its faults is too great, and the outcast's only recourse is the preservation of individual integrity.

Because other critics focused on only one group--either poor whites, Blacks, or women (no significant work had been done on criminals)--I studied all of the groups in depth, concentrating on the human qualities which strengthen individual characters. I noted the attributes of individuals in each group, relating their qualities of endurance to those of the other socially outcast people. This cross-reference suggests that man's strength lies in his acceptance of shared responsibility, and these outcast figures succeed through the preservation of a humanistic value system and through the retention of individual dignity. From this vantage point, they counter man's weaknesses with the inner strength necessary to bear the burden of their humanity.

This study of Faulkner's people on society's fringes confirms his growing concern with mankind's ultimate salvation. With the qualities he notes in these social outcasts--humor, compassion, forgiveness, dignity, integrity, love, and moral action--mankind will not merely survive or endure; it will prevail. [Order No. 77-24,232; 210 pages. DAI, 38A (Nov.-Dec. 1977), 2789-90.]

369 Faulkner's Sartoris: A Comprehensive Study / Merle Wallace KEISER, New York University, 1977 (James W. Tuttleton).

This dissertation is a comprehensive study of William Faulkner's third novel, Sartoris, with emphasis upon setting, structure, themes, characters, and style. It contains also a review of the cutting of the Flags papers to form the novel published as Sartoris in 1929. With assistance from the biography of Faulkner by Joseph Blotner, the 1973 edition of Flags in the Dust by Douglas Day, the bibliographical dissertations by Stephen Neal Dennis and Melvin Reed Roberts, as well as from other critical and historical materials, the dissertation makes a fresh assessment of Sartoris.

The complexity of the novel, its diffuse nature and crowded condition, results from Faulkner's attempt to picture the stream of life. He complicates the creation of the illusion of reality by using the method of reality itself, which method he explains with his metaphor of "thirteen ways of looking at a blackbird." The reader, in making the "fourteenth image," must sift the raw data, along with the characters, and judge the worth of the reflecting consciousnesses. If one understands, for example, that the first twenty-four pages of Sartoris unroll for the reader through the musing of old Bayard, the "Carolina" Bayard story becomes comprehensible as the romantic embroideries of Miss Jenny mixed with the biases and prejudices of old Bayard.

Sartoris possesses a poetical structure incapable of logical analysis, although it was wrought by a painstaking craftsman who put his materials through fifteen identifiable levels of revision. Poetically, the shape of the novel is that of polarity and tension and accommodation. Careful examination reveals also the geometric forms: the circle, the line, and the web. The circle represents concrete time with its circadian rhythms and progression of the seasons; the line, abstract time with its yesterday, today, and tomorrow strung like beads on a string; and the web, the interrelatedness of the human community.

In the artistic design of the novel, the elements of structure, themes, characterizations, and style penetrate and permeate each other as if in concrete, heterogeneous time. Thus, the novel accomplishes being a demonstration of its own meanings. Sartoris is a poem in prose, William Faulkner's Inferno, Paradise Lost, Old Testament hell, and classical Hades. It is a study of a small community in a fallen world as a microcosm of the human condition. It is about time and community and continuity, and some threats to these concepts facing modern man. On the other hand, there are some affirmations in those representative acts of love and hope and compassion and sacrifice, the banners in the "dust," a Mississippi country term for "dusk," or twilight. In poetic terms, the novel becomes a theory of society, with the Mississippi county a moribund, not a Utopian social model. The land and its people present, however, with the Faulknerian ambiguities, ironies, and satire playing over them, a theory of education capable of transforming the community into an integrated and slowly progressing social order.

What exercised William Faulkner and set the demon of creation upon him included greed, exploitation, and injustice. In northern Mississippi, the first settlers exploited the Indians; the aristocrats exploited the sharecroppers and the small farmers, and they all exploited the Negroes. There was no justice, and there could be none as long as there was, in Frye's words, "no power to realize the possibilities of human life." The guilt over which the author brooded stemmed from the violence and vainglory inherent in the dream of opening up the land to development; and the expiation of the guilt reaches to the third and fourth generations, and perhaps even to the fifth.

Sartoris operates on several levels, with the plot lines running close to the earth. Without exact correspondences in objective reality, classical, Biblical, Shakespearean, romantic, and modern allusions run through the novel, teasing the imagination and enlarging the meanings. A major finding of this study is that the structure and the themes of the novel rest squarely on the imagery, particularly that of the Bergson metaphors associated with time; that of decay, death, ghosts, and hell; and that of the corn and other seeds and cuttings associated with continuity. Many critics appear to have missed the unity of Sartoris, finding instead only excesses in its crowded condition and its seeming diffusion of imagery. The present study finds, however, that there is unity in diversity when the focus is on the community of Jefferson as the "little town" of Keats' "Ode on a Grecian Urn," arrested in art from the duration of "slow Time."

Sartoris is not a treatise on the "Lost Generation," or a diatribe on the "Lost Cause," or even a lament for the "Lost Eden." As a matter of fact, none of these is really lost. For Faulkner contends that the present drags along with it the past, swollen into legend and ritual, and possessing both crippling and ennobling power, and that these together prefigure the future. With change in individuals and social institutions inevitable, the implication of Sartoris is that in this twilight, or "dust" of civilization, man must direct change, consciously eliminate crippling injustice and violence, and retain the ennobling aspects of tradition, such as honor, decorum, responsibility, and neighborliness. [Order No. 7808537; 326 pages. DAI, 38A (May-June 1978), 7333-34.]

370 The Artist in Shadow: Quentin Compson in William Faulkner's The Sound and the Fury / Jimmy Lee KELLY, University of North Carolina at Chapel Hill, 1977 (Louis D. Rubin, Jr.).

The object of this study is to identify and analyze some of the key elements that entered into William Faulkner's creation of Quentin Compson and the Quentin section of The Sound and the Fury.

Quentin does not have a consistent and clear-cut voice of his own, as do Benjy and Jason, but, rather, his voice is an amalgam of many voices. In creating Quentin, Faulkner drew upon a profound knowledge of literary tradition and used extensively the voices of T. S. Eliot and James Joyce. Many of Quentin's attitudes and much of his language are an unexamined expression of the received ideas of his region. Intrenched ideas enter into his remarks on the South, blacks, family and personal honor, and social and sexual behavior. Quentin is victimized by verbal systems generated by the myths of his culture. The highly experimental nature of the Quentin section is dictated by Faulkner's desire to make prose recapitulate a tortured mind and so Quentin's voice is often an immediate rendering of his psychological state. Elements of Faulkner's own life enter strongly into his creation of Quentin. Many of Faulkner's own frustrations in love, war, and artistic ambition contribute to the portrait. Quentin's parents played a major role in shaping Quentin's thought and language.

He uses his mother's idiom as an idiom for pain and condemnation and his father's as an idiom for cynicism and disillusionment. At times these two idioms are conjoined in a linguistic process that mirrors Quentin's biological origins. Quentin also employs his brothers' idioms. Benjy's voice is the idiom for isolation and a primitive kind of poetry, while Jason's voice is the idiom for sarcasm and story-telling. Most important is the voice of the artist, a voice that closely resembles Faulkner's own. It is here that Quentin comes closest to establishing a voice and an identity of his own. Quentin consistently uses poetic devices and develops two primary sets of images, a set drawn from nature and a set that treats the problems of perception. If Quentin had recognized the artistic impulse within himself, it might have been his salvation.
[Order No. 7810468; 232 pages. DAI, 39A (July-Aug. 1978), 279-80.]

371 The Multilinear Novel: A Structural Analysis of Novels by Dos Passos, Doblin, Faulkner, and Kieppen / Kathleen Lenore KOMAR, Princeton University, 1977 (Theodore J. Ziolkowski).

This dissertation deals with twentieth-century novels in which the narrative surface is fragmented, split up into several separate lines of narration. I have labelled this type of structurally complex text the multilinear novel. My first goal is to define the multilinear novel as a literary subgenre, to describe its emergence, development, and place in literary history. My second goal is to refine methods of analyzing the fragmented structures of such texts by using narrative matrices which display the surface features of these books and enable the critic to keep the entire novel in view at one time.

This work is built upon earlier typological studies but adds to them a more detailed analysis of individual texts that exemplify different varieties of multilinearity. Chapter I examines the cultural and historical factors which provided the impetus for the emergence of multilinear novels early in this century as well as more strictly literary background such as the demise of the omniscient narrator and the abandonment of chronological sequencing and the causality implied by it. Chapters II through V present analyses of four individual texts which serve as a representative sampling of the structural possibilities of multilinearity. Chapter II concerns Dos Passos' Manhattan Transfer, an early example of multilinearity of parallel plot lines. Of the four novels under consideration, Manhattan Transfer employs the simplest multilinear structure based primarily upon a principle of repetition of specific passages, incidents, and images across the lives of many characters. In Chapter III Doblin's Berlin Alexanderplatz represents a variation of the basic multilinear type used by Dos Passos. Doblin uses parallel patterns of development in biblical and literary allusions to reinforce the central plot line of Franz Biberkipf's personal story while creating a structural dissonance by using conflicting patterns of documentary material and interpolated narratives. In As I Lay Dying, examined in Chapter IV, Faulkner reveals another variation of the multilinear model by employing two symmetrical patterns, one of the fulfillment of a mythic plot and the other of a range of human consciousness as presented in his fifteen different narrators, to create the basic axes of the novel's structure and to generate the comic and tragic tensions that torment the Bundren family. In Chapter V Koeppen's Tauben im Gras represents a return to the technique of repetition and parallel plot lines used by Dos Passos. Koeppen, however, counterbalances the darker repetition of entrapment, disillusion, and despair with the repeated life patterns of couples who succeed in personal, social, racial, and cultural reconciliations.

Finally, in the conclusion to the dissertation, I investigate what these novels share in the realms of theme, structure, and technique. I consider the replacement of a single, omniscient narrator by direct structural manipulation of the texts' characters and themes and the implications of this new form of authorial control. I then attempt to elucidate the further problems that the subgenre of multilinear novels creates for the reader and to outline more clearly the larger literary and cultural dilemmas that generated them. [Order No. 77-21,461; 190 pages. DAI, 38A (Sept.-Oct. 1977), 2101.]

372 Faulkner's Commedia: An Interpretation of The Sound and the Fury, Sanctuary, As I Lay Dying, and Light in August / Charles Lance LYDAY, Vanderbilt University, 1977 (Thomas D. Young).

Northop Frye's four-fold theory of archetypal criticism provides a useful framework for understanding four of William Faulkner's greatest novels. The Sound and the Fury illustrates the tragic movement from innocence to experience. Sanctuary belongs to the depraved world of irony and satire. As I Lay Dying exemplifies the comic movement from death to rebirth. And Light in August, although it portrays a fallen world, is best understood as a version of pastoral. Together, the four novels constitute what Frye calls the total quest myth, which rolls from birth to death and back to rebirth.

The Sound and the Fury, the tragedy of the Compson family, embodies the tragic myth but includes a variety of modes within its larger tragic vision. Benjy's section belongs to the mythos of pastoral romance; he functions as the natural man against whom the civilized man is measured and judged. Jason's section belongs to the mythos of irony and satire; he functions as the satirist who, despising the irrationality of others, is irrational himself. Quentin's section, standing between the two, belongs to the tragic mythos. Benjy and Jason embody, respectively, the "dream of innocence" and the "fact of guilt," which meet and clash within Quentin and figuratively tear him apart. The first three sections also reveal the tragedy of Caddy Compson, and the fourth section recapitulates the themes of the first three sections, ending not on a note of hope, but on a note of meaningless despair.

Sanctuary continues this note of despair and belongs wholly to the mythos of irony. The story of Temple Drake depicts a "hell-on-earth," and this vision is reinforced by an elaborate parallel with Dante's Inferno. Sanctuary begins with the entrance of Horace Benbow, Faulkner's Dante, into the "darkwood" of the Old Frenchman place, and climaxes with Popeye, Faulkner's Satan, on the scaffold. This modern "journey through the underworld" concerns the discovery and nature of evil. Its world is almost totally depraved, yet the fountainhead of this evil, Popeye, is finally revealed as the ultimate victim and prisoner of his universe.

As I Lay Dying exemplifies the upward, or comic, movement in the cycle. Beginning where Sanctuary ends, As I Lay Dying portrays a journey to the "promised land." While Sanctuary concerns Horace Benbow's discovery of evil, As I Lay Dying involves Addie Bundren's search for salvation. Like The Sound and the Fury, As I Lay Dying portrays a family conflict. Jewel and Darl embody, respectively, the heroic and ironic attitudes but their brother Cash successfully unites the opposing values of thought and action. While The Sound and the Fury is about the disintegration of a family, As I Lay Dying portrays the rebirth of a family, which is seen especially in the father Anse, who is completely rejuvenated.

Light in August, representing a further stage in the cycle, is a pastoral, not that it portrays a world of bucolic innocence, but in that, as William Empson employs the term, it involves a contrast between simple and complex ways of life. Lena Grove is closely associated with Nature and functions as the pastoral norm against which corrupt humanity is judged. Joe Christmas, whose world is a paved street, is a tragic version of the mythic hero of romance. The mythic hero normally undergoes a symbolic death-and-rebirth, but Faulkner gives the rebirth to Gail Hightower, who achieves a kind of salvation. Byron Bunch undergoes a comic rebirth. Through his portrayal of the lives of these characters and their impact on the community of Jefferson, Faulkner creates a vision of the interdependence of mankind in a good, though certainly imperfect, society. [Order No. 7812428; 304 pages. DAI, 39A (July-Aug. 1978), 886.]

373 Faulkner's Trilogy: A Reevaluation / Richard David MCDOWELL, Tulane University, 1977 (Richard P. Adams).

This study reevaluates William Faulkner's Snopes trilogy, The Hamlet, The Town, and The Mansion, in the light of the implications of his statements that "Life is motion" and that the aim of the artist is "to arrest motion." Special attention is given to his claim that the Snopeses have responded to progress "and have coped with it pretty well"--a statement which implies that the Snopeses are more dynamic characters than they are commonly assumed to be. Each of the three novels is treated as an individual work as well as a part of the trilogy in order that the artistic merits of each may be discussed.

In The Hamlet Faulkner successfully arrests motion in print by using a variety of technical devices to create impressions of energy and force that are thwarted or blocked by static obstacles so that the stoppages render the motion more apparent. The mythical method is not only his primary tool for shaping and ordering the novel but also one of his principal tools for arresting motion. The Grail legend and older fertility myths are among the several mythical patterns that operate in the novel. An ironic fertility comedy that succeeds both structurally and stylistically, The Hamlet treats the individual's search for personal value in a spiritual wasteland. The central structural metaphor is the marriage of Flem Snopes to Eula Varner, a marriage of Hades to Persephone, of ironic Grail knight to Grail maiden. Flem, who combines both dynamic and static qualities, serves Faulkner's artistic purposes especially well. In the context of the trilogy, The Hamlet records the early stages of the assimilation of the relatively primitive Snopes clan into the established culture of Yoknapatawpha. The Snopeses of The Hamlet are sufficiently diverse to defy the critical stereotype implied by the term "Snopesism."

In The Town and The Mansion, Faulkner's artistry is less sure, and he neglects many of his most effective tools, including the mythical method. As a result, the later novels are esthetically inferior to The Hamlet. Faulkner apparently wished to strengthen the symbol of Snopes as corrupt exploiter; he does so but sacrifices the diversity of the clan as projected in The Hamlet. In The Town and The Mansion, Faulkner fulfills the fictional premises of certain of the Snopes characters who first appear in The Hamlet; as he introduces new Snopeses, however, the clan as a whole does approach the stereotype of "Snopesism." The Snopeses cope with progress "pretty well" in the sense that they enjoy the dynamic possibilities of men who have not fully acquired the forms and conventions of society and, hence, are free to act as more civilized men who recognize and acknowledge authority cannot. But, when confronted with the authority of society, the Snopeses as a group do not prove to be dynamic characters. In The Town and The Mansion, Faulkner initiates a consistent pattern of introducing and then eliminating the exploiter--a pattern which, although thematically clear, is not true to his earlier conception of the clan. The result is paradoxically a weakening of the thematic unity of the trilogy. What begins as a story of cultural assimilation modulates into one of the elimination of Snopes. [Order No. 7800599; 370 pages. DAI, 38A (March-April 1978), 5481-82.]

374 The Two Patrimonies of Isaac McCaslin: Responsibilities to Secular and Liminal Time in Faulkner's Go Down, Moses / Robert Emmett MAGUIRE, University of Dallas, 1977 (Louise S. Cowan).

Part IV of "The Bear" is the climax of William Faulkner's novel Go Down, Moses. In this section the protagonist, Isaac McCaslin, chooses to renounce his familial patrimony--the McCaslin farm. Most critics regard his action as an escape from secular responsibility. I argue, on the contrary, that Ike has been marked by the wilderness (the numinous mask of God), to be the sucessor, not to his natural father Theophilus McCaslin, but to Sam Fathers, whose patrimony is stewardship over the liminal communitas of the wilderness.

While reviewing "The Tedious and Shabby Chronicle" of human history (Chapter One of the dissertation), Ike explains that he has had a conversion experience which revealed that God has chosen him to share in the divine work of saving the earth by building up the "communal anonymity of brotherhood" (the Christian community.) He does so by dedicating himself to fostering the ritual hunt in the woods because the hunt serves as a school of virtue where men annually renew the bonds of brotherhood.

Furthermore, the novel portrays Isaac's renunciation as instrumental to his being a vessel of "A Wisdom Beyond Even That Learned Through Suffering" (Chapter Two), namely, a knowledge of the permanent structures (or paradigms) both of human nature and of the divine plan for creation.

The renunciation is a sacrifice which immortalizes his relationship to the woods in their eternal dimension as a sign of God's mysterious presence in the world. The sacrifice enables Ike to act primarily in the paradigmatic realm of existence which goes beyond the limits of society. His renunciation is therefore consistent with his call to an office centered outside the political order. Now Isaac can understand Keats' words addressed to him by his cousin Cass: "Forever Wilt Thou Love and She Be Fair" (Chapter Three).

Therefore Ike can say to Cass, "Sam Fathers Set Me Free" (Chapter Four). Sam confirmed Ike as a steward of liminal communitas, that is, of a ritual threshold to a communal state where men temporarily encounter one another in the wholeness of their unique personalities rather than as role players in the hierarchical structure of secular society.

Finally, Faulkner shows "How Much It Takes to Compound a Man" (Chapter Five) whose renunciation detaches him from life's transience while still enabling him to remain active in the world as a mediator of transcendent order. Hence, the puzzling aspects of Isaac's course of action, so much debated by commentators on the novel, are explainable when one sees his choice as not so much a rejection of the civic and familial bonds but as a commitment to their renewal through a communitas which is open to that divine source of human order and which imperfectly but genuinely participates in Christianity's hope for perfect brotherhood at time's end. [Order No. 7823623; 361 pages. DAI, 39A (Nov.-Dec. 1978), 3582.

375 Flannery O'Connor's American Models: Her Work in Relation to that of Hawthorne, James, Faulkner, and West / Margaret Louise MARKS, Duke University, 1977 (Victor Strandberg).

"Flannery O'Connor's American Models" is a study of O'Connor's work in its relationship to the writings of four American novelists--Nathaniel Hawthorne, Henry James, William Faulkner, and Nathanael West--all of whom her essays and lectures show her to have admired. The dissertation is not a comprehensive study. It seeks, first, to show what O'Connor had in common with the four models and what she may have perceived them to share with each other and, second, to delineate some of the ways in which O'Connor used the models' work in her own.

Chapter I, the Introduction, examines what O'Connor identified as perhaps her most crucial artistic problem: the distance she felt, because she was a committed Catholic Christian, between herself and the modern secular audience. She faced the task of rendering believably in fiction what she often called "mystery" to readers who had largely eliminated such concerns from their lives. The chapter then explores Hawthorne, James, Faulkner, and West as writers who dealt in some fashion with the mysterious and who thus could offer O'Connor apt models for her work. The appropriateness of the Romance for the writer dealing with mystery is an important concern of Chapter I, as it is of the whole study.

Chapter II, on O'Connor and Hawthorne, examines O'Connor's own assertion that she was, like Hawthorne, a writer of Romance and was thus his literary descendant. The two writers had in common their interest in sin and guilt as a thematic concern and the use of Romance to depict that concern. Two Romance techniques in the use of which O'Connor followed Hawthorne were the grotesque and the manipulation of atmosphere to suggest movement between the realistic world and the world of Romance. Among O'Connor's grotesque characters, her scientists, artist, and intellectuals seem to be closest in affinity with the work and spirit of Hawthorne.

Chapter III explores O'Connor's work in relation to that of James, in whose writing she found an admirable blend of Novel and Romance. O'Connor was, like James, a depictor of manners, specifically manners in change and conflict; and her type character of the Displaced Person has affinities with James's American-in-Europe. O'Connor often said that mystery must be shown, in fiction, through manners, a concept she learned from James. Much of Chapter III is devoted to this and other critical ideas which O'Connor seems to have gleaned from Jamesian criticism.

O'Connor's and Faulkner's sharing of a Southern historical sense and of an interest in the poor as material for fiction forms the subject of Chapter IV. O'Connor frequently said of the poor that they live with little padding between themselves and "the raw forces of life" and that they thus dramatize the mystery of human existence. Her treatment of the poor is often close to Faulkner's. Her second novel, The Violent Bear It Away, seems to owe a debt to Faulkner's story of the heroic poor, As I Lay Dying; and much of Chapter IV concerns the relationship of the two books.

Chapter V, on O'Connor and West, deals primarily with O'Connor's use of West's Miss Lonelyhearts in her own Wise Blood and with the repercussions which her early dramatizations of the modern prophet or saint had in her later work. West's work provided another important model for O'Connor's use of the grotesque; and his influence helps to account for her most explicit treatments of the problems of belief in a secular world.

The Conclusion, Chapter VI, recalls O'Connor's character types--the prophet, the double, the visionary, the child, the grotesque--who seem particularly related to the works of Hawthorne, James, Faulkner, and West. The final chapter also summarizes ways in which O'Connor seems to have made use of her models in her own quest to write about "the mystery of our position on earth." [Order No. 7731679; 213 pages. DAI, 38A (Jan.-Feb. 1978), 4830.]

376 William Faulkner's Thomas Sutpen, Quentin Compson, Joe Christmas: A Study of the Hero-Archetype / Bernice Berger MILLER, University of Florida, 1977 (Gordon E. Bigelow).

In all the great mass of Faulkner criticism, no one has systematically applied Jungian concepts to a study of his writings. This study examines three of Faulkner's major characters in terms of the Jungian hero-archetype: Thomas Sutpen of Absalom, Absalom!, Quentin Compson of The Sound and the Fury, and Joe Christmas of Light in August. The archetypes are deep-rooted, intangible forces in the collective unconscious propelling the characters to deed or thought. Jung describes the hero-archetype as a symbolic representation of the psyche's process of growth through several stages to an integration of personality called individuation. Emphasis in this study is therefore upon the unconscious motivations of the characters' action rather than on surface behavior. The hero (psyche) in this process of growth encounters archetypes such as his Shadow, all aspects of the Archetypal Feminine (particularly his Anima), the Wise Old Man, and any number of archetypal images such as a cave, house, fish, woods, blood.

Each of the three characters represents a different stage in the process of psychic growth, and taken together, they represent that entire process. Thomas Sutpen is an archetypally numinous figure whose mysterious origins and power resemble those in Jung's concept of an invincible god. But his inability to accept his own Shadow nature, symbolized by his mulatto son Charles Bon, results in a failure to go beyond the beginning stage of psychic growth. Quentin Compson fails to deal with the Archetypal Feminine in his nature, as represented by his sister Caddy, and thus his level of growth, though more advanced than Sutpen's, still falls short of completion. Joe Christmas completes his pattern of growth, because his quest leads him ultimately to a final ritualistic scene of submission where he experiences a realization of Self, individuation. [Order No. 7806732; 164 pages. DAI, 38A (May-June 1978), 6728.]

377 Humanistic and Legal Values in Some Works of Faulkner / Ralph Eugene MILLIS, University of Iowa, 1977 (William C. Murray).

One of the major conflicts in Faulkner's work is between the external forces of civil and social law and the humanistic moral values of the individual conscience. In his Yoknapatawpha world Faulkner characteristically portrays law--the imperatives of social order--as a morally debilitating artificial restraint on man's life. As a result, those characters who attempt to find fulfillment in the world either must transcend or resist, rather than obey or accept, the demands of civil and social law in favor of a higher order based upon what Faulkner has termed in his Nobel Prize address, "the old verities and truths of the heart, the old universal truths lacking which any story is ephemeral and doomed--love and honor and pity and pride and compassion and sacrifice." Furthermore, those characters who resist civil law recognize, or in some cases dimly sense, that justice resides in their individual moral responses to the pressures of an immoral system and not in any attempt to overhaul tne system itself.

Within such works as Sanctuary, Requiem for a Nun, The Unvanquished, Intruder in the Dust, The Hamlet, The Town, and The Mansion certain major characters react in different ways and with varying degrees of success to the constant conflict between humanistic and legalistic values: Temple Drake uses the legal system to violate the humanistic impulse; Nancy Mannigoe transcends a corrupt life by exalting faith and suffering as antidotes to human "sin"; Mink Snopes lives by a code of elemental justice derived from the violence of the South's frontier past; Horace Benbow is fatally caught in a system of sterile cultural archetypes which do not take into account the reality of human nature; Gavin Stevens, the most complex of all, typifies the sensitive man, ultimately forced by his own imperfections to acknowledge the primacy of humanism over legalism. These characters serve to prove that Faulkner's humanistic vision is not so much influenced by the concepts of human perfectibility and ideal justice as it is by the acquiring of painful self-knowledge and the efficacy of the admission of mea culpa. Their experiences prove that only by subordinating the "absolutes" of civil law to the higer, unchanging considerations of human nobility, love, and compassion can "justice" be obtained. Accordingly, as these works show, true humanity resides not in those artificial rules and sanctions of society often divorced from morality; rather, only by following the feelings, the dictates, the "laws" of human conscience and emotions can the humanistic vision be affirmed at the expense of sterile legalism. [Order No. 77-28,493; 229 pages. DAI, 38A (Jan.-Feb. 1978), 4170.]

378 Ring Composition: The Structural Unity of William Faulkner's Go Down, Moses / Kossia ORLOFF, University of Iowa, 1977 (Adalaide Morris).

The purpose of this study is to present a new way of reading William Faulkner's Go Down, Moses. It argues that because Go Down, Moses is a ring composition it is a coherent novel, not, as critics have usually held, a collection of loosely related stories.

Ring composition is essentially achronological, and in Go Down, Moses Faulkner has juxtaposed the stories against each other to emphasize thematic relationships rather than chronological development. He thereby focuses the reader's attention on the significant correspondences which bind the stories together.

Further, as the name "ring composition" implies, Go Down, Moses is circular and consequently symmetrical. The one structural pattern which creates the symmetry is chiasmus: the thematically systematic sequential arrangement of parts in the first half leading to the center is precisely the same in the second half but in reversed order. Because the structural momentum of chiasmus calls attention to the structurally centered sequence-- "The Old People"--Faulkner puts in this space the one narrative sequence which refracts light on all that has gone before and comes after. The narrative of "The Old People," then, provides the reader with the key to the novel's thematic coherence: the tension between love and pride, not a tension limited to race or time or condition.

Because of the formal symmetry provided by chiasmus, each story in the first half is structurally balanced by one in the second. Faulkner turns this structure to advantage by creating thematic correspondence between each set of characters: Buck and Sophonsiba in "Was" balance Gavin and Miss Worsham in "Go Down, Moses"; Lucas in "The Fire and the Hearth" balances Isaac in "Delta Autumn"; and Rider in "Pantaloon in Black" balances Isaac in "The Bear." Since the cast of characters in any two balanced stories is different, again the emphasis is on thematic relationships.

These correspondences both structurally and thematically serve to make Go Down, Moses a coherent novel because the symmetry structurally binds together discrete sequences and thematically connects seemingly unrelated characters. Because it is the structure of ring composition which creates these correspondences, it is by this means that Faulkner reveals his ideational purpose in placing characters in particular structural relationships. It is not only the overall structure which educated the reader to Faulkner's perspective. All of the stories in Go Down, Moses are ring compositions which contain smaller ones, and all perform the same functions described above.

Chapter I describes the structural properties of ring composition and analyzes the second paragraph of "Was" to demonstrate how Faulkner uses the structure both to bring coherence to the seemingly unrelated pieces of information it contains and also to educate his audience as to his own point of view toward Isaac McCaslin's choices.

The remaining three chapters demonstrate that knowledge of Go Down, Moses as a ring composition provides one with important insights into the novel's thematic and structural coherence. Chapter II examines the ring composition of "The Old People," locates its center, and demonstrates that therein lies the one theme which embraces all of the other ones. Chapter III explicates the thematic correspondence of each symmetrical pair of stories. Chapter IV illuminates how ring composition brings into coherence contiguous stories which seem to have little in common. Both Chapters III and IV reconfirm the central tension of the novel and disclose Faulkner's own tragic point of view with respect to the human condition. [Order No. 77-28,499; 197 pages. DAI, 38A (Jan.-Feb. 1978), 4184.]

379 Narcissus Observed: The Pastoral Elegiac in Woolf, Faulkner, Fitzgerald, and Graeme Gibson / James Robert RUPPEL, University of Toronto, Canada, 1977.

The thesis consists of four chapters, each a study of a modern novel--namely, Graeme Gibson's Five Legs, Fitzgerald's The Great Gatsby, Faulkner's The Sound and the Fury, and Virginia Woolf's Mrs. Dalloway. Though this must at first appear an odd miscellany, the object of the juxtapositioning is to demonstrate a generic relationship between these novels as variations in the pastoral elegiac mode, a long-standing poetic tradition most influentially carried into the twentieth century by Eliot in The Waste Land. In fact, each of these novels shows to some extent the influence of Eliot and the Frazerian myth of the dying scapegoat god lying behind his work. Hopefully the works of the four writers chosen (and the silent spectre of Eliot) are in the end mutually illuminating.

The commentary on each novel explores some of the major thematic concerns of pastoral elegy. There is first of all the perspective effect of "double vision," the implied contrast between golden and fallen world (often past and present) which underlies the very idea of pastoral. This effect is in the present cases complicated by a sort of schizoided narcissism in which the world has been absorbed into the self, yet is at the same time disquieteningly alien from it. The traditional suggestion of the "doubling" between mourner and mourned and the treatment of the landscape as an image of the speaker's state of mind are taken up in terms of the "myths" of modern psychological theory--the Freudian dynamics of projection and identification, Laing's ontological insecurity, Erikson's identity crisis. Rites of fertility and passage have become the sexual confusions of prolonged adolescence.

The internalization of the pastoral mode into a study of consciousness is reflected in the narrative techniques used in the novels under discussion. In Gibson two first-personal worlds overlap; in Fitzgerald there is a central narrator whose vision mirrors his personality; in Faulkner there are four self-absorbed sections; in Woolf the consciousness of an "omniscient" narrator pervades the novel, breaking down the lines of distinction between individual characters. A common tendency is for the reader to be drawn into the novels as something of a participant in their self-exploration--the image of the drowned sailor found in each of them we may invoke as a symbol of this submersion of self in its own element.

The artist too is contained in his own art. Not only do the biographical hints of these works point us to the idea of a portrait of the artist, but thematically as well they can be read as about their own creation, and oddly enough, usually their own failure. The only resolution to this thematic stasis of self-reflection is the very creation of these novels themselves. [Canadian Dissertation, DAI, 39A (Jan.-Feb. 1979), 4249.]

380 William Faulkner's World War I and Flying Short Fiction: An Imaginative Appropriation of History / Nancy Belcher SEDERBERG, University of South Carolina, 1977 (Donald J. Greiner).

This study is a close examination of Faulkner's twelve short stories about World War I and flying. The basic orientation is thematic, though attention is also given to such topics as symbolism, narrative techniques, style, structure, and sources and analogues, as well as revisions among the various versions. The stories have been paired in approximate chronological order to emphasize central thematic interconnections and developments. In Chapter I, the two apprenticeship stories "Landing in Luck" and the unpublished "Love" are discussed, with special attention to the unifying theme of the nature of courage. Chapter II focuses on the two most surrealistic of the stories: "The Leg" and "Crevasse," in which the war serves as a catalyst for a symbolic nightmare and descent into hell. The third chapter develops the themes of the clashes between choice and chance and provincial and war values. Chapter IV discusses the best known of Faulkner's war stories, "All the Dead Pilots" and "Ad Astra," as exemplifications of the themes of ideals versus reality and of internecine conflicts among races, ranks, and individuals. The chapter on "Honor" and "Death Drag" emphasizes the psychic death and deracination of the pilots in the post-war world. The last chapter on "Turnabout" and the unpublished "With Caution and Dispatch" explores the themes of man versus machines and the differing perspectives of youth and age. Finally, the concluding chapter is an attempt to illuminate further interconnections among the war and aviation stories and to place them within the larger context of Faulkner's fiction.

The basic conclusion of this study is that this group of stories confounds the commentators that they are either romantic, especially in their treatment of the aviators as modern knights of the air, or indistinguishable from the whole class of "lost generation" fiction in their aura of disillusionment and pessimistic philosophy of the futility and waste of war. Although Faulkner clearly identifies with certain of his characters--particularly the pilots--they never become mere projections of his own personal legends; rather, he retains enough distance to view them with simultaneous sympathy and detachment. Conversely, complete nihilism also never prevails. Almost every story portrays a shifting dialectic between romanticism and realism, myths and the mundane: between the perspectives of youth and age, Americans and Europeans, or callow, inexperienced characters and veterans. Finally, these stories frustrate any classification that differentiates literature from history or life. A simplistic biographical approach has been too prevalent among critics who prefer to view Faulkner's protagonists merely as personas rather than as distinct literary creations. Although Faulkner never underwent active service or even probably flew during this period (prior to 1933), he did have first-hand contact with veterans in New Haven and during his R.A.F. training in Toronto in 1918 and with pilots in New Orleans and Memphis. Faulkner's greatest experience of both the war and flying, however, was literary--a result of his extensive reading of newspapers, magazines, memoirs, novels, and poetry. Both the Great War and flying, like the complex knowledge of Southern society and custom that infuses his Yoknapatawpha fiction, are the catalysts for his own imaginative appropriation of history. [Order No. 7801179; 408 pages. DAI, 38A (March-April 1978), 5484.]

381 Literary Continuity Traced Through the Progression in the Use of Time in Wordsworth, Faulkner, Virginia Woolf, T.S. Eliot, and Yeats / Nazan Feride SENGELLI, George Peabody College for Teachers, 1977 (Eva Touster).

This study explores the continuity of literature through the use of time in the works of Wordsworth, Faulkner, Virginia Woolf, T.S. Eliot, and Yeats. A pattern of development towards the ultimate expression of the eternal moment in the works of each of these artists has been investigated. The pattern of development unfolds as the study moves from Wordsworth's concept of "spots of time" to duration novels of Faulkner and Woolf, and to the theme of time-lessness in the poetry of Eliot and Yeats. The works discussed in this study are Wordsworth's The Prelude, Faulkner's The Sound and the Fury, As I Lay Dying, and Absalom, Absalom!, Woolf's Orlando, To the Lighthouse, and Mrs. Dalloway, Eliot's Four Quartets, and Yeats' Byzantium poems.

Wordsworth is able to recapture the lost vision of eternity at certain moments when the imagination brings "the radiance which was once so bright" into the present. Those moments occur at the intersection of two different time series. At those "spots of time" the poet gets a glimpse of an order in the universe which he cannot find in the natural world. But the vision is temporary, because the moment is fleeting.

Faulkner concentrates on the expression of the internal consciousness of those characters who seek to achieve an ideal order in their universe but cannot because of their intense subjectivity. The method of stream of consciousness is used to convey the continuity of existence. Faulkner's sense of time is thus durational when he focuses on the individual experience of time.

Virginia Woolf is also involved with the subjective experience of the human mind, but at the same time she is seeking for an objective reality beyond that mind which she seems to be engrossed in. She reaches "moments of reality" within the flow and flux of life at the end of her novels.

Eliot realizes that in order to reach permanence and overcome change and flux, he must transcend the temporal. He achieves the "still point" through a pattern, a balance of tension, a reconciliation of opposites, and the image of the Christian God at the center.

Yeats also transcends the temporal to find permanence in the creation of art. His pursuit of art may be seen as the substitute for the spiritual quest of Eliot. Like Eliot he accepts the paradox of man in time and his aspiration for eternity. He finds the reality which would embrace both concepts of time and timelessness in art. [Order No. 77-25,132; 156 pages. DAI, 38A (Nov.-Dec. 1977), 2766.]

382 The South in Motley: A Study of the Fool Tradition in Selected Works by Faulkner, McCullers, and O'Connor / Joy Farmer SHAW, University of Virginia, 1977 (Douglas T. Day).

This study deals with the fool tradition and fool figures in Faulkner's The Sound and the Fury, McCullers' The Heart Is a Lonely Hunter, and O'Connor's "The Life You Save May Be Your Own," "A Temple of the Holy Ghost," "The Comforts of Home," "Revelation," and The Violent Bear It Away. Its purpose is to examine the varying ways each author shapes the fool figure to fit the story of Southern displacement he is seeking to relate.

Chapters I and II establish the fundamentals of the fool tradition at the same time that they deal in depth with The Sound and the Fury. Chapter I focuses on Benjy and explores his literary and historical antecedents: the court jester, Shakespeare's great clowns, and sacrificial and scapegoat figures of fertility festivals, to name just a few. It concludes with a discussion of Benjy as the perfect emblem of a family, and indeed an entire culture, displaced by time from its remembered Eden.

Chapter II examines the relationship of the novel's other characters with the man in traditional motley, and demonstrates that no one, not even Dilsey, is exempt from the appellation "fool." Because, however, folly can be either life-enhancing or life-defeating, the chapter distinguishes between characters who are fools in a temporal sense (that is, blind to their worldly welfare) and characters who are fools in an eternal sense (that is, blind to the interests of their immortal souls.) A lengthy section on Quentin attempts to alert the reader to the humor in Part II of The Sound and the Fury, and to establish a relationship between Quentin and Hamlet on the basis of their unsuccessful efforts to play the fool. This chapter concludes with a discussion of doubling in the novel, since one of the chief characteristics of the fool is his double nature.

Chapter III deals with clown pairs and demonstrates how Antonapoulos and Singer are cast in the respective roles of knave and dupe throughout The Heart Is a Lonely Hunter. The essay then discusses Mick, Jake, and Dr. Copeland, displaced people who achieve a momentary sense of belonging when they find a center for their lives in Singer, and through Singer, in Antonapoulos. The way they respond to the mutes is shown to be typical of audience response during a comedy routine calling for a clown pair.

Also examined in Chapter III is the breakdown of the fool show when Antonapoulos, who releases the revitalizing powers of chaos, finally dies and Singer, who channels this chaos to others, commits suicide. The remainder of the chapter deals with the realm which the fool show leaves open even after the show's illusion has been dispelled and the real horror behind the illusion been revealed. This realm is possibility; and the concluding argument seeks to prove that this ostensibly pessimistic novel ends optimistically because each character is left with the possible.

Chapter IV deals with O'Connor's theological use of the fool figure as a symbol of man's displacement as a result of the Fall, and as the embodiment of man's opportunity to accept God's grace. Along with Chapter III, it constitutes an effort on the part of this author to show how two Southern novelists have been able to build on the writings of Faulkner, whose Benjy is the fool done to completion, without being limited or overshadowed by them. [Order No. 77-28,627; 257 pages. DAI, 38A (Jan.-Feb. 1978), 4162.]

383 Suggestions of Death-Anxiety in the Life of William Faulkner / Jerold Howard STOCK, West Virginia University, 1977 (Ruel E. Foster)

During one of his classroom conferences as writer-in-residence at the University of Virginia, William Faulkner spoke of "the burden which man carries all his life . . . the knowledge of death." This burden I call anxiety over death—more precisely, painful or apprehensive uneasiness of mind at the thought of death; more concisely, death-anxiety. My paper answers the question: to what extent was Faulkner talking about himself when he spoke in effect of man suffering all his life from death-anxiety? To find the answer, I devoted a chapter apiece to the strongest suggestions of death-anxiety in Faulkner's childhood, adolescence, young manhood, prime, early middle age, later middle age, and old age. This procedure yielded the answer that Faulkner was speaking largely of his own life and torment when he spoke of man's lifelong death-anxiety. More specifically, he very possibly suffered from this anxiety in childhood, very probably in adolescence, almost certainly in his young manhood and prime, and certainly thereafter.

Had my paper done nothing more than answer the question of whether and how long Faulkner suffered from death-anxiety, its contribution to Faulkner studies would have been modest at best. What makes it of significant value to these studies is that, in the course of answering this question, it takes a small but definite step toward answering one of the most important Faulkner questions of all: what was the enigmatic Mississippian really like? It does so because countless suggestions of death-anxiety consist of showing that as many Faulkner enigmas are persuasively explained by assuming this anxiety on his part. The question of his enigmatic personality is so important because no art, of course, is uninfluenced by the personality of the artist. Thus, to understand Faulkner better is to understand his art better. My paper shows that Faulkner's death-anxiety is a key to this better understanding.

My paper, finally, also contributes appreciably to Faulkner studies by showing that a generally accepted answer to another major Faulkner question is inaccurate. I refer to the question of Faulkner's philosophy and the answer that he is a humanist, one whose supreme value is man. My paper shows that he is more accurately characterized as a vitalist, one whose supreme value is life. It does so because a recurrent suggestion of death-anxiety consists of innumerable statements clearly implying that life rather than man or even art is his summum bonum--statements predictable and hence suggestive of one suffering from death-anxiety.

In sum, my paper shows that Faulkner suffered at least much of his life from death-anxiety, that this anxiety is a key to his personality and so to his art, and that he is more accurately termed a vitalist than a humanist. It thus implies that no future attempt, whether biographical or critical, to solve the enigma that is William Faulkner will wholly succeed if it ignores his anxiety over death or assumes--too readily at least--that his supreme value is man. [Order No. 77-22,751; 236 pages. DAI, 38A (Sept.-Oct. 1977), 2130-31.]

384 The French and Faulkner: The Reception of William Faulkner's Writing in France and its Influence on Modern French Literature / Phiet Qui TRAN, University of Texas at Austin, 1977 (William M. Stott).

An outstanding phenomenon in the history of Franco-American relationships was the vogue of the American novel between the two wars in France. By "the American novel" the French meant especially the writing of five American novelists--Dos Passos, Hemingway, Faulkner, Caldwell, and Steinbeck--whose technical innovations and whose treatment of violence, brutality, and pessimism fascinated the French. American techniques, French critics claimed, helped their fellow-writers solve what they called the crisis of the French novel; American themes responded to the prevailing French mood of the post-war years.

Of these cinq grands, as the French called these American novelists, Faulkner was the most important. The only modern American writer to have received constant serious and scholarly attention from French critics, he was also one of the strongest contemporary influences on French writing. The themes that Faulkner was concerned with in his novels--tragedy, despair, prejudice, hope, and salvation--were close to the French experience. In addition two major French literary schools--Existentialism and the New Novel--were influenced by Faulkner's themes and techniques. The former picked up from Faulkner ideas such as the contingent and the absurd; the latter drew upon his concepts of time and consciousness and borrowed and extended his techniques to deal with these problems. [Order No. 77-29,110; 210 pages. DAI, 38A (Jan.-Feb. 1978), 4162.]

385 The Uncreating World: Creators of Fiction in William Faulkner's Major Novels / Gillian Jennifer WILSON, University of California at Santa Barbara, 1977 (Lawrence Wilson).

Faulkner once said that moral responsibility is the curse man had to accept from the gods in order to gain from them the right to dream. The argument, developed from a series of Faulkner's novels, examines this right to dream, specifically as it reveals the author's use of the fictive process as a subject matter for his own fiction.

Faulkner does not merely create fictions for himself; he also portrays characters who create fictions as a way of ordering and understanding experience. His purpose is to identify the creative imagination as it submits to the pressure of the past and fashions out of history designs for the future. His male characters, in particular, are incorrigible dreamers. They fabricate images, historical and mythical, which give them the illusion of understanding the irony which lurks in human events. Moreover, their verbal creations become artifacts, like Keats' "Grecian Urn," capable of withstanding the onslaught of time and of offering a measure of immortality to those, like Quentin Compson and Harry Wilbourne, who cannot bear that the "is" of the flesh will become "was." The style reveals this temporal suspension.

Words may be vehicles for moral perception, and for the artistic process, but they also betray, since out of them arise fictions which lead their creator away from the very experience he is trying to grasp: he suffers from the illusion that he can control the universe by describing it. Addie Bundren noted the inadequacy of language as a means of describing experience. Language always forces action into fixed patterns of a mythical or historical heritage which may have obsolesced. Thus, the words, on the one hand, allow each character moral vision through the historical imagination; on the other, they doom him to recreate and repeat the myth of the past, as if it were destiny. Each character discovers for himself the inadequacies of a world without order; we discover for him the tragedy of imposing his own fiction of order and meaning upon what is apparently inchoate and chaotic. There appears to be no resolution. Man is doomed to failure if he adopts, through his language, his myths and historical patterns, and doomed to moral vacuity if he rejects them; hence the irony which frequently pervades Faulkner's works.

The reader, participating in the creation of verbal fictions, behaves like the characters who espouse them and must suffer a parallel disillusionment. Only those, like Dilsey and Lena, who love and accept without thinking about it, achieve something like the wisdom of a still tongue. But Dilsey and Lena are also mythical figures about whom ordinary people dream and who may prove unavailable in nature and unreliable in art. Faulkner suggests that the word and the deed must always be in conflict with each other; hence the tension created between an apparently traditional morality and the intransigence of the style used to describe it. [Order No. 7807032; 321 pages. DAI, 38A (May-June 1978), 6719.]

386 Faulkner: The Transfiguration of Biography / Judith Bryand WITTEN-BERG, Brown University, 1977 (Hyatt H. Waggoner) no DAI entry.

387 William Faulkner's Mosquitoes: An Introduction and Annotations to the Novel / Edwin Turner ARNOLD, III, University of South Carolina, 1978 (James B. Meriwether).

Mosquitoes was William Faulkner's second novel. It has generally been considered as among the least of his works, an anomaly to be excused or ignored. However, although it is the work of a young writer, at times beset by the weaknesses of an early work, it would be a mistake to dismiss the book as the unimportant product of a novice. It is an ambitious, experimental work which represents the culmination of over ten years of study and writing and may be read as the summation of Faulkner's intellectual and artistic growth as he entered the fourth decade of his life. It is the one work which leads most directly to The Sound and the Fury and is the first in which Faulkner established his credo as an artist. The purpose of this study is to examine Mosquitoes as an indication of Faulkner's development as an artist and as a reflection of the works and traditions which went into this growth. Annotations cover literary allusions and influences, historical and mythological events and personages, geographical identifications, and matters of text where such information sheds light on the published novel. A collation of the substantive variants between the surviving typescript and the 1927 first edition is also included as an appendix to the dissertation. [Order No. 7907583; 377 pages. DAI, 39A (March-April 1979), 6125.]

388 The Textual History and Definitive Textual Apparatus for Soldiers' Pay: A Bibliographic Study of William Faulkner's First Novel / Francis John BOSHA, Marquette University, 1978 (Joseph Schwartz).

The publication of William Faulkner's first novel, Soldiers' Pay, was beset with a problem that would recur with the publication of many of his later works: he was unable to resist the many editorial emendations that were imposed on his texts. As one close friend and publisher of Faulkner's recently speculated in a letter to this author, Faulkner "was so damn glad to get those two books [Soldiers' Pay and Mosquitoes] published that he accepted a great deal of whatever [Liveright editor] Tom Smith did with his manuscript." This dissertation traces the textual history of Soldiers' Pay from its inception through to its publication in this country and England. Also, in a textual apparatus, this study seeks to establish the definitive text of the novel by suggesting emendations to the copy-text which have been determined by a careful collation of the two extant typescripts and the first American edition of the novel.

The dissertation is divided into three parts: the History of the Text, the Textual Apparatus, and the Appendices. The first part contains sections on the inception of Soldiers' Pay, and traces the roots of the novel to Faulkner's war poems of 1919 and certain of his sketches, some unpublished, and his essay "Literature and War" that were written between 1920 and 1925. The composition section covers the period from January through June 1925 when Faulkner actually wrote Soldiers' Pay. Faulkner's process of writing is discussed here, as is the influence of Sherwood Anderson and the role of Faulkner's Oxford friends, Phil Stone, Edith Brown Douds, and Grace Hudson, played in the preparation of the novel. Certain of the conclusions drawn in this section are based on an examination of the unpublished correspondence of Anderson, which is part of the Newberry Library's Sherwood Anderson Collection, and correspondence between this author and Mrs. Douds and Mrs. Hudson. The publication section covers the period from late June 1925 to February 1926, when the novel was first published, and discusses the reception Faulkner's manuscript received at the Liveright offices. Also, the fact that after he submitted his manuscript, Faulkner had little control during the pre-publication preparation of Soldiers' Pay, is treated in this section. The last section in the History describes the following texts of Soldiers' Pay that were consulted to prepare this study: the earlier, 345 page unbound typescript, which is part of the New York Public Library's Henry W. and Albert A. Berg Collection; the later, 476-page bound typescript, which is part of the William Faulkner Collection of the University of Virginia's Alderman Library and which serves as the copy-text of the textual apparatus; and the 1926 Boni & Liveright and 1930 Chatto and Windus first editions, the later American and English printings and the Liveright, Penguin, and Signet paperbound editions.

The second part of this dissertation is the Textual Apparatus, and consists of a table of suggested emendations to the copy-text, keyed to the American first edition; explanatory notes to the emendations are included where necessary. The remainder of the Apparatus is an historical collation which isolates every textual variant occuring among the two typescripts and the American first edition, and is accompanied by pertinent textual notes.

There are also six appendices, which include a listing of the word counts Faulkner kept throughout the composition of the later typescript, and a transcription of the two pages of holograph notes in which Faulkner sketched many of the novel's major scenes. A third appendix establishes the stages in which Faulkner actually wrote the novel, and is followed by a textual appendix which reproduces the pages Faulkner rejected in the course of composition. The fifth appendix is a collation of the American and English first editions, and the last appendix establishes the readings for words hyphenated at line-end in the copy-text and the American first edition. [Order No. 7905169; 711 pages. DAI, 39A (March-April 1979), 5509.]

389 Beyond the Meaning of History: The Quest for a Southern Myth in Faulkner's Characters / Kathleen Shine CAIN, Marquette University, 1978 (Joseph M. Schwartz).

In an effort to substitute for a God who apparently has ceased to exist for them, many of Faulkner's protagonists attempt to invest their existence with cosmic significance by mythologizing the history of the South. These characters ultimately fail because they ask too much of their world. The only heroes who succeed are those who take life one day at a time, refusing to concern themselves with the universal implications of their actions.

Quentin Compson, in The Sound and the Fury and Absalom, Absalom!, is the paradigm of the Faulknerian failure. Magnifying the sins of his sister beyond all proportion, Quentin assumes the twin roles of judge and redeemer, and through his suicide seeks to purge Caddy of her guilt. His chivalric act, reminiscent of the "Golden Age" of the South, is meaningless.

Living in that "Golden Age," Thomas Sutpen of Absalom, Absalom! attempts to transcend time through his great "design" namely the dynasty which will leave its indelible mark upon the Southern soil. The only mark actually left, however, is the charred remains of Sutpen's ancestral mansion, and his only remaining descendant is a witless idiot.

The heritage left by the ancestors of Ike McCaslin in "The Bear" is stained by outrageous sin. Repudiating this heritage, Ike seeks purity in the wilderness--the wilderness which slowly vanishes after the death of its god, Old Ben. Deifying a mortal creature and relinquishing his ties with his fellow man, Ike fails to atone for the sins of his fathers.

Even accepted tradition becomes meaningless when ritual is followed solely for its own sake. In As I Lay Dying the selfish motives of the Bundrens belie the sincerity of their perilous funeral journey. Similarly, Charlotte and Harry's adherence to the ritual of romantic love in The Wild Palms causes them to destroy the child of that love. (In "Old Man" the opposite occurs: a child is born, but the significance of the event is lost on the convict.)

The hopelessness of the above works is borne out in Light in August, in which the Christ figure's death serves only to reinforce the hatred of the community, for Joe Christmas, rather than assuming their guilt, shares in it. In A Fable the crucifixion is without hope as well--Christ fails to rise again as true God-Man; instead he becomes Everyman as he is laid to rest in the Tomb of the Unknown Soldier. The message is clear: the Christian myth is a lie.

Virtually the only positive characters in Faulkner's work are Bayard Sartoris (The Unvanquished) and Chick Mallison (Intruder in the Dust,) each of whom finds success because he attempts only that which is within his power. Bayard meets his father's killer and Chick proves the accused Lucas innocent without trying to alter the social structure of the community. These two leave the mythologizing to others, and thus they do not fail. [Order No. 7905170; 146 pages. DAI, 39A (March-April 1979), 5509-10.]

390 The Fatal Arc: The Evolution of Tragic Image and Idea in Three Novels by William Faulkner / John Lloyd DODDS, Loyola University of Chicago, 1978 (Stanley A. Clayes).

In an interview at the University of Virginia, William Faulkner proposed that "every writer in a way is writing one story . . . there's one thing in man's condition that seems to him the most moving, the most tragic." This dissertation traces in three novels--Sartoris, Light in August, and Absalom, Absalom!--the evolution of the tragic vision which informs this "one story."

In particular, I try to demonstrate two things: that the pattern of ideas and images embodying Faulkner's tragic vision in these novels constitutes an effective unifying structure for each novel and that this pattern helps us account for the maturing of this vision from Sartoris through Absalom. Sartoris, I argue, is an ironic romantic tragedy, Light in August, a naturalistic tragedy, and Absalom, Absalom!, a tragedy along more classical lines.

In each of these novels, the basic pattern of the tragedy is essentially the same. Impelled by particular energies, the tragic hero chooses a course of action to achieve a particular goal, but his energies, inevitably in conflict with himself and his environment, bring him to tragic goals. Ambivalent, divided by this conflict, the hero attempts to avoid the conflict and its source by seeking or erecting a sanctuary from what he understands to be the forces threatening him. In every novel, however, this sanctuary fails; with the failure, the protagonist is forced out, exposed to the conflict he sought to evade, in a process that creates the tragic fate implicit in his energies from the beginning.

The maturing of this pattern can be traced in the evolution of the themes central to the tragedy and in the images that present these themes, especially those images in the dense purple passages so often neglected and sometimes condemned by critics. These themes are: the duality inherent in the tragic hero; the complex energies born of this duality; the hero's opposition to the harmonious order and motion of all living things; the outrages against self and others that result from his defiance; the tragic arc--hubris leading to hamartia, peripety and fall; and primal injustice, that force checking the hero which we sense at work in his fate and which the tragic structure of the novel enacts. In a particular novel these themes are given substance by particular constellations of images. In other novels, Faulkner expands, refines, or makes these same themes more complex by adding new images to the constellations, by shifting the configuration of images, or by developing new aspects of imagery used earlier. Images and themes evolve within the basic tragic pattern, producing the different final effect of each novel.

I have divided my analysis into three chapters for each of the novels. The first chapter on each novel is primarily a study of characterization, of primal energy; the second, dealing with sanctuaries and social centers, considers milieu and plot; the third distinguishes the nature of fate in each novel and the final effect of the tragedy. In a concluding chapter I argue, first, that the evolution of Faulkner's tragic vision also presents the growth of his artistic powers, and, second, that this vision is in force even when, in a novel like The Hamlet, Faulkner's aims are comic; tragic figures and imagery in a comic context heighten the reality of the comedy and give weight to comic themes. [Order No. 7807066; 437 pages. DAI, 38A (May-June 1978), 6722-23.]

391 Psychic Transformation through Memory-Work and Negation in William Faulkner's Absalom, Absalom! / Eileen Marie DONOHUE, University of Notre Dame, 1978 (Carvel Collins).

William Faulkner's Absalom, Absalom! is the story of the psychic transformation of Quentin Compson, a twentieth-century Hamlet figure, from an immature young man resisting life's complexity to a psychologically old young man inclined toward death. Quentin's extended "to be, or not to be" entails an erosthanatos tension played out as the inner conflict of Quentin's three selves, first through negation, resistance, and repression, later through memory-work and psycho-catharsis, and always through the medium of the Sutpen story. Preoccupied by death, Quentin weighs the risk of dreams to come against the "calamity of so long life." In the Sutpen story, once willing to confront it, he seeks signs of love that might make life worth living. Instead he finds such archetypal evils as human exploitation, incest, and miscegenation. Psychologically, Quentin becomes anachronistic: a young man on the threshold of adult life but oriented toward death rather than toward growth and procreation.

Quentin's inner conflict determines the form of the novel. The book's most irreducible structural element, its language, is pervasively negative in tenor in order to indicate the centrality of the ultimate negation, death. The "notlanguage" of Absalom, Absalom! not only reveals death as the work's center and Quentin's major preoccupation, but makes of it a metaphor for certain epiphanic moments capable of transforming or destroying a person. Quentin's inner turmoil results from his resistance to such a moment of discovery and its meaning. Another function of the negative modality is to signify the removal of Quentin's repressions. Finally, the book's "notlanguage" hints at a pre-speech level of consciousness, preparing the reader to see in portions of the book (Chapters III and V, perhaps) the transition of repressed, unconscious material into consciousness through memory-work and association.

Further, Quentin's inner struggle determines the conformation of characters in Absalom, Absalom!. The definition of these "notpeople" is achieved not only through negative verbal assessments and negative actions, but also through their attitudes toward death and impermanence. As Quentin uses the Sutpen story to test his notions of reality, he encounters people positioned along a hypothetical spectrum ranging from fear of impermanence to conviction that man's greatest curse is to be born.

In another sense--one in which the term "notpeople" designates the various strata of Quentin's personality, the three Quentins of the book's third page--Quentin's pre-speech "duel" signifies the larger pattern of the book. His psychic thrusts and parries echo in the verbal duels of various characters, including Quentin and Henry. The verbal duels establish the book's shape as stichomythic and its movement as vortical, with death the vacuum at its center. The centripetal force of the Sutpen story, most fully signified in Quentin's chiastic dialogue with Henry, relentlessly drives Quentin to his climactic statement hinting ironically at his readiness for death. Likewise, the novel's centripetal force, which moves the reader toward the mysterious Chapter V, generates maximum reader participation.

While in the first four chapters of the book Quentin is a reluctant non-listener repressing all-too familiar material, in the last four he engages in memory-work which retrieves repressed, forgotten content from the shadowy world of the unconscious and restores it to consciousness. The process consists in the activation of memory-traces, similar to the recovery of repressed material in psychoanalysis, largely by association.

Through inner monologues, flashbacks, the filtering of another's words through his consciousness, and repeated visualizations, Quentin slowly confronts the reality he has fled so long. Previously familiar, it now appears estranged and menacing by reason of repetition; the result is an air of uncanniness.

Quentin's experience at Harvard thus attenuates his epiphanic instant at Sutpen's Hundred. At its end he understands that, like Rosa, he is incapable of crossing the emotional threshold into mature adulthood. Rosa's death is a signal of his own.

Absalom, Absalom! is consequently a fully autonomous psychological novel expressive of "the human heart in conflict with itself"; it is a modern Hamlet's "to be, or not to be." [Order No. 7815534; 213 pages. DAI, 39A (Sept.-Oct. 1978), 1546.]

392 Faulkner's Men and Women: A Critical Study of Male-Female Relationships in His Early Yoknapatawpha County Novels / Robert H. EGOLF, Lehigh University, 1978 (James R. Frakes).

The male-female relationships in William Faulkner's early Yoknapatawpha County novels--Sartoris, The Sound and the Fury, As I Lay Dying, and Light in August--reflect a decadent and futile response to love and "the old verities and truths of the heart." Through careful analysis of the male-female relationships, this study discusses the reasons for such loveless alliances and indicates reasons for Faulkner's creation of these misalliances.

The study of Sartoris is supplemented with a comparative analysis of Flags in the Dust. The male-female relationships form a continuous chain of weak and malformed links. Obsessed with his dead brother, young Bayard Sartoris is unable to transfer his love for his brother to Narcissa. Narcissa, confronted with a conflict between her love for her brother, Horace, and her love for her husband, is also unable to transfer her affections and compassion. These characters cannot form positive relationships because they are obsessed with the past and are actually seeking sibling-substitutes.

In The Sound and the Fury the members of the Compson family are not compatible and sharing because they are in conflict. Caddy's love is thwarted and turns sour because she is neither loved nor allowed to love. Quentin, because of his twisted love for Caddy, takes his own life in a desperate attempt to annihilate love, guilt, and Caddy. Jason, who as a child is rebuked and as a man is dominated by his mother, learns to survive by shunning all relationships. Finally the family dissolves to scattered people who have resorted to living alone in cold, selfish, and disillusioned worlds.

Faulkner presents another view of a family in turmoil and on the verge of collapse in As I Lay Dying. Each character has a personal and selfish motive for making the journey to fulfill Addie's revengeful request, but as the journey unfolds it seems to signal the deracination of the family. However, in the end the family is stronger because the members have learned to sacrifice and to live together.

In Light in August male-female relationships exist among characters not related by blood. These relationships develop because of the characters' needs and desires either to escape or to solve a personal dilemma. Joe Christmas finds permanent escape at the hands of Percy Grimm because Joe has lived a life of not knowing who or what he is. Lena, in contrast to Joe, knows her purpose and pursues her goals to find a father for her child and to form a family unit. Byron Bunch is able to bring meaning to his life because of his feelings for Lena and his desire to be with her.

Faulkner's early Yoknapatawpha County novels deal with love, pity, honor, and compassion through characters who are either able to overcome and endure the obstacles of obsessions, envy, greed, vanity, and lust. The characters are confronted with barriers that must be removed to experience compassionate and companionable relationships. [Order No. 7904303; 262 pages. DAI, 39A (Jan.-Feb. 1979), 4946-47.]

393 Innocence and Experience in Selected Major Fiction of William Faulkner / Robert Ira GREENE, Indiana University, 1978 (Terence Martin).

In a country founded as a religious haven, it is not surprising that "innocence" is a concern often reflected in its fictions. Yet, although innocence is guiltlessness if defined theologically, it is ignorance if defined humanistically, a state of "not-knowing" that demands enlightenment. Indeed, the archetypal Innocent, pre-lapsarian Adam, is as important for his failure of understanding and his exclusion from experience as he is for his embodiment of guiltlessness. This suggests that innocence can be limitation as much as inviolate guiltlessness, and insofar as William Faulkner was a self-professed "humanist," his novels often do not reflect this bias.

In the four "major" novels surveyed here, The Sound and the Fury, Light in August, As I Lay Dying, and Go Down, Moses, Faulkner consistently exposes the inadequacies of a partial vision of experience. Normally, the characters "innocent" in this sense are trapped in a too-narrow construction of experience, a failure to recognize change. In the ways that these "innocent" characters choose ceremony, ritual, or obsession over adaptation to movement, they are finally all egotists. For example, Quentin Compson's entrapment in the past, Joe Christmas' inability to tolerate racial ambiguities (like himself,) and Darl Bundren's morbid preoccupations with identity and time freeze their personalities, injure others, and isolate them in solipsistic worlds akin to Benjy Compson's.

Yet, it is also clear that each of these characters is attractive to Faulkner: they are all moral mirrors of sorts for their communities and they all live close to the myths and archetypes that underlie the experience of their societies, particularly those of heroism and resurrection. Generally, the heroic doom that this type of Faulkner "innocent" suffers tests and can regenerate the assumptions and values of his society. Excluded from normal experience, he somehow manages to illuminate its bare spots and revitalize it. Although such characters pervert Faulkner's "eternal verities," they are often the agents of their continual reinterpretation.

Furthermore, Faulkner is not wholly "humanistic"; from The Sound and the Fury on, the "innocents" are not always grandly tragic isolates who cannot deal effectively with space and time. In their ranks are also characters like Dilsey, who embody the theologically-defined innocence of orthodox Christianity. Their "innocence" is fullness rather than limitation, a coupling of Paul Tillich's "courage to be" with Simone Weil's courage of self-denial rather than (using Paul Ricoeur's language) the imprisonment in the terminology of human fault that marked the innocence of characters like Quentin and Christmas. Yet, Dilsey is, finally, dull; she inspires us more than charms us.

However, by the time of Go Down, Moses, the gulf between the tragic, grand "innocence" of Quentin and the comic, dull "innocence" of Dilsey is somewhat narrowed. Although the aesthetics of Go Down, Moses make it inferior to and less bold than the earlier great works, Faulkner's seemingly hardening religious sensibility and his cooling intensity lead him to draw the "comic" and the "tragic" innocent figures closer together by incorporating in one character, Ike McCaslin, both the failure of innocence when it is ritualized and its redemptive power.

Through him, the old comic cultural myth of American innocence again expresses itself, although Faulkner continues to warn us about its oversimplifications. In general, the problem of innocence runs throughout the Faulkner novels as both obsessive failure and romantic idyll, a goal for experience and an index of its tragic misappropriation. [Order No. 7916889; 304 pages. DAI, 40A (July-Aug. 1979), 852-53.]

394 Comedy in Faulkner's Fiction / Elizabeth Tracy HAYES, Syracuse University, 1978 (David Owen).

Although surprisingly neglected as an area of study, comedy affects Faulkner's fiction profoundly. Besides considerably lightening the tone of his prose, comedy frequently provides a new perspective upon the characters and an indirect, humorous presentation of theme. Most important, the presence and frequency of comedy indicates Faulkner's "comic" view of man, a view held in the face of all the forces of decay, sterility, and destruction presented in his work.

To understand the influence of comedy upon Faulkner's fiction, one must examine the particular types of comedy that Faulkner employs, the ways in which they are used, and the frequency with which they occur in his work. Some of his comedy is "pure"; more--perhaps two-thirds--contains serious, pathetic, or painful elements which qualify the comedy and diminish the humorous effect. Whether muted or "pure," comedy appears in and influences most of the fiction Faulkner produced.

This dissertation is an analytical survey of seven types of comedy in Faulkner's fiction (the tall tale, black humor, surrealistic humor, humor of the absurd, low comedy, comedy of ritual, and comic conclusions to non-comic works), focusing upon the thematic, structural, and tonal effects of the comedy. Chief among the points of discussion are the elements of the individual types of comedy, Faulkner's sometimes distinctive use of particular types, the frequency with which individual types are used in a work or in the Faulkner canon, the context in which the comic situation is placed, the weight of the situation in the work as a whole, and the humor of the individual comic passages.

The methodology is to analyze, using the above points of discussion, examples of each category of comedy from a number of Faulkner's works, including fifteen novels and selected short stories. The rationale for such a study is clear: so broad is the range of Faulkner's comedy, so high its quality, and so important its effect upon his fiction, that understanding the comedy is vital for an appreciation of America's greatest twentieth-century writer. [Order No. 7914220; 241 pages. DAI, 40A (July-Aug. 1979), 256-57.]

395 The Unity of Collected Stories of William Faulkner / Michael Allen HAYNES, Ball State University, 1978 (Joseph F. Trimmer).

Collected Stories of William Faulkner, published in 1950 and awarded the National Book Award for Fiction in 1951, is more than an arbitrarily arranged selection of representative stories. Indeed, it is remarkably similar in form and theme to many of Faulkner's novels, especially Go Down, Moses, and can profitably be read as a unified work.

Like Go Down, Moses, As I Lay Dying, Light in August, and other Faulkner novels, Collected Stories is structured around a center, in this case a theme: the relationship between man and his environment. The six chapters of Collected Stories and the stories within each chapter are arranged in a "counter-pointed" fashion; together, they offer myriad ways of looking at the central theme.

Each chapter of the work is unified thematically, and each ultimately has relevance to the theme of man in relationship to his environment. "The Country" is set in rural Yoknapatawpha County and concerns the idea of self-assertion. Most of the people of the country are close to the land and its lessons, and are independent and self-sufficient, but also have a sense of community responsibility. Thus, the world of "The Country" is ideal, a world where the relationship between man and his environment is a close one. In "The Village," set in more populated areas, especially Jefferson, Mississippi, the theme of isolation is dominant. The land is not in evidence in "The Village," and the people have neither the sense of community responsibility found in "The Country," nor real independence. The majority of the characters in "The Village" suffer some form of isolation, self-imposed, imposed by others, or both.

"The Wilderness" concerns the early days of Yoknapatawpha County and its original inhabitants, the Indians. A part of "The Wilderness" develops an almost idyllic picture, a picture of man living a life close to the land and to his fellow man. But a part of "The Wilderness" concerns the decline in values and traditions that accompanied the misuse of the land. As the Indians become more materialistic (under the influence of the encroaching white culture), they lose their moral and physical uprightness. "The Wasteland," on the other hand, is all negative. Set in a time of war, "The Wasteland" portrays a world where man is alienated from his environment. The land had been destroyed, and the men who participate in the war have lost their sense of purpose, of meaning.

Rearranged chronologically, the first four chapters of Collected Stories would give a historical picture of the decline of the relationship between man and his environment. The last two chapters of the work, "The Middle Ground" and "Beyond," do not fit into a chronological pattern, but both extend the central theme of Collected Stories into new territories.

The people of "The Middle Ground" are caught in some kind of "middle" position--between two people, two ideas, two value systems--and are forced to take action. "Beyond" transcends ordinary time and place, expanding the central theme of Collected Stories into territories like the after-life, the mind of the insane, and the world of the imagination.

Together, the forty-two stories of Collected Stories form an exhaustive examination of the theme of man and his relationship to his environment; though they can be read as representative stories from the Faulkner canon, they gain new meaning if approached as a unified whole. [Order No. 7821106; 326 pages. DAI, 39A (Nov.-Dec. 1978), 2938.]

396 The Influence of William Faulkner in Four Latin American Novelists
[Agustín Yáñez, José Donoso, Alvaro Cepeda Samudio, and Gabriel García Márquez]. / Joan Loyd HERNANDEZ, Louisiana State University and Agricultural and Mechanical College, 1978 (Alfredo R. Lozada).

The purpose of this study was to examine the influence of the Southern writer, William Faulkner, in the works of selected writers of Latin America: Agustín Yáñez, José Donoso, Alvaro Cepeda Samudio, and Gabriel García Márquez. It is a continuation of earlier work of Dr. James East Irby, "La Influencia de William Faulkner en Cuatro Narradores Hispanoamericanos," published in 1956. [Order No. 7911573; 282 pages. DAI, 39A (May-June 1979), 6756.]

397 Psychic Displacement and Adaptation in the Novels of Dickens and
Faulkner / Linda Sue KAUFFMAN, University of California at Santa Barbara, 1978 (Patrick J. McCarthy).

While some of the similarities in the work of Dickens and Faulkner have already been noticed, scholars fail to recognize the closeness of the parallels and their profound significance, for two of the greatest novelists of the 19th and 20th centuries share similar mental, moral, and artistic temperaments.

As against the current interest in structure in the novel, Faulkner's primary interest, like Dickens', is in people. The supremacy of character in the novel is thus implicit in my argument; I focus on the people in the novels of Dickens and Faulkner. Similarities in theme and technique--as well as specific examples of direct influence--will emerge, but most important are the affinities in the characters, for what Faulkner loves above all in Dickens are "those people he wrote about and what they did."

Emerging from their interest in similar kinds of characters is a fundamental moral vision which Faulkner shares with Dickens. Both novelists affirm the necessity of fellowship while recognizing the barriers which prevent men and women from acknowledging kinship. They see crime and wealth as insidiously and pervasively connected in a materialistic and rigidly caste-conscious society. Their portrayal of characters who aggressively pursue respectability and gentility further reveals that the worlds of 19th-century England and Yoknapatawpha County are more similar than different. Dickens and Faulkner both portray obsessive characters who share the same impulse to negate and to destroy, who are outraged solipsists, and who are imprisoned by crippling systems of thought which divide men on the basis of wealth or religion or color or social codes. Faulkner once spoke of "the simple things which all human beings want . . . to be loved and to love," and reflected that no natural instinct can be repressed: "You can mash it down but it comes up somewhere else and very likely in a tragic form." Similar patterns of psychic displacement can be found throughout both novelists' work. Calvinists like Mrs. Clennam and Rosa Coldfield, parasites like Chevy Slyme and Clarence Snopes, caste-builders like Thomas Sutpen and William Dorrit, and tyrants like Josiah Bounderby and Jason Compson appear with astonishing frequency in Dickens and Faulkner.

Yet in contrast to the rigid characters who inflict all kinds of psychic damage on others and themselves, their heroic characters remain flexible, adapting to changes in fortune and the times. Faulkner once described Sairey Gamp as one of his favorite characters in fiction. Her resemblance to Reba Rivers makes Faulkner's debt indisputable: both women are thoroughly familiar with the sordidness of life, but approach life with gusto and affirm their humanity. Where Sairey and Reba assume responsibility for individuals, Sissy Jupe and Dilsey take responsibility for entire families and belong to a community of grace which celebrates its interrelation. In Bleak House and the Snopes trilogy, the scope of responsibility encompasses all levels of society. Although Esther Summerson and Linda Snopes Kohl are scarred by evil, they act as agents of Providence. In the tragic worlds of Little Dorrit and Absalom, Absalom!, the wise passiveness of Amy Dorrit and Judith Sutpen is the better part of virtue.

Amid myriad forms of psychic displacement, these heroines adapt, taking responsibility for their fellows and celebrating the interdependence of the human family. While acknowledging the enormous differences which distinguish Faulkner's work from Dickens', a study of their fictional worlds illuminates the moral vision they share. In recognizing the endless interworking of good and evil, of tragedy and comedy, of despair and faith, Faulkner succeeded in ranking with Dickens as the most passionate humanist of his time. [Order No. 7824180; 262 pages. DAI, 39A (Nov.-Dec. 1978), 3573-74.]

398 Scenes from Yoknapatawpha: A Study of People and Places in the Real and Imaginary Worlds of William Faulkner / Emma Jo Grimes MARSHALL, University of Alabama, 1978 (David J. Masoner).

The theme for the study was William Faulkner and his Yoknapatawpha stories. The research was undertaken as a creative project in the interest of a more effective treatment of Faulkner's writing in college English classes. The study explored the relationship between Faulkner's fictional county of Yoknapatawpha and the reality of his own environment in northwest Mississippi. The study sought to determine how the actuality of Lafayette County and Oxford, Mississippi provided a basis for Faulkner's legend of Yoknapatawpha County and Jefferson. A further purpose of the study was to draw parallels between people, places, and events which occur in his Yoknapatawpha stories.

The study contained: (1) eighty-three photographs, many of which are from the private collections belonging to certain members of William Faulkner's family; (2) identification of each photograph and its connection with William Faulkner's family; (3) commentary based on personal communications with family members and personal friends of Faulkner, relating the photographs to an event, person, or place known to Faulkner; (4) commentary based on research of biographical and critical material about Faulkner, and a comprehensive reading of Faulkner's own writing, relating the photographs to incidents, people, and places occurring in Faulkner's fiction; (5) a chart of the Faulkner family genealogy; and (6) a discussion of additional actual events and people, of which no pictures were available, that may have served Faulkner as source material for his fiction.

Included in this study were photographs of paintings done by John Faulkner, William Faulkner's brother. These paintings illustrate various scenes from William Faulkner's writing.

The conclusions of the study were: (1) William Faulkner frequently drew upon members of his family and other people he knew as he created the characters for his stories set in Yoknapatawpha County; (2) in many instances, Faulkner seemed to transpose actual people into fictional characters with only a minor effort to disguise them; (3) in other instances, the fictional characters only bear a slight resemblance to the persons who inspired their creation; and (4) many places and events in the Yoknapatawpha saga have their counterparts in the reality of northwest Mississippi.

The conclusions drawn from the study did not suggest that Faulkner's achievement can only be appreciated by relating his imaginary world to his real world; however, the impressions which came to Faulkner through his past, through his ancestry, and through associations with the land and people of his native region recognizably influenced and shaped his body of fiction set in Yoknapatawpha County. [Order No. 7819197; 342 pages. DAI, 39A (Sept.-Oct. 1978), 2276.]

399 Verbal-Visual Simultaneity in Faulkner's The Sound and the Fury: A Literary Montage Filmscript for Quentin / Frances Elam NEIDHARDT, East Texas State University, 1978 (William T. Jack).

Purpose of the Study: The two-part work is a creative exploration intended to relate the arts of literature and film within the concept of "simultaneity," a medium involving space, time, and metaphysics. Essentially epistemological in approach, the inquiry sought to test the hypothesis that subjective or "irrational" verbal expression, when operating within a spatiotemporal fusion that dissolves linear barriers, can attain a dynamic iconography that is both plastically valid and personally meaningful. New constructs of reality seemed possible if visual and verbal forms could be recognized as bearing primary structural affinities when they are released within a fluid time-space notion that allows verbal forms to express spatiality, visual forms to express temporality, and verbal-visual forms to join in a necessary alliance.

Procedure: In order to explore the potential meeting of verbal and visual forms on the level of psychic time, two endeavors, one theoretical and one creative, were initiated.

Part I frames a theory of "verbal-visual simultaneity" (V-VS.) Development of the theory involved examination of its three components--visual, verbal, and verbal-visual creations. These components were treated, sequentially, as dynamic aesthetic processes consciously manifested "in" space and acted on "in" time, their deeper purpose being the giving of new meaning to the self.

Philosophic grounding for these creations was found in Susanne K. Langer's notion of art as "living form" and in Henri Bergson's idea of psychic duration (la duree.) Through Langer and Bergson the holistic direction of the study is established.

Design grounding was found in the formal aspects of two- and three-dimensional visual art, in literature, and in film, or four-dimensional art. These works, primarily from the modernist period in Russia, Europe, and America, are presented as illustrations of the theory and as contributory forces to the evolving definition of "visual-verbal simultaneity." Special emphases are placed on Faulkner's Quentin monologue in The Sound and the Fury, as Eisenstein's film montage through which he devised an "inner film monologue" which he sought to employ by adapting verbal stream of consciousness.

Part II presents June Second 1910 Anno Domini. It is a piece that seeks to make visible the deeper aspects of Faulkner's major work. The process of visualizing the novel in terms of a filmscript to be read independently and/or to serve as an intermediate step between the novel and a technical shooting script is made possible through the film concepts of Soviet montage. The script utilizes narrative, intellectual, and emotional cutting. Designed in fourteen sequences, the script is experimental and metaphoric in its approach to filmic texture and color, rhythm and sound. It presents The Sound and the Fury in a manner which, though in some ways entirely new, essentially adheres to Faulkner's plot, characters, and to his apocalyptic sensibility and his consciously wrought symphonic design.

Findings: Inquiry into the components of "verbal-visual simultaneity" gave rise to a tentative theory: V-VS is a spatial-temporal art principle through which fluid configurations that are metaphorically and subjectively realized can arise from the dynamic and necessary interaction of plastic verbal and visual art forms. The literary montage filmscript demonstrated that a verbal creation wherein the dynamics of time and motion and their relation to emotion are central and formal elements (i.e., a stream-of-consciousness novel) can be adapted to visual form.

Conclusion: New constructs of reality are possible if creators of visual and verbal art forms recognize primary psychic and structural affinities existing in spatio-temporal simultaneity and consciously work to create a dynamic iconology based on these commonalities. Further, the psychic depths of narrative expression can be made visual within the fourth dimension and can profitably be structured within a literary montage format. [Order No. 7816621; 169 pages. DAI, 39A (Sept. - Oct. 1978), 1165.]

400 Women as Victims in the Novels of Charles Dickens and William Faulkner / Evelyn Matthews ROMIG, Rice University, 1978 (Monroe K. Spears).

The female victim is a significant figure in the novels of Dickens and Faulkner. Her victimization can be a result of misfortune, cruelty and selfishness in others, or her own lack of self-knowledge and responsible behavior; her survival depends on how she learns to know herself and adapt to a hostile world. In this, female victims are important counterparts of Dickens' and Faulkner's better-known male protagonists, and both authors develop major female characters more than is readily acknowledged by many critics. In fact, characters like Esther Summerson, Caddy Compson, Little Dorrit, and Rosa Coldfield overshadow the action and narration in novels ostensibly concerned with many figures.

In David Copperfield, Light in August, As I Lay Dying, Our Mutual Friend, and Sanctuary, the victimized woman is often an unhappy wife or sweetheart, and domestic conflict between male and female wills is a central theme. Misused sexual attractiveness, mercenary motives for marriage, and romances that are merely "mistaken impulses of undisciplined hearts" are chronicled, and structures of traditional romance are inverted to show that love assures no happy endings in real domestic life. Victimized children are an unsurprising consequence in families who begin on weak foundations, and "motherless" girls like Florence Dombey, Caddy Compson, and Little Nell must fill adult needs and expectations too soon. In such novels, structure again echoes theme in the inversion of the fairy tale: in the real world the young hero (or heroine) is ill-equipped in terms of strength of will to provide salvation for cursed houses and doomed families.

Too much strength of will can also cause victimization, and Miss Rosa Coldfield in Absalom, Absalom! and Miss Havisham in Great Expectations are examples of the extreme will: frozen in behaviors of the past, obsessed with tragic events, they can neither change nor forgive, and determined to perpetuate the memory of their sorrows, the two old women isolate themselves in unreal worlds of vengeance and bitterness. Unable to accept that their victimization is no more cataclysmic than other human sufferings, they try to recreate their self-tormented lives as myth, repeating their stories to impressionable listeners.

In Bleak House, Little Dorrit, and the Snopes trilogy these patterns are interwoven, creating worlds of victimization. Domestic misery becomes social unrest; selfish wills, weak or strong, contribute to a dark vision of a hostile world. The individual, though, who begins this chain of suffering is also the key to a humanistic view of man's salvation. Each person (and especially the woman who nurtures children, and thus the future) must move and serve: to truly know oneself, one must yield to the demands of time and society, and act in accordance with the nature of things as they are. Inbedded in this shared view is an important difference between Dickens and Faulkner, for while Faulkner interprets the nature of things as literal nature (man's agrarian ties to the land) and thus is more concerned with eternal cycles and the past, Dickens' constant, in the face of Victorian industrial growth and change, was human behavior, the nature of man that must be perpetually dealt with--thus his focus on the present. [Order No. 7814797; 158 pages. DAI, 39A (Sept. - Oct. 1978), 1600.]

401 Narrative Mode in the Novels of William Faulkner / Hugh Michael RUPPERSBURG, University of South Carolina, 1978 (James B. Meriwether).

Throughout his career William Faulkner followed the practice of never placing his ideas into the mouth or mind of a character in his fiction. Essentially, Faulkner never speaks, and what his characters say represents only their own opinions, not those of their creator. This "doctrine of impersonality," which led Faulkner to withdraw completely from his fiction, results in narrative techniques which place emphasis on the individual perceptions of characters, who are always shown to be fallible and imperfect. The traditional definition of "point of view" is not, however, specific enough to describe these strategies; a better term is "narrative mode," which encompasses a wide range of narrative elements.

Faulkner made much use of characters as narrators and as focal characters (whose thoughts are relayed by an external, uninvolved narrator.) An external narrator becomes important, yet his voice still cannot be equated with the author's. The most significant effect of such techniques is in characterization. Numerous views, none completely accurate, may be given of one individual: he may be described objectively by the external narrator or subjectively by other characters; as a character-narrator or focal character he may speak or think about himself. This kind of narrative method also tends to create a thematic contrast between the single individual and the community, the world in which he lives.

In Light in August, for example, the perceptions of certain individuals, primarily Joe Christmas, are contrasted with the general beliefs of the Jefferson townspeople. Individuals are depicted as a combination of what they believe about themselves and what the community believes. No one has a "correct" view, and one of the novel's main themes is that the "truth" of human character is simply unknowable. In Pylon the often mistaken perspective of the Reporter is used to symbolize the breakdown of communication in the modern world, of the basic bonds which unite a community. Emphasis is placed on the illusory nature of truth, which is also a concern in Absalom, Absalom!, in which individuals over a period of three generations and seventy-five years attempt to discover the facts of Thomas Sutpen's life. Though no character ever discovers the truth, each is affected by it. The personalities of character-narrators directly influence the content of their narratives. Absalom employs such complex narrative mode techniques as the transmission of knowledge over long periods of time, the hearer-teller relationship, the tendency to focus on the listener rather than the character-narrator talking to him, and the use of one focal character, Quentin, who receives all the knowledge which the novel reveals. In Requiem for a Nun narrative emphasis focused on individual perceptions by allowing characters to stand alone, speaking independently and interacting with each other. The effect is of drama, but the method is that of a novel. In fact, the dramatic sections employ such a fictional device as an external narrator. The prose sections demonstrate that past history has a specific, demonstrable effect on the actions and dilemmas of the individual in the present.

Faulkner intended that narrative mode be an unobtrusive technique which would emphasize the more important elements of character, plot, and theme. His doctrine of impersonality enabled him to stress the importance of the individual, his perceptions and experiences. But it also places an obligation on the reader, forcing him to become involved in evaluating character strengths and weaknesses, to enter the novel as an active participant rather than a passive observer. Faulkner's achievement as a narrative artist undoubtedly places him alongside James Joyce and Herman Melville as the greatest of modern novelists in the English language. [Order No. 7816526; 343 pages. DAI, 39A (Sept.-Oct. 1978), 1576.]

402 The Social Role of Faulkner's Women: A Materialist Interpretation /
Carol Ann TWIGG, State University of New York at Buffalo, 1978 (William C. Fischer).

There are numerous episodes in the fiction of William Faulkner which dramatize the problematic nature of women's role in society. Faulkner's strong sense of how inherited patterns of thought influence the present establishes the cultural perimeters within which his female characters act. His fiction is filled with women who hold various positions in relation to the traditional female role--women who are destroyed by it, women who uphold it, and women who attempt to escape from it. Yet the critical response has generally been to view Faulkner's female characters as essentially one-sided in their representation, a response reflecting larger cultural issues concerning women's social status.

A combination of particular historical circumstances and material conditions have produced a traditional concept of the appropriate role for women in society, a concept which has been sustained by an ideology of male supremacy. Woman's sphere of activity has been limited by her exclusion from socially productive work, making her economically dependent on men, and by her vulnerability to unwanted pregnancies, keeping her subject to her biological role and preventing her from a consistent relation to socially productive work. Women are forced into a narrow, restricted role in life and prevented from fulfilling any potential which we normally define as human. Her ability to make choices and her capability for autonomous action are unnaturally limited by a deterministic view of what is possible for her.

My dissertation will develop a theory of the source of women's social position and a critique of male supremacist ideology. This theoretical chapter will provide the context in which Faulkner's female characters will be discussed. It will point out the limitations of the traditional critical view of Faulkner's women--and by inference the predominant cultural attitude toward women--demonstrating how material factors present in these characters' lives affect their ability to think and act. It will specifically examine the female characters of Absalom, Absalom!, which provide the historical context of attitudes toward women in Faulkner's fiction, Sanctuary, whose women are victimized by those attitudes, and The Wild Palms, whose central character attempts to break out of the traditional role. It will, of necessity, involve an interdisciplinary approach, drawing from women's social and political history. [Order No. 7817087; 210 pages. DAI, 39A (Sept.-Oct. 1978), 1578.]

403 The "Feeder" Motif in Selected Fiction of William Faulkner and Flannery O'Connor / Delores Cole WASHBURN, Texas Tech University, 1978 (Everett A. Gillis).

Numerous special studies of the history of Southern life reveal a sociological phenomenon which may for convenience be called the "Feeder." At the center of the family in the antebellum South, which shows the Feeder in her purest role, was a person, wife or mother, who provided the physical nourishment of her family and of guests or other persons attached to her home, achieving, at the same time among the members of the family, a sense of social well-being. During the Civil War the Feeder often, in the absence of husband or sons away at war, became the sole provider for her family.

Within the increasingly more industrialized and urbanized South of the post-bellum period, however, the Feeder sometimes relinquished her responsibilities to a black servant or other surrogate trained in the skills necessary for the Feeder role. During the same period food formerly supplied by domestic sources became available at the supermarket, and national foodchains drastically reduced the Feeder's personal labor in the preparation of daily meals. In the twentieth century the Feeder role has become increasingly less personalized as the Feeder has turned to commercially prepared foods or to restaurant fare to provide her family's needs.

The fiction of both William Faulkner and Flannery O'Connor reflect the role of the Feeder primarily against the background of the changing patterns of Southern home and community life of the antebellum and contemporary periods. In Faulkner's The Unvanquished Granny Rosa Millard appears as the traditional matriarch and Feeder of the Sartoris clan during the Civil War, being succeeded afterward by Aunt Jenny DuPre, who assumes the Feeding role in the latter part of the Sartoris saga. In the Compson clan in The Sound and the Fury Mrs. Compson relinquishes the Feeding role properly hers as a wife and mother to Dilsey Gibson, a Negro servant, who performs this service for her. Other surrogate feeders, principally Byron Bunch and Joanna Burden, appear in Light in August. In the same novel the deterioration of the Feeder role against the background of an industrialized and urbanized South, is suggested by the success or failure of the persons just designated in the Feeder role.

The fiction of Flannery O'Connor is centered primarily in the period of a modern technological culture. In the novel The Violent Bear It Away the principal Feeder, Mason Tarwater, attempts to provide food and spiritual well-being for his clan. But his nephew, George Rayber, tends to substitute his own services for his kin, his efforts reflecting an affinity for commercial feeding as opposed to the more traditional role of his uncle. In many respects Feeding activities in this novel reflect strongly spiritual overtones. Two of O'Connor's short stories, "A View of the Woods," and "Greenleaf," from Everything That Rises Must Converge, reveal the thwarted impulses of the Feeder in the modern age as represented by Mrs. Pitts and Mrs. May. In "The Life You Save May Be Your Own" and "Good Country People," from A Good Man Is Hard To Find, which also reflect an increasingly materialistic society, Mrs. Crater and Mrs. Hopewell, as Feeders, crassly neglect their Feeding responsibilities and the well-being of their children.

As may be seen in the present study, the fictional representation of the Feeder role in the work of Faulkner and O'Connor closely reflects the basic cultural development of Southern life as the region gradually changed from an agrarian to an industrialized environment. As is also shown, the Feeder motif functions as a mirror, symbol, and technical device within the works included in the study. [Order No. 7917326; 449 pages. DAI, 40A (July-Aug. 1979), 861.]

404 Faulkner's Sartoris Family and the Problem of Human Freedom / Robert Henry WEBKING, University of Virginia, 1978 (Delba Winthrop).

In this country we claim that all men should have some voice in government because all men are free human beings. This important claim of freedom merits close examination by political theorists, and William Faulkner causes us to consider it with care in his books The Unvanquished and Sartoris.

The novels are about an aristocratic Southern family, the Sartoris family. The Unvanquished takes place during the Civil War and Reconstruction, and its principal character is a Confederate Colonel named John Sartoris. Colonel Sartoris displays great courage and prudence in fighting for the losing Confederate cause. After the war he continues to fight for the South by killing carpetbaggers and establishing the "night riders" in order to keep the Negroes in their inferior position. Colonel Sartoris claims that he is fighting in the name of human freedom, and Faulkner seems to agree that Sartoris' actions are justified in terms of that end.

Sartoris is set in the years immediately following World War I. It is the story of the descendents of the Confederate Colonel and their attempt to live up to the standard that he has given them. Yet these twentieth-century Sartorises, Faulkner shows, do not know what freedom is. They are often courageous and daring in the manner of their noble ancestors, but there is no direction to their courageous motion. In Sartoris we are presented with an argument that human freedom is impossible, that men have no ability to resist the total control of nature. Faulkner disagrees with this conclusion and continues to claim that men like John Sartoris are free, that some men can shape their own destinies and therewith endow dignity upon mankind as a whole. But in the modern political community, Faulkner demonstrates, this understanding of human freedom has been lost.

Faulkner's purpose in writing his epic of the Sartoris family is to lead his reader to an appreciation of the possibilities of human action. He seeks to supply the teaching about freedom and dignity whose lack has led to the debasement of man. He wishes to inform potentially great men of what greatness entails, and he wishes to teach other men to respect that greatness. [Order No. 7916342; 210 pages. DAI, 40A (July-Aug. 1979), 1062.]

405 A Topographical Study of Thomas Hardy and William Faulkner / John Thomas WHATLEY, Yale University, 1978 (J. Hillis Miller).

Thomas Hardy and William Faulkner create imaginary worlds whose landscapes are so clearly defined that they can be mapped. Because Hardy uses the fictional area of England known as Wessex as the setting of his major novels and since Faulkner repeatedly focuses his novels on life in the apocryphal region of Mississippi known as Yoknapatawpha County, certain patterns of topographical description and certain relationships between character and environment recur in each man's works. This dissertation examines these recurring patterns of landscape description and landscape perception in an attempt to discover each novelist's own unique idea of the spatial form of the world, an idea which reveals the overall structure of consciousness in his works. In Hardy's or Faulkner's novels the perception of the landscape influences such diverse concerns as the use of topographical metaphors, the significance of certain places or kinds of places, the expression of time, and even the style and plot organization of the individual work. While methodological concerns tend to be suppressed in this dissertation, any examination of the meaning of the landscape must be viewed, as the Introduction suggests, against a background of such thinkers as Martin Heidegger, Gaston Bachelard, or Jean-Pierre Richard, who have probed the meaning of man's perception of space or examined the landscape's function as a structuring principle in literature.

Chapter One studies Faulkner's repeated use of a scene in which a character stands on a hill that reveals three distinct topographical areas: the hill itself, a clearly defined area in a valley before the character, and a prospect of misty hills which encircle the valley and merge in the distance with a river. Each of these areas has a number of characteristics which are peculiar to it, but Faulkner defines the general meaning of all three areas in terms of an opposition between the horizontal plane of space, which represents life, motion, and sexuality, and the vertical plane, which represents death, idealism, an inability to deal with life's problems, and art. A character's reaction to a hill scene demonstrates his relationship to the two significant planes of space and reveals the essential elements of his being, especially his relationship to the past. Faulkner's hill scenes freeze motion and reveal the past and future to be immanent in the landscape. This spatialized temporal structure revealed on the hill dominates the form and style of Faulkner's novels.

Chapter Two explores the landscape descriptions which always appear in the opening chapters of Hardy's novels. While the characters' perceptions of these landscapes reveal their relationships to their surroundings, Hardy also uses these descriptive scenes to indicate the true significance of those surroundings to the reader. Each of these landscape descriptions has implications which develop through the whole course of the novel it introduces, and Hardy's use of these scenes from novel to novel demonstrates the evolving tendencies of his fiction. Moreover, the landscape descriptions always contain a moving human figure which symbolizes Hardy's idea that the temporal, moral, social, and emotional courses of a character's career can be measured in terms of his movement across the topography. This linear conception of time influences the plot structure of Hardy's novels.

In the last two chapters of this dissertation, the topographical structures developed in the preceding chapters are used to give detailed readings of The Mayor of Casterbridge and Light in August. The dissertation concludes with a short Afterword and a Selected Bibliography of Hardy and Faulkner criticism and of topographical approaches to literature. [Order No. 7819498; 376 pages. DAI, 39A (Sept.-Oct. 1978), 2266.]

406 A Fable of the Invincible Dust: Faulkner's Vision of Man in A Fable /
    Chung-Hei Kim YUN, Syracuse University, 1978 (David Owen).

This dissertation is a study and re-examination of Faulkner's novel, A Fable. Due to the apparent framework Faulkner employs in this novel, A Fable has been interpreted as an account of Christ's crucifixion and resurrection retold in the modern setting. I have taken A Fable purely as a "fable," which Faulkner so explicitly states in the title--an allegory or a visibilia (the concrete reality of man) that reveals an Invisibilia (the abstract internal reality of man) which transcends any cultural and prescribed religious boundary, thus encompassing the universal human condition. In accordance with this primary assumption, I intend to demonstrate that Faulkner's A Fable extends beyond "a fable" of human destiny within the Judeo-Christian-Western Weltanschauung, and that the vision of man Faulkner chisels out in this novel comprehends that of both East and West, Christianity and Hindu-Buddhism.

The essence of Faulkner's vision of man is eloquently expressed in his phrase, "the invincible dust," referring to man. This oxymoron stands as a metaphor for the ineradicable human condition.

War and mutiny, two opposing forces in the novel, stand as external counterparts of man's inner conflict and struggle; the battleground during World War I stands for the human heart in conflict.

Circumscribed by space and time, against the "furious immobility" of human condition, man ever mutinies; to live is to mutiny. The mutiny led by the Corporal becomes the culminating embodiment of the inherent spirit of mutiny lodged in that "invincible dust."

Various modes through which man encounters reality bound by his "squirrel cage" and "the common clay" are discussed. Some dwell in the caves of their past; some flee from their past as well as present to the moral desert in "another country" in "another time," and some flee from the present to the ever beckoning dreams from beyond now. Whiteness of life, thus, is transformed into a "many-colored dome" reflecting the dreams and illusions man fabricates. The grand dream or illusion of man is to witness the miracle of transubstantiation--transformation of the perishable clay into the imperishable essence, the metamorphosis of the "common clay."

In the Passion Week of life, there are always the agonies of Gethsemane, of temptation, of crucifixion, and the splendor of resurrection. The miracle of resurrection, however, is brought down from the supernatural and the divine to the natural and humanistic level in A Fable. Metamorphosis of clay is possible without actual miracle of resurrection; one can transcend the squirrel cage without being out of it. This mystery of paradox in life is embodied in the figure of the terribly scarred British runner, the invincible dust.

The last chapter of the novel, "Tomorrow," returns to the beginning of another Passion Week on the seamless cycle of wheel of life, which encompasses the dust invincible, laughter and tears, good and evil, "two articulations," and both "yin" and "yang." [Order No. 7914269; 166 pages. DAI, 40A (July 1979), 261.]

407 The Trilogy as Experimental Form: Faulkner's Snopes Trilogy, Dos Passos' U.S.A., and Sartre's Les Chemins De La Liberté / Peter Glenn CHRISTENSEN, State University of New York at Binghamton, 1979 (Haskell Block).

This dissertation is an examination of the use that three major twentieth-century novelists have made of the novel trilogy. The works under discussion are John Dos Passos' U.S.A., William Faulkner's Snopes trilogy, and Jean-Paul Sartre's Les Chemins de la liberté. Each of these novel trilogies is composed of three autonomous novels which also function as one whole.

The first chapter provides background information on the origins of the trilogy in the Western literary tradition, the significance of the number three (Jungian perspective,) and the growth of the novel trilogy as a form since Balzac. In tracing the changes that the novel trilogy has undergone, works by Balzac, Beckett, Broch, Joyce Cary, Gide, Capek, Calvino, and Goytisolo are discussed.

A historical thread connects the works of Dos Passos and Faulkner to those of Sartre. During the 1930s, Sartre was an avid reader of both American authors, and wrote two essays on Faulkner and one on Dos Passos. Although Sartre had reservations about Faulkner's writings, he believed that

Dos Passos was the greatest novelist of his time.

Chapter Two unravels the different relationships among the four modes of vision in U.S.A. These are the narratives, biographies, Camera Eyes, and newsreels. In each novel of U.S.A., The 42nd Parallel (1930), 1919 (1932), and The Big Money (1936), a different mode of vision is stressed. In the first novel, it is the narratives; in the second, the biographies; and, in the third, the Camera Eyes. The narrative plot becomes looser and less important in each volume. Dos Passos' look at American history, beginning with the turn of the century, stops short of the 1929 stock market crash. Instead, it ends with the traumatizing social questioning raised by the execution of Sacco and Vanzetti.

Chapter Three sketches the genesis of Faulkner's The Hamlet (1940), The Town (1957), and The Mansion (1959). Various interruptions, often financial difficulties, prevented Faulkner from writing the last two volumes shortly after his work on The Hamlet. The trilogy as finally written is quite different from the original plan, and certain discrepancies between volumes remain. Faulkner capitalizes on the change in point-of-view from novel to novel. The Hamlet is told by an omniscient narrator, and the reader never has any more information than the narrator does. The Town is a dialogue between the three Snopes watchers, Gavin Stevens, Chick Mallison, and V.K. Ratliff. The reader plays a major part in structuring the dialogue. The information given by all three men is added together. In The Mansion, the reader is forced to choose between the information presented by the various narrators. The conflicting ideas on God, Providence, and destiny call into question the significance of the death of Flem Snopes. The conclusion is that men are "poor sons of bitches."

Chapter Four examines Jean-Paul Sartre's unfinished sequence novel, Les Chemins de la liberté, composed of L'Age de raison (1945), Le Sursis (1945), La Mort dans l'âme (1949), and two chapters entitled "Drôle d'amitié" from the projected novel, La Dernière Chance, of which two additional chapters have been written. Les Chemins de la liberté is Sartre's attempt to find his way toward his literary characters from the God-like powers of the narrator.

Chapter Five consolidates the relationships among the novelists and examines Sartre's essays from the 1930s on Dos Passos and Faulkner. Of the three authors, Faulkner handled the trilogy form the most skillfully. Novel trilogies vary so markedly in structure that it is impossible to provide a set of characteristics applicable to each one. Nevertheless, most successful trilogies use the third volume to combine contrasting plots or themes from the first two novels.

The appendix discusses three novel tetralogies, Claude Mauriac's Le Dialogue Intérieur, Clauder Ollier's Le Jeu de l'enfant, and Lawrence Durrell's Alexandria Quartet, and suggests a possible relationship between the trilogy and tetralogy forms. [Order No. 7923439; 383 pages. DAI, 40A (Sept.-Oct. 1979), 2045-46.]

408 Repetition and Structure: A Study of William Faulkner and Claude Simon / Margot Evelyn COBLEY, University of British Columbia (Canada), 1979 (Dr. Frederic Grover).

This study focuses on repetition as a literary device and documents its findings with examples from William Faulkner's Absalom, Absalom! and Claude Simon's La Route des Flandres. It distinguishes between the following kinds of repetition: (1) immediate repetition of words where two or more identical or near-identical words succeed each other immediately; (2) interrupted repetition of words or sentences where some material separates two or more occurrences of the same or similar words (sentences); (3) repetitive patterns in the narrative structure which take the form of (a) simple duplication of episodes, characters, narrators; (b) repetition as a retardation device in the suspense structure of Absalom, Absalom!; (c) repetition in the fragmented structure of

La Route des Flandres; (d) doubling of characters in repetitive behavioral patterns; and (4) repetition and intertextuality where literary allusions draw attention to the "copy mechanism" which connects a text with a precoded cultural system. These divisions form the major chapters of this study; they move from the smallest to the largest units of the fictional text and follow an analogical rather than a causal pattern.

The major purpose of repetition in Absalom, Absalom! and La Route des Flandres is to perform such functions as ambiguities; formal transitions between episodes; the relationship between main narrative and digressions; narrative pace, temporal stratifications, narrative voices, thematic associations; the relationship between fact and fiction; narrative progression; the symmetrical arrangement of narrative fragments; the doubling of characters and narrators in structural and psychoanalytic terms; representation and nonreferentiality in literature. As a result, repetition in Absalom, Absalom! and La Route des Flandres: (1) conforms to conventional usage in some instances and exploits experimental possibilities in others; (2) contributes both to narrative continuity and discontinuity; (3) functions as an ordering, stabilizing device but acts as a subversive agent when it erodes the coherence it supposedly establishes and maintains; (4) challenges literary conventions by blurring the distinctions between such categories as character and narrator, past and present, time of narration and time of the narrative, main story and narrative frame; (5) challenges assumptions about human nature by undermining the concept of the independent and isolated human individual; and (6) challenges assumptions about the nature of creativity by questioning the possibility of original (ex nihilo) literary production. Most critics discuss repetition in terms of sameness and "spatial form." Assuming that a word or phrase, when repeated, is identical to its previous occurrences, they conclude that the aim of repetition is to abolish time by space. But this study makes difference rather than sameness the main focus and accounts for the effect on repetition of intervening material. This new perspective corrects the overemphasis that the "spatial form" orthodoxy places on analogical relationships. When repetitive devices are analyzed both temporally and spatially, Faulkner and Simon are seen to go beyond spatial form to exploit repetition through breaks in the narrative sequence. Continuities and discontinuities thus complement each other in ways that differ significantly from "spatial form" interpretations. [DAI, (May 1980), 5851-52.]

409 An Index to the Characters in the Published and Unpublished Fiction of William Faulkner / Thomas Earle DASHER, University of South Carolina, 1979 (James B. Meriwether).

This index to characters and names in the published and unpublished fiction of William Faulkner is in two parts. The first, divided into novels, short stories, and unpublished fiction, lists the characters within each individual work. The second is an index of all named characters. Within each division of the first part of the index, works are listed alphabetically. The characters and names in each work are divided into fictional, unnamed, historical, Biblical, and mythic/literary. The master index of named characters is a conflation of all the fictional, historical, Biblical, mythic, and literary characters and names which appear in all the fiction. All characters are identified as clearly and succinctly as possible without interpretation of their roles in the work.

Each fictional character is indexed on every page on which he appears whether he is referred to by name or pronoun. If he is mentioned more than once on a page, this is not indicated. The character is listed by the name to which he is referred in the work itself with nicknames and titles included in parentheses. No names are inferred from one work to another. For example, characters and events similar to Rider's story in "Pantaloon in Black" are referred to in Requiem for a Nun. These characters appear under the unnamed characters in Requiem. If more than one name is used in a work, they are cross-referenced within the work; women who are referred to both by maiden and married names appear under the married name with maiden name cross-referenced. When several generations with the same name appear in a work, Roman numerals differentiate among them. Unnamed family relations of named characters are listed with the named characters; for example, in The Unvanquished, Col. John Sartoris' first wife, never named, is listed under "Sartoris, Col. John" as "his wife," with page references. The index of all named characters lists only those characters who are named in the individual works. In the case of characters with the same surname, those with the least identification are listed first.

Some unnamed characters, such as the Tall Convict in The Wild Palms and the Reporter in Pylon, should obviously be indexed. Other unnamed characters who figure prominently in the work or who help the reader locate significant scenes within the work are also listed. For example, the man who pulls the knife on Jewel Bundren as the Bundrens enter Jefferson in As I Lay Dying is indexed. Unnamed characters are listed only with the work in which they appear.

Faulkner often refers to historical figures in his fiction. Those who are merely referred to, such as Jack Dempsey, are not divided from the few historical characters who actually appear in the fiction, such as General Nathan Bedford Forrest in "My Grandmother Millard." All historical figures are listed by full given name, regardless of how Faulkner refers to them, followed by their birth and death dates, if known, and the pages on which they appear. Faulkner's spelling of these names is in parentheses if it varies from the standard spelling. Biblical, literary, and mythic names which are mentioned in the fiction are also indexed. [Order No. 7920030; 579 pages. DAI, 40A (Sept.-Oct. 1979), 1466.]

410 A Critical and Textual Study of William Faulkner's Flags in the Dust / George Frederick HAYHOE, University of South Carolina, 1979 (James B. Meriwether).

William Faulkner's third novel, Flags in the Dust, was completed in 1927, but it was refused by a number of publishers until Harcourt, Brace agreed to publish the book, provided that Faulkner's friend, Ben Wasson, cut it to 110,000 words. The novel was published under the title Sartoris in 1929. Random House finally published Flags in 1973, and in a reset Vintage paperback edition in 1974, but both of these texts are seriously flawed. This dissertation provides a critical reading of the novel, established the text of the novel on the basis of the manuscript and typescript which survive in the Faulkner collection at the University of Virginia, and surveys critical opinion of Sartoris and Flags in the Dust from 1929 to the present.

The body of the dissertation is a critical study of Flags in the Dust. The introduction establishes the need for such a study, paying particular attention to the history of the novel's composition and publication, and the problems which it poses editorially and critically, and attempts to explain how and why Faulkner came to write the book. A chapter of the dissertation is devoted to a reading of each of Flags' five books, paying particular attention to authorial revisions, characterization, and the inter-relation of subplots to the main plot. The conclusion provides a critical estimate of the book's significance as a novel and considers its importance in Faulkner's development as a novelist.

The first five appendices concern the text of the novel. Appendix A provides a newly-edited version of Faulkner's manuscript introduction to Flags, previously published as "William Faulkner's Essay on the Composition of Sartoris." A historical collation of variants between the typescript of the novel and the two published editions is found in Appendix B. Appendix C contains a table of suggested emendations to the 1973 Random House text, as well as those common to the 1974 Vintage text; Appendix D is a table of additional suggested emendations to the Vintage edition. Both appendices B and C contain textual notes. The text established in Appendix C is used in the critical discussion of the novel. Appendix E is a transcription of Faulkner's rejected manuscript opening to the novel.

An annotated bibliography comprises Appendix F. Included are reviews, critical books, articles, and dissertations which consider Sartoris and Flags in the Dust. [Order No. 8002253; 566 pages. DAI, 40A (Jan. 1980), 4036.]

411 The Making of a Novelist: William Faulkner's Career to the Writing of The Sound and the Fury / Martin Lewis KREISWIRTH, University of Toronto (Canada), 1979.

In 1928 when William Faulkner (according to his subsequent account) closed his doors to publishers and began writing The Sound and the Fury only for himself, it seemed as if he was beginning his literary career anew. For him the novel was a decisive turning point, unique in its conception, composition, and execution, and critical studies of his development have insisted almost unanimously upon the singularity of this first--and perhaps greatest-- of his major achievements, emphasizing the degree to which it differs in substance, technique, and accomplishment from the works which preceded it. Close examination of the early stages of Faulkner's career tends to suggest, however, that The Sound and the Fury is more intimately related to its antecedents than has been formerly thought, and that its very uniqueness depends upon a transmutation of themes, narrative strategies, and actual scenes from those earlier works. Underlying the strikingly obvious technical differences between The Sound and the Fury and its predecessors is a fundamental similarity in creative procedure involving very much the same kind of borrowing and reworking of previously explored materials.

While critics have viewed The Sound and the Fury in terms of sudden creative leap, the process by which Faulkner became a novelist capable of its achievement was in fact a very gradual one. From the beginning of his career, Faulkner later stated, he set out to learn all he could about the craft of writing, and his early literary education included a great deal of reading of both speculative and imaginative works as well as a programme of creative exercises based, to a large extent, upon that reading. The derivative poetry and deliberately varied prose of the early nineteen-twenties provide evidence of this self-conscious, and largely self-imposed, apprenticeship. Much of Faulkner's verse--including his first published work, The Marble Faun--involves the imitation and creative examination of existing literary texts and reveals, on the one hand, his initial dependence upon late romantic styles, on the other, an innovative and independent approach to literary form already clearly evident in The Marble Faun. The heterogeneous prose pieces written during this period, although less obviously derivative, point to a similar concern for aesthetic self-education and reflect the young writer's deliberate attempt to explore the full technical range of his newly adopted medium.

Faulkner's first novel, Soldiers' Pay, can be seen as the result, or more properly the extension, of these prose explorations. In the process of developing an extended narrative structure, he transcended the merely experimental and discovered how his prodigious facility could be translated into viable organizational strategies, some of which were to prove important for his future work. This restless experimentation continued with Mayday, Mosquitoes, and the unfinished novel, "Elmer," texts which added new techniques to Faulkner's growing repertoire, but which were perhaps of greater long-term importance in showing him what he would have to leave behind.

Throughout this period of apprenticeship Faulkner learned from both positive and negative experiences, and there can be little doubt that the failure of Mosquitoes in some sense caused him to change his basic subject matter and call his muse home. In writing Flags in the Dust, "Father Abraham," and the related Yoknapatawpha stories, Faulkner for the first time turned squarely toward his native region and began to create that vast and densely imagined fictional world which was to occupy him for the remainder of his career and provide a secure basis for his subsequent creative adventures. In writing The Sound and the Fury he was able to draw freely upon that already-established setting and context, just as he was in a position to adapt narrative strategies from "Elmer" and Soldiers' Pay and organizational procedures from The Marble Faun and so arrive at a cumulative and totally transformed synthesis of aspects of his genius for which he had previously found only brief and fragmentary expression. [DAI, 40A (June 1980), 6280.]

412 Present Past: Hawthorne, Faulkner, and the Problem of History / Roger Warren LUNDIN, University of Connecticut, 1979 (Milton R. Stern).

Since the first explorers landed on its shores almost half a millennium ago, America has been a land blessed--some would say cursed--by a tradition of prophetic millennialism. And, as the last several decades of our scholarship have shown, America has also had a distinct literature to give voice to its visions of apocalyptic glory. That literature has cultivated and worshipped its image of America as a vast and virgin land offering Western man a radical break with the corrupt history of the Old World.

Yet, alongside this corporate image of America as either an apocalyptic kingdom or a self-yielding paradise, there has grown up a sharply different understanding of American history and destiny. This countervailing view has found its outlet in a literature highly anti-millennial in spirit and implicitly, if not overtly, Christian in its understanding of nature and history.

Nathaniel Hawthorne and William Faulkner worked in the mainstream of this counter-tradition. Throughout their fiction, Hawthorne and Faulkner show a profound awareness of man's historicity. That is, they define man as a creature bound and limited by his existence within history: a creature saddled with an inescapable moral past, with a keen sense of time's fleeting present, and with a painful awareness of his own inevitable death. Hawthorne and Faulkner saw that this consciousness of history may free man from forces which claim final authority over him. But they also sensed that man's historicity implies that all his judgments are partial and limited, all his actions tainted by guilt, his beliefs produced by his desires, his hopes destined for the grave.

There is scant room for corporate American millennialism or unbounded romantic optimism within such a conservative view of human possibilities. And though Hawthorne dwelt upon his own historical consciousness, he could not rest within the confines of his vision. He demanded of life something more than history alone could offer. He believed, especially in his final years, that he had found it in the domestic mythology he fabricated around his life with his wife, Sophia. In individual chapters, my dissertation examines each of Hawthorne's four major novels. It explores the artistic disintegration which is only hinted at in The Scarlet Letter's vague hope for a feminine "angel and apostle of the coming revelation," but which is plainly proclaimed in The Marble Faun's desperate vision of America as a land of purity and innocence.

Faulkner adheres to the vision of historicity far more consistently and ruthlessly than does Hawthorne. All is given to history in Faulkner's fiction. Faulkner seeks to bear the burden of his own bleak perspective, not by returning to an older order of faith, not by escaping to a realm of pure but futile fantasies, but by stubbornly clinging to the category of hope. In each of the three novels I discuss in separate chapters--The Sound and the Fury, Light in August, and Absalom, Absalom!--Faulkner strives to desacralize all human claims to finality within history and, in turn, to discover grounds for the hope man must have as he struggles with the hard realities of that history.

My dissertation, then, seeks to explore the often observed similarities between Hawthorne and Faulkner. I see them as two of our greatest anti-millennial prophets, yet I recognize vast differences in their separate responses to the understanding they shared of man's historicity. [Order No. 7917361; 262 pages. DAI, 40A (Sept.-Oct. 1979), 1469-70.]

413 The Development of the Black Character in the Fiction of William Faulkner / Sandra Delores MILLOY, University of Michigan, 1979 (Joseph Blotner).

This study focuses on the positive changes in William Faulkner's attitude toward and treatment of black people in his fiction. It traces the development of Faulkner's portrayal of black character from a poorly-conceived stereotype to a fully-realized individual. Chapter One considers Faulkner within the family context and Faulkner, the non-fictionist. It explains to what extent the Faulkner family and the South formed Faulkner's personal beliefs about black people and influenced his literary presentation of them. Chapter Two deals with the Southern literary tradition out of which Faulkner grew and began to write. In this chapter, I show how Faulkner included in his fiction some of the stereotyped black characters and some of the stereotyped notions about Blacks that Southern literature and Southern society had taught him. Chapter Three shows to what extent Faulkner succeeded in destroying the popular black stereotypes and in creating sharply individualized black characters. Chapter Four is devoted to the Mississippi love-hate mystique from which William Faulkner and many of his humane white characters suffer.

Faulkner begins his depiction of black character with the popular black stereotypes. However, he gradually rejects these figures and creates black individuals. Several times during the course of thirty-five years, Faulkner succeeds in destroying certain black stereotypes. The positive changes in his presentation of Blacks are occasioned by the changes in his attitude toward black people in general. As a result of the dramatic contemporary social and political developments in the South, Faulkner became increasingly aware of and incensed by the social injustices suffered by Negroes. He expressed his views on the "race question" in a series of speeches, essays, and letters to the editors of newspapers and magazines. Many of these ideas found their way into his fiction and affected his portrayal of black characters.

Faulkner's attitude toward black people and his literary presentation of them change, but these changes are not systematic. His most realistic and heroic black character is not created at the end, but near the middle, of his career. A close scrutiny of Faulkner's fiction and non-fiction will show that the changes in his attitude toward Blacks are by no means revolutionary. Faulkner comes to sympathize with the "Black cause" but he does not abandon all of the stereotyped and negative attitudes toward black people that he had inherited from his family and his region. Although he creates several memorable black individuals, his body of fiction is never free of black stereotypes.

Faulkner, the private citizen, remained paternalistic, ultimately unable to believe in the intrinsic equality of Blacks, as his continuing non-fictional writings and public statements reveal. As for Faulkner the artist, black stereotypes can be found throughout his fiction. Even though Faulkner is to be praised for his ambitious attempt to transcend such stereotypes in American literature and create realistic, responsible black individuals, his vision of Blacks seriously limited his portrayal of the diversity of black life. [Order No. 7916780; 243 pages. DAI, 40A (July-Aug. 1979), 856.]

414 1. Emerson's "Self-Reliance" from Journal to Essay. 2. Faulkner's Early Writing: The Discomfort of the Text. 3. Tom Jones in London /

William Halsey PLUMMER, Jr., State University of New Jersey (New Brunswick), 1979 (Richard Poirier).

1. Emerson's "Self-Reliance" From Journal to Essay. This essay examines the career of the language of "Self-Reliance" from its first formulation in the journals through its use in the lectures to its status in the finished essay. It is posited here that an Emersonian essay is best experienced as a "course" of verbal events whose turns and tropes are staggered to jolt the reader to his own unacknowledged potential. The first section considers "Self-Reliance" against the backdrop of Emerson's own spiritual life in 1840, when the essay itself was composed; the conclusion is that, unlike "Spiritual Laws" and "Circles," "Self-Reliance" does not dramatize its author's crisis in "self-trust." The second section examines how, in the journals, Emerson works up strong, positive sentences: that is, by a species of "self-indignation" and "self-remonstration." The final section is a longer musing on Emerson's triumphs and failures of expression in "Self-Reliance": his ambivalence towards low, vigorous language; his desire for "universal signs," which leads him to subtract "voice" from the essay.

2. Faulkner's Early Writing: The Discomfort of the Text. Faulkner's early novels are troubled, not merely ill-executed. Contemporary reviewers spoke repeatedly of their "discomfort" in reading the early work, induced by what they took to be Faulkner's own lack of ease. The first section of this essay examines Faulkner's early critical writing: the conclusion is that a conspiracy of influences (exerted by such as critics Willard Huntington Wright and William Stanley Braithwaite, and by the New Orleans Double Dealer) deterred Faulkner from turning to his own more congenial native materials until his third novel, Flags in the Dust. The section examines Soldiers' Pay, a prototypical war novel with only one truly Faulknerian character: Januarius Jones, who is a register of obsessive (sex and death) and artistic interests Faulkner is not yet able to accommodate in his fiction. In the early work Faulkner assumes attitudes of sophistication that are inimical to his art.

3. Tom Jones in London. In the spring of 1778, even as he was beginning the London books of Tom Jones, Fielding announced in his two-penny weekly, The Jacobite's Journal, that he was swearing off irony as an overall narrative strategy. The repercussions of this announcement are felt in Tom Jones. Fielding's "best reader" in the first two-thirds of Tom Jones is an accomplice to the narrator's ironies, many of which are at the expense of a hypothetical dull reader. With the disavowal of irony as an overall narrative strategy, the best reader is all at sea. Fielding continues to employ what William Empson has called "double irony," but such a device is dependent upon an overall confederacy between reader and narrator, and "double irony" degenerates from moral complexity into moral relativism. Having sworn off the language of burlesque, Fielding seeks a new language and finds it in the fashionable genres of "weeping sentimental comedy" and "bourgeois tragedy." In addition, he no longer burlesques but borrows certain of Samuel Richardson's attitudes and devices in Clarissa. [Order No. 7928439; 130 pages. DAI, 40A (Jan. 1980), 4029.]

415 The Economy of Memory in Faulkner's Yoknapatawpha / Thomas Branch PRUIT, University of Dallas, 1979 (Melvin Bradford).

Memory is understood in this dissertation to be derivative of the memoria of the classical rhetorical-ethical tradition, especially as it is used by Cicero and Quintilian. The first rule for the ancient orator regarding memory is to assign those things to be remembered to a particular place, and the second rule is to assign those places in a particular order. For the ancient teacher of ethics the study of prudence begins with memory: one must first remember examples of virtue before one can begin to practice and to know virtue, to be virtuous. In discovering Yoknapatawpha County Faulkner rediscovered the traditional memoria. For Faulkner, remembrance is an activity essential to the attainment of manhood. It involves a redemption of the past and a deepening of the present.

The argument is divided into three sections. The first section introduces the idea of the classical memoria through an examination of Cicero (De Inventione, De Oratore, Tusculan Disputations), Quintilian (Institutio Oratoria), and the anonymous author of the Ad Herennium. Important also to this part of the argument are Fustel de Coulanges' The Ancient City, and Frances Yates' The Art of Memory. Following this examination of Cicero et al., the argument passes to a discussion of the rhetorical theory of Richard Weaver who serves to make articulate in general terms much of what Faulkner imbeds in images and action.

The second section of the argument involves a discussion of five Faulkner novels: The Sound and the Fury, The Unvanquished, Go Down, Moses, The Reivers, and Absalom, Absalom! respectively. Fundamentally, this section treats the relation of memory and time, from the concern with personal time in The Sound and the Fury to the relation of memory to historical time in Absalom, Absalom!. The three middle chapters of this section deal with the tripartite progression in the process of remembrance for the normative Faulknerian hero. From the confrontation with doom brought on by defeat in The Unvanquished arises the possibility of true suffering which, in turn, provides the basis for a genuine memoria. In Go Down, Moses, turning from catastrophe to the relation to the earth, memory is considered in terms of the two major symbols associated with it, the hunt and the hearth. Beyond one's confrontation with doom and one's relation to the land is one's relation to a traditional code of behavior especially as it finds itself beleaguered by a myriad of inimical elements pressuring it to compromise and ultimately dissolve. The Reivers is considered as the depiction of an attempt to preserve a traditional code of behavior through two major symbols, the horse and the car.

The third section of the argument shifts the relation of memory from time to space as it considers Intruder in the Dust. The significance of Charles Mallison's act of graverobbing is considered in terms of memory. In addition, the speeches of Gavin Stevens are considered as an integral part of the progression of Mallison's character from boyhood to manhood. The practical, social role of memory, explored and made manifest in Intruder in the Dust, is perhaps its most beneficial aspect, as it achieves both personal and civic virtue. [Order No. 7924837; 346 pages. DAI, 40A (Nov. 1979), 1647.]

AUTHOR INDEX

Adamowski, Thomas Henry 145
Addison, Bill Kaler 194
Aiken, David Hubert 309
Akin, Warren, IV 310
Allredge, Betty Jean Edwards 336
Antoniadis, Roxandra Illiaschenko 169
Archer, Lewis Franklin 114
Arnold, Edwin Turner, III 387
Arthur, Christopher Edward 337
Backman, Melvin Abraham 47
Ballenger, Sara E. 38
Ballew, Steven Early 278
Bamberg, Robert D. 51
Barbour, Brian Michael 146
Barricklow, Gary Edwin 338
Bartheleme, Helen Moore 339
Bassett, John Earl 195
Beauchamp, Fay Elizabeth 279
Beasley, William M. 30
Bedell, George Chester 147
Bellue, John Vernon 311
Berets, Ralph Adolph 148
Berk, Lynn Marie Lipphart 223
Berner, Robert Leslie 48
Berrone, Louis C., Jr. 247
Berry, Thomas E. 6
Bickham, Robert S. 52
Billingslea, Oliver La Fayette 196
Blair, Arthur Hadfield 312
Bluefarb, Samuel 109
Bond, Christopher James 280
Bosha, Francis John 388
Bradford, Melvin Eustace 122
Brady, Emily Kuempel 60
Brady, Ruth Annette Huntington Hartmann 197
Bricker, Emil Stanley 198
Brogunier, Joseph Edward 149
Broughton, Panthea Reid 199
Brown, May Cameron 313
Brown, William Richard 102
Brylowski, Walter Marion 84
Buck, Lynn Dillon 340
Burggraf, David Leroy 314
Burns, Mattie Ann 281
Butterworth, Abner Keen, Jr. 170

Byrne, Mary Ellen 341
Byrne, Sister Mary Enda 123
Cain, Kathleen Shine 389
Callen, Shirley Parker 61
Cantrell, William Frank 171
Cantrill, Dante Kenneth 282
Carey, Glenn Owaroff 62
Carnes, Frank Ferrell 124
Carothers, James B. 172
Carpenter, Thomas P. 3
Castille, Philip Dubuisson 361
Cater, Althea C. 4
Cavanaugh, Hilayne E. 362
Chavkin, Allan Richard 363
Chisholm, W. C. 85
Christensen, Peter Glenn 407
Chung, Hae-Ja Kim 248
Ciancie, Ralph A. 86
Clark, Anderson Aubrey 315
Clark, Edward Depriest, Sr. 224
Clark, William Bedford 249
Clark, Winifred 200
Coale, Samuel Chase 173
Cobley, Evelyn Margot 408
Coffee, Jessie Alma 201
Collins, Robert George 63
Colson, Theodore Lewis 115
Corridori, Edward L. 202
Corwin, Ronald Lloyd 342
Coulombe, Joseph Michael 174
Cox, Leland Holcombe, Jr. 364
Creighton, Joanne Vanish 150
Crigler, John Peyton, III 343
Crow, Peter Glenn 250
Culley, Margaret Mary Mulvehill 225
Curto, Josephine J. 151
Dasher, Thomas Earle 409
Davenport, F. Garvin, Jr. 116
Davis, Roger Lewis 203
Davis, Thadious Marie 344
Dean, Charles Wilbur, Jr. 316
Dean, Sharon Welch 251
Degenfelder, E. Pauline Sutta 226
Degroot, Elizabeth M. 117
Dennis, Stephen Neal 152
Desmond, John Francis 204

Author Index

Despain, Norma LaRene 317
Devlin, Albert J. 175
Diffey, C. T. 103
Dike, Donald Albyn 15
Ditsky, John Michael 118
Dodds, John Lloyd 390
Donohoe, Eileen Marie 391
Doster, William Clark 22
Dowell, Bobby Ray 64
Downey, Elizabeth Ann 227
Dunlap, Mary Montgomery 176
Eaglin, Patrick Gerald 365
Eberly, Ralph Dunbar 12
Egolf, Robert H. 392
Elder, John Clark 252
Elkin, Stanley Lawrence 53
Emerson, O. B. 65
England, Kenneth 1
Ewell, Barbara Nelle 153
Fadiman, Regina Kobacker 177
Farnham, James Franklin 66
Fazio, Rocco Roberto 87
Ferguson, Robert Clark 205
Ficken, Carl Frederick Wilhelm 228
Fitzgerald, James Randolph 253
Fletcher, Mary Dell 283
Flory, Joseph Weldon 229
Folks, Jeffrey Jay 366
Foran, Donald James 254
Ford, Daniel Gordon 255
Foster, Ruel Elton 2
Fowler, Doreen Ferlaino 284
Franklin, Rosemary Futrelle 125
Friedling, Sheila 256
Friend, George Leroy 88
Garson, Helen Sylvia 119
Gegerias, Mary 126
Gernes, Sonia Grace 318
Gill, Linda Gerson 319
Gladstein, Mimi Reisel 257
Gold, Joseph 39
Goddenberger, Mary Ellen Marshall 345
Goren, Leyla Melek 72
Graves, Allen Wallace 16
Greene, Robert Ira 394
Gregg, Alvin Lanier 154
Gregory, Charles Thomas 127
Gregory, Nancy Eileen 320
Gresham, Jewell Handy 178
Gribbin, Daniel Vernon 258
Grimwood, James Michael 346
Grove, James Leland 128
Guetti, James Lawrence 89
Hafner, John Henry 155
Hamblin, Bobby Wayne 347
Harrington, Catherine S. 73
Harter, Carol Ann Clancey 179
Harwick, Robert Duane 104
Hawkins, Ewell Otis, Jr. 54
Hayes, Elizabeth Tracy 394
Hayhoe, George Frederick 410
Haynes, Michael Allen 395
Hedin, Anne Miller 321
Heller, Terry L. 259
Hepburn, Kenneth William 129
Hernandez, Joan Loyd 396
Higgins, Claire M. 17
Hinchcliffe, A. P. 74
Hinchey, John Joseph 285
Hinkle, Diane Leonard 206
Hoadley, Frank Mitchell 23
Hochberg, Mark Robert 180
Hochstettler, David 230
Hodges, Elizabeth Lowther 156
Hofammann, Albert G., Jr. 9
Hoff, Patricia Joanne 130
Holden, Sarah Holland 367
Holmes, Edward Morris 67
Honeywell, Arthur J. 18
Hornback, Vernon Theodore, Jr. 75
Howell, John Michael 76
Hunt, John W., Jr. 55
Hutcheon, Philip Loring 286
Hyde, Monique Raymonde 207
Ilacqua, Alma Aquilino 287
Jaffe, Evelyn 368
Jenkins, Lee Clinton 260
Johnson, Beulah V. 24
Jordan, Peter Wilson 288
Josephs, Mary Jim 261
Kartiganer, Donald Mordecai 90
Kauffman, Linda Sue 397
Keiser, Merle Wallace 369
Kelly, Jimmy Lee 370
Kerlin, Charles Martin, Jr. 131
Kibler, James Everett, Jr. 181
Kirk, Robert Warner 40
Knox, Robert Hilton 41
Komar, Kathleen Lenore 371
Kondravy, Connie Ranck 322
Kornfeld, Milton Herbert 183
Korenman, Joan Smolin 182
Kreiswirth, Martin Lewis 411
Labatt, Blair Plowman, Jr. 289
Lampl, Nancy Williams 348
Lang, Eleanor Marianne 184
Lannon, John Michael 131
Lawson, Lewis Allen 91
Lawson, Richard Alan 110

Author Index

Leaska, Mitchell A. 157
Lehan, Richard D. 42
Lennox, Sara Jane King 262
Levins, Lynn Gartrell 263
Levit, Donald Jay 158
Libby, Anthony Peter 159
Lilly, Paul Raymond, Jr. 208
Lincoln, Ruth Thompson 264
Little, Matthew Wood 323
Lloyd, James Barlow 324
Longley, John Lewis, Jr. 31
Loughrey, Rev. Thomas Francis 68
Lowrey, Perrin Holmes 32
Lundin, Roger Warren 412
Lyday, Charles Lance 372
McAlexander, Hubert Horton 265
McClelland, Benjamin Wright 232
McCorquodale, Marjorie Kimball 25
McDowell, Richard David 373
McHaney, Thomas Lafayette 160
McLaughlin, C. D. 69
Macmillan, Duane Johnson 233
MacMillan, Kenneth Douglas 234
McWilliams, David Dean 161
Maguire, Robert Emmett 374
Makuck, Peter Landers 209
Malin, Irving Mesmin 35
Mallone, Helen H. 325
Manley, Justine M. 290
Marks, Margaret Louise 375
Marshall, Emma Jo Grimes 398
Mascitelli, David William 132
Massey, Tom Malcolm 162
Matthews, John Thomas 349
Matton, Collin Gilles 291
Meeks, Elizabeth Lorraine 105
Mellard, James Milton 92
Memmott, Albert James 266
Meriwether, James B. 36
Meyer, Norma Lee 210
Mikules, Thomas Leonard 37
Miller, Bernice Berger 376
Milliner, Gladys Welch 185
Millis, Ralph Eugene 377
Milloy, Sandra Delores 413
Milum, Richard Allen 235
Miner, Ward L. 10
Mirabelli, Eugene, Jr. 93
Moore, Robert Henry 236
Moreland, Agnes Louise 49
Momberger, Philip 186
Moriarty, Jane V. 19
Mortimer, Gail Linda 350
Moses, Henry Clay, III 133
Murphree, John Wilson, Jr. 326

Murray, Trudy Kehret 292
Musil, Robert Kirkland 187
Nadeau, Robert L. 188
Neidhardt, Frances Elam 399
Newhall, Eric Luther 327
Nigliazzo, Marc Anthony 267
Nilon, Charles Hampton 11
Nochimson, Martha 351
Norris, Nancy Rife 211
Oldenburg, Egbert William 111
Oppewall, Peter 56
Orloff, Kossia 378
Ott, Friedrich Peter 134
Overly, Dorothy N. 7
Page, Sally Rigsbee 163
Palumbo, Donald Emanuel 352
Parr, Susan Dale Resneck 237
Pastore, Philip Edward 164
Pate, Frances Willard 165
Patten, Catherine Mary 238
Peabody, Henry Wooten 239
Pearson, Theresa Lee 353
Peek, Charles Arthur 212
Penick, Edwin A., Jr. 20
Perry, Thomas Edmund 293
Peters, Erskine Alvin 354
Peterson, Richard Frank 166
Petesch, Donald Anthony 135
Pieper, Janet Leah Steffen 355
Pierce, Constance Mae 240
Pindell, Richard Philip 213
Pires, Sister Mary Dolorine, SS. CC. 189
Pisani, Assunta Sarnacchiaro 356
Player, Raleigh Preston, Jr. 106
Ploegstra, Henry Alden 112
Plummer, William Halsey, Jr. 414
Polek, Fran James 136
Polk, Noel Earl 214
Pollock, Agnes Schelling 107
Powell, Irma Anne 167
Pruit, Thomas Branch 415
Radomski, James Louis 294
Ramsey, William Currie 215
Randolph, Linda Scott 328
Reed, Richard Allen 216
Reirdon, Suzanne Renshaw 295
Reynolds, Gordon Duncan 268
Richards, Lewis Alva 77
Richardson, Harold Edward 78
Richardson, Kenneth E. 70
Rigsby, Carol Anne Roscoe 269
Rinaldi, Nicholas Michael 79
Riskin, Myra Jehlen 137
Robbins, Deborah Lynn 357

Author Index

Roberts, James L. 33
Roberts, Melvin Reed 296
Robinson, Evalyne Carter 217
Rodnon, Stewart 57
Rollyson, Carl Edmund, Jr. 329
Romig, Evelyn Matthews 400
Rose, Maxine Smith 270
Rosenman, John Brown 190
Ross, Maude Cardwell 94
Ross, Stephen Moodey 241
Routh, Michael Perry 271
Rower, Ann Doniger 297
Rubel, Warren Gunther 95
Rudensky, Bernice J. 298
Ruppel, James Robert 379
Ruppersburg, Hugh Michael 401
Samway, Patrick H. 299
Savarese, Sister Paul Christi 242
Scanlan, Margaret Christine Trieschmann 243
Schendler, Sylvan 26
Schermbrucker, William Gerald 272
Schlumpf, Otto Norman 300
Schultz, William James 138
Sederberg, Nancy Belcher 380
Sengelli, Nazan Feride 381
Serafin, Sister Joan Michael, F. S. E. 139
Serruya, Barbara Booth 301
Shanaghan, Father Malachy Michael, O. S. B. 50
Shaw, Joy Farmer 382
Shelton, Frank Wilsey 218
Sidney, George R. 43
Siegel, Roslyn 302
Simon, John Kenneth 80
Simpson, Hassell Algernon 71
Skenazy, Paul V. 203
Slabey, Robert M. 58
Slade, John Howard 304
Slatoff, Walter Jacob 27
Smith, Don Noel 191
Smith, H. M. 44
Smith, Kearney Isaac 273
Smith, Stella P. 358
Solomon, Robert H. 330
Springer, Anne M. 45
Stein, Randolph Edward 108
Steinberg, Aaron 81
Stephenson, Shelby Dean 305
Stewart, David Hugh 46
Stock, Jerold Howard 383
Stonum, Gary Lee 274
Strauss, Mary Therese 192
Stubbelfield, Charles F. 140
Sullivan, Barbara White 141
Sullivan, William Patrick 59
Sutton, George William 120
Swiggart, Charles P. 21
Tanner, Jimmie Eugene 96
Taylor, Walter Fuller, Jr. 97
Thomas, Frank Howard, III 244
Thompson, Evelyn Joyce 245
Toles, George Edward, Jr. 359
Tololyan, Khachig 331
Tran, Phiet Qui 384
Trimmer, Joseph Francis 142
Tritschler, Donald Hubert 34
Trowbridge, William Leigh 332
Tumulty, Rev. Michael J. 275
Twigg, Carol Ann 402
Ulrey, Pamela Anne 82
Vickery, Olga Weetland 13
Vorpahl, Ben Merchant 113
Wall, Carey Gail 98
Washburn, Delores Cole 403
Waters, Maureen Anne 333
Watson, James Gray 143
Webb, Gerald Fred 246
Webking, Robert Henry 404
Wee, Morris Owen 306
Weeks, Willis Earl 276
Weingrat, C. L. 99
Weinstein, Arnold Louis 144
Wenstrand, Thomas E. 121
Westbrook, Andrew Jackson 193
Weybright, Myron Duane 219
Whately, John Thomas 405
Whitaker, Charles Francis 307
White, John Owen 220
Whittenberg, Judith Bryant 386
Whittington, Joseph Richard 83
Wigley, Joseph Alexander 28
Wiley, Electa C. 100
Williams, David Larry 277
Williams, Philip Eugene 101
Wilson, Gillian Jennifer 385
Wilson, Herman O. 29
Winkel, Carol Ann Groening 308
Winn, Harlan Harbour, III 334
Wittenberg, Judith Bryant 386
Wormley, Margaret J. 5
Wouters, A. F. M. 8
Yamada, Agnes Akiko 221
Yep, Laurence Michael 335
Yonce, Margaret Janis 222
Yun, Chug-Hei Kim 406
Ziegfeld, Richard Evan 360
Zink, Karl E. 14
Zrime, Marie-Antoinette Untereiner 168

DIRECTOR INDEX

Adams, Hazard 84
Adams, Richard P. 61, 76, 361, 373
Adams, Robert M. 89
Allen, Gay Wilson 118
Allen, Robert L. 121
Anderson, Charles R. 186
Antush, John V. 247
Apple, Alfred, Jr. 159
Arthos, John 12, 27
Bacon, W. A. 28
Bader, Arno L. 56
Baker, Carlos H. 346, 354
Ball, Roland C. 161
Banta, Martha 318
Bargill, Oscar 31
Beatty, Richard Croom 1, 2, 30
Bennett, George N. 124
Benson, Carl 255, 281
Benstock, Bernard 166
Bent, Rudyard Kipling 100
Berryman, Charles B. 254
Berthoff, Warner B. 285
Bigelow, Gordon E. 188, 376
Blair, Walter 7, 32
Blessing, Richard 282
Block, Haskell 407
Blotner, Joseph 413
Boatright, Mody C. 94
Bone, Robert A. 178, 333
Bradford, Melvin 415
Bradley, E. Sculley 10, 45
Brooks, Cleanth 343
Brown, Clavin S. 156
Champigny, Robert 207
Cargill, Oscar 31, 57, 81
Carlock, Mary Sue 358
Chase, Richard 47, 49, 59
Church, Margaret 307
Clark, Harry Hayden 11
Clayes, Stanley A. 390
Colacurcio, Michael J. 133
Collins, Carvel 391
Colvert, James B. 273
Cowan, Louise S. 374
Cozada, Alfred R. 396

Cunliffe, Marcus 74
Davis, Joe Lee 4
Day, Douglas 382
Day, Robert A. 351
Delgarno, Emily K. 344
Dowden, Wilfred S. 286
Downer, James W. 85
Durham, Philip C. 203, 327
Eberhart, Wilfred 217
Elconin, Victor A. 23, 83, 204
Elderry, B. R. M., Jr. 29
Elias, Robert 180
Ellmann, Richard 26, 34
Emerson, O. B. 270
Enck, John J. 91
Engel, Monroe 93
Falk, Eugene H. 206
Ferrell, Wilfred A. 220, 276
Feidelson, Charles, Jr. 252
Fiedler, Leslie A. 335, 350
Fischer, William C. 402
Flanagan, John T. 53, 62, 88
Folsom, James K. 368
Foster, Ruel E. 383
Frakes, James R. 184, 322, 392
Frenz, Horst 38
Fritz, A. J. 96
Frohock, Wilbur M. 144, 168
Gale, Robert L. 143, 192
Galloway, David D. 226
Giannone, Richard 208
Gillis, Everett A. 403
Gindin, James 148, 352
Gorman, Thomas R. 290
Gose, Ellito 234
Gower, Herschel 315
Graham, Philip 92
Greenhut, Morris 46
Greiner, Donald J. 380
Grier, Edward F. 175
Griffith, Frank Clark 33
Gross, Eugene 278
Gross, Harvey S. 63
Grover, Frederic 408
Guerard, Allens J. 41

Director Index

Hadley, Paul E. 77
Hafley, James 275
Hagopian, John V. 179
Hagstrum, Jean H. 187
Hakutani, Yoshinobu 294
Hall, James W. 48
Handy, William J. 221, 336
Harter, Carol Clancy 314
Harvey, Robert D. 201
Haugh, Robert F. 106, 191, 225
Haugh, L. Robert 104
Hayes, Curtis W. 210
Hayman, David 243
Heimert, Alan 365
Hendy, Andrew J. Von see Von Hendy
Heston, Lillia A. 219
Hilen, Andrew R., Jr. 73
Hill, Archibald A. 154
Hill, Hamlin 109, 323
Hiltner, Seword 55
Hoffman, Daniel 211
Hoffman, Frederick J. 39, 42
Hoffmann, Frederick J. 13
Holland, Lawrence B. 274, 349
Holman, C. Hugh 218, 263, 312
Hopper, Stanley 114
Horsford, Howard 87, 195
Houck, Charles L. 326
Howard, Alan 359
Howard, Leon 37, 107, 267, 301
Hume, Robert A. 162
Isle, Walter 367
James, Stuart 64, 69, 239
Jepsen, Laura 153
Johnson, David M. 353
Johnson, Manly 200
Justus, James H. 145, 235, 264, 366
Kapstein, Israel J. 60
Kartiganer, Donald 292
Kay, Wallace G. 123
Kinney, Arthur F. 231, 316
Knapp, Joseph George, S. J. 242
Krieger, Murray 268
Kuehl, John R. 238
Kummer, George 205
Kunst, Arthur E. 262
Lacy, James M. 295
Langford, Gerald 296, 337, 339
Lecky, Eleazer 136
Lemon, Lee T. 212
Levenson, Jacob 172, 289
Levin, David 321
Levin, Harry 134

Lewis, Arthur O. 44
Lewis, Richard W. B. 80
Lucid, Robert F. 279
Ludwig, Jack 309
Lutwack, Leonard 119
Lynn, Kenneth S. 72, 128
Lyons, John O. 256
McCarthy, Patrick J. 397
McCullen, J. T., Jr. 245
McElderry, Bruce R., Jr. 40, 78
McHaney, Thomas 313
McKeon, Richard P. 18
McLaughlin, Charles A. 317
McNamee, Maurice Basil, S. J. 189
Male, Roy R. See Fritz, A. J. 96
Marshall, Thomas F. 190, 202
Martin, Ronald E. 308
Martin, Terence 394
Masoner, David J. 398
Mather, T. R. 5
Mercier, Vivan 169
Meriwether, James B. 160, 170, 171, 176, 181, 214, 222, 228, 320, 364, 384, 401, 409, 410
Mignon, Charles W. 362
Miller, James, Jr. 112, 158
Miller, J. Hillis 405
Milligate, Michael H. 269, 329
Mills, Gordon 135
Montesi, Albert Joseph 75
Moore, Jack B. 325
Moore, Rayburn S. 253
Morris, Adalaide 378
Moses, William R. 138
Moser, Thomas C. 241, 304
Murray, William C. 377
Nevius, Blake R. 177
Nicoloff, Philip L. 251
Nilon, Charles 131
Noble, David W. 116
Nye, Russel B. 261
O'Connor, W. V. 99
Outler, Albert Cook 20
Owen, David H. 15, 224, 230, 287, 395, 406
Pearce, Roy Harvey 319
Pearson, Norman H. 21
Perrin, Porter G. 16
Philbrick, Thomas L. 244
Phillips, William 129
Pickett, Roy 338
Pilkington, John 120, 324, 328, 347
Pochmann, Henry A. 19
Poiner, Richard 414
Porte, Joel 182

Poteat, William H. 147
Powers, Lyall H. 150, 198, 248
Prescott, Joseph 311
Price, Martin 213
Pugh, Griffith T. 71, 151, 167, 246
Ramsey, Earl 309
Ranald, Ralph A. 79
Richardson, Lyon N. 66
Rideout, Walter B. 113, 155, 196, 234, 236, 237, 265, 271, 305
Ridgely, Joseph V. 127
Robbins, J. Albert 232
Roberts, James L. 345, 355
Roeder, Robert E. 227
Roppolo, Joseph Patrick 110, 185
Rosenblatt, Louise M. 17, 24, 157
Rossby, William 341
Roudiez, Leon S. 126
Rouse, H. B. 102
Rubin, Louis D., Jr. 258, 299
Rudolph, Earle Leighton 54, 95
Rueckert, William 293
Sacks, Sheldon 259, 298
Sale, William 51, 82
Sandeen, Ernest 50, 58, 68
Schmitter, Dean M. 260
Scholes, Robert 331
Schwartz, Joseph M. 291, 388, 389
Scowcrott, Richard P. 35
Seelye, John D. 288
Shaaber, Mattias A. 9
Shaver, Claude L. 130
Shrell, Darwin 249
Slabey, Robert M. 139
Sears, Sallie 340
Seeves, Pascal 141
Slatoff, Walter J. 152
Smith, Henry Hash 137
Solomon, Roger B. 348
Spears, Monroe K. 400
Spiller, Robert E. 101
Stade, George 297
Stafford, William T. 142, 174, 223
Stegner, Wallace 98
Stein, Arnold 14
Stern, Milton R. 412
Sterrett, Marvin D. 105
Stewart, David H. 111
Stewart, John 319
Stewart, Randall 65
Stillinger, Jack 363
Stone, A. E. 97

Stott, William M. 384
Strandberg, Victor 250, 375
Suggart, Peter 183
Swiggart, Peter 342
Tedlock, E. W., Jr. 43, 52
Teunissen, John J. 277
Thompson, H. W. 8
Thornton, Weldon 199, 215
Thorp, Willard 36
Tomlinson, A. C. 103
Touster, Eva 381
Trawbridge, Hoyt 257
Trimmer, Joseph F. 395
Turner, Arlin 132, 163
Turpie, Mary C. 194
Tuttleton, James W. 369
Twining, E. S. 140
Varner, John G. 197
Vincent, Howard P. 146, 209
Von Hendy, Andrew J. 306
Waggoner, Hyatt H. 67, 90, 173, 284, 386
Walcutt, Charles C. 302
Warfel, Harry R. 22, 164
Warren, Austin 115
Watkins, Floyd C. 125, 165, 216
Watt, Ian P. 203
Wegelin, Christof 334
Weimer, David R. 280
Weinstein, Arnold, L. 356
Wells, Arvin R. 108
Wheeler, Otis B. 283
Whitebread, Thomas B. 193
Whitehead, Lee M. 272
Wickes, George 70
Willson, Lawrence 300, 385
Wilson, A. Leslie 360
Winthrop, Delba 404
Winters, Yvor 3
Wright, George T. 149, 266
Young, Philip 229, 240, 330
Young, Thomas Daniel 122, 332, 372
Ziolkowski, Theodore J. 371

TITLE INDEX

Abstraction and Insularity in the Fiction of WF 199
The Achievement of Gavin Stevens 176
Affirming the Void: Futilitarianism in the Fiction of Conrad and F 286
Against the Limitations of Rationalism: Undercurrent in the Works of WF 351
America in Literature 8
The American Novel in France 19
The American Novel in Germany: A Study of the Critical Reception of Eight American Novelists Between the Two World Wars 45
An Analysis of Style: The Application of Sector Analysis to Examples of American Prose Fiction 121
An Analysis of the Imagery of WF's Absalom, Absalom! 28
An Analysis of WF's Major Techniques of Comedy 151
An Application of Script Analysis to Four of WF's Women Characters 295
'And By Bergson, Obviously': F's The Sound and the Fury, As I Lay Dying, and Absalom, Absalom! from a Bergsonian Perspective 237
The Apprenticeship of WF: The Early Short Stories and the First Three Novels 93
Archetypes in the Major Novels of Thomas Hardy and Their Literary Application 117
As I Lay Dying: A Study of the Poor White in F 190
The Barrier of Words: A Study of WF's Distrust of Language 223
Bergsonian Dynamism in the Writings of WF 61
Beyond the Meaning of History: The Quest for a Southern Myth in F's Characters 389
The Bible as a Novel: A Comparative Study of Two Modernized Versions of Biblical Stories: Zola's La Faute de L'Abee Mouret and F's A Fable 156
The Biblical View of History: Hawthorne, Mark Twain, F, and Eliot 101
Black Characters in F's Fiction 355
The Bystander in F's Fiction 234
The Cavalier Spirit in F's Fiction 235
Changes in the Novel: A Structuralist Comparison of Middlemarch, The Confidence-Man, and Absalom, Absalom! 367
Characters in Crisis: Communication and the Idea of Self in F 357
The Characters of Hawthorne and F: A Typology of Sinners 115
Christian Historical Analogues in the Fiction of WF and Flannery O'Connor 264
Chronicles of Children: WF's Short Fiction 159
A Chronology of WF's Yoknapatawpha County 216
Cinematic Techniques in the Novels of WF 242
Clairvoyance, Vision, and Imagination in the Fiction of WF 125
Classical Myth in the Novels of WF 330
Coleridge's Definition of the Poet and the Works of Herman Melville and WF 114
Comedy in F's Fiction 395
The Commitment of Self in the Works of WF 193

Title Index

Confronting the Ghost: Quentin Compson's Struggle with His Heritage in F's Absalom, Absalom! 306
A Contextual Approach to the Teaching of Two Novels by WF at College Level 105
Coordinate Structure in Four F Novels 215
The Cosmographic Strain in Narrative: From Homer to F, Joyce, and Butor 331
Courtly Love in the Writings of WF 315
Creation of Atmosphere in the Novels of Hawthorne, F, and Julien Green 168
Creative Responses to Time in the Novels of WF 349
A Critical Analysis of the Fictional Techniques of WF 50
A Critical and Textual Study of WF's A Fable 170
A Critical and Textual Study of WF's 'Flags in the Dust' 410
A Critical and Textual Study of WF's Light in August 228
The Critical Reception of American Fiction in the Netherlands, 1900-1953 56
The Critical Reception of WF's Work in the United States: 1926-1950 32
A Critical Study of F's Early Sketches and Collected Stories 186
The Current of Time in the Novels of WF 107
The Darkening Window: Four Problematic American Novels 359
A Darker Freedom: The Villain in the Novels of Hawthorne, James, and F 183
Darkness to Appall: Destructive Designs and Patterns in Some Characters of WF 127
The Decline of the Southern Gentleman Character as He Is Illustrated in Novels by Present-Day Southern Novelists 1
The Decomposing Form: Studies in F, Woolf, and Beckett 348
The Demonic Paradox; Studies in F's Imagery" 340
The Design of F's Light in August: A Comprehensive Study 191
The Development of Narrative Technique in the Apprenticeship Fiction of WF 342
The Development of the Black Character in the Fiction of WF 413
The Development of Women Characters in the Works of WF 281
A Dialect Study of F Country, Arkansas 130
The Diaphoric Structure and Unity of WF's Go Down, Moses 179
The Dickens' World and Yoknapatawpha County: A Study of Character and Society in Dickens and F 145
Difficult Contemporary Short Stories: WF, Katherine Anne Porter, Dylan Thomas, Eudora Welty, and Virginia Woolf 16
Duality in the Novels of WF and Fyodor Dostoevsky 198
Dubliners and Go Down, Moses: The Short Story Composite 150
Earth, Air, Fire and Water: The Elements in F's Fiction 240
The Economy of Memory in F's Yoknapatawpha 415
Emphases and Modes of Organization in the Fiction of WF: A Study in Patterns of Rhetoric and Perception 27
The Endless Jar: 'Contraries' in WF 221
Endure and Prevail: F's Social Outcasts 368
The Escape Motif in the Modern American Novel: Mark Twain to Carson McCullers 109
Eschatological Thought in F's Yoknapatawpha Novels 225
Essays on F: Style, Use of History, Film Adaptations on His Fiction 226
The Evolution of an Artist: A Genetic Study of WF's The Hamlet 301
The Evolution of Patterns of Characterization from F's Soldiers' Pay (1926) Through Absalom, Absalom! (1936) 358
The Existential Absurd in F's Snopes Trilogy 220
Existentialism and the Modern American Novel 42
An Exploration of the Literary Relationship Between Sherwood Anderson and

Title Index

WF 123
A Fable of the Invincible Dust: F's Vision of Man in A Fable 406
The Failure of the Imagination: A Study of Melville, Conrad, and F 89
Faith, Identity, and Perception--Three Existential Crises in Modern Fiction and Their Artistic Reconciliation: A Comparison of the Fiction of Dostoevsky, Joyce, Kafka, and F from the Perspective of the Works of Sartre and Camus (Volumes I-III) 352
The Fallen Women in American Naturalistic Fiction: From Crane to F 119
The Family in the Novels of Wharton, F, Cather, Lewis, and Dreiser 218
The Fatal Art: The Evolution of Tragic Image and Idea in Three Novels by WF 390
The Fatal Illusions: Self, Sex, Race, and Religion in WF's World 178
F and American Humor: Tradition and Innovations 323
F and the Concept of Excellence 287
F and the Negro 81
F and the Storyteller 289
F in Hollywood: A Study of His Career as a Scenarist 43
F's Absalom, Absalom! and Dickens: A Study of Time and Change Correspondences 247
F's Black Characters: A Comparative Study 302
F's Changing Vision: Narrative Progress Toward Affirmation 284
F's Characters of Sensibility 132
F's Comic Spirit 64
F's Commedia: An Interpretation of The Sound and the Fury, Sanctuary, As I Lay Dying, and Light in August 372
F's Conflicting Galaxies: A Study in Literary Polarity 9
F's Crime Fiction: His Use of the Detective Story and the Thriller 288
F's Decline 146
F's Doctrine of Nature: A Study of the 'Endurance' Theme in the Yoknapatawpha Fiction 122
F's Early Heroines 361
F's Early Short Story Career 343
F's Early Writings: The Discomfort of the Text 414
F's Females: The Thematic Function of Women in the Yoknapatawpha Cycle 162
F's 'Flags in the Dust' and 'Sartoris': A Comparative Study of the Typescript and the Originally Published Novel 296
F's Grecian Urn 182
F's Indians 267
F's Initiation Stories: An Approach to the Major Works 239
F's Late Short Fiction 171
F's Light in August: Sources and Revisions 177
F's Men and Women: A Critical Study of Male-Female Relationships in His Early Yoknapatawpha County Novels 392
F's Military World 312
F's Narrative Voices in The Sound and the Fury 319
F's Negro: Art and the Southern Context, 1926-1936 344
F's Psychology of Individualism: A Fictional Principle and Light in August 278
F's Readers 195
F's Rhetoric 98
F's Sanctuary and Requiem for a Nun: Songs of Innocence and Experience 82
F's Sartoris: A Comprehensive Study 369
F's Sartoris Family and the Problem of Human Freedom 404
F's Sense of History: Criticism of the Magnolia Myth in the Novels of WF 227

Title Index

F's South: Myth and History in the Novel 137
F's Study of Youth 322
F's Style and Its Relation to Theme: A Stylistic Study of Two Stories from Go Down, Moses 308
F's Tragic Heroes 31
F's Trilogy: A Revaluation 377
F's Twice-Told Tales: His Re-Use of His Material 67
F's Un-Christlike Christians: Biblical Allusions in the Novels 201
F's Uses of the Classics 139
F's Vitalistic Vision: A Close Study of Eight Novels 250
F's Young Males: From Futility to Responsibility 276
F's Young Protagonists: The Innocent and the Damned 185
F, Stasis, and Keats' 'Ode to a Grecian Urn' 362
F Studies in France: 1953-1969 209
F: The Transfiguration of Biography 380
The 'Feeder' Motif in Selected Fiction of WF and Flannery O'Connor 403
The Fiction of WF and Uwe Johnson 262
Flanner O'Connor's American Models: Her Work in Relation to That of Hawthorne, James, F, and West 375
The Form and Meaning of the Impressionist Novel 99
Four Critical Interpretations in the Modern Novel 63
The Fourteenth View: A Study of Ambiguity in WF's Light in August 192
A Freight of Faith and Hope: A Study of the Quest in the American Novel 140
The French and F: The Reception of WF's Writing in France and Its Influence on Modern French Literature 384
Freudian Influence in the American Autobiographical Novel 2
From Genesis to Revelation: The Grand Design of F's Absalom, Absalom! 270
From Tradition to Technique: Development of Character in Joyce and F 123
The Function of Stock Humor and Grotesque Humor in F's Major Novels 290
The Fury and the Design: Realism of Being and Knowing in Four Novels of WF 87
A Gallery of Grotesques: The Alienation Theme in the Works of Hawthorne, Twain, Anderson, F, and Wolfe 141
Game-Consciousness and Game-Metaphor in the Work of WF 79
The Genesis and Unity of F's 'Big Woods' 314
The Glance of the Idiot: A Thematic Study of F and Modern French Fiction 80
The Grotesque in Modern American Fiction: An Existential Theory 86
The Grotesque in Recent Southern Fiction 91
The Grotesque in the Fiction of WF 205
A Handbook of Yoknapatawpha 54
Hawthorne and F: The Continuity of a Dark American Tradition 184
History as Perception, History as Obsession: F's Development of a Theme 265
History as Voice and Metaphor: A Study of Tate, Warren, and F 133
A History of the Recent Translations of the American Novel into Spanish 6
The Human Comedies of Honoré de Balzac and WF: Similarities and Differences 169
Humanistic and Legal Values in Some Works of F 377
Humor in F's Novels: Its Development, Forms and Functions 92
Humor in Novels of WF 104
Humorous Characterization and Tradition of the Jonsonian Comedy of Manners in WF's Early Fiction 324
The Hunting Metaphor in Hemingway and F 261
Images of the Negro in the Novels of WF 260
Immediacy, Suspense, and Meaning in WF's The Sound and the Fury: An Ex-

Title Index

periment in Critical Analysis 12
Implausible Motion: Generation and Regeneration in the Novels of WF 285
Inarticulate Characters in Modern American Fiction: A Study of Fitzgerald, Hemingway, and F 203
The Indestructible Woman in the Works of F, Hemingway, and Steinbeck 257
An Index and Encyclopedia of the Characters in the Fictional Works of WF 40
An Index to the Characters in the Published and Unpublished Fiction of WF 409
The Individual and the Community: Values in the Novels of WF 90
The Influence of WF on Four Latin American Novelists 396
The Influence of WF on Michael Butor 161
Innocence and Experience in Selected Major Fiction of WF 394
An Inquiry into the Nature of Plot in the 20th Century Novel 18
The Irrational Narrator in Virginia Woolf's The Waves, WF's The Sound and the Fury, and Gunter Grass' The Tin Drum 148
Jeffersonian Agrarianism in F's Yoknapatawpha: The Evolution of Social and Economic Standard 246
The Jefferson Urn: F's Literary Sources and Influences 149
Joyce, F, O'Connor: Conceptual Approach to Major Characters 309
Kenneth Burke's Structuralism: A Structural Description of Narrative and Technique in F's Fiction of the Southern Aristocracy 338
Kierkegaard and F: Modalities of Existence 147
Knowing in the Novels of WF 293
Land-Character Relationships in Selected Works of F's Yoknapatawpha Saga 325
Land-Nostalgia in the Novels of F, Cather, and Steinbeck 118
Levels of Consciousness: Women in the Stream of Consciousness Novels of Joyce, Woolf, and F 336
Levels of Maturity: The Theme of Striving in the Novels of WF 88
Life in Motion: Gentell and Vernacular Attitudes in the Works of the Southwestern American Humorists, Mark Twain, and WF 131
Literary Continuity Traced Through the Progression in the Use of Time in Wordsworth, F, Virginia Woolf, T. S. Eliot, and Yeats 381
The Literary F: His Indebtedness to Conrad, Lawrence, Hemingway, and Other Modern Novelists 60
The Literary Styles of Jean-Paul Sartre and WF: An Analysis, Comparison, and Contrast 77
The Literature of the Air: Themes and Imagery in the Works of F, Saint-Exupéry, and Gaiser 134
Lost Ladies: The Isolated Heroine in the Fiction of Hawthorne, James, Fitzgerald, Hemingway, and F 251
The Making of a Novelist: WF's Career to the Writing of The Sound and the Fury 411
The Making of Sartoris: A Description and Discussion of the Manuscript and Composite Typescript of WF's Third Novel 152
Man in His Struggle: Structure, Technique, and Theme in F's Snopes Trilogy 167
Man's Enduring Chronicle: A Study of Myth in the Novels of WF 84
The Material of Abnormal Psychology in Some Contemporary English and American Novels 3
Men of Thought, Men of Action: A Pattern of Contrasts in F's Major Novels 258
A Methodology for the Study of Philosophy in Literature: Philosophy and Symbol in Selected Works of WF and Thomas Mann 360
Michel Butor and WF: Some Structures and Techniques 126

Title Index

The Monument and the Plain: The Art of Mythic Consciousness in WF's Absalom, Absalom! 196
Moral Values of the American Woman as Presented in Three Major American Authors (Hawthorne, Henry James, and WF) 94
Moses, Its Sources, Revisions, and Structures 112
Motion and Statis Theme as Structuring Principle in the Art of WF 188
Motion in Yoknapatawpha County: Theme and Point of View in the Novels of WF 138
The Multilinear Novel: A Structural Analysis of Novels by Dos Passos, Döblin, F, and Koeppen 371
The Mystery of Significance and the Enigma of Time: An Analysis of the Thematic Structures of F's The Sound and the Fury and Claude Simon's L'Herbe 206
Myth and Dream in the Novels of WF 332
The Myth of Southern History: 20th Century Variations 116
Names of Characters in F's Mississippi 165
Narcissus Observed: The Pastoral Elegiac in Woolf, F, Fitzgerald, and Graeme Gibson 379
Narrative Forms in the Modern Southern Novel 180
Narrative Mode in the Novels of WF 401
The Negro Character in the Fiction of WF 106
Negro Characterization in the American Novel: A Historical Survey of Work by White Authors 44
The Negro in Southern Fiction, 1920-1940 5
Neither We from Them Nor They from Us: An Interpretation of Go Down, Moses 310
The New Rhetoric of F's Heroes in His Later Work 229
The New South and Five Southern Novelists, 1920-1950 30
The Non-Yoknapatawpha Novels of WF: An Examination of Soldiers' Pay, Mosquitoes, Pylon, The Wild Palms, and A Fable 233
Not Only to Survive But to Prevail: A Study of WF's Search for a Redeemer of Modern Man 232
The Novels of WF: Patterns of Perspective 13
On the Aesthetics of F's Fiction 124
Ontological Implications in F's Major Novels 264
The Origins and Importance of the Initiation Story in 20th Century British and American Fiction 52
Out of that Generous Land: A Study of the Scope of the Novel Based on America from Cooper to F 103
Parent-Child Relationships in the Works of WF 175
The Past in the Works of WF 194
Pastoral and Parody: The Making of F's Anthology Novels 346
Patterns of Initiation in WF's Go Down, Moses 110
Perspectives of WF: The Author and His Work as Reflected in Surveys of American History, Works on Southern Life and History, and Works and Comments by Mississippians 236
The Pilgrimage of WF: A Study of F's Fiction, 1929-1942 47
The Place of The Unvanquished in WF's Yoknapatawpha Series 36
Plantation and Frontier: A View of Southern Fiction 51
Plot Manipulation and Kaleidoscoping of Time as Sources of Tragic Perception in WF's Absalom, Absalom! 189
Plot Materials and Narrative Form in F's Early Fiction 366
Point of View as a Mode of Thematic Definition in Conrad and F 248
Portrait of the Artist in Motion: A Study of the Artist-Surrogates in the Novels of WF 142

Title Index

Possibilities of Place: The Fiction of WF 337
Present, Past: Hawthorne, F, and the Problem of History 412
Primitivism in the Fiction of WF 120
Prisons and Prisoners in the Works of WF 327
The Problem of Character in the Development of Theme in the Novels and Short Stories of WF 7
Problems of Perception in the Modern Novel: The Representation of Consciousness in the Works of Henry James, Gertrude Stein, and WF 256
Psychic Displacement and Adaptation in the Novels of Dickens and F 397
Psychic Transformation Through Memorywork and Negation in WF's Absalom, Absalom! 391
Psychological Approaches to the Narrative Personality in the Novels of WF 307
Psychological Rebirth in Selected Works by Nathaniel Hawthorne, Stephen Crane, Henry James, WF, and Ralph Ellison 268
Pylon: The Doomed Quest: A Critical and Textual Study of WF's Neglected Allegory 339
Quentin Compson as Narrative Voice in the Works of WF 313
Quest for Faith: A Study of Destructive and Creative Force in the Novels of WF 70
The Quest for Sacred Space: Setting in the Novels of WF 202
A Question of Responsibility: The Villain in the Yoknapatawpha Fiction of WF 328
The Racing Impotence: Humor in the Novels of Dostoevsky, F, and Beckett 356
The Reality of Gothic Terror in F 197
The Reception of the American Novel in German Periodicals, 1947-1957 38
The Reconstructive Mode in Fiction: A Study of F and the French New Novel 144
The Regional Novel of the South: The Dilemma of Innocence 83
The Relationship of Storyteller to Community in the Southwest Humorists, Mark Twain and WF 318
Religion in Yoknapatawpha County 69
The Religion Symbolism in F's Novels 200
Religious Themes and Symbolism in the Novels of WF 53
Repetition and Structure: A Study of WF and Claude Simon 408
Rhetoric of Loss: An Analysis of F's Perceptual Style 350
The Rhetoric of Multiple Points of View in Selecting Contemporary Novels 157
Ring Composition: The Structural Unity of WF's Go Down, Moses 378
The Ritual of Survival: Landscape in Conrad and F 213
A Road to WF: A Reading of Southern Fiction 37
The Role of the South in the Fiction of WF, Carson McCullers, Flannery O'Connor, and William Styron 173
The Role of Women in F's Yoknapatawpha 333
The Role of Women in Three of F's Families 291
The Roles of the Negro in WF's Fiction 97
The Roles of the Negro in WF's Public and Private World 217
Scenes from Yoknapatawpha: A Study of People and Places in the Real and Imaginary Worlds of WF 398
The Search for Identity of F's Black Characters 244
The Secular Imagination: The Continuity of the Secular Romantic Tradition of Wordsworth and Keats in Stevens, F, Roethke, and Bellow 363
The Self as History: Studies in Adams, F, Ellison, Belyj, Pasternak 321
Self-Communion: The Early Novels of WF 335

Title Index

Sentence Patterns in The Sound and the Fury 85
The Serpent of Lust in the Southern Garden: The Theme of Miscegenation in Cable, Twain, F, and Warren 249
The Short Stories of WF 71
Short Story Cycles of Hemingway, Steinbeck, F, and O'Connor 334
Silence and the Impeccable Language: A Study of WF's Philosophy of Language 208
Sinbad in New Orleans: Early Short Fiction by WF--An Annotated Edition 364
The Signboard for New Hope: F's As I Lay Dying 212
The Single Vision: A Study of the Philosophy and the Forms of Its Presentation in the Works of WF 39
Six Grotesques in Three F Novels 224
'The Snopes Dilemma': Morality and Amorality in F's Snopes Trilogy 143
Social Attitudes in Five Contemporary Southern Novelists: Erskine Caldwell, WF, Ellen Glasgow, Caroline Gordon, and T. S. Stribling 4
The Social Role of F's Women: A Materialistic Interpretation 402
Soldiers' Pay: A Critical Study of WF's First Novel 222
Soldiers' Pay to The Sound and the Fury: Development of Poetic in the Early Novels of WF 129
Some Aspects of the Treatment of Negro Characters by Five Representative American Novelists: Cooper, Melville, Tourgee, Glasgow, F 11
Some Romantic Elements in the Works of WF 273
The Sound and the Fury: An Archetypal Reading 353
The South in Motley: A Study of the Fool Tradition in Selected Works by F, McCullers, and O'Connor 382
Southern Fiction and the Quest for Identity 73
Sports, Sporting Codes, and Sportsmanship in the Works of Ring Lardner, James T. Farrell, Ernest Hemingway, and WF 57
The Story of All Things: F's Yoknapatawpha County as Cosmology by Way of Light in August 271
Strange Textures of Vision: A Study of the Significance of Mannered Fictional Techniques in Six Selected Novels of D. H. Lawrence, WF, and Patrick White Together With a Theoretical Introduction on The Novel of Vision 272
Stream of Consciousness Variation in F: A Redefinition 317
The Structural Function of the Christ Figure in the Fiction of WF 95
Structural Principles in WF's Go Down, Moses 280
The Structure and Meaning of WF's A Fable 164
A Study of F's Presentation of Some Problems That Relate to Negroes 49
A Study of Humor in the Fiction of WF 29
A Study of Metaphor and Simile in the American Literary Novel and the American Popular Novel, 1911-1940 17
A Study of Tensiveness in Selected Novels of WF 219
A Study of the Early Versions of F's The Town and The Mansion 320
A Study of the Noble Savage Myth in Characterization of the Negro in Selected American Literary Works 100
A Study of the Text of WF's The Hamlet 181
A Study of WF's A Fable 304
A Study of WF's As I Lay Dying Based on the Manuscript and Text 238
A Study of WF's Informal Dialect Theory and His Use of Dialect Markers in Eight Novels 326
Style and Dialect in Light in August and Other Works by WF 154
Such Stuff as Dreams Are Made on: History, Myth and the Comic Vision of Mark Twain and WF 113
Suggestions of Death--Anxiety in the Life of WF 383
Symbolism in the American Novel, 1850-1960: An Examination of the Findings

Title Index

of Recent Literary Critics in Respect of the Novels of Hawthorne, Melville, James, Hemingway, and F 74
Syntactic Features of WF's Narrative Style 210
A Textual and Critical Evaluation for the Manuscripts and Typescripts of WF's Intruder in the Dust 299
A Textual and Critical Study of WF's Requiem for a Nun 214
The Textual History and Definitive Textual Apparatus for Soldiers' Pay: A Bibliographic Study of WF's First Novel 388
Theme and Characterization in F's Snopes Trilogy 135
The Theme of Responsibility in the Later Fiction of WF 48
The Theme of Revenge in the Fiction of WF 266
A Theological Critique of the Interpretation of Man in the Fiction and Drama of WF, Ernest Hemingway, Jean-Paul Sartre, and Albert Camus 20
They Who Endure and Prevail: Characters of WF 66
Time and Identity in the Novels of WF 136
Time and Structure in the Novels of WF 21
Time as Character in the Fiction of James Joyce and WF 166
To Move in Time: A Study of the Structure of F's As I Lay Dying, Light in August, and Absalom, Absalom! 153
Told by an Idiot: Toward an Understanding of Modern Fiction Through an Analysis of the Works of WF and John Barth 282
A Topographical Study of Thomas Hardy and WF 405
Towards a New Objectivity: Essays on the Body and Native in F, Lawrence, and Mann 252
The Treatment of the Negro Woman as a Major Character in American Novels, 1900-1950 24
Tricked by Words: Syntax and Style in F's As I Lay Dying 292
Trilogy as Experimental Form: F's Snopes Trilogy, Dos Passos' U. S. A., and Sartre's Les Chemins de la Liberté 407
The Trilogy as Form in Modern American Fiction 174
The Twentieth Century Impressionistic Novel: Conrad and F 96
The Two Patrimonies of Isaac McCaslin: Responsibilities to Secular and Liminal Time in F's Go Down, Moses 374
The Unalterable Doom: Tragedy in Four Novels of WF 298
The Uncreating Word: Creators of Fiction in WF's Major Novels 385
The Unity of Collected Stories of WF 395
Uses of the Past in the Novels of WF 329
Uses of Time in Four Novels by WF 255
Values and Love in the Fiction of WF 68
The Vanishing Community: Studies in Some Late Novels by WF 269
Visions and Revisions: A Study of the Obtuse Narrator in American Fiction from Brackden Brown to F 128
The Visual Imagination of WF 187
The Waste Land Tradition in the American Novel 76
Whorls of Form in F's Fiction 34
WF and Claude Simon: A Stylistic Study 207
WF and Existentialism 25
WF and Mikhail Sholokhov: A Comparative Study of Two Representatives of the Regional Conscience, Their Affinities and Meanings 46
WF and the Community 59
WF and the Mythology of Women 277
WF and the Negro 22
WF and the Search for Lost Time: Three Aspects of Literary Deformation 243
WF and the Terror of History: Myth, History, and Moral Freedom in the Yoknapatawpha Cycle 75

Title Index

WF: An International Novelist 72
WF: An Interpretation 35
WF as a Literary Naturalist 311
WF: A Study in Spatial Form 231
WF: A Thematic Study 33
WF: Critic of Society 62
WF: From Past to Self-Discovery: A Study of His Life and Work Through Sartoris (1929) 78
WF: Myth-Maker and Morals-Monger: Esthetics and Ethics in Yoknapatawpha County 300
WF's Absalom, Absalom! 41
WF's Absalom, Absalom!: An Exercise in Affirmation 254
WF's A Fable 26
WF's A Fable: A Fragmented Christ 230
WF's Compleat Woman 345
WF's Early Experiments with Narrative Technique 111
WF's Literary Reputation in America 65
WF's Literary Reputation in Britain, with A Checklist of Criticism, 1929-1972 253
WF's Mosquitoes: An Introduction and Annotations to the Novel 387
WF's Narrators 155
WF's Rendering of Modern Experience: A Theological Analysis 55
WF's Romantic Heritage: Beyond America 316
WF's Short Stories 172
WF's The Hamlet: Its Revisions and Structure 158
WF's Theory of Fiction 347
WF's The Wild Palms: A Textual and Critical Study 160
WF's Thomas Sutpen, Quentin Compson, Joe Christmas: A Study of the Hero-Archetype 376
WF's Trilogy 211
WF: Studies in Form and Idea 14
WF's Use of the Material of Abnormal Psychology in Characterization 102
WF's Use of the Tragic Mulatto Myth 279
WF's Uses of Elaboration and Multiple Story Lines 259
WF's World War I and Flying Short Fiction: An Imaginative Appropriation of History 380
WF's Yoknapatawpha: The Land of Broken Dreams 245
WF: The Calvinistic Sensibility 283
WF: The Dynamics of Form 274
WF: The Heroic Design of Yoknapatawpha 263
WF: The Search for Reality 365
WF: 'The Waste Land' Phase 58
WF, V. K. Ratliff, and the Snopes Saga (1925-1940) 203
Woman in the Works of WF 163
Women as Victims in the Novels of Charles Dickens and WF 400
Work in Counterpoint: F's The Wild Palms 297
The World of F's Imagination 15
A World of Voices: 'Talking' in the Novels of WF 241
The World of WF 10
The World Outside Yoknapatawpha: A Study of Five Novels by WF 108
The World View of WF 23
The Yoknapatawpha World and Black Being 354
Youth and Innocence in the Novels of WF 275

UNIVERSITY INDEX

Arizona State University 220, 276
Auburn University 255, 281
Ball State University 326, 395
Boston College 306
Boston University 5, 344
Brandeis University 183, 342
Brown University 60, 67, 90, 173, 284, 331, 356, 386
Bryn Mawr College 310
Case Western Reserve University 66, 205, 226, 348
City University of New York 302, 351
Claremont University 70
Columbia University 47, 49, 59, 121, 126, 127, 178, 260, 297, 333
Cornell University 8, 51, 82, 89, 133, 152, 180, 337
Drew University 114
Duke University 132, 147, 163, 250, 375
Emory University 97, 125, 165, 216
Florida State University 71, 151, 153, 167, 246
Fordham University 79, 208, 247
George Peabody College for Teachers 381
Georgia State University 313
Harvard University 41, 72, 93, 128, 134, 144, 168, 182, 285, 365
Indiana University 38, 145, 207, 218, 229, 232, 235, 264, 366, 394
Johns Hopkins University 186, 274, 349
Kansas State University 138
Kent State University 146, 166, 190, 202, 209, 294
Lehigh University 184, 322, 392
Louisiana State University & Agricultural & Mechanical College 130, 249, 283, 396
Loyola University of Chicago 390
Marquette University 291, 388, 389
Michigan State University 84, 261
New York University 17, 24, 31, 57, 81, 117, 118, 157, 238, 369

Northwestern University 26, 28, 34, 187, 219, 357
Ohio State University 217
Ohio University 107, 314
Pennsylvania State University 44, 240, 330
Princeton University 36, 346, 354, 371
Purdue University 142, 174, 223, 307
Rice University 286, 367, 400
Rutgers University 280
St. John's University 275
St. Louis University 75, 189, 242
Stanford University 3, 35, 98, 159, 203, 241, 304
State University of Iowa 33
State University of New Jersey 414
State University of New York, Binghamton 179, 407
State University of New York, Buffalo 335, 350, 402
State University of New York, Stony Brook 309, 340
Syracuse University 15, 224, 230, 287, 395, 406
Temple University 341
Texas Tech University 245, 358, 403
Tulane University 61, 76, 110, 185, 361, 373
University of Alabama 270, 398
University of Arkansas 54, 95, 100, 102
University of Bristol, England 103
University of British Columbia, Canada 233, 272, 408
University of California, Berkeley 137
University of California, Davis 99
University of California, Irvine 268
University of California, Los Angeles 37, 107, 177, 203, 301, 327
University of California, San Diego 319

University Index

University of California, Santa Barbara 300, 385, 397
University of Chicago 7, 18, 32, 112, 155, 158, 259, 290, 298, 323
University of Colorado 131, 169, 368
University of Connecticut 288, 317, 412
University of Dallas 374, 415
University of Delaware 308
University of Denver 63, 64, 69, 140, 227, 239
University of Florida 22, 164, 188, 376
University of Georgia 141, 156, 253, 273
University of Houston 105
University of Illinois 53, 62, 88
University of Illinois, Urbana-Champaign 263
University of Iowa 243, 377, 378
University of Kansas 175
University of Maryland 119
University of Massachusetts 231, 277, 316
University of Michigan 4, 12, 27, 46, 56, 85, 106, 111, 115, 149, 150, 191, 198, 225, 248, 352, 413
University of Minnesota 116, 149, 194, 266
University of Mississippi 31, 120, 328, 347
University of Nebraska 104, 210, 212
University of Nebraska, Lincoln 345, 355, 362
University of Nevada 162, 201, 338
University of New Hampshire 251
University of New Mexico 43, 52, 109, 257, 267, 353
University of North Carolina, Chapel Hill 199, 206, 215, 218, 258, 263, 299, 312
University of Notre Dame 50, 58, 68, 139, 391
University of Oklahoma 23, 83, 96, 204
University of Oregon 161, 221, 334, 336
University of Pennsylvania 9, 10, 45, 101, 211, 279
University of Pittsburgh 6, 86, 143, 192, 244
University of Rochester 87, 195, 293
University of Southern California 29, 40, 77, 78, 136, 254
University of South Carolina 160, 170, 171, 176, 181, 222, 228, 241, 320, 364, 380, 387, 401, 409, 410
University of South Florida 325
University of Southern Mississippi 123
University of Texas, Austin 25, 92, 94, 135, 154, 193, 197, 296, 339, 360, 384
University of Toronto, Canada 269, 329, 379, 411
University of Tulsa 200
University of Virginia 172, 289, 321, 359, 382, 404
University of Washington 14, 16, 48, 73, 129, 282, 292, 312
University of Wisconsin 11, 13, 19, 39, 42, 91, 113, 155, 196, 234, 236, 237, 256, 262, 265, 271, 305
Vanderbilt University 1, 2, 30, 65, 122, 124, 315, 332, 372
Victoria University of Manchester, England 74
Wayne State University 311
West Virginia University 383
Yale University 20, 21, 80, 213, 252, 343, 405

SUBJECT INDEX

Absalom, Absalom! (1936) 28, 41, 87, 153, 189, 196, 224, 237, 239, 243, 247, 250, 254, 255, 270, 272, 306, 358, 367, 391
The Absurd 220
Aesthetics 124, 300
Affirmation 254, 284
Alienation 141
Allegory 339
Ambiguity 192
Anthology novels 346
Apprenticeship 93
Archetypes 117
Aristocracy, Southern 30, 338
Artist-surrogates 142
As I Lay Dying (1930) 36, 54, 69, 75, 87, 122, 138, 145, 153, 162, 176, 190, 212, 216, 225, 237, 238, 245, 246, 250, 272, 292, 372, 392, 398
Biblical allusions 156, 201
Biblical view 101
Bibliography (British) 253
Bibliographical and textual study 388
"Big Woods" 314
Black women 24
Blacks (or black characters) 5, 11, 22, 44, 49, 81, 97, 100, 106, 217, 244, 260, 302, 354, 355, 413
Body and nature 252
Burke, Kenneth 338
Bystanders 234
Calvinism 283
Cavalier spirit 235
Characterization 1, 7, 40, 66, 100, 102, 115, 123, 127, 132, 201, 358
Characters--Index 409
Children 159
Christ figure 95, 230
Christianity 201, 204
Christmas, Joe 376
Cinematic techniques 242
Clairvoyance 125
Classical myth 139, 330

Collected Stories of William Faulkner (1950) 186, 395
Comic vision 64, 151, 169, 324, 395
Commitment 193
Communication 357
Community 59, 90, 269, 318
Compson, Quentin 306, 313, 370, 376, 399
Conceptual approaches 309
The Confidence-Man (Melville) 367
Consciousness 256
Continuity 381
"Contraries" 221
Contrast 258
Courtly love 315
Creative force 70
Crime fiction 288
The Damned 185
A dark tradition 184
Death 383
Decline 146
Destructive force 70
Dialect 130, 154, 326
Dream 332
Duality 198
Dubliners (Joyce) 150
Early novels 129, 342, 355, 364, 366, 414
Emphases 27
Endurance 122
Escape 109
Eschatology 225
Ethics 300
Excellence, the concept of 287
Existentialism 42, 86, 147, 220, 264, 352
Experience 83, 185, 275, 394
A Fable (1954) 26, 108, 156, 164, 170, 230, 233, 304, 406
Faith 70, 140, 352
Family 175, 218, 291
F and Adams 321
F and Anderson 141, 341
F and Balzac 169

F and Barth 282
F and Beckett 348, 356
F and Bellow 363
F and Belyj 321
F and Bergson 61, 237
F and Brown 128
F and Butor 126, 161, 331
F and Cable 249
F and Caldwell 4
F and Camus 352
F and Cather 118, 218
F and Coleridge 114
F and Conrad 60, 89, 96, 213, 248, 286
F and Cooper 11, 103
F and Crane 119, 268
F and Dickens 145, 274, 397, 400
F and Döblin 371
F and Donoso 396
F and Dos Passos 371, 407
F and Dostoevsky 198, 352, 356
F and Dreiser 218
F and Eliot (George) 367
F and Eliot (T.S.) 101
F and Ellison 268, 321
F and Farrell 57
F and Fitzgerald 203, 251, 379
F and Gaiser 134
F and García Márquez 396
F and Glasgow 4, 11
F and Gordon 4
F and Grass 148
F and Green 168
F and Hardy 117, 405
F and Hawthorne 74, 94, 101, 115, 141, 168, 183, 184, 251, 268, 375, 412
F and Hemingway 20, 57, 60, 74, 203, 251, 257, 261, 334
F and Homer 331
F and James 74, 94, 256, 268, 375, 813
F and Johnson 382
F and Jonson 324
F and Joyce 123, 150, 166, 309, 331, 336, 352
F and Kafka 123, 150, 166, 336, 352
F and Keats 362, 363
F and Kierkegaard 147
F and Koeppen 371
F and Lardner 57
F and Lawrence 252, 272
F and Lewis 218
F and McCullers 173, 382
F and Mann 252, 360

F and Melville 11, 74, 89, 114, 367
F and O'Connor 173, 204, 310, 334, 375, 382, 403
F and Paskernak 321
F and Porter 16
F and Proust 243
F and Roethke 363
F and Saint-Exupery 134
F and Samudio 396
F and Sartre 20, 77, 352, 407
F and Sholokhov 46
F and Simon 206, 207, 408
F and Stein 256
F and Steinbeck 118, 257, 334
F and Stevens 363
F and Stribling 4
F and Styron 173
F and Tate 133
F and the French 384
F and Thomas 16
F and Tourgee 11
F and Twain 101, 113, 131, 249, 318
F and Warren 133, 249
F and Welty 16
F and West 375
F and Wharton 218
F and White 272
F and Wolfe 16, 141, 148, 336, 348, 379, 381
F and Wordsworth 363, 381
F and Yánez 396
F and Zola 156
F and the French new fiction 144
F and modern fiction 80
F as an international novelist 72
F as a scenarist 43
F Country, Arkansas 130
F studies in France 19, 209
F studies in Germany 45
F studies in the Netherlands 56
La Faute de l'Abbe Mouret (Zola) 156
Feeder motif 403
Fiction, theory of 347
Films 226
First three novels [Soldiers' Pay, Mosquitoes, and Sartoris] 93
Five Legs 379
"Flags in the Dust" 296, 410
The Fool tradition 382
Forms 14, 34, 39, 231, 274, 348
Four elements (earth, air, fire, and water) 240

Subject Index

Freedom, a darker 183
Freedom, human 404
Freedom, moral 75
Freudian influence 2
Frontier 51
French literature 384
Futilitarianism 286
Game-metaphor 79
Genteel and vernacular attitudes 131
Ghost 306
Gibson, Graeme 379
Go Down, Moses (1942) 110, 150, 179, 239, 250, 280, 308, 310, 374, 378
Gothic terror 197
The Great Gatsby (Fitzgerald) 379
Grotesques 86, 91, 141, 205, 224
Growth as a writer 47
The Hamlet (1940) 50, 135, 143, 158, 167, 174, 181, 203, 211, 215, 220, 243, 250, 301, 326, 373
Heritage 306
Hero-archetype 376
Heroes, tragic 31
Heroes, young 185
Heroines 251, 361
History 75, 101, 113, 137, 226, 227, 236, 265, 412
History (World War I) 380
Hollywood 43
Hope 140, 212
Human comedy 169
Humor 29, 92, 104, 131, 290, 318, 324, 356
Hunting metaphor 261
Idea 14
Identity 73, 136, 244, 352
Idiot 80
Imagery 28, 340, 390
Imagination 15, 89, 125, 187, 363
Impressionist novel 99
Inarticulate characters 203
Indians 267
Individualism 90, 278
Influence 149
Initiation 52, 110, 239
Innocence and experience 83, 185, 275, 394
Insularity 199
Intruder in the Dust (1948) 239, 299, 305, 326
Jeffersonian agrarianism 246
Knowing 293
Landscape 213

Land-character 325
Land-nostalgia 118
Language 208, 223
Late novels 269
"Life in motion" 131, 188
Light in August (1932) 36, 50, 54, 69, 75, 87, 122, 138, 145, 153, 154, 176, 177, 191, 192, 216, 224, 225, 228, 239, 245, 246, 250, 255, 271, 278, 305, 326, 372, 392, 398
Literary deformation 243
Literary polarity 9
Literature of the air 134
Love 68
McCaslin, Isaac 374
McCullers, Carson 173
Magnolia myth 227
Male-female relationships 392
Man's image 20, 406
Man's struggle (Snopes trilogy) 167
The Mansion (1959) 135, 143, 167, 174, 203, 211, 220, 243, 320, 373
Manuscript (Intruder in the Dust) 299
Manuscript (Sartoris) 152
Meaning (A Fable) 164
Memory 391, 415
Metaphor 17
Middlemarch (G. Eliot) 367
Military World 312
Miscegenation 249
Mississippi 165
Mrs. Dalloway (Woolf) 379
Modern experience 55
Modern man 232
Montage 399
Morality and amorality 143
Moses 112
Mosquitoes (1927) 93, 108, 233, 387
Motion and statis theme 112, 188
Multilinear novels 371
Myth 75, 84, 113, 196, 332
Myth, classical 330
Myth, mulatto 279
Myth, Southern 389
Myth and history 137
Narrative techniques 111, 128, 155, 180, 307, 313, 319, 331, 342, 395, 401
Naturalism 119, 311
Nature 122, 252
Negation 391

Negroes see Blacks
Noble savage myth 100
Non-Yoknapatawpha novels 108
Ontology 264
Organization 27
Parent-child relationship 175
Parody 340
Past 78, 194, 329
Pastoral 340, 379
Peace officers 305
Perception 352
Perspective 13
Philosophy and literature 39, 360
Place 337
Plantation and frontier 51
Plot 18
The Poetic 129
Point of view 138, 157, 248
Poor white 190
Primitivism 120
Prisons and prisoners 327
Psychic adaptation 397
Psychic displacement 397
Psychic transformation 391
Psychology, abnormal 3, 102
Psychology of individualism 278
Public and private worlds 217
Pylon (1935) 108, 233, 339
Race 178
Rationalism 351
Ratliff, V.K. 203
Reading public 195
Reconstructive mode 144
A redeemer 232
Regional conscience 46
Regional novel 83
The Reivers (1962) 239, 250, 326
Religion 53, 69, 178
Reputation 32, 56, 65
Reputation in Britain 48, 253
Requiem for a Nun 82, 214
Responsibility 328
Revenge 266
Revisions 159, 177
Rhetoric 27, 98, 157
Romanticism 273, 316, 363
Sacred space 202
Saint-Exupéry, Antoine de 134
Sanctuary (1931) 82, 250, 255, 359, 372
Sartoris 36, 54, 69, 75, 78, 93, 122, 138, 145, 152, 154, 162, 176, 216, 225, 243, 245, 246, 296, 326, 369, 392, 398, 404
Sartoris family 404

Subject Index

The Search for Lost Time (Proust) 243
Self-communion 335
Self-discovery 78, 178, 193, 321, 357
Sentence patterns 85
Setting 202
Sex 178
Sheriffs 305
Short stories 7, 16, 71, 93, 150, 159, 171, 172, 334, 380
Short stories (World War I and flying) 380
Simile 17
Sinners 115
Snopes trilogy 135, 143, 167, 174, 203, 211, 373, 407
Social attitude 4
Social criticism 62
Social outcasts 368
Soldiers' Pay (1926) 87, 93, 108, 129, 222, 233, 358, 388
The Sound and the Fury (1929) 12, 36, 54, 75, 85, 87, 122, 129, 138, 145, 148, 154, 206, 215, 216, 224, 225, 237, 243, 245, 246, 250, 255, 319, 326, 353, 370, 372, 379, 392, 399, 411
Sources 67, 149, 177
South 1, 30, 116, 137, 173, 236, 338, 382, 389
Southern aristocracy 1, 30, 338
Southern myth 389
Spanish translation 6
Sports 51
Stasis 131, 188, 362
Stevens, Gavin 176
Storyteller 289, 318
Stream of consciousness 317
Striving, the theme of 88
Structure 21, 87, 126, 153, 158, 179, 206, 215, 312, 371, 408
Structuralism 338
Structure (A Fable) 164
Style 77, 121, 154, 207, 226, 294, 308, 350
Sutpen, Thomas 376
Symbolism 74
Syntactic features 210, 292
Techniques 50, 126, 272
"Tensiveness" 219
Textual study--general 160, 228, 388
Textual study--A Fable 170
Textual study--"Flags in the Dust"

327